T0336834

Probability and Computing

Randomization and probabilistic techniques play an important role in modern computer science, with applications ranging from combinatorial optimization and machine learning to communication networks and secure protocols.

This textbook provides an indispensable teaching tool to accompany a one- or two-semester course for advanced undergraduate or beginning graduate students in computer science and applied mathematics. It offers a comprehensive introduction to the role of randomization and probabilistic techniques in modern computer science, in particular to techniques and paradigms used in the development and probabilistic analysis of algorithms and for data analyses. It assumes only an elementary background in discrete mathematics and gives a rigorous yet accessible treatment of the material, with numerous examples and applications.

The first half of the book covers core material, including random sampling, expectations, Markov's inequality, Chebyshev's inequality, Chernoff bounds, balls-and-bins models, the probabilistic method, and Markov chains. In the second half, the authors delve into more advanced topics such as continuous probability, applications of limited independence, entropy, Markov chain Monte Carlo methods, coupling, martingales, and balanced allocations.

This greatly expanded new edition includes several newly added chapters and sections, covering topics including normal distributions, sample complexity, VC dimension, Rademacher complexity, power laws and related distributions, cuckoo hashing, and applications of the Lovász Local Lemma. New material relevant to machine learning and big data analysis enables students to learn up-to-date techniques and applications. Among the many new exercises and examples are programming-related exercises that provide students with practical experience and training related to the theoretical concepts covered in the text.

Michael Mitzenmacher is a Professor of Computer Science in the School of Engineering and Applied Sciences at Harvard University, where he was also the Area Dean for Computer Science from 2010 to 2013. Michael has authored or co-authored over 200 conference and journal publications on a variety of topics, including algorithms for the Internet, efficient hash-based data structures, erasure and error-correcting codes, power laws, and compression. His work on low-density parity-check codes shared the 2002 IEEE Information Theory Society Best Paper Award and won the 2009 ACM SIGCOMM Test of Time Award. He is an ACM Fellow, and was elected as the Chair of the ACM Special Interest Group on Algorithms and Computation Theory in 2015.

Eli Upfal is a Professor of Computer Science at Brown University, where he was also the department chair from 2002 to 2007. Prior to joining Brown in 1998, he was a researcher and project manager at the IBM Almaden Research Center, and a Professor of Applied Mathematics and Computer Science at the Weizmann Institute of Science. His main research interests are randomized algorithms, probabilistic analysis of algorithms, and computational statistics, with applications ranging from combinatorial and stochastic optimization, computational biology, and computational finance. He is a Fellow of both the IEEE and the ACM.

Probability and Computing

Randomization and Probabilistic Techniques in Algorithms and Data Analysis

Second Edition

Michael Mitzenmacher   Eli Upfal

CAMBRIDGE UNIVERSITY PRESS

Shaftesbury Road, Cambridge CB2 8EA, United Kingdom

One Liberty Plaza, 20th Floor, New York, NY 10006, USA

477 Williamstown Road, Port Melbourne, VIC 3207, Australia

314–321, 3rd Floor, Plot 3, Splendor Forum, Jasola District Centre, New Delhi – 110025, India

103 Penang Road, #05–06/07, Visioncrest Commercial, Singapore 238467

Cambridge University Press is part of Cambridge University Press & Assessment,
a department of the University of Cambridge.

We share the University's mission to contribute to society through the pursuit of
education, learning and research at the highest international levels of excellence.

www.cambridge.org
Information on this title: www.cambridge.org/9781107154889

10.1017/9781316651124

First published 2017
7th printing 2022

A catalogue record for this publication is available from the British Library

Library of Congress Cataloging-in-Publication data
Names: Mitzenmacher, Michael, 1969– author. | Upfal, Eli, 1954– author.
Title: Probability and computing / Michael Mitzenmacher Eli Upfal.
Description: Second edition. | Cambridge, United Kingdom ;
New York, NY, USA : Cambridge University Press, [2017] |
Includes bibliographical references and index.
Identifiers: LCCN 2016041654 | ISBN 9781107154889
Subjects: LCSH: Algorithms. | Probabilities. | Stochastic analysis.
Classification: LCC QA274.M574 2017 | DDC 518/.1 – dc23
LC record available at https://lccn.loc.gov/2016041654

ISBN   978-1-107-15488-9   Hardback

Additional resources for this publication at www.cambridge.org/Mitzenmacher.

To

Stephanie, Michaela, Jacqueline, and Chloe
M.M.

Liane, Tamara, and Ilan
E.U.

Contents

Note: Asterisks indicate advanced material for this chapter.

Preface to the Second Edition

In the ten years since the publication of the first edition of this book, probabilistic methods have become even more central to computer science, rising with the growing importance of massive data analysis, machine learning, and data mining. Many of the successful applications of these areas rely on algorithms and heuristics that build on sophisticated probabilistic and statistical insights. Judicious use of these tools requires a thorough understanding of the underlying mathematical concepts. Most of the new material in this second edition focuses on these concepts.

The ability in recent years to create, collect, and store massive data sets, such as the World Wide Web, social networks, and genome data, lead to new challenges in modeling and analyzing such structures. A good foundation for models and analysis comes from understanding some standard distributions. Our new chapter on the normal distribution (also known as the Gaussian distribution) covers the most common statistical distribution, as usual with an emphasis on how it is used in settings in computer science, such as for tail bounds. However, an interesting phenomenon is that in many modern data sets, including social networks and the World Wide Web, we do not see normal distributions, but instead we see distributions with very different properties, most notably unusually heavy tails. For example, some pages in the World Wide Web have an unusually large number of pages that link to them, orders of magnitude larger than the average. The new chapter on power laws and related distributions covers specific distributions that are important for modeling and understanding these kinds of modern data sets.

Machine learning is one of the great successes of computer science in recent years, providing efficient tools for modeling, understanding, and making predictions based on large data sets. A question that is often overlooked in practical applications of machine learning is the accuracy of the predictions, and in particular the relation between accuracy and the sample size. A rigorous introduction to approaches to these important questions is presented in a new chapter on sample complexity, VC dimension, and Rademacher averages.

We have also used the new edition to enhance some of our previous material. For example, we present some of the recent advances on algorithmic variations of the powerful Lovász local lemma, and we have a new section covering the wonderfully named and increasingly useful hashing approach known as cuckoo hashing. Finally, in addition to all of this new material, the new edition includes updates and corrections, and many new exercises.

We thank the many readers who sent us corrections over the years – unfortunately, too many to list here!

Preface to the First Edition

Why Randomness?

Why should computer scientists study and use randomness? Computers appear to behave far too unpredictably as it is! Adding randomness would seemingly be a disadvantage, adding further complications to the already challenging task of efficiently utilizing computers.

Science has learned in the last century to accept randomness as an essential component in modeling and analyzing nature. In physics, for example, Newton's laws led people to believe that the universe was a deterministic place; given a big enough calculator and the appropriate initial conditions, one could determine the location of planets years from now. The development of quantum theory suggests a rather different view; the universe still behaves according to laws, but the backbone of these laws is probabilistic. "God does not play dice with the universe" was Einstein's anecdotal objection to modern quantum mechanics. Nevertheless, the prevailing theory today for subparticle physics is based on random behavior and statistical laws, and randomness plays a significant role in almost every other field of science ranging from genetics and evolution in biology to modeling price fluctuations in a free-market economy.

Computer science is no exception. From the highly theoretical notion of probabilistic theorem proving to the very practical design of PC Ethernet cards, randomness and probabilistic methods play a key role in modern computer science. The last two decades have witnessed a tremendous growth in the use of probability theory in computing. Increasingly more advanced and sophisticated probabilistic techniques have been developed for use within broader and more challenging computer science applications. In this book, we study the fundamental ways in which randomness comes to bear on computer science: randomized algorithms and the probabilistic analysis of algorithms.

Randomized algorithms: Randomized algorithms are algorithms that make random choices during their execution. In practice, a randomized program would use values generated by a random number generator to decide the next step at several branches of its execution. For example, the protocol implemented in an Ethernet card uses random numbers to decide when it next tries to access the shared Ethernet communication medium. The randomness is useful for breaking symmetry, preventing different cards from repeatedly accessing the medium at the same time. Other commonly used applications of randomized algorithms include Monte Carlo simulations and primality testing in cryptography. In these and many other important applications, randomized algorithms are significantly more efficient than the best known deterministic solutions. Furthermore, in most cases the randomized algorithms are also simpler and easier to program.

These gains come at a price; the answer may have some probability of being incorrect, or the efficiency is guaranteed only with some probability. Although it may seem unusual to design an algorithm that may be incorrect, if the probability of error is sufficiently small then the improvement in speed or memory requirements may well be worthwhile.

Probabilistic analysis of algorithms: Complexity theory tries to classify computation problems according to their computational complexity, in particular distinguishing between easy and hard problems. For example, complexity theory shows that the Traveling Salesman problem is NP-hard. It is therefore very unlikely that we will ever know an algorithm that can solve any instance of the Traveling Salesman problem in time that is subexponential in the number of cities. An embarrassing phenomenon for the classical worst-case complexity theory is that the problems it classifies as hard to compute are often easy to solve in practice. Probabilistic analysis gives a theoretical explanation for this phenomenon. Although these problems may be hard to solve on some set of pathological inputs, on most inputs (in particular, those that occur in real-life applications) the problem is actually easy to solve. More precisely, if we think of the input as being randomly selected according to some probability distribution on the collection of all possible inputs, we are very likely to obtain a problem instance that is easy to solve, and instances that are hard to solve appear with relatively small probability. Probabilistic analysis of algorithms is the method of studying how algorithms perform when the input is taken from a well-defined probabilistic space. As we will see, even NP-hard problems might have algorithms that are extremely efficient on almost all inputs.

The Book

This textbook is designed to accompany one- or two-semester courses for advanced undergraduate or beginning graduate students in computer science and applied mathematics. The study of randomized and probabilistic techniques in most leading universities has moved from being the subject of an advanced graduate seminar meant for theoreticians to being a regular course geared generally to advanced undergraduate and beginning graduate students. There are a number of excellent advanced, research-oriented books on this subject, but there is a clear need for an introductory textbook. We hope that our book satisfies this need.

The textbook has developed from courses on probabilistic methods in computer science taught at Brown (CS 155) and Harvard (CS 223) in recent years. The emphasis in these courses and in this textbook is on the probabilistic techniques and paradigms, not on particular applications. Each chapter of the book is devoted to one such method or technique. Techniques are clarified though examples based on analyzing randomized algorithms or developing probabilistic analysis of algorithms on random inputs. Many of these examples are derived from problems in networking, reflecting a prominent trend in the networking field (and the taste of the authors).

The book contains fourteen chapters. We may view the book as being divided into two parts, where the first part (Chapters 1–7) comprises what we believe is core material. The book assumes only a basic familiarity with probability theory, equivalent to what is covered in a standard course on discrete mathematics for computer scientists. Chapters 1–3 review this elementary probability theory while introducing some interesting applications. Topics covered include random sampling, expectation, Markov's inequality, variance, and Chebyshev's inequality. If the class has sufficient background in probability, then these chapters can be taught quickly. We do not suggest skipping them, however, because they introduce the concepts of randomized algorithms and probabilistic analysis of algorithms and also contain several examples that are used throughout the text.

Chapters 4–7 cover more advanced topics, including Chernoff bounds, balls-and-bins models, the probabilistic method, and Markov chains. The material in these chapters is more challenging than in the initial chapters. Sections that are particularly challenging (and hence that the instructor may want to consider skipping) are marked with an asterisk. The core material in the first seven chapters may constitute the bulk of a quarter- or semester-long course, depending on the pace.

The second part of the book (Chapters 8–17) covers additional advanced material that can be used either to fill out the basic course as necessary or for a more advanced second course. These chapters are largely self-contained, so the instructor can choose the topics best suited to the class. The chapters on continuous probability and entropy are perhaps the most appropriate for incorporating into the basic course. Our introduction to continuous probability (Chapter 8) focuses on uniform and exponential distributions, including examples from queueing theory. Our examination of entropy (Chapter 10) shows how randomness can be measured and how entropy arises naturally in the context of randomness extraction, compression, and coding.

Chapters 11 and 12 cover the Monte Carlo method and coupling, respectively; these chapters are closely related and are best taught together. Chapter 13, on martingales, covers important issues on dealing with dependent random variables, a theme that continues in a different vein in Chapter 15 is the development of pairwise independence and derandomization. Finally, the chapter on balanced allocations (Chapter 17) covers a topic close to the authors' hearts and ties in nicely with Chapter 5 concerning analysis of balls-and-bins problems.

The order of the subjects, especially in the first part of the book, corresponds to their relative importance in the algorithmic literature. Thus, for example, the study of Chernoff bounds precedes more fundamental probability concepts such as Markov chains. However, instructors may choose to teach the chapters in a different order. A course with more emphasis on general stochastic processes, for example, may teach Markov chains (Chapter 7) immediately after Chapters 1–3, following with the chapter on balls, bins, and random graphs (Chapter 5, omitting the Hamiltonian cycle example). Chapter 6 on the probabilistic method could then be skipped, following instead with continuous probability and the Poisson process (Chapter 8). The material from Chapter 4 on Chernoff bounds, however, is needed for most of the remaining material.

Most of the exercises in the book are theoretical, but we have included some programming exercises – including two more extensive exploratory assignments that require some programming. We have found that occasional programming exercises are often helpful in reinforcing the book's ideas and in adding some variety to the course.

We have decided to restrict the material in this book to methods and techniques based on rigorous mathematical analysis; with few exceptions, all claims in this book are followed by full proofs. Obviously, many extremely useful probabilistic methods do not fall within this strict category. For example, in the important area of Monte Carlo methods, most practical solutions are heuristics that have been demonstrated to be effective and efficient by experimental evaluation rather than by rigorous mathematical analysis. We have taken the view that, in order to best apply and understand the strengths and weaknesses of heuristic methods, a firm grasp of underlying probability theory and rigorous techniques – as we present in this book – is necessary. We hope that students will appreciate this point of view by the end of the course.

Acknowledgments

Our first thanks go to the many probabilists and computer scientists who developed the beautiful material covered in this book. We chose not to overload the textbook with numerous references to the original papers. Instead, we provide a reference list that includes a number of excellent books giving background material as well as more advanced discussion of the topics covered here.

The book owes a great deal to the comments and feedback of students and teaching assistants who took the courses CS 155 at Brown and CS 223 at Harvard. In particular we wish to thank Aris Anagnostopoulos, Eden Hochbaum, Rob Hunter, and Adam Kirsch, all of whom read and commented on early drafts of the book.

Special thanks to Dick Karp, who used a draft of the book in teaching CS 174 at Berkeley during fall 2003. His early comments and corrections were most valuable in improving the manuscript. Peter Bartlett taught CS 174 at Berkeley in spring 2004, also providing many corrections and useful comments.

We thank our colleagues who carefully read parts of the manuscript, pointed out many errors, and suggested important improvements in content and presentation: Artur Czumaj, Alan Frieze, Claire Kenyon, Joe Marks, Salil Vadhan, Eric Vigoda, and the anonymous reviewers who read the manuscript for the publisher.

We also thank Rajeev Motwani and Prabhakar Raghavan for allowing us to use some of the exercises in their excellent book *Randomized Algorithms*.

We are grateful to Lauren Cowles of Cambridge University Press for her editorial help and advice in preparing and organizing the manuscript.

Writing of this book was supported in part by NSF ITR Grant no. CCR-0121154.

CHAPTER ONE

Events and Probability

This chapter introduces the notion of randomized algorithms and reviews some basic concepts of probability theory in the context of analyzing the performance of simple randomized algorithms for verifying algebraic identities and finding a minimum cut-set in a graph.

1.1. Application: Verifying Polynomial Identities

Computers can sometimes make mistakes, due for example to incorrect programming or hardware failure. It would be useful to have simple ways to double-check the results of computations. For some problems, we can use randomness to efficiently verify the correctness of an output.

Suppose we have a program that multiplies together monomials. Consider the problem of verifying the following identity, which might be output by our program:

$$(x+1)(x-2)(x+3)(x-4)(x+5)(x-6) \stackrel{?}{\equiv} x^6 - 7x^3 + 25.$$

There is an easy way to verify whether the identity is correct: multiply together the terms on the left-hand side and see if the resulting polynomial matches the right-hand side. In this example, when we multiply all the constant terms on the left, the result does not match the constant term on the right, so the identity cannot be valid. More generally, given two polynomials $F(x)$ and $G(x)$, we can verify the identity

$$F(x) \stackrel{?}{\equiv} G(x)$$

by converting the two polynomials to their canonical forms $\left(\sum_{i=0}^{d} c_i x^i \right)$; two polynomials are equivalent if and only if all the coefficients in their canonical forms are equal. From this point on let us assume that, as in our example, $F(x)$ is given as a product $F(x) = \prod_{i=1}^{d}(x - a_i)$ and $G(x)$ is given in its canonical form. Transforming $F(x)$ to its canonical form by consecutively multiplying the ith monomial with the product of

1

the first $i - 1$ monomials requires $\Theta(d^2)$ multiplications of coefficients. We assume in what follows that each multiplication can be performed in constant time, although if the products of the coefficients grow large then it could conceivably require more than constant time to add and multiply numbers together.

So far, we have not said anything particularly interesting. To check whether the computer program has multiplied monomials together correctly, we have suggested multiplying the monomials together again to check the result. Our approach for checking the program is to write another program that does essentially the same thing we expect the first program to do. This is certainly one way to double-check a program: write a second program that does the same thing, and make sure they agree. There are at least two problems with this approach, both stemming from the idea that there should be a difference between checking a given answer and recomputing it. First, if there is a bug in the program that multiplies monomials, the same bug may occur in the checking program. (Suppose that the checking program was written by the same person who wrote the original program!) Second, it stands to reason that we would like to check the answer in less time than it takes to try to solve the original problem all over again.

Let us instead utilize randomness to obtain a faster method to verify the identity. We informally explain the algorithm and then set up the formal mathematical framework for analyzing the algorithm.

Assume that the maximum degree, or the largest exponent of x, in $F(x)$ and $G(x)$ is d. The algorithm chooses an integer r uniformly at random in the range $\{1, \ldots, 100d\}$, where by "uniformly at random" we mean that all integers are equally likely to be chosen. The algorithm then computes the values $F(r)$ and $G(r)$. If $F(r) \neq G(r)$ the algorithm decides that the two polynomials are not equivalent, and if $F(r) = G(r)$ the algorithm decides that the two polynomials are equivalent.

Suppose that in one computation step the algorithm can generate an integer chosen uniformly at random in the range $\{1, \ldots, 100d\}$. Computing the values of $F(r)$ and $G(r)$ can be done in $O(d)$ time, which is faster than computing the canonical form of $F(r)$. The randomized algorithm, however, may give a wrong answer.

How can the algorithm give the wrong answer?

If $F(x) \equiv G(x)$, then the algorithm gives the correct answer, since it will find that $F(r) = G(r)$ for any value of r.

If $F(x) \not\equiv G(x)$ and $F(r) \neq G(r)$, then the algorithm gives the correct answer since it has found a case where $F(x)$ and $G(x)$ disagree. Thus, when the algorithm decides that the two polynomials are not the same, the answer is always correct.

If $F(x) \not\equiv G(x)$ and $F(r) = G(r)$, the algorithm gives the wrong answer. In other words, it is possible that the algorithm decides that the two polynomials are the same when they are not. For this error to occur, r must be a root of the equation $F(x) - G(x) = 0$. The degree of the polynomial $F(x) - G(x)$ is no larger than d and, by the fundamental theorem of algebra, a polynomial of degree up to d has no more than d roots. Thus, if $F(x) \not\equiv G(x)$, then there are no more than d values in the range $\{1, \ldots, 100d\}$ for which $F(r) = G(r)$. Since there are $100d$ values in the range $\{1, \ldots, 100d\}$, the chance that the algorithm chooses such a value and returns a wrong answer is no more than $1/100$.

2

1.2. Axioms of Probability

We turn now to a formal mathematical setting for analyzing the randomized algorithm. Any probabilistic statement must refer to the underlying probability space.

Definition 1.1: *A probability space has three components:*

1. *a sample space Ω, which is the set of all possible outcomes of the random process modeled by the probability space;*
2. *a family of sets $\mathcal{F}$ representing the allowable events, where each set in $\mathcal{F}$ is a subset[1] of the sample space Ω; and*
3. *a probability function $\Pr : \mathcal{F} \to \mathbf{R}$ satisfying Definition 1.2.*

An element of Ω is called a *simple* or *elementary* event.

In the randomized algorithm for verifying polynomial identities, the sample space is the set of integers $\{1, \ldots, 100d\}$. Each choice of an integer r in this range is a simple event.

Definition 1.2: *A probability function is any function $\Pr : \mathcal{F} \to \mathbf{R}$ that satisfies the following conditions:*

1. *for any event E, $0 \leq \Pr(E) \leq 1$;*
2. *$\Pr(\Omega) = 1$; and*
3. *for any finite or countably infinite sequence of pairwise mutually disjoint events $E_1, E_2, E_3, \ldots,$*

$$\Pr\left(\bigcup_{i \geq 1} E_i\right) = \sum_{i \geq 1} \Pr(E_i).$$

In most of this book we will use *discrete* probability spaces. In a discrete probability space the sample space Ω is finite or countably infinite, and the family $\mathcal{F}$ of allowable events consists of all subsets of Ω. In a discrete probability space, the probability function is uniquely defined by the probabilities of the simple events.

Again, in the randomized algorithm for verifying polynomial identities, each choice of an integer r is a simple event. Since the algorithm chooses the integer uniformly at random, all simple events have equal probability. The sample space has $100d$ simple events, and the sum of the probabilities of all simple events must be 1. Therefore each simple event has probability $1/100d$.

Because events are sets, we use standard set theory notation to express combinations of events. We write $E_1 \cap E_2$ for the occurrence of both E_1 and E_2 and write $E_1 \cup E_2$ for the occurrence of either E_1 or E_2 (or both). For example, suppose we roll two dice. If E_1 is the event that the first die is a 1 and E_2 is the event that the second die is a 1, then $E_1 \cap E_2$ denotes the event that both dice are 1 while $E_1 \cup E_2$ denotes the event that at least one of the two dice lands on 1. Similarly, we write $E_1 - E_2$ for the occurrence

---

[1] In a discrete probability space $\mathcal{F} = 2^{\Omega}$. Otherwise, and introductory readers may skip this point, since the events need to be measurable, $\mathcal{F}$ must include the empty set and be closed under complement and union and intersection of countably many sets (a σ-algebra).

3

of an event that is in E_1 but not in E_2. With the same dice example, $E_1 - E_2$ consists of the event where the first die is a 1 and the second die is not. We use the notation $\bar{E}$ as shorthand for $\Omega - E$; for example, if E is the event that we obtain an even number when rolling a die, then $\bar{E}$ is the event that we obtain an odd number.

Definition 1.2 yields the following obvious lemma.

Lemma 1.1: *For any two events E_1 and E_2,*

$$\Pr(E_1 \cup E_2) = \Pr(E_1) + \Pr(E_2) - \Pr(E_1 \cap E_2).$$

Proof: From the definition,

$$\Pr(E_1) = \Pr(E_1 - (E_1 \cap E_2)) + \Pr(E_1 \cap E_2),$$
$$\Pr(E_2) = \Pr(E_2 - (E_1 \cap E_2)) + \Pr(E_1 \cap E_2),$$
$$\Pr(E_1 \cup E_2) = \Pr(E_1 - (E_1 \cap E_2)) + \Pr(E_2 - (E_1 \cap E_2)) + \Pr(E_1 \cap E_2).$$

The lemma easily follows. ■

A consequence of Definition 1.2 is known as the *union bound*. Although it is very simple, it is tremendously useful.

Lemma 1.2: *For any finite or countably infinite sequence of events $E_1, E_2, \ldots,$*

$$\Pr\left(\bigcup_{i \geq 1} E_i\right) \leq \sum_{i \geq 1} \Pr(E_i).$$

Notice that Lemma 1.2 differs from the third part of Definition 1.2 in that Definition 1.2 is an equality and requires the events to be pairwise mutually disjoint.

Lemma 1.1 can be generalized to the following equality, often referred to as the *inclusion–exclusion principle*.

Lemma 1.3: *Let $E_1, \ldots, E_n$ be any n events. Then*

$$\Pr\left(\bigcup_{i=1}^{n} E_i\right) = \sum_{i=1}^{n} \Pr(E_i) - \sum_{i<j} \Pr(E_i \cap E_j) + \sum_{i<j<k} \Pr(E_i \cap E_j \cap E_k)$$
$$- \cdots + (-1)^{\ell+1} \sum_{i_1 < i_2 < \cdots < i_\ell} \Pr\left(\bigcap_{r=1}^{\ell} E_{i_r}\right) + \cdots.$$

The proof of the inclusion–exclusion principle is left as Exercise 1.7.

We showed before that the only case in which the algorithm may fail to give the correct answer is when the two input polynomials $F(x)$ and $G(x)$ are not equivalent; the algorithm then gives an incorrect answer if the random number it chooses is a root of the polynomial $F(x) - G(x)$. Let E represent the event that the algorithm failed to give the correct answer. The elements of the set corresponding to E are the roots of the polynomial $F(x) - G(x)$ that are in the set of integers $\{1, \ldots, 100d\}$. Since the polynomial has no more than d roots it follows that the event E includes no more than

d simple events, and therefore

$$\Pr(\text{algorithm fails}) = \Pr(E) \le \frac{d}{100d} = \frac{1}{100}.$$

It may seem unusual to have an algorithm that can return the wrong answer. It may help to think of the correctness of an algorithm as a goal that we seek to optimize in conjunction with other goals. In designing an algorithm, we generally seek to minimize the number of computational steps and the memory required. Sometimes there is a trade-off; there may be a faster algorithm that uses more memory or a slower algorithm that uses less memory. The randomized algorithm we have presented gives a trade-off between correctness and speed. Allowing algorithms that may give an incorrect answer (but in a systematic way) expands the trade-off space available in designing algorithms. Rest assured, however, that not all randomized algorithms give incorrect answers, as we shall see.

For the algorithm just described, the algorithm gives the correct answer 99% of the time even when the polynomials are not equivalent. Can we improve this probability? One way is to choose the random number r from a larger range of integers. If our sample space is the set of integers $\{1, \ldots, 1000d\}$, then the probability of a wrong answer is at most $1/1000$. At some point, however, the range of values we can use is limited by the precision available on the machine on which we run the algorithm.

Another approach is to repeat the algorithm multiple times, using different random values to test the identity. The property we use here is that the algorithm has a *one-sided error*. The algorithm may be wrong only when it outputs that the two polynomials are equivalent. If any run yields a number r such that $F(r) \ne G(r)$, then the polynomials are not equivalent. Thus, if we repeat the algorithm a number of times and find $F(r) \ne G(r)$ in at least one round of the algorithm, we know that $F(x)$ and $G(x)$ are not equivalent. The algorithm outputs that the two polynomials are equivalent only if there is equality for all runs.

In repeating the algorithm we repeatedly choose a random number in the range $\{1, \ldots, 100d\}$. Repeatedly choosing random numbers according to a given distribution is generally referred to as *sampling*. In this case, we can repeatedly choose random numbers in the range $\{1, \ldots, 100d\}$ in two ways: we can sample either *with replacement* or *without replacement*. Sampling with replacement means that we do not remember which numbers we have already tested; each time we run the algorithm, we choose a number uniformly at random from the range $\{1, \ldots, 100d\}$ regardless of previous choices, so there is some chance we will choose an r that we have chosen on a previous run. Sampling without replacement means that, once we have chosen a number r, we do not allow the number to be chosen on subsequent runs; the number chosen at a given iteration is uniform over all previously unselected numbers.

Let us first consider the case where sampling is done with replacement. Assume that we repeat the algorithm k times, and that the input polynomials are not equivalent. What is the probability that in all k iterations our random sampling from the set $\{1, \ldots, 100d\}$ yields roots of the polynomial $F(x) - G(x)$, resulting in a wrong output by the algorithm? If $k = 1$, we know that this probability is at most $d/100d = 1/100$.

5

If $k = 2$, it seems that the probability that the first iteration finds a root is at most $1/100$ and the probability that the second iteration finds a root is at most $1/100$, so the probability that both iterations find a root is at most $(1/100)^2$. Generalizing, for any k, the probability of choosing roots for k iterations would be at most $(1/100)^k$.

To formalize this, we introduce the notion of *independence*.

Definition 1.3: *Two events E and F are independent if and only if*

$$\Pr(E \cap F) = \Pr(E) \cdot \Pr(F).$$

More generally, events $E_1, E_2, \ldots, E_k$ are mutually independent if and only if, for any subset $I \subseteq [1, k]$,

$$\Pr\left(\bigcap_{i \in I} E_i\right) = \prod_{i \in I} \Pr(E_i).$$

If our algorithm samples with replacement then in each iteration the algorithm chooses a random number uniformly at random from the set $\{1, \ldots, 100d\}$, and thus the choice in one iteration is independent of the choices in previous iterations. For the case where the polynomials are not equivalent, let E_i be the event that, on the ith run of the algorithm, we choose a root r_i such that $F(r_i) - G(r_i) = 0$. The probability that the algorithm returns the wrong answer is given by

$$\Pr(E_1 \cap E_2 \cap \cdots \cap E_k).$$

Since $\Pr(E_i)$ is at most $d/100d$ and since the events $E_1, E_2, \ldots, E_k$ are independent, the probability that the algorithm gives the wrong answer after k iterations is

$$\Pr(E_1 \cap E_2 \cap \cdots \cap E_k) = \prod_{i=1}^{k} \Pr(E_i) \leq \prod_{i=1}^{k} \frac{d}{100d} = \left(\frac{1}{100}\right)^k.$$

The probability of making an error is therefore at most exponentially small in the number of trials.

Now let us consider the case where sampling is done without replacement. In this case the probability of choosing a given number is *conditioned* on the events of the previous iterations.

Definition 1.4: *The conditional probability that event E occurs given that event F occurs is*

$$\Pr(E \mid F) = \frac{\Pr(E \cap F)}{\Pr(F)}.$$

The conditional probability is well-defined only if $\Pr(F) > 0$.

Intuitively, we are looking for the probability of $E \cap F$ within the set of events defined by F. Because F defines our restricted sample space, we normalize the probabilities by dividing by $\Pr(F)$, so that the sum of the probabilities of all events is 1. When $\Pr(F) > 0$, the definition can also be written in the useful form

$$\Pr(E \mid F) \Pr(F) = \Pr(E \cap F).$$

Notice that, when E and F are independent and $\Pr(F) \neq 0$, we have

$$\Pr(E \mid F) = \frac{\Pr(E \cap F)}{\Pr(F)} = \frac{\Pr(E) \Pr(F)}{\Pr(F)} = \Pr(E).$$

This is a property that conditional probability should have; intuitively, if two events are independent, then information about one event should not affect the probability of the second event.

Again assume that we repeat the algorithm k times and that the input polynomials are not equivalent. What is the probability that in all the k iterations our random sampling from the set $\{1, \ldots, 100d\}$ yields roots of the polynomial $F(x) - G(x)$, resulting in a wrong output by the algorithm?

As in the analysis with replacement, we let E_i be the event that the random number r_i chosen in the ith iteration of the algorithm is a root of $F(x) - G(x)$; again, the probability that the algorithm returns the wrong answer is given by

$$\Pr(E_1 \cap E_2 \cap \cdots \cap E_k).$$

Applying the definition of conditional probability, we obtain

$$\Pr(E_1 \cap E_2 \cap \cdots \cap E_k) = \Pr(E_k \mid E_1 \cap E_2 \cap \cdots \cap E_{k-1}) \cdot \Pr(E_1 \cap E_2 \cap \cdots \cap E_{k-1}),$$

and repeating this argument gives

$$\begin{aligned}
\Pr(E_1 &\cap E_2 \cap \cdots \cap E_k) \\
&= \Pr(E_1) \cdot \Pr(E_2 \mid E_1) \cdot \Pr(E_3 \mid E_1 \cap E_2) \cdots \Pr(E_k \mid E_1 \cap E_2 \cap \cdots \cap E_{k-1}).
\end{aligned}$$

Can we bound $\Pr(E_j \mid E_1 \cap E_2 \cap \cdots \cap E_{j-1})$? Recall that there are at most d values r for which $F(r) - G(r) = 0$; if trials 1 through $j - 1 < d$ have found $j - 1$ of them, then when sampling without replacement there are only $d - (j - 1)$ values out of the $100d - (j - 1)$ remaining choices for which $F(r) - G(r) = 0$. Hence

$$\Pr(E_j \mid E_1 \cap E_2 \cap \cdots \cap E_{j-1}) \leq \frac{d - (j - 1)}{100d - (j - 1)},$$

and the probability that the algorithm gives the wrong answer after $k \leq d$ iterations is bounded by

$$\Pr(E_1 \cap E_2 \cap \cdots \cap E_k) \leq \prod_{j=1}^{k} \frac{d - (j - 1)}{100d - (j - 1)} \leq \left(\frac{1}{100}\right)^k.$$

Because $(d - (j - 1))/(100d - (j - 1)) < d/100d$ when $j > 1$, our bounds on the probability of making an error are actually slightly better without replacement. You may also notice that, if we take $d + 1$ samples without replacement and the two polynomials are not equivalent, then we are guaranteed to find an r such that $F(r) - G(r) \neq 0$. Thus, in $d + 1$ iterations we are guaranteed to output the correct answer. However, computing the value of the polynomial at $d + 1$ points takes $\Theta(d^2)$ time using the standard approach, which is no faster than finding the canonical form deterministically.

Since sampling without replacement appears to give better bounds on the probability of error, why would we ever want to consider sampling *with* replacement? In some cases, sampling with replacement is significantly easier to analyze, so it may be worth considering for theoretical reasons. In practice, sampling with replacement is often simpler to code and the effect on the probability of making an error is almost negligible, making it a desirable alternative.

1.3. Application: Verifying Matrix Multiplication

We now consider another example where randomness can be used to verify an equality more quickly than the known deterministic algorithms. Suppose we are given three $n \times n$ matrices $\mathbf{A}$, $\mathbf{B}$, and $\mathbf{C}$. For convenience, assume we are working over the integers modulo 2. We want to verify whether

$$\mathbf{AB} = \mathbf{C}.$$

One way to accomplish this is to multiply $\mathbf{A}$ and $\mathbf{B}$ and compare the result to $\mathbf{C}$. The simple matrix multiplication algorithm takes $\Theta(n^3)$ operations. There exist more sophisticated algorithms that are known to take roughly $\Theta(n^{2.37})$ operations.

Once again, we use a randomized algorithm that allows for faster verification – at the expense of possibly returning a wrong answer with small probability. The algorithm is similar in spirit to our randomized algorithm for checking polynomial identities. The algorithm chooses a random vector $\bar{r} = (r_1, r_2, \ldots, r_n) \in \{0, 1\}^n$. It then computes $\mathbf{AB}\bar{r}$ by first computing $\mathbf{B}\bar{r}$ and then $\mathbf{A}(\mathbf{B}\bar{r})$, and it also computes $\mathbf{C}\bar{r}$. If $\mathbf{A}(\mathbf{B}\bar{r}) \neq \mathbf{C}\bar{r}$, then $\mathbf{AB} \neq \mathbf{C}$. Otherwise, it returns that $\mathbf{AB} = \mathbf{C}$.

The algorithm requires three matrix-vector multiplications, which can be done in time $\Theta(n^2)$ in the obvious way. The probability that the algorithm returns that $\mathbf{AB} = \mathbf{C}$ when they are actually not equal is bounded by the following theorem.

Theorem 1.4: *If $\mathbf{AB} \neq \mathbf{C}$ and if $\bar{r}$ is chosen uniformly at random from $\{0, 1\}^n$, then*

$$\Pr(\mathbf{AB}\bar{r} = \mathbf{C}\bar{r}) \leq \frac{1}{2}.$$

Proof: Before beginning, we point out that the sample space for the vector $\bar{r}$ is the set $\{0, 1\}^n$ and that the event under consideration is $\mathbf{AB}\bar{r} = \mathbf{C}\bar{r}$. We also make note of the following simple but useful lemma.

Lemma 1.5: *Choosing $\bar{r} = (r_1, r_2, \ldots, r_n) \in \{0, 1\}^n$ uniformly at random is equivalent to choosing each r_i independently and uniformly from $\{0, 1\}$.*

Proof: If each r_i is chosen independently and uniformly at random, then each of the 2^n possible vectors $\bar{r}$ is chosen with probability 2^{-n}, giving the lemma. ∎

Let $\mathbf{D} = \mathbf{AB} - \mathbf{C} \neq 0$. Then $\mathbf{AB}\bar{r} = \mathbf{C}\bar{r}$ implies that $\mathbf{D}\bar{r} = 0$. Since $\mathbf{D} \neq 0$ it must have some nonzero entry; without loss of generality, let that entry be d_{11}.

For $\mathbf{D}\bar{r} = 0$, it must be the case that

$$\sum_{j=1}^{n} d_{1j} r_j = 0$$

or, equivalently,

$$r_1 = -\frac{\sum_{j=2}^{n} d_{1j} r_j}{d_{11}}. \tag{1.1}$$

Now we introduce a helpful idea. Instead of reasoning about the vector $\bar{r}$, suppose that we choose the r_k independently and uniformly at random from $\{0, 1\}$ in order, from r_n down to r_1. Lemma 1.5 says that choosing the r_k in this way is equivalent to choosing a vector $\bar{r}$ uniformly at random. Now consider the situation just before r_1 is chosen. At this point, the right-hand side of Eqn. (1.1) is determined, and there is at most one choice for r_1 that will make that equality hold. Since there are two choices for r_1, the equality holds with probability at most $1/2$, and hence the probability that $\mathbf{AB}\bar{r} = \mathbf{C}\bar{r}$ is at most $1/2$. By considering all variables besides r_1 as having been set, we have reduced the sample space to the set of two values $\{0, 1\}$ for r_1 and have changed the event being considered to whether Eqn. (1.1) holds. ∎

This idea is called the *principle of deferred decisions*. When there are several random variables, such as the r_i of the vector $\bar{r}$, it often helps to think of some of them as being set at one point in the algorithm with the rest of them being left random – or deferred – until some further point in the analysis. Formally, this corresponds to conditioning on the revealed values; when some of the random variables are revealed, we must condition on the revealed values for the rest of the analysis. We will see further examples of the principle of deferred decisions later in the book.

To formalize this argument, we first introduce a simple fact, known as the law of total probability.

Theorem 1.6 [Law of Total Probability]: *Let $E_1, E_2, \ldots, E_n$ be mutually disjoint events in the sample space Ω, and let $\bigcup_{i=1}^{n} E_i = \Omega$. Then*

$$\Pr(B) = \sum_{i=1}^{n} \Pr(B \cap E_i) = \sum_{i=1}^{n} \Pr(B \mid E_i) \Pr(E_i).$$

Proof: Since the events E_i $(i = 1, \ldots, n)$ are disjoint and cover the entire sample space Ω, it follows that

$$\Pr(B) = \sum_{i=1}^{n} \Pr(B \cap E_i).$$

Further,

$$\sum_{i=1}^{n} \Pr(B \cap E_i) = \sum_{i=1}^{n} \Pr(B \mid E_i) \Pr(E_i)$$

by the definition of conditional probability. ∎

Now, using this law and summing over all collections of values $(x_2, x_3, x_4, \ldots, x_n) \in \{0, 1\}^{n-1}$ yields

$$
\begin{aligned}
\Pr(\mathbf{AB}\bar{r} = \mathbf{C}\bar{r}) \\
&= \sum_{(x_2,\ldots,x_n) \in \{0,1\}^{n-1}} \Pr\left((\mathbf{AB}\bar{r} = \mathbf{C}\bar{r}) \cap ((r_2, \ldots, r_n) = (x_2, \ldots, x_n))\right) \\
&\leq \sum_{(x_2,\ldots,x_n) \in \{0,1\}^{n-1}} \Pr\left(\left(r_1 = -\frac{\sum_{j=2}^{n} d_{1j} r_j}{d_{11}}\right) \cap ((r_2, \ldots, r_n) = (x_2, \ldots, x_n))\right) \\
&= \sum_{(x_2,\ldots,x_n) \in \{0,1\}^{n-1}} \Pr\left(r_1 = -\frac{\sum_{j=2}^{n} d_{1j} r_j}{d_{11}}\right) \cdot \Pr((r_2, \ldots, r_n) = (x_2, \ldots, x_n)) \\
&\leq \sum_{(x_2,\ldots,x_n) \in \{0,1\}^{n-1}} \frac{1}{2} \Pr((r_2, \ldots, r_n) = (x_2, \ldots, x_n)) \\
&= \frac{1}{2}.
\end{aligned}
$$

Here we have used the independence of r_1 and $(r_2, \ldots, r_n)$ in the fourth line. ∎

To improve on the error probability of Theorem 1.4, we can again use the fact that the algorithm has a one-sided error and run the algorithm multiple times. If we ever find an $\bar{r}$ such that $\mathbf{AB}\bar{r} \neq \mathbf{C}\bar{r}$, then the algorithm will correctly return that $\mathbf{AB} \neq \mathbf{C}$. If we always find $\mathbf{AB}\bar{r} = \mathbf{C}\bar{r}$, then the algorithm returns that $\mathbf{AB} = \mathbf{C}$ and there is some probability of a mistake. Choosing $\bar{r}$ with replacement from $\{0, 1\}^n$ for each trial, we obtain that, after k trials, the probability of error is at most 2^{-k}. Repeated trials increase the running time to $\Theta(kn^2)$.

Suppose we attempt this verification 100 times. The running time of the randomized checking algorithm is still $\Theta(n^2)$, which is faster than the known deterministic algorithms for matrix multiplication for sufficiently large n. The probability that an incorrect algorithm passes the verification test 100 times is at most 2^{-100}, an astronomically small number. In practice, the computer is much more likely to crash during the execution of the algorithm than to return a wrong answer.

An interesting related problem is to evaluate the gradual change in our confidence in the correctness of the matrix multiplication as we repeat the randomized test. Toward that end we introduce Bayes' law.

Theorem 1.7 [Bayes' Law]: *Assume that $E_1, E_2, \ldots, E_n$ are mutually disjoint events in the sample space Ω such that $\bigcup_{i=1}^{n} E_i = \Omega$. Then*

$$
\Pr(E_j \mid B) = \frac{\Pr(E_j \cap B)}{\Pr(B)} = \frac{\Pr(B \mid E_j) \Pr(E_j)}{\sum_{i=1}^{n} \Pr(B \mid E_i) \Pr(E_i)}.
$$

As a simple application of Bayes' law, consider the following problem. We are given three coins and are told that two of the coins are fair and the third coin is biased, landing heads with probability 2/3. We are not told which of the three coins is biased. We permute the coins randomly, and then flip each of the coins. The first and second coins come up heads, and the third comes up tails. What is the probability that the first coin is the biased one?

The coins are in a random order and so, before our observing the outcomes of the coin flips, each of the three coins is equally likely to be the biased one. Let E_i be the event that the ith coin flipped is the biased one, and let B be the event that the three coin flips came up heads, heads, and tails.

Before we flip the coins we have $\Pr(E_i) = 1/3$ for all i. We can also compute the probability of the event B conditioned on E_i:

$$\Pr(B \mid E_1) = \Pr(B \mid E_2) = \frac{2}{3} \cdot \frac{1}{2} \cdot \frac{1}{2} = \frac{1}{6},$$

and

$$\Pr(B \mid E_3) = \frac{1}{2} \cdot \frac{1}{2} \cdot \frac{1}{3} = \frac{1}{12}.$$

Applying Bayes' law, we have

$$\Pr(E_1 \mid B) = \frac{\Pr(B \mid E_1)\,\Pr(E_1)}{\sum_{i=1}^{3}\Pr(B \mid E_i)\,\Pr(E_i)} = \frac{2}{5}.$$

Thus, the outcome of the three coin flips increases the likelihood that the first coin is the biased one from $1/3$ to $2/5$.

Returning now to our randomized matrix multiplication test, we want to evaluate the increase in confidence in the matrix identity obtained through repeated tests. In the Bayesian approach one starts with a *prior* model, giving some initial value to the model parameters. This model is then modified, by incorporating new observations, to obtain a *posterior* model that captures the new information.

In the matrix multiplication case, if we have no information about the process that generated the identity then a reasonable prior assumption is that the identity is correct with probability $1/2$. If we run the randomized test once and it returns that the matrix identity is correct, how does this change our confidence in the identity?

Let E be the event that the identity is correct, and let B be the event that the test returns that the identity is correct. We start with $\Pr(E) = \Pr(\bar{E}) = 1/2$, and since the test has a one-sided error bounded by $1/2$, we have $\Pr(B \mid E) = 1$ and $\Pr(B \mid \bar{E}) \leq 1/2$. Applying Bayes' law yields

$$\Pr(E \mid B) = \frac{\Pr(B \mid E)\,\Pr(E)}{\Pr(B \mid E)\,\Pr(E) + \Pr(B \mid \bar{E})\,\Pr(\bar{E})} \geq \frac{1/2}{1/2 + 1/2 \cdot 1/2} = \frac{2}{3}.$$

Assume now that we run the randomized test again and it again returns that the identity is correct. After the first test, I may naturally have revised my prior model, so that I believe $\Pr(E) \geq 2/3$ and $\Pr(\bar{E}) \leq 1/3$. Now let B be the event that the new test returns that the identity is correct; since the tests are independent, as before we have $\Pr(B \mid E) = 1$ and $\Pr(B \mid \bar{E}) \leq 1/2$. Applying Bayes' law then yields

$$\Pr(E \mid B) \geq \frac{2/3}{2/3 + 1/3 \cdot 1/2} = \frac{4}{5}.$$

In general: if our prior model (before running the test) is that $\Pr(E) \geq 2^i/(2^i + 1)$ and if the test returns that the identity is correct (event B), then

$$\Pr(E \mid B) \geq \frac{\dfrac{2^i}{2^i + 1}}{\dfrac{2^i}{2^i + 1} + \dfrac{1}{2}\dfrac{1}{2^i + 1}} = \frac{2^{i+1}}{2^{i+1} + 1} = 1 - \frac{1}{2^{i+1} + 1}.$$

Thus, if all 100 calls to the matrix identity test return that the identity is correct, our confidence in the correctness of this identity is at least $1 - 1/(2^{101} + 1)$.

1.4. Application: Naïve Bayesian Classifier

A *naïve Bayesian classifier* is a supervised learning algorithm that classifies objects by estimating conditional probabilities using Bayes' law in a simplified ("naïve") probabilistic model. While the independence assumptions that would justify the approach are significant oversimplifications, this method proves very effective in many practical applications such as subject classification of text documents and junk e-mail filtering. It also provides an example of a deterministic algorithm that is based on the probabilistic concept of conditional probability.

Assume that we are given a collection of n training examples

$$\{(D_1, c(D_1)), (D_2, c(D_2)), \ldots, (D_n, c(D_n))\},$$

where each D_i is represented as a features vector $x^i = (x^i_1, \ldots, x^i_m)$. Here D_i is an object, such as a text document, and an object has features $(X_1, X_2, \ldots, X_m)$, where feature X_j can take a value from a set of possibilities F_j. By $x^i = (x^i_1, \ldots, x^i_m)$ we mean that for D_i we have $X_1 = x^i_1, \ldots, X_m = x^i_m$. For example, if D_i is a text document, and we have a list of important keywords, the X_j could be Boolean features where $x^i_j = 1$ if the jth listed keyword appears in D_i and $x^i_j = 0$ otherwise. In this case, the feature vector of the document would just correspond to the set of keywords it contains. Finally, we have a set $C = \{c_1, c_2, \ldots, c_t\}$ of possible classifications for the object, and $c(D_i)$ is the classification of D_i. For example, the classification set C could be a collection of labels such as {"spam", "no-spam"}. Given a document, corresponding to a web page or e-mail, we might want to classify the document according to the keywords the document contains.

The classification paradigm assumes that the training set is a sample from an unknown distribution in which the classification of an object is a function of the m features. The goal is, given a new document, to return an accurate classification. More generally, we can instead return a vector $(z_1, z_2, \ldots, z_t)$, where z_j is an estimate of the probability that $c(D_i) = c_j$ based on the training set. If we want to return just the most likely classification, we can return the c_j with the highest value of z_j.

Suppose to begin that we had a very, very large training set. Then for each vector $y = (y_1, \ldots, y_m)$ and each classification c_j, we could use the training set to compute the empirical conditional probability that an object with a features vector y is classified C_j:

$$p_{y,j} = \frac{\{|i \ : \ x^i = y, \ c(D_i) = c_j|\}}{\{|i \ : \ x^i = y)|\}}.$$

Assuming that a new object D^* with a features vector x^* has the same distribution as the training set, then $p_{x^*,j}$ is an empirical estimate for the conditional probability

$$\Pr(c(D^*) = c_j \mid x^* = (x_1^*, \ldots, x_m^*)).$$

Indeed, we could compute these values ahead of time in a large lookup table and simply return the vector $(z_1, z_2, \ldots, z_t) = (p_{x^*,1}, p_{x^*,2}, \ldots, p_{x^*,t})$ after computing the features vector x^* from the object.

The difficulty in this approach is that we need to obtain accurate estimates of a large collection of conditional probabilities, corresponding to all possible combination of values of the m features. Even if each feature has just two values we would need to estimate 2^m conditional probabilities per class, which would generally require $\Omega(|C|2^m)$ samples.

The training process is faster and requires significantly fewer examples if we assume a "naïve" model in which the m features are independent. In that case we have for

$$\Pr(c(D^*) = c_j \mid x^*) = \frac{\Pr(x^* \mid c(D^*) = c_j) \cdot \Pr(c(D^*) = c_j)}{\Pr(x^*)} \qquad (1.2)$$

$$= \frac{\prod_{k=1}^m \Pr(x_k^* = x_i \mid c(D^*) = c_j) \cdot \Pr(c(D^*) = c_j)}{\Pr(x^*)}. \qquad (1.3)$$

Here x_k^* is the kth component of the features vector x^* of object D^*. Notice that the denominator is independent of c_j, and can be treated as just a normalizing constant factor.

With a constant number of possible values per feature, we only need to learn estimates for $O(m|C|)$ probabilities. In what follows, we use $\hat{\Pr}$ to denote *empirical probabilities*, which are the relative frequency of events in our training set of examples. This notation emphasizes that we are taking estimates of these probabilities as determined from the training set. (In practice, one often makes slight modifications, such as adding $1/2$ to the numerator in each of the fractions to guarantee that no empirical probability equals 0.)

The training process is simple:

- For each classification class c_j, keep track of the fraction of objects classified as c_j to compute

$$\hat{\Pr}(c(D^*) = c_j) = \frac{|\{i \mid c(D_i) = c_j\}|}{|D|},$$

where $|D|$ is the number of objects in the training set.

- For each feature X_k and feature value x_k keep track of the fraction of objects with that feature value that are classified as c_j, to compute

$$\hat{\Pr}(x_k^* = x_k \mid c(D^*) = c_j) = \frac{|\{i \ : \ x_k^i = x_k, c(D_i) = c_j\}|}{\{i \mid c(D_i) = c_j\}|}.$$

Naïve Bayes Classifier Algorithm

Input: Set of possible classifications C, set of features and feature values $F_1, \ldots, F_m$, and a training set of classified items $\mathcal{D}$.

Training Phase:

1. For each category $c \in C$, feature $k = 1, \ldots, m$, and feature value $x_k \in F_k$ compute

$$\hat{\Pr}(x_k^* = x_k \mid c(D^*) = c) = \frac{|\{i \,:\, x_k^i = x_k, c(D_i) = c\}|}{\{i \mid c(D_i) = c\}|}.$$

2. For each category $c \in C$, compute

$$\hat{\Pr}(c(D^*) = c) = \frac{|\{i \mid c(D_i) = c\}|}{|D|}.$$

Classifying a new item D^*:

1. To compute the most likely classification for $x^* = x = (x_1, \ldots, x_m)$

$$c(D^*) = \arg\max_{c_j \in C} \left(\prod_{k=1}^m \hat{\Pr}(x_k^* = x_k \mid c(D^*) = c_j)\right) \hat{\Pr}(c(D^*) = c_j).$$

2. To compute a classification distribution:

$$\hat{\Pr}(c(D^*) = c_j) = \frac{\left(\prod_{k=1}^m \hat{\Pr}(x_k^* = x_k \mid c(D^*) = c_j)\right) \hat{\Pr}(c(D^*) = c_j)}{\hat{\Pr}(x^* = x)}.$$

Algorithm 1.1: Naïve Bayes Classifier.

Once we train the classifier, the classification of a new object D^* with features vector $x^* = (x_1^*, \ldots, x_m^*)$ is computed by calculating

$$\left(\prod_{k=1}^m \hat{\Pr}(x_k^* = x_k \mid c(D^*) = c_j)\right) \hat{\Pr}(c(D^*) = c_j)$$

for each c_j and taking the classification with the highest value.

In practice, the products may lead to underflow values; an easy solution to that problem is to instead compute the logarithm of the above expression. Estimates of the entire probability vector can be found by normalizing appropriately. (Alternatively, instead of normalizing, one could provide probability estimates by also computing estimates for $\Pr(x^* = x)$ from the sample data. Under our independence assumption $\Pr(x^* = (x_1^*, \ldots, x_m^*)) = \prod_{k=1}^m \Pr(x_k^* = x_k)$, and one could estimate the denominator of Equation 1.2 with the product of the corresponding estimates.)

The naïve Bayesian classifier is efficient and simple to implement due to the "naïve" assumption of independence. This assumption may lead to misleading outcomes when the classification depends on combinations of features. As a simple example consider a collection of items characterized by two Boolean features X and Y. If $X = Y$ the item is in class A, and otherwise it is in class B. Assume further that for each value of X and Y the training set has an equal number of items in each class. All the conditional probabilities computed by the classifier equal 0.5, and therefore the classifier is not better than a coin flip in this example. In practice such phenomena are rare and the naïve Bayesian classifier is often very effective.

1.5. Application: A Randomized Min-Cut Algorithm

A *cut-set* in a graph is a set of edges whose removal breaks the graph into two or more connected components. Given a graph $G = (V, E)$ with n vertices, the minimum cut – or *min-cut* – problem is to find a minimum cardinality cut-set in G. Minimum cut problems arise in many contexts, including the study of network reliability. In the case where nodes correspond to machines in the network and edges correspond to connections between machines, the min-cut is the smallest number of edges that can fail before some pair of machines cannot communicate. Minimum cuts also arise in clustering problems. For example, if nodes represent Web pages (or any documents in a hypertext-based system) and two nodes have an edge between them if the corresponding nodes have a hyperlink between them, then small cuts divide the graph into clusters of documents with few links between clusters. Documents in different clusters are likely to be unrelated.

We shall proceed by making use of the definitions and techniques presented so far in order to analyze a simple randomized algorithm for the min-cut problem. The main operation in the algorithm is *edge contraction*. In contracting an edge (u, v) we merge the two vertices u and v into one vertex, eliminate all edges connecting u and v, and retain all other edges in the graph. The new graph may have parallel edges but no self-loops. Examples appear in Figure 1.1, where in each step the dark edge is being contracted.

The algorithm consists of $n - 2$ iterations. In each iteration, the algorithm picks an edge from the existing edges in the graph and contracts that edge. There are many possible ways one could choose the edge at each step. Our randomized algorithm chooses the edge uniformly at random from the remaining edges.

Each iteration reduces the number of vertices in the graph by one. After $n - 2$ iterations, the graph consists of two vertices. The algorithm outputs the set of edges connecting the two remaining vertices.

It is easy to verify that any cut-set of a graph in an intermediate iteration of the algorithm is also a cut-set of the original graph. On the other hand, not every cut-set of the original graph is a cut-set of a graph in an intermediate iteration, since some edges of the cut-set may have been contracted in previous iterations. As a result, the output of the algorithm is always a cut-set of the original graph but not necessarily the minimum cardinality cut-set (see Figure 1.1).

We now establish a lower bound on the probability that the algorithm returns a correct output.

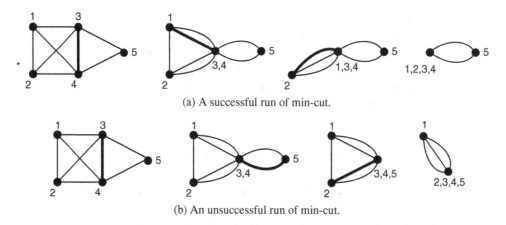

(a) A successful run of min-cut.

(b) An unsuccessful run of min-cut.

Figure 1.1: An example of two executions of min-cut in a graph with minimum cut-set of size 2.

Theorem 1.8: *The algorithm outputs a min-cut set with probability at least* $2/(n(n-1))$.

Proof: Let k be the size of the min-cut set of G. The graph may have several cut-sets of minimum size. We compute the probability of finding one specific such set C.

Since C is a cut-set in the graph, removal of the set C partitions the set of vertices into two sets, S and $V - S$, such that there are no edges connecting vertices in S to vertices in $V - S$. Assume that, throughout an execution of the algorithm, we contract only edges that connect two vertices in S or two vertices in $V - S$, but not edges in C. In that case, all the edges eliminated throughout the execution will be edges connecting vertices in S or vertices in $V - S$, and after $n - 2$ iterations the algorithm returns a graph with two vertices connected by the edges in C. We may therefore conclude that, if the algorithm never chooses an edge of C in its $n - 2$ iterations, then the algorithm returns C as the minimum cut-set.

This argument gives some intuition for why we choose the edge at each iteration uniformly at random from the remaining existing edges. If the size of the cut C is small and if the algorithm chooses the edge uniformly at each step, then the probability that the algorithm chooses an edge of C is small – at least when the number of edges remaining is large compared to C.

Let E_i be the event that the edge contracted in iteration i is not in C, and let $F_i = \bigcap_{j=1}^{i} E_j$ be the event that no edge of C was contracted in the first i iterations. We need to compute $\Pr(F_{n-2})$.

We start by computing $\Pr(E_1) = \Pr(F_1)$. Since the minimum cut-set has k edges, all vertices in the graph must have degree k or larger. If each vertex is adjacent to at least k edges, then the graph must have at least $nk/2$ edges. The first contracted edge is chosen uniformly at random from the set of all edges. Since there are at least $nk/2$ edges in the graph and since C has k edges, the probability that we do not choose an edge of C in the first iteration is given by

$$\Pr(E_1) = \Pr(F_1) \geq 1 - \frac{2k}{nk} = 1 - \frac{2}{n}.$$

16

Let us suppose that the first contraction did not eliminate an edge of C. In other words, we condition on the event F_1. Then, after the first iteration, we are left with an $(n-1)$-node graph with minimum cut-set of size k. Again, the degree of each vertex in the graph must be at least k, and the graph must have at least $k(n-1)/2$ edges. Thus,

$$\Pr(E_2 \mid F_1) \geq 1 - \frac{k}{k(n-1)/2} = 1 - \frac{2}{n-1}.$$

Similarly,

$$\Pr(E_i \mid F_{i-1}) \geq 1 - \frac{k}{k(n-i+1)/2} = 1 - \frac{2}{n-i+1}.$$

To compute $\Pr(F_{n-2})$, we use

$$\begin{aligned}
\Pr(F_{n-2}) &= \Pr(E_{n-2} \cap F_{n-3}) = \Pr(E_{n-2} \mid F_{n-3}) \cdot \Pr(F_{n-3}) \\
&= \Pr(E_{n-2} \mid F_{n-3}) \cdot \Pr(E_{n-3} \mid F_{n-4}) \cdots \Pr(E_2 \mid F_1) \cdot \Pr(F_1) \\
&\geq \prod_{i=1}^{n-2} \left(1 - \frac{2}{n-i+1}\right) = \prod_{i=1}^{n-2} \left(\frac{n-i-1}{n-i+1}\right) \\
&= \left(\frac{n-2}{n}\right)\left(\frac{n-3}{n-1}\right)\left(\frac{n-4}{n-2}\right) \cdots \left(\frac{4}{6}\right)\left(\frac{3}{5}\right)\left(\frac{2}{4}\right)\left(\frac{1}{3}\right) \\
&= \frac{2}{n(n-1)}. \qquad\blacksquare
\end{aligned}$$

Since the algorithm has a one-sided error, we can reduce the error probability by repeating the algorithm. Assume that we run the randomized min-cut algorithm $n(n-1)\ln n$ times and output the minimum size cut-set found in all the iterations. The probability that the output is not a min-cut set is bounded by

$$\left(1 - \frac{2}{n(n-1)}\right)^{n(n-1)\ln n} \leq e^{-2\ln n} = \frac{1}{n^2}.$$

In the first inequality we have used the fact that $1 - x \leq e^{-x}$.

1.6. Exercises

Exercise 1.1: We flip a fair coin ten times. Find the probability of the following events.

(a) The number of heads and the number of tails are equal.
(b) There are more heads than tails.
(c) The ith flip and the $(11-i)$th flip are the same for $i = 1, \ldots, 5$.
(d) We flip at least four consecutive heads.

Exercise 1.2: We roll two standard six-sided dice. Find the probability of the following events, assuming that the outcomes of the rolls are independent.

(a) The two dice show the same number.
(b) The number that appears on the first die is larger than the number on the second.

(c) The sum of the dice is even.

(d) The product of the dice is a perfect square.

Exercise 1.3: We shuffle a standard deck of cards, obtaining a permutation that is uniform over all 52! possible permutations. Find the probability of the following events.

(a) The first two cards include at least one ace.

(b) The first five cards include at least one ace.

(c) The first two cards are a pair of the same rank.

(d) The first five cards are all diamonds.

(e) The first five cards form a full house (three of one rank and two of another rank).

Exercise 1.4: We are playing a tournament in which we stop as soon as one of us wins n games. We are evenly matched, so each of us wins any game with probability $1/2$, independently of other games. What is the probability that the loser has won k games when the match is over?

Exercise 1.5: After lunch one day, Alice suggests to Bob the following method to determine who pays. Alice pulls three six-sided dice from her pocket. These dice are not the standard dice, but have the following numbers on their faces:

- die A – 1, 1, 6, 6, 8, 8;
- die B – 2, 2, 4, 4, 9, 9;
- die C – 3, 3, 5, 5, 7, 7.

The dice are fair, so each side comes up with equal probability. Alice explains that she and Bob will each pick up one of the dice. They will each roll their die, and the one who rolls the lowest number loses and will buy lunch. So as to take no advantage, Alice offers Bob the first choice of the dice.

(a) Suppose that Bob chooses die A and Alice chooses die B. Write out all of the possible events and their probabilities, and show that the probability that Alice wins is greater than $1/2$.

(b) Suppose that Bob chooses die B and Alice chooses die C. Write out all of the possible events and their probabilities, and show that the probability that Alice wins is greater than $1/2$.

(c) Since die A and die B lead to situations in Alice's favor, it would seem that Bob should choose die C. Suppose that Bob does choose die C and Alice chooses die A. Write out all of the possible events and their probabilities, and show that the probability that Alice wins is still greater than $1/2$.

Exercise 1.6: Consider the following balls-and-bin game. We start with one black ball and one white ball in a bin. We repeatedly do the following: choose one ball from the bin uniformly at random, and then put the ball back in the bin with another ball of the same color. We repeat until there are n balls in the bin. Show that the number of white balls is equally likely to be any number between 1 and $n - 1$.

Exercise 1.7: **(a)** Prove Lemma 3, the inclusion–exclusion principle.

(b) Prove that, when ℓ is odd,

$$\Pr\left(\bigcup_{i=1}^{n} E_i\right) \leq \sum_{i=1}^{n} \Pr(E_i) - \sum_{i<j} \Pr(E_i \cap E_j) + \sum_{i<j<k} \Pr(E_i \cap E_j \cap E_k)$$
$$- \cdots + (-1)^{\ell+1} \sum_{i_1 < i_2 < \cdots < i_\ell} \Pr(E_{i_1} \cap \cdots \cap E_{i_\ell}).$$

(c) Prove that, when ℓ is even,

$$\Pr\left(\bigcup_{i=1}^{n} E_i\right) \geq \sum_{i=1}^{n} \Pr(E_i) - \sum_{i<j} \Pr(E_i \cap E_j) + \sum_{i<j<k} \Pr(E_i \cap E_j \cap E_k)$$
$$- \cdots + (-1)^{\ell+1} \sum_{i_1 < i_2 < \cdots < i_\ell} \Pr(E_{i_1} \cap \cdots \cap E_{i_\ell}).$$

Exercise 1.8: I choose a number uniformly at random from the range $[1, 1{,}000{,}000]$. Using the inclusion–exclusion principle, determine the probability that the number chosen is divisible by one or more of 4, 6, and 9.

Exercise 1.9: Suppose that a fair coin is flipped n times. For $k > 0$, find an upper bound on the probability that there is a sequence of $\log_2 n + k$ consecutive heads.

Exercise 1.10: I have a fair coin and a two-headed coin. I choose one of the two coins randomly with equal probability and flip it. Given that the flip was heads, what is the probability that I flipped the two-headed coin?

Exercise 1.11: I am trying to send you a single bit, either a 0 or a 1. When I transmit the bit, it goes through a series of n relays before it arrives to you. Each relay flips the bit independently with probability p.

(a) Argue that the probability you receive the correct bit is

$$\sum_{k=0}^{\lfloor n/2 \rfloor} \binom{n}{2k} p^{2k} (1-p)^{n-2k}.$$

(b) We consider an alternative way to calculate this probability. Let us say the relay has *bias* q if the probability it flips the bit is $(1-q)/2$. The bias q is therefore a real number in the range $[-1, 1]$. Prove that sending a bit through two relays with bias q_1 and q_2 is equivalent to sending a bit through a single relay with bias $q_1 q_2$.

(c) Prove that the probability you receive the correct bit when it passes through n relays as described before (a) is

$$\frac{1 + (1-2p)^n}{2}.$$

Exercise 1.12: The following problem is known as the Monty Hall problem, after the host of the game show "Let's Make a Deal". There are three curtains. Behind one curtain is a new car, and behind the other two are goats. The game is played as follows.

19

The contestant chooses the curtain that she thinks the car is behind. Monty then opens one of the other curtains to show a goat. (Monty may have more than one goat to choose from; in this case, assume he chooses which goat to show uniformly at random.) The contestant can then stay with the curtain she originally chose or switch to the other unopened curtain. After that, the location of the car is revealed, and the contestant wins the car or the remaining goat. Should the contestant switch curtains or not, or does it make no difference?

Exercise 1.13: A medical company touts its new test for a certain genetic disorder. The false negative rate is small: if you have the disorder, the probability that the test returns a positive result is 0.999. The false positive rate is also small: if you do not have the disorder, the probability that the test returns a positive result is only 0.005. Assume that 2% of the population has the disorder. If a person chosen uniformly from the population is tested and the result comes back positive, what is the probability that the person has the disorder?

Exercise 1.14: I am playing in a racquetball tournament, and I am up against a player I have watched but never played before. I consider three possibilities for my prior model: we are equally talented, and each of us is equally likely to win each game; I am slightly better, and therefore I win each game independently with probability 0.6; or he is slightly better, and thus he wins each game independently with probability 0.6. Before we play, I think that each of these three possibilities is equally likely.

In our match we play until one player wins three games. I win the second game, but he wins the first, third, and fourth. After this match, in my posterior model, with what probability should I believe that my opponent is slightly better than I am?

Exercise 1.15: Suppose that we roll ten standard six-sided dice. What is the probability that their sum will be divisible by 6, assuming that the rolls are independent? (*Hint:* Use the principle of deferred decisions, and consider the situation after rolling all but one of the dice.)

Exercise 1.16: Consider the following game, played with three standard six-sided dice. If the player ends with all three dice showing the same number, she wins. The player starts by rolling all three dice. After this first roll, the player can select any one, two, or all of the three dice and re-roll them. After this second roll, the player can again select any of the three dice and re-roll them one final time. For questions (a)–(d), assume that the player uses the following optimal strategy: if all three dice match, the player stops and wins; if two dice match, the player re-rolls the die that does not match; and if no dice match, the player re-rolls them all.

(a) Find the probability that all three dice show the same number on the first roll.
(b) Find the probability that exactly two of the three dice show the same number on the first roll.
(c) Find the probability that the player wins, conditioned on exactly two of the three dice showing the same number on the first roll.

(d) By considering all possible sequences of rolls, find the probability that the player wins the game.

Exercise 1.17: In our matrix multiplication algorithm, we worked over the integers modulo 2. Explain how the analysis would change if we worked over the integers modulo k for $k > 2$.

Exercise 1.18: We have a function $F : \{0, \ldots, n-1\} \to \{0, \ldots, m-1\}$. We know that, for $0 \leq x, y \leq n-1$, $F((x+y) \bmod n) = (F(x) + F(y)) \bmod m$. The only way we have for evaluating F is to use a lookup table that stores the values of F. Unfortunately, an Evil Adversary has changed the value of $1/5$ of the table entries when we were not looking.

Describe a simple randomized algorithm that, given an input z, outputs a value that equals $F(z)$ with probability at least $1/2$. Your algorithm should work for every value of z, regardless of what values the Adversary changed. Your algorithm should use as few lookups and as little computation as possible.

Suppose I allow you to repeat your initial algorithm three times. What should you do in this case, and what is the probability that your enhanced algorithm returns the correct answer?

Exercise 1.19: Give examples of events where $\Pr(A \mid B) < \Pr(A)$, $\Pr(A \mid B) = \Pr(A)$, and $\Pr(A \mid B) > \Pr(A)$.

Exercise 1.20: Show that, if $E_1, E_2, \ldots, E_n$ are mutually independent, then so are $\bar{E}_1, \bar{E}_2, \ldots, \bar{E}_n$.

Exercise 1.21: Give an example of three random events X, Y, Z for which any pair are independent but all three are not mutually independent.

Exercise 1.22: **(a)** Consider the set $\{1, \ldots, n\}$. We generate a subset X of this set as follows: a fair coin is flipped independently for each element of the set; if the coin lands heads then the element is added to X, and otherwise it is not. Argue that the resulting set X is equally likely to be any one of the 2^n possible subsets.

(b) Suppose that two sets X and Y are chosen independently and uniformly at random from all the 2^n subsets of $\{1, \ldots, n\}$. Determine $\Pr(X \subseteq Y)$ and $\Pr(X \cup Y = \{1, \ldots, n\})$. (*Hint:* Use the part (a) of this problem.)

Exercise 1.23: There may be several different min-cut sets in a graph. Using the analysis of the randomized min-cut algorithm, argue that there can be at most $n(n-1)/2$ distinct min-cut sets.

Exercise 1.24: Generalizing on the notion of a cut-set, we define an r-way cut-set in a graph as a set of edges whose removal breaks the graph into r or more connected components. Explain how the randomized min-cut algorithm can be used to find minimum r-way cut-sets, and bound the probability that it succeeds in one iteration.

21

Exercise 1.25: To improve the probability of success of the randomized min-cut algorithm, it can be run multiple times.

(a) Consider running the algorithm twice. Determine the number of edge contractions and bound the probability of finding a min-cut.

(b) Consider the following variation. Starting with a graph with n vertices, first contract the graph down to k vertices using the randomized min-cut algorithm. Make copies of the graph with k vertices, and now run the randomized algorithm on this reduced graph ℓ times, independently. Determine the number of edge contractions and bound the probability of finding a minimum cut.

(c) Find optimal (or at least near-optimal) values of k and ℓ for the variation in (b) that maximize the probability of finding a minimum cut while using the same number of edge contractions as running the original algorithm twice.

Exercise 1.26: Tic-tac-toe always ends up in a tie if players play optimally. Instead, we may consider random variations of tic-tac-toe.

(a) First variation: Each of the nine squares is labeled either X or O according to an independent and uniform coin flip. If only one of the players has one (or more) winning tic-tac-toe combinations, that player wins. Otherwise, the game is a tie. Determine the probability that X wins. (You may want to use a computer program to help run through the configurations.)

(b) Second variation: X and O take turns, with the X player going first. On the X player's turn, an X is placed on a square chosen independently and uniformly at random from the squares that are still vacant; O plays similarly. The first player to have a winning tic-tac-toe combination wins the game, and a tie occurs if neither player achieves a winning combination. Find the probability that each player wins. (Again, you may want to write a program to help you.)

CHAPTER TWO

Discrete Random Variables and Expectation

In this chapter, we introduce the concepts of discrete random variables and expectation and then develop basic techniques for analyzing the expected performance of algorithms. We apply these techniques to computing the expected running time of the well-known Quicksort algorithm. In analyzing two versions of Quicksort, we demonstrate the distinction between the analysis of randomized algorithms, where the probability space is defined by the random choices made by the algorithm, and the *probabilistic analysis* of deterministic algorithms, where the probability space is defined by some probability distribution on the inputs.

Along the way we define the Bernoulli, binomial, and geometric random variables, study the expected size of a simple branching process, and analyze the expectation of the coupon collector's problem – a probabilistic paradigm that reappears throughout the book.

2.1. Random Variables and Expectation

When studying a random event, we are often interested in some value associated with the random event rather than in the event itself. For example, in tossing two dice we are often interested in the sum of the two dice rather than the separate value of each die. The sample space in tossing two dice consists of 36 events of equal probability, given by the ordered pairs of numbers $\{(1, 1), (1, 2), \ldots, (6, 5), (6, 6)\}$. If the quantity we are interested in is the sum of the two dice, then we are interested in 11 events (of unequal probability): the 11 possible outcomes of the sum. Any such function from the sample space to the real numbers is called a random variable.

Definition 2.1: *A random variable X on a sample space Ω is a real-valued (measurable) function on Ω; that is, $X : \Omega \to \mathbb{R}$. A discrete random variable is a random variable that takes on only a finite or countably infinite number of values.*

Since random variables are functions, they are usually denoted by a capital letter such as X or Y, while real numbers are usually denoted by lowercase letters.

For a discrete random variable X and a real value a, the event "$X = a$" includes all the basic events of the sample space in which the random variable X assumes the value a. That is, "$X = a$" represents the set $\{s \in \Omega \mid X(s) = a\}$. We denote the probability of that event by

$$\Pr(X = a) = \sum_{s \in \Omega : X(s) = a} \Pr(s).$$

If X is the random variable representing the sum of the two dice, then the event $X = 4$ corresponds to the set of basic events $\{(1, 3), (2, 2), (3, 1)\}$. Hence

$$\Pr(X = 4) = \frac{3}{36} = \frac{1}{12}.$$

The definition of independence that we developed for events extends to random variables.

Definition 2.2: *Two random variables X and Y are independent if and only if*

$$\Pr((X = x) \cap (Y = y)) = \Pr(X = x) \cdot \Pr(Y = y)$$

for all values x and y. Similarly, random variables $X_1, X_2, \ldots, X_k$ are mutually independent if and only if, for any subset $I \subseteq [1, k]$ and any values x_i, $i \in I$,

$$\Pr\left(\bigcap_{i \in I}(X_i = x_i)\right) = \prod_{i \in I} \Pr(X_i = x_i).$$

A basic characteristic of a random variable is its *expectation*, which is also often called the *mean*. The expectation of a random variable is a weighted average of the values it assumes, where each value is weighted by the probability that the variable assumes that value.

Definition 2.3: *The expectation of a discrete random variable X, denoted by $E[X]$, is given by*

$$E[X] = \sum_i i \Pr(X = i),$$

where the summation is over all values in the range of X. The expectation is finite if $\sum_i |i| \Pr(X = i)$ converges; otherwise, the expectation is unbounded.

For example, the expectation of the random variable X representing the sum of two dice is

$$E[X] = \frac{1}{36} \cdot 2 + \frac{2}{36} \cdot 3 + \frac{3}{36} \cdot 4 + \cdots + \frac{1}{36} \cdot 12 = 7.$$

You may try using symmetry to give simpler argument for why $E[X] = 7$.

As an example of where the expectation of a discrete random variable is unbounded, consider a random variable X that takes on the value 2^i with probability $1/2^i$ for $i = 1, 2, \ldots$. The expected value of X is

$$E[X] = \sum_{i=1}^{\infty} \frac{1}{2^i} 2^i = \sum_{i=1}^{\infty} 1 = \infty.$$

Here we use the somewhat informal notation $E[X] = \infty$ to express that $E[X]$ is unbounded.

2.1.1. *Linearity of Expectations*

A key property of expectation that significantly simplifies its computation is the *linearity of expectations*. By this property, the expectation of the sum of random variables is equal to the sum of their expectations. Formally, we have the following theorem.

Theorem 2.1 [Linearity of Expectations]: *For any finite collection of discrete random variables $X_1, X_2, \ldots, X_n$ with finite expectations,*

$$E\left[\sum_{i=1}^{n} X_i\right] = \sum_{i=1}^{n} E[X_i].$$

Proof: We prove the statement for two random variables X and Y; the general case follows by induction. The summations that follow are understood to be over the ranges of the corresponding random variables:

$$
\begin{aligned}
E[X + Y] &= \sum_i \sum_j (i + j) \Pr((X = i) \cap (Y = j)) \\
&= \sum_i \sum_j i \Pr((X = i) \cap (Y = j)) + \sum_i \sum_j j \Pr((X = i) \cap (Y = j)) \\
&= \sum_i i \sum_j \Pr((X = i) \cap (Y = j)) + \sum_j j \sum_i \Pr((X = i) \cap (Y = j)) \\
&= \sum_i i \Pr(X = i) + \sum_j j \Pr(Y = j) \\
&= E[X] + E[Y].
\end{aligned}
$$

The first equality follows from Definition 1.2. In the penultimate equation we have used Theorem 1.6, the Law of Total Probability. ∎

We now use this property to compute the expected sum of two standard dice. Let $X = X_1 + X_2$, where X_i represents the outcome of die i for $i = 1, 2$. Then

$$E[X_i] = \frac{1}{6} \sum_{j=1}^{6} j = \frac{7}{2}.$$

Applying the linearity of expectations, we have

$$E[X] = E[X_1] + E[X_2] = 7.$$

It is worth emphasizing that linearity of expectations holds for any collection of random variables, even if they are *not* independent! For example, consider again the previous example and let the random variable $Y = X_1 + X_1^2$. We have

$$\mathbf{E}[Y] = \mathbf{E}[X_1 + X_1^2] = \mathbf{E}[X_1] + \mathbf{E}[X_1^2],$$

even though X_1 and X_1^2 are clearly dependent. As an exercise, you may verify this identity by considering the six possible outcomes for X_1.

Linearity of expectations also holds for countably infinite summations in certain cases. Specifically, it can be shown that

$$\mathbf{E}\left[\sum_{i=1}^{\infty} X_i\right] = \sum_{i=1}^{\infty} \mathbf{E}[X_i]$$

whenever $\sum_{i=1}^{\infty} \mathbf{E}[|X_i|]$ converges. The issue of dealing with the linearity of expectations with countably infinite summations is further considered in Exercise 2.29.

This chapter contains several examples in which the linearity of expectations significantly simplifies the computation of expectations. One result related to the linearity of expectations is the following simple lemma.

Lemma 2.2: *For any constant c and discrete random variable X,*

$$\mathbf{E}[cX] = c\mathbf{E}[X].$$

Proof: The lemma is obvious for $c = 0$. For $c \neq 0$,

$$
\begin{aligned}
\mathbf{E}[cX] &= \sum_j j \Pr(cX = j) \\
&= c \sum_j (j/c) \Pr(X = j/c) \\
&= c \sum_k k \Pr(X = k) \\
&= c\mathbf{E}[X].
\end{aligned}
$$
∎

2.1.2. Jensen's Inequality

Suppose that we choose the length X of a side of a square uniformly at random from the range $[1, 99]$. What is the expected value of the area? We can write this as $\mathbf{E}[X^2]$. It is tempting to think of this as being equal to $\mathbf{E}[X]^2$, but a simple calculation shows that this is not correct. In fact, $\mathbf{E}[X]^2 = 2500$ whereas $\mathbf{E}[X^2] = 9950/3 > 2500$.

More generally, we can prove that $\mathbf{E}[X^2] \geq (\mathbf{E}[X])^2$. Consider $Y = (X - \mathbf{E}[X])^2$. The random variable Y is nonnegative and hence its expectation must also be nonnegative. Therefore,

$$
\begin{aligned}
0 \leq \mathbf{E}[Y] &= \mathbf{E}[(X - \mathbf{E}[X])^2] \\
&= \mathbf{E}[X^2 - 2X\mathbf{E}[X] + (\mathbf{E}[X])^2] \\
&= \mathbf{E}[X^2] - 2\mathbf{E}[X\mathbf{E}[X]] + (\mathbf{E}[X])^2 \\
&= \mathbf{E}[X^2] - (\mathbf{E}[X])^2.
\end{aligned}
$$

To obtain the penultimate line, we used the linearity of expectations. To obtain the last line we used Lemma 2.2 to simplify $\mathbf{E}[X\mathbf{E}[X]] = \mathbf{E}[X] \cdot \mathbf{E}[X]$.

The fact that $\mathbf{E}[X^2] \geq (\mathbf{E}[X])^2$ is an example of a more general theorem known as Jensen's inequality. Jensen's inequality shows that, for any convex function f, we have $\mathbf{E}[f(X)] \geq f(\mathbf{E}[X])$.

Definition 2.4: *A function $f : \mathbf{R} \rightarrow \mathbf{R}$ is said to be convex if, for any x_1, x_2 and $0 \leq \lambda \leq 1$,*

$$f(\lambda x_1 + (1 - \lambda)x_2) \leq \lambda f(x_1) + (1 - \lambda)f(x_2).$$

Visually, a convex function f has the property that, if you connect two points on the graph of the function by a straight line, this line lies on or above the graph of the function. The following fact, which we state without proof, is often a useful alternative to Definition 2.4.

Lemma 2.3: *If f is a twice differentiable function, then f is convex if and only if $f''(x) \geq 0$.*

Theorem 2.4 [Jensen's Inequality]: *If f is a convex function, then*

$$\mathbf{E}[f(X)] \geq f(\mathbf{E}[X]).$$

Proof: We prove the theorem assuming that f has a Taylor expansion. Let $\mu = \mathbf{E}[X]$. By Taylor's theorem there is a value c such that

$$f(x) = f(\mu) + f'(\mu)(x - \mu) + \frac{f''(c)(x - \mu)^2}{2}$$
$$\geq f(\mu) + f'(\mu)(x - \mu),$$

since $f''(c) > 0$ by convexity. Taking expectations of both sides and applying linearity of expectations and Lemma 2.2 yields the result:

$$\mathbf{E}[f(X)] \geq \mathbf{E}[f(\mu) + f'(\mu)(X - \mu)]$$
$$= \mathbf{E}[f(\mu)] + f'(\mu)(\mathbf{E}[X] - \mu)$$
$$= f(\mu) = f(\mathbf{E}[X]). \qquad \blacksquare$$

An alternative proof of Jensen's inequality, which holds for any random variable X that takes on only finitely many values, is presented in Exercise 2.10.

2.2. The Bernoulli and Binomial Random Variables

Suppose that we run an experiment that succeeds with probability p and fails with probability $1 - p$.

Let Y be a random variable such that

$$Y = \begin{cases} 1 & \text{if the experiment succeeds,} \\ 0 & \text{otherwise.} \end{cases}$$

The variable Y is called a *Bernoulli* or an *indicator* random variable. Note that, for a Bernoulli random variable,

$$\mathbf{E}[Y] = p \cdot 1 + (1 - p) \cdot 0 = p = \Pr(Y = 1).$$

For example, if we flip a fair coin and consider the outcome "heads" a success, then the expected value of the corresponding indicator random variable is $1/2$.

Consider now a sequence of n independent coin flips. What is the distribution of the number of heads in the entire sequence? More generally, consider a sequence of n independent experiments, each of which succeeds with probability p. If we let X represent the number of successes in the n experiments, then X has a *binomial distribution*.

Definition 2.5: *A binomial random variable X with parameters n and p, denoted by $B(n, p)$, is defined by the following probability distribution on $j = 0, 1, 2, \ldots, n$:*

$$\Pr(X = j) = \binom{n}{j} p^j (1 - p)^{n-j}.$$

That is, the binomial random variable X equals j when there are exactly j successes and $n - j$ failures in n independent experiments, each of which is successful with probability p.

As an exercise, you should show that Definition 2.5 ensures that $\sum_{j=0}^{n} \Pr(X = j) = 1$. This is necessary for the binomial random variable to have a valid probability function, according to Definition 1.2.

The binomial random variable arises in many contexts, especially in sampling. As a practical example, suppose that we want to gather data about the packets going through a router by postprocessing them. We might want to know the approximate fraction of packets from a certain source or of a certain data type. We do not have the memory available to store all of the packets, so we choose to store a random subset – or *sample* – of the packets for later analysis. If each packet is stored with probability p and if n packets go through the router each day, then the number of sampled packets each day is a binomial random variable X with parameters n and p. If we want to know how much memory is necessary for such a sample, a natural starting point is to determine the expectation of the random variable X.

Sampling in this manner arises in other contexts as well. For example, by sampling the program counter while a program runs, one can determine what parts of a program are taking the most time. This knowledge can be used to aid dynamic program optimization techniques such as binary rewriting, where the executable binary form of a program is modified while the program executes. Since rewriting the executable as the program runs is expensive, sampling helps the optimizer to determine when it will be worthwhile.

What is the expectation of a binomial random variable X? We can compute it directly from the definition as

$$
\begin{aligned}
\mathbf{E}[X] &= \sum_{j=0}^{n} j \binom{n}{j} p^j (1-p)^{n-j} \\
&= \sum_{j=0}^{n} j \frac{n!}{j!\,(n-j)!} p^j (1-p)^{n-j} \\
&= \sum_{j=1}^{n} \frac{n!}{(j-1)!\,(n-j)!} p^j (1-p)^{n-j} \\
&= np \sum_{j=1}^{n} \frac{(n-1)!}{(j-1)!\,((n-1)-(j-1))!} p^{j-1} (1-p)^{(n-1)-(j-1)} \\
&= np \sum_{k=0}^{n-1} \frac{(n-1)!}{k!\,((n-1)-k)!} p^k (1-p)^{(n-1)-k} \\
&= np \sum_{k=0}^{n-1} \binom{n-1}{k} p^k (1-p)^{(n-1)-k} \\
&= np,
\end{aligned}
$$

where the last equation uses the binomial identity

$$
(x+y)^n = \sum_{k=0}^{n} \binom{n}{k} x^k y^{n-k}.
$$

The linearity of expectations allows for a significantly simpler argument. If X is a binomial random variable with parameters n and p, then X is the number of successes in n trials, where each trial is successful with probability p. Define a set of n indicator random variables $X_1, \ldots, X_n$, where $X_i = 1$ if the ith trial is successful and 0 otherwise. Clearly, $\mathbf{E}[X_i] = p$ and $X = \sum_{i=1}^{n} X_i$ and so, by the linearity of expectations,

$$
\mathbf{E}[X] = \mathbf{E}\left[\sum_{i=1}^{n} X_i \right] = \sum_{i=1}^{n} \mathbf{E}[X_i] = np.
$$

The linearity of expectations makes this approach of representing a random variable by a sum of simpler random variables, such as indicator random variables, extremely useful.

2.3. Conditional Expectation

Just as we have defined conditional probability, it is useful to define the *conditional expectation* of a random variable. The following definition is quite natural.

Definition 2.6:
$$E[Y \mid Z = z] = \sum_y y \Pr(Y = y \mid Z = z),$$

where the summation is over all y in the range of Y.

The definition states that the conditional expectation of a random variable is, like the expectation, a weighted sum of the values it assumes. The difference is that now each value is weighted by the *conditional probability* that the variable assumes that value. One can similarly define the conditional expectation of a random variable Y conditioned on an event $\mathcal{E}$ as

$$E[Y \mid \mathcal{E}] = \sum_y y \Pr(Y = y \mid \mathcal{E}).$$

For example, suppose that we independently roll two standard six-sided dice. Let X_1 be the number that shows on the first die, X_2 the number on the second die, and X the sum of the numbers on the two dice. Then

$$E[X \mid X_1 = 2] = \sum_x x \Pr(X = x \mid X_1 = 2) = \sum_{x=3}^{8} x \cdot \frac{1}{6} = \frac{11}{2}.$$

As another example, consider $E[X_1 \mid X = 5]$:

$$E[X_1 \mid X = 5] = \sum_{x=1}^{4} x \Pr(X_1 = x \mid X = 5)$$

$$= \sum_{x=1}^{4} x \frac{\Pr(X_1 = x \cap X = 5)}{\Pr(X = 5)} = \sum_{x=1}^{4} x \frac{1/36}{4/36} = \frac{5}{2}.$$

The following natural identity follows from Definition 2.6.

Lemma 2.5: *For any random variables X and Y,*

$$E[X] = \sum_y \Pr(Y = y) E[X \mid Y = y],$$

where the sum is over all values in the range of Y and all of the expectations exist.

Proof:
$$\sum_y \Pr(Y = y) E[X \mid Y = y] = \sum_y \Pr(Y = y) \sum_x x \Pr(X = x \mid Y = y)$$

$$= \sum_x \sum_y x \Pr(X = x \mid Y = y) \Pr(Y = y)$$

$$= \sum_x \sum_y x \Pr(X = x \cap Y = y)$$

$$= \sum_x x \Pr(X = x) = E[X]. \qquad \blacksquare$$

The linearity of expectations also extends to conditional expectations. This is clarified in Lemma 2.6, whose proof is left as Exercise 2.11.

Lemma 2.6: *For any finite collection of discrete random variables $X_1, X_2, \ldots, X_n$ with finite expectations and for any random variable Y,*

$$\mathbf{E}\left[\sum_{i=1}^{n} X_i \mid Y = y\right] = \sum_{i=1}^{n} \mathbf{E}[X_i \mid Y = y].$$

Perhaps somewhat confusingly, the conditional expectation is also used to refer to the following random variable.

Definition 2.7: *The expression $\mathbf{E}[Y \mid Z]$ is a random variable $f(Z)$ that takes on the value $\mathbf{E}[Y \mid Z = z]$ when $Z = z$.*

We emphasize that $\mathbf{E}[Y \mid Z]$ is *not* a real value; it is actually a function of the random variable Z. Hence $\mathbf{E}[Y \mid Z]$ is itself a function from the sample space to the real numbers and can therefore be thought of as a random variable.

In the previous example of rolling two dice,

$$\mathbf{E}[X \mid X_1] = \sum_{x} x \Pr(X = x \mid X_1) = \sum_{x=X_1+1}^{X_1+6} x \cdot \frac{1}{6} = X_1 + \frac{7}{2}.$$

We see that $\mathbf{E}[X \mid X_1]$ is a random variable whose value depends on X_1.

If $\mathbf{E}[Y \mid Z]$ is a random variable, then it makes sense to consider its expectation $\mathbf{E}[\mathbf{E}[Y \mid Z]]$. In our example, we found that $\mathbf{E}[X \mid X_1] = X_1 + 7/2$. Thus

$$\mathbf{E}[\mathbf{E}[X \mid X_1]] = \mathbf{E}\left[X_1 + \frac{7}{2}\right] = \frac{7}{2} + \frac{7}{2} = 7 = \mathbf{E}[X].$$

More generally, we have the following theorem.

Theorem 2.7:

$$\mathbf{E}[Y] = \mathbf{E}[\mathbf{E}[Y \mid Z]].$$

Proof: From Definition 2.7 we have $\mathbf{E}[Y \mid Z] = f(Z)$, where $f(Z)$ takes on the value $\mathbf{E}[Y \mid Z = z]$ when $Z = z$. Hence

$$\mathbf{E}[\mathbf{E}[Y \mid Z]] = \sum_{z} \mathbf{E}[Y \mid Z = z] \Pr(Z = z).$$

The right-hand side equals $\mathbf{E}[Y]$ by Lemma 2.5. ∎

We now demonstrate an interesting application of conditional expectations. Consider a program that includes one call to a process S. Assume that each call to process S recursively spawns new copies of the process S, where the number of new copies is a binomial random variable with parameters n and p. We assume that these random variables are independent for each call to S. What is the expected number of copies of the process S generated by the program?

To analyze this recursive spawning process, we introduce the idea of *generations*. The initial process S is in generation 0. Otherwise, we say that a process S is in generation i if it was spawned by another process S in generation $i - 1$. Let Y_i denote the number of S processes in generation i. Since we know that $Y_0 = 1$, the number of processes in generation 1 has a binomial distribution. Thus,

$$\mathbf{E}[Y_1] = np.$$

Similarly, suppose we knew that the number of processes in generation $i - 1$ was y_{i-1}, so $Y_{i-1} = y_{i-1}$. Let Z_k be the number of copies spawned by the kth process spawned in the $(i - 1)$th generation for $1 \le k \le y_{i-1}$. Each Z_k is a binomial random variable with parameters n and p. Then

$$\mathbf{E}[Y_i \mid Y_{i-1} = y_{i-1}] = \mathbf{E}\left[\sum_{k=1}^{y_{i-1}} Z_k \mid Y_{i-1} = y_{i-1} \right]$$

$$= \sum_{j \ge 0} j \Pr\left(\sum_{k=1}^{y_{i-1}} Z_k = j \mid Y_{i-1} = y_{i-1} \right)$$

$$= \sum_{j \ge 0} j \Pr\left(\sum_{k=1}^{y_{i-1}} Z_k = j \right)$$

$$= \mathbf{E}\left[\sum_{k=1}^{y_{i-1}} Z_k \right]$$

$$= \sum_{k=1}^{y_{i-1}} \mathbf{E}[Z_k]$$

$$= y_{i-1} np.$$

In the third line we have used that the Z_k are all independent binomial random variables; in particular, the value of each Z_k is independent of Y_{i-1}, allowing us to remove the conditioning. In the fifth line, we have applied the linearity of expectations.

Applying Theorem 2.7, we can compute the expected size of the ith generation inductively. We have

$$\mathbf{E}[Y_i] = \mathbf{E}[\mathbf{E}[Y_i \mid Y_{i-1}]] = \mathbf{E}[Y_{i-1} np] = np \mathbf{E}[Y_{i-1}].$$

By induction on i, and using the fact that $Y_0 = 1$, we then obtain

$$\mathbf{E}[Y_i] = (np)^i.$$

The expected total number of copies of process S generated by the program is given by

$$\mathbf{E}\left[\sum_{i \ge 0} Y_i \right] = \sum_{i \ge 0} \mathbf{E}[Y_i] = \sum_{i \ge 0} (np)^i.$$

If $np \ge 1$ then the expectation is unbounded; if $np < 1$, the expectation is $1/(1 - np)$. Thus, the expected number of processes generated by the program is bounded if and only if the expected number of processes spawned by each process is less than 1.

The process analyzed here is a simple example of a *branching process*, a probabilistic paradigm extensively studied in probability theory.

2.4. The Geometric Distribution

Suppose that we flip a coin until it lands on heads. What is the distribution of the number of flips? This is an example of a *geometric distribution*, which arises in the following situation: we perform a sequence of independent trials until the first success, where each trial succeeds with probability p.

Definition 2.8: *A geometric random variable X with parameter p is given by the following probability distribution on $n = 1, 2, \ldots,$:*

$$\Pr(X = n) = (1 - p)^{n-1}p.$$

That is, for the geometric random variable X to equal n, there must be $n - 1$ failures, followed by a success.

As an exercise, you should show that the geometric random variable satisfies

$$\sum_{n \geq 1} \Pr(X = n) = 1.$$

Again, this is necessary for the geometric random variable to have a valid probability function, according to Definition 1.2.

In the context of our example from Section 2.2 of sampling packets on a router, if packets are sampled with probability p, then the number of packets transmitted after the last sampled packet until and including the next sampled packet is given by a geometric random variable with parameter p.

Geometric random variables are said to be *memoryless* because the probability that you will reach your first success n trials from now is independent of the number of failures you have experienced. Informally, one can ignore past failures because they do not change the distribution of the number of future trials until first success. Formally, we have the following statement.

Lemma 2.8: *For a geometric random variable X with parameter p and for $n > 0$,*

$$\Pr(X = n + k \mid X > k) = \Pr(X = n).$$

Proof:

$$
\begin{aligned}
\Pr(X = n + k \mid X > k) &= \frac{\Pr((X = n + k) \cap (X > k))}{\Pr(X > k)} \\
&= \frac{\Pr(X = n + k)}{\Pr(X > k)} \\
&= \frac{(1 - p)^{n+k-1}p}{\sum_{i=k}^{\infty}(1 - p)^i p} \\
&= \frac{(1 - p)^{n+k-1}p}{(1 - p)^k} \\
&= (1 - p)^{n-1}p \\
&= \Pr(X = n).
\end{aligned}
$$

The fourth equality uses the fact that, for $0 < x < 1$, $\sum_{i=k}^{\infty} x^i = x^k/(1 - x)$. ∎

We now turn to computing the expectation of a geometric random variable. When a random variable takes values in the set of natural numbers $\mathbf{N} = \{0, 1, 2, 3, \ldots\}$, there is an alternative formula for calculating its expectation.

Lemma 2.9: *Let X be a discrete random variable that takes on only nonnegative integer values. Then*

$$\mathbf{E}[X] = \sum_{i=1}^{\infty} \Pr(X \geq i).$$

Proof:

$$\sum_{i=1}^{\infty} \Pr(X \geq i) = \sum_{i=1}^{\infty} \sum_{j=i}^{\infty} \Pr(X = j)$$

$$= \sum_{j=1}^{\infty} \sum_{i=1}^{j} \Pr(X = j)$$

$$= \sum_{j=1}^{\infty} j \Pr(X = j)$$

$$= \mathbf{E}[X].$$

The interchange of (possibly) infinite summations is justified, since the terms being summed are all nonnegative. ∎

For a geometric random variable X with parameter p,

$$\Pr(X \geq i) = \sum_{n=i}^{\infty} (1 - p)^{n-1} p = (1 - p)^{i-1}.$$

Hence

$$\mathbf{E}[X] = \sum_{i=1}^{\infty} \Pr(X \geq i)$$

$$= \sum_{i=1}^{\infty} (1 - p)^{i-1}$$

$$= \frac{1}{1 - (1 - p)}$$

$$= \frac{1}{p}.$$

Thus, for a fair coin where $p = 1/2$, on average it takes two flips to see the first heads.

There is another approach to finding the expectation of a geometric random variable X with parameter p – one that uses conditional expectations and the memoryless property of geometric random variables. Recall that X corresponds to the number of flips until the first heads given that each flip is heads with probability p. Let $Y = 0$ if the first flip is tails and $Y = 1$ if the first flip is heads. By the identity from Lemma 2.5,

$$\mathbf{E}[X] = \Pr(Y = 0)\mathbf{E}[X \mid Y = 0] + \Pr(Y = 1)\mathbf{E}[X \mid Y = 1]$$
$$= (1 - p)\mathbf{E}[X \mid Y = 0] + p\mathbf{E}[X \mid Y = 1].$$

If $Y = 1$ then $X = 1$, so $\mathbf{E}[X \mid Y = 1] = 1$. If $Y = 0$, then $X > 1$. In this case, let the number of remaining flips (after the first flip until the first heads) be Z. Then, by the linearity of expectations,

$$\mathbf{E}[X] = (1 - p)\mathbf{E}[Z + 1] + p \cdot 1 = (1 - p)\mathbf{E}[Z] + 1.$$

By the memoryless property of geometric random variables, Z is also a geometric random variable with parameter p. Hence $\mathbf{E}[Z] = \mathbf{E}[X]$, since they both have the same distribution. We therefore have

$$\mathbf{E}[X] = (1 - p)\mathbf{E}[Z] + 1 = (1 - p)\mathbf{E}[X] + 1,$$

which yields $\mathbf{E}[X] = 1/p$.

This method of using conditional expectations to compute an expectation is often useful, especially in conjunction with the memoryless property of a geometric random variable.

2.4.1. *Example: Coupon Collector's Problem*

The coupon collector's problem arises from the following scenario. Suppose that each box of cereal contains one of n different coupons. Once you obtain one of every type of coupon, you can send in for a prize. Assuming that the coupon in each box is chosen independently and uniformly at random from the n possibilities and that you do not collaborate with others to collect coupons, how many boxes of cereal must you buy before you obtain at least one of every type of coupon? This simple problem arises in many different scenarios and will reappear in several places in the book.

Let X be the number of boxes bought until at least one of every type of coupon is obtained. We now determine $\mathbf{E}[X]$. If X_i is the number of boxes bought while you had exactly $i - 1$ different coupons, then clearly $X = \sum_{i=1}^{n} X_i$.

The advantage of breaking the random variable X into a sum of n random variables X_i, $i = 1, \ldots, n$, is that each X_i is a geometric random variable. When exactly $i - 1$ coupons have been found, the probability of obtaining a new coupon is

$$p_i = 1 - \frac{i - 1}{n}.$$

Hence, X_i is a geometric random variable with parameter p_i, and

$$\mathbf{E}[X_i] = \frac{1}{p_i} = \frac{n}{n - i + 1}.$$

Using the linearity of expectations, we have that

$$E[X] = E\left[\sum_{i=1}^{n} X_i\right]$$

$$= \sum_{i=1}^{n} E[X_i]$$

$$= \sum_{i=1}^{n} \frac{n}{n-i+1}$$

$$= n \sum_{i=1}^{n} \frac{1}{i}.$$

The summation $\sum_{i=1}^{n} 1/i$ is known as the *harmonic number* $H(n)$, and as we show next, $H(n) = \ln n + \Theta(1)$. Thus, for the coupon collector's problem, the expected number of random coupons required to obtain all n coupons is $n \ln n + \Theta(n)$.

Lemma 2.10: *The harmonic number $H(n) = \sum_{i=1}^{n} 1/i$ satisfies $H(n) = \ln n + \Theta(1)$.*

Proof: Since $1/x$ is monotonically decreasing, we can write

$$\ln n = \int_{x=1}^{n} \frac{1}{x} \, dx \le \sum_{k=1}^{n} \frac{1}{k}$$

and

$$\sum_{k=2}^{n} \frac{1}{k} \le \int_{x=1}^{n} \frac{1}{x} \, dx = \ln n.$$

This is clarified in Figure 2.1, where the area below the curve $f(x) = 1/x$ corresponds to the integral and the areas of the shaded regions correspond to the summations $\sum_{k=1}^{n} 1/k$ and $\sum_{k=2}^{n} 1/k$.

Hence $\ln n \le H(n) \le \ln n + 1$, proving the claim. ■

As a simple application of the coupon collector's problem, suppose that packets are sent in a stream from a source host to a destination host along a fixed path of routers. The host at the destination would like to know which routers the stream of packets has passed through, in case it finds later that some router damaged packets that it processed. If there is enough room in the packet header, each router can append its identification number to the header, giving the path. Unfortunately, there may not be that much room available in the packet header.

Suppose instead that each packet header has space for exactly one router identification number, and this space is used to store the identification of a router chosen uniformly at random from all of the routers on the path. This can actually be accomplished easily; we consider how in Exercise 2.18. Then, from the point of view of the destination host, determining all the routers on the path is like a coupon collector's problem. If there are n routers along the path, then the expected number of packets in

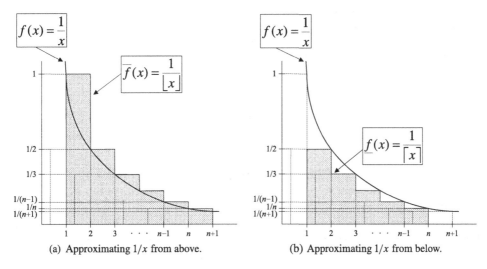

(a) Approximating $1/x$ from above.　　　(b) Approximating $1/x$ from below.

Figure 2.1: Approximating the area above and below $f(x) = 1/x$.

the stream that must arrive before the destination host knows all of the routers on the path is $nH(n) = n \ln n + \Theta(n)$.

2.5. Application: The Expected Run-Time of Quicksort

Quicksort is a simple – and, in practice, very efficient – sorting algorithm. The input is a list of n numbers $x_1, x_2, \ldots, x_n$. For convenience, we will assume that the numbers are distinct. A call to the Quicksort function begins by choosing a *pivot* element from the set. Let us assume the pivot is x. The algorithm proceeds by comparing every other element to x, dividing the list of elements into two sublists: those that are less than x and those that are greater than x. Notice that if the comparisons are performed in the natural order, from left to right, then the order of the elements in each sublist is the same as in the initial list. Quicksort then recursively sorts these sublists.

In the worst case, Quicksort requires $\Omega(n^2)$ comparison operations. For example, suppose our input has the form $x_1 = n$, $x_2 = n - 1$, $\ldots$, $x_{n-1} = 2$, $x_n = 1$. Suppose also that we adopt the rule that the pivot should be the first element of the list. The first pivot chosen is then n, so Quicksort performs $n - 1$ comparisons. The division has yielded one sublist of size 0 (which requires no additional work) and another of size $n - 1$, with the order $n - 1, n - 2, \ldots, 2, 1$. The next pivot chosen is $n - 1$, so Quicksort performs $n - 2$ comparisons and is left with one group of size $n - 2$ in the order $n - 2, n - 3, \ldots, 2, 1$. Continuing in this fashion, Quicksort performs

$$(n - 1) + (n - 2) + \cdots + 2 + 1 = \frac{n(n - 1)}{2} \text{comparisons.}$$

This is not the only bad case that leads to $\Omega(n^2)$ comparisons; similarly poor performance occurs if the pivot element is chosen from among the smallest few or the largest few elements each time.

37

Quicksort Algorithm:

Input: A list $S = \{x_1, \ldots, x_n\}$ of n distinct elements over a totally ordered universe.

Output: The elements of S in sorted order.

1. If S has one or zero elements, return S. Otherwise continue.
2. Choose an element of S as a pivot; call it s.
3. Compare every other element of S to x in order to divide the other elements into two sublists:
   (a) S_1 has all the elements of S that are less than x;
   (b) S_2 has all those that are greater than x.
4. Use Quicksort to sort S_1 and S_2.
5. Return the list S_1, x, S_2.

Algorithm 2.1: Quicksort.

We clearly made a bad choice of pivots for the given input. A reasonable choice of pivots would require many fewer comparisons. For example, if our pivot always splits the list into two sublists of size at most $\lceil n/2 \rceil$, then the number of comparisons $C(n)$ would obey the following recurrence relation:

$$C(n) \le 2C(\lceil n/2 \rceil) + \Theta(n).$$

The solution to this equation yields $C(n) = O(n \log n)$, which is the best possible result for comparison-based sorting. In fact, any sequence of pivot elements that always split the input list into two sublists each of size at least cn for some constant c would yield an $O(n \log n)$ running time.

This discussion provides some intuition for how we would like pivots to be chosen. In each iteration of the algorithm there is a good set of pivot elements that split the input list into two almost equal sublists; it suffices if the sizes of the two sublists are within a constant factor of each other. There is also a bad set of pivot elements that do not split up the list significantly. If good pivots are chosen sufficiently often, Quicksort will terminate quickly. How can we guarantee that the algorithm chooses good pivot elements sufficiently often? We can resolve this problem in one of two ways.

First, we can change the algorithm to choose the pivots randomly. This makes Quicksort a randomized algorithm; the randomization makes it extremely unlikely that we repeatedly choose the wrong pivots. We demonstrate shortly that the expected number of comparisons made by a simple randomized Quicksort is $2n \ln n + O(n)$, matching (up to constant factors) the $\Omega(n \log n)$ bound for comparison-based sorting. Here, the expectation is over the random choice of pivots.

A second possibility is that we can keep our deterministic algorithm, using the first list element as a pivot, but consider a probabilistic model of the inputs. A *permutation* of a set of n distinct items is just one of the $n!$ orderings of these items. Instead of looking for the worst possible input, we assume that the input items are given to us in a random order. This may be a reasonable assumption for some applications; alternatively, this could be accomplished by ordering the input list according to a randomly

38

chosen permutation before running the deterministic Quicksort algorithm. In this case, we have a deterministic algorithm but a *probabilistic analysis* based on a model of the inputs. We again show in this setting that the expected number of comparisons made is $2n \ln n + O(n)$. Here, the expectation is over the random choice of inputs.

The same techniques are generally used both in analyses of randomized algorithms and in probabilistic analyses of deterministic algorithms. Indeed, in this application the analysis of the randomized Quicksort and the probabilistic analysis of the deterministic Quicksort under random inputs are essentially the same.

Let us first analyze Random Quicksort, the randomized algorithm version of Quicksort.

Theorem 2.11: *Suppose that, whenever a pivot is chosen for Random Quicksort, it is chosen independently and uniformly at random from all possibilities. Then, for any input, the expected number of comparisons made by Random Quicksort is $2n \ln n + O(n)$.*

Proof: Let $y_1, y_2, \ldots, y_n$ be the same values as the input values $x_1, x_2, \ldots, x_n$ but sorted in increasing order. For $i < j$, let X_{ij} be a random variable that takes on the value 1 if y_i and y_j are compared at any time over the course of the algorithm, and 0 otherwise. Then the total number of comparisons X satisfies

$$X = \sum_{i=1}^{n-1} \sum_{j=i+1}^{n} X_{ij},$$

and

$$\mathbf{E}[X] = \mathbf{E}\left[\sum_{i=1}^{n-1} \sum_{j=i+1}^{n} X_{ij} \right]$$

$$= \sum_{i=1}^{n-1} \sum_{j=i+1}^{n} \mathbf{E}[X_{ij}]$$

by the linearity of expectations.

Since X_{ij} is an indicator random variable that takes on only the values 0 and 1, $\mathbf{E}[X_{ij}]$ is equal to the probability that X_{ij} is 1. Hence all we need to do is compute the probability that two elements y_i and y_j are compared. Now, y_i and y_j are compared if and only if either y_i or y_j is the first pivot selected by Random Quicksort from the set $Y^{ij} = \{y_i, y_{i+1}, \ldots, y_{j-1}, y_j\}$. This is because if y_i (or y_j) is the first pivot selected from this set, then y_i and y_j must still be in the same sublist, and hence they will be compared. Similarly, if neither is the first pivot from this set, then y_i and y_j will be separated into distinct sublists and so will not be compared.

Since our pivots are chosen independently and uniformly at random from each sublist, it follows that, the first time a pivot is chosen from Y^{ij}, it is equally likely to be any element from this set. Thus the probability that y_i or y_j is the first pivot selected from Y^{ij}, which is the probability that $X_{ij} = 1$, is $2/(j - i + 1)$. Using the substitution

$k = j - i + 1$ then yields

$$\mathbf{E}[X] = \sum_{i=1}^{n-1} \sum_{j=i+1}^{n} \frac{2}{j-i+1}$$

$$= \sum_{i=1}^{n-1} \sum_{k=2}^{n-i+1} \frac{2}{k}$$

$$= \sum_{k=2}^{n} \sum_{i=1}^{n+1-k} \frac{2}{k}$$

$$= \sum_{k=2}^{n} (n+1-k)\frac{2}{k}$$

$$= \left((n+1) \sum_{k=2}^{n} \frac{2}{k} \right) - 2(n-1)$$

$$= (2n+2) \sum_{k=1}^{n} \frac{1}{k} - 4n.$$

Notice that we used a rearrangement of the double summation to obtain a clean form for the expectation.

Recalling that the summation $H(n) = \sum_{k=1}^{n} 1/k$ satisfies $H(n) = \ln n + \Theta(1)$, we have $\mathbf{E}[X] = 2n \ln n + \Theta(n)$. ∎

Next we consider the deterministic version of Quicksort, on random input. We assume that the order of the elements in each recursively constructed sublist is the same as in the initial list.

Theorem 2.12: *Suppose that, whenever a pivot is chosen for Quicksort, the first element of the sublist is chosen. If the input is chosen uniformly at random from all possible permutations of the values, then the expected number of comparisons made by Deterministic Quicksort is $2n \ln n + O(n)$.*

Proof: The proof is essentially the same as for Random Quicksort. Again, y_i and y_j are compared if and only if either y_i or y_j is the first pivot selected by Quicksort from the set Y^{ij}. Since the order of elements in each sublist is the same as in the original list, the first pivot selected from the set Y^{ij} is just the first element from Y^{ij} in the input list, and since all possible permutations of the input values are equally likely, every element in Y^{ij} is equally likely to be first. From this, we can again use linearity of expectations in the same way as in the analysis of Random Quicksort to obtain the same expression for $\mathbf{E}[X]$. ∎

2.6. Exercises

Exercise 2.1: Suppose we roll a fair k-sided die with the numbers 1 through k on the die's faces. If X is the number that appears, what is $\mathbf{E}[X]$?

Exercise 2.2: A monkey types on a 26-letter keyboard that has lowercase letters only. Each letter is chosen independently and uniformly at random from the alphabet. If the monkey types 1,000,000 letters, what is the expected number of times the sequence "proof" appears?

Exercise 2.3: Give examples of functions f and random variables X where $E[f(X)] < f(E[X])$, $E[f(X)] = f(E[X])$, and $E[f(X)] > f(E[X])$.

Exercise 2.4: Prove that $E[X^k] \geq E[X]^k$ for any even integer $k \geq 1$.

Exercise 2.5: If X is a $B(n, 1/2)$ random variable with $n \geq 1$, show that the probability that X is even is $1/2$.

Exercise 2.6: Suppose that we independently roll two standard six-sided dice. Let X_1 be the number that shows on the first die, X_2 the number on the second die, and X the sum of the numbers on the two dice.

(a) What is $E[X \mid X_1 \text{ is even}]$?
(b) What is $E[X \mid X_1 = X_2]$?
(c) What is $E[X_1 \mid X = 9]$?
(d) What is $E[X_1 - X_2 \mid X = k]$ for k in the range $[2, 12]$?

Exercise 2.7: Let X and Y be independent geometric random variables, where X has parameter p and Y has parameter q.

(a) What is the probability that $X = Y$?
(b) What is $E[\max(X, Y)]$?
(c) What is $\Pr(\min(X, Y) = k)$?
(d) What is $E[X \mid X \leq Y]$?

You may find it helpful to keep in mind the memoryless property of geometric random variables.

Exercise 2.8: (a) Alice and Bob decide to have children until either they have their first girl or they have $k \geq 1$ children. Assume that each child is a boy or girl independently with probability $1/2$ and that there are no multiple births. What is the expected number of female children that they have? What is the expected number of male children that they have?

(b) Suppose Alice and Bob simply decide to keep having children until they have their first girl. Assuming that this is possible, what is the expected number of boys that they have?

Exercise 2.9: (a) Suppose that we roll twice a fair k-sided die with the numbers 1 through k on the die's faces, obtaining values X_1 and X_2. What is $E[\max(X_1, X_2)]$? What is $E[\min(X_1, X_2)]$?

41

(b) Show from your calculations in part (a) that

$$\mathbf{E}[\max(X_1, X_2)] + \mathbf{E}[\min(X_1, X_2)] = \mathbf{E}[X_1] + \mathbf{E}[X_2]. \qquad (2.1)$$

(c) Explain why Eqn. (2.1) must be true by using the linearity of expectations instead of a direct computation.

Exercise 2.10: **(a)** Show by induction that if $f : \mathbf{R} \to \mathbf{R}$ is convex then, for any $x_1, x_2, \ldots, x_n$ and $\lambda_1, \lambda_2, \ldots, \lambda_n$ with $\sum_{i=1}^{n} \lambda_i = 1$,

$$f\left(\sum_{i=1}^{n} \lambda_i x_i\right) \leq \sum_{i=1}^{n} \lambda_i f(x_i). \qquad (2.2)$$

(b) Use Eqn. (2.2) to prove that if $f : \mathbf{R} \to \mathbf{R}$ is convex then

$$\mathbf{E}[f(X)] \geq f(\mathbf{E}[X])$$

for any random variable X that takes on only finitely many values.

Exercise 2.11: Prove Lemma 2.6.

Exercise 2.12: We draw cards uniformly at random with replacement from a deck of n cards. What is the expected number of cards we must draw until we have seen all n cards in the deck? If we draw $2n$ cards, what is the expected number of cards in the deck that are not chosen at all? Chosen exactly once?

Exercise 2.13: **(a)** Consider the following variation of the coupon collector's problem. Each box of cereal contains one of $2n$ different coupons. The coupons are organized into n pairs, so that coupons 1 and 2 are a pair, coupons 3 and 4 are a pair, and so on. Once you obtain one coupon from every pair, you can obtain a prize. Assuming that the coupon in each box is chosen independently and uniformly at random from the $2n$ possibilities, what is the expected number of boxes you must buy before you can claim the prize?

(b) Generalize the result of the problem in part (a) for the case where there are kn different coupons, organized into n disjoint sets of k coupons, so that you need one coupon from every set.

Exercise 2.14: The geometric distribution arises as the distribution of the number of times we flip a coin until it comes up heads. Consider now the distribution of the number of flips X until the kth head appears, where each coin flip comes up heads independently with probability p. Prove that this distribution is given by

$$\Pr(X = n) = \binom{n-1}{k-1} p^k (1-p)^{n-k}$$

for $n \geq k$. (This is known as the *negative binomial* distribution.)

Exercise 2.15: For a coin that comes up heads independently with probability p on each flip, what is the expected number of flips until the kth heads?

Exercise 2.16: Suppose we flip a coin n times to obtain a sequence of flips X_1, $X_2, \ldots, X_n$. A *streak* of flips is a consecutive subsequence of flips that are all the same. For example, if X_3, X_4, and X_5 are all heads, there is a streak of length 3 starting at the third flip. (If X_6 is also heads, then there is also a streak of length 4 starting at the third flip.)

(a) Let n be a power of 2. Show that the expected number of streaks of length $\log_2 n + 1$ is $1 - o(1)$.
(b) Show that, for sufficiently large n, the probability that there is no streak of length at least $\lfloor \log_2 n - 2 \log_2 \log_2 n \rfloor$ is less than $1/n$. (*Hint:* Break the sequence of flips up into disjoint blocks of $\lfloor \log_2 n - 2 \log_2 \log_2 n \rfloor$ consecutive flips, and use that the event that one block is a streak is independent of the event that any other block is a streak.)

Exercise 2.17: Recall the recursive spawning process described in Section 2.3. Suppose that each call to process S recursively spawns new copies of the process S, where the number of new copies is 2 with probability p and 0 with probability $1 - p$. If Y_i denotes the number of copies of S in the ith generation, determine $\mathbf{E}[Y_i]$. For what values of p is the expected total number of copies bounded?

Exercise 2.18: The following approach is often called *reservoir sampling*. Suppose we have a sequence of items passing by one at a time. We want to maintain a sample of one item with the property that it is uniformly distributed over all the items that we have seen at each step. Moreover, we want to accomplish this without knowing the total number of items in advance or storing all of the items that we see.

Consider the following algorithm, which stores just one item in memory at all times. When the first item appears, it is stored in the memory. When the kth item appears, it replaces the item in memory with probability $1/k$. Explain why this algorithm solves the problem.

Exercise 2.19: Suppose that we modify the reservoir sampling algorithm of Exercise 2.18 so that, when the kth item appears, it replaces the item in memory with probability $1/2$. Describe the distribution of the item in memory.

Exercise 2.20: A permutation on the numbers $[1, n]$ can be represented as a function $\pi : [1, n] \to [1, n]$, where $\pi(i)$ is the position of i in the ordering given by the permutation. A fixed point of a permutation $\pi : [1, n] \to [1, n]$ is a value for which $\pi(x) = x$. Find the expected number of fixed points of a permutation chosen uniformly at random from all permutations.

Exercise 2.21: Let $a_1, a_2, \ldots, a_n$ be a random permutation of $\{1, 2, \ldots, n\}$, equally likely to be any of the $n!$ possible permutations. When sorting the list $a_1, a_2, \ldots, a_n$, the element a_i must move a distance of $|a_i - i|$ places from its current position to reach

43

its position in the sorted order. Find

$$\mathbf{E}\left[\sum_{i=1}^{n} |a_i - i|\right],$$

the expected total distance that elements will have to be moved.

Exercise 2.22: Let $a_1, a_2, \ldots, a_n$ be a list of n distinct numbers. We say that a_i and a_j are *inverted* if $i < j$ but $a_i > a_j$. The *Bubblesort* sorting algorithm swaps pairwise adjacent inverted numbers in the list until there are no more inversions, so the list is in sorted order. Suppose that the input to Bubblesort is a random permutation, equally likely to be any of the $n!$ permutations of n distinct numbers. Determine the expected number of inversions that need to be corrected by Bubblesort.

Exercise 2.23: *Linear insertion* sort can sort an array of numbers in place. The first and second numbers are compared; if they are out of order, they are swapped so that they are in sorted order. The third number is then placed in the appropriate place in the sorted order. It is first compared with the second; if it is not in the proper order, it is swapped and compared with the first. Iteratively, the kth number is handled by swapping it downward until the first k numbers are in sorted order. Determine the expected number of swaps that need to be made with a linear insertion sort when the input is a random permutation of n distinct numbers.

Exercise 2.24: We roll a standard fair die over and over. What is the expected number of rolls until the first pair of consecutive sixes appears? (*Hint:* The answer is not 36.)

Exercise 2.25: A blood test is being performed on n individuals. Each person can be tested separately, but this is expensive. Pooling can decrease the cost. The blood samples of k people can be pooled and analyzed together. If the test is negative, this one test suffices for the group of k individuals. If the test is positive, then each of the k persons must be tested separately and thus $k + 1$ total tests are required for the k people.

Suppose that we create n/k disjoint groups of k people (where k divides n) and use the pooling method. Assume that each person has a positive result on the test independently with probability p.

(a) What is the probability that the test for a pooled sample of k people will be positive?
(b) What is the expected number of tests necessary?
(c) Describe how to find the best value of k.
(d) Give an inequality that shows for what values of p pooling is better than just testing every individual.

Exercise 2.26: A permutation $\pi : [1, n] \to [1, n]$ can be represented as a set of cycles as follows. Let there be one vertex for each number i, $i = 1, \ldots, n$. If the permutation maps the number i to the number $\pi(i)$, then a directed arc is drawn from vertex i to vertex $\pi(i)$. This leads to a graph that is a set of disjoint cycles. Notice that some of the cycles could be self-loops. What is the expected number of cycles in a random permutation of n numbers?

Exercise 2.27: Consider the following distribution on the integers $x \geq 1$: $\Pr(X = x)$ $= (6/\pi^2)x^{-2}$. This is a valid distribution, since $\sum_{k=1}^{\infty} k^{-2} = \pi^2/6$. What is its expectation?

Exercise 2.28: Consider a simplified version of roulette in which you wager x dollars on either red or black. The wheel is spun, and you receive your original wager plus another x dollars if the ball lands on your color; if the ball doesn't land on your color, you lose your wager. Each color occurs independently with probability $1/2$. (This is a simplification because real roulette wheels have one or two spaces that are neither red nor black, so the probability of guessing the correct color is actually less than $1/2$.)

The following gambling strategy is a popular one. On the first spin, bet 1 dollar. If you lose, bet 2 dollars on the next spin. In general, if you have lost on the first $k - 1$ spins, bet 2^{k-1} dollars on the kth spin. Argue that by following this strategy you will eventually win a dollar. Now let X be the random variable that measures your maximum loss before winning (i.e., the amount of money you have lost before the play on which you win). Show that $\mathbf{E}[X]$ is unbounded. What does it imply about the practicality of this strategy?

Exercise 2.29: Prove that, if $X_0, X_1, \ldots$ is a sequence of random variables such that

$$\sum_{j=0}^{\infty} \mathbf{E}[|X_j|]$$

converges, then the linearity of expectations holds:

$$\mathbf{E}\left[\sum_{j=0}^{\infty} X_j\right] = \sum_{j=0}^{\infty} \mathbf{E}[X_j].$$

Exercise 2.30: In the roulette problem of Exercise 2.28, we found that with probability 1 you eventually win a dollar. Let X_j be the amount you win on the jth bet. (This might be 0 if you have already won a previous bet.) Determine $\mathbf{E}[X_j]$ and show that, by applying the linearity of expectations, you find your expected winnings are 0. Does the linearity of expectations hold in this case? (Compare with Exercise 2.29.)

Exercise 2.31: A variation on the roulette problem of Exercise 2.28 is the following. We repeatedly flip a fair coin. You pay j dollars to play the game. If the first head comes up on the kth flip, you win $2^k/k$ dollars. What are your expected winnings? How much would you be willing to pay to play the game?

Exercise 2.32: You need a new staff assistant, and you have n people to interview. You want to hire the best candidate for the position. When you interview a candidate, you can give them a score, with the highest score being the best and no ties being possible.

45

You interview the candidates one by one. Because of your company's hiring practices, after you interview the kth candidate, you either offer the candidate the job before the next interview or you forever lose the chance to hire that candidate. We suppose the candidates are interviewed in a random order, chosen uniformly at random from all $n!$ possible orderings.

We consider the following strategy. First, interview m candidates but reject them all; these candidates give you an idea of how strong the field is. After the mth candidate, hire the first candidate you interview who is better than all of the previous candidates you have interviewed.

(a) Let E be the event that we hire the best assistant, and let E_i be the event that ith candidate is the best and we hire him. Determine $\Pr(E_i)$, and show that

$$\Pr(E) = \frac{m}{n} \sum_{j=m+1}^{n} \frac{1}{j-1}.$$

(b) Bound $\sum_{j=m+1}^{n} \frac{1}{j-1}$ to obtain

$$\frac{m}{n}(\ln n - \ln m) \le \Pr(E) \le \frac{m}{n}(\ln(n-1) - \ln(m-1)).$$

(c) Show that $m(\ln n - \ln m)/n$ is maximized when $m = n/e$, and explain why this means $\Pr(E) \ge 1/e$ for this choice of m.

CHAPTER THREE

Moments and Deviations

In this and the next chapter we examine techniques for bounding the *tail distribution*, the probability that a random variable assumes values that are far from its expectation. In the context of analysis of algorithms, these bounds are the major tool for estimating the failure probability of algorithms and for establishing high probability bounds on their run-time. In this chapter we study Markov's and Chebyshev's inequalities and demonstrate their application in an analysis of a randomized median algorithm. The next chapter is devoted to the Chernoff bound and its applications.

3.1. Markov's Inequality

Markov's inequality, formulated in the next theorem, is often too weak to yield useful results, but it is a fundamental tool in developing more sophisticated bounds.

Theorem 3.1 [Markov's Inequality]: *Let X be a random variable that assumes only nonnegative values. Then, for all $a > 0$,*

$$\Pr(X \geq a) \leq \frac{\mathbf{E}[X]}{a}.$$

Proof: For $a > 0$, let

$$I = \begin{cases} 1 & \text{if } X \geq a, \\ 0 & \text{otherwise,} \end{cases}$$

and note that, since $X \geq 0$,

$$I \leq \frac{X}{a}. \tag{3.1}$$

Because I is a 0–1 random variable, $\mathbf{E}[I] = \Pr(I = 1) = \Pr(X \geq a)$.

Taking expectations in (3.1) thus yields

$$\Pr(X \geq a) = \mathbf{E}[I] \leq \mathbf{E}\left[\frac{X}{a}\right] = \frac{\mathbf{E}[X]}{a}. \qquad \blacksquare$$

For example, suppose we use Markov's inequality to bound the probability of obtaining more than $3n/4$ heads in a sequence of n fair coin flips. Let

$$X_i = \begin{cases} 1 & \text{if the } i\text{th coin flip is heads,} \\ 0 & \text{otherwise,} \end{cases}$$

and let $X = \sum_{i=1}^{n} X_i$ denote the number of heads in the n coin flips. Since $\mathbf{E}[X_i] = \Pr(X_i = 1) = 1/2$, it follows that $\mathbf{E}[X] = \sum_{i=1}^{n} \mathbf{E}[X_i] = n/2$. Applying Markov's inequality, we obtain

$$\Pr(X \geq 3n/4) \leq \frac{\mathbf{E}[X]}{3n/4} = \frac{n/2}{3n/4} = \frac{2}{3}.$$

3.2. Variance and Moments of a Random Variable

Markov's inequality gives the best tail bound possible when all we know is the expectation of the random variable and that the variable is nonnegative (see Exercise 3.16). It can be improved upon if more information about the distribution of the random variable is available.

Additional information about a random variable is often expressed in terms of its *moments*. The expectation is also called the *first moment* of a random variable. More generally, we define the moments of a random variable as follows.

Definition 3.1: *The kth moment of a random variable X is $\mathbf{E}[X^k]$.*

A significantly stronger tail bound is obtained when the second moment ($\mathbf{E}[X^2]$) is also available. Given the first and second moments, one can compute the *variance* and *standard deviation* of the random variable. Intuitively, the variance and standard deviation offer a measure of how far the random variable is likely to be from its expectation.

Definition 3.2: *The* variance *of a random variable X is defined as*

$$\mathbf{Var}[X] = \mathbf{E}[(X - \mathbf{E}[X])^2] = \mathbf{E}[X^2] - (\mathbf{E}[X])^2.$$

The standard deviation *of a random variable X is*

$$\sigma[X] = \sqrt{\mathbf{Var}[X]}.$$

The two forms of the variance in the definition are equivalent, as is easily seen by using the linearity of expectations. Keeping in mind that $\mathbf{E}[X]$ is a constant, we have

$$\begin{aligned} \mathbf{E}[(X - \mathbf{E}[X])^2] &= \mathbf{E}[X^2 - 2X\mathbf{E}[X] + \mathbf{E}[X]^2] \\ &= \mathbf{E}[X^2] - 2\mathbf{E}[X\mathbf{E}[X]] + \mathbf{E}[X]^2 \\ &= \mathbf{E}[X^2] - 2\mathbf{E}[X]\mathbf{E}[X] + \mathbf{E}[X]^2 \\ &= \mathbf{E}[X^2] - (\mathbf{E}[X])^2. \end{aligned}$$

If a random variable X is constant – so that it always assumes the same value – then its variance and standard deviation are both zero. More generally, if a random variable X takes on the value $k\mathbf{E}[X]$ with probability $1/k$ and the value 0 with probability

48

$1 - 1/k$, then its variance is $(k - 1)(E[X])^2$ and its standard deviation is $\sqrt{k - 1}E[X]$. These cases help demonstrate the intuition that the variance (and standard deviation) of a random variable are small when the random variable assumes values close to its expectation and are large when it assumes values far from its expectation.

We have previously seen that the expectation of the sum of two random variables is equal to the sum of their individual expectations. It is natural to ask whether the same is true for the variance. We find that the variance of the sum of two random variable has an extra term, called the covariance.

Definition 3.3: *The* covariance *of two random variables X and Y is*

$$\mathbf{Cov}(X, Y) = \mathbf{E}[(X - \mathbf{E}[X])(Y - \mathbf{E}[Y])].$$

Theorem 3.2: *For any two random variables X and Y,*

$$\mathbf{Var}[X + Y] = \mathbf{Var}[X] + \mathbf{Var}[Y] + 2\,\mathbf{Cov}(X, Y).$$

Proof:

$$
\begin{aligned}
\mathbf{Var}[X + Y] &= \mathbf{E}[(X + Y - \mathbf{E}[X + Y])^2] \\
&= \mathbf{E}[(X + Y - \mathbf{E}[X] - \mathbf{E}[Y])^2] \\
&= \mathbf{E}[(X - \mathbf{E}[X])^2 + (Y - \mathbf{E}[Y])^2 + 2(X - \mathbf{E}[X])(Y - \mathbf{E}[Y])] \\
&= \mathbf{E}[(X - \mathbf{E}[X])^2] + \mathbf{E}[(Y - \mathbf{E}[Y])^2] + 2\mathbf{E}[(X - \mathbf{E}[X])(Y - \mathbf{E}[Y])] \\
&= \mathbf{Var}[X] + \mathbf{Var}[Y] + 2\,\mathbf{Cov}(X, Y). \qquad \blacksquare
\end{aligned}
$$

The extension of this theorem to a sum of any finite number of random variables is proven in Exercise 3.14.

The variance of the sum of two (or any finite number of) random variables does equal the sum of the variances when the random variables are independent. Equivalently, if X and Y are independent random variables, then their covariance is equal to zero. To prove this result, we first need a result about the expectation of the product of independent random variables.

Theorem 3.3: *If X and Y are two independent random variables, then*

$$\mathbf{E}[X \cdot Y] = \mathbf{E}[X] \cdot \mathbf{E}[Y].$$

Proof: In the summations that follow, let i take on all values in the range of X, and let j take on all values in the range of Y:

$$
\begin{aligned}
\mathbf{E}[X \cdot Y] &= \sum_i \sum_j (i \cdot j) \cdot \Pr((X = i) \cap (Y = j)) \\
&= \sum_i \sum_j (i \cdot j) \cdot \Pr(X = i) \cdot \Pr(Y = j) \\
&= \left(\sum_i i \cdot \Pr(X = i) \right)\left(\sum_j j \cdot \Pr(Y = j) \right) \\
&= \mathbf{E}[X] \cdot \mathbf{E}[Y],
\end{aligned}
$$

where the independence of X and Y is used in the second line. $\blacksquare$

Unlike the linearity of expectations, which holds for the sum of random variables whether they are independent or not, the result that the expectation of the product of two (or more) random variables is equal to the product of their expectations does not necessarily hold if the random variables are dependent. To see this, let Y and Z each correspond to fair coin flips, with Y and Z taking on the value 0 if the flip is heads and 1 if the flip is tails. Then $\mathbf{E}[Y] = \mathbf{E}[Z] = 1/2$. If the two flips are independent, then $Y \cdot Z$ is 1 with probability $1/4$ and 0 otherwise, so indeed $\mathbf{E}[Y \cdot Z] = \mathbf{E}[Y] \cdot \mathbf{E}[Z]$. Suppose instead that the coin flips are dependent in the following way: the coins are tied together, so Y and Z either both come up heads or both come up tails together. Each coin considered individually is still a fair coin flip, but now $Y \cdot Z$ is 1 with probability $1/2$ and so $\mathbf{E}[Y \cdot Z] \neq \mathbf{E}[Y] \cdot \mathbf{E}[Z]$.

Corollary 3.4: *If X and Y are independent random variables, then*

$$\mathbf{Cov}(X, Y) = 0$$

and

$$\mathbf{Var}[X + Y] = \mathbf{Var}[X] + \mathbf{Var}[Y].$$

Proof:

$$\begin{aligned}
\mathbf{Cov}(X, Y) &= \mathbf{E}[(X - \mathbf{E}[X])(Y - \mathbf{E}[Y])] \\
&= \mathbf{E}[X - \mathbf{E}[X]] \cdot \mathbf{E}[Y - \mathbf{E}[Y]] \\
&= 0.
\end{aligned}$$

In the second equation we have used the fact that, since X and Y are independent, so are $X - \mathbf{E}[X]$ and $Y - \mathbf{E}[Y]$ and hence Theorem 3.3 applies. For the last equation we use the fact that, for any random variable Z,

$$\mathbf{E}[(Z - \mathbf{E}[Z])] = \mathbf{E}[Z] - \mathbf{E}[\mathbf{E}[Z]] = 0.$$

Since $\mathbf{Cov}(X, Y) = 0$, we have $\mathbf{Var}[X + Y] = \mathbf{Var}[X] + \mathbf{Var}[Y]$. ∎

By induction we can extend the result of Corollary 3.4 to show that the variance of the sum of any finite number of independent random variables equals the sum of their variances.

Theorem 3.5: *Let $X_1, X_2, \ldots, X_n$ be mutually independent random variables. Then*

$$\mathbf{Var}\left[\sum_{i=1}^{n} X_i \right] = \sum_{i=1}^{n} \mathbf{Var}[X_i].$$

3.2.1. *Example: Variance of a Binomial Random Variable*

The variance of a binomial random variable X with parameters n and p can be determined directly by computing $\mathbf{E}[X^2]$:

$$
\mathbf{E}[X^2] = \sum_{j=0}^{n} \binom{n}{j} p^j (1-p)^{n-j} j^2
$$

$$
= \sum_{j=0}^{n} \frac{n!}{(n-j)! \, j!} p^j (1-p)^{n-j} ((j^2 - j) + j)
$$

$$
= \sum_{j=0}^{n} \frac{n! \, (j^2 - j)}{(n-j)! \, j!} p^j (1-p)^{n-j} + \sum_{j=0}^{n} \frac{n! \, j}{(n-j)! \, j!} p^j (1-p)^{n-j}
$$

$$
= n(n-1)p^2 \sum_{j=2}^{n} \frac{(n-2)!}{(n-j)! \, (j-2)!} p^{j-2} (1-p)^{n-j}
$$

$$
+ np \sum_{j=1}^{n} \frac{(n-1)!}{(n-j)! \, (j-1)!} p^{j-1} (1-p)^{n-j}
$$

$$
= n(n-1)p^2 + np.
$$

Here we have simplified the summations by using the binomial theorem. We conclude that

$$
\begin{aligned}
\mathbf{Var}[X] &= \mathbf{E}[X^2] - (\mathbf{E}[X])^2 \\
&= n(n-1)p^2 + np - n^2 p^2 \\
&= np - np^2 \\
&= np(1-p).
\end{aligned}
$$

An alternative derivation makes use of independence. Recall from Section 2.2 that a binomial random variable X can be represented as the sum of n independent Bernoulli trials, each with success probability p. Such a Bernoulli trial Y has variance

$$
\mathbf{E}[(Y - \mathbf{E}[Y])^2] = p(1-p)^2 + (1-p)(-p)^2 = p - p^2 = p(1-p).
$$

By Theorem 3.5, the variance of X is then $np(1-p)$.

3.3. Chebyshev's Inequality

Using the expectation and the variance of the random variable, one can derive a significantly stronger tail bound known as Chebyshev's inequality.

Theorem 3.6 [Chebyshev's Inequality]: *For any $a > 0$,*

$$
\Pr(|X - \mathbf{E}[X]| \geq a) \leq \frac{\mathbf{Var}[X]}{a^2}.
$$

Proof: We first observe that

$$\Pr(|X - \mathbf{E}[X]| \geq a) = \Pr((X - \mathbf{E}[X])^2 \geq a^2).$$

Since $(X - \mathbf{E}[X])^2$ is a nonnegative random variable, we can apply Markov's inequality to prove:

$$\Pr((X - \mathbf{E}[X])^2 \geq a^2) \leq \frac{\mathbf{E}[(X - \mathbf{E}[X])^2]}{a^2} = \frac{\mathbf{Var}[X]}{a^2}. \qquad \blacksquare$$

The following useful variants of Chebyshev's inequality bound the deviation of the random variable from its expectation in terms of a constant factor of its standard deviation or expectation.

Corollary 3.7: *For any $t > 1$,*

$$\Pr(|X - \mathbf{E}[X]| \geq t \cdot \sigma[X]) \leq \frac{1}{t^2} \quad and$$

$$\Pr(|X - \mathbf{E}[X]| \geq t \cdot \mathbf{E}[X]) \leq \frac{\mathbf{Var}[X]}{t^2(\mathbf{E}[X])^2}.$$

Let us again consider our coin-flipping example, and this time use Chebyshev's inequality to bound the probability of obtaining more than $3n/4$ heads in a sequence of n fair coin flips. Recall that $X_i = 1$ if the ith coin flip is heads and 0 otherwise, and that $X = \sum_{i=1}^{n} X_i$ denotes the number of heads in the n coin flips. To use Chebyshev's inequality we need to compute the variance of X. Observe first that, since X_i is a 0–1 random variable,

$$\mathbf{E}[(X_i)^2] = \mathbf{E}[X_i] = \frac{1}{2}.$$

Thus,

$$\mathbf{Var}[X_i] = \mathbf{E}[(X_i)^2] - (\mathbf{E}[X_i])^2 = \frac{1}{2} - \frac{1}{4} = \frac{1}{4}.$$

Now, since $X = \sum_{i=1}^{n} X_i$ and the X_i are independent, we can use Theorem 3.5 to compute

$$\mathbf{Var}[X] = \mathbf{Var}\left[\sum_{i=1}^{n} X_i\right] = \sum_{i=1}^{n} \mathbf{Var}[X_i] = \frac{n}{4}.$$

Applying Chebyshev's inequality then yields

$$\Pr(X \geq 3n/4) \leq \Pr(|X - \mathbf{E}[X]| \geq n/4)$$
$$\leq \frac{\mathbf{Var}[X]}{(n/4)^2}$$
$$= \frac{n/4}{(n/4)^2}$$
$$= \frac{4}{n}.$$

In fact, we can do slightly better. Chebyshev's inequality yields that $4/n$ is actually a bound on the probability that X is either smaller than $n/4$ or larger than $3n/4$, so by symmetry the probability that X is greater than $3n/4$ is actually $2/n$. Chebyshev's inequality gives a significantly better bound than Markov's inequality for large n.

3.3.1. *Example: Coupon Collector's Problem*

We apply Markov's and Chebyshev's inequalities to the coupon collector's problem. Recall that the time X to collect n coupons has expectation nH_n, where $H_n = \sum_{i=1}^{n} 1/n = \ln n + O(1)$. Hence Markov's inequality yields

$$\Pr(X \geq 2nH_n) \leq \frac{1}{2}.$$

To use Chebyshev's inequality, we need to find the variance of X. Recall again from Section 2.4.1 that $X = \sum_{i=1}^{n} X_i$, where the X_i are geometric random variables with parameter $(n - i + 1)/n$. In this case, the X_i are independent because the time to collect the ith coupon does not depend on how long it took to collect the previous $i - 1$ coupons. Hence

$$\mathbf{Var}[X] = \mathbf{Var}\left[\sum_{i=1}^{n} X_i \right] = \sum_{i=1}^{n} \mathbf{Var}[X_i],$$

so we need to find the variance of a geometric random variable.

Let Y be a geometric random variable with parameter p. As we saw in Section 2.4, $\mathbf{E}[X] = 1/p$. We calculate $\mathbf{E}[Y^2]$. The following trick proves useful. We know that, for $0 < x < 1$,

$$\frac{1}{1 - x} = \sum_{i=0}^{\infty} x^i.$$

Taking derivatives, we find:

$$\frac{1}{(1 - x)^2} = \sum_{i=0}^{\infty} ix^{i-1}$$

$$= \sum_{i=0}^{\infty} (i + 1)x^i;$$

$$\frac{2}{(1 - x)^3} = \sum_{i=0}^{\infty} i(i - 1)x^{i-2}$$

$$= \sum_{i=0}^{\infty} (i + 1)(i + 2)x^i.$$

We can conclude that

$$\sum_{i=1}^{\infty} i^2 x^i = \sum_{i=0}^{\infty} i^2 x^i$$

$$= \sum_{i=0}^{\infty} (i+1)(i+2)x^i - 3\sum_{i=0}^{\infty} (i+1)x^i + \sum_{i=0}^{\infty} x^i$$

$$= \frac{2}{(1-x)^3} - 3\frac{1}{(1-x)^2} + \frac{1}{(1-x)}$$

$$= \frac{x^2 + x}{(1-x)^3}.$$

We now use this to find

$$\mathbf{E}[Y^2] = \sum_{i=1}^{\infty} p(1-p)^{i-1} i^2$$

$$= \frac{p}{1-p} \sum_{i=1}^{\infty} (1-p)^i i^2$$

$$= \frac{p}{1-p} \frac{(1-p)^2 + (1-p)}{p^3}$$

$$= \frac{2-p}{p^2}.$$

Finally, we reach

$$\mathbf{Var}[Y] = \mathbf{E}[Y^2] - \mathbf{E}[Y]^2$$

$$= \frac{2-p}{p^2} - \frac{1}{p^2}$$

$$= \frac{1-p}{p^2}.$$

We have just proven the following useful lemma.

Lemma 3.8: *The variance of a geometric random variable with parameter p is* $(1-p)/p^2$.

For a geometric random variable Y, $\mathbf{E}[Y^2]$ can also be derived using conditional expectations. We use that Y corresponds to the number of flips until the first heads, where each flip is heads with probability p. Let $X = 0$ if the first flip is tails and $X = 1$ if the first flip is heads. By Lemma 2.5,

$$\mathbf{E}[Y^2] = \Pr(X = 0)\mathbf{E}[Y^2 \mid X = 0] + \Pr(X = 1)\mathbf{E}[Y^2 \mid X = 1]$$
$$= (1-p)\mathbf{E}[Y^2 \mid X = 0] + p\mathbf{E}[Y^2 \mid X = 1].$$

54

If $X = 1$, then $Y = 1$ and so $\mathbf{E}[Y^2 \mid X = 1] = 1$. If $X = 0$, then $Y > 1$. In this case, let the number of remaining flips after the first flip until the first head be Z. Then

$$\begin{aligned}\mathbf{E}[Y^2] &= (1 - p)\mathbf{E}[(Z + 1)^2] + p \cdot 1 \\ &= (1 - p)\mathbf{E}[Z^2] + 2(1 - p)\mathbf{E}[Z] + 1\end{aligned} \tag{3.2}$$

by the linearity of expectations. By the memoryless property of geometric random variables, Z is also a geometric random variable with parameter p. Hence $\mathbf{E}[Z] = 1/p$ and $\mathbf{E}[Z^2] = \mathbf{E}[Y^2]$. Plugging these values into Eqn. (3.2), we have

$$\mathbf{E}[Y^2] = (1 - p)\mathbf{E}[Y^2] + \frac{2(1 - p)}{p} + 1 = (1 - p)\mathbf{E}[Y^2] + \frac{2 - p}{p},$$

which yields $\mathbf{E}[Y^2] = (2 - p)/p^2$, matching our other derivation.

We return now to the question of the variance in the coupon collector's problem. We simplify the argument by using the upper bound $\mathbf{Var}[Y] \leq 1/p^2$ for a geometric random variable, instead of the exact result of Lemma 3.8. Then

$$\mathbf{Var}[X] = \sum_{i=1}^{n} \mathbf{Var}[X_i] \leq \sum_{i=1}^{n} \left(\frac{n}{n - i + 1}\right)^2 = n^2 \sum_{i=1}^{n} \left(\frac{1}{i}\right)^2 \leq \frac{\pi^2 n^2}{6}.$$

Here we have used the identity

$$\sum_{i=1}^{\infty} \left(\frac{1}{i}\right)^2 = \frac{\pi^2}{6}.$$

Now, by Chebyshev's inequality,

$$\Pr(|X - nH_n| \geq nH_n) \leq \frac{n^2 \pi^2/6}{(nH_n)^2} = \frac{\pi^2}{6(H_n)^2} = O\left(\frac{1}{\ln^2 n}\right).$$

In this case, Chebyshev's inequality again gives a much better bound than Markov's inequality. But it is still a fairly weak bound, as we can see by considering instead a fairly simple union bound argument.

Consider the probability of not obtaining the ith coupon after $n \ln n + cn$ steps. This probability is

$$\left(1 - \frac{1}{n}\right)^{n(\ln n + c)} < e^{-(\ln n + c)} = \frac{1}{e^c n}.$$

By a union bound, the probability that some coupon has not been collected after $n \ln n + cn$ steps is only e^{-c}. In particular, the probability that all coupons are not collected after $2n \ln n$ steps is at most $1/n$, a bound that is significantly better than what can be achieved even with Chebyshev's inequality.

3.4. Median and Mean

Let X be a random variable. The *median* of X is defined to be any value m such that

$$\Pr(X \leq m) \geq 1/2 \quad \text{and} \quad \Pr(X \geq m) \geq 1/2.$$

For example, for a discrete random variable that is uniformly distributed over an odd number of distinct, sorted values $x_1, x_2, \ldots, x_{2k+1}$, the median is the middle value x_{k+1}. For a discrete random variable that is uniformly distributed over an even number of values $x_1, x_2, \ldots, x_{2k}$, any value in the range (x_k, x_{k+1}) would be a median.

The expectation $\mathbf{E}[X]$ and the median are usually different numbers. For distributions with a unique median that are symmetric around either the mean or median, the median is equal to the mean. For some distributions, the median can be easier to work with than the mean, and in some settings it is a more natural quantity to work with.

The following theorem gives an alternate characterization of the mean and median:

Theorem 3.9: *For any random variable X with finite expectation $\mathbf{E}[X]$ and finite median m,*

1. the expectation $\mathbf{E}[X]$ is the value of c that minimizes the expression

$$\mathbf{E}[(X - c)^2],$$

and

2. the median m is a value of c that minimizes the expression

$$\mathbf{E}[|X - c|].$$

Proof: The first result follows from linearity of expectations.

$$\mathbf{E}[(X - c)^2] = \mathbf{E}[X^2] - 2c\mathbf{E}[X] + c^2,$$

and taking the derivative with respect to c shows that $c = \mathbf{E}[X]$ yields the minimum.

For the second result, we want to show that that for any value c that is not a median and for any median m, we have $\mathbf{E}[|X - c|] > \mathbf{E}[|X - m|]$, or equivalently that $\mathbf{E}[|X - c| - |X - m|] > 0$. In that case the value of c that minimizes $\mathbf{E}[|X - c|]$ will be a median. (In fact, as a by-product, we show that for any two medians m and m', $\mathbf{E}[|X - m|] = \mathbf{E}[|X - m'|]$.)

Let us take the case where $c > m$ for a median m, and c is not a median, so $\Pr(X \geq c) < 1/2$. A similar argument holds for any value of c such that $\Pr(X \leq c) < 1/2$.

For $x \geq c$, $|x - c| - |x - m| = m - c$. For $m < x < c$, $|x - c| - |x - m| = c + m - 2x > m - c$. Finally, for $x \leq m$, $|x - c| - |x - m| = c - m$. Combining the three cases, we have

$$\mathbf{E}[|X - c| - |X - m|]$$
$$= \Pr(X \geq c)(m - c) + \sum_{x:m<x<c} \Pr(X = x)(c + m - 2x) + \Pr(X \leq m)(c - m).$$

We now consider two cases. If $\Pr(m < X < c) = 0$, then

$$\mathbf{E}[|X - c| - |X - m|] = \Pr(X \geq c)(m - c) + \Pr(X \leq m)(c - m)$$
$$> \frac{1}{2}(m - c) + \frac{1}{2}(c - m)$$
$$= 0,$$

where the inequality comes from $\Pr(X \geq c) < 1/2$ and $m < c$. (Note here that if c were another median, so $\Pr(X \geq c) = 1/2$, we would obtain $\mathbf{E}[|X - c| - |X - m|] = 0$, as stated earlier.)

If $\Pr(m < X < c) \neq 0$, then

$$\mathbf{E}[|X - c| - |X - m|]$$
$$= \Pr(X \geq c)(m - c) + \sum_{x:m<x<c} \Pr(X = x)(c + m - 2x) + \Pr(X \leq m)(c - m)$$
$$> \Pr(X > m)(m - c) + \Pr(X \leq m)(c - m)$$
$$> \frac{1}{2}(m - c) + \frac{1}{2}(c - m)$$
$$= 0,$$

where here the first inequality comes from $c + m - 2x > m - c$ for any value of x with non-zero probability in the range $m < x < c$. (This case cannot hold if c and m are both medians, as in this case we cannot have $\Pr(X \geq m) = 1/2$ and $\Pr(X \geq c) = 1/2$.) ∎

Interestingly, for well-behaved random variables, the median and the mean cannot deviate from each other too much.

Theorem 3.10: *If X is a random variable with finite standard deviation σ, expectation μ, and median m, then*

$$|\mu - m| \leq \sigma.$$

Proof: The proof follows from the following sequence:

$$|\mu - m| = |\mathbf{E}[X] - m|$$
$$= |\mathbf{E}[X - m]|$$
$$\leq \mathbf{E}[|X - m|]$$
$$\leq \mathbf{E}[|X - \mu|]$$
$$\leq \sqrt{\mathbf{E}[(X - \mu)^2]}$$
$$= \sigma.$$

Here the first inequality follows from Jensen's inequality, the second inequality follows from the result that the median minimizes $\mathbf{E}[|X - c|]$, and the third inequality is again Jensen's inequality. ∎

In Exercise 3.19, we suggest another way of proving this result.

3.5. Application: A Randomized Algorithm for Computing the Median

Given a set S of n elements drawn from a totally ordered universe, the *median* of S is an element m of S such that at least $\lfloor n/2 \rfloor$ elements in S are less than or equal to m and at least $\lfloor n/2 \rfloor + 1$ elements in S are greater than or equal to m. If the elements in S are distinct, then m is the ($\lceil n/2 \rceil$)th element in the sorted order of S. Note that the median of a set is similar to but slightly different from the the median of a random variable defined in Section 3.4.

The median can be easily found deterministically in $O(n \log n)$ steps by sorting, and there is a relatively complex deterministic algorithm that computes the median in $O(n)$ time. Here we analyze a randomized linear time algorithm that is significantly simpler than the deterministic one and yields a smaller constant factor in the linear running time. To simplify the presentation, we assume that n is odd and that the elements in the input set S are distinct. The algorithm and analysis can be easily modified to include the case of a multi-set S (see Exercise 3.24) and a set with an even number of elements.

3.5.1. *The Algorithm*

The main idea of the algorithm involves *sampling*, which we first discussed in Section 1.2. The goal is to find two elements that are close together in the sorted order of S and that have the median lie between them. Specifically, we seek two elements $d, u \in S$ such that:

1. $d \le m \le u$ (the median m is between d and u); and
2. for $C = \{s \in S : d \le s \le u\}$, $|C| = o(n/\log n)$ (the total number of elements between d and u is small).

Sampling gives us a simple and efficient method for finding two such elements.

We claim that, once these two elements are identified, the median can easily be found in linear time with the following steps. The algorithm counts (in linear time) the number ℓ_d of elements of S that are smaller than d and then sorts (in sublinear, or $o(n)$, time) the set C. Notice that, since $|C| = o(n/ \log n)$, the set C can be sorted in time $o(n)$ using any standard sorting algorithm that requires $O(m \log m)$ time to sort m elements. The ($\lfloor n/2 \rfloor - \ell_d + 1$)th element in the sorted order of C is m, since there are exactly $\lfloor n/2 \rfloor$ elements in S that are smaller than that value ($\lfloor n/2 - \ell_d \rfloor$ in the set C and ℓ_d in $S - C$).

To find the elements d and u, we sample with replacement a multi-set R of $\lceil n^{3/4} \rceil$ elements from S. Recall that sampling with replacement means each element in R is chosen uniformly at random from the set S, independent of previous choices. Thus, the same element of S might appear more than once in the multi-set R. Sampling without replacement might give marginally better bounds, but both implementing and analyzing it are significantly harder. It is worth noting that we assume that an element can be sampled from S in constant time.

Since R is a random sample of S we expect m, the median element of S, to be close to the median element of R. We therefore choose d and u to be elements of R surrounding the median of R.

We require all the steps of our algorithm to work *with high probability*, by which we mean with probability at least $1 - O(1/n^c)$ for some constant $c > 0$. To guarantee that with high probability the set C includes the median m, we fix d and u to be respectively the $\lfloor n^{3/4}/2 - \sqrt{n} \rfloor$th and the $\lceil n^{3/4}/2 + \sqrt{n} \rceil$th elements in the sorted order of R. With

---

Randomized Median Algorithm:

Input: A set S of n elements over a totally ordered universe.

Output: The median element of S, denoted by m.

1. Pick a (multi-)set R of $\lceil n^{3/4} \rceil$ elements in S, chosen independently and uniformly at random with replacement.
2. Sort the set R.
3. Let d be the $\left(\lfloor \frac{1}{2} n^{3/4} - \sqrt{n} \rfloor \right)$th smallest element in the sorted set R.
4. Let u be the $\left(\lceil \frac{1}{2} n^{3/4} + \sqrt{n} \rceil \right)$th smallest element in the sorted set R.
5. By comparing every element in S to d and u, compute the set
   $C = \{x \in S : d \le x \le u\}$ and the numbers $\ell_d = |\{x \in S : x < d\}|$ and
   $\ell_u = |\{x \in S : x > u\}|$.
6. If $\ell_d > n/2$ or $\ell_u > n/2$ then FAIL.
7. If $|C| \le 4n^{3/4}$ then sort the set C, otherwise FAIL.
8. Output the $(\lfloor n/2 \rfloor - \ell_d + 1)$th element in the sorted order of C.

Algorithm 3.1: Randomized median algorithm.

this choice, the set C includes all the elements of S that are between the $2\sqrt{n}$ sample points surrounding the median of R. The analysis will clarify that the choice of the size of R and the choices for d and u are tailored to guarantee both that (a) the set C is large enough to include m with high probability and (b) the set C is sufficiently small so that it can be sorted in sublinear time with high probability.

A formal description of the procedure is presented as Algorithm 3.1. In what follows, for convenience we treat $\sqrt{n}$ and $n^{3/4}$ as integers.

3.5.2. *Analysis of the Algorithm*

Based on our previous discussion, we first prove that – regardless of the random choices made throughout the procedure – the algorithm (a) always terminates in linear time and (b) outputs either the correct result or FAIL.

Theorem 3.11: *The randomized median algorithm terminates in linear time, and if it does not output FAIL then it outputs the correct median element of the input set S.*

Proof: Correctness follows because the algorithm could only give an incorrect answer if the median were not in the set C. But then either $\ell_d > n/2$ or $\ell_u > n/2$ and thus step 6 of the algorithm guarantees that, in these cases, the algorithm outputs FAIL. Similarly, as long as C is sufficiently small, the total work is only linear in the size of S. Step 7 of the algorithm therefore guarantees that the algorithm does not take more than linear time; if the sorting might take too long, the algorithm outputs FAIL without sorting. ∎

The interesting part of the analysis that remains after Theorem 3.11 is bounding the probability that the algorithm outputs FAIL. We bound this probability by identifying three "bad" events such that, if none of these bad events occurs, the algorithm does not fail. In a series of lemmas, we then bound the probability of each of these events and show that the sum of these probabilities is only $O(n^{-1/4})$.

Consider the following three events:

$\mathcal{E}_1 : Y_1 = |\{r \in R \mid r \le m\}| < \frac{1}{2}n^{3/4} - \sqrt{n}$;
$\mathcal{E}_2 : Y_2 = |\{r \in R \mid r \ge m\}| < \frac{1}{2}n^{3/4} - \sqrt{n}$;
$\mathcal{E}_3 : |C| > 4n^{3/4}$.

Lemma 3.12: *The randomized median algorithm fails if and only if at least one of $\mathcal{E}_1$, $\mathcal{E}_2$, or $\mathcal{E}_3$ occurs.*

Proof: Failure in step 7 of the algorithm is equivalent to the event $\mathcal{E}_3$. Failure in step 6 of the algorithm occurs if and only if $\ell_d > n/2$ or $\ell_u > n/2$. But for $\ell_d > n/2$, the $\left(\frac{1}{2}n^{3/4} - \sqrt{n}\right)$th smallest element of R must be larger than m; this is equivalent to the event $\mathcal{E}_1$. Similarly, $\ell_u > n/2$ is equivalent to the event $\mathcal{E}_2$. ∎

Lemma 3.13:

$$\Pr(\mathcal{E}_1) \le \frac{1}{4}n^{-1/4}.$$

Proof: Define a random variable X_i by

$$X_i = \begin{cases} 1 & \text{if the } i\text{th sample is less than or equal to the median,} \\ 0 & \text{otherwise.} \end{cases}$$

The X_i are independent, since the sampling is done with replacement. Because there are $(n - 1)/2 + 1$ elements in S that are less than or equal to the median, the probability that a randomly chosen element of S is less than or equal to the median can be written as

$$\Pr(X_i = 1) = \frac{(n - 1)/2 + 1}{n} = \frac{1}{2} + \frac{1}{2n}.$$

The event $\mathcal{E}_1$ is equivalent to

$$Y_1 = \sum_{i=1}^{n^{3/4}} X_i < \frac{1}{2}n^{3/4} - \sqrt{n}.$$

Since Y_1 is the sum of Bernoulli trials, it is a binomial random variable with parameters $n^{3/4}$ and $1/2 + 1/2n$. Hence, using the result of Section 3.2.1 yields

$$\mathbf{Var}[Y_1] = n^{3/4}\left(\frac{1}{2} + \frac{1}{2n}\right)\left(\frac{1}{2} - \frac{1}{2n}\right)$$

$$= \frac{1}{4}n^{3/4} - \frac{1}{4n^{5/4}}$$

$$< \frac{1}{4}n^{3/4}.$$

Applying Chebyshev's inequality then yields

$$\Pr(\mathcal{E}_1) = \Pr\left(Y_1 < \frac{1}{2}n^{3/4} - \sqrt{n}\right)$$
$$\leq \Pr\left(|Y_1 - \mathbf{E}[Y_1]| > \sqrt{n}\right)$$
$$\leq \frac{\mathbf{Var}[Y_1]}{n}$$
$$< \frac{\frac{1}{4}n^{3/4}}{n} = \frac{1}{4}n^{-1/4}.$$

We similarly obtain the same bound for the probability of the event $\mathcal{E}_2$. We now bound the probability of the third bad event, $\mathcal{E}_3$.

Lemma 3.14:

$$\Pr(\mathcal{E}_3) \leq \frac{1}{2}n^{-1/4}.$$

Proof: If $\mathcal{E}_3$ occurs, so $|C| > 4n^{3/4}$, then at least one of the following two events occurs:

$\mathcal{E}_{3,1}$: at least $2n^{3/4}$ elements of C are greater than the median;
$\mathcal{E}_{3,2}$: at least $2n^{3/4}$ elements of C are smaller than the median.

Let us bound the probability that the first event occurs; the second will have the same bound by symmetry. If there are at least $2n^{3/4}$ elements of C above the median, then the order of u in the sorted order of S was at least $\frac{1}{2}n + 2n^{3/4}$ and thus the set R has at least $\frac{1}{2}n^{3/4} - \sqrt{n}$ samples among the $\frac{1}{2}n - 2n^{3/4}$ largest elements in S.

Let X be the number of samples among the $\frac{1}{2}n - 2n^{3/4}$ largest elements in S. Let $X = \sum_{i=1}^{n^{3/4}} X_i$, where

$$X_i = \begin{cases} 1 & \text{if the } i\text{th sample is among the } \frac{1}{2}n - 2n^{3/4} \text{ largest elements in } S, \\ 0 & \text{otherwise.} \end{cases}$$

Again, X is a binomial random variable, and we find

$$\mathbf{E}[X] = \frac{1}{2}n^{3/4} - 2\sqrt{n}$$

and

$$\mathbf{Var}[X] = n^{3/4}\left(\frac{1}{2} - 2n^{-1/4}\right)\left(\frac{1}{2} + 2n^{-1/4}\right) = \frac{1}{4}n^{3/4} - 4n^{1/4} < \frac{1}{4}n^{3/4}.$$

Applying Chebyshev's inequality yields

$$\Pr(\mathcal{E}_{3,1}) = \Pr\left(X \geq \frac{1}{2}n^{3/4} - \sqrt{n}\right) \tag{3.3}$$

$$\leq \Pr\left(|X - \mathbf{E}[X]| \geq \sqrt{n}\right) \leq \frac{\mathbf{Var}[X]}{n} < \frac{\frac{1}{4}n^{3/4}}{n} = \frac{1}{4}n^{-1/4}. \tag{3.4}$$

Similarly,

$$\Pr(\mathcal{E}_{3,2}) \leq \frac{1}{4}n^{-1/4}$$

and

$$\Pr(\mathcal{E}_3) \leq \Pr(\mathcal{E}_{3,1}) + \Pr(\mathcal{E}_{3,2}) \leq \frac{1}{2}n^{-1/4}. \qquad \blacksquare$$

Combining the bounds just derived, we conclude that the probability that the algorithm outputs FAIL is bounded by

$$\Pr(\mathcal{E}_1) + \Pr(\mathcal{E}_2) + \Pr(\mathcal{E}_3) \leq n^{-1/4}.$$

This yields the following theorem.

Theorem 3.15: *The probability that the randomized median algorithm fails is bounded by $n^{-1/4}$.*

By repeating Algorithm 3.1 until it succeeds in finding the median, we can obtain an iterative algorithm that never fails but has a random running time. The samples taken in successive runs of the algorithm are independent, so the success of each run is independent of other runs, and hence the number of runs until success is achieved is a geometric random variable. As an exercise, you may wish to show that this variation of the algorithm (that runs until it finds a solution) still has linear expected running time.

Randomized algorithms that may fail or return an incorrect answer are called *Monte Carlo* algorithms. The running time of a Monte Carlo algorithm often does not depend on the random choices made. For example, we showed in Theorem 3.11 that the randomized median algorithm always terminates in linear time, regardless of its random choices.

A randomized algorithm that always returns the right answer is called a *Las Vegas* algorithm. We have seen that the Monte Carlo randomized algorithm for the median can be turned into a Las Vegas algorithm by running it repeatedly until it succeeds. Again, turning it into a Las Vegas algorithm means the running time is variable, although the expected running time is still linear.

3.6. Exercises

Exercise 3.1: Let X be a number chosen uniformly at random from $[1, n]$. Find **Var**$[X]$.

Exercise 3.2: Let X be a number chosen uniformly at random from $[-k, k]$. Find **Var**$[X]$.

Exercise 3.3: Suppose that we roll a standard fair die 100 times. Let X be the sum of the numbers that appear over the 100 rolls. Use Chebyshev's inequality to bound $\Pr(|X - 350| \geq 50)$.

Exercise 3.4: Prove that, for any real number c and any discrete random variable X, **Var**$[cX] = c^2$ **Var**$[X]$.

Exercise 3.5: Given any two random variables X and Y, by the linearity of expectations we have $\mathbf{E}[X - Y] = \mathbf{E}[X] - \mathbf{E}[Y]$. Prove that, when X and Y are independent, $\mathbf{Var}[X - Y] = \mathbf{Var}[X] + \mathbf{Var}[Y]$.

Exercise 3.6: For a coin that comes up heads independently with probability p on each flip, what is the variance in the number of flips until the kth head appears?

Exercise 3.7: A simple model of the stock market suggests that, each day, a stock with price q will increase by a factor $r > 1$ to qr with probability p and will fall to q/r with probability $1 - p$. Assuming we start with a stock with price 1, find a formula for the expected value and the variance of the price of the stock after d days.

Exercise 3.8: Suppose that we have an algorithm that takes as input a string of n bits. We are told that the expected running time is $O(n^2)$ if the input bits are chosen independently and uniformly at random. What can Markov's inequality tell us about the worst-case running time of this algorithm on inputs of size n?

Exercise 3.9: (a) Let X be the sum of Bernoulli random variables, $X = \sum_{i=1}^{n} X_i$. The X_i do not need to be independent. Show that

$$\mathbf{E}[X^2] = \sum_{i=1}^{n} \Pr(X_i = 1)\mathbf{E}[X \mid X_i = 1]. \tag{3.5}$$

Hint: Start by showing that

$$\mathbf{E}[X^2] = \sum_{i=1}^{n} \mathbf{E}[X_i X],$$

and then apply conditional expectations.

(b) Use Eqn. (3.5) to provide another derivation for the variance of a binomial random variable with parameters n and p.

Exercise 3.10: For a geometric random variable X, find $\mathbf{E}[X^3]$ and $\mathbf{E}[X^4]$. (*Hint:* Use Lemma 2.5.)

Exercise 3.11: Recall the Bubblesort algorithm of Exercise 2.22. Determine the variance of the number of inversions that need to be corrected by Bubblesort.

Exercise 3.12: Find an example of a random variable with finite expectation and unbounded variance. Give a clear argument showing that your choice has these properties.

Exercise 3.13: Find an example of a random variable with finite jth moments for $1 \leq j \leq k$ but an unbounded $(k + 1)$th moment. Give a clear argument showing that your choice has these properties.

Exercise 3.14: Prove that, for any finite collection of random variables $X_1, X_2, \ldots, X_n$,

$$\mathbf{Var}\left[\sum_{i=1}^{n} X_i\right] = \sum_{i=1}^{n} \mathbf{Var}[X_i] + 2\sum_{i=1}^{n}\sum_{j>i} \mathbf{Cov}(X_i, X_j).$$

Exercise 3.15: Let the random variable X be representable as a sum of random variables $X = \sum_{i=1}^{n} X_i$. Show that, if $\mathbf{E}[X_i X_j] = \mathbf{E}[X_i]\mathbf{E}[X_j]$ for every pair of i and j with $1 \le i < j \le n$, then $\mathbf{Var}[X] = \sum_{i=1}^{n} \mathbf{Var}[X_i]$.

Exercise 3.16: This problem shows that Markov's inequality is as tight as it could possibly be. Given a positive integer k, describe a random variable X that assumes only nonnegative values such that

$$\Pr(X \ge k\mathbf{E}[X]) = \frac{1}{k}.$$

Exercise 3.17: Can you give an example (similar to that for Markov's inequality in Exercise 3.16) that shows that Chebyshev's inequality is tight? If not, explain why not.

Exercise 3.18: Show that, for a random variable X with standard deviation $\sigma[X]$ and any positive real number t:

(a) $\Pr(X - \mathbf{E}[X] \ge t\sigma[X]) \le \dfrac{1}{1+t^2}$;

(b) $\Pr(|X - \mathbf{E}[X]| \ge t\sigma[X]) \le \dfrac{2}{1+t^2}$.

Exercise 3.19: Using Exercise 3.18, show that $|\mu - m| \le \sigma$ for a random variable with finite standard deviation σ, expectation μ, and median m.

Exercise 3.20: Let Y be a nonnegative integer-valued random variable with positive expectation. Prove

$$\frac{\mathbf{E}[Y]^2}{\mathbf{E}[Y^2]} \le \Pr[Y \ne 0] \le \mathbf{E}[Y].$$

Exercise 3.21: **(a)** Chebyshev's inequality uses the variance of a random variable to bound its deviation from its expectation. We can also use higher moments. Suppose that we have a random variable X and an even integer k for which $\mathbf{E}[(X - \mathbf{E}[X])^k]$ is finite. Show that

$$\Pr\left(|X - \mathbf{E}[X]| > t\sqrt[k]{\mathbf{E}[(X - \mathbf{E}[X])^k]}\right) \le \frac{1}{t^k}.$$

(b) Why is it difficult to derive a similar inequality when k is odd?

Exercise 3.22: A fixed point of a permutation $\pi\ [1, n] \to [1, n]$ is a value for which $\pi(x) = x$. Find the variance in the number of fixed points of a permutation chosen uniformly at random from all permutations. (*Hint:* Let X_i be 1 if $\pi(i) = i$, so that $\sum_{i=1}^{n} X_i$

64

is the number of fixed points. You cannot use linearity to find $\mathbf{Var}\left[\sum_{i=1}^{n} X_i\right]$, but you can calculate it directly.)

Exercise 3.23: Suppose that we flip a fair coin n times to obtain n random bits. Consider all $m = \binom{n}{2}$ pairs of these bits in some order. Let Y_i be the exclusive-or of the ith pair of bits, and let $Y = \sum_{i=1}^{m} Y_i$ be the number of Y_i that equal 1.

(a) Show that each Y_i is 0 with probability $1/2$ and 1 with probability $1/2$.
(b) Show that the Y_i are not mutually independent.
(c) Show that the Y_i satisfy the property that $\mathbf{E}[Y_i Y_j] = \mathbf{E}[Y_i]\mathbf{E}[Y_j]$.
(d) Using Exercise 3.15, find $\mathbf{Var}[Y]$.
(e) Using Chebyshev's inequality, prove a bound on $\Pr(|Y - \mathbf{E}[Y]| \geq n)$.

Exercise 3.24: Generalize the median-finding algorithm for the case where the input S is a multi-set. Bound the error probability and the running time of the resulting algorithm.

Exercise 3.25: Generalize the median-finding algorithm to find the kth largest item in a set of n items for any given value of k. Prove that your resulting algorithm is correct, and bound its running time.

Exercise 3.26: The weak law of large numbers states that, if $X_1, X_2, X_3, \ldots$ are independent and identically distributed random variables with mean μ and standard deviation σ, then for any constant $\varepsilon > 0$ we have

$$\lim_{n \to \infty} \Pr\left(\left|\frac{X_1 + X_2 + \cdots + X_n}{n} - \mu\right| > \varepsilon\right) = 0.$$

Use Chebyshev's inequality to prove the weak law of large numbers.

CHAPTER FOUR

Chernoff and Hoeffding Bounds

This chapter introduces large deviation bounds commonly called Chernoff and Hoeffding bounds. These bounds are extremely powerful, giving exponentially decreasing bounds on the tail distribution. These bounds are derived by applying Markov's inequality to the moment generating function of a random variable. We start this chapter by defining and discussing the properties of the moment generating function. We then derive Chernoff bounds for the binomial distribution and other related distributions, using a set balancing problem as an example, and the Hoeffding bound for sums of bounded random variables. To demonstrate the power of Chernoff bounds, we apply them to the analysis of randomized packet routing schemes on the hypercube and butterfly networks.

4.1. Moment Generating Functions

Before developing Chernoff bounds, we discuss the special role of the moment generating function $\mathbf{E}[e^{tX}]$.

Definition 4.1: *The* moment generating function *of a random variable X is*

$$M_X(t) = \mathbf{E}[e^{tX}].$$

We are mainly interested in the existence and properties of this function in the neighborhood of zero.

The function $M_X(t)$ captures all of the moments of X.

Theorem 4.1: *Let X be a random variable with moment generating function $M_X(t)$. Under the assumption that exchanging the expectation and differentiation operands is legitimate, for all $n > 1$ we then have*

$$\mathbf{E}[X^n] = M_X^{(n)}(0),$$

where $M_X^{(n)}(0)$ is the nth derivative of $M_X(t)$ evaluated at $t = 0$.

Proof: Assuming that we can exchange the expectation and differentiation operands, then

$$M_X^{(n)}(t) = \mathbf{E}[X^n e^{tX}].$$

Computed at $t = 0$, this expression yields

$$M_X^{(n)}(0) = \mathbf{E}[X^n]. \qquad \blacksquare$$

The assumption that expectation and differentiation operands can be exchanged holds whenever the moment generating function exists in a neighborhood of zero, which will be the case for all distributions considered in this book.

As a specific example, consider a geometric random variable X with parameter p, as in Definition 2.8. Then, for $t < -\ln(1 - p)$,

$$M_X(t) = \mathbf{E}[e^{tX}]$$

$$= \sum_{k=1}^{\infty} (1 - p)^{k-1} p e^{tk}$$

$$= \frac{p}{1 - p} \sum_{k=1}^{\infty} (1 - p)^k e^{tk}$$

$$= \frac{p}{1 - p} ((1 - (1 - p)e^t)^{-1} - 1).$$

It follows that

$$M_X^{(1)}(t) = p(1 - (1 - p)e^t)^{-2} e^t \quad \text{and}$$

$$M_X^{(2)}(t) = 2p(1 - p)(1 - (1 - p)e^t)^{-3} e^{2t} + p(1 - (1 - p)e^t)^{-2} e^t.$$

Evaluating these derivatives at $t = 0$ and using Theorem 4.1 gives $\mathbf{E}[X] = 1/p$ and $\mathbf{E}[X^2] = (2 - p)/p^2$, matching our previous calculations from Section 2.4 and Section 3.3.1.

Another useful property is that the moment generating function of a random variable (or, equivalently, all of the moments of the variable) uniquely defines its distribution. However, the proof of the following theorem is beyond the scope of this book.

Theorem 4.2: *Let X and Y be two random variables. If*

$$M_X(t) = M_Y(t)$$

for all $t \in (-\delta, \delta)$ for some $\delta > 0$, then X and Y have the same distribution.

One application of Theorem 4.2 is in determining the distribution of a sum of independent random variables.

Theorem 4.3: *If X and Y are independent random variables, then*

$$M_{X+Y}(t) = M_X(t)M_Y(t).$$

Proof:

$$M_{X+Y}(t) = \mathbf{E}[e^{t(X+Y)}] = \mathbf{E}[e^{tX} e^{tY}] = \mathbf{E}[e^{tX}]\mathbf{E}[e^{tY}] = M_X(t)M_Y(t).$$

67

Here we have used that X and Y are independent – and hence e^{tX} and e^{tY} are independent – to conclude that $\mathbf{E}[e^{tX}e^{tY}] = \mathbf{E}[e^{tX}]\mathbf{E}[e^{tY}]$. ∎

Thus, if we know $M_X(t)$ and $M_Y(t)$ and if we recognize the function $M_X(t)M_Y(t)$ as the moment generating function of a known distribution, then that must be the distribution of $X + Y$ when Theorem 4.2 applies. We will see examples of this in subsequent sections and in the exercises.

4.2. Deriving and Applying Chernoff Bounds

The Chernoff bound for a random variable X is obtained by applying Markov's inequality to e^{tX} for some well-chosen value t. From Markov's inequality, we can derive the following useful inequality: for any $t > 0$,

$$\Pr(X \geq a) = \Pr(e^{tX} \geq e^{ta}) \leq \frac{\mathbf{E}[e^{tX}]}{e^{ta}}.$$

In particular,

$$\Pr(X \geq a) \leq \min_{t>0} \frac{\mathbf{E}[e^{tX}]}{e^{ta}}.$$

Similarly, for any $t < 0$,

$$\Pr(X \leq a) = \Pr(e^{tX} \geq e^{ta}) \leq \frac{\mathbf{E}[e^{tX}]}{e^{ta}}.$$

Hence

$$\Pr(X \leq a) \leq \min_{t<0} \frac{\mathbf{E}[e^{tX}]}{e^{ta}}.$$

Bounds for specific distributions are obtained by choosing appropriate values for t. While the value of t that minimizes $\mathbf{E}[e^{tX}]/e^{ta}$ gives the best possible bounds, often one chooses a value of t that gives a convenient form. Bounds derived from this approach are generally referred to collectively as *Chernoff bounds*. When we speak of a Chernoff bound for a random variable, it could actually be one of many bounds derived in this fashion.

4.2.1. *Chernoff Bounds for the Sum of Poisson Trials*

We now develop the most commonly used version of the Chernoff bound: for the tail distribution of a sum of independent 0–1 random variables, which are also known as *Poisson trials*. (Poisson trials differ from Poisson random variables, which will be discussed in Section 5.3.) The distributions of the random variables in Poisson trials are not necessarily identical. *Bernoulli trials* are a special case of Poisson trials where the independent 0–1 random variables have the same distribution; in other words, all trials are Poisson trials that take on the value 1 with the same probability. Also recall that the binomial distribution gives the number of successes in n independent Bernoulli trials. Our Chernoff bound will hold for the binomial distribution and also for the more general setting of the sum of Poisson trials.

Let $X_1, \ldots, X_n$ be a sequence of independent Poisson trials with $\Pr(X_i = 1) = p_i$. Let $X = \sum_{i=1}^{n} X_i$, and let

$$\mu = \mathbf{E}[X] = \mathbf{E}\left[\sum_{i=1}^{n} X_i\right] = \sum_{i=1}^{n} \mathbf{E}[X_i] = \sum_{i=1}^{n} p_i.$$

For a given $\delta > 0$, we are interested in bounds on $\Pr(X \geq (1+\delta)\mu)$ and $\Pr(X \leq (1-\delta)\mu)$ – that is, the probability that X deviates from its expectation μ by $\delta\mu$ or more. To develop a Chernoff bound we need to compute the moment generating function of X. We start with the moment generating function of each X_i:

$$\begin{aligned}
M_{X_i}(t) &= \mathbf{E}[e^{tX_i}] \\
&= p_i e^t + (1 - p_i) \\
&= 1 + p_i(e^t - 1) \\
&\leq e^{p_i(e^t - 1)},
\end{aligned}$$

where in the last inequality we have used the fact that, for any y, $1 + y \leq e^y$. Applying Theorem 4.3, we take the product of the n generating functions to obtain

$$\begin{aligned}
M_X(t) &= \prod_{i=1}^{n} M_{X_i}(t) \\
&\leq \prod_{i=1}^{n} e^{p_i(e^t - 1)} \\
&= \exp\left\{\sum_{i=1}^{n} p_i(e^t - 1)\right\} \\
&= e^{(e^t - 1)\mu}.
\end{aligned}$$

Now that we have determined a bound on the moment generating function, we are ready to develop concrete versions of the Chernoff bound for a sum of Poisson trials. We start with bounds on the deviation above the mean.

Theorem 4.4: *Let $X_1, \ldots, X_n$ be independent Poisson trials such that $\Pr(X_i = 1) = p_i$. Let $X = \sum_{i=1}^{n} X_i$ and $\mu = \mathbf{E}[X]$. Then the following Chernoff bounds hold:*

1. for any $\delta > 0$,

$$\Pr(X \geq (1+\delta)\mu) \leq \left(\frac{e^\delta}{(1+\delta)^{(1+\delta)}}\right)^\mu; \tag{4.1}$$

2. for $0 < \delta \leq 1$,

$$\Pr(X \geq (1+\delta)\mu) \leq e^{-\mu\delta^2/3}; \tag{4.2}$$

3. for $R \geq 6\mu$,

$$\Pr(X \geq R) \leq 2^{-R}. \tag{4.3}$$

The first bound of the theorem is the strongest, and it is from this bound that we derive the other two bounds, which have the advantage of being easier to state and compute with in many situations.

Proof: Applying Markov's inequality, for any $t > 0$ we have

$$\Pr(X \geq (1 + \delta)\mu) = \Pr(e^{tX} \geq e^{t(1+\delta)\mu})$$
$$\leq \frac{\mathbf{E}[e^{tX}]}{e^{t(1+\delta)\mu}}$$
$$\leq \frac{e^{(e^t-1)\mu}}{e^{t(1+\delta)\mu}}.$$

For any $\delta > 0$, we can set $t = \ln(1 + \delta) > 0$ to get Eqn. (4.1):

$$\Pr(X \geq (1 + \delta)\mu) \leq \left(\frac{e^\delta}{(1 + \delta)^{(1+\delta)}} \right)^\mu.$$

To obtain Eqn. (4.2) we need to show that, for $0 < \delta \leq 1$,

$$\frac{e^\delta}{(1 + \delta)^{(1+\delta)}} \leq e^{-\delta^2/3}.$$

Taking the logarithm of both sides, we obtain the equivalent condition

$$f(\delta) = \delta - (1 + \delta) \ln(1 + \delta) + \frac{\delta^2}{3} \leq 0.$$

Computing the derivatives of $f(\delta)$, we have:

$$f'(\delta) = 1 - \frac{1 + \delta}{1 + \delta} - \ln(1 + \delta) + \frac{2}{3}\delta$$
$$= -\ln(1 + \delta) + \frac{2}{3}\delta;$$
$$f''(\delta) = -\frac{1}{1 + \delta} + \frac{2}{3}.$$

We see that $f''(\delta) < 0$ for $0 \leq \delta < 1/2$ and that $f''(\delta) > 0$ for $\delta > 1/2$. Hence $f'(\delta)$ first decreases and then increases over the interval $[0, 1]$. Since $f'(0) = 0$ and $f'(1) < 0$, we can conclude that $f'(\delta) \leq 0$ in the interval $[0, 1]$. Since $f(0) = 0$, it follows that $f(\delta) \leq 0$ in that interval, proving Eqn. (4.2).

To prove Eqn. (4.3), let $R = (1 + \delta)\mu$. Then, for $R \geq 6\mu$, $\delta = R/\mu - 1 \geq 5$. Hence, using Eqn. (4.1),

$$\Pr(X \geq (1 + \delta)\mu) \leq \left(\frac{e^\delta}{(1 + \delta)^{(1+\delta)}} \right)^\mu$$
$$\leq \left(\frac{e}{1 + \delta} \right)^{(1+\delta)\mu}$$
$$\leq \left(\frac{e}{6} \right)^R$$
$$\leq 2^{-R}. \qquad \blacksquare$$

We obtain similar results bounding the deviation below the mean.

Theorem 4.5: *Let $X_1, \ldots, X_n$ be independent Poisson trials such that $\Pr(X_i = 1) = p_i$. Let $X = \sum_{i=1}^{n} X_i$ and $\mu = \mathbf{E}[X]$. Then, for $0 < \delta < 1$:*

1.
$$\Pr(X \leq (1 - \delta)\mu) \leq \left(\frac{e^{-\delta}}{(1 - \delta)^{(1-\delta)}} \right)^{\mu}; \tag{4.4}$$

2.
$$\Pr(X \leq (1 - \delta)\mu) \leq e^{-\mu\delta^2/2}. \tag{4.5}$$

Again, the bound of Eqn. (4.4) is stronger than Eqn. (4.5), but the latter is generally easier to use and sufficient in most applications.

Proof: Using Markov's inequality, for any $t < 0$ we have

$$\Pr(X \leq (1 - \delta)\mu) = \Pr(e^{tX} \geq e^{t(1-\delta)\mu})$$
$$\leq \frac{\mathbf{E}[e^{tX}]}{e^{t(1-\delta)\mu}}$$
$$\leq \frac{e^{(e^t - 1)\mu}}{e^{t(1-\delta)\mu}}.$$

For $0 < \delta < 1$, we set $t = \ln(1 - \delta) < 0$ to get Eqn. (4.4):

$$\Pr(X \leq (1 - \delta)\mu) \leq \left(\frac{e^{-\delta}}{(1 - \delta)^{(1-\delta)}} \right)^{\mu}.$$

To prove Eqn. (4.5) we must show that, for $0 < \delta < 1$,

$$\frac{e^{-\delta}}{(1 - \delta)^{(1-\delta)}} \leq e^{-\delta^2/2}.$$

Taking the logarithm of both sides, we obtain the equivalent condition

$$f(\delta) = -\delta - (1 - \delta) \ln(1 - \delta) + \frac{\delta^2}{2} \leq 0$$

for $0 < \delta < 1$.

Differentiating $f(\delta)$ yields

$$f'(\delta) = \ln(1 - \delta) + \delta,$$
$$f''(\delta) = -\frac{1}{1 - \delta} + 1.$$

Since $f''(\delta) < 0$ in the range $(0, 1)$ and since $f'(0) = 0$, we have $f'(\delta) \leq 0$ in the range $[0, 1)$. Therefore, $f(\delta)$ is nonincreasing in that interval. Since $f(0) = 0$, it follows that $f(\delta) \leq 0$ when $0 < \delta < 1$, as required. ∎

Often the following form of the Chernoff bound, which is derived immediately from Eqn. (4.2) and Eqn. (4.4), is used.

Corollary 4.6: *Let $X_1, \ldots, X_n$ be independent Poisson trials such that $\Pr(X_i = 1) = p_i$. Let $X = \sum_{i=1}^{n} X_i$ and $\mu = \mathbf{E}[X]$. For $0 < \delta < 1$,*

$$\Pr(|X - \mu| \geq \delta\mu) \leq 2e^{-\mu\delta^2/3}. \tag{4.6}$$

In practice we often do not have the exact value of $\mathbf{E}[X]$. Instead we can use $\mu \geq \mathbf{E}[X]$ in Theorem 4.4 and $\mu \leq \mathbf{E}[X]$ in Theorem 4.5 (see Exercise 4.7).

4.2.2. *Example: Coin Flips*

Let X be the number of heads in a sequence of n independent fair coin flips. Applying the Chernoff bound of Eqn. (4.6), we have

$$\Pr\left(\left|X - \frac{n}{2}\right| \geq \frac{1}{2}\sqrt{6n \ln n}\right) \leq 2 \exp\left\{-\frac{1}{3}\frac{n}{2}\frac{6\ln n}{n}\right\}$$
$$= \frac{2}{n}.$$

This demonstrates that the concentration of the number of heads around the mean $n/2$ is very tight; most of the time, the deviations from the mean are on the order of $O(\sqrt{n \ln n})$.

To compare the power of this bound to Chebyshev's bound, consider the probability of having no more than $n/4$ heads or no fewer than $3n/4$ heads in a sequence of n independent fair coin flips. In the previous chapter, we used Chebyshev's inequality to show that

$$\Pr\left(\left|X - \frac{n}{2}\right| \geq \frac{n}{4}\right) \leq \frac{4}{n}.$$

Already, this bound is worse than the Chernoff bound just calculated for a significantly larger event! Using the Chernoff bound in this case, we find that

$$\Pr\left(\left|X - \frac{n}{2}\right| \geq \frac{n}{4}\right) \leq 2 \exp\left\{-\frac{1}{3}\frac{n}{2}\frac{1}{4}\right\}$$
$$\leq 2e^{-n/24}.$$

Thus, Chernoff's technique gives a bound that is exponentially smaller than the bound obtained using Chebyshev's inequality.

4.2.3. *Application: Estimating a Parameter*

Suppose that we are interested in evaluating the probability that a particular gene mutation occurs in the population. Given a DNA sample, a lab test can determine if it carries the mutation. However, the test is expensive and we would like to obtain a relatively reliable estimate from a small number of samples.

Let p be the unknown value that we are trying to estimate. Assume that we have n samples and that $X = \tilde{p}n$ of these samples have the mutation. Given a sufficiently large number of samples, we expect the value p to be close to the sampled value $\tilde{p}$. We express this intuition using the concept of a confidence interval.

Definition 4.2: *A $1 - \gamma$ confidence interval for a parameter p is an interval $[\tilde{p} - \delta, \tilde{p} + \delta]$ such that*

$$\Pr(p \in [\tilde{p} - \delta, \tilde{p} + \delta]) \geq 1 - \gamma.$$

Notice that, instead of predicting a single value for the parameter, we give an interval that is likely to contain the parameter. If p can take on any real value, it may not make sense to try to pin down its exact value from a finite sample, but it does make sense to estimate it within some small range.

Naturally we want both the interval size 2δ and the error probability γ to be as small as possible. We derive a trade-off between these two parameters and the number of samples n. In particular, given that among n samples (chosen uniformly at random from the entire population) we find the mutation in exactly $X = \tilde{p}n$ samples, we need to find values of δ and γ for which

$$\Pr(p \in [\tilde{p} - \delta, \tilde{p} + \delta]) = \Pr(np \in [n(\tilde{p} - \delta), n(\tilde{p} + \delta)]) \geq 1 - \gamma.$$

Now $X = n\tilde{p}$ has a binomial distribution with parameters n and p, so $\mathbf{E}[X] = np$. If $p \notin [\tilde{p} - \delta, \tilde{p} + \delta]$ then we have one of the following two events:

1. if $p < \tilde{p} - \delta$, then $X = n\tilde{p} > n(p + \delta) = \mathbf{E}[X](1 + \delta/p)$;
2. if $p > \tilde{p} + \delta$, then $n\tilde{p} < n(p - \delta) = \mathbf{E}[X](1 - \delta/p)$.

We can apply the Chernoff bounds in Eqns. (4.2) and (4.5) to compute

$$\Pr(p \notin [\tilde{p} - \delta, \tilde{p} + \delta]) = \Pr\left(X < np\left(1 - \frac{\delta}{p}\right)\right) + \Pr\left(X > np\left(1 + \frac{\delta}{p}\right)\right) \quad (4.7)$$

$$< e^{-np(\delta/p)^2/2} + e^{-np(\delta/p)^2/3} \quad (4.8)$$

$$= e^{-n\delta^2/2p} + e^{-n\delta^2/3p}. \quad (4.9)$$

The bound given in Eqn. (4.9) is not useful because the value of p is unknown. A simple solution is to use the fact that $p \leq 1$, yielding

$$\Pr(p \notin [\tilde{p} - \delta, \tilde{p} + \delta]) < e^{-n\delta^2/2} + e^{-n\delta^2/3}.$$

Setting $\gamma = e^{-n\delta^2/2} + e^{-n\delta^2/3}$, we obtain a trade-off between δ, n, and the error probability γ.

We can apply other Chernoff bounds, such as those in Exercises 4.13 and 4.16, to obtain better bounds. We return to the subject of parameter estimation when we discuss the Monte Carlo method in Chapter 11.

4.3. Better Bounds for Some Special Cases

We can obtain stronger bounds using a simpler proof technique for some special cases of symmetric random variables.

We consider first the sum of independent random variables when each variable assumes the value 1 or -1 with equal probability.

Theorem 4.7: *Let $X_1, \ldots, X_n$ be independent random variables with*

$$\Pr(X_i = 1) = \Pr(X_i = -1) = \frac{1}{2}.$$

Let $X = \sum_{i=1}^{n} X_i$. For any $a > 0$,

$$\Pr(X \geq a) \leq e^{-a^2/2n}.$$

Proof: For any $t > 0$,

$$\mathbf{E}[e^{tX_i}] = \frac{1}{2}e^t + \frac{1}{2}e^{-t}.$$

To estimate $\mathbf{E}[e^{tX_i}]$, we observe that

$$e^t = 1 + t + \frac{t^2}{2!} + \cdots + \frac{t^i}{i!} + \cdots$$

and

$$e^{-t} = 1 - t + \frac{t^2}{2!} + \cdots + (-1)^i \frac{t^i}{i!} + \cdots,$$

using the Taylor series expansion for e^t. Thus,

$$\begin{aligned}
\mathbf{E}[e^{tX_i}] &= \frac{1}{2}e^t + \frac{1}{2}e^{-t} \\
&= \sum_{i \geq 0} \frac{t^{2i}}{(2i)!} \\
&\leq \sum_{i \geq 0} \frac{(t^2/2)^i}{i!} \\
&= e^{t^2/2}.
\end{aligned}$$

Using this estimate yields

$$\mathbf{E}[e^{tX}] = \prod_{i=1}^{n} \mathbf{E}[e^{tX_i}] \leq e^{t^2 n/2}$$

and

$$\Pr(X \geq a) = \Pr(e^{tX} \geq e^{ta}) \leq \frac{\mathbf{E}[e^{tX}]}{e^{ta}} \leq e^{t^2 n/2 - ta}.$$

Setting $t = a/n$, we obtain

$$\Pr(X \geq a) \leq e^{-a^2/2n}.$$

By symmetry we also have

$$\Pr(X \leq -a) \leq e^{-a^2/2n}.$$

Combining the two results yields our next corollary.

Corollary 4.8: *Let $X_1, \ldots, X_n$ be independent random variables with*

$$\Pr(X_i = 1) = \Pr(X_i = -1) = \frac{1}{2}.$$

Let $X = \sum_{i=1}^{n} X_i$. Then, for any $a > 0$,

$$\Pr(|X| \geq a) \leq 2e^{-a^2/2n}.$$

Applying the transformation $Y_i = (X_i + 1)/2$ allows us to prove the following.

Corollary 4.9: *Let $Y_1, \ldots, Y_n$ be independent random variables with*

$$\Pr(Y_i = 1) = \Pr(Y_i = 0) = \frac{1}{2}.$$

Let $Y = \sum_{i=1}^{n} Y_i$ and $\mu = \mathbf{E}[Y] = n/2$.

1. For any $a > 0$,

$$\Pr(Y \geq \mu + a) \leq e^{-2a^2/n}.$$

2. For any $\delta > 0$,

$$\Pr(Y \geq (1 + \delta)\mu) \leq e^{-\delta^2\mu}. \tag{4.10}$$

Proof: Using the notation of Theorem 4.7, we have

$$Y = \sum_{i=1}^{n} Y_i = \frac{1}{2}\left(\sum_{i=1}^{n} X_i\right) + \frac{n}{2} = \frac{1}{2}X + \mu.$$

Applying Theorem 4.7 yields

$$\Pr(Y \geq \mu + a) = \Pr(X \geq 2a) \leq e^{-4a^2/2n},$$

proving the first part of the corollary. The second part follows from setting $a = \delta\mu = \delta n/2$. Again applying Theorem 4.7, we have

$$\Pr(Y \geq (1 + \delta)\mu) = \Pr(X \geq 2\delta\mu) \leq e^{-2\delta^2\mu^2/n} = e^{-\delta^2\mu}. \qquad \blacksquare$$

Note that the constant in the exponent of the bound of Eqn. (4.10) is 1 instead of the 1/3 in the bound of Eqn. (4.2).

Similarly, we have the following result.

Corollary 4.10: *Let $Y_1, \ldots, Y_n$ be independent random variables with*

$$\Pr(Y_i = 1) = \Pr(Y_i = 0) = \frac{1}{2}.$$

Let $Y = \sum_{i=1}^{n} Y_i$ and $\mu = \mathbf{E}[Y] = n/2$.

1. For any $0 < a < \mu$,

$$\Pr(Y \leq \mu - a) \leq e^{-2a^2/n}.$$

2. For any $0 < \delta < 1$,

$$\Pr(Y \leq (1 - \delta)\mu) \leq e^{-\delta^2\mu}. \tag{4.11}$$

4.4. Application: Set Balancing

Given an $n \times m$ matrix $\mathbf{A}$ with entries in $\{0, 1\}$, let

$$\begin{pmatrix} a_{11} & a_{12} & \cdots & a_{1m} \\ a_{21} & a_{22} & \cdots & a_{2m} \\ \vdots & \vdots & \ddots & \vdots \\ a_{n1} & a_{n2} & \cdots & a_{nm} \end{pmatrix} \begin{pmatrix} b_1 \\ b_2 \\ \vdots \\ b_m \end{pmatrix} = \begin{pmatrix} c_1 \\ c_2 \\ \vdots \\ c_n \end{pmatrix}.$$

Suppose that we are looking for a vector $\bar{b}$ with entries in $\{-1, 1\}$ that minimizes

$$\|\mathbf{A}\bar{b}\|_\infty = \max_{i=1,\ldots,n} |c_i|.$$

This problem arises in designing statistical experiments. Each column of the matrix $\mathbf{A}$ represents a subject in the experiment and each row represents a feature. The vector $\bar{b}$ partitions the subjects into two disjoint groups, so that each feature is roughly as balanced as possible between the two groups. One of the groups serves as a control group for an experiment that is run on the other group.

Our randomized algorithm for computing a vector $\bar{b}$ is extremely simple. We randomly choose the entries of $\bar{b}$, with $\Pr(b_i = 1) = \Pr(b_i = -1) = 1/2$. The choices for different entries are independent. Surprisingly, although this algorithm ignores the entries of the matrix $\mathbf{A}$, the following theorem shows that $\|\mathbf{A}\bar{b}\|_\infty$ is likely to be only $O(\sqrt{m \ln n})$. This bound is fairly tight. In Exercise 4.15 you are asked to show that, when $m = n$, there exists a matrix $\mathbf{A}$ for which $\|\mathbf{A}\bar{b}\|_\infty$ is $\Omega(\sqrt{n})$ for any choice of $\bar{b}$.

Theorem 4.11: *For a random vector $\bar{b}$ with entries chosen independently and with equal probability from the set $\{-1, 1\}$,*

$$\Pr\left(\|\mathbf{A}\bar{b}\|_\infty \geq \sqrt{4m \ln n}\right) \leq \frac{2}{n}.$$

Proof: Consider the ith row $\bar{a}_i = a_{i,1}, \ldots, a_{i,m}$, and let k be the number of 1s in that row. If $k \leq \sqrt{4m \ln n}$, then clearly $|\bar{a}_i \cdot \bar{b}| = |c_i| \leq \sqrt{4m \ln n}$. On the other hand, if $k > \sqrt{4m \ln n}$ then we note that the k nonzero terms in the sum

$$Z_i = \sum_{j=1}^{m} a_{i,j} b_j$$

are independent random variables, each with probability $1/2$ of being either $+1$ or -1.

Now using the Chernoff bound of Corollary 4.8 and the fact that $m \geq k$,

$$\Pr\left(|Z_i| > \sqrt{4m \ln n}\right) \leq 2e^{-4m \ln n/2k} \leq \frac{2}{n^2}.$$

By the union bound, the probability that the bound fails for any row is at most $2/n$. ∎

4.5. The Hoeffding Bound

Hoeffding's bound extends the Chernoff bound technique to general random variables with a bounded range.

Theorem 4.12 [Hoeffding Bound]: *Let $X_1, \ldots, X_n$ be independent random variables such that for all $1 \le i \le n$, $\mathbf{E}[X_i] = \mu$ and $\Pr(a \le X_i \le b) = 1$. Then*

$$\Pr\left(\left| \frac{1}{n} \sum_{i=1}^{n} X_i - \mu \right| \ge \epsilon \right) \le 2e^{-2n\epsilon^2/(b-a)^2}.$$

Proof: The proof relies on the following bound for the moment generating function, which we prove first.

Lemma 4.13 [Hoeffding's Lemma]: *Let X be a random variable such that $\Pr(X \in [a, b]) = 1$ and $\mathbf{E}[X] = 0$. Then for every $\lambda > 0$,*

$$\mathbf{E}[e^{\lambda X}] \le e^{\lambda^2 (b-a)^2/8}.$$

Proof: Before beginning, note that since $\mathbf{E}[X] = 0$, if $a = 0$ then $b = 0$ and the statement is trivial. Hence we may assume $a < 0$ and $b > 0$.

Since $f(x) = e^{\lambda x}$ is a convex function, for any $\alpha \in (0, 1)$,

$$f(\alpha a + (1 - \alpha)b) \le \alpha e^{\lambda a} + (1 - \alpha)e^{\lambda b}.$$

For $x \in [a, b]$, let $\alpha = \frac{b-x}{b-a}$; then $x = \alpha a + (1 - \alpha)b$ and we have

$$e^{\lambda x} \le \frac{b - x}{b - a}e^{\lambda a} + \frac{x - a}{b - a}e^{\lambda b}.$$

We consider $e^{\lambda X}$ and take expectations. Using the fact that $\mathbf{E}[X] = 0$, we have

$$\mathbf{E}[e^{\lambda X}] \le \mathbf{E}\left[\frac{b - X}{b - a}e^{\lambda a} \right] + \mathbf{E}\left[\frac{X - a}{b - a}e^{\lambda b} \right]$$

$$= \frac{b}{b - a}e^{\lambda a} - \frac{\mathbf{E}[X]}{b - a}e^{\lambda a} - \frac{a}{b - a}e^{\lambda b} + \frac{\mathbf{E}[X]}{b - a}e^{\lambda b}$$

$$= \frac{b}{b - a}e^{\lambda a} - \frac{a}{b - a}e^{\lambda b}.$$

We now require some manipulation of this final expression. Let $\phi(t) = -\theta t + \ln(1 - \theta + \theta e^t)$, for $\theta = \frac{-a}{b-a} > 0$. Then

$$e^{\phi(\lambda(b-a))} = e^{-\theta\lambda(b-a)}(1 - \theta + \theta e^{\lambda(b-a)})$$

$$= e^{\lambda a}(1 - \theta + \theta e^{\lambda(b-a)})$$

$$= e^{\lambda a}\left(\frac{b}{b - a} - \frac{a}{b - a}e^{\lambda(b-a)} \right)$$

$$= \frac{b}{b - a}e^{\lambda a} - \frac{a}{b - a}e^{\lambda b},$$

which equals the upper bound we derived for $\mathbf{E}[e^{\lambda X}]$. It is not hard to verify that $\phi(0) = \phi'(0) = 0$, and $\phi''(t) \le 1/4$ for all t. By Taylor's theorem, for any $t > 0$ there is a

77

$t' \in [0, t]$ such that

$$\phi(t) = \phi(0) + t\phi'(0) + \frac{1}{2}t^2\phi''(t') \le \frac{1}{8}t^2.$$

Thus, for $t = \lambda(b - a)$, we have

$$\phi(\lambda(b - a)) \le \frac{\lambda^2(b - a)^2}{8}.$$

It follows that

$$\mathbf{E}[e^{\lambda X}] \le e^{\phi(\lambda(b-a))} \le e^{\lambda^2(b-a)^2/8}. \qquad \blacksquare$$

We now return to the proof of Theorem 4.12. Let $Z_i = X_i - \mathbf{E}[X_i]$ and $Z = \frac{1}{n}\sum_{i=1}^{n} Z_i$.

For any $\lambda > 0$, by Markov's inequality,

$$\Pr(Z \ge \epsilon) = \Pr(e^{\lambda Z} \ge e^{\lambda\epsilon}) \le e^{-\lambda\epsilon}\mathbf{E}[e^{\lambda Z}] \le e^{-\lambda\epsilon}\prod_{i=1}^{n}\mathbf{E}[e^{\lambda Z_i/n}]$$

$$\le e^{-\lambda\epsilon}\prod_{i=1}^{n}e^{\lambda^2(b-a)^2/n^2} \le e^{-\lambda\epsilon + \lambda^2(b-a)^2/8n},$$

where for the key second to last inequality we have used Hoeffding's Lemma with the fact that Z_i/n is bounded between $(a - \mu)/n$ and $(b - \mu)/n$. Setting $\lambda = \frac{4n\epsilon}{(b-a)^2}$ gives

$$\Pr\left(\frac{1}{n}\sum_{i=1}^{n} X_i - \mu \ge \epsilon\right) = \Pr(Z \ge \epsilon) \le e^{-2n\epsilon^2/(b-a)^2}.$$

Applying the same argument for $\Pr(Z \le -\epsilon)$ with $\lambda = -\frac{4n\epsilon}{(b-a)^2}$ gives

$$\Pr\left(\frac{1}{n}\sum_{i=1}^{n} X_i - \mu \le -\epsilon\right) = \Pr(Z \le -\epsilon) \le e^{-2n\epsilon^2/(b-a)^2}.$$

Applying a union bound on the two cases gives the theorem. $\qquad \blacksquare$

The proof of the following more general version of the bound is left as an exercise (Exercise 4.20).

Theorem 4.14: *Let $X_1, \ldots, X_n$ be independent random variables with $\mathbf{E}[X_i] = \mu_i$ and $\Pr(a_i \le X_i \le b_i) = 1$ for constants a_i and b_i. Then*

$$\Pr\left(\left|\sum_{i=1}^{n} X_i - \sum_{i=1}^{n}\mu_i\right| \ge \epsilon\right) \le 2e^{-2\epsilon^2/\sum_{i=1}^{n}(b_i-a_i)^2}.$$

Note that Theorem 4.12 bounds the deviation of the average of the n random variables while Theorem 4.14 bounds the deviation of the sum of the variables.

Examples:

1. Consider n independent random variables $X_1, \ldots, X_n$ such that X_i is uniformly distributed in $\{0, \ldots, \ell\}$. For all i, $\mu = \mathbf{E}[X_i] = \ell/2$, and

$$\Pr\left(\left|\frac{1}{n}\sum_{i=1}^{n} X_i - \frac{\ell}{2}\right| \geq \epsilon\right) \leq 2e^{-2n\epsilon^2/\ell^2}.$$

In particular,

$$\Pr\left(\left|\frac{1}{n}\sum_{i=1}^{n} X_i - \mu\right| \geq \delta\mu\right) \leq 2e^{-n\delta^2/2}.$$

2. Consider n independent random variables $Y_1, \ldots, Y_n$ such that Y_i is uniformly distributed in $\{0, i\}$. Let $Y = \sum_{i=1}^{n} Y_i$. Then $\mathbf{E}[Y_i] = i/2$, and $\mu = \mathbf{E}[Y] = \sum_{i=1}^{n} i/2 = n(n+1)/4$. Applying Theorem 4.14 with $c_i = i$ we have

$$\Pr\left(\left|Y - \frac{n(n+1)}{4}\right| \geq \epsilon\right) \leq 2e^{-2\epsilon^2/\sum_{i=1}^{n} c_i^2} = 2e^{-2\epsilon^2/(n(n+1)(2n+1)/6)}$$

$$= 2e^{-12\epsilon^2/(n(n+1)(2n+1))}.$$

We can conclude

$$\Pr(|Y - \mu| \geq \delta\mu) \leq 2e^{-12\delta^2 n^2(n+1)^2/(16n(n+1)(2n+1))} \leq 2e^{-3n\delta^2/8}.$$

4.6.* Application: Packet Routing in Sparse Networks

A fundamental problem in parallel computing is how to communicate efficiently over sparse communication networks. We model a communication network by a directed graph on N nodes. Each node is a routing switch. A directed edge models a communication channel, which connects two adjacent routing switches. We consider a synchronous computing model in which (a) an edge can carry one packet in each time step and (b) a packet can traverse no more than one edge per step. We assume that switches have buffers or queues to store packets waiting for transmission through each of the switch's outgoing edges.

Given a network topology, a *routing algorithm* specifies, for each pair of nodes, a route – or a sequence of edges – connecting the pair in the network. The algorithm may also specify a queuing policy for ordering packets in the switches' queues. For example, the First In First Out (FIFO) policy orders packets by their order of arrival. The Furthest To Go (FTG) policy orders packets in decreasing order of the number of edges they must still cross in the network.

Our measure of the performance of a routing algorithm on a given network topology is the maximum time – measured as the number of parallel steps – required to route an arbitrary *permutation routing* problem, where each node sends exactly one packet and each node is the address of exactly one packet.

Of course, routing a permutation can be done in just one parallel step if the network is a complete graph connecting all of the nodes to each other. Practical considerations, however, dictate that a network for a large-scale parallel machine must be sparse.

Each node can be connected directly to only a few neighbors, and most packets must traverse intermediate nodes en route to their final destination. Since an edge may be on the path of more than one packet and since each edge can process only one packet per step, parallel packet routing on sparse networks may lead to congestion and bottlenecks. The practical problem of designing an efficient communication scheme for parallel computers leads to an interesting combinatorial and algorithmic problem: designing a family of sparse networks connecting any number of processors, together with a routing algorithm that routes an arbitrary permutation request in a small number of parallel steps.

We discuss here a simple and elegant randomized routing technique and then use Chernoff bounds to analyze its performance on the hypercube network and the butterfly network. We first analyze the case of routing a permutation on a hypercube, a network with N processors and $O(N \log N)$ edges. We then present a tighter argument for the butterfly network, which has N nodes and only $O(N)$ edges.

4.6.1. Permutation Routing on the Hypercube

Let $\mathcal{N} = \{0 \le i \le N - 1\}$ be the set of processors in our parallel machine and assume that $N = 2^n$ for some integer n. Let $\bar{x} = (x_1, \ldots, x_n)$ be the binary representation of the number $0 \le x \le N - 1$.

Definition 4.3: *The n-dimensional* hypercube *(or n-cube) is a network with $N = 2^n$ nodes such that node x has a direct connection to node y if and only if $\bar{x}$ and $\bar{y}$ differ in exactly one bit.*

See Figure 4.1. Note that the total number of directed edges in the n-cube is nN, since each node is adjacent to n outgoing and n ingoing edges. Also, the diameter of the network is n; that is, there is a directed path of length up to n connecting any two nodes in the network, and there are pairs of nodes that are not connected by any shorter path.

The topology of the hypercube allows for a simple bit-fixing routing mechanism, as shown in Algorithm 4.1. When determining which edge to cross next, the algorithm simply considers each bit in order and crosses the edge if necessary.

Although it seems quite natural, using only the bit-fixing routes can lead to high levels of congestion and poor performance, as shown in Exercise 4.22. There are certain permutations on which the bit-fixing routes behave poorly. It turns out, as we will show, that these routes perform well if each packet is being sent from a source to a destination chosen uniformly at random. This motivates the following approach: first route each packet to a randomly chosen intermediate point, and then route it from this intermediate point to its final destination.

It may seem unusual to first route packets to a random intermediate point. In some sense, this is similar in spirit to our analysis of Quicksort in Section 2.5. We found there that for a list already sorted in reverse order, Quicksort would take $\Omega(n^2)$ comparisons, whereas the expected number of comparisons for a randomly chosen permutation is only $O(n \log n)$. Randomizing the data can lead to a better running time for Quicksort.

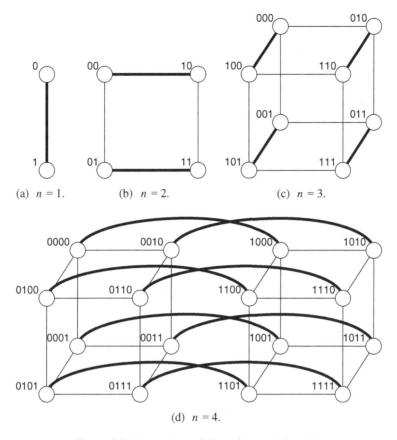

(a) $n = 1$.   (b) $n = 2$.   (c) $n = 3$.

(d) $n = 4$.

Figure 4.1: Hypercubes of dimensions 1, 2, 3, and 4.

---

n-Cube Bit-Fixing Routing Algorithm:

1. Let $\bar{a}$ and $\bar{b}$ be the origin and the destination of the packet.

2. For $i = 1$ to n, do:

   (a) If $a_i \neq b_i$ then traverse the edge $(b_1, \ldots, b_{i-1}, a_i, \ldots, a_n) \rightarrow (b_1, \ldots, b_{i-1}, b_i, a_{i+1}, \ldots, a_n)$.

Algorithm 4.1: n-Cube bit-fixing routing algorithm.

Here, too, randomizing the routes that packets take – by routing them through a random intermediate point – avoids bad initial permutations and leads to good expected performance.

The two-phase routing algorithm (Algorithm 4.2) is executed in parallel by all the packets. The random choices are made independently for each packet. Our analysis holds for any queueing policy that obeys the following natural requirement: if a queue is not empty at the beginning of a time step, some packet is sent along the edge associated with that queue during that time step. We prove that this routing strategy achieves asymptotically optimal parallel time.

Two-Phase Routing Algorithm:

Phase I – Route the packet to a randomly chosen node in the network using the bit-fixing route.

Phase II – Route the packet from its random location to its final destination using the bit-fixing route.

Algorithm 4.2: Two-phase routing algorithm.

Theorem 4.15: *Given an arbitrary permutation routing problem, with probability $1 - O(N^{-1})$ the two-phase routing scheme of Algorithm 4.2 routes all packets to their destinations on the n-cube in $O(n) = O(\log N)$ parallel steps.*

Proof: We first analyze the run-time of Phase I. To simplify the analysis we assume that no packet starts the execution of Phase II before all packets have finished the execution of Phase I. We show later that this assumption can be removed.

We emphasize a fact that we use implicitly throughout. If a packet is routed to a randomly chosen node $\bar{x}$ in the network, we can think of $\bar{x} = (x_1, \ldots, x_n)$ as being generated by setting each x_i independently to be 0 with probability $1/2$ and 1 with probability $1/2$.

For a given packet M, let $T_1(M)$ be the number of steps for M to finish Phase I. For a given edge e, let $X_1(e)$ denote the total number of packets that traverse edge e during Phase I.

In each step of executing Phase I, packet M is either traversing an edge or waiting in a queue while some other packet traverses an edge on M's route. This simple observation relates the routing time of M to the total number of packet transitions through edges on the path of M, as follows.

Lemma 4.16: *Let $e_1, \ldots, e_m$ be the $m \leq n$ edges traversed by a packet M in Phase I. Then*

$$T_1(M) \leq \sum_{i=1}^{m} X_1(e_i).$$

Let us call any path $P = (e_1, e_2, \ldots, e_m)$ of $m \leq n$ edges that follows the bit-fixing algorithm a *possible packet path*. We denote the corresponding nodes by $v_0, v_1, \ldots, v_m$ with $e_i = (v_{i-1}, v_i)$. Following the definition of $T_1(M)$, for any possible packet path P we let

$$T_1(P) = \sum_{i=1}^{m} X_1(e_i).$$

By Lemma 4.16, the probability that Phase I takes more than T steps is bounded by the probability that, for some possible packet path P, $T_1(P) \geq T$. Note that there are at most $2^n \cdot 2^n = 2^{2n}$ possible packet paths, since there are 2^n possible origins and 2^n possible destinations.

To prove the theorem, we need a high-probability bound on $T_1(P)$. Since $T_1(P)$ equals the summation $\sum_{i=1}^{n} X_1(e_i)$, it would be natural to try to use a Chernoff bound. The difficulty here is that the $X_1(e_i)$ are not independent random variables, since a packet that traverses an edge is likely to traverse one of its adjacent edges. To circumvent this difficulty, we first use a Chernoff bound to prove that, with high probability, no more than $6n$ different packets cross any edge of P. We then condition on this event to derive a high-probability bound on the total number of transitions these packets make through edges of the path P, again using a Chernoff bound.[1]

Let us now fix a specific possible packet path P with m edges. To obtain a high-probability bound on the number of packets that cross an edge of P, let us call a packet *active* at a node v_{i-1} on the path P if it reaches v_{i-1} and has the possibility of crossing edge e_i to v_i. That is, if v_{i-1} and v_i differ in the jth bit then – in order for a packet to be active at v_{i-1} – its jth bit cannot have been fixed by the bit-fixing algorithm when it reaches v_{i-1}. We may also call a packet active if it is active at some vertex on the path P. We bound the total number of active packets.

For $k = 1, \ldots, N$, let H_k be a 0–1 random variable such that $H_k = 1$ if the packet starting at node k is active and $H_k = 0$ otherwise. Notice that the H_k are independent because (a) each H_k depends only on the choice of the intermediate destination of the packet starting at node k and (b) these choices are independent for all packets. Let $H = \sum_{k=1}^{N} H_k$ be the total number of active packets.

We first bound $\mathbf{E}[H]$. Consider all the active packets at v_{i-1}. Assume that $v_{i-1} = (b_1, \ldots, b_{j-1}, a_j, a_{j+1}, \ldots, a_n)$ and $v_i = (b_1, \ldots, b_{j-1}, b_j, a_{j+1}, \ldots, a_n)$. Then only packets that start at one of the addresses $(*, \ldots, *, a_j, \ldots, a_n)$, where $*$ stands for either a 0 or a 1, can reach v_{i-1} before the jth bit is fixed. Similarly, each of these packets actually reaches v_{i-1} only if its random destination is one of the addresses $(b_1, \ldots, b_{j-1}, *, \ldots, *)$. Thus, there are no more than 2^{j-1} possible active packets at v_{i-1}, and the probability that each of these packets is actually active at v_{i-1} is $2^{-(j-1)}$. Hence the expected number of active packets per vertex is 1 and, since we need only consider the m vertices $v_0, \ldots, v_{m-1}$, it follows by linearity of expectations that

$$\mathbf{E}[H] \le m \cdot 1 \le n.$$

Since H is the sum of independent 0–1 random variables, we can apply the Chernoff bound (we use the bound of Eqn. (4.3)) to prove

$$\Pr(H \ge 6n \ge 6\mathbf{E}[H]) \le 2^{-6n}.$$

The high-probability bound for H can help us obtain a bound for $T_1(P)$ as follows. Using

$$\Pr(A) = \Pr(A \mid B)\,\Pr(B) + \Pr(A \mid \bar{B})\,\Pr(\bar{B})$$
$$\le \Pr(B) + \Pr(A \mid \bar{B}),$$

---

[1] This approach overestimates the time to finish a phase. In fact, there is a deterministic argument showing that, in this setting, the delay of a packet on a path is bounded by the number of different packets that traverse edges of the path, and hence there is no need to bound the total number of traversals of these packets on the path. However, in the spirit of this book we prefer to present the probabilistic argument.

we find for a given possible packet path P that

$$\Pr(T_1(P) \geq 30n) \leq \Pr(H \geq 6n) + \Pr(T_1(P) \geq 30n \mid H < 6n)$$
$$\leq 2^{-6n} + \Pr(T_1(P) \geq 30n \mid H < 6n).$$

Hence if we show

$$\Pr(T_1(P) \geq 30n \mid H < 6n) \leq 2^{-3n-1},$$

we then have

$$\Pr(T_1(P) \geq 30n) \leq 2^{-3n},$$

which proves sufficient for our purposes.

We therefore need to bound the conditional probability $\Pr(T_1(P) \geq 30n \mid H \leq 6n)$. In other words, conditioning on having no more than $6n$ active packets that might use edges of P, we need a bound on the total number of transitions that these packets take through edges of P.

We first observe that, if a packet leaves the path, it cannot return to that path in this phase of the routing algorithm. Indeed, assume that the active packet was at v_i and that it moved to $w \neq v_{i+1}$. The smallest index bit in which v_{i+1} and w differ cannot be fixed later in this phase, so the route of the packet and the path P cannot meet again in this phase.

Now suppose we have an active packet on our path P at node v_i. What is the probability that the packet crosses e_i? Let us think of our packet as fixing the bits in the binary representation of its destination one at a time by independent random coin flips. The nodes of the edge e_i differ in one bit (say, the jth bit) in this representation. It is therefore clear that the probability of the packet crossing edge e_i is at most $1/2$, since to cross this edge it must choose the appropriate value for the jth bit. (In fact, the probability might be less than $1/2$; the packet might cross some other edge before choosing the value of the jth bit.)

To obtain our bound, let us view as a *trial* each point in the algorithm where an active packet at a node v_i on the path P might cross edge e_i. The trial is successful if the packet leaves the path but a failure if the packet stays on the path. Since the packet leaves the path on a successful trial, if there are at most $6n$ active packets then there can be at most $6n$ successes. Each trial is successful, independently, with probability at least $1/2$. The number of trials is itself a random variable, which we use in our bound of $T_1(P)$.

We claim that the probability that the active packets cross edges of P more than $30n$ times is less than the probability that a fair coin flipped $36n$ times comes up heads fewer than $6n$ times. To see this, think of a coin being flipped for each trial, with heads corresponding to a success. The coin is biased to come up heads with the proper probability for each trial, but this probability is always at least $1/2$ and the coins are independent for each trial. Each failure (tails) corresponds to an active packet crossing an edge, but once there have been $6n$ successes we know there are no more active packets left that can cross an edge of the path. Using a fair coin instead of a coin possibly biased in favor of success can only lessen the probability that the active packets cross edges of

P more than $30n$ times, as can be shown easily by induction (on the number of biased coins).

Letting Z be the number of heads in $36n$ fair coin flips, we now apply the Chernoff bound of Eqn. (4.5) to prove:

$$\Pr(T_1(P) \geq 30n \mid H \leq 6n) \leq \Pr(Z \leq 6n) \leq e^{-18n(2/3)^2/2} = e^{-4n} \leq 2^{-3n-1}.$$

It follows that

$$\Pr(T_1(P) \geq 30n) \leq \Pr(H \geq 6n) + \Pr(T_1(P) \geq 30n \mid H \leq 6n) \leq 2^{-3n},$$

as we wanted to show. Because there are at most 2^{2n} possible packet paths in the hypercube, the probability that there is *any* possible packet path for which $T_1(P) \geq 30n$ is bounded by

$$2^{2n}2^{-3n} = 2^{-n} = O(N^{-1}).$$

This completes the analysis of Phase I. Consider now the execution of Phase II, assuming that all packets completed their Phase I route. In this case, Phase II can be viewed as running Phase I backwards: instead of packets starting at a given origin and going to a random destination, they start at a random origin and end at a given destination. Hence no packet spends more than $30n$ steps in Phase II with probability $1 - O(N^{-1})$.

In fact, we can remove the assumption that packets begin Phase II only after Phase I has completed. The foregoing argument allows us to conclude that the total number of packet traversals across the edges of any packet path during Phase I and Phase II together is bounded by $60n$ with probability $1 - O(N^{-1})$. Since a packet can be delayed only by another packet traversing that edge, we find that every packet completes both Phase I and Phase II after $60n$ steps with probability $1 - O(N^{-1})$ regardless of how the phases interact, concluding the proof of Theorem 4.15 ∎

Note that the run-time of the routing algorithm is optimal up to a constant factor, since the diameter of the hypercube is n. However, the network is not fully utilized because $2nN$ directed edges are used to route just N packets. At any give time, at most $1/2n$ of the edges are actually being used. This issue is addressed in the next section.

4.6.2. *Permutation Routing on the Butterfly*

In this section we adapt the result for permutation routing on the hypercube networks to routing on butterfly networks, yielding a significant improvement in network utilization. Specifically, our goal in this section is to route a permutation on a network with N nodes and $O(N)$ edges in $O(\log N)$ parallel time steps. Recall that the hypercube network had N nodes but $\Omega(N \log N)$ edges. Although the argument will be similar in spirit to that for the hypercube network, there is some additional complexity to the argument for the butterfly network.

We work on the wrapped butterfly network, defined as follows.

Definition 4.4: *The* wrapped butterfly network *has $N = n2^n$ nodes. The nodes are arranged in n columns and 2^n rows. A node's address is a pair (x, r), where $1 \leq x \leq 2^n$*

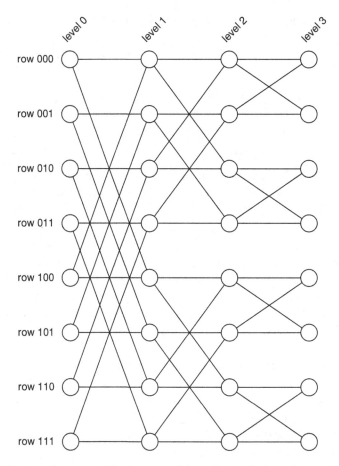

Figure 4.2: The butterfly network. In the wrapped butterfly, levels 0 and 3 are collapsed into one level.

is the row number and $0 \leq r \leq n-1$ is the column number of the node. Node (x, r) is connected to node (y, s) if and only if $s = r + 1 \bmod n$ and either:

1. $x = y$ (the "direct" edge); or
2. x and y differ in precisely the sth bit in their binary representation (the "flip" edge).

See Figure 4.2. To see the relation between the wrapped butterfly and the hypercube, observe that by collapsing the n nodes in each row of the wrapped butterfly into one "super node" we obtain an n-cube network. Using this correspondence, one can easily verify that there is a unique directed path of length n connecting node (x, r) to any other node (w, r) in the same column. This path is obtained by bit fixing: first fixing bits $r + 1$ to n, then bits 1 to r. See Algorithm 4.3. Our randomized permutation routing algorithm on the butterfly consists of three phases, as shown in Algorithm 4.4.

Unlike our analysis of the hypercube, our analysis here cannot simply bound the number of active packets that possibly traverse edges of a path. Given the path of a packet, the expected number of other packets that share edges with this path when

---

Wrapped Butterfly Bit-Fixing Routing Algorithm:

1. Let (x, r) and (y, r) be the origin and the destination of a packet.
2. For $i = 0$ to $n - 1$, do:
   (a) $j = ((i + r) \bmod n) + 1$;
   (b) if $a_j = b_j$ then traverse the direct edge to column $j \bmod n$, else traverse the flip edge to column $j \bmod n$.

Algorithm 4.3: Wrapped butterfly bit-fixing routing algorithm.

Three-Phase Routing Algorithm:

For a packet sent from node (x, r) to node (y, s):

Phase I – Choose a random $w \in [1, \ldots, 2^n]$. Route the packet from node (x, r) to node (w, r) using the bit-fixing route.
Phase II – Route the packet to node (w, s) using direct edges.
Phase III – Route the packet from node (w, s) to node (y, s) using the bit-fixing route.

Algorithm 4.4: Three-phase routing algorithm.

routing a random permutation on the butterfly network is $\Omega(n^2)$ and not $O(n)$ as in the n-cube. To obtain an $O(n)$ routing time, we need a more refined analysis technique that takes into account the order in which packets traverse edges.

Because of this, we need to consider the priority policy that the queues use when there are several packets waiting to use the edge. A variety of priority policies would work here; we assume the following rules.

1. The priority of a packet traversing an edge is $(i - 1)n + t$, where i is the current phase of the packet and t is the number of edge traversals the packet has already executed in this phase.
2. If at any step more than one packet is available to traverse an edge, the packet with the smallest priority number is sent first.

Theorem 4.17: *Given an arbitrary permutation routing problem on the wrapped butterfly with $N = n2^n$ nodes, with probability $1 - O(N^{-1})$ the three-phase routing scheme of Algorithm 4.4 routes all packets to their destinations in $O(n) = O(\log N)$ parallel steps.*

Proof: The priority rule in the edge queues guarantees that packets in a phase cannot delay packets in earlier phases. Because of this, in our forthcoming analysis we can consider the time for each phase to complete separately and then add these times to bound the total time for the three-phase routing scheme to complete.

We begin by considering the second phase. We first argue that with high probability each row transmits at most $4n$ packets in the second phase. To see this, let X_w be the number of packets whose intermediate row choice is w in the three-phase routing algorithm. Then X_w is the sum of 0–1 independent random variables, one for each packet, and $\mathbf{E}[X_w] = n$. Hence, we can directly apply the Chernoff bound of Eqn. (4.1) to find

$$\Pr(X_w \geq 4n) \leq \left(\frac{e^3}{4^4}\right)^n \leq 3^{-2n}.$$

There are 2^n possible rows w. By the union bound, the probability that any row has more than $4n$ packets is only $2^n \cdot 3^{-2n} = O(N^{-1})$.

We now argue that, if each row has at most $4n$ packets for the second phase, then the second phase takes at most $5n$ steps to complete. Combined with our previous observations, this means the second phase takes at most $5n$ steps with probability $1 - O(N^{-1})$. To see this, note that in the second phase the routing has a special structure: each packet moves from edge to edge along its row. Because of the priority rule, each packet can be delayed only by packets already in a queue when it arrives. Therefore, to place an upper bound on the number of packets that delay a packet p, we can bound the total number of packets found in each queue when p arrives at the queue. But in Phase II, the number of other packets that an arriving packet finds in a queue cannot increase in size over time, since at each step a queue sends a packet and receives at most one packet. (It is worth considering the special case when a queue becomes empty at some point in Phase II; this queue can receive another packet at some later step, but the number of packets an arriving packet will find in the queue after that point is always zero.) Since there are at most $4n$ packets total in the row to begin with, p finds at most $4n$ packets that delay it as it moves from queue to queue. Since each packet moves at most n times in the second phase, the total time for the phase is $5n$ steps.

We now consider the other phases. The first and third phases are again the same by symmetry, so we consider just the first phase. Our analysis will use a delay sequence argument. ∎

Definition 4.5: *A delay sequence for an execution of Phase I is a sequence of n edges $e_1, \ldots, e_n$ such that either $e_i = e_{i+1}$ or e_{i+1} is an outgoing edge from the end vertex of e_i. The sequence $e_1, \ldots, e_n$ has the further property that e_i is (one of) the last edges to transmit packets with priority up to i among e_{i+1} and the two incoming edges of e_{i+1}.*

The relation between the delay sequence and the time for Phase I to complete is given by the following lemma.

Lemma 4.18: *For a given execution of Phase I and delay sequence $e_1, \ldots, e_n$, let t_i be the number of packets with priority i sent through edge e_i. Let T_i be the time that edge e_i finishes sending all packets with priority number up to i, so that T_n is the earliest time at which all packets passing through e_n during Phase I have passed through it. Then:*

1. $T_n \leq \sum_{i=1}^n t_i$.
2. If the execution of Phase I takes T steps, then there is a delay sequence for this execution for which $\sum_{i=1}^n t_i \geq T$.

Proof: By the design of the delay sequence, at time T_i the queue of e_{i+1} already holds all of the packets that it will need to subsequently transmit with priority $i + 1$, and at that time it has already finished transmitting all packets with priority numbers up to i. Thus,

$$T_{i+1} \le T_i + t_{i+1}.$$

Since $T_1 = t_1$, we have

$$
\begin{aligned}
T_n &\le T_{n-1} + t_n \\
&\le T_{n-2} + t_{n-1} + t_n \\
&\le \sum_{i=1}^{n} t_i,
\end{aligned}
$$

proving the first part of the lemma.

For the second part, assume that Phase I took T steps and let e be an edge that transmitted a packet at time T. We can construct a delay sequence with $e_n = e$ by choosing e_{n-1} to be the edge among e and its two incoming edges that last transmits packets of priority $n - 1$, and similarly choosing e_{n-2} down to e_1. By the first part of the lemma, $\sum_{i=1}^{n} t_i \ge T$. ∎

Returning to the proof of Theorem 4.17, we now show that the probability of a delay sequence with $T \ge 40n$ is only $O(N^{-1})$. We call any sequence of edges $e_1, \ldots, e_n$ such that either $e_i = e_{i+1}$ or e_{i+1} is an outgoing edge from the end vertex of e_i a *possible delay sequence*. For a given execution and a possible delay sequence, let t_i be the number of packets with priority i sent through e_i. Let $T = \sum_{i=1}^{n} t_i$. We first bound $\mathbf{E}[T]$. Consider the edge $e_i = v \to v'$. Packets with priority i pass through this edge only if their source is at distance $i - 1$ from v. There are precisely 2^{i-1} nodes that are connected to v by a directed path of length $i - 1$. Since packets are sent in Phase I to random destinations, the probability that each of these nodes sends a packet that traverses edge e_i is 2^{-i}, giving

$$\mathbf{E}[t_i] = 2^{i-1}2^{-i} = \frac{1}{2} \quad \text{and} \quad \mathbf{E}[T] = \frac{n}{2}.$$

The motivation for using the delay sequence argument should now be clear. Each possible delay sequence defines a random variable T, where $\mathbf{E}[T] = n/2$. The maximum of T over all delay sequences bounds the run-time of the phase. So we need a bound on T that holds with sufficiently high probability to cover all possible delay sequences. A high-probability bound on T can now be obtained using an argument similar to the one used in the proof of Theorem 4.15. We first bound the number of different packets that contribute to edge traversals counted in T.

For $j = 1, \ldots, N$, let $H_j = 1$ if any traversal of the packet sent by node j is counted in T; otherwise, $H_j = 0$. Clearly, $H = \sum_{j=1}^{N} H_j \le T$ and $\mathbf{E}[H] \le \mathbf{E}[T] = n/2$, where the H_j are independent random variables. Applying the Chernoff bound of Eqn. (4.3) therefore yields

$$\Pr(H \ge 5n) \le 2^{-5n}.$$

Conditioning on the event $H \le 5n$, we now proceed to prove a bound on T, following the same line as in the proof of Theorem 4.15. Given a packet u with at least one traversal counted in T, we consider how many additional traversals of u are counted in T. Specifically, if u is counted in t_i then we consider the probability that it is counted in t_{i+1}. We distinguish between two cases as follows.

1. If $e_{i+1} = e_i$ then u cannot be counted in t_{i+1}, since its traversal with priority $i + 1$ is in the next column. Similarly, it cannot be counted in any t_j, $j > i$.
2. If $e_{i+1} \neq e_i$, then the probability that u continues through e_{i+1} (and is counted in t_{i+1}) is at most $1/2$. If it does not continue through e_{i+1}, then it cannot intersect with the delay sequence in any further traversals in this phase.

As in the proof of Theorem 4.15, the probability that $T \geq 40n$ is less than the probability that a fair coin flipped $40n$ times comes up heads fewer than $5n$ times. (Keep in mind that, in this case, the first traversal by each packet in H must be counted as contributing to T.) Letting Z be the number of heads in $40n$ fair coin flips, we now apply the Chernoff bound (4.5) to prove

$$\Pr(T \geq 40n \mid H \leq 5n) \leq \Pr(Z \leq 5n) \leq e^{-20n(3/4)^2/2} \leq 2^{-5n}.$$

We conclude that

$$\Pr(T \geq 40n) \leq \Pr(T \geq 40n \mid H \leq 5n) + \Pr(H \geq 5n) \leq 2^{-5n+1}.$$

There are no more than $2N3^{n-1} \leq n2^n3^n$ possible delay sequences, since a sequence can start in any one of the $2N$ edges of the network, and by Definition 4.5, if e_i is the ith edge in the sequence, there are only three possible assignments for e_{i+1}. Thus, the probability that, in the execution of Phase I, there is a delay sequence with $T \geq 40n$ is bounded above (using the union bound) by

$$n2^n3^n2^{-5n+1} \leq O(N^{-1}).$$

Since Phase III is entirely similar to Phase I and since Phase II also finishes in $O(n)$ steps with probability $1 - O(N^{-1})$, we have that the three-phase routing algorithm finishes in $O(n)$ steps with probability $1 - O(N^{-1})$.

4.7. Exercises

Exercise 4.1: Alice and Bob play checkers often. Alice is a better player, so the probability that she wins any given game is 0.6, independent of all other games. They decide to play a tournament of n games. Bound the probability that Alice loses the tournament using a Chernoff bound.

Exercise 4.2: We have a standard six-sided die. Let X be the number of times that a 6 occurs over n throws of the die. Let p be the probability of the event $X \geq n/4$. Compare the best upper bounds on p that you can obtain using Markov's inequality, Chebyshev's inequality, and Chernoff bounds.

Exercise 4.3: (a) Determine the moment generating function for the binomial random variable $B(n, p)$.

(b) Let X be a $B(n, p)$ random variable and Y a $B(m, p)$ random variable, where X and Y are independent. Use part (a) to determine the moment generating function of $X + Y$.

(c) What can we conclude from the form of the moment generating function of $X + Y$?

Exercise 4.4: Determine the probability of obtaining 55 or more heads when flipping a fair coin 100 times by an explicit calculation, and compare this with the Chernoff bound. Do the same for 550 or more heads in 1000 flips.

Exercise 4.5: We plan to conduct an opinion poll to find out the percentage of people in a community who want its president impeached. Assume that every person answers either yes or no. If the actual fraction of people who want the president impeached is p, we want to find an estimate X of p such that

$$\Pr(|X - p| \leq \varepsilon p) > 1 - \delta$$

for a given ε and δ, with $0 < \varepsilon, \delta < 1$.

We query N people chosen independently and uniformly at random from the community and output the fraction of them who want the president impeached. How large should N be for our result to be a suitable estimator of p? Use Chernoff bounds, and express N in terms of p, ε, and δ. Calculate the value of N from your bound if $\varepsilon = 0.1$ and $\delta = 0.05$ and if you know that p is between 0.2 and 0.8.

Exercise 4.6: **(a)** In an election with two candidates using paper ballots, each vote is independently misrecorded with probability $p = 0.02$. Use a Chernoff bound to give an upper bound on the probability that more than 4% of the votes are misrecorded in an election of 1,000,000 ballots.

(b) Assume that a misrecorded ballot always counts as a vote for the other candidate. Suppose that candidate A received 510,000 votes and that candidate B received 490,000 votes. Use Chernoff bounds to upper bound the probability that candidate B wins the election owing to misrecorded ballots. Specifically, let X be the number of votes for candidate A that are misrecorded and let Y be the number of votes for candidate B that are misrecorded. Bound $\Pr((X > k) \cup (Y < \ell))$ for suitable choices of k and ℓ.

Exercise 4.7: Throughout the chapter we implicitly assumed the following extension of the Chernoff bound. Prove that it is true.

Let $X = \sum_{i=1}^{n} X_i$, where the X_i are independent 0–1 random variables. Let $\mu = E[X]$. Choose any μ_L and μ_H such that $\mu_L \leq \mu \leq \mu_H$. Then, for any $\delta > 0$,

$$\Pr(X \geq (1 + \delta)\mu_H) \leq \left(\frac{e^{\delta}}{(1 + \delta)^{(1+\delta)}} \right)^{\mu_H}.$$

Similarly, for any $0 < \delta < 1$,

$$\Pr(X \leq (1 - \delta)\mu_L) \leq \left(\frac{e^{-\delta}}{(1 - \delta)^{(1-\delta)}} \right)^{\mu_L}.$$

91

Exercise 4.8: We show how to construct a random permutation π on $[1, n]$, given a black box that outputs numbers independently and uniformly at random from $[1, k]$ where $k \geq n$. If we compute a function $f[1, n] \to [1, k]$ with $f(i) \neq f(j)$ for $i \neq j$, this yields a permutation; simply output the numbers $[1, n]$ according to the order of the $f(i)$ values. To construct such a function f, do the following for $j = 1, \ldots, n$: choose $f(j)$ by repeatedly obtaining numbers from the black box and setting $f(j)$ to the first number found such that $f(j) \neq f(i)$ for $i < j$.

Prove that this approach gives a permutation chosen uniformly at random from all permutations. Find the expected number of calls to the black box that are needed when $k = n$ and $k = 2n$. For the case $k = 2n$, argue that the probability that each call to the black box assigns a value of $f(j)$ to some j is at least $1/2$. Based on this, use a Chernoff bound to bound the probability that the number of calls to the black box is at least $4n$.

Exercise 4.9: Suppose that we can obtain independent samples $X_1, X_2, \ldots$ of a random variable X and that we want to use these samples to estimate $\mathbf{E}[X]$. Using t samples, we use $\left(\sum_{i=1}^{t} X_i\right)/t$ for our estimate of $\mathbf{E}[X]$. We want the estimate to be within $\varepsilon \mathbf{E}[X]$ from the true value of $\mathbf{E}[X]$ with probability at least $1 - \delta$. We may not be able to use Chernoff's bound directly to bound how good our estimate is if X is not a 0–1 random variable, and we do not know its moment generating function. We develop an alternative approach that requires only having a bound on the variance of X. Let $r = \sqrt{\mathbf{Var}[X]}/\mathbf{E}[X]$.

(a) Show using Chebyshev's inequality that $O(r^2/\varepsilon^2\delta)$ samples are sufficient to solve the problem.

(b) Suppose that we need only a weak estimate that is within $\varepsilon \mathbf{E}[X]$ of $\mathbf{E}[X]$ with probability at least $3/4$. Argue that $O(r^2/\varepsilon^2)$ samples are enough for this weak estimate.

(c) Show that, by taking the median of $O(\log(1/\delta))$ weak estimates, we can obtain an estimate within $\varepsilon \mathbf{E}[X]$ of $\mathbf{E}[X]$ with probability at least $1 - \delta$. Conclude that we need only $O((r^2 \log(1/\delta))/\varepsilon^2)$ samples.

Exercise 4.10: A casino is testing a new class of simple slot machines. Each game, the player puts in \$1, and the slot machine is supposed to return either \$3 to the player with probability $4/25$, \$100 with probability $1/200$, or nothing with all remaining probability. Each game is supposed to be independent of other games.

The casino has been surprised to find in testing that the machines have lost \$10,000 over the first million games. Derive a Chernoff bound for the probability of this event. You may want to use a calculator or program to help you choose appropriate values as you derive your bound.

Exercise 4.11: Consider a collection $X_1, \ldots, X_n$ of n independent integers chosen uniformly from the set $\{0, 1, 2\}$. Let $X = \sum_{i=1}^{n} X_i$ and $0 < \delta < 1$. Derive a Chernoff bound for $\Pr(X \geq (1 + \delta)n)$ and $\Pr(X \leq (1 - \delta)n)$.

Exercise 4.12: Consider a collection $X_1, \ldots, X_n$ of n independent geometrically distributed random variables with mean 2. Let $X = \sum_{i=1}^{n} X_i$ and $\delta > 0$.

(a) Derive a bound on $\Pr(X \geq (1 + \delta)(2n))$ by applying the Chernoff bound to a sequence of $(1 + \delta)(2n)$ fair coin tosses.

(b) Directly derive a Chernoff bound on $\Pr(X \geq (1 + \delta)(2n))$ using the moment generating function for geometric random variables.

(c) Which bound is better?

Exercise 4.13: Let $X_1, \ldots, X_n$ be independent Poisson trials such that $\Pr(X_i = 1) = p$. Let $X = \sum_{i=1}^{n} X_i$, so that $\mathbf{E}[X] = pn$. Let

$$F(x, p) = x \ln(x/p) + (1 - x) \ln((1 - x)/(1 - p)).$$

(a) Show that, for $1 \geq x > p$,

$$\Pr(X \geq xn) \leq e^{-nF(x,p)}.$$

(b) Show that, when $0 < x, p < 1$, we have $F(x, p) - 2(x - p)^2 \geq 0$. (*Hint:* Take the second derivative of $F(x, p) - 2(x - p)^2$ with respect to x.)

(c) Using parts (a) and (b), argue that

$$\Pr(X \geq (p + \varepsilon)n) \leq e^{-2n\varepsilon^2}.$$

(d) Use symmetry to argue that

$$\Pr(X \leq (p - \varepsilon)n) \leq e^{-2n\varepsilon^2},$$

and conclude that

$$\Pr(|X - pn| \geq \varepsilon n) \leq 2e^{-2n\varepsilon^2}.$$

Exercise 4.14: Modify the proof of Theorem 4.4 to show the following bound for a weighted sum of Poisson trials. Let $X_1, \ldots, X_n$ be independent Poisson trials such that $\Pr(X_i) = p_i$ and let $a_1, \ldots, a_n$ be real numbers in $[0, 1]$. Let $X = \sum_{i=1}^{n} a_i X_i$ and $\mu = \mathbf{E}[X]$. Then the following Chernoff bound holds: for any $\delta > 0$,

$$\Pr(X \geq (1 + \delta)\mu) \leq \left(\frac{e^\delta}{(1 + \delta)^{(1+\delta)}} \right)^\mu.$$

Prove a similar bound for the probability that $X \leq (1 - \delta)\mu$ for any $0 < \delta < 1$.

Exercise 4.15: Let $X_1, \ldots, X_n$ be independent random variables such that

$$\Pr(X_i = 1 - p_i) = p_i \quad \text{and} \quad \Pr(X_i = -p_i) = 1 - p_i.$$

Let $X = \sum_{i=1}^{n} X_i$. Prove

$$\Pr(|X| \geq a) \leq 2e^{-2a^2/n}.$$

Hint: You may need to assume the inequality

$$p_i e^{\lambda(1-p_i)} + (1 - p_i)e^{-\lambda p_i} \leq e^{\lambda^2/8}.$$

This inequality is difficult to prove directly.

93

Exercise 4.16: Let $X_1, \ldots, X_n$ be independent Poisson trials such that $\Pr(X_i = 1) = p_i$. Let $X = \sum_{i=1}^n a_i X_i$ and $\mu = \mathbf{E}[X]$. Use the result of Exercise 4.15 to prove that if $|a_i| \le 1$ for all $1 \le i \le n$, then for any $0 < \delta < 1$,

$$\Pr(|X - \mu| \ge \delta\mu) \le 2e^{-2\delta^2\mu^2/n}.$$

Exercise 4.17: Suppose that we have n jobs to distribute among m processors. For simplicity, we assume that m divides n. A job takes 1 step with probability p and $k > 1$ steps with probability $1 - p$. Use Chernoff bounds to determine upper and lower bounds (that hold with high probability) on when all jobs will be completed if we randomly assign exactly n/m jobs to each processor.

Exercise 4.18: In many wireless communication systems, each receiver listens on a specific frequency. The bit $b(t)$ sent at time t is represented by a 1 or -1. Unfortunately, noise from other nearby communications can affect the receiver's signal. A simplified model of this noise is as follows. There are n other senders, and the ith has strength $p_i \le 1$. At any time t, the ith sender is also trying to send a bit $b_i(t)$ that is represented by 1 or -1. The receiver obtains the signal $s(t)$ given by

$$s(t) = b(t) + \sum_{i=1}^n p_i b_i(t).$$

If $s(t)$ is closer to 1 than -1, the receiver assumes that the bit sent at time t was a 1; otherwise, the receiver assumes that it was a -1.

Assume that all the bits $b_i(t)$ can be considered independent, uniform random variables. Give a Chernoff bound to estimate the probability that the receiver makes an error in determining $b(t)$.

Exercise 4.19: Recall that a function f is said to be *convex* if, for any x_1, x_2 and for $0 \le \lambda \le 1$,

$$f(\lambda x_1 + (1 - \lambda)x_2) \le \lambda f(x_1) + (1 - \lambda)f(x_2).$$

(a) Let Z be a random variable that takes on a (finite) set of values in the interval $[0, 1]$, and let $p = \mathbf{E}[Z]$. Define the Bernoulli random variable X by $\Pr(X = 1) = p$ and $\Pr(X = 0) = 1 - p$. Show that $\mathbf{E}[f(Z)] \le \mathbf{E}[f(X)]$ for any convex function f.
(b) Use the fact that $f(x) = e^{tx}$ is convex for any $t \ge 0$ to obtain a Chernoff bound for the sum of n independent random variables with distribution Z as in part (a), based on a Chernoff bound for independent Poisson trials.

Exercise 4.20: Prove Theorem 4.14.

Exercise 4.21: We prove that the Randomized Quicksort algorithm sorts a set of n numbers in time $O(n \log n)$ with high probability. Consider the following view of Randomized Quicksort. Every point in the algorithm where it decides on a pivot element is called a *node*. Suppose the size of the set to be sorted at a particular node is s. The node is called *good* if the pivot element divides the set into two parts, each of size not exceeding $2s/3$. Otherwise the node is called *bad*. The nodes can be thought of as forming a tree in which the root node has the whole set to be sorted and its children have the two sets formed after the first pivot step and so on.

(a) Show that the number of good nodes in any path from the root to a leaf in this tree is not greater than $c \log_2 n$, where c is some positive constant.

(b) Show that, with high probability (greater than $1 - 1/n^2$), the number of nodes in a given root to leaf path of the tree is not greater than $c' \log_2 n$, where c' is another constant.

(c) Show that, with high probability (greater than $1 - 1/n$), the number of nodes in the longest root to leaf path is not greater than $c' \log_2 n$. (*Hint:* How many nodes are there in the tree?)

(d) Use your answers to show that the running time of Quicksort is $O(n \log n)$ with probability at least $1 - 1/n$.

Exercise 4.22: Consider the bit-fixing routing algorithm for routing a permutation on the n-cube. Suppose that n is even. Write each source node s as the concatenation of two binary strings a_s and b_s each of length $n/2$. Let the destination of s's packet be the concatenation of b_s and a_s. Show that this permutation causes the bit-fixing routing algorithm to take $\Omega(\sqrt{N})$ steps.

Exercise 4.23: Consider the following modification to the bit-fixing routing algorithm for routing a permutation on the n-cube. Suppose that, instead of fixing the bits in order from 1 to n, each packet chooses a random order (independent of other packets' choices) and fixes the bits in that order. Show that there is a permutation for which this algorithm requires $2^{\Omega(n)}$ steps with high probability.

Exercise 4.24: Assume that we use the randomized routing algorithm for the n-cube network (Algorithm 4.2) to route a total of up to $p2^n$ packets, where each node is the source of no more than p packets and each node is the destination of no more than p packets.

(a) Give a high-probability bound on the run-time of the algorithm.

(b) Give a high-probability bound on the maximum number of packets at any node at any step of the execution of the routing algorithm.

Exercise 4.25: Show that the expected number of packets that traverse any edge on the path of a given packet when routing a random permutation on the wrapped butterfly network of $N = n2^n$ nodes is $\Omega(n^2)$.

Exercise 4.26: In this exercise, we design a randomized algorithm for the following packet routing problem. We are given a network that is an undirected connected graph G, where nodes represent processors and the edges between the nodes represent wires. We are also given a set of N packets to route. For each packet we are given a source node, a destination node, and the exact route (path in the graph) that the packet should take from the source to its destination. (We may assume that there are no loops in the path.) In each time step, at most one packet can traverse an edge. A packet can wait at any node during any time step, and we assume unbounded queue sizes at each node.

A *schedule* for a set of packets specifies the timing for the movement of packets along their respective routes. That is, it specifies which packet should move and which should wait at each time step. Our goal is to produce a schedule for the packets that tries to minimize the total time and the maximum queue size needed to route all the packets to their destinations.

(a) The dilation d is the maximum distance traveled by any packet. The congestion c is the maximum number of packets that must traverse a single edge during the entire course of the routing. Argue that the time required for any schedule should be at least $\Omega(c + d)$.

(b) Consider the following unconstrained schedule, where many packets may traverse an edge during a single time step. Assign each packet an integral delay chosen randomly, independently, and uniformly from the interval $[1, \lceil \alpha c / \log(Nd) \rceil]$, where α is a constant. A packet that is assigned a delay of x waits in its source node for x time steps; then it moves on to its final destination through its specified route without ever stopping. Give an upper bound on the probability that more than $O(\log(Nd))$ packets use a particular edge e at a particular time step t.

(c) Again using the unconstrained schedule of part (b), show that the probability that more than $O(\log(Nd))$ packets pass through any edge at any time step is at most $1/(Nd)$ for a sufficiently large α.

(d) Use the unconstrained schedule to devise a simple randomized algorithm that, with high probability, produces a schedule of length $O(c + d \log(Nd))$ using queues of size $O(\log(Nd))$ and following the constraint that at most one packet crosses an edge per time step.

CHAPTER FIVE

Balls, Bins, and Random Graphs

In this chapter, we focus on one of the most basic of random processes: m balls are thrown randomly into n bins, each ball landing in a bin chosen independently and uniformly at random. We use the techniques we have developed previously to analyze this process and develop a new approach based on what is known as the Poisson approximation. We demonstrate several applications of this model, including a more sophisticated analysis of the coupon collector's problem and an analysis of the Bloom filter data structure. After introducing a closely related model of random graphs, we show an efficient algorithm for finding a Hamiltonian cycle on a random graph with sufficiently many edges. Even though finding a Hamiltonian cycle is NP-hard in general, our result shows that, for a randomly chosen graph, the problem is solvable in polynomial time with high probability.

5.1. Example: The Birthday Paradox

Sitting in lecture, you notice that there are 30 people in the room. Is it more likely that some two people in the room share the same birthday or that no two people in the room share the same birthday?

We can model this problem by assuming that the birthday of each person is a random day from a 365-day year, chosen independently and uniformly at random for each person. This is obviously a simplification; for example, we assume that a person's birthday is equally likely to be any day of the year, we avoid the issue of leap years, and we ignore the possibility of twins! As a model, however, it has the virtue of being easy to understand and analyze.

One way to calculate this probability is to directly count the configurations where two people do not share a birthday. It is easier to think about the configurations where people do not share a birthday than about configurations where some two people do. Thirty days must be chosen from the 365; there are $\binom{365}{30}$ ways to do this. These 30 days can be assigned to the people in any of the 30! possible orders. Hence there are $\binom{365}{30}$ 30! configurations where no two people share the same birthday, out of the 365^{30}

ways the birthdays could occur. Thus, the probability is

$$\frac{\binom{365}{30} 30!}{365^{30}}. \tag{5.1}$$

We can also calculate this probability by considering one person at a time. The first person in the room has a birthday. The probability that the second person has a different birthday is $(1 - 1/365)$. The probability that the third person in the room then has a birthday different from the first two, given that the first two people have different birthdays, is $(1 - 2/365)$. Continuing on, the probability that the kth person in the room has a different birthday than the first $k - 1$, assuming that the first $k - 1$ have different birthdays, is $(1 - (k - 1)/365)$. So the probability that 30 people all have different birthdays is the product of these terms, or

$$\left(1 - \frac{1}{365}\right) \cdot \left(1 - \frac{2}{365}\right) \cdot \left(1 - \frac{3}{365}\right) \cdots \left(1 - \frac{29}{365}\right).$$

You can check that this matches the expression (5.1).

Calculations reveal that (to four decimal places) this product is 0.2937, so when 30 people are in the room there is more than a 70% chance that two share the same birthday. A similar calculation shows that only 23 people need to be in the room before it is more likely than not that two people share a birthday.

More generally, if there are m people and n possible birthdays then the probability that all m have different birthdays is

$$\left(1 - \frac{1}{n}\right) \cdot \left(1 - \frac{2}{n}\right) \cdot \left(1 - \frac{3}{n}\right) \cdots \left(1 - \frac{m-1}{n}\right) = \prod_{j=1}^{m-1} \left(1 - \frac{j}{n}\right).$$

Using that $1 - k/n \approx e^{-k/n}$ when k is small compared to n, we see that if m is small compared to n then

$$\prod_{j=1}^{m-1} \left(1 - \frac{j}{n}\right) \approx \prod_{j=1}^{m-1} e^{-j/n}$$

$$= \exp\left\{-\sum_{j=1}^{m-1} \frac{j}{n}\right\}$$

$$= e^{-m(m-1)/2n}$$

$$\approx e^{-m^2/2n}.$$

Hence the value for m at which the probability that m people all have different birthdays is $1/2$ is approximately given by the equation

$$\frac{m^2}{2n} = \ln 2,$$

or $m = \sqrt{2n \ln 2}$. For the case $n = 365$, this approximation gives $m = 22.49$ to two decimal places, matching the exact calculation quite well.

Quite tight and formal bounds can be established using bounds in place of the approximations just derived, an option that is considered in Exercise 5.3. The following simple arguments, however, give loose bounds and good intuition. Let us consider each person one at a time, and let E_k be the event that the kth person's birthday does not match any of the birthdays of the first $k - 1$ people. Then the probability that the first k people fail to have distinct birthdays is

$$\Pr(\bar{E}_1 \cup \bar{E}_2 \cup \cdots \cup \bar{E}_k) \leq \sum_{i=1}^{k} \Pr(\bar{E}_i)$$

$$\leq \sum_{i=1}^{k} \frac{i-1}{n}$$

$$= \frac{k(k-1)}{2n}.$$

If $k \leq \sqrt{n}$ this probability is less than $1/2$, so with $\lfloor \sqrt{n} \rfloor$ people the probability is at least $1/2$ that all birthdays will be distinct.

Now assume that the first $\lceil \sqrt{n} \rceil$ people all have distinct birthdays. Each person after that has probability at least $\sqrt{n}/n = 1/\sqrt{n}$ of having the same birthday as one of these first $\lceil \sqrt{n} \rceil$ people. Hence the probability that the next $\lceil \sqrt{n} \rceil$ people all have different birthdays than the first $\lceil \sqrt{n} \rceil$ people is at most

$$\left(1 - \frac{1}{\sqrt{n}}\right)^{\lceil \sqrt{n} \rceil} < \frac{1}{e} < \frac{1}{2}.$$

Hence, once there are $2\lceil \sqrt{n} \rceil$ people, the probability is at most $1/e$ that all birthdays will be distinct.

5.2. Balls into Bins

5.2.1. *The Balls-and-Bins Model*

The birthday paradox is an example of a more general mathematical framework that is often formulated in terms of balls and bins. We have m balls that are thrown into n bins, with the location of each ball chosen independently and uniformly at random from the n possibilities. What does the distribution of the balls in the bins look like? The question behind the birthday paradox is whether or not there is a bin with two balls.

There are several interesting questions that we could ask about this random process. For example, how many of the bins are empty? How many balls are in the fullest bin? Many of these questions have applications to the design and analysis of algorithms.

Our analysis of the birthday paradox showed that, if m balls are randomly placed into n bins then, for some $m = \Omega(\sqrt{n})$, at least one of the bins is likely to have more than one ball in it. Another interesting question concerns the maximum number of balls in a bin, or the maximum *load*. Let us consider the case where $m = n$, so that the number of balls equals the number of bins and the average load is 1. Of course the maximum possible load is n, but it is very unlikely that all n balls land in the same bin. We seek an upper bound that holds with probability tending to 1 as n grows large. We can show that the maximum load is more than $3 \ln n / \ln \ln n$ with probability at most $1/n$ for sufficiently large n via a direct calculation and a union bound. This is a very loose bound; although the maximum load is in fact $\Omega(\ln n / \ln \ln n)$ with probability close to 1 (as we show later), the constant factor 3 we use here is chosen to simplify the argument and could be reduced with more care.

Lemma 5.1: *When n balls are thrown independently and uniformly at random into n bins, the probability that the maximum load is more than $3 \ln n / \ln \ln n$ is at most $1/n$ for n sufficiently large.*

Proof: The probability that bin 1 receives at least M balls is at most

$$\binom{n}{M} \left(\frac{1}{n} \right)^M.$$

This follows from a union bound; there are $\binom{n}{M}$ distinct sets of M balls, and for any set of M balls the probability that all land in bin 1 is $(1/n)^M$. We now use the inequalities

$$\binom{n}{M} \left(\frac{1}{n} \right)^M \leq \frac{1}{M!} \leq \left(\frac{e}{M} \right)^M.$$

Here the second inequality is a consequence of the following general bound on factorials: since

$$\frac{k^k}{k!} < \sum_{i=0}^{\infty} \frac{k^i}{i!} = e^k,$$

we have

$$k! > \left(\frac{k}{e} \right)^k.$$

Applying a union bound again allows us to find that, for $M \geq 3 \ln n / \ln \ln n$, the probability that any bin receives at least M balls is bounded above by

$$n \left(\frac{e}{M} \right)^M \leq n \left(\frac{e \ln \ln n}{3 \ln n} \right)^{3 \ln n / \ln \ln n}$$

$$\leq n \left(\frac{\ln \ln n}{\ln n} \right)^{3 \ln n / \ln \ln n}$$

$$= e^{\ln n} (e^{\ln \ln \ln n - \ln \ln n})^{3 \ln n / \ln \ln n}$$

$$= e^{-2 \ln n + 3(\ln n)(\ln \ln \ln n)/\ln \ln n}$$

$$\leq \frac{1}{n}$$

for n sufficiently large. ∎

5.2.2. *Application: Bucket Sort*

Bucket sort is an example of a sorting algorithm that, under certain assumptions on the input, breaks the $\Omega(n \log n)$ lower bound for standard comparison-based sorting. For example, suppose that we have a set of $n = 2^m$ elements to be sorted and that each element is an integer chosen independently and uniformly at random from the range $[0, 2^k)$, where $k \geq m$. Using Bucket sort, we can sort the numbers in expected time $O(n)$. Here the expectation is over the choice of the random input, since Bucket sort is a completely deterministic algorithm.

Bucket sort works in two stages. In the first stage, we place the elements into n buckets. The jth bucket holds all elements whose first m binary digits correspond to the number j. For example, if $n = 2^{10}$, bucket 3 contains all elements whose first 10 binary digits are 0000000011. When $j < \ell$, the elements of the jth bucket all come before the elements in the ℓth bucket in the sorted order. Assuming that each element can be placed in the appropriate bucket in $O(1)$ time, this stage requires only $O(n)$ time. Because of the assumption that the elements to be sorted are chosen uniformly, the number of elements that land in a specific bucket follows a binomial distribution $B(n, 1/n)$. Buckets can be implemented using linked lists.

In the second stage, each bucket is sorted using any standard quadratic time algorithm (such as Bubblesort or Insertion sort). Concatenating the sorted lists from each bucket in order gives us the sorted order for the elements. It remains to show that the expected time spent in the second stage is only $O(n)$.

The result relies on our assumption regarding the input distribution. Under the uniform distribution, Bucket sort falls naturally into the balls and bins model: the elements are balls, buckets are bins, and each ball falls uniformly at random into a bin.

Let X_j be the number of elements that land in the jth bucket. The time to sort the jth bucket is then at most $c(X_j)^2$ for some constant c. The expected time spent sorting in the second stage is at most

$$\mathbf{E}\left[\sum_{j=1}^{n} c(X_j)^2\right] = c\sum_{j=1}^{n} \mathbf{E}[X_j^2] = cn\mathbf{E}[X_1^2],$$

where the first equality follows from the linearity of expectations and the second follows from symmetry, as $\mathbf{E}[X_j^2]$ is the same for all buckets.

Since X_1 is a binomial random variable $B(n, 1/n)$, using the results of Section 3.2.1 yields

$$\mathbf{E}[X_1^2] = \frac{n(n-1)}{n^2} + 1 = 2 - \frac{1}{n} < 2.$$

Hence the total expected time spent in the second stage is at most $2cn$, so Bucket sort runs in expected linear time.

5.3. The Poisson Distribution

We now consider the probability that a given bin is empty in the balls and bins model with m balls and n bins as well as the expected number of empty bins. For the first bin

101

to be empty, it must be missed by all m balls. Since each ball hits the first bin with probability $1/n$, the probability the first bin remains empty is

$$\left(1 - \frac{1}{n}\right)^m \approx e^{-m/n};$$

of course, by symmetry this probability is the same for all bins. If X_i is a random variable that is 1 when the ith bin is empty and 0 otherwise, then $\mathbf{E}[X_i] = (1 - 1/n)^m$. Let X be a random variable that represents the number of empty bins. Then, by the linearity of expectations,

$$\mathbf{E}[X] = \mathbf{E}\left[\sum_{i=1}^{n} X_i\right] = \sum_{i=1}^{n} \mathbf{E}[X_i] = n\left(1 - \frac{1}{n}\right)^m \approx ne^{-m/n}.$$

Thus, the expected fraction of empty bins is approximately $e^{-m/n}$. This approximation is very good even for moderately size values of m and n, and we use it frequently throughout this chapter.

We can generalize the preceding argument to find the expected fraction of bins with r balls for any constant r. The probability that a given bin has r balls is

$$\binom{m}{r}\left(\frac{1}{n}\right)^r\left(1 - \frac{1}{n}\right)^{m-r} = \frac{1}{r!}\frac{m(m-1)\cdots(m-r+1)}{n^r}\left(1 - \frac{1}{n}\right)^{m-r}.$$

When m and n are large compared to r, the second factor on the right-hand side is approximately $(m/n)^r$, and the third factor is approximately $e^{-m/n}$. Hence the probability p_r that a given bin has r balls is approximately

$$p_r \approx \frac{e^{-m/n}(m/n)^r}{r!}, \tag{5.2}$$

and the expected number of bins with exactly r balls is approximately np_r. We formalize this relationship in Section 5.3.1.

The previous calculation naturally leads us to consider the following distribution.

Definition 5.1: *A discrete Poisson random variable X with parameter μ is given by the following probability distribution on $j = 0, 1, 2, \ldots$:*

$$\Pr(X = j) = \frac{e^{-\mu}\mu^j}{j!}.$$

(Note that Poisson random variables differ from Poisson trials, discussed in Section 4.2.1.)

Let us verify that the definition gives a proper distribution in that the probabilities sum to 1:

$$\sum_{j=0}^{\infty} \Pr(X = j) = \sum_{j=0}^{\infty} \frac{e^{-\mu}\mu^j}{j!}$$

$$= e^{-\mu}\sum_{j=0}^{\infty} \frac{\mu^j}{j!}$$

$$= 1,$$

where we have used the Taylor expansion $e^x = \sum_{j=0}^{\infty}(x^j/j!)$.

Next we show that the expectation of this random variable is μ:

$$\mathbf{E}[X] = \sum_{j=0}^{\infty} j \Pr(X = j)$$

$$= \sum_{j=1}^{\infty} j \frac{e^{-\mu}\mu^j}{j!}$$

$$= \mu \sum_{j=1}^{\infty} \frac{e^{-\mu}\mu^{j-1}}{(j-1)!}$$

$$= \mu \sum_{j=0}^{\infty} \frac{e^{-\mu}\mu^j}{j!}$$

$$= \mu.$$

In the context of throwing m balls into n bins, the distribution of the number of balls in a bin is approximately Poisson with $\mu = m/n$, which is exactly the average number of balls per bin, as one might expect.

An important property of Poisson distributions is given in the following lemma.

Lemma 5.2: *The sum of a finite number of independent Poisson random variables is a Poisson random variable.*

Proof: We consider two independent Poisson random variables X and Y with means μ_1 and μ_2; the case of more random variables is simply handled by induction. Now

$$\Pr(X + Y = j) = \sum_{k=0}^{j} \Pr((X = k) \cap (Y = j - k))$$

$$= \sum_{k=0}^{j} \frac{e^{-\mu_1}\mu_1^k}{k!} \frac{e^{-\mu_2}\mu_2^{(j-k)}}{(j-k)!}$$

$$= \frac{e^{-(\mu_1+\mu_2)}}{j!} \sum_{k=0}^{j} \frac{j!}{k!\,(j-k)!} \mu_1^k \mu_2^{(j-k)}$$

$$= \frac{e^{-(\mu_1+\mu_2)}}{j!} \sum_{k=0}^{j} \binom{j}{k} \mu_1^k \mu_2^{(j-k)}$$

$$= \frac{e^{-(\mu_1+\mu_2)}(\mu_1 + \mu_2)^j}{j!}.$$

In the last equality we used the binomial theorem to simplify the summation. ∎

We can also prove Lemma 5.2 using moment generating functions.

Lemma 5.3: *The moment generating function of a Poisson random variable with parameter μ is*

$$M_x(t) = e^{\mu(e^t - 1)}.$$

Proof: For any t,

$$\mathbf{E}[e^{tX}] = \sum_{k=0}^{\infty} \frac{e^{-\mu}\mu^k}{k!} e^{tk} = e^{\mu(e^t-1)} \sum_{k=0}^{\infty} \frac{e^{-\mu e^t}(\mu e^t)^k}{k!} = e^{\mu(e^t-1)}. \qquad \blacksquare$$

Given two independent Poisson random variables X and Y with means μ_1 and μ_2, we apply Theorem 4.3 to prove

$$M_{X+Y}(t) = M_X(t) \cdot M_Y(t) = e^{(\mu_1+\mu_2)(e^t-1)},$$

which is the moment generating function of a Poisson random variable with mean $\mu_1 + \mu_2$. By Theorem 4.2, the moment generating function uniquely defines the distribution, and hence the sum $X + Y$ is a Poisson random variable with mean $\mu_1 + \mu_2$.

We can also use the moment generating function of the Poisson distribution to prove that $\mathbf{E}[X^2] = \lambda(\lambda + 1)$ and $\mathbf{Var}[X] = \lambda$ (see Exercise 5.5).

Next we develop a Chernoff bound for Poisson random variables that we will use later in this chapter.

Theorem 5.4: *Let X be a Poisson random variable with parameter μ.*

1. *If $x > \mu$, then*

$$\Pr(X \geq x) \leq \frac{e^{-\mu}(e\mu)^x}{x^x};$$

2. *If $x < \mu$, then*

$$\Pr(X \leq x) \leq \frac{e^{-\mu}(e\mu)^x}{x^x}.$$

3. *For $\delta > 0$,*

$$\Pr(X \geq (1+\delta)\mu) \leq \left(\frac{e^{\delta}}{(1+\delta)^{(1+\delta)}}\right)^{\mu};$$

4. *For $0 < \delta < 1$,*

$$\Pr(X \leq (1-\delta)\mu) \leq \left(\frac{e^{-\delta}}{(1-\delta)^{(1-\delta)}}\right)^{\mu}.$$

Proof: For any $t > 0$ and $x > \mu$,

$$\Pr(X \geq x) = \Pr(e^{tX} \geq e^{tx}) \leq \frac{\mathbf{E}[e^{tX}]}{e^{tx}}.$$

Plugging in the expression for the moment generating function of the Poisson distribution, we have

$$\Pr(X \geq x) \leq e^{\mu(e^t-1)-xt}.$$

Choosing $t = \ln(x/\mu) > 0$ gives

$$\Pr(X \geq x) \leq e^{x-\mu-x\ln(x/\mu)}$$
$$= \frac{e^{-\mu}(e\mu)^x}{x^x}.$$

For any $t < 0$ and $x < \mu$,

$$\Pr(X \le x) = \Pr(e^{tX} \ge e^{tx}) \le \frac{\mathbf{E}[e^{tX}]}{e^{tx}}.$$

Hence

$$\Pr(X \le x) \le e^{\mu(e^t - 1) - xt}.$$

Choosing $t = \ln(x/\mu) < 0$, it follows that

$$\Pr(X \le x) \le e^{x - \mu - x \ln(x/\mu)}$$
$$= \frac{e^{-\mu}(e\mu)^x}{x^x}.$$

The alternate forms of the bound given in parts 3 and 4 follow immediately from parts 1 and 2. ∎

5.3.1. *Limit of the Binomial Distribution*

We have shown that, when throwing m balls randomly into n bins, the probability p_r that a bin has r balls is approximately the Poisson distribution with mean m/n. In general, the Poisson distribution is the limit distribution of the binomial distribution with parameters n and p, when n is large and p is small. More precisely, we have the following limit result.

Theorem 5.5: *Let X_n be a binomial random variable with parameters n and p, where p is a function of n and $\lim_{n \to \infty} np = \lambda$ is a constant that is independent of n. Then, for any fixed k,*

$$\lim_{n \to \infty} \Pr(X_n = k) = \frac{e^{-\lambda} \lambda^k}{k!}.$$

This theorem directly applies to the balls-and-bins scenario. Consider the situation where there are m balls and n bins, where m is a function of n and $\lim_{m \to \infty} m/n = \lambda$. Let X_m be the number of balls in a specific bin. Then X_m is a binomial random variable with parameters m and $1/n$. Theorem 5.5 thus applies and says that

$$\lim_{m \to \infty} \Pr(X_m = r) = \frac{e^{-m/n}(m/n)^r}{r!},$$

matching the approximation of Eqn. (5.2).

Before proving Theorem 5.5, we describe some of its applications. Distributions of this type arise frequently and are often modeled by Poisson distributions. For example, consider the number of spelling or grammatical mistakes in a book, including this book. One model for such mistakes is that each word is likely to have an error with some very small probability p. The number of errors is then a binomial random variable with large n and small p that can therefore be treated as a Poisson random variable. As another example, consider the number of chocolate chips inside a chocolate chip cookie. One possible model is to split the volume of the cookie into a large number of small disjoint compartments, so that a chip lands in each compartment with some probability p. With this model, the number of chips in a cookie roughly follows a Poisson distribution.

We will see similar applications of the Poisson distribution in continuous settings in Chapter 8.

Proof of Theorem 5.5: We can write

$$\Pr(X_n = k) = \binom{n}{k} p^k (1-p)^{n-k}.$$

In what follows, we make use of the bound that, for $|x| \leq 1$,

$$e^x(1-x^2) \leq 1 + x \leq e^x, \tag{5.3}$$

which follows from the Taylor series expansion of e^x. (This is left as Exercise 5.7.) Then

$$\Pr(X_n = k) \leq \frac{n^k}{k!} p^k \frac{(1-p)^n}{(1-p)^k}$$

$$\leq \frac{(np)^k}{k!} \frac{e^{-pn}}{1-pk}$$

$$= \frac{e^{-pn}(np)^k}{k!} \frac{1}{1-pk}.$$

The second line follows from the first by Eqn. (5.3) and the fact that $(1-p)^k \geq 1 - pk$ for $k \geq 0$. Also,

$$\Pr(X_n = k) \geq \frac{(n-k+1)^k}{k!} p^k (1-p)^n$$

$$\geq \frac{((n-k+1)p)^k}{k!} e^{-pn}(1-p^2)^n$$

$$\geq \frac{e^{-pn}((n-k+1)p)^k}{k!}(1-p^2 n),$$

where in the second inequality we applied Eqn. (5.3) with $x = -p$.

Combining, we have

$$\frac{e^{-pn}(np)^k}{k!} \frac{1}{1-pk} \geq \Pr(X_n = k) \geq \frac{e^{-pn}((n-k+1)p)^k}{k!}(1-p^2 n).$$

In the limit, as n approaches infinity, p approaches zero because the limiting value of pn is the constant λ. Hence $1/(1-pk)$ approaches 1, $1 - p^2 n$ approaches 1, and the difference between $(n-k+1)p$ and np approaches 0. It follows that

$$\lim_{n\to\infty} \frac{e^{-pn}(np)^k}{k!} \frac{1}{1-pk} = \frac{e^{-\lambda}\lambda^k}{k!}$$

and

$$\lim_{n\to\infty} \frac{e^{-pn}((n-k+1)p)^k}{k!}(1-p^2 n) = \frac{e^{-\lambda}\lambda^k}{k!}.$$

Since $\lim_{n\to\infty} \Pr(X_n = k)$ lies between these two values, the theorem follows. ∎

5.4. The Poisson Approximation

The main difficulty in analyzing balls-and-bins problems is handling the dependencies that naturally arise in such systems. For example, if we throw m balls into n bins and find that bin 1 is empty, then it is less likely that bin 2 is empty because we know that the m balls must now be distributed among $n - 1$ bins. More concretely: if we know the number of balls in the first $n - 1$ bins, then the number of balls in the last bin is completely determined. The loads of the various bins are not independent, and independent random variables are generally much easier to analyze, since we can apply Chernoff bounds. It is therefore useful to have a general way to circumvent these sorts of dependencies.

We have already shown that, after throwing m balls independently and uniformly at random into n bins, the distribution of the number of balls in a given bin is approximately Poisson with mean m/n. We would like to say that the joint distribution of the number of balls in *all* the bins is well approximated by assuming the load at *each* bin is an *independent* Poisson random variable with mean m/n. This would allow us to treat bin loads as independent random variables. We show here that we can do this when we are concerned with sufficiently rare events. Specifically, we show in Corollary 5.9 that taking the probability of an event using this Poisson approximation for all of the bins and multiplying it by $e\sqrt{m}$ gives an upper bound for the probability of the event when m balls are thrown into n bins. For rare events, this extra $e\sqrt{m}$ factor will not be significant. To achieve this result, we now introduce some technical machinery.

Suppose that m balls are thrown into n bins independently and uniformly at random, and let $X_i^{(m)}$ be the number of balls in the ith bin, where $1 \le i \le n$. Let $Y_1^{(m)}, \ldots, Y_n^{(m)}$ be independent Poisson random variables with mean m/n. We derive a useful relationship between these two sets of random variables. Tighter bounds for specific problems can often be obtained with more detailed analysis, but this approach is quite general and easy to apply.

The difference between throwing m balls randomly and assigning each bin a number of balls that is Poisson distributed with mean m/n is that, in the first case, we know there are m balls in total, whereas in the second case we know only that m is the expected number of balls in all of the bins. But suppose when we use the Poisson distribution we end up with m balls. In this case, we do indeed have that the distribution is the same as if we threw m balls into n bins randomly.

Theorem 5.6: *The distribution of* $(Y_1^{(m)}, \ldots, Y_n^{(m)})$ *conditioned on* $\sum_i Y_i^{(m)} = k$ *is the same as* $(X_1^{(k)}, \ldots, X_n^{(k)})$, *regardless of the value of m.*

Proof: When throwing k balls into n bins, the probability that $(X_1^{(k)}, \ldots, X_n^{(k)}) = (k_1, \ldots, k_n)$ for any $k_1, \ldots, k_n$ satisfying $\sum_i k_i = k$ is given by

$$\frac{\binom{k}{k_1; k_2; \ldots; k_n}}{n^k} = \frac{k!}{(k_1!)(k_2!) \cdots (k_n!)n^k}.$$

Now, for any $k_1, \ldots, k_n$ with $\sum_i k_i = k$, consider the probability that

$$\left(Y_1^{(m)}, \ldots, Y_n^{(m)}\right) = (k_1, \ldots, k_n)$$

107

conditioned on $(Y_1^{(m)}, \ldots, Y_n^{(m)})$ satisfying $\sum_i Y_i^{(m)} = k$:

$$\Pr\left((Y_1^{(m)}, \ldots, Y_n^{(m)}) = (k_1, \ldots, k_n) \mid \sum_{i=1}^{n} Y_i^{(m)} = k\right)$$

$$= \frac{\Pr\left((Y_1^{(m)} = k_1) \cap (Y_1^{(m)} = k_2) \cap \cdots \cap (Y_n^{(m)} = k_n)\right)}{\Pr\left(\sum_{i=1}^{n} Y_i^{(m)} = k\right)}.$$

The probability that $Y_i^{(m)} = k_i$ is $e^{-m/n}(m/n)^{k_i}/k_i!$, since the $Y_i^{(m)}$ are independent Poisson random variables with mean m/n. Also, by Lemma 5.2, the sum of the $Y_i^{(m)}$ is itself a Poisson random variable with mean m. Hence

$$\frac{\Pr\left((Y_1^{(m)} = k_1) \cap (Y_1^{(m)} = k_2) \cap \cdots \cap (Y_n^{(m)} = k_n)\right)}{\Pr\left(\sum_{i=1}^{n} Y_i^{(m)} = k\right)} = \frac{\prod_{i=1}^{n} e^{-m/n}(m/n)^{k_i}/k_i!}{e^{-m}m^k/k!}$$

$$= \frac{k!}{(k_1!)(k_2!) \cdots (k_n!)n^k},$$

proving the theorem. ∎

With this relationship between the two distributions, we can prove strong results about *any* function on the loads of the bins.

Theorem 5.7: Let $f(x_1, \ldots, x_n)$ be a nonnegative function. Then

$$\mathbf{E}[f(X_1^{(m)}, \ldots, X_n^{(m)})] \le e\sqrt{m}\,\mathbf{E}[f(Y_1^{(m)}, \ldots, Y_n^{(m)})]. \tag{5.4}$$

Proof: We have that

$$\mathbf{E}[f(Y_1^{(m)}, \ldots, Y_n^{(m)})] = \sum_{k=0}^{\infty} \mathbf{E}\left[f(Y_1^{(m)}, \ldots, Y_n^{(m)}) \mid \sum_{i=1}^{n} Y_i^{(m)} = k\right] \Pr\left(\sum_{i=1}^{n} Y_i^{(m)} = k\right)$$

$$\ge \mathbf{E}\left[f(Y_1^{(m)}, \ldots, Y_n^{(m)}) \mid \sum_{i=1}^{n} Y_i^{(m)} = m\right] \Pr\left(\sum_{i=1}^{n} Y_i^{(m)} = m\right)$$

$$= \mathbf{E}[f(X_1^{(m)}, \ldots, X_n^{(m)})] \Pr\left(\sum Y_i^{(m)} = m\right),$$

where the last equality follows from the fact that the joint distribution of the $Y_i^{(m)}$ given $\sum_{i=1}^{n} Y_i^{(m)} = m$ is exactly that of the $X_i^{(m)}$, as shown in Theorem 5.6. Since $\sum_{i=1}^{n} Y_i^{(m)}$ is Poisson distributed with mean m, we now have

$$\mathbf{E}[f(Y_1^{(m)}, \ldots, Y_n^{(m)})] \ge \mathbf{E}[f(X_1^{(m)}, \ldots, X_n^{(m)})]\frac{m^m e^{-m}}{m!}.$$

We use the following loose bound on $m!$, which we prove as Lemma 5.8:

$$m! < e\sqrt{m}\left(\frac{m}{e}\right)^m.$$

This yields

$$\mathbf{E}[f(Y_1^{(m)}, \ldots, Y_n^{(m)})] \ge \mathbf{E}[f(X_1^{(m)}, \ldots, X_n^{(m)})]\frac{1}{e\sqrt{m}},$$

and the theorem is proven. ∎

We prove the upper bound we used for factorials, which closely matches the loose lower bound we used in Lemma 5.1.

Lemma 5.8:

$$n! \leq e\sqrt{n}\left(\frac{n}{e}\right)^n. \tag{5.5}$$

Proof: We use the fact that

$$\ln(n!) = \sum_{i=1}^{n} \ln i.$$

We first claim that, for $i \geq 2$,

$$\int_{i-1}^{i} \ln x \, dx \geq \frac{\ln(i-1) + \ln i}{2}.$$

This follows from the fact that $\ln x$ is concave, since its second derivative is $-1/x^2$, which is always negative. Therefore,

$$\int_{1}^{n} \ln x \, dx \geq \sum_{i=1}^{n} \ln i - \frac{\ln n}{2}$$

or, equivalently,

$$n \ln n - n + 1 \geq \ln(n!) - \frac{\ln n}{2}.$$

The result now follows simply by exponentiating. ∎

Theorem 5.7 holds for any nonnegative function on the number of balls in the bins. In particular, if the function is the indicator function that is 1 if some event occurs and 0 otherwise, then the theorem gives bounds on the probability of events. Let us call the scenario in which the number of balls in the bins are taken to be independent Poisson random variables with mean m/n the *Poisson case,* and the scenario where m balls are thrown into n bins independently and uniformly at random the *exact case.*

Corollary 5.9: *Any event that takes place with probability p in the Poisson case takes place with probability at most $pe\sqrt{m}$ in the exact case.*

Proof: Let f be the indicator function of the event. In this case, $\mathbf{E}[f]$ is just the probability that the event occurs, and the result follows immediately from Theorem 5.7. ∎

This is a quite powerful result. It says that any event that happens with small probability in the Poisson case also happens with small probability in the exact case, where balls are thrown into bins. Since in the analysis of algorithms we often want to show that certain events happen with small probability, this result says that we can utilize an

109

analysis of the Poisson approximation to obtain a bound for the exact case. The Poisson approximation is easier to analyze because the numbers of balls in each bin are independent random variables.[1]

We can actually do even a little bit better in many natural cases. Part of the proof of the following theorem is outlined in Exercises 5.14 and 5.15.

Theorem 5.10: *Let $f(x_1, \ldots, x_n)$ be a nonnegative function such that $\mathbf{E}[f(X_1^{(m)}, \ldots, X_n^{(m)})]$ is either monotonically increasing or monotonically decreasing in m. Then*

$$\mathbf{E}[f(X_1^{(m)}, \ldots, X_n^{(m)})] \le 2\mathbf{E}[f(Y_1^{(m)}, \ldots, Y_n^{(m)})]. \tag{5.6}$$

The following corollary is immediate.

Corollary 5.11: *Let $\mathcal{E}$ be an event whose probability is either monotonically increasing or monotonically decreasing in the number of balls. If $\mathcal{E}$ has probability p in the Poisson case, then $\mathcal{E}$ has probability at most $2p$ in the exact case.*

To demonstrate the utility of this corollary, we again consider the maximum load problem for the case $m = n$. We have shown via a union bound argument that the maximum load is at most $3 \ln n / \ln \ln n$ with high probability. Using the Poisson approximation, we prove the following almost-matching lower bound on the maximum load.

Lemma 5.12: *When n balls are thrown independently and uniformly at random into n bins, the maximum load is at least $\ln n / \ln \ln n$ with probability at least $1 - 1/n$ for n sufficiently large.*

Proof: In the Poisson case, the probability that bin 1 has load at least $M = \ln n / \ln \ln n$ is at least $1/eM!$, which is the probability it has load exactly M. In the Poisson case, all bins are independent, so the probability that no bin has load at least M is at most

$$\left(1 - \frac{1}{eM!}\right)^n \le e^{-n/(eM!)}.$$

We now need to choose M so that $e^{-n/(eM!)} \le n^{-2}$, for then (by Theorem 5.7) we will have that the probability that the maximum load is not at least M in the exact case is at most $e\sqrt{n}/n^2 < 1/n$. This will give the lemma. Because the maximum load is clearly monotonically increasing in the number of balls, we could also apply the slightly better Theorem 5.10, but this would not affect the argument substantially.

It therefore suffices to show that $M! \le n/2e \ln n$, or equivalently that $\ln M! \le \ln n - \ln \ln n - \ln(2e)$. From our bound of Eqn. (5.5), it follows that

$$M! \le e\sqrt{M}\left(\frac{M}{e}\right)^M \le M\left(\frac{M}{e}\right)^M$$

---

[1] There are other ways to handle the dependencies in the balls-and-bins model. In Chapter 13 we describe a more general way to deal with dependencies (using martingales) that applies here. Also, there is a theory of negative dependence that applies to balls-and-bins problems that also allows these dependencies to be dealt with nicely.

when n (and hence $M = \ln n / \ln \ln n$) are suitably large. Hence, for n suitably large,

$$\begin{aligned}
\ln M! &\leq M \ln M - M + \ln M \\
&= \frac{\ln n}{\ln \ln n}(\ln \ln n - \ln \ln \ln n) - \frac{\ln n}{\ln \ln n} + (\ln \ln n - \ln \ln \ln n) \\
&\leq \ln n - \frac{\ln n}{\ln \ln n} \\
&\leq \ln n - \ln \ln n - \ln(2e),
\end{aligned}$$

where in the last two inequalities we have used the fact that $\ln \ln n = o(\ln n / \ln \ln n)$. ∎

5.4.1.* *Example: Coupon Collector's Problem, Revisited*

The coupon collector's problem introduced in Section 2.4.1 can be thought of as a balls-and-bins problem. Recall that in this problem there are n different types of coupons, each cereal box yields a coupon chosen independently and uniformly at random from the n types, and you need to buy cereal boxes until you collect one of each coupon. If we think of coupons as bins and cereal boxes as balls, the question becomes: If balls are thrown independently and uniformly at random into bins, how many balls are thrown until all bins have at least one ball? We showed in Section 2.4.1 that the expected number of cereal boxes necessary is $nH(n) \approx n \ln n$; in Section 3.3.1 we showed that, if there are $n \ln n + cn$ cereal boxes, then the probability that not all coupons are collected is at most e^{-c}. These results translate immediately to the balls-and-bins setting. The expected number of balls that must be thrown before each bin has at least one ball is $nH(n)$, and when $n \ln n + cn$ balls are thrown the probability that not all bins have at least one ball is e^{-c}.

We have seen in Chapter 4 that Chernoff bounds yield concentration results for sums of independent 0–1 random variables. We will use here a Chernoff bound for the Poisson distribution to obtain much stronger results for the coupon collector's problem.

Theorem 5.13: *Let X be the number of coupons observed before obtaining one of each of n types of coupons. Then, for any constant c,*

$$\lim_{n \to \infty} \Pr[X > n \ln n + cn] = 1 - e^{-e^{-c}}.$$

This theorem states that, for large n, the number of coupons required should be very close to $n \ln n$. For example, over 98% of the time the number of coupons required lies between $n \ln n - 4n$ and $n \ln n + 4n$. This is an example of a *sharp threshold*, where the random variable is closely concentrated around its mean.

Proof: We look at the problem as a balls-and-bins problem. We begin by considering the Poisson approximation, and then demonstrate that the Poisson approximation gives the correct answer in the limit. For the Poisson approximation, we suppose that the number of balls in each bin is a Poisson random variable with mean $\ln n + c$, so that the expected total number of balls is $m = n \ln n + cn$. The probability that a specific bin is empty is then

$$e^{-(\ln n + c)} = \frac{e^{-c}}{n}.$$

111

Since all bins are independent under the Poisson approximation, the probability that no bin is empty is

$$\left(1 - \frac{e^{-c}}{n}\right)^{n} \approx e^{-e^{-c}}.$$

The last approximation is appropriate in the limit as n grows large, so we apply it here.

To show the Poisson approximation is accurate, we undertake the following steps. Consider the experiment where each bin has a Poisson number of balls, each with mean $\ln n + c$. Let $\mathcal{E}$ be the event that no bin is empty, and let X be the number of balls thrown. We have seen that

$$\lim_{n \to \infty} \Pr(\mathcal{E}) = e^{-e^{-c}}.$$

We use $\Pr(\mathcal{E})$ by splitting it as follows:

$$
\begin{aligned}
\Pr(\mathcal{E}) &= \Pr\left(\mathcal{E} \cap \left(|X - m| \le \sqrt{2m \ln m}\right)\right) + \Pr\left(\mathcal{E} \cap \left(|X - m| > \sqrt{2m \ln m}\right)\right) \\
&= \Pr\left(\mathcal{E} \mid |X - m| \le \sqrt{2m \ln m}\right) \cdot \Pr\left(|X - m| \le \sqrt{2m \ln m}\right) \\
&\quad + \Pr\left(\mathcal{E} \mid |X - m| > \sqrt{2m \ln m}\right) \cdot \Pr\left(|X - m| > \sqrt{2m \ln m}\right). \quad (5.7)
\end{aligned}
$$

This representation proves helpful once we establish two facts. First, we show that $\Pr\left(|X - m| > \sqrt{2m \ln m}\right)$ is $o(1)$; that is, the probability that in the Poisson case the number of balls thrown deviates significantly from its mean m is $o(1)$. This guarantees that the second term in the summation on the right of Eqn. (5.7) is $o(1)$. Second, we show that

$$\left| \Pr\left(\mathcal{E} \mid |X - m| \le \sqrt{2m \ln m}\right) - \Pr(\mathcal{E} \mid X = m) \right| = o(1).$$

That is, the difference between our experiment coming up with exactly m balls or just almost m balls makes an asymptotically negligible difference in the probability that every bin has a ball. With these two facts, Eqn. (5.7) becomes

$$
\begin{aligned}
\Pr(\mathcal{E}) &= \Pr\left(\mathcal{E} \mid |X - m| \le \sqrt{2m \ln m}\right) \cdot \Pr\left(|X - m| \le \sqrt{2m \ln m}\right) \\
&\quad + \Pr\left(\mathcal{E} \mid |X - m| > \sqrt{2m \ln m}\right) \cdot \Pr\left(|X - m| > \sqrt{2m \ln m}\right) \\
&= \Pr\left(\mathcal{E} \mid |X - m| \le \sqrt{2m \ln m}\right) \cdot (1 - o(1)) + o(1) \\
&= \Pr(\mathcal{E} \mid X = m)(1 - o(1)) + o(1),
\end{aligned}
$$

and hence

$$\lim_{n \to \infty} \Pr(\mathcal{E}) = \lim_{n \to \infty} \Pr(\mathcal{E} \mid X = m).$$

But from Theorem 5.6, the quantity on the right is equal to the probability that every bin has at least one ball when m balls are thrown randomly, since conditioning on m total balls with the Poisson approximation is equivalent to throwing m balls randomly into the n bins. As a result, the theorem follows once we have shown these two facts.

To show that $\Pr\left(|X - m| > \sqrt{2m \ln m}\right)$ is $o(1)$, consider that X is a Poisson random variable with mean m, since it is a sum of independent Poisson random variables. We use the Chernoff bound for the Poisson distribution (Theorem 5.4) to bound this probability, writing the bound as

$$\Pr(X \geq x) \leq e^{x-m-x\ln(x/m)}.$$

For $x = m + \sqrt{2m \ln m}$, we use that $\ln(1 + z) \geq z - z^2/2$ for $z \geq 0$ to show

$$\Pr\left(X > m + \sqrt{2m \ln m}\right) \leq e^{\sqrt{2m \ln m}-(m+\sqrt{2m \ln m})\ln(1+\sqrt{2\ln m/m})}$$

$$\leq e^{\sqrt{2m \ln m}-(m+\sqrt{2m \ln m})(\sqrt{2\ln m/m}-\ln m/m)}$$

$$= e^{-\ln m+\sqrt{2m \ln m}(\ln m/m)} = o(1).$$

A similar argument holds if $x < m$, so $\Pr\left(|X - m| > \sqrt{2m \ln m}\right) = o(1)$.

We now show the second fact, that

$$\left|\Pr\left(\mathcal{E} \mid |X - m| \leq \sqrt{2m \ln m}\right) - \Pr(\mathcal{E} \mid X = m)\right| = o(1).$$

Note that $\Pr(\mathcal{E} \mid X = k)$ is increasing in k, since this probability corresponds to the probability that all bins are nonempty when k balls are thrown independently and uniformly at random. The more balls that are thrown, the more likely all bins are nonempty. It follows that

$$\Pr\left(\mathcal{E} \mid X = m - \sqrt{2m \ln m}\right) \leq \Pr\left(\mathcal{E} \mid |X - m| \leq \sqrt{2m \ln m}\right)$$

$$\leq \Pr\left(\mathcal{E} \mid X = m + \sqrt{2m \ln m}\right).$$

Hence we have the bound

$$\left|\Pr(\mathcal{E} \mid |X - m| \leq \sqrt{2m \ln m}) - \Pr(\mathcal{E} \mid X = m)\right|$$

$$\leq \Pr\left(\mathcal{E} \mid X = m + \sqrt{2m \ln m}\right) - \Pr\left(\mathcal{E} \mid X = m - \sqrt{2m \ln m}\right),$$

and we show the right-hand side is $o(1)$. This is the difference between the probability that all bins receive at least one ball when $m - \sqrt{2m \ln m}$ balls are thrown and when $m + \sqrt{2m \ln m}$ balls are thrown. This difference is equivalent to the probability of the following experiment: we throw $m - \sqrt{2m \ln m}$ balls and there is still at least one empty bin, but after throwing an additional $2\sqrt{2m \ln m}$ balls, all bins are nonempty. In order for this to happen, there must be at least one empty bin after $m - \sqrt{2m \ln m}$ balls; the probability that one of the next $2\sqrt{2m \ln m}$ balls covers this bin is at most $\left(2\sqrt{2m \ln m}\right)/n = o(1)$ by the union bound. Hence this difference is $o(1)$ as well. ∎

5.5. Application: Hashing

5.5.1. *Chain Hashing*

The balls-and-bins-model is also useful for modeling *hashing*. For example, consider the application of a password checker, which prevents people from using common, easily cracked passwords by keeping a dictionary of unacceptable passwords. When a user tries to set up a password, the application would like to check if the requested password is part of the unacceptable set. One possible approach for a password checker would be to store the unacceptable passwords alphabetically and do a binary search on the dictionary to check if a proposed password is unacceptable. A binary search would require $\Theta(\log m)$ time for m words.

113

Another possibility is to place the words into bins and then search the appropriate bin for the word. The words in a bin would be represented by a linked list. The placement of words into bins is accomplished by using a *hash function.* A hash function *f* from a universe *U* into a range $[0, n - 1]$ can be thought of as a way of placing items from the universe into *n* bins. Here the universe *U* would consist of possible password strings. The collection of bins is called a *hash table.* This approach to hashing is called *chain hashing,* since items that fall in the same bin are chained together in a linked list.

Using a hash table turns the dictionary problem into a balls-and-bins problem. If our dictionary of unacceptable passwords consists of *m* words and the range of the hash function is $[0, n - 1]$, then we can model the distribution of words in bins with the same distribution as *m* balls placed randomly in *n* bins. We are making a rather strong assumption by presuming that our hash function maps words into bins in a fashion that appears random, so that the location of each word is independent and identically distributed. There is a great deal of theory behind designing hash functions that appear random, and we will not delve into that theory here. We simply model the problem by assuming that hash functions are random. In other words, we assume that (a) for each $x \in U$, the probability that $f(x) = j$ is $1/n$ (for $0 \le j \le n - 1$) and that (b) the values of $f(x)$ for each *x* are independent of each other. Notice that this does not mean that every evaluation of $f(x)$ yields a different random answer! The value of $f(x)$ is fixed for all time; it is just equally likely to take on any value in the range.

Let us consider the search time when there are *n* bins and *m* words. To search for an item, we first hash it to find the bin that it lies in and then search sequentially through the linked list for it. If we search for a word that is not in our dictionary, the expected number of words in the bin the word hashes to is m/n. If we search for a word that is in our dictionary, the expected number of other words in that word's bin is $(m - 1)/n$, so the expected number of words in the bin is $1 + (m - 1)/n$. If we choose $n = m$ bins for our hash table, then the expected number of words we must search through in a bin is constant. If the hashing takes constant time, then the total expected time for the search is constant.

The maximum time to search for a word, however, is proportional to the maximum number of words in a bin. We have shown that when $n = m$ this maximum load is $\Theta(\ln n / \ln \ln n)$ with probability close to 1, and hence with high probability this is the maximum search time in such a hash table. While this is still faster than the required time for standard binary search, it is much slower than the average, which can be a drawback for many applications.

Another drawback of chain hashing can be wasted space. If we use *n* bins for *n* items, several of the bins will be empty, potentially leading to wasted space. The space wasted can be traded off against the search time by making the average number of words per bin larger than 1.

5.5.2. *Hashing: Bit Strings*

If we want to save space instead of time, we can use hashing in another way. Again, we consider the problem of keeping a dictionary of unsuitable passwords. Assume that a password is restricted to be eight ASCII characters, which requires 64 bits (8 bytes) to represent. Suppose we use a hash function to map each word into a 32-bit string. This string will serve as a short *fingerprint* for the word; just as a fingerprint is a succinct way of identifying people, the fingerprint string is a succinct way of identifying a word. We keep the fingerprints in a sorted list. To check if a proposed password is unacceptable, we calculate its fingerprint and look for it on the list, say by a binary search.[2] If the fingerprint is on the list, we declare the password unacceptable.

In this case, our password checker may not give the correct answer! It is possible for a user to input an acceptable password, only to have it rejected because its fingerprint matches the fingerprint of an unacceptable password. Hence there is some chance that hashing will yield a *false positive*: it may falsely declare a match when there is not an actual match. The problem is that – unlike fingerprints for human beings – our fingerprints do not uniquely identify the associated word. This is the only type of mistake this algorithm can make; it does *not* allow a password that is in the dictionary of unsuitable passwords. In the password application, allowing false positives means our algorithm is overly conservative, which is probably acceptable. Letting easily cracked passwords through, however, would probably not be acceptable.

To place the problem in a more general context, we describe it as an *approximate set membership* problem. Suppose we have a set $S = \{s_1, s_2, \ldots, s_m\}$ of m elements from a large universe U. We would like to represent the elements in such a way that we can quickly answer queries of the form "is x an element of S?" We would also like the representation to take as little space as possible. In order to save space, we would be willing to allow occasional mistakes in the form of false positives. Here the unallowable passwords correspond to our set S.

How large should the range of the hash function used to create the fingerprints be? Specifically, if we are working with bits, how many bits should we use to create a fingerprint? Obviously, we want to choose the number of bits that gives an acceptable probability for a false positive match. The probability that an acceptable password has a fingerprint that is different from any specific unallowable password in S is $(1 - 1/2^b)$. It follows that if the set S has size m and if we use b bits for the fingerprint, then the probability of a false positive for an acceptable password is $1 - (1 - 1/2^b)^m \geq 1 - e^{-m/2^b}$. If we want this probability of a false positive to be less than a constant c, we need

$$e^{-m/2^b} \geq 1 - c,$$

which implies that

$$b \geq \log_2 \frac{m}{\ln(1/(1 - c))}.$$

That is, we need $b = \Omega(\log_2 m)$ bits. On the other hand, if we use $b = 2\log_2 m$ bits, then the probability of a false positive falls to

$$1 - \left(1 - \frac{1}{m^2}\right)^m < \frac{1}{m}.$$

---

[2] In this case the fingerprints will be uniformly distributed over all 32-bit strings. There are faster algorithms for searching over sets of numbers with this distribution, just as Bucket sort allows faster sorting than standard comparison-based sorting when the elements to be sorted are from a uniform distribution, but we will not concern ourselves with this point here.

In our example, if our dictionary has $2^{16} = 65{,}536$ words, then using 32 bits when hashing yields a false positive probability of just less than $1/65{,}536$.

5.5.3. *Bloom Filters*

We can generalize the hashing ideas of Sections 5.5.1 and 5.5.2 to achieve more interesting trade-offs between the space required and the false positive probability. The resulting data structure for the approximate set membership problem is called a *Bloom filter.*

A Bloom filter consists of an array of n bits, $A[0]$ to $A[n-1]$, initially all set to 0. A Bloom filter uses k independent random hash functions $h_1, \ldots, h_k$ with range $\{0, \ldots, n-1\}$. We make the usual assumption for analysis that these hash functions map each element in the universe to a random number independently and uniformly over the range $\{0, \ldots, n-1\}$. Suppose that we use a Bloom filter to represent a set $S = \{s_1, s_2, \ldots, s_m\}$ of m elements from a large universe U. For each element $s \in S$, the bits $A[h_i(s)]$ are set to 1 for $1 \leq i \leq k$. A bit location can be set to 1 multiple times, but only the first change has an effect. To check if an element x is in S, we check whether all array locations $A[h_i(x)]$ for $1 \leq i \leq k$ are set to 1. If not, then clearly x is not a member of S, because if x were in S then all locations $A[h_i(x)]$ for $1 \leq i \leq k$ would be set to 1 by construction. If all $A[h_i(x)]$ are set to 1, we assume that x is in S, although we could be wrong. We would be wrong if all of the positions $A[h_i(x)]$ were set to 1 by elements of S even though x is not in the set. Hence Bloom filters may yield false positives. Figure 5.1 shows an example.

The probability of a false positive for an element not in the set – the *false positive probability* – can be calculated in a straightforward fashion, given our assumption that the hash functions are random. After all the elements of S are hashed into the Bloom filter, the probability that a specific bit is still 0 is

$$\left(1 - \frac{1}{n}\right)^{km} \approx e^{-km/n}.$$

We let $p = e^{-km/n}$. To simplify the analysis, let us temporarily assume that a fraction p of the entries are still 0 after all of the elements of S are hashed into the Bloom filter.

The probability of a false positive is then

$$\left(1 - \left(1 - \frac{1}{n}\right)^{km}\right)^k \approx (1 - e^{-km/n})^k = (1 - p)^k.$$

We let $f = (1 - e^{-km/n})^k = (1 - p)^k$. From now on, for convenience we use the asymptotic approximations p and f to represent (respectively) the probability that a bit in the Bloom filter is 0 and the probability of a false positive.

Suppose that we are given m and n and wish to optimize the number of hash functions k in order to minimize the false positive probability f. There are two competing forces: using more hash functions gives us more chances to find a 0-bit for an element that is not a member of S, but using fewer hash functions increases the fraction of 0-bits

Start with an array of 0s.

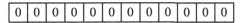

Each element of S is hashed k times; each
hash gives an array location to set to 1.

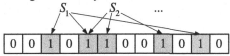

To check if y is in S, check the k hash
locations. If a 0 appears, y is not in S.

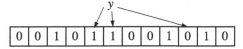

If only 1s appear, conclude that y is in S.
This may yield false positives.

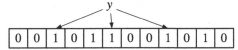

Figure 5.1: Example of how a Bloom filter functions.

in the array. The optimal number of hash functions that minimizes f as a function of k is easily found taking the derivative. Let $g = k \ln(1 - e^{-km/n})$, so that $f = e^g$ and minimizing the false positive probability f is equivalent to minimizing g with respect to k. We find

$$\frac{dg}{dk} = \ln(1 - e^{-km/n}) + \frac{km}{n} \frac{e^{-km/n}}{1 - e^{-km/n}}.$$

It is easy to check that the derivative is zero when $k = (\ln 2) \cdot (n/m)$ and that this point is a global minimum. In this case the false positive probability f is $(1/2)^k \approx (0.6185)^{n/m}$. The false positive probability falls exponentially in n/m, the number of bits used per item. In practice, of course, k must be an integer, so the best possible choice of k may lead to a slightly higher false positive rate.

A Bloom filter is like a hash table, but instead of storing set items we simply use one bit to keep track of whether or not an item hashed to that location. If $k = 1$, we have just one hash function and the Bloom filter is equivalent to a hashing-based fingerprint system, where the list of the fingerprints is stored in a 0–1 bit array. Thus Bloom filters can be seen as a generalization of the idea of hashing-based fingerprints. As we saw when using fingerprints, to get even a small constant probability of a false positive required $\Omega(\log m)$ fingerprint bits per item. In many practical applications, $\Omega(\log m)$ bits per item can be too many. Bloom filters allow a constant probability of a false positive while keeping n/m, the number of bits of storage required per item, constant. For many applications, the small space requirements make a constant probability of error acceptable. For example, in the password application, we may be willing to accept false positive rates of 1% or 2%.

Bloom filters are highly effective even if $n = cm$ for a small constant c, such as $c = 8$. In this case, when $k = 5$ or $k = 6$ the false positive probability is just over 0.02. This contrasts with the approach of hashing each element into $\Theta(\log m)$ bits. Bloom filters require significantly fewer bits while still achieving a very good false positive probability.

It is also interesting to frame the optimization another way. Consider f, the probability of a false positive, as a function of p. We find

$$
\begin{aligned}
f &= (1 - p)^k \\
&= (1 - p)^{(-\ln p)(n/m)} \\
&= (e^{-\ln(p)\ln(1-p)})^{n/m}.
\end{aligned}
\tag{5.8}
$$

From the symmetry of this expression, it is easy to check that $p = 1/2$ minimizes the false positive probability f. Hence the optimal results are achieved when each bit of the Bloom filter is 0 with probability $1/2$. An optimized Bloom filter looks like a random bit string.

To conclude, we reconsider our assumption that the fraction of entries that are still 0 after all of the elements of S are hashed into the Bloom filter is p. Each bit in the array can be thought of as a bin, and hashing an item is like throwing a ball. The fraction of entries that are still 0 after all of the elements of S are hashed is therefore equivalent to the fraction of empty bins after mk balls are thrown into n bins. Let X be the number of such bins when mk balls are thrown. The expected fraction of such bins is

$$
p' = \left(1 - \frac{1}{n}\right)^{km}.
$$

The events of different bins being empty are not independent, but we can apply Corollary 5.9, along with the Chernoff bound of Eqn. (4.6), to obtain

$$
\Pr(|X - np'| \geq \varepsilon n) \leq 2e\sqrt{n}e^{-n\varepsilon^2/3p'}.
$$

Actually, Corollary 5.11 applies as well, since the number of 0-entries – which corresponds to the number of empty bins – is monotonically decreasing in the number of balls thrown. The bound tells us that the fraction of empty bins is close to p' (when n is reasonably large) and that p' is very close to p. Our assumption that the fraction of 0-entries in the Bloom filter is p is therefore quite accurate for predicting actual performance.

5.5.4. Breaking Symmetry

As our last application of hashing, we consider how hashing provides a simple way to break symmetry. Suppose that n users want to utilize a resource, such as time on a supercomputer. They must use the resource sequentially, one at a time. Of course, each user wants to be scheduled as early as possible. How can we decide a permutation of the users quickly and fairly?

118

If each user has an identifying name or number, hashing provides one possible solution. Hash each user's identifier into 2^b bits, and then take the permutation given by the sorted order of the resulting numbers. That is, the user whose identifier gives the smallest number when hashed comes first, and so on. For this approach to work, we do not want two users to hash to the same value, since then we must decide again how to order these users.

If b is sufficiently large, then with high probability the users will all obtain distinct hash values. One can analyze the probability that two hash values collide by using the analysis from Section 5.1 for the birthday paradox; hash values correspond to birthdays. We here use a simpler analysis based just on using a union bound. There are $\binom{n}{2}$ pairs of users. The probability that any specific pair has the same hash value is $1/2^b$. Hence the probability that any pair has the same hash value is at most

$$\binom{n}{2}\frac{1}{2^b} = \frac{n(n-1)}{2^{b+1}}.$$

Choosing $b = 3\log_2 n - 1$ guarantees success with probability at least $1 - 1/n$.

This solution is extremely flexible, making it useful for many situations in distributed computing. For example, new users can easily be added into the schedule at any time, as long as they do not hash to the same number as another scheduled user.

A related problem is *leader election*. Suppose that instead of trying to order all of the users, we simply want to fairly choose a leader from them. Again, if we have a suitably random hash function then we can simply take the user whose hash value is the smallest. An analysis of this scheme is left as Exercise 5.26.

5.6. Random Graphs

5.6.1. *Random Graph Models*

There are many NP-hard computational problems defined on graphs: Hamiltonian cycle, independent set, vertex cover, and so forth. One question worth asking is whether these problems are hard for most inputs or just for a relatively small fraction of all graphs. *Random graph* models provide a probabilistic setting for studying such questions.

Most of the work on random graphs has focused on two closely related models, $G_{n,p}$ and $G_{n,N}$. In $G_{n,p}$ we consider all undirected graphs on n distinct vertices $v_1, v_2, \ldots, v_n$. A graph with a given set of m edges has probability

$$p^m(1-p)^{\binom{n}{2}-m}.$$

One way to generate a random graph in $G_{n,p}$ is to consider each of the $\binom{n}{2}$ possible edges in some order and then independently add each edge to the graph with probability p.

119

The expected number of edges in the graph is therefore $\binom{n}{2} p$, and each vertex has expected degree $(n-1)p$.

In the $G_{n,N}$ model, we consider all undirected graphs on n vertices with exactly N edges. There are $\left(\binom{\binom{n}{2}}{N} \right)$ possible graphs, each selected with equal probability. One way to generate a graph uniformly from the graphs in $G_{n,N}$ is to start with a graph with no edges. Choose one of the $\binom{n}{2}$ possible edges uniformly at random and add it to the edges in the graph. Now choose one of the remaining $\binom{n}{2} - 1$ possible edges independently and uniformly at random and add it to the graph. Similarly, continue choosing one of the remaining unchosen edges independently and uniformly at random until there are N edges.

The $G_{n,p}$ and $G_{n,N}$ models are related; when $p = N/\binom{n}{2}$, the number of edges in a random graph in $G_{n,p}$ is concentrated around N, and conditioned on a graph from $G_{n,p}$ having N edges, that graph is uniform over all the graphs from $G_{n,N}$. The relationship is similar to the relationship between throwing m balls into n bins and having each bin have a Poisson distributed number of balls with mean m/n.

Here, for example is one way of formalizing the relationship between the $G_{n,p}$ and $G_{n,N}$ models. A graph property is a property that holds for a graph regardless of how the vertices are labeled, so it holds for all possible isomorphisms of the graph. We say that a graph property is monotone increasing if whenever the property holds for $G = (V, E)$ it holds also for any graph $G' = (V, E')$ with $E \subseteq E'$; monotone decreasing graph properties are defined similarly. For example, the property that a graph is connected is a monotone increasing graph property, as is the property that a graph contains a connected component of at least k vertices for any particular value of k. The property that a graph is a tree, however, is not a monotone graph property, although the property that the graph contains no cycles is a monotone decreasing graph property. We have the following lemma:

Lemma 5.14: *For a given monotone increasing graph property let $P(n, N)$ be the probability that the property holds for a graph in $G_{n,N}$ and $P(n, p)$ the probability that it holds for a graph in $G_{n,p}$. Let $p^+ = (1 + \epsilon)N/\binom{n}{2}$ and $p^- = (1 - \epsilon)N/\binom{n}{2}$ for a constant $1 > \epsilon > 0$. Then*

$$P(n, p^-) - e^{-O(N)} \le P(n, N) \le P(n, p^+) + e^{-O(N)}.$$

Proof: Let X be a random variable giving the number of edges that occur when a graph is chosen from G_{n,p^-}. Conditioned on $X = k$, a random graph from G_{n,p^-} is equivalent to a graph from $G_{n,k}$, since the k edges chosen are equally likely to be any subset of k edges. Hence

$$P(n, p^-) = \sum_{k=0}^{\binom{n}{2}} P(n, k) \Pr(X = k).$$

In particular,

$$P(n, p^-) = \sum_{k \le N} P(n, k) \Pr(X = k) + \sum_{k > N} P(n, k) \Pr(X = k).$$

120

Also, for a monotone increasing graph property, $P(n, k) \leq P(n, N)$ for $k \leq N$. Hence

$$P(n, p^-) \leq \Pr(X \leq N)P(n, N) + \Pr(X > N) \leq P(n, N) + \Pr(X > N).$$

However, $\Pr(X > N)$ can be bounded by a standard Chernoff bound; X is the sum of $\binom{n}{2}$ independent Bernoulli random variables, and hence by Theorem 4.4

$$\Pr(X > N) = \Pr\left(X > \frac{1}{1-\epsilon}\mathbf{E}[X]\right) \leq \Pr(X > (1+\epsilon)\mathbf{E}[X]) \leq e^{-(1-\epsilon)\epsilon^2 N/3}.$$

Here we have used that $\frac{1}{1-\epsilon} > 1 + \epsilon$ for $0 < \epsilon < 1$.

Similarly,

$$P(n, p^+) = \sum_{k<N} P(n, k)\Pr(X = k) + \sum_{k \geq N} P(n, k)\Pr(X = k),$$

so

$$P(n, p^+) \geq \Pr(X \geq N)P(n, N) \geq P(n, N) - \Pr(X < N).$$

By Theorem 4.5

$$\Pr(X > N) = \Pr\left(X < \frac{1}{1+\epsilon}\mathbf{E}[X]\right) \leq \Pr\left(X < \left(1 + \frac{\epsilon}{2}\right)\mathbf{E}[X]\right) \leq e^{-(1+\epsilon)\epsilon^2 N/8},$$

where here we have used that $\frac{1}{1+\epsilon} < 1 - \epsilon/2$ for $0 < \epsilon < 1$. ∎

A similar result holds for monotone decreasing properties. Another formalization of the relationship between the graph models is given as Exercise 5.18.

There are many additional similarities between random graphs and the balls-and-bins model. Throwing edges into the graph as in the $G_{n,N}$ model is like throwing balls into bins. However, since each edge has two endpoints, each edge is like throwing two balls at once into two different bins. The pairing defined by the edges adds a rich structure that does not exist in the balls-and-bins model. Yet we can often utilize the relation between the two models to simplify analysis in random graph models. For example, in the coupon collector's problem we found that when we throw $n \ln n + cn$ balls, the probability that there are no empty bins converges to $e^{-e^{-c}}$ as n grows to infinity. Similarly, we have the following theorem for random graphs, which is left as Exercise 5.20.

Theorem 5.15: *Let $N = \frac{1}{2}(n \ln n + cn)$. Then the probability that there are no isolated vertices (vertices with degree 0) in $G_{n,N}$ converges to $e^{-e^{-c}}$ as n grows to infinity.*

5.6.2. *Application: Hamiltonian Cycles in Random Graphs*

A Hamiltonian path in a graph is a path that traverses each vertex exactly once. A Hamiltonian cycle is a cycle that traverses each vertex exactly once. We show an interesting connection between random graphs and balls-and-bins problems by analyzing a simple and efficient algorithm for finding Hamiltonian cycles in random graphs. The algorithm is randomized, and its probabilistic analysis is over both the input distribution and the random choices of the algorithm. Finding a Hamiltonian cycle in a graph

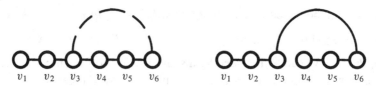

Figure 5.2: The rotation of the path $v_1, v_2, v_3, v_4, v_5, v_6$ with the edge (v_6, v_3) yields a new path $v_1, v_2, v_3, v_6, v_5, v_4$.

is an NP-hard problem. However, our analysis of this algorithm shows that finding a Hamiltonian cycle is not hard for suitably randomly selected graphs, even though it may be hard to solve in general.

Our algorithm will make use of a simple operation called a *rotation*. Let G be an undirected graph. Suppose that

$$P = v_1, v_2, \ldots, v_k$$

is a simple path in G and that (v_k, v_i) is an edge of G. Then

$$P' = v_1, v_2, \ldots, v_i, v_k, v_{k-1}, \ldots, v_{i+2}, v_{i+1}$$

is also a simple path, which we refer to as the rotation of P with the rotation edge (v_k, v_i); see Figure 5.2.

We first consider a simple, natural algorithm that proves challenging to analyze. We assume that our input is presented as a list of adjacent edges for each vertex in the graph, with the edges of each list being given in a random order according to independent and uniform random permutations. Initially, the algorithm chooses an arbitrary vertex to start the path; this is the initial *head* of the path. The head is always one of the endpoints of the path. From this point on, the algorithm either "grows" the path deterministically from the head, or rotates the path – as long as there is an adjacent edge remaining on the head's list. See Algorithm 5.1.

The difficulty in analyzing this algorithm is that, once the algorithm views some edges in the edge lists, the distribution of the remaining edges is conditioned on the edges the algorithm has already seen. We circumvent this difficulty by considering a modified algorithm that, though less efficient, avoids this conditioning issue and so is easier to analyze for the random graphs we consider. See Algorithm 5.2. Each vertex v keeps two lists. The list used-edges(v) contains edges adjacent to v that have been used in the course of the algorithm while v was the head; initially this list is empty. The list unused-edges(v) contains other edges adjacent to v that have not been used.

We initially analyze the algorithm assuming a specific model for the initial unused-edges lists. We subsequently relate this model to the $G_{n,p}$ model for random graphs. Assume that each of the $n - 1$ possible edges connected to a vertex v is initially on the unused-edges list for vertex v independently with some probability q. We also assume these edges are in a random order. One way to think of this is that, before beginning the algorithm, we create the unused-edges list for each vertex v by inserting each possible edge (v, u) with probability q; we think of the corresponding graph G as being the graph including all edges that were inserted on some unused-edges list. Notice that

---

Hamiltonian Cycle Algorithm:

Input: A graph $G = (V, E)$ with n vertices.

Output: A Hamiltonian cycle, or failure.

1. Start with a random vertex as the head of the path.
2. Repeat the following steps until the rotation edge closes a Hamiltonian cycle or the unused-edges list of the head of the path is empty:
   (a) Let the current path be $P = v_1, v_2, \ldots, v_k$, where v_k is the head, and let (v_k, u) be the first edge in the head's list.
   (b) Remove (v_k, u) from the head's list and u's list.
   (c) If $u \neq v_i$ for $1 \leq i \leq k$, add $u = v_{k+1}$ to the end of the path and make it the head.
   (d) Otherwise, if $u = v_i$, rotate the current path with (v_k, v_i) and set v_{i+1} to be the head. (This step closes the Hamiltonian path if $k = n$ and the chosen edge is (v_n, v_1).)
3. Return a Hamiltonian cycle if one was found or failure if no cycle was found.

Algorithm 5.1: Hamiltonian cycle algorithm.

Modified Hamiltonian Cycle Algorithm:

Input: A graph $G = (V, E)$ with n vertices and associated edge lists.

Output: A Hamiltonian cycle, or failure.

1. Start with a random vertex as the head of the path.
2. Repeat the following steps until the rotation edge closes a Hamiltonian cycle or the unused-edges list of the head of the path is empty:
   (a) Let the current path be $P = v_1, v_2, \ldots, v_k$, with v_k being the head.
   (b) Execute i, ii, or iii with probabilities $1/n$, $|\text{used-edges}(v_k)|/n$, and $1 - 1/n - |\text{used-edges}(v_k)|/n$, respectively:
      i. Reverse the path, and make v_1 the head.
      ii. Choose uniformly at random an edge from used-edges(v_k); if the edge is (v_k, v_i), rotate the current path with (v_k, v_i) and set v_{i+1} to be the head. (If the edge is (v_k, v_{k-1}), then no change is made.)
      iii. Select the first edge from unused-edges(v_k), call it (v_k, u). If $u \neq v_i$ for $1 \leq i \leq k$, add $u = v_{k+1}$ to the end of the path and make it the head. Otherwise, if $u = v_i$, rotate the current path with (v_k, v_i) and set v_{i+1} to be the head. (This step closes the Hamiltonian path if $k = n$ and the chosen edge is (v_n, v_1).)
   (c) Update the used-edges and unused-edges lists appropriately.
3. Return a Hamiltonian cycle if one was found or failure if no cycle was found.

Algorithm 5.2: Modified Hamiltonian cycle algorithm.

this means an edge (v, u) could initially be on the unused-edges list for v but not for u. Also, when an edge (v, u) is first used in the algorithm, if v is the head then it is removed just from the unused-edges list of v; if the edge is on the unused-edges list for u, it remains on this list.

By choosing the rotation edge from either the used-edges list or the unused-edges list with appropriate probabilities and then reversing the path with some small probability in each step, we modify the rotation process so that the next head of the list is chosen uniformly at random from among all vertices of the graph. Once we establish this property, the progress of the algorithm can be analyzed through a straightforward application of our analysis of the coupon collector's problem.

The modified algorithm appears wasteful; reversing the path or rotating with one of the used edges cannot increase the path length. Also, we may not be taking advantage of all the possible edges of G at each step. The advantage of the modified algorithm is that it proves easier to analyze, owing to the following lemma.

Lemma 5.16: *Suppose the modified Hamiltonian cycle algorithm is run on a graph chosen using the described model. Let V_t be the head vertex after the tth step. Then, for any vertex u, as long as at the tth step there is at least one unused edge available at the head vertex,*

$$\Pr(V_{t+1} = u \mid V_t = u_t, V_{t-1} = u_{t-1}, \ldots, V_0 = u_0) = 1/n.$$

That is, the head vertex can be thought of as being chosen uniformly at random from all vertices at each step, regardless of the history of the process.

Proof: Consider the possible cases when the path is $P = v_1, v_2, \ldots, v_k$.

The only way v_1 can become the head is if the path is reversed, so $V_{t+1} = v_1$ with probability $1/n$.

If $u = v_{i+1}$ is a vertex that lies on the path and (v_k, v_i) is in used-edges(v_k), then the probability that $V_{t+1} = u$ is

$$\frac{|\text{used-edges}(v_k)|}{n} \frac{1}{|\text{used-edges}(v_k)|} = \frac{1}{n}.$$

If u is not covered by one of the first two cases then we use the fact that, when an edge is chosen from unused-edges(v_k), the adjacent vertex is uniform over all the $n - |\text{used-edges}(v_k)| - 1$ remaining vertices. This follows from the principle of deferred decisions. Our initial setup required the unused-edges list for v_k to be constructed by including each possible edge with probability q and randomizing the order of the list. This is equivalent to choosing X neighboring vertices for v_k, where X is a $B(n-1, q)$ random variable and the X vertices are chosen uniformly at random without replacement. Because v_k's list was determined independently from the lists of the other vertices, the history of the algorithm tells us nothing about the remaining edges in unused-edges(v_k), and the principle of deferred decisions applies. Hence any edge in v_k's unused-edges list that we have not seen is by construction equally likely to connect to any of the $n - |\text{used-edges}(v_k)| - 1$ remaining possible neighboring vertices.

If $u = v_{i+1}$ is a vertex on the path but (v_k, v_i) is not in used-edges(v_k), then the probability that $V_{t+1} = u$ is the probability that the edge (v_k, v_i) is chosen from unused-edges(v_k) as the next rotation edge, which is

$$\left(1 - \frac{1}{n} - \frac{|\text{used-edges}(v_k)|}{n}\right)\left(\frac{1}{n - |\text{used-edges}(v_k)| - 1}\right) = \frac{1}{n}. \qquad (5.9)$$

Finally, if u is not on the path, then the probability that $V_{t+1} = u$ is the probability that the edge (v_{k+1}, u) is chosen from unused-edges(v_k). But this has the same probability as in Eqn. (5.9). ∎

For Algorithm 5.2, the problem of finding a Hamiltonian path looks exactly like the coupon collector's problem; the probability of finding a new vertex to add to the path when there are k vertices left to be added is k/n. Once all the vertices are on the path, the probability that a cycle is closed in each rotation is $1/n$. Hence, if no list of unused-edges is exhausted then we can expect a Hamiltonian path to be formed in about $O(n \ln n)$ rotations, with about another $O(n \ln n)$ rotations to close the path to form a Hamiltonian cycle. More concretely, we can prove the following theorem.

Theorem 5.17: *Suppose the input to the modified Hamiltonian cycle algorithm initially has unused-edge lists where each edge (v, u) with $u \neq v$ is placed on v's list independently with probability $q \geq 20 \ln n / n$. Then the algorithm successfully finds a Hamiltonian cycle in $O(n \ln n)$ iterations of the repeat loop (step 2) with probability $1 - O(n^{-1})$.*

Note that we did not assume that the input random graph has a Hamiltonian cycle. A corollary of the theorem is that, with high probability, a random graph chosen in this way has a Hamiltonian cycle.

Proof of Theorem 5.17: Consider the following two events.

$\mathcal{E}_1$: The algorithm ran for $3n \ln n$ steps with no unused-edges list becoming empty, but it failed to construct a Hamiltonian cycle.

$\mathcal{E}_2$: At least one unused-edges list became empty during the first $3n \ln n$ iterations of the loop.

For the algorithm to fail, either event $\mathcal{E}_1$ or $\mathcal{E}_2$ must occur. We first bound the probability of $\mathcal{E}_1$. Lemma 5.16 implies that, as long as there is no empty unused-edges list in the first $3n \ln n$ iterations of step 2 of Algorithm 5.2, in each iteration the next head of the path is uniform among the n vertices of the graph. To bound $\mathcal{E}_1$, we therefore consider the probability that more than $3n \ln n$ iterations are required to find a Hamiltonian cycle when the head is chosen uniformly at random each iteration.

The probability that the algorithm takes more than $2n \ln n$ iterations to find a Hamiltonian path is exactly the probability that a coupon collector's problem on n types requires more than $2n \ln n$ coupons. The probability that any specific coupon type has not been found among $2n \ln n$ random coupons is

$$\left(1 - \frac{1}{n}\right)^{2n \ln n} \leq e^{-2 \ln n} = \frac{1}{n^2}.$$

By the union bound, the probability that any coupon type is not found is at most $1/n$.

In order to complete a Hamiltonian path to a cycle the path must close, which it does at each step with probability $1/n$. Hence the probability that the path does not become a cycle within the next $n \ln n$ iterations is

$$\left(1 - \frac{1}{n}\right)^{n \ln n} \le e^{-\ln n} = \frac{1}{n}.$$

Thus we have shown that

$$\Pr(\mathcal{E}_1) \le \frac{2}{n}.$$

Next we bound $\Pr(\mathcal{E}_2)$, the probability that an unused-edges list is empty in the first $3n \ln n$ iterations. We consider two subevents as follows.

$\mathcal{E}_{2a}$: At least $9 \ln n$ edges were removed from the unused-edges list of at least one vertex in the first $3n \ln n$ iterations of the loop.

$\mathcal{E}_{2b}$: At least one vertex had fewer than $10 \ln n$ edges initially in its unused-edges list.

For $\mathcal{E}_2$ to occur, either $\mathcal{E}_{2a}$ or $\mathcal{E}_{2b}$ must occur. Hence

$$\Pr(\mathcal{E}_2) \le \Pr(\mathcal{E}_{2a}) + \Pr(\mathcal{E}_{2b}).$$

Let us first bound $\Pr(\mathcal{E}_{2a})$. Exactly one edge is used in each iteration of the loop. From the proof of Lemma 5.16 we have that, at each iteration, the probability that a given vertex v is the head of the path is $1/n$, independently at each step. Hence the number of times X that v is the head during the first $3n \ln n$ steps is a binomial random variable $B(3n \ln n, 1/n)$, and this dominates the number of edges taken from v's unused-edges list.

Using the Chernoff bound of Eqn. (4.1) with $\delta = 2$ and $\mu = 3 \ln n$ for the binomial random variable $B(3n \ln n, 1/n)$, we have

$$\Pr(X \ge 9 \ln n) \le \left(\frac{e^2}{27}\right)^{3 \ln n} \le \frac{1}{n^2}.$$

By taking a union bound over all vertices, we find $\Pr(\mathcal{E}_{2a}) \le 1/n$.

Next we bound $\Pr(\mathcal{E}_{2b})$. The expected number of edges Y initially in a vertex's unused-edges list is at least $(n-1)q \ge (20(n-1)\ln n)/n \ge 19 \ln n$ for sufficiently large n. Using Chernoff bounds again (Eqn. (4.5)), the probability that any vertex initially has $10 \ln n$ edges or fewer on its list is at most

$$\Pr(Y \le 10 \ln n) \le e^{-(19 \ln n)(9/19)^2/2} \le \frac{1}{n^2},$$

and by the union bound the probability that any vertex has too few adjacent edges is at most $1/n$. Thus,

$$\Pr(\mathcal{E}_{2b}) \le \frac{1}{n}$$

and hence

$$\Pr(\mathcal{E}_2) \le \frac{2}{n}.$$

In total, the probability that the algorithm fails to find a Hamiltonian cycle in $3n \ln n$ iterations is bounded by

$$\Pr(\mathcal{E}_1) + \Pr(\mathcal{E}_2) \le \frac{4}{n}. \qquad \blacksquare$$

We did not make an effort to optimize the constants in the proof. There is, however, a clear trade-off; with more edges, one could achieve a lower probability of failure.

We are left with showing how our algorithm can be applied to graphs in $G_{n,p}$. We show that, as long as p is known, we can partition the edges of the graph into edge lists that satisfy the requirements of Theorem 5.17.

Corollary 5.18: *By initializing edges on the unused-edges lists appropriately, Algorithm 5.2 will find a Hamiltonian cycle on a graph chosen randomly from $G_{n,p}$ with probability $1 - O(1/n)$ whenever $p \ge (40 \ln n)/n$.*

Proof: We partition the edges of our input graph from $G_{n,p}$ as follows. Let $q \in [0, 1]$ be such that $p = 2q - q^2$. Consider any edge (u, v) in the input graph. We execute exactly one of the following three possibilities: with probability $q(1 - q)/(2q - q^2)$ we place the edge on u's unused-edges list but not on v's; with probability $q(1 - q)/(2q - q^2)$ we initially place the edge on v's unused-edges list but not on u's; and with the remaining probability $q^2/(2q - q^2)$ the edge is placed on both unused-edges lists.

Now, for any possible edge (u, v), the probability that it is initially placed in the unused-edges list for v is

$$p\left(\frac{q(1 - q)}{2q - q^2} + \frac{q^2}{2q - q^2}\right) = q.$$

Moreover, the probability that an edge (u, v) is initially placed on the unused-edges list for both u and v is $pq^2/(2q - q^2) = q^2$, so these two placements are independent events. Since each edge (u, v) is treated independently, this partitioning fulfills the requirements of Theorem 5.17 provided the resulting q is at least $20 \ln n/n$. When $p \ge (40 \ln n)/n$ we have $q \ge p/2 \ge (20 \ln n)/n$, and the result follows. $\qquad \blacksquare$

In Exercise 5.27, we consider how to use Algorithm 5.2 even in the case where p is not known in advance, so that the edge lists must be initialized without knowledge of p.

5.7. Exercises

Exercise 5.1: For what values of n is $(1 + 1/n)^n$ within 1% of e? Within 0.0001% of e? Similarly, for what values of n is $(1 - 1/n)^n$ within 1% of $1/e$? Within 0.0001%?

Exercise 5.2: Suppose that Social Security numbers were issued uniformly at random, with replacement. That is, your Social Security number would consist of just nine randomly generated digits, and no check would be made to ensure that the same number was not issued twice. Sometimes, the last four digits of a Social Security number are used as a password. How many people would you need to have in a room before it was more likely than not that two had the same last four digits? How many numbers could be issued before it would be more likely than not that there is a duplicate number? How would you answer these two questions if Social Security numbers had 13 digits? Try to give exact numerical answers.

Exercise 5.3: Suppose that balls are thrown randomly into n bins. Show, for some constant c_1, that if there are $c_1 \sqrt{n}$ balls then the probability that no two land in the same bin is at most $1/e$. Similarly, show for some constant c_2 (and sufficiently large n) that, if there are $c_2 \sqrt{n}$ balls, then the probability that no two land in the same bin is at least $1/2$. Make these constants as close to optimal as possible. *Hint:* You may want to use the facts that

$$e^{-x} \geq 1 - x$$

and

$$e^{-x-x^2} \leq 1 - x \quad \text{for} \quad x \leq \frac{1}{2}.$$

Exercise 5.4: In a lecture hall containing 100 people, you consider whether or not there are three people in the room who share the same birthday. Explain how to calculate this probability exactly, using the same assumptions as in our previous analysis.

Exercise 5.5: Use the moment generating function of the Poisson distribution to compute the second moment and the variance of the distribution.

Exercise 5.6: Let X be a Poisson random variable with mean μ, representing the number of errors on a page of this book. Each error is independently a grammatical error with probability p and a spelling error with probability $1 - p$. If Y and Z are random variables representing the number of grammatical and spelling errors (respectively) on a page of this book, prove that Y and Z are Poisson random variables with means μp and $\mu(1 - p)$, respectively. Also, prove that Y and Z are independent.

Exercise 5.7: Use the Taylor expansion

$$\ln(1 + x) = x - \frac{x^2}{2} + \frac{x^3}{3} - \frac{x^4}{4} + \cdots$$

to prove that, for any x with $|x| \leq 1$,

$$e^x(1 - x^2) \leq 1 + x \leq e^x.$$

Exercise 5.8: Suppose that n balls are thrown independently and uniformly at random into n bins.

(a) Find the conditional probability that bin 1 has one ball given that exactly one ball fell into the first three bins.

(b) Find the conditional expectation of the number of balls in bin 1 under the condition that bin 2 received no balls.

(c) Write an expression for the probability that bin 1 receives more balls than bin 2.

Exercise 5.9: Our analysis of Bucket sort in Section 5.2.2 assumed that n elements were chosen independently and uniformly at random from the range $[0, 2^k)$. Suppose instead that n elements are chosen independently from the range $[0, 2^k)$ according to a distribution with the property that any number $x \in [0, 2^k)$ is chosen with probability at most $a/2^k$ for some fixed constant $a > 0$. Show that, under these conditions, Bucket sort still requires linear expected time.

Exercise 5.10: Consider the probability that every bin receives exactly one ball when n balls are thrown randomly into n bins.

(a) Give an upper bound on this probability using the Poisson approximation.

(b) Determine the *exact* probability of this event.

(c) Show that these two probabilities differ by a multiplicative factor that equals the probability that a Poisson random variable with parameter n takes on the value n. Explain why this is implied by Theorem 5.6.

Exercise 5.11: Consider throwing m balls into n bins, and for convenience let the bins be numbered from 0 to $n - 1$. We say there is a k-*gap* starting at bin i if bins $i, i + 1, \ldots, i + k - 1$ are all empty.

(a) Determine the expected number of k-gaps.

(b) Prove a Chernoff-like bound for the number of k-gaps. (*Hint:* If you let $X_i = 1$ when there is a k-gap starting at bin i, then there are dependencies between X_i and X_{i+1}; to avoid these dependencies, you might consider X_i and X_{i+k}.)

Exercise 5.12: The following problem models a simple distributed system wherein agents contend for resources but "back off" in the face of contention. Balls represent agents, and bins represent resources.

The system evolves over rounds. Every round, balls are thrown independently and uniformly at random into n bins. Any ball that lands in a bin by itself is *served* and removed from consideration. The remaining balls are thrown again in the next round. We begin with n balls in the first round, and we finish when every ball is served.

(a) If there are b balls at the start of a round, what is the expected number of balls at the start of the next round?

(b) Suppose that every round the number of balls served was exactly the expected number of balls to be served. Show that all the balls would be served in $O(\log \log n)$ rounds. (*Hint:* If x_j is the expected number of balls left after j rounds, show and use that $x_{j+1} \leq x_j^2/n$.)

Exercise 5.13: Suppose that we vary the balls-and-bins process as follows. For convenience let the bins be numbered from 0 to $n - 1$. There are $\log_2 n$ players. Each player randomly chooses a starting location ℓ uniformly from $[0, n - 1]$ and then places one ball in each of the bins numbered $\ell \bmod n$, $\ell + 1 \bmod n$, ..., $\ell + n/\log_2 n - 1 \bmod n$. Argue that the maximum load in this case is only $O(\log\log n/\log\log\log n)$ with probability that approaches 1 as $n \to \infty$.

Exercise 5.14: We prove that if Z is a Poisson random variable of mean μ, where $\mu \geq 1$ is an integer, then $\Pr(Z \geq \mu) \geq 1/2$.

(a) Show that $\Pr(Z = \mu + h) \geq \Pr(Z = \mu - h - 1)$ for $0 \leq h \leq \mu - 1$.
(b) Using part (a), argue that $\Pr(Z \geq \mu) \geq 1/2$.
(c) Show that $\Pr(Z \leq \mu) \leq 1/2$ for all integers μ from 1 to 10 by explicitly performing the calculation. (This is in fact true for all integers $\mu \geq 1$, but it is more difficult to prove.)

Exercise 5.15: **(a)** In Theorem 5.7 we showed that, for any nonnegative functions f,

$$\mathbf{E}\left[f\left(Y_1^{(m)}, \ldots, Y_n^{(m)}\right)\right] \geq \mathbf{E}\left[f\left(X_1^{(m)}, \ldots, X_n^{(m)}\right)\right] \Pr\left(\sum Y_i^{(m)} = m\right).$$

Prove that if $\mathbf{E}[f(X_1^{(m)}, \ldots, X_n^{(m)})]$ is monotonically increasing in m, then

$$\mathbf{E}\left[f\left(Y_1^{(m)}, \ldots, Y_n^{(m)}\right)\right] \geq \mathbf{E}\left[f\left(X_1^{(m)}, \ldots, X_n^{(m)}\right)\right] \Pr\left(\sum Y_i^{(m)} \geq m\right),$$

again under the condition that f is nonnegative. Make a similar statement for the case when $\mathbf{E}[f(X_1^{(m)}, \ldots, X_n^{(m)})]$ is monotonically decreasing in m.
(b) Using part (a) and Exercise 5.14, prove Theorem 5.10 for the case that $\mathbf{E}[f(X_1^{(m)}, \ldots, X_n^{(m)})]$ is monotonically increasing.

Exercise 5.16: We consider another way to obtain Chernoff-like bounds in the setting of balls and bins without using Theorem 5.7. Consider n balls thrown randomly into n bins. Let $X_i = 1$ if the ith bin is empty and 0 otherwise. Let $X = \sum_{i=1}^{n} X_i$. Let Y_i, $i = 1, \ldots, n$, be independent Bernoulli random variables that are 1 with probability $p = (1 - 1/n)^n$. Let $Y = \sum_{i=1}^{n} Y_i$.

(a) Show that $\mathbf{E}[X_1 X_2 \cdots X_k] \leq \mathbf{E}[Y_1 Y_2 \cdots Y_k]$ for any $k \geq 1$.
(b) Show that $\mathbf{E}[e^{tX}] \leq \mathbf{E}[e^{tY}]$ for all $t \geq 0$. (*Hint:* Use the expansion for e^x and compare $\mathbf{E}[X^k]$ to $\mathbf{E}[Y^k]$.)
(c) Derive a Chernoff bound for $\Pr(X \geq (1 + \delta)\mathbf{E}[X])$.

Exercise 5.17: Let G be a random graph generated using the $G_{n,p}$ model.

(a) A *clique* of k vertices in a graph is a subset of k vertices such that all $\binom{k}{2}$ edges between these vertices lie in the graph. For what value of p, as a function of n, is the expected number of cliques of five vertices in G equal to 1?
(b) A $K_{3,3}$ graph is a complete bipartite graph with three vertices on each side. In other words, it is a graph with six vertices and nine edges; the six distinct vertices are arranged in two groups of three, and the nine edges connect each of the nine pairs

of vertices with one vertex in each group. For what value of p, as a function of n, is the expected number of $K_{3,3}$ subgraphs of G equal to 1?

(c) For what value of p, as a function of n, is the expected number of Hamiltonian cycles in the graph equal to 1?

Exercise 5.18: Theorem 5.7 shows that any event that occurs with small probability in the balls-and-bins setting where the number of balls in each bin is an independent Poisson random variable also occurs with small probability in the standard balls-and-bins model. Prove a similar statement for random graphs: Every event that happens with small probability in the $G_{n,p}$ model also happens with small probability in the $G_{n,N}$ model for $N = \binom{n}{2} p$.

Exercise 5.19: An undirected graph on n vertices is *disconnected* if there exists a set of $k < n$ vertices such that there is no edge between this set and the rest of the graph. Otherwise, the graph is said to be *connected*. Show that there exists a constant c such that if $N \geq cn \log n$ then, with probability $1 - o(1)$, a graph randomly chosen from $G_{n,N}$ is connected.

Exercise 5.20: Prove Theorem 5.15.

Exercise 5.21: **(a)** Let $f(n)$ be the expected number of random edges that must be added before an empty undirected graph with n vertices becomes connected. (Connectedness is defined in Exercise 5.19.) That is, suppose that we start with a graph on n vertices with zero edges and then repeatedly add an edge, chosen uniformly at random from all edges not currently in the graph, until the graph becomes connected. If X_n represents the number of edges added, then $f(n) = \mathbf{E}[X_n]$.

Write a program to estimate $f(n)$ for a given value of n. Your program should track the connected components of the graph as you add edges until the graph becomes connected. You will probably want to use a disjoint set data structure, a topic covered in standard undergraduate algorithms texts. You should try $n = 100, 200, 300, 400, 500, 600, 700, 800, 900,$ and 1000. Repeat each experiment 100 times, and for each value of n compute the average number of edges needed. Based on your experiments, suggest a function $h(n)$ that you think is a good estimate for $f(n)$.

(b) Modify your program for the problem in part (a) so that it also keeps track of isolated vertices. Let $g(n)$ be the expected number of edges added before there are no more isolated vertices. What seems to be the relationship between $f(n)$ and $g(n)$?

Exercise 5.22: In hashing with *open addressing,* the hash table is implemented as an array and there are no linked lists or chaining. Each entry in the array either contains one hashed item or is empty. The hash function defines, for each key k, a *probe sequence* $h(k, 0), h(k, 1), \ldots$ of table locations. To insert the key k, we first examine the sequence of table locations in the order defined by the key's probe sequence until we find an empty location; then we insert the item at that position. When searching for an item in the hash table, we examine the sequence of table locations in the order defined by the key's probe sequence until either the item is found or we have found an empty location in the sequence. If an empty location is found, this means the item is not present in the table.

An open-address hash table with $2n$ entries is used to store n items. Assume that the table location $h(k, j)$ is uniform over the $2n$ possible table locations and that all $h(k, j)$ are independent.

(a) Show that, under these conditions, the probability of an insertion requiring more than k probes is at most 2^{-k}.

(b) Show that, for $i = 1, 2, \ldots, n$, the probability that the ith insertion requires more than $2 \log n$ probes is at most $1/n^2$.

Let the random variable X_i denote the number of probes required by the ith insertion. You have shown in part (b) that $\Pr(X_i > 2 \log n) \leq 1/n^2$. Let the random variable $X = \max_{1 \leq i \leq n} X_i$ denote the maximum number of probes required by any of the n insertions.

(c) Show that $\Pr(X > 2 \log n) \leq 1/n$.

(d) Show that the expected length of the longest probe sequence is $\mathbf{E}[X] = O(\log n)$.

Exercise 5.23: Bloom filters can be used to estimate set differences. Suppose you have a set X and I have a set Y, both with n elements. For example, the sets might represent our 100 favorite songs. We both create Bloom filters of our sets, using the same number of bits m and the same k hash functions. Determine the expected number of bits where our Bloom filters differ as a function of m, n, k, and $|X \cap Y|$. Explain how this could be used as a tool to find people with the same taste in music more easily than comparing lists of songs directly.

Exercise 5.24: Suppose that we wanted to extend Bloom filters to allow deletions as well as insertions of items into the underlying set. We could modify the Bloom filter to be an array of counters instead of an array of bits. Each time an item is inserted into a Bloom filter, the counters given by the hashes of the item are increased by one. To delete an item, one can simply decrement the counters. To keep space small, the counters should be a fixed length, such as 4 bits.

Explain how errors can arise when using fixed-length counters. Assuming a setting where one has at most n elements in the set at any time, m counters, k hash functions, and counters with b bits, explain how to bound the probability that an error occurs over the course of t insertions or deletions.

Exercise 5.25: Suppose that you built a Bloom filter for a dictionary of words with $m = 2^b$ bits. A co-worker building an application wants to use your Bloom filter but has only 2^{b-1} bits available. Explain how your colleague can use your Bloom filter to avoid rebuilding a new Bloom filter using the original dictionary of words.

Exercise 5.26: For the leader election problem alluded to in Section 5.5.4, we have n users, each with an identifier. The hash function takes as input the identifier and outputs a b-bit hash value, and we assume that these values are independent and uniformly distributed. Each user hashes its identifier, and the leader is the user with the smallest hash value. Give lower and upper bounds on the number of bits b necessary to ensure that a unique leader is successfully chosen with probability p. Make your bounds as tight as possible.

Exercise 5.27: Consider Algorithm 5.2, the modified algorithm for finding Hamiltonian cycles. We have shown that the algorithm can be applied to find a Hamiltonian cycle with high probability in a graph chosen randomly from $G_{n,p}$, when p is known and sufficiently large, by initially placing edges in the edge lists appropriately. Argue that the algorithm can similarly be applied to find a Hamiltonian cycle with high probability on a graph chosen randomly from $G_{n,N}$ when $N = c_1 n \ln n$ for a suitably large constant c_1. Argue also that the modified algorithm can be applied even when p is not known in advance as long as p is at least $c_2 \ln n/n$ for a suitably large constant c_2.

5.8. An Exploratory Assignment

Part of the research process in random processes is first to understand what is going on at a high level and then to use this understanding in order to develop formal mathematical proofs. In this assignment, you will be given several variations on a basic random process. To gain insight, you should perform experiments based on writing code to simulate the processes. (The code should be very short, a few pages at most.) After the experiments, you should use the results of the simulations to guide you to make conjectures and prove statements about the processes. You can apply what you have learned up to this point, including probabilistic bounds and analysis of balls-and-bins problems.

Consider a complete binary tree with $N = 2^n - 1$ nodes. Here n is the depth of the tree. Initially, all nodes are *unmarked*. Over time, via processes that we shall describe, nodes becomes *marked*.

All of the processes share the same basic form. We can think of the nodes as having unique identifying numbers in the range of $[1, N]$. Each unit of time, I *send* you the identifier of a node. When you receive a sent node, you mark it. Also, you invoke the following *marking rule,* which takes effect before I send out the next node.

- If a node and its sibling are marked, its parent is marked.
- If a node and its parent are marked, the other sibling is marked.

The marking rule is applied *recursively as much as possible* before the next node is sent. For example, in Figure 5.3, the marked nodes are filled in. The arrival of the node labeled by an X will allow you to mark the remainder of the nodes, as you apply the marking rule first up and then down the tree. Keep in mind that you always apply the marking rule as much as possible.

Now let us consider the different ways in which I might be sending you the nodes.

Process 1: Each unit of time, I send the identifier of a node chosen *independently and uniformly at random from all of the N nodes*. Note that I might send you a node that is already marked, and in fact I may send a useless node that I have already sent.

133

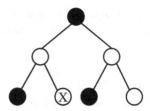

Figure 5.3: The arrival of X causes all other nodes to be marked.

Process 2: Each unit of time I send the identifier of a node chosen uniformly at random from those nodes *that I have not yet sent*. Again, a node that has already been marked might arrive, but each node will be sent at most once.

Process 3: Each unit of time I send the identifier of a node chosen uniformly at random from those nodes *that you have not yet marked*.

We want to determine how many time steps are needed before all the nodes are marked for each of these processes. Begin by writing programs to simulate the sending processes and the marking rule. Run each process ten times for each value of n in the range [10, 20]. Present the data from your experiments in a clear, easy-to-read fashion and explain your data suitably. A tip: You may find it useful to have your program print out the last node that was sent before the tree became completely marked.

1. For the first process, prove that the expected number of nodes sent is $\Omega(N \log N)$. How well does this match your simulations?
2. For the second process, you should find that almost all N nodes must be sent before the tree is marked. Show that, with constant probability, at least $N - 2\sqrt{N}$ nodes must be sent.
3. The behavior of the third process might seem a bit unusual. Explain it with a proof.

After answering these questions, you may wish to consider other facts you could prove about these processes.

CHAPTER SIX

The Probabilistic Method

The *probabilistic method* is a way of proving the existence of objects. The underlying principle is simple: to prove the existence of an object with certain properties, we demonstrate a sample space of objects in which the probability is positive that a randomly selected object has the required properties. If the probability of selecting an object with the required properties is positive, then the sample space must contain such an object, and therefore such an object exists. For example, if there is a positive probability of winning a million-dollar prize in a raffle, then there must be at least one raffle ticket that wins that prize.

Although the basic principle of the probabilistic method is simple, its application to specific problems often involves sophisticated combinatorial arguments. In this chapter we study a number of techniques for constructing proofs based on the probabilistic method, starting with simple counting and averaging arguments and then introducing two more advanced tools, the Lovász local lemma and the second moment method.

In the context of algorithms we are generally interested in explicit constructions of objects, not merely in proofs of existence. In many cases the proofs of existence obtained by the probabilistic method can be converted into efficient randomized construction algorithms. In some cases, these proofs can be converted into efficient deterministic construction algorithms; this process is called *derandomization*, since it converts a probabilistic argument into a deterministic one. We give examples of both randomized and deterministic construction algorithms arising from the probabilistic method.

6.1. The Basic Counting Argument

To prove the existence of an object with specific properties, we construct an appropriate probability space S of objects and then show that the probability that an object in S with the required properties is selected is strictly greater than 0.

For our first example, we consider the problem of coloring the edges of a graph with two colors so that there are no large cliques with all edges having the same color.

Let K_n be a complete graph (with all $\binom{n}{2}$ edges) on n vertices. A clique of k vertices in K_n is a complete subgraph K_k.

Theorem 6.1: *If $\binom{n}{k}2^{-\binom{k}{2}+1} < 1$ then it is possible to color the edges of K_n with two colors so that it has no monochromatic K_k subgraph.*

Proof: Define a sample space consisting of all possible colorings of the edges of K_n using two colors. There are $2^{\binom{n}{2}}$ possible colorings, so if one is chosen uniformly at random then the probability of choosing each coloring in our probability space is $2^{-\binom{n}{2}}$. A nice way to think about this probability space is: if we color each edge of the graph independently, with each edge taking each of the two colors with probability $1/2$, then we obtain a random coloring chosen uniformly from this sample space. That is, we flip an independent fair coin to determine the color of each edge.

Fix an arbitrary ordering of all of the $\binom{n}{k}$ different k-vertex cliques of K_n, and for $i = 1, \ldots, \binom{n}{k}$ let A_i be the event that clique i is monochromatic. Once the first edge in clique i is colored, the remaining $\binom{k}{2} - 1$ edges must all be given the same color. It follows that

$$\Pr(A_i) = 2^{-\binom{k}{2}+1}.$$

Using a union bound then yields

$$\Pr\left(\bigcup_{i=1}^{\binom{n}{k}} A_i\right) \leq \sum_{i=1}^{\binom{n}{k}} \Pr(A_i) = \binom{n}{k} 2^{-\binom{k}{2}+1} < 1,$$

where the last inequality follows from the assumptions of the theorem. Hence

$$\Pr\left(\bigcap_{i=1}^{\binom{n}{k}} \overline{A_i}\right) = 1 - \Pr\left(\bigcup_{i=1}^{\binom{n}{k}} A_i\right) > 0.$$

Since the probability of choosing a coloring with no monochromatic k-vertex clique from our sample space is strictly greater than 0, there must exist a coloring with no monochromatic k-vertex clique. ∎

As an example, consider whether the edges of K_{1000} can be 2-colored in such a way that there is no monochromatic K_{20}. Our calculations are simplified if we note that, for $n \leq 2^{k/2}$ and $k \geq 3$,

$$\binom{n}{k} 2^{-\binom{k}{2}+1} \leq \frac{n^k}{k!} 2^{-(k(k-1)/2)+1}$$

$$\leq \frac{2^{k/2+1}}{k!}$$

$$< 1.$$

Observing that for our example $n = 1000 \leq 2^{10} = 2^{k/2}$, we see that by Theorem 6.1 there exists a 2-coloring of the edges of K_{1000} with no monochromatic K_{20}.

Can we use this proof to design an efficient algorithm to construct such a coloring? Let us consider a general approach that gives a randomized construction algorithm. First, we require that we can efficiently sample a coloring from the sample space. In this case sampling is easy, because we can simply color each edge independently with a randomly chosen color. In general, however, there might not be an efficient sampling algorithm.

If we have an efficient sampling algorithm, the next question is: How many samples must we generate before obtaining a sample that satisfies our requirements? If the probability of obtaining a sample with the desired properties is p and if we sample independently at each trial, then the number of samples needed before finding a sample with the required properties is a geometric random variable with expectation $1/p$. Hence we need that $1/p$ be polynomial in the problem size in order to have an algorithm that finds a suitable sample in polynomial expected time.

If $p = 1 - o(1)$, then sampling once gives a Monte Carlo construction algorithm that is incorrect with probability $o(1)$. In our specific example of finding a coloring on a graph of 1000 vertices with no monochromatic K_{20}, we know that the probability that a random coloring has a monochromatic K_{20} is at most

$$\frac{2^{20/2+1}}{20!} < 8.5 \cdot 10^{-16}.$$

Hence we have a Monte Carlo algorithm with a small probability of failure.

If we want a Las Vegas algorithm – that is, one that always gives a correct construction – then we need a third ingredient. We require a polynomial time procedure for verifying that a sample object satisfies the requirements; then we can test samples until we find one that does so. An upper bound on the expected time for this construction can be found by multiplying together the expected number of samples $1/p$ by the sum of an upper bound on the time to generate each sample and an upper bound on the time to check each sample.[1] For the coloring problem, there is a polynomial time verification algorithm when k is a constant: simply check all $\binom{n}{k}$ cliques and make sure they are not monochromatic. It does not seem that this approach can be extended to yield polynomial time algorithms when k grows with n.

6.2. The Expectation Argument

As we have seen, in order to prove that an object with certain properties exists, we can design a probability space from which an element chosen at random yields an object with the desired properties with positive probability. A similar and sometimes easier approach for proving that such an object exists is to use an averaging argument. The intuition behind this approach is that, in a discrete probability space, a random variable must with positive probability assume at least one value that is no greater than its expectation and at least one value that is not smaller than its expectation.

---

[1] Sometimes the time to generate or check a sample may itself be a random variable. In this case, Wald's equation (discussed in Chapter 13) may apply.

For example, if the expected value of a raffle ticket is \$3, then there must be at least one ticket that ends up being worth no more than \$3 and at least one that ends up being worth no less than \$3.

More formally, we have the following lemma.

Lemma 6.2: *Suppose we have a probability space S and a random variable X defined on S such that $\mathbf{E}[X] = \mu$. Then $\Pr(X \geq \mu) > 0$ and $\Pr(X \leq \mu) > 0$.*

Proof: We have

$$\mu = \mathbf{E}[X] = \sum_x x \Pr(X = x),$$

where the summation ranges over all values in the range of X. If $\Pr(X \geq \mu) = 0$, then

$$\mu = \sum_x x \Pr(X = x) = \sum_{x < \mu} x \Pr(X = x) < \sum_{x < \mu} \mu \Pr(X = x) = \mu,$$

giving a contradiction. Similarly, if $\Pr(X \leq \mu) = 0$ then

$$\mu = \sum_x x \Pr(X = x) = \sum_{x > \mu} x \Pr(X = x) > \sum_{x > \mu} \mu \Pr(X = x) = \mu,$$

again yielding a contradiction. ∎

Thus, there must be at least one instance in the sample space of S for which the value of X is at least μ and at least one instance for which the value of X is no greater than μ.

6.2.1. *Application: Finding a Large Cut*

We consider the problem of finding a large cut in an undirected graph. A cut is a partition of the vertices into two disjoint sets, and the *value* of a cut is the weight of all edges crossing from one side of the partition to the other. Here we consider the case where all edges in the graph have the same weight 1. The problem of finding a maximum cut is NP-hard. Using the probabilistic method, we show that the value of the maximum cut must be at least $1/2$ the number of edges in the graph.

Theorem 6.3: *Given an undirected graph G with m edges, there is a partition of V into two disjoint sets A and B such that at least $m/2$ edges connect a vertex in A to a vertex in B. That is, there is a cut with value at least $m/2$.*

Proof: Construct sets A and B by randomly and independently assigning each vertex to one of the two sets. Let $e_1, \ldots, e_m$ be an arbitrary enumeration of the edges of G. For $i = 1, \ldots, m$, define X_i such that

$$X_i = \begin{cases} 1 & \text{if edge } i \text{ connects } A \text{ to } B, \\ 0 & \text{otherwise.} \end{cases}$$

The probability that edge e_i connects a vertex in A to a vertex in B is $1/2$, and thus

$$\mathbf{E}[X_i] = \frac{1}{2}.$$

138

Let $C(A, B)$ be a random variable denoting the value of the cut corresponding to the sets A and B. Then

$$\mathbf{E}[C(A, B)] = \mathbf{E}\left[\sum_{i=1}^{m} X_i\right] = \sum_{i=1}^{m} \mathbf{E}[X_i] = m \cdot \frac{1}{2} = \frac{m}{2}.$$

Since the expectation of the random variable $C(A, B)$ is $m/2$, there exists a partition A and B with at least $m/2$ edges connecting the set A to the set B. ∎

We can transform this argument into an efficient algorithm for finding a cut with value at least $m/2$. We first show how to obtain a Las Vegas algorithm. In Section 6.3, we show how to construct a deterministic polynomial time algorithm.

It is easy to randomly choose a partition as described in the proof. The expectation argument does not give a lower bound on the probability that a random partition has a cut of value at least $m/2$. To derive such a bound, let

$$p = \Pr\left(C(A, B) \geq \frac{m}{2}\right),$$

and observe that $C(A, B) \leq m$. Then

$$\frac{m}{2} = \mathbf{E}[C(A, B)]$$
$$= \sum_{i < m/2} i \Pr(C(A, B) = i) + \sum_{i \geq m/2} i \Pr(C(A, B) = i)$$
$$\leq (1 - p)\left(\frac{m}{2} - 1\right) + pm,$$

which implies that

$$p \geq \frac{1}{m/2 + 1}.$$

The expected number of samples before finding a cut with value at least $m/2$ is therefore just $m/2 + 1$. Testing to see if the value of the cut determined by the sample is at least $m/2$ can be done in polynomial time simply by counting the edges crossing the cut. We therefore have a Las Vegas algorithm for finding the cut.

6.2.2. Application: Maximum Satisfiability

We can apply a similar argument to the maximum satisfiability (MAXSAT) problem. In a logical formula, a *literal* is either a Boolean variable or the negation of a Boolean variable. We use $\bar{x}$ to denote the negation of the variable x. A satisfiability (SAT) problem, or a SAT formula, is a logical expression that is the conjunction (AND) of a set of clauses, where each clause is the disjunction (OR) of literals. For example, the following expression is an instance of SAT:

$$(x_1 \vee \bar{x_2} \vee \bar{x_3}) \wedge (\bar{x_1} \vee \bar{x_3}) \wedge (x_1 \vee x_2 \vee x_4) \wedge (x_4 \vee \bar{x_3}) \wedge (x_4 \vee \bar{x_1}).$$

A solution to an instance of a SAT formula is an assignment of the variables to the values True and False so that all the clauses are satisfied. That is, there is at least one true literal in each clause. For example, assigning x_1 to True, x_2 to False, x_3 to False, and x_4 to True satisfies the preceding SAT formula. In general, determining if a SAT formula has a solution is NP-hard.

A related goal, given a SAT formula, is satisfying as many of the clauses as possible. In what follows, let us assume that no clause contains both a variable and its complement, since in this case the clause is always satisfied.

Theorem 6.4: *Given a set of m clauses, let k_i be the number of literals in the ith clause for $i = 1, \ldots, m$. Let $k = \min_{i=1}^{m} k_i$. Then there is a truth assignment that satisfies at least*

$$\sum_{i=1}^{m} (1 - 2^{-k_i}) \geq m(1 - 2^{-k})$$

clauses.

Proof: Assign values independently and uniformly at random to the variables. The probability that the ith clause with k_i literals is satisfied is at least $(1 - 2^{-k_i})$. The expected number of satisfied clauses is therefore at least

$$\sum_{i=1}^{m} (1 - 2^{-k_i}) \geq m(1 - 2^{-k}),$$

and there must be an assignment that satisfies at least that many clauses. ∎

The foregoing argument can also be easily transformed into an efficient randomized algorithm; the case where all $k_i = k$ is left as Exercise 6.1.

6.3. Derandomization Using Conditional Expectations

The probabilistic method can yield insight into how to construct deterministic algorithms. As an example, we apply the *method of conditional expectations* in order to *derandomize* the algorithm of Section 6.2.1 for finding a large cut.

Recall that we find a partition of the n vertices V of a graph into sets A and B by placing each vertex independently and uniformly at random in one of the two sets. This gives a cut with expected value $\mathbf{E}[C(A, B)] \geq m/2$. Now imagine placing the vertices deterministically, one at a time, in an arbitrary order $v_1, v_2, \ldots, v_n$. Let x_i be the set where v_i is placed (so x_i is either A or B). Suppose that we have placed the first k vertices, and consider the expected value of the cut if the *remaining* vertices are then placed independently and uniformly into one of the two sets. We write this quantity as $\mathbf{E}[C(A, B) \mid x_1, x_2, \ldots, x_k]$; it is the conditional expectation of the value of the cut given the locations $x_1, x_2, \ldots, x_k$ of the first k vertices. We show inductively how to place the next vertex so that

$$\mathbf{E}[C(A, B) \mid x_1, x_2, \ldots, x_k] \leq \mathbf{E}[C(A, B) \mid x_1, x_2, \ldots, x_{k+1}].$$

140

It follows that

$$\mathbf{E}[C(A, B)] \le \mathbf{E}[C(A, B) \mid x_1, x_2, \ldots, x_n].$$

The right-hand side is the value of the cut determined by our placement algorithm, since if $x_1, x_2, \ldots, x_n$ are all determined then we have a cut of the graph. Hence our algorithm returns a cut whose value is at least $\mathbf{E}[C(A, B)] \ge m/2$.

The base case in the induction is

$$\mathbf{E}[C(A, B) \mid x_1] = \mathbf{E}[C(A, B)],$$

which holds by symmetry because it does not matter where we place the first vertex.

We now prove the inductive step, that

$$\mathbf{E}[C(A, B) \mid x_1, x_2, \ldots, x_k] \le \mathbf{E}[C(A, B) \mid x_1, x_2, \ldots, x_{k+1}]. \tag{6.1}$$

Consider placing v_{k+1} randomly, so that it is placed in A or B with probability $1/2$ each, and let Y_{k+1} be a random variable representing the set where it is placed. Then

$$\mathbf{E}[C(A, B) \mid x_1, x_2, \ldots, x_k] = \frac{1}{2}\mathbf{E}[C(A, B) \mid x_1, x_2, \ldots, x_k, Y_{k+1} = A]$$

$$+ \frac{1}{2}\mathbf{E}[C(A, B) \mid x_1, x_2, \ldots, x_k, Y_{k+1} = B].$$

It follows that

$$\max\left(\mathbf{E}[C(A, B) \mid x_1, x_2, \ldots, x_k, Y_{k+1} = A], \mathbf{E}[C(A, B) \mid x_1, x_2, \ldots, x_k, Y_{k+1} = B]\right)$$
$$\ge \mathbf{E}[C(A, B) \mid x_1, x_2, \ldots, x_k].$$

Therefore, all we have to do is compute the two quantities $\mathbf{E}[C(A, B) \mid x_1, x_2, \ldots, x_k, Y_{k+1} = A]$ and $\mathbf{E}[C(A, B) \mid x_1, x_2, \ldots, x_k, Y_{k+1} = B]$ and then place the v_{k+1} in the set that yields the larger expectation. Once we do this, we will have a placement satisfying

$$\mathbf{E}[C(A, B) \mid x_1, x_2, \ldots, x_k] \le \mathbf{E}[C(A, B) \mid x_1, x_2, \ldots, x_{k+1}].$$

To compute $\mathbf{E}[C(A, B) \mid x_1, x_2, \ldots, x_k, Y_{k+1} = A]$, note that the conditioning gives the placement of the first $k + 1$ vertices. We can therefore compute the number of edges among these vertices that contribute to the value of the cut. For all other edges, the probability that it will later contribute to the cut is $1/2$, since this is the probability its two endpoints end up on different sides of the cut. By linearity of expectations, $\mathbf{E}[C(A, B) \mid x_1, x_2, \ldots, x_k, Y_{k+1} = A]$ is the number of edges crossing the cut whose endpoints are both among the first $k + 1$ vertices, plus half of the remaining edges. This is easy to compute in linear time. The same is true for $\mathbf{E}[C(A, B) \mid x_1, x_2, \ldots, x_k, Y_{k+1} = B]$.

In fact, from this argument, we see that the larger of the two quantities is determined just by whether v_{k+1} has more neighbors in A or in B. All edges that do not have v_{k+1} as an endpoint contribute the same amount to the two expectations. Our derandomized algorithm therefore has the following simple form: Take the vertices in some order. Place the first vertex arbitrarily in A. Place each successive vertex to maximize the number of edges crossing the cut. Equivalently, place each vertex on the side with fewer neighbors, breaking ties arbitrarily. This is a simple greedy algorithm, and our analysis shows that it always guarantees a cut with at least $m/2$ edges.

6.4. Sample and Modify

Thus far we have used the probabilistic method to construct random structures with the desired properties directly. In some cases it is easier to work indirectly, breaking the argument into two stages. In the first stage we construct a random structure that does not have the required properties. In the second stage we then modify the random structure so that it does have the required property. We give two examples of this sample-and-modify technique.

6.4.1. *Application: Independent Sets*

An *independent set* in a graph G is a set of vertices with no edges between them. Finding the largest independent set in a graph is an NP-hard problem. The following theorem shows that the probabilistic method can yield bounds on the size of the largest independent set of a graph.

Theorem 6.5: *Let $G = (V, E)$ be a connected graph on n vertices with $m \geq n/2$ edges. Then G has an independent set with at least $n^2/4m$ vertices.*

Proof: Let $d = 2m/n \geq 1$ be the average degree of the vertices in G. Consider the following randomized algorithm.

1. Delete each vertex of G (together with its incident edges) independently with probability $1 - 1/d$.
2. For each remaining edge, remove it and one of its adjacent vertices.

The remaining vertices form an independent set, since all edges have been removed. This is an example of the sample-and-modify technique. We first sample the vertices, and then we modify the remaining graph.

Let X be the number of vertices that survive the first step of the algorithm. Since the graph has n vertices and since each vertex survives with probability $1/d$, it follows that

$$\mathbf{E}[X] = \frac{n}{d}.$$

Let Y be the number of edges that survive the first step. There are $nd/2$ edges in the graph, and an edge survives if and only if its two adjacent vertices survive. Thus

$$\mathbf{E}[Y] = \frac{nd}{2}\left(\frac{1}{d}\right)^2 = \frac{n}{2d}.$$

The second step of the algorithm removes all the remaining edges and at most Y vertices. When the algorithm terminates, it outputs an independent set of size at least

$X - Y$, and

$$\mathbf{E}[X - Y] = \frac{n}{d} - \frac{n}{2d} = \frac{n}{2d}.$$

The expected size of the independent set generated by the algorithm is at least $n/2d$, so the graph has an independent set with at least $n/2d = n^2/4m$ vertices.   ∎

6.4.2. *Application: Graphs with Large Girth*

As another example we consider the *girth* of a graph, which is the length of its smallest cycle. Intuitively we expect dense graphs to have small girth. We can show, however, that there are dense graphs with relatively large girth.

Theorem 6.6: *For any integer $k \geq 3$, for n sufficiently large there is a graph with n nodes, at least $\frac{1}{4}n^{1+1/k}$ edges, and girth at least k.*

Proof: We first sample a random graph $G \in G_{n,p}$ with $p = n^{1/k-1}$. Let X be the number of edges in the graph. Then

$$\mathbf{E}[X] = p \binom{n}{2} = \frac{1}{2}\left(1 - \frac{1}{n}\right)n^{1/k+1}.$$

Let Y be the number of cycles in the graph of length at most $k - 1$. Any specific possible cycle of length i, where $3 \leq i \leq k - 1$, occurs with probability p^i. Also, there are $\binom{n}{i}\frac{(i-1)!}{2}$ possible cycles of length i; to see this, first consider choosing the i vertices, then consider the possible orders, and finally keep in mind that reversing the order yields the same cycle. Hence,

$$\mathbf{E}[Y] = \sum_{i=3}^{k-1} \binom{n}{i} \frac{(i-1)!}{2} p^i \leq \sum_{i=3}^{k-1} n^i p^i = \sum_{i=3}^{k-1} n^{i/k} < kn^{(k-1)/k}.$$

We modify the original randomly chosen graph G by eliminating one edge from each cycle of length up to $k - 1$. The modified graph therefore has girth at least k. When n is sufficiently large, the expected number of edges in the resulting graph is

$$\mathbf{E}[X - Y] \geq \frac{1}{2}\left(1 - \frac{1}{n}\right)n^{1/k+1} - kn^{(k-1)/k} \geq \frac{1}{4}n^{1/k+1}.$$

Hence there exists a graph with at least $\frac{1}{4}n^{1+1/k}$ edges and girth at least k.   ∎

6.5. The Second Moment Method

The second moment method is another useful way to apply the probabilistic method. The standard approach typically makes use of the following inequality, which is easily derived from Chebyshev's inequality.

Theorem 6.7: *If X is an integer-valued random variable, then*

$$\Pr(X = 0) \leq \frac{\mathbf{Var}[X]}{(\mathbf{E}[X])^2}. \tag{6.2}$$

143

Proof:

$$\Pr(X = 0) \le \Pr(|X - \mathbf{E}[X]| \ge \mathbf{E}[X]) \le \frac{\mathbf{Var}[X]}{(\mathbf{E}[X])^2}. \qquad \blacksquare$$

6.5.1. *Application: Threshold Behavior in Random Graphs*

The second moment method can be used to prove the threshold behavior of certain random graph properties. That is, in the $G_{n,p}$ model it is often the case that there is a *threshold function f* such that: (a) when p is just less than $f(n)$, almost no graph has the desired property; whereas (b) when p is just larger than $f(n)$, almost every graph has the desired property. We present here a relatively simple example.

Theorem 6.8: *In $G_{n,p}$, suppose that $p = f(n)$, where $f(n) = o(n^{-2/3})$. Then, for any $\varepsilon > 0$ and for sufficiently large n, the probability that a random graph chosen from $G_{n,p}$ has a clique of four or more vertices is less than ε. Similarly, if $f(n) = \omega(n^{-2/3})$ then, for sufficiently large n, the probability that a random graph chosen from $G_{n,p}$ does not have a clique with four or more vertices is less than ε.*

Proof: We first consider the case in which $p = f(n)$ and $f(n) = o(n^{-2/3})$. Let $C_1, \ldots, C_{\binom{n}{4}}$ be an enumeration of all the subsets of four vertices in G. Let

$$X_i = \begin{cases} 1 & \text{if } C_i \text{ is a 4-clique,} \\ 0 & \text{otherwise.} \end{cases}$$

Let

$$X = \sum_{i=1}^{\binom{n}{4}} X_i,$$

so that

$$\mathbf{E}[X] = \binom{n}{4} p^6.$$

In this case $\mathbf{E}[X] = o(1)$, which means that $\mathbf{E}[X] < \varepsilon$ for sufficiently large n. Since X is a nonnegative integer-valued random variable, it follows that $\Pr(X \ge 1) \le \mathbf{E}[X] < \varepsilon$. Hence, the probability that a random graph chosen from $G_{n,p}$ has a clique of four or more vertices is less than ε.

We now consider the case when $p = f(n)$ and $f(n) = \omega(n^{-2/3})$. In this case, $\mathbf{E}[X] \to \infty$ as n grows large. This in itself is not sufficient to conclude that, with high probability, a graph chosen random from $G_{n,p}$ has a clique of at least four vertices. We can, however, use Theorem 6.7 to prove that $\Pr(X = 0) = o(1)$ in this case. To do so we must show that $\mathbf{Var}[X] = o((\mathbf{E}[X])^2)$. Here we shall bound the variance directly; an alternative approach is given as Exercise 6.12.

We begin with the following useful formula.

Lemma 6.9: *Let Y_i, $i = 1, \ldots, m$, be 0–1 random variables, and let $Y = \sum_{i=1}^{m} Y_i$. Then*

$$\mathbf{Var}[Y] \le \mathbf{E}[Y] + \sum_{1 \le i, j \le m; i \ne j} \mathbf{Cov}(Y_i, Y_j).$$

Proof: For any sequence of random variables $Y_1, \ldots, Y_m$,

$$\mathbf{Var}\left[\sum_{i=1}^{m} Y_i\right] = \sum_{i=1}^{m} \mathbf{Var}[Y_i] + \sum_{1 \leq i, j \leq m; i \neq j} \mathbf{Cov}(Y_i, Y_j).$$

This is the generalization of Theorem 3.2 to m variables.

When Y_i is a 0–1 random variable, $\mathbf{E}[Y_i^2] = \mathbf{E}[Y_i]$ and so

$$\mathbf{Var}[Y_i] = \mathbf{E}[Y_i^2] - (\mathbf{E}[Y_i])^2 \leq \mathbf{E}[Y_i],$$

giving the lemma. ∎

We wish to compute

$$\mathbf{Var}[X] = \mathbf{Var}\left[\sum_{i=1}^{\binom{n}{4}} X_i\right].$$

Applying Lemma 6.9, we see that we need to consider the covariance of the X_i. If $|C_i \cap C_j| = 0$ then the corresponding cliques are disjoint, and it follows that X_i and X_j are independent. Hence, in this case, $\mathbf{E}[X_i X_j] - \mathbf{E}[X_i]\mathbf{E}[X_j] = 0$. The same is true if $|C_i \cap C_j| = 1$.

If $|C_i \cap C_j| = 2$, then the corresponding cliques share one edge. For both cliques to be in the graph, the eleven corresponding edges must appear in the graph. Hence, in this case $\mathbf{E}[X_i X_j] - \mathbf{E}[X_i]\mathbf{E}[X_j] \leq \mathbf{E}[X_i X_j] \leq p^{11}$. There are $\binom{n}{6}$ ways to choose the six vertices and $\binom{6}{2;2;2}$ ways to split them into C_i and C_j (because we choose two vertices for $C_i \cap C_j$, two for C_i alone, and two for C_j alone).

If $|C_i \cap C_j| = 3$, then the corresponding cliques share three edges. For both cliques to be in the graph, the nine corresponding edges must appear in the graph. Hence, in this case $\mathbf{E}[X_i X_j] - \mathbf{E}[X_i]\mathbf{E}[X_j] \leq \mathbf{E}[X_i X_j] \leq p^9$. There are $\binom{n}{5}$ ways to choose the five vertices, and $\binom{5}{3;1;1}$ ways to split them into C_i and C_j.

Finally, recall again that $\mathbf{E}[X] = \binom{n}{4}p^6$ and $p = f(n) = \omega(n^{-2/3})$. Therefore,

$$\mathbf{Var}[X] \leq \binom{n}{4}p^6 + \binom{n}{6}\binom{6}{2;2;2}p^{11} + \binom{n}{5}\binom{5}{3;1;1}p^9 = o(n^8 p^{12}) = o((\mathbf{E}[X])^2),$$

since

$$(\mathbf{E}[X])^2 = \left(\binom{n}{4}p^6\right)^2 = \Theta(n^8 p^{12}).$$

Theorem 6.7 now applies, showing that $\Pr(X = 0) = o(1)$ and thus the second part of the theorem. ∎

6.6. The Conditional Expectation Inequality

For a sum of Bernoulli random variables, we can derive an alternative to the second moment method that is often easier to apply.

Theorem 6.10: *Let $X = \sum_{i=1}^n X_i$, where each X_i is a 0–1 random variable. Then*

$$\Pr(X > 0) \geq \sum_{i=1}^n \frac{\Pr(X_i = 1)}{\mathbf{E}[X \mid X_i = 1]}. \tag{6.3}$$

Notice that the X_i need not be independent for Eqn. (6.3) to hold.

Proof: Let $Y = 1/X$ if $X > 0$, with $Y = 0$ otherwise. Then

$$\Pr(X > 0) = \mathbf{E}[XY].$$

However,

$$\mathbf{E}[XY] = \mathbf{E}\left[\sum_{i=1}^n X_i Y\right]$$

$$= \sum_{i=1}^n \mathbf{E}[X_i Y]$$

$$= \sum_{i=1}^n \left(\mathbf{E}[X_i Y \mid X_i = 1]\Pr(X_i = 1) + \mathbf{E}[X_i Y \mid X_i = 0]\Pr(X_i = 0)\right)$$

$$= \sum_{i=1}^n \mathbf{E}[Y \mid X_i = 1]\Pr(X_i = 1)$$

$$= \sum_{i=1}^n \mathbf{E}[1/X \mid X_i = 1]\Pr(X_i = 1)$$

$$\geq \sum_{i=1}^n \frac{\Pr(X_i = 1)}{\mathbf{E}[X \mid X_i = 1]}.$$

The key step is from the third to the fourth line, where we use conditional expectations in a fruitful way by taking advantage of the fact that $\mathbf{E}[X_i Y \mid X_i = 0] = 0$. The last line makes use of Jensen's inequality, with the convex function $f(x) = 1/x$. ∎

We can use Theorem 6.10 to give an alternate proof of Theorem 6.8. Specifically, if $p = f(n) = \omega(n^{-2/3})$, we use Theorem 6.10 to show that, for any constant $\varepsilon > 0$ and for sufficiently large n, the probability that a random graph chosen from $G_{n,p}$ does not have a clique with four or more vertices is less than ε.

As in the proof of Theorem 6.8, let $X = \sum_{i=1}^{\binom{n}{4}} X_i$, where X_i is 1 if the subset of four vertices C_i is a 4-clique and 0 otherwise. For a specific X_j, we have $\Pr(X_j = 1) = p^6$. Using the linearity of expectations, we compute

$$\mathbf{E}[X \mid X_j = 1] = \mathbf{E}\left[\sum_{i=1}^{\binom{n}{4}} X_i \,\middle|\, X_j = 1\right] = \sum_{i=1}^{\binom{n}{4}} \mathbf{E}[X_i \mid X_j = 1].$$

Conditioning on $X_j = 1$, we now compute $\mathbf{E}[X_i \mid X_j = 1]$ by using that, for a 0–1 random variable,

$$\mathbf{E}[X_i \mid X_j = 1] = \Pr(X_i = 1 \mid X_j = 1).$$

There are $\binom{n-4}{4}$ sets of vertices C_i that do not intersect C_j. Each corresponding X_i is 1 with probability p^6. Similarly, $X_i = 1$ with probability p^6 for the $4\binom{n-4}{3}$ sets C_i that have one vertex in common with C_j.

For the remaining cases, we have $\Pr(X_i = 1 \mid X_j = 1) = p^5$ for the $6\binom{n-4}{2}$ sets C_i that have two vertices in common with C_j and $\Pr(X_i = 1 \mid X_j = 1) = p^3$ for the $4\binom{n-4}{1}$ sets C_i that have three vertices in common with C_j. Summing, we have

$$\mathbf{E}[X \mid X_j = 1] = \sum_{i=1}^{\binom{n}{4}} \mathbf{E}[X_i \mid X_j = 1]$$

$$= 1 + \binom{n-4}{4} p^6 + 4\binom{n-4}{3} p^6 + 6\binom{n-4}{2} p^5 + 4\binom{n-4}{1} p^3.$$

Applying Theorem 6.10 yields

$$\Pr(X > 0) \geq \frac{\binom{n}{4} p^6}{1 + \binom{n-4}{4} p^6 + 4\binom{n-4}{3} p^6 + 6\binom{n-4}{2} p^5 + 4\binom{n-4}{1} p^3},$$

which approaches 1 as n grows large when $p = f(n) = \omega(n^{-2/3})$.

6.7. The Lovász Local Lemma

One of the most elegant and useful tools in applying the probabilistic method is the Lovász Local Lemma. Let $E_1, \ldots, E_n$ be a set of bad events in some probability space. We want to show that there is an element in the sample space that is not included in any of the bad events.

This would be easy to do if the events were mutually independent. Recall that events $E_1, E_2, \ldots, E_n$ are mutually independent if and only if, for *any* subset $I \subseteq [1, n]$,

$$\Pr\left(\bigcap_{i \in I} E_i\right) = \prod_{i \in I} \Pr(E_i).$$

Also, if $E_1, \ldots, E_n$ are mutually independent then so are $\bar{E}_1, \ldots, \bar{E}_n$. (This was left as Exercise 1.20.) If $\Pr(E_i) < 1$ for all i, then

$$\Pr\left(\bigcap_{i=1}^{n} \bar{E}_i\right) = \prod_{i=1}^{n} \Pr(\bar{E}_i) > 0,$$

and there is an element of the sample space that is not included in any bad event.

Mutual independence is too much to ask for in many arguments. The Lovász local lemma generalizes the preceding argument to the case where the n events are not mutually independent but the dependency is limited. Specifically, following from the definition of mutual independence, we say that an event E_{n+1} is *mutually independent* of the events $E_1, E_2, \ldots, E_n$ if, for any subset $I \subseteq [1, n]$,

$$\Pr\left(E_{n+1} \mid \bigcap_{j \in I} E_j\right) = \Pr(E_{n+1}).$$

The dependency between events can be represented in terms of a dependency graph.

Definition 6.1: *A* dependency graph *for a set of events* $E_1, \ldots, E_n$ *is a graph* $G = (V, E)$ *such that* $V = \{1, \ldots, n\}$ *and, for* $i = 1, \ldots, n$, *event* E_i *is mutually independent of the events* $\{E_j \mid (i, j) \notin E\}$. *The* degree *of the dependency graph is the maximum degree of any vertex in the graph.*

We discuss first a special case, the symmetric version of the Lovász Local Lemma, which is more intuitive and is sufficient for most algorithmic applications.

Theorem 6.11 [Lovász Local Lemma]: *Let* $E_1, \ldots, E_n$ *be a set of events, and assume that the following hold:*

1. for all i, $\Pr(E_i) \leq p$;
2. the degree of the dependency graph given by $E_1, \ldots, E_n$ *is bounded by* d;
3. $4dp \leq 1$.

Then

$$\Pr\left(\bigcap_{i=1}^{n} \bar{E}_i\right) > 0.$$

Proof: Let $S \subset \{1, \ldots, n\}$. We prove by induction on $s = 0, \ldots, n - 1$ that, if $|S| \leq s$, then for all $k \notin S$ we have

$$\Pr\left(E_k \mid \bigcap_{j \in S} \bar{E}_j\right) \leq 2p.$$

For this expression to be well-defined when S is not empty, we need $\Pr\left(\bigcap_{j \in S} \bar{E}_j\right) > 0$.

The base case $s = 0$ follows from the assumption that $\Pr(E_k) \leq p$. To perform the inductive step, we first show that $\Pr\left(\bigcap_{j \in S} \bar{E}_j\right) > 0$. This is true when $s = 1$, because $\Pr(\bar{E}_j) \geq 1 - p > 0$. For $s > 1$, without loss of generality let $S = \{1, 2, \ldots, s\}$. Then

$$\Pr\left(\bigcap_{i=1}^{s} \bar{E}_i\right) = \prod_{i=1}^{s} \Pr\left(\bar{E}_i \mid \bigcap_{j=1}^{i-1} \bar{E}_j\right)$$

$$= \prod_{i=1}^{s}\left(1 - \Pr\left(E_i \mid \bigcap_{j=1}^{i-1} \bar{E}_j\right)\right)$$

$$\geq \prod_{i=1}^{s}(1 - 2p) > 0.$$

In obtaining the last line we used the induction hypothesis.

For the rest of the induction, let $S_1 = \{j \in S \mid (k, j) \in E\}$ and $S_2 = S - S_1$. If $S_2 = S$ then E_k is mutually independent of the events $\bar{E}_i$, $i \in S$, and

$$\Pr\left(E_k \mid \bigcap_{j \in S} \bar{E}_j\right) = \Pr(E_k) \leq p.$$

We continue with the case $|S_2| < s$. It will be helpful to introduce the following notation. Let F_S be defined by

$$F_S = \bigcap_{j \in S} \bar{E}_j,$$

and similarly define F_{S_1} and F_{S_2}. Notice that $F_S = F_{S_1} \cap F_{S_2}$.

Applying the definition of conditional probability yields

$$\Pr(E_k \mid F_S) = \frac{\Pr(E_k \cap F_S)}{\Pr(F_S)}. \tag{6.4}$$

Applying the definition of conditional probability to the numerator of Eqn. (6.4), we obtain

$$\Pr(E_k \cap F_S) = \Pr(E_k \cap F_{S_1} \cap F_{S_2})$$
$$= \Pr(E_k \cap F_{S_1} \mid F_{S_2}) \Pr(F_{S_2}).$$

The denominator can be written as

$$\Pr(F_S) = \Pr(F_{S_1} \cap F_{S_2})$$
$$= \Pr(F_{S_1} \mid F_{S_2}) \Pr(F_{S_2}).$$

Canceling the common factor, which we have already shown to be nonzero, yields

$$\Pr(E_k \mid F_S) = \frac{\Pr(E_k \cap F_{S_1} \mid F_{S_2})}{\Pr(F_{S_1} \mid F_{S_2})}. \tag{6.5}$$

Note that Eqn. (6.5) is valid even when $S_2 = \emptyset$.

Since the probability of an intersection of events is bounded by the probability of any one of the events and since E_k is independent of the events in S_2, we can bound the numerator of Eqn. (6.5) by

$$\Pr(E_k \cap F_{S_1} \mid F_{S_2}) \leq \Pr(E_k \mid F_{S_2}) = \Pr(E_k) \leq p.$$

Because $|S_2| < |S| = s$, we can apply the induction hypothesis to

$$\Pr(E_i \mid F_{S_2}) = \Pr\left(E_i \mid \bigcap_{j \in S_2} \bar{E}_j\right).$$

Using also the fact that $|S_1| \le d$, we establish a lower bound on the denominator of Eqn. (6.5) as follows:

$$\Pr(F_{S_1} \mid F_{S_2}) = \Pr\left(\bigcap_{i \in S_1} \bar{E}_i \mid \bigcap_{j \in S_2} \bar{E}_j \right)$$

$$\ge 1 - \sum_{i \in S_1} \Pr\left(E_i \mid \bigcap_{j \in S_2} \bar{E}_j \right)$$

$$\ge 1 - \sum_{i \in S_1} 2p$$

$$\ge 1 - 2pd$$

$$\ge \frac{1}{2}.$$

Using the upper bound for the numerator and the lower bound for the denominator, we prove the induction:

$$\Pr(E_k \mid F_S) = \frac{\Pr(E_k \cap F_{S_1} \mid F_{S_2})}{\Pr(F_{S_1} \mid F_{S_2})}$$

$$\le \frac{p}{1/2} = 2p.$$

The theorem follows from

$$\Pr\left(\bigcap_{i=1}^{n} \bar{E}_i \right) = \prod_{i=1}^{n} \Pr\left(\bar{E}_i \mid \bigcap_{j=1}^{i-1} \bar{E}_j \right)$$

$$= \prod_{i=1}^{n} \left(1 - \Pr\left(E_i \mid \bigcap_{j=1}^{i-1} \bar{E}_j \right) \right)$$

$$\ge \prod_{i=1}^{n} (1 - 2p) > 0. \qquad \blacksquare$$

6.7.1. *Application: Edge-Disjoint Paths*

Assume that n pairs of users need to communicate using edge-disjoint paths on a given network. Each pair $i = 1, \ldots, n$ can choose a path from a collection F_i of m paths. We show using the Lovász local lemma that, if the possible paths do not share too many edges, then there is a way to choose n edge-disjoint paths connecting the n pairs.

Theorem 6.12: *If any path in F_i shares edges with no more than k paths in F_j, where $i \ne j$ and $8nk/m \le 1$, then there is a way to choose n edge-disjoint paths connecting the n pairs.*

Proof: Consider the probability space defined by each pair choosing a path independently and uniformly at random from its set of m paths. Define $E_{i,j}$ to represent the event that the paths chosen by pairs i and j share at least one edge. Since a path in F_i shares edges with no more than k paths in F_j,

$$p = \Pr(E_{i,j}) \leq \frac{k}{m}.$$

Let d be the degree of the dependency graph. Since event $E_{i,j}$ is independent of all events $E_{i',j'}$ when $i' \notin \{i, j\}$ and $j' \notin \{i, j\}$, we have $d < 2n$. Since

$$4dp < \frac{8nk}{m} \leq 1,$$

all of the conditions of the Lovász Local Lemma are satisfied, proving

$$\Pr\left(\bigcap_{i \neq j} \bar{E}_{i,j}\right) > 0.$$

Hence, there is a choice of paths such that the n paths are edge disjoint. ∎

6.7.2. Application: Satisfiability

As a second example, we return to the satisfiability question. For the k-satisfiability (k-SAT) problem, the formula is restricted so that each clause has exactly k literals. Again, we assume that no clause contains both a literal and its negation, as these clauses are trivial. We prove that any k-SAT formula in which no variable appears in too many clauses has a satisfying assignment.

Theorem 6.13: *If no variable in a k-SAT formula appears in more than $T = 2^k/4k$ clauses, then the formula has a satisfying assignment.*

Proof: Consider the probability space defined by giving a random assignment to the variables. For $i = 1, \ldots, m$, let E_i denote the event that the ith clause is not satisfied by the random assignment. Since each clause has k literals,

$$\Pr(E_i) = 2^{-k}.$$

The event E_i is mutually independent of all of the events related to clauses that do not share variables with clause i. Because each of the k variables in clause i can appear in no more than $T = 2^k/4k$ clauses, the degree of the dependency graph is bounded by $d \leq kT \leq 2^{k-2}$.

In this case,

$$4dp \leq 4 \cdot 2^{k-2}2^{-k} \leq 1,$$

so we can apply the Lovász Local Lemma to conclude that

$$\Pr\left(\bigcap_{i=1}^{m} \bar{E}_i\right) > 0;$$

hence there is a satisfying assignment for the formula. ∎

151

6.8.* Explicit Constructions Using the Local Lemma

The Lovász Local Lemma proves that a random element in an appropriately defined sample space has a nonzero probability of satisfying our requirement. However, this probability might be too small for an algorithm that is based on simple sampling. The number of objects that we need to sample before we find an element that satisfies our requirements might be exponential in the problem size.

In a number of interesting applications, the existential result of the Lovász Local Lemma can be used to derive efficient construction algorithms. Although the details differ in the specific applications, many known algorithms are based on a common two-phase scheme. In the first phase, a subset of the variables of the problem are assigned random values; the remaining variables are deferred to the second stage. The subset of variables that are assigned values in the first stage is chosen so that:

1. using the Local Lemma, one can show that the random partial solution fixed in the first phase can be extended to a full solution of the problem without modifying any of the variables fixed in the first phase; and
2. the dependency graph H between events defined by the variables deferred to the second phase has, with high probability, only small connected components.

When the dependency graph consists of connected components, a solution for the variables of one component can be found independently of the other components. Thus, the first phase of the two-phase algorithm breaks the original problem into smaller subproblems. Each of the smaller subproblems can then be solved independently in the second phase by an exhaustive search.

6.8.1. *Application: A Satisfiability Algorithm*

We demonstrate this technique in an algorithm for finding a satisfying assignment for a k-SAT formula. The explicit construction result will be significantly weaker than the existence result proven in the previous section. In particular, we obtain a polynomial time algorithm only for the case when k is a constant. This result is still interesting, since for $k \geq 3$ the problem of k-satisfiability is NP-complete. For notational convenience we treat here only the case where k is an even constant with $k \geq 12$; the case where k is a sufficiently large odd constant is similar.

Consider a k-SAT formula $\mathcal{F}$, with k an even constant, such that each variable appears in no more than $T = 2^{\alpha k}$ clauses for some constant $\alpha > 0$ determined in the proof. Let $x_1, \ldots, x_\ell$ be the ℓ variables and $C_1, \ldots, C_m$ the m clauses of $\mathcal{F}$.

Following the outline suggested in Section 6.8, our algorithm for finding a satisfying assignment for $\mathcal{F}$ has two phases. Some of the variables are fixed at the first phase, and the remaining variables are deferred to the second phase. While executing the first phase, we call a clause C_i *dangerous* if both the following conditions hold:

1. $k/2$ literals of the clause C_i have been fixed; and
2. C_i is not yet satisfied.

Phase I can be described as follows. Consider the variables $x_1, \ldots, x_\ell$ sequentially. If x_i is not in a dangerous clause, assign it independently and uniformly at random a value in $\{0, 1\}$.

A clause is a *surviving* clause if it is not satisfied by the variables fixed in phase I. Note that a surviving clause has no more than $k/2$ of its variables fixed in the first phase. A *deferred* variable is a variable that was not assigned a value in the first phase. In phase II, we use exhaustive search in order to assign values to the deferred variables and so complete a satisfying assignment for the formula.

In the next two lemmas we show that:

1. the partial solution computed in phase I can be extended to a full satisfying assignment of $\mathcal{F}$, and
2. with high probability, the exhaustive search in phase II is completed in time that is polynomial in m.

Lemma 6.14: *There is an assignment of values to the deferred variables such that all the surviving clauses are satisfied.*

Proof: Let $H = (V, E)$ be a graph on m nodes, where $V = \{1, \ldots, m\}$, and let $(i, j) \in E$ if and only if $C_i \cap C_j \neq \emptyset$. That is, H is the dependency graph for the original problem. Let $H' = (V', E')$ be a graph with $V' \subseteq V$ and $E' \subseteq E$ such that (a) $i \in V'$ if and only if C_i is a surviving clause and (b) $(i, j) \in E'$ if and only if C_i and C_j share a deferred variable. In the following discussion we do not distinguish between node i and clause i.

Consider the probability space defined by assigning a random value in $\{0, 1\}$ independently to each deferred variable. The assignment of values to the nondeferred variables in phase I, together with the random assignment of values to the deferred variables, defines an assignment to all the ℓ variables. For $i = 1, \ldots, m$, let E_i be the event that surviving clause C_i is not satisfied by this assignment. Associate the event E_i with node i in V'. The graph H' is then the dependency graph for this set of events.

A surviving clause has at least $k/2$ deferred variables, so

$$p = \Pr(E_i) \leq 2^{-k/2}.$$

A variable appears in no more than T clauses; therefore, the degree of the dependency graph is bounded by

$$d = kT \leq k2^{\alpha k}.$$

For any $k \geq 12$, there is a corresponding suitably small constant $\alpha > 0$ so that

$$4dp = 4k2^{\alpha k}2^{-k/2} \leq 1$$

and so, by the Lovász Local Lemma, there is an assignment for the deferred variables that – together with the assignment of values to variables in phase I – satisfies the formula. ∎

The assignment of values to a subset of the variables in phase I partitions the problem into as many as m independent subformulas, so that each deferred variable appears in only one subformula. The subformulas are given by the connected components of H'. If we can show that each connected component in H' has size $O(\log m)$, then each subformula will have no more than $O(k \log m)$ deferred variables. An exhaustive search of all the possible assignments for all variables in each subformula can then be done in polynomial time. Hence we focus on the following lemma.

Lemma 6.15: *All connected components in H' are of size $O(\log m)$ with probability $1 - o(1)$.*

Proof: Consider a connected component R of r vertices in H. If R is a connected component in H', then all its r nodes are surviving clauses. A surviving clause is either a dangerous clause or it shares at least one deferred variable with a dangerous clause (i.e., it has a neighbor in H' that is a dangerous clause). The probability that a given clause is dangerous is at most $2^{-k/2}$, since exactly $k/2$ of its variables were given random values in phase I yet none of these values satisfied the clause. The probability that a given clause survives is the probability that either this clause or at least one of its direct neighbors is dangerous, which is bounded by

$$(d+1)2^{-k/2},$$

where again $d = kT > 1$.

If the survival of individual clauses were independent events then we would be in excellent shape. However, from our description here it is evident that such events are not independent. Instead, we identify a subset of the vertices in R such that the survival of the clauses represented by the vertices of this subset are independent events. A *4-tree* S of a connected component R in H is defined as follows:

1. S is a rooted tree;
2. any two nodes in S are at distance at least 4 in H;
3. there can be an edge in S only between two nodes with distance exactly 4 between them in H;
4. any node of R is either in S or is at distance 3 or less from a node in S.

Considering the nodes in a 4-tree proves useful because the event that a node u in a 4-tree survives and the event that another node v in a 4-tree survives are actually independent. Any clause that could cause u to survive has distance at least 2 from any clause that could cause v to survive. Clauses at distance 2 share no variables, and hence the events that they are dangerous are independent. We can take advantage of this independence to conclude that, for any 4-tree S, the probability that the nodes in the 4-tree survive is at most

$$((d+1)2^{-k/2})^{|S|}.$$

A maximal 4-tree S of a connected component R is the 4-tree with the largest possible number of vertices. Since the degree of the dependency graph is bounded by d, there are no more than

$$d + d(d-1) + d(d-1)(d-1) \le d^3 - 1$$

nodes at distance 3 or less from any given vertex. We therefore claim that a maximal 4-tree of R must have at least r/d^3 vertices. Otherwise, when we consider the vertices of the maximal 4-tree S and all neighbors within distance 3 or less of these vertices, we obtain fewer than r vertices. Hence there must be a vertex of distance at least 4 from all vertices in S. If this vertex has distance exactly 4 from some vertex in S, then it can be added to S and thus S is not maximal, yielding a contradiction. If its distance is larger than 4 from all vertices in S, consider any path that brings it closer to S; such a path must eventually pass through a vertex of distance at least 4 from all vertices in S and of distance 4 from some vertex in S, again contradicting the maximality of S.

To show that with probability $1 - o(1)$ there is no connected component R of size $r \geq c \log_2 m$ for some constant c in H', we show that there is no 4-tree of H of size r/d^3 that survives with probability $1 - o(1)$. Since a surviving connected component R would have a maximal 4-tree of size r/d^3, the absence of such a 4-tree implies the absence of such a component.

We need to count the number of 4-trees of size $s = r/d^3$ in H. We can choose the root of the 4-tree in m ways. A tree with root v is uniquely defined by an Eulerian tour that starts and ends at v and traverses each edge of the tree twice, once in each direction. Since an edge of S represents a path of length 4 in H, at each vertex in the 4-tree the Eulerian path can continue in as many as d^4 different ways, and therefore the number of 4-trees of size $s = r/d^3$ in H is bounded by

$$m(d^4)^{2s} = md^{8r/d^3}.$$

The probability that the nodes of each such 4-tree survive in H' is at most

$$((d+1)2^{-k/2})^s = ((d+1)2^{-k/2})^{r/d^3}.$$

Hence the probability that H' has a connected component of size r is bounded by

$$md^{8r/d^3}((d+1)2^{-k/2})^{r/d^3} \leq m2^{(rk/d^3)(8\alpha+2\alpha-1/2)} = o(1)$$

for $r \geq c \log_2 m$ and for a suitably large constant c and a sufficiently small constant $\alpha > 0$. $\blacksquare$

Thus, we have the following theorem.

Theorem 6.16: *Consider a k-SAT formula with m clauses, where $k \geq 12$ is an even constant and each variable appears in up to $2^{\alpha k}$ clauses for a sufficiently small constant $\alpha > 0$. Then there is an algorithm that finds a satisfying assignment for the formula in expected time that is polynomial in m.*

Proof: As we have described, if the first phase partitions the problem into subformulas involving only $O(k \log m)$ variables, then a solution can be found by solving each subformula exhaustively in time that is polynomial in m. The probability of the first phase partitioning the problem appropriately is $1 - o(1)$, so we need only run phase I a constant number of times on average before obtaining a good partition. The theorem follows. $\blacksquare$

6.9. Lovász Local Lemma: The General Case

For completeness we include the statement and proof of the general case of the Lovász Local Lemma.

Theorem 6.17: *Let $E_1, \ldots, E_n$ be a set of events in an arbitrary probability space, and let $G = (V, E)$ be the dependency graph for these events. Assume there exist $x_1, \ldots, x_n \in [0, 1]$ such that, for all $1 \leq i \leq n$,*

$$\Pr(E_i) \leq x_i \prod_{(i,j)\in E} (1 - x_j).$$

Then

$$\Pr\left(\bigcap_{i=1}^{n} \bar{E}_i\right) \geq \prod_{i=1}^{n} (1 - x_i).$$

Proof: Let $S \subseteq \{1, \ldots, n\}$. We prove by induction on $s = 0, \ldots, n$ that, if $|S| \leq s$, then for all k we have

$$\Pr\left(E_k \mid \bigcap_{j\in S} \bar{E}_j\right) \leq x_k.$$

As in the case of the symmetric version of the Local Lemma, we must be careful that the conditional probability is well-defined. This follows using the same approach as in the symmetric case, so we focus on the rest of the induction.

The base case $s = 0$ follows from the assumption that

$$\Pr(E_k) \leq x_k \prod_{(k,j)\in E} (1 - x_j) \leq x_k.$$

For the inductive step, let $S_1 = \{j \in S \mid (k, j) \in E\}$ and $S_2 = S - S_1$. If $S_2 = S$ then E_k is mutually independent of the events $\bar{E}_i$, $i \in S$, and

$$\Pr\left(E_k \mid \bigcap_{j\in S} \bar{E}_j\right) = \Pr(E_k) \leq x_k.$$

We continue with the case $|S_2| < s$. We again use the notation

$$F_S = \bigcap_{j\in S} \bar{E}_j$$

and define F_{S_1} and F_{S_2} similarly, so that $F_S = F_{S_1} \cap F_{S_2}$.

Applying the definition of conditional probability yields

$$\Pr(E_k \mid F_S) = \frac{\Pr(E_k \cap F_S)}{\Pr(F_S)}. \tag{6.6}$$

By once again applying the definition of conditional probability, the numerator of Eqn. (6.6) can be written as

$$\Pr(E_k \cap F_S) = \Pr(E_k \cap F_{S_1} \mid F_{S_2}) \Pr(F_{S_2})$$

and the denominator as

$$\Pr(F_S) = \Pr(F_{S_1} \mid F_{S_2}) \Pr(F_{S_2}).$$

156

Canceling the common factor then yields

$$\Pr(E_k \mid F_S) = \frac{\Pr(E_k \cap F_{S_1} \mid F_{S_2})}{\Pr(F_{S_1} \mid F_{S_2})}. \tag{6.7}$$

Since the probability of an intersection of events is bounded by the probability of each of the events and since E_k is independent of the events in S_2, we can bound the numerator of Eqn. (6.7) by

$$\Pr(E_k \cap F_{S_1} \mid F_{S_2}) \leq \Pr(E_k \mid F_{S_2}) = \Pr(E_k) \leq x_k \prod_{(k,j) \in E} (1 - x_j).$$

To bound the denominator of Eqn. (6.7), let $S_1 = \{j_1, \ldots, j_r\}$. Applying the induction hypothesis, we have

$$\Pr(F_{S_1} \mid F_{S_2}) = \Pr \left(\bigcap_{j \in S_1} \bar{E}_j \mid \bigcap_{j \in S_2} \bar{E}_j \right)$$

$$= \prod_{i=1}^{r} \left(1 - \Pr \left(E_{j_i} \mid \left(\bigcap_{t=1}^{i-1} \bar{E}_{j_t} \right) \cap \left(\bigcap_{j \in S_2} \bar{E}_j \right) \right) \right)$$

$$\geq \prod_{i=1}^{r} (1 - x_{j_i})$$

$$\geq \prod_{(k,j) \in E} (1 - x_j).$$

Using the upper bound for the numerator and the lower bound for the denominator, we can prove the induction hypothesis:

$$\Pr \left(E_k \mid \bigcap_{j \in S} \bar{E}_j \right) = \Pr(E_k \mid F_S)$$

$$= \frac{\Pr(E_k \cap F_{S_1} \mid F_{S_2})}{\Pr(F_{S_1} \mid F_{S_2})}$$

$$\leq \frac{x_k \prod_{(k,j) \in E} (1 - x_j)}{\prod_{(k,j) \in E} (1 - x_j)}$$

$$= x_k.$$

The theorem now follows from:

$$\Pr(\bar{E}_1, \ldots, \bar{E}_n) = \prod_{i=1}^{n} \Pr(\bar{E}_i \mid \bar{E}_1, \ldots, \bar{E}_{i-1})$$

$$= \prod_{i=1}^{n} (1 - \Pr(E_i \mid \bar{E}_1, \ldots, \bar{E}_{i-1}))$$

$$\geq \prod_{i=1}^{n} (1 - x_i) > 0.$$

∎

157

6.10.* The Algorithmic Lovász Local Lemma

Recently, there have been several advances in extending the Lovász Local Lemma. We briefly summarize the key points here, and start by looking again to the k-SAT problem to provide an example of these ideas in action.

We have shown previously that if no variable in a k-SAT formula appears in more than $2^k/(4k)$ clauses, then the formula has a satisfying assignment, and we have shown that if each variable appears in no more that $2^{\alpha k}$ clauses for some constant α a solution can be found in expected polynomial time. Here we provide an improved result which again provides a solution in expected polynomial time.

Theorem 6.18: *Suppose that every clause in a k-SAT formula shares one or more variables with at most $2^{k-3} - 1$ other clauses. Then a solution for the formula exists and can be found in expected time that is polynomial in the number of clauses m.*

Before starting the proof, we informally describe our algorithm. As before, let $x_1, x_2, \ldots, x_\ell$ be the ℓ variables and $C_1, C_2, \ldots, C_m$ be the m clauses in the formula. We begin by choosing a random truth assignment (uniformly at random). We then look for a clause C_i that is unsatisfied; if no such clause exists we are done. If such a clause exists, we look specifically at the variables in the clause, and randomly choose a new truth assignment for those variables. Doing so will hopefully "fix" the clause C_i so that it is satisfied, but it may not; even worse, it may end up causing a clause C_j that shares a variable with C_i to become unsatisfied. We recursively fix these neighboring clauses, so that when the recursion is finished, we have that C_i is satisfied and we have not damaged any clause by making it become unsatisfied. We therefore have improved the situation by satisfying at least one previously unsatisfied clause. We then continue to the next unsatisfied clause; we have to do this at most m times.

The underlying question that we need to answer to show that this algorithm works is how we know that the recursion we have described stops successfully. Perhaps it simply goes on forever, or for an exponential amount of time. The proof we provide shows that this cannot be the case through a new type of argument. Specifically, we show that if such bad recursions occur with non-trivial probability, then one could compress a random string of n independent, unbiased flips into much fewer than n bits. That should seem impossible, and it is. While compression is a theme we cover in much more detail in Chapter 10, we explain the compression result we need here in the proof of the theorem. All we need is that a string of r random bits, where each bit is chosen independently and uniformly at random, cannot be compressed so that the average length of the representation over all choices of the r random bits is less than $r - 2$.

To see that this must be true, assume the best possible setting for us, where we don't have to worry about the "end" of our compressed sequence, but can use each string of bits of length less than r to represent one of the 2^r possible strings we aim to compress. That is, we won't worry that one compressed string might be "0" and another one might be "00", in which case it might be hard to distinguish whether "00" was meant to represent a single compressed string, or two copies of the string represented by "0". (Essentially, a compressed string can be terminated for free; this allowance can only hurt us in our argument.) Still, each string of $s < r$ bits can only represent a single possible string of length r. Hence we have available one string of length 0 (the empty string), two strings of length 1, and so on. There are only $2^r - 1$ strings of length less than r; even if we count only those in computing the average length of the compressed string, which again can only hurt us, the average length would be at least

$$\sum_{i=1}^{r-1} \frac{1}{2^{r-i}} \cdot i \geq r - 2.$$

The same compression fact naturally holds true for any collection of 2^r equally likely strings; they do not have to be limited to strings of r random bits.

Given this fact, our proof proceeds as follows.

Proof of Theorem 6.18: The algorithm we use is explicitly provided as the k-Satisfiability Algorithm below.

---

k-Satisfiability Algorithm (Using Algorithmic LLL):

Input: A collection $C_1, C_2, \ldots, C_m$ of clauses for a k-SAT formula over n variables.

Output: A truth assignment for these variables.

Main routine:

1. Start with a random assignment.
2. While some C_i is not satisfied:
   (a) choose the unsatisfied C_i with the smallest value of i;
   (b) enter i in binary using $\lceil \log_2 m \rceil$ bits in the history;
   (c) use localcorrect on clause C_i.

localcorrect(C):

1. Resample new values for every variable in clause C.
2. While some C_j that shares a variable with C (including possibly C itself) is not satisfied
   (a) choose the unsatisfied C_j sharing a variable with C with the smallest value of j;
   (b) enter "0" followed by j in binary using $k - 3$ bits in the history;
   (c) use localcorrect on clause C_j.
3. Enter "1" in the history.

We note the algorithm produces a history, which we use in the analysis of the algorithm.

It is important to realize that while a clause can become satisfied and unsatisfied again multiple times through the recursive process, when we return to the main routine and complete the call to localcorrect, we have satisfied the clause C_i that localcorrect was called on from the main routine, and further any clause that was previously satisfied has stayed satisfied because of the recursion. What we wish to show is that the recursive process has to stop.

Our analysis makes use of the fact that our algorithm makes use of a random string. We provide two different ways to describe how our algorithm runs.

We can think of our algorithm as being described by the random string of bits it uses. It takes n bits to initially assign random truth values to each of the variables. After that, it takes k bits to resample values for a clause each time localcorrect is called. Let us refer to each time localcorrect is called as a round. Then one way to describe our algorithm's actions for j rounds is with the random string of $n + jk$ bits used by the algorithm.

But here is another way of describing how our algorithm works. We keep track of the "history" of the algorithm as shown in the algorithm. The history includes a list of the clauses that localcorrect is called on by the main routine. The history also includes a list of the recursive calls to localcorrect, in a slightly non-obvious way. First, we note that the algorithm uses a flag bit 0 and a flag bit 1 to mark the start and end of recursive calls, so the algorithm tracks the stack of recursive calls in a natural way. Second, instead of the natural approach of using $\lceil \log_2 m \rceil$ bits to represent the index of the clause in our recursive calls, the algorithm uses only $k - 3$ bits. We now explain why only $k - 3$ bits are needed. Since there are at most 2^{k-3} possible clauses that share a variable with the current clause (including the current clause itself) that could be the next one called, the clause can be represented by an index of $k - 3$ bits. (Imagine having an ordered list of the up to 2^{k-3} clauses that share a variable with each clause; we just need the index into that list.) Finally, our history will also include the current truth assignment of n bits. Note that the current truth assignment can be thought of as in an separate updatable storage area for the history; every time the truth assignment is updated, so is this part of the history.

We now show that when the algorithm has run j rounds, we can recover the random string of $n + jk$ bits that the algorithm has used from the history we have described. Start with the current truth assignment, and break the history up, using the flags that mark invocations of localcorrect. We can use the history to determine the sequence of recursive calls, and what clauses localcorrect was called on. Then, going backwards through the history, we know at each step which clause was being resampled. For that clause to have to be resampled, it must have been unsatisfied previously. But there is only *one* setting of the variables that makes a clause unsatisfied, and hence we know what the truth values for those variables were before the clause was resampled. We can therefore update the current truth assignment so that it represents the truth assignment before the resampling, and continue backwards through the process. Repeating this action, we can determine the original truth assignment, and since at each step we can determine what variable values were changed and what their values were on each resampling, we recover the whole string of $n + jk$ random bits.

Our history takes at most $n + m\lceil \log_2 m \rceil + j(k - 1)$ bits; here we use the fact that each resampling uses at most $k - 1$ bits, including the two bits that may be necessary as flags for the start and end of the recursion given by that resampling. For large enough j, our history yields a compressed form of the the random string used to run the algorithm, since only $k - 1$ bits are used to represent each resampling in the history instead of the k bits used by the algorithm.

Now suppose there were no truth assignment, in which case the algorithm would run forever. Then after a large enough number of rounds J, the history will be at most

$n + m\lceil \log_2 m \rceil + J(k - 1)$ bits, while the random string running the algorithm would be $n + Jk$ bits. By our result on compressing random strings, we must have

$$n + m\lceil \log_2 m \rceil + J(k - 1) \geq n + Jk - 2.$$

Hence

$$J \leq m\lceil \log_2 m \rceil + 2.$$

This contradicts that the algorithm can run forever, so there must be a truth assignment.

Similarly, the number of rounds J is more than $m\lceil \log_2 m \rceil + 2 + i$ with probability at most 2^{-i}. To see this, suppose the probability of lasting to this round is greater than 2^{-i}. Again consider the algorithm after $J = m\lceil \log_2 m \rceil + 2 + i$ rounds, so the history will be at most $n + m\lceil \log_2 m \rceil + J(k - 1)$ bits. The algorithm can also be described by the $n + Jk$ random bits that led to the current state. As there are at least 2^{n+Jk} random bit strings of this length, and the probability of lasting at least this many rounds is greater than 2^{-i} by assumption, there are at least 2^{n+Jk-i} random bit strings associated with reaching this round. By our result on compressing random strings, it requires more than $n + Jk - i - 2$ bits on average to represent the at least 2^{n+Jk-i} random bit strings associated with reaching this round. But the history, as we have already argued, provides a representation of these random bit strings, in that we can reconstruct the algorithm's random bit string from the history. The number of bits the history uses is only

$$n + m\lceil \log_2 m \rceil + J(k - 1) = n + Jk - i - 2,$$

a contradiction.

Since the probability of lasting more than $m\lceil \log_2 m \rceil + 2 + i$ is at most 2^{-i}, we can bound the expected number of rounds by

$$m\lceil \log_2 m \rceil + 2 + \sum_{i=1}^{\infty} i2^{-i}.$$

The expected number rounds used by the algorithm is thus at most $m\lceil \log_2 m \rceil + 4$.

The work done in each resampling round can easily be made to be polynomial in m, so the total expected time to find an assigment can be made polynomial in m as well. ∎

While already surprising, the proof above can be improved slightly. A more careful encoding shows that the expected number of rounds required can be reduced to $O(m)$ instead of $O(m \log m)$. This is covered in the Exercise 6.21.

The algorithmic approach we have used for the satisfiability problem in the proof of Theorem 6.18 can be extended further to obtain an algorithmic version of the Lovász local lemma, which we now describe. Let us suppose that we have a collection of n events $E_1, E_2, \ldots, E_n$ that depend on a collection of ℓ mutually independent variables $y_1, y_2, \ldots, y_\ell$. The dependency graph on events has an edge between two events if they both depend on at least one shared variable y_i. The idea is that at each step if there is an event that is unsatisfied, we resample only the random variables on which that event depends. As with the k-Satisfiability Algorithm using the algorithmic Lovász

Local Lemma, this resampling process has to be ordered carefully to ensure progress. If the dependencies are not too great, then the right resampling algorithm terminates with a solution.

The symmetric version is easier to state.

Theorem 6.19: *Let $E_1, E_2, \ldots, E_n$ be a set of events in an arbitrary probability space that are determined by mutually independent random variables $y_1, y_2, \ldots, y_\ell$, and let $G = (V, E)$ be the dependency graph for these events. Suppose the following conditions hold for values d and p:*

1. each event E_i is adjacent to at most d other events in the dependency graph, or equivalently, there are only d other events that also depend on one or more of the y_j that E_i depends on;
2. $\Pr(E_i) \le p$;
3. $ep(d + 1) \le 1$.

Then there exists an assignment of the y_i so that the event $\cap_{i=1}^n \bar{E}_i$ holds, and a resampling algorithm with the property that the expected number of times the algorithm resamples the event E_i in finding such an assignment is at most $1/d$. Hence the expected total number of resampling steps taken by the algorithm is at most n/d.

However, we also have a corresponding theorem for the asymmetric version.

Theorem 6.20: *Let $E_1, E_2, \ldots, E_n$ be a set of events in an arbitrary probability space that are determined by mutually independent random variables $y_1, y_2, \ldots, y_\ell$, and let $G = (V, E)$ be the dependency graph for these events. Assume there exist $x_1, x_2, \ldots, x_n \in [0, 1]$ such that, for all $1 \le i \le n$*

$$\Pr(E_i) \le x_i \prod_{(i,j) \in E} (1 - x_j).$$

Then there exists an assignment of the y_i so that the event $\cap_{i=1}^n \bar{E}_i$ holds, and a resampling algorithm with the property that the expected number of times the algorithm resamples the event E_i in finding such an assignment is at most $x_i/(1 - x_i)$. Hence the expected total number of resampling steps taken by the algorithm is at most $\sum_{i=1}^n x_i/(1 - x_i)$.

The proofs of these theorems are beyond the scope of the book. Similar to the algorithm for satisfiability based on resampling given above, the proof relies on bounding the expected number of resamplings that occur over the course of the algorithm.

6.11. Exercises

Exercise 6.1: Consider an instance of SAT with m clauses, where every clause has exactly k literals.

(a) Give a Las Vegas algorithm that finds an assignment satisfying at least $m(1 - 2^{-k})$ clauses, and analyze its expected running time.

(b) Give a derandomization of the randomized algorithm using the method of conditional expectations.

Exercise 6.2:

(a) Prove that, for every integer n, there exists a coloring of the edges of the complete graph K_n by two colors so that the total number of monochromatic copies of K_4 is at most $\binom{n}{4} 2^{-5}$.

(b) Give a randomized algorithm for finding a coloring with at most $\binom{n}{4} 2^{-5}$ monochromatic copies of K_4 that runs in expected time polynomial in n.

(c) Show how to construct such a coloring deterministically in polynomial time using the method of conditional expectations.

Exercise 6.3: Given an n-vertex undirected graph $G = (V, E)$, consider the following method of generating an independent set. Given a permutation σ of the vertices, define a subset $S(\sigma)$ of the vertices as follows: for each vertex i, $i \in S(\sigma)$ if and only if no neighbor j of i precedes i in the permutation σ.

(a) Show that each $S(\sigma)$ is an independent set in G.

(b) Suggest a natural randomized algorithm to produce σ for which you can show that the expected cardinality of $S(\sigma)$ is

$$\sum_{i=1}^{n} \frac{1}{d_i + 1},$$

where d_i denotes the degree of vertex i.

(c) Prove that G has an independent set of size at least $\sum_{i=1}^{n} 1/(d_i + 1)$.

Exercise 6.4: Consider the following two-player game. The game begins with k tokens placed at the number 0 on the integer number line spanning $[0, n]$. Each round, one player, called the *chooser*, selects two disjoint and nonempty sets of tokens A and B. (The sets A and B need not cover all the remaining tokens; they only need to be disjoint.) The second player, called the *remover*, takes all the tokens from one of the sets off the board. The tokens from the other set all move up one space on the number line from their current position. The chooser wins if any token ever reaches n. The remover wins if the chooser finishes with one token that has not reached n.

(a) Give a winning strategy for the chooser when $k \geq 2^n$.

(b) Use the probabilistic method to show that there must exist a winning strategy for the remover when $k < 2^n$.

(c) Explain how to use the method of conditional expectations to derandomize the winning strategy for the remover when $k < 2^n$.

Exercise 6.5: We have shown using the probabilistic method that, if a graph G has n nodes and m edges, then there exists a partition of the n nodes into sets A and B such that at least $m/2$ edges cross the partition. Improve this result slightly: show that there exists a partition such that at least $mn/(2n - 1)$ edges cross the partition.

Exercise 6.6: We can generalize the problem of finding a large cut to finding a large k-cut. A k-cut is a partition of the vertices into k disjoint sets, and the value of a cut is the weight of all edges crossing from one of the k sets to another. In Section 6.2.1 we considered 2-cuts when all edges had the same weight 1, showing via the probabilistic method that any graph G with m edges has a cut with value at least $m/2$. Generalize this argument to show that any graph G with m edges has a k-cut with value at least $(k-1)m/k$. Show how to use derandomization (following the argument of Section 6.3) to give a deterministic algorithm for finding such a cut.

Exercise 6.7: A hypergraph H is a pair of sets (V, E), where V is the set of vertices and E is the set of hyperedges. Every hyperedge in E is a subset of V. In particular, an r-uniform hypergraph is one where the size of each edge is r. For example, a 2-uniform hypergraph is just a standard graph. A dominating set in a hypergraph H is a set of vertices $S \subset V$ such that $e \cap S \neq \emptyset$ for every edge $e \in E$. That is, S hits every edge of the hypergraph.

Let $H = (V, E)$ be an r-uniform hypergraph with n vertices and m edges. Show that there is a dominating set of size at most $np + (1-p)^r m$ for every real number $0 \leq p \leq 1$. Also, show that there is a dominating set of size at most $(m + n \ln r)/r$.

Exercise 6.8: Prove that, for every integer n, there exists a way to 2-color the edges of K_x so that there is no monochromatic clique of size k when

$$x = n - \binom{n}{k} 2^{1 - \binom{k}{2}}.$$

(*Hint:* Start by 2-coloring the edges of K_n, then fix things up.)

Exercise 6.9: A *tournament* is a graph on n vertices with exactly one directed edge between each pair of vertices. If vertices represent players, then each edge can be thought of as the result of a match between the two players: the edge points to the winner. A *ranking* is an ordering of the n players from best to worst (ties are not allowed). Given the outcome of a tournament, one might wish to determine a ranking of the players. A ranking is said to *disagree* with a directed edge from y to x if y is ahead of x in the ranking (since x beat y in the tournament).

(a) Prove that, for every tournament, there exists a ranking that disagrees with at most 50% of the edges.
(b) Prove that, for sufficiently large n, there exists a tournament such that every ranking disagrees with at least 49% of the edges in the tournament.

Exercise 6.10: A family of subsets $\mathcal{F}$ of $\{1, 2, \ldots, n\}$ is called an *antichain* if there is no pair of sets A and B in $\mathcal{F}$ satisfying $A \subset B$.

(a) Give an example of $\mathcal{F}$ where $|\mathcal{F}| = \binom{n}{\lfloor n/2 \rfloor}$.
(b) Let f_k be the number of sets in $\mathcal{F}$ with size k. Show that

$$\sum_{k=0}^{n} \frac{f_k}{\binom{n}{k}} \leq 1.$$

164

(*Hint:* Choose a random permutation of the numbers from 1 to n, and let $X_k = 1$ if the first k numbers in your permutation yield a set in $\mathcal{F}$. If $X = \sum_{k=0}^{n} X_k$, what can you say about X?)

(c) Argue that $|\mathcal{F}| \leq \binom{n}{\lfloor n/2 \rfloor}$ for any antichain $\mathcal{F}$.

Exercise 6.11: Consider a graph in $G_{n,p}$ with n vertices and each pair of vertices independently connected by an edge with probability p. We prove a threshold for the existence of triangles in the graph.

Let $t_1, \ldots, t_{\binom{n}{3}}$ be an enumeration of all triplets of three vertices in the graph. Let $X_i = 1$ if the the three edges of the triplet t_i appear in the graph, so that t_i forms a triangle in the graph. Otherwise $X_i = 0$. Let $X = \sum_{i=1}^{\binom{n}{3}} X_i$.

(a) Compute $\mathbf{E}[X]$.
(b) Use (a) to show that if $pn \to 0$ then $\Pr(X > 0) \to 0$.
(c) Show that $\mathbf{Var}[X_i] \leq p^3$.
(d) Show that $\mathbf{Cov}(X_i, X_j) = p^5 - p^6$ for $O(n^4)$ pairs $i \neq j$, otherwise $\mathbf{Cov}(X_i, X_j) = 0$.
(e) Show that $\mathbf{Var}[X] = O(n^3 p^3 + n^4(p^5 - p^6))$.
(f) Conclude that if p is such that $pn \to \infty$ then $\Pr(X = 0) \to 0$.

Exercise 6.12: In Section 6.5.1, we bounded the variance of the number of 4-cliques in a random graph in order to demonstrate the second moment method. Show how to calculate the variance directly by using the equality from Exercise 3.9: for $X = \sum_{i=1}^{n} X_i$ the sum of Bernoulli random variables,

$$\mathbf{E}[X^2] = \sum_{i=1}^{n} \Pr(X_i = 1)\mathbf{E}[X \mid X_i = 1].$$

Exercise 6.13: Consider the problem of whether graphs in $G_{n,p}$ have cliques of constant size k. Suggest an appropriate threshold function for this property. Generalize the argument used for cliques of size 4, using either the second moment method or the conditional expectation inequality, to prove that your threshold function is correct for cliques of size 5.

Exercise 6.14: Consider a graph in $G_{n,p}$, with $p = c \ln n / n$. Use the second moment method or the conditional expectation inequality to prove that if $c < 1$ then, for any constant $\varepsilon > 0$ and for n sufficiently large, the graph has isolated vertices with probability at least $1 - \varepsilon$.

Exercise 6.15: Consider a graph in $G_{n,p}$, with $p = 1/n$. Let X be the number of triangles in the graph, where a triangle is a clique with three edges. Show that

$$\Pr(X \geq 1) \leq 1/6$$

and that

$$\lim_{n \to \infty} \Pr(X \geq 1) \geq 1/7.$$

(*Hint:* Use the conditional expectation inequality.)

165

Exercise 6.16: Consider the set-balancing problem of Section 4.4. We claim that there is an $n \times n$ matrix $\mathbf{A}$ for which $\|\mathbf{A}\bar{b}\|_\infty$ is $\Omega(\sqrt{n})$ for any choice of $\bar{b}$. For convenience here we assume that n is even.

(a) We have shown in Eqn. (5.5) that

$$n! \le e\sqrt{n}\left(\frac{n}{e}\right)^n.$$

Using similar ideas, show that

$$n! \ge a\sqrt{n}\left(\frac{n}{e}\right)^n$$

for some positive constant a.

(b) Let $b_1, b_2, \ldots, b_{m/2}$ all equal 1, and let $b_{m/2+1}, b_{m/2+2}, \ldots, b_m$ all equal -1. Let $Y_1, Y_2, \ldots, Y_m$ each be chosen independently and uniformly at random from $\{0, 1\}$. Show that there exists a positive constant c such that, for sufficiently large m,

$$\Pr\left(\left|\sum_{i=1}^m b_i Y_i\right| > c\sqrt{m}\right) > \frac{1}{2}.$$

(*Hint:* Condition on the number of Y_i that are equal to 1.)

(c) Let $b_1, b_2, \ldots, b_m$ each be equal to either 1 or -1. Let $Y_1, Y_2, \ldots, Y_m$ each be chosen independently and uniformly at random from $\{0, 1\}$. Show that there exists a positive constant c such that, for sufficiently large m,

$$\Pr\left(\left|\sum_{i=1}^m b_i Y_i\right| > c\sqrt{m}\right) > \frac{1}{2}.$$

(d) Prove that there exists a matrix $\mathbf{A}$ for which $\|\mathbf{A}\bar{b}\|_\infty$ is $\Omega(\sqrt{n})$ for any choice of $\bar{b}$.

Exercise 6.17: Use the Lovász Local Lemma to show that, if

$$4\binom{k}{2}\binom{n}{k-2}2^{1-\binom{k}{2}} \le 1,$$

then it is possible to color the edges of K_n with two colors so that it has no monochromatic K_k subgraph.

Exercise 6.18: Use the general form of the Lovász Local Lemma to prove that the symmetric version of Theorem 6.11 can be improved by replacing the condition $4dp \le 1$ by the weaker condition $ep(d+1) \le 1$.

Exercise 6.19: Let $G = (V, E)$ be an undirected graph and suppose each $v \in V$ is associated with a set $S(v)$ of $8r$ colors, where $r \ge 1$. Suppose, in addition, that for each $v \in V$ and $c \in S(v)$ there are at most r neighbors u of v such that c lies in $S(u)$. Prove that there is a proper coloring of G assigning to each vertex v a color from its class $S(v)$ such that, for any edge $(u, v) \in E$, the colors assigned to u and v are different.

You may want to let $A_{u,v,c}$ be the event that u and v are both colored with color c and then consider the family of such events.

Exercise 6.20: A k-uniform hypergraph is an ordered pair $G = (V, E)$, but edges consist of sets of k (distinct) vertices, instead of just 2. (So a 2-uniform hypergraph is just what we normally call a graph.) A hypergraph is k-regular if all vertices have degree k; that is, they are in k hypergraph edges.

Show that for sufficiently large k, the vertices of a k-uniform, k-regular hypergraph can be 2-colored so that no edge is monochromatic. What's the smallest value of k you can achieve?

Exercise 6.21: In our description of the k-Satisfiability Algorithm using the algorithmic Lovász local lemma, we used $\lceil \log_2 m \rceil$ bits in the history to represent each clause called in the main routine. Instead, however, we could simply record in the history which clauses are initially unsatisfied with an array of m bits. Explain any other changes you need to make in the algorithm in order to properly record a history that you can "reverse" to obtain the initial assignment, and explain how this allows one to modify the proof of Theorem 6.18 so that only $O(m)$ rounds are needed in expectation.

Exercise 6.22: Implement the algorithmic Lovász Local Lemma for the following scenario. Consider a 9-SAT formula where each variable appears in 8 clauses. Set up a formula with 112,500 variables and 100,000 clauses in the following manner: set up 8 copies of each of the 112,500 variables (900,000 total variables), permute them, and use the ordering to assign the variables to the 100,000 clauses. (If any clauses share a variable, which is likely to happen, try to locally correct for this by swapping one copy to another clause.) Then assign a random "sign" to each variable – with probability $1/2$, use $\bar{x}$ instead of x. This gives a formula that satisfies the conditions of Theorem 6.18.

Your implementation of the algorithmic Lovász Local Lemma does not need to keep track of the history. However, you should track how many times the local correction procedure is required before termination. Repeat this experiment with 100 different formulas derived from the process above, and report on the distribution of the number of local corrections required. Note that you may want to take some care to make the local correction step efficient in order to have your program run effectively.

CHAPTER SEVEN

Markov Chains and Random Walks

Markov chains provide a simple but powerful framework for modeling random processes. We start this chapter with the basic definitions related to Markov chains and then show how Markov chains can be used to analyze simple randomized algorithms for the 2-SAT and 3-SAT problems. Next we study the long-term behavior of Markov chains, explaining the classifications of states and conditions for convergence to a stationary distribution. We apply these techniques to analyzing simple gambling schemes and a discrete version of a Markovian queue. Of special interest is the limiting behavior of random walks on graphs. We prove bounds on the covering time of a graph and use this bound to develop a simple randomized algorithm for the s–t connectivity problem. Finally, we apply Markov chain techniques to resolve a subtle probability problem known as Parrondo's paradox.

7.1. Markov Chains: Definitions and Representations

A *stochastic process* $\mathbf{X} = \{X(t) : t \in T\}$ is a collection of random variables. The index t often represents time, and in that case the process $\mathbf{X}$ models the value of a random variable X that changes over time.

We call $X(t)$ the *state* of the process at time t. In what follows, we use X_t interchangeably with $X(t)$. If, for all t, X_t assumes values from a countably infinite set, then we say that $\mathbf{X}$ is a *discrete space* process. If X_t assumes values from a finite set then the process is *finite*. If T is a countably infinite set we say that $\mathbf{X}$ is a *discrete time* process.

In this chapter we focus on a special type of discrete time, discrete space stochastic process $X_0, X_1, X_2, \ldots$ in which the value of X_t depends on the value of X_{t-1} but *not* on the sequence of states that led the system to that value.

Definition 7.1: *A discrete time stochastic process $X_0, X_1, X_2, \ldots$ is a Markov chain if*[1]

$$\Pr(X_t = a_t \mid X_{t-1} = a_{t-1}, X_{t-2} = a_{t-2}, \ldots, X_0 = a_0) = \Pr(X_t = a_t \mid X_{t-1} = a_{t-1})$$
$$= P_{a_{t-1}, a_t}.$$

---

[1] Strictly speaking, this is a time-homogeneous Markov chain; this will be the only type we study in this book.

This definition expresses that the state X_t depends on the previous state X_{t-1} but is independent of the particular history of how the process arrived at state X_{t-1}. This is called the *Markov property* or *memoryless property,* and it is what we mean when we say that a chain is *Markovian.* It is important to note that the Markov property does not imply that X_t is independent of the random variables $X_0, X_1, \ldots, X_{t-2}$; it just implies that any dependency of X_t on the past is captured in the value of X_{t-1}.

Without loss of generality, we can assume that the discrete state space of the Markov chain is $\{0, 1, 2, \ldots, n\}$ (or $\{0, 1, 2, \ldots\}$ if it is countably infinite). The transition probability

$$P_{i,j} = \Pr(X_t = j \mid X_{t-1} = i)$$

is the probability that the process moves from i to j in one step. The Markov property implies that the Markov chain is uniquely defined by the one-step *transition matrix*:

$$\mathbf{P} = \begin{pmatrix} P_{0,0} & P_{0,1} & \cdots & P_{0,j} & \cdots \\ P_{1,0} & P_{1,1} & \cdots & P_{1,j} & \cdots \\ \vdots & \vdots & \ddots & \vdots & \ddots \\ P_{i,0} & P_{i,1} & \cdots & P_{i,j} & \cdots \\ \vdots & \vdots & \ddots & \vdots & \ddots \end{pmatrix}.$$

That is, the entry in the ith row and jth column is the transition probability $P_{i,j}$. It follows that, for all i, $\sum_{j \geq 0} P_{i,j} = 1$.

This transition matrix representation of a Markov chain is convenient for computing the distribution of future states of the process. Let $p_i(t)$ denote the probability that the process is at state i at time t. Let $\bar{p}(t) = (p_0(t), p_1(t), p_2(t), \ldots)$ be the vector giving the distribution of the state of the chain at time t. Summing over all possible states at time $t - 1$, we have

$$p_i(t) = \sum_{j \geq 0} p_j(t-1) P_{j,i}$$

or[2]

$$\bar{p}(t) = \bar{p}(t-1)\mathbf{P}.$$

We represent the probability distribution as a row vector and multiply $\bar{p}\mathbf{P}$ instead of $\mathbf{P}\bar{p}$ to conform with the interpretation that starting with a distribution $\bar{p}(t-1)$ and applying the operand $\mathbf{P}$, we arrive at the distribution $\bar{p}(t)$.

For any $m \geq 0$, we define the m-step transition probability

$$P_{i,j}^m = \Pr(X_{t+m} = j \mid X_t = i)$$

as the probability that the chain moves from state i to state j in exactly m steps.

Conditioning on the first transition from i, we have

$$P_{i,j}^m = \sum_{k \geq 0} P_{i,k} P_{k,j}^{m-1}. \tag{7.1}$$

---

[2] Operations on vectors are generalized to a countable number of elements in the natural way.

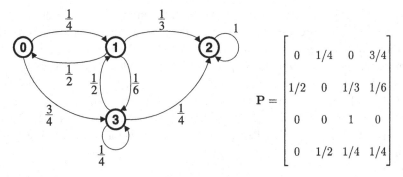

Figure 7.1: A Markov chain (*left*) and the corresponding transition matrix (*right*).

Let $\mathbf{P^{(m)}}$ be the matrix whose entries are the m-step transition probabilities, so that the entry in the ith row and jth column is $P_{i,j}^m$. Then, applying Eqn. (7.1) yields

$$\mathbf{P^{(m)}} = \mathbf{P} \cdot \mathbf{P^{(m-1)}};$$

by induction on m,

$$\mathbf{P^{(m)}} = \mathbf{P^m}.$$

Thus, for any $t \geq 0$ and $m \geq 1$,

$$\bar{p}(t + m) = \bar{p}(t)\mathbf{P^m}.$$

Another useful representation of a Markov chain is by a directed, weighted graph $D = (V, E, w)$. The set of vertices of the graph is the set of states of the chain. There is a directed edge $(i, j) \in E$ if and only if $P_{i,j} > 0$, in which case the weight $w(i, j)$ of the edge (i, j) is given by $w(i, j) = P_{i,j}$. Self-loops, where an edge starts and ends at the same vertex, are allowed. Again, for each i we require that $\sum_{j:(i,j)\in E} w(i, j) = 1$. A sequence of states visited by the process is represented by a directed path on the graph. The probability that the process follows this path is the product of the weights of the path's edges.

Figure 7.1 gives an example of a Markov chain and the correspondence between the two representations. Let us consider how we might calculate with each representation the probability of going from state 0 to state 3 in exactly three steps. With the graph, we consider all the paths that go from state 0 to state 3 in exactly three steps. There are only four such paths: 0–1–0–3, 0–1–3–3, 0–3–1–3, and 0–3–3–3. The probabilities that the process follows each of these paths are 3/32, 1/96, 1/16, and 3/64, respectively. Summing these probabilities, we find that the total probability is 41/192. Alternatively, we can simply compute

$$\mathbf{P}^3 = \begin{bmatrix} 3/16 & 7/48 & 29/64 & 41/192 \\ 5/48 & 5/24 & 79/144 & 5/36 \\ 0 & 0 & 1 & 0 \\ 1/16 & 13/96 & 107/192 & 47/192 \end{bmatrix}.$$

170

2-SAT Algorithm:

1. Start with an arbitrary truth assignment.
2. Repeat up to $2mn^2$ times, terminating if all clauses are satisfied:
   (a) Choose an arbitrary clause that is not satisfied.
   (b) Choose uniformly at random one of the literals in the clause and switch the value of its variable.
3. If a valid truth assignment has been found, return it.
4. Otherwise, return that the formula is unsatisfiable.

Algorithm 7.1: 2-SAT algorithm.

The entry $P_{0,3}^3 = 41/192$ gives the correct answer. The matrix is also helpful if we want to know the probability of ending in state 3 after three steps when we begin in a state chosen uniformly at random from the four states. This can be computed by calculating

$$(1/4, 1/4, 1/4, 1/4)\mathbf{P}^3 = (17/192, 47/384, 737/1152, 43/288);$$

here the last entry, $43/288$, is the required answer.

7.1.1. *Application: A Randomized Algorithm for 2-Satisfiability*

Recall from Section 6.2.2 that an input to the general satisfiability (SAT) problem is a Boolean formula given as the conjunction (AND) of a set of clauses, where each clause is the disjunction (OR) of literals and where a literal is a Boolean variable or the negation of a Boolean variable. A solution to an instance of a SAT formula is an assignment of the variables to the values True (T) and False (F) such that all the clauses are satisfied. The general SAT problem is NP-hard. We analyze here a simple randomized algorithm for 2-SAT, a restricted case of the problem that is solvable in polynomial time.

For the k-satisfiability (k-SAT) problem, the satisfiability formula is restricted so that each clause has exactly k literals. Hence an input for 2-SAT has exactly two literals per clause. The following expression is an instance of 2-SAT:

$$(x_1 \vee \overline{x_2}) \wedge (\overline{x_1} \vee \overline{x_3}) \wedge (x_1 \vee x_2) \wedge (x_4 \vee \overline{x_3}) \wedge (x_4 \vee \overline{x_1}). \tag{7.2}$$

One natural approach to finding a solution for a 2-SAT formula is to start with an assignment, look for a clause that is not satisfied, and change the assignment so that the clause becomes satisfied. If there are two literals in the clause, then there are two possible changes to the assignment that will satisfy the clause. Our 2-SAT algorithm (Algorithm 7.1) decides which of these changes to try randomly. In the algorithm, n denotes the number of variables in the formula and m is an integer parameter that determines the probability that the algorithm terminates with a correct answer.

In the instance given in (7.2), if we begin with all variables set to False then the clause $(x_1 \vee x_2)$ is not satisfied. The algorithm might therefore choose this clause and then select x_1 to be set to True. In this case the clause $(x_4 \vee \overline{x_1})$ would be unsatisfied and the algorithm might switch the value of a variable in that clause, and so on.

If the algorithm terminates with a truth assignment, it clearly returns a correct answer. The case where the algorithm does not find a truth assignment requires some care, and we will return to this point later. Assume for now that the formula is satisfiable and that the algorithm will actually run as long as necessary to find a satisfying truth assignment.

We are mainly interested in the number of iterations of the while-loop executed by the algorithm. We refer to each time the algorithm changes a truth assignment as a *step*. Since a 2-SAT formula has $O(n^2)$ distinct clauses, each step can be executed in $O(n^2)$ time. Faster implementations are possible but we do not consider them here. Let S represent a satisfying assignment for the n variables and let A_i represent the variable assignment after the ith step of the algorithm. Let X_i denote the number of variables in the current assignment A_i that have the same value as in the satisfying assignment S. When $X_i = n$, the algorithm terminates with a satisfying assignment. In fact, the algorithm could terminate before X_i reaches n if it finds another satisfying assignment, but for our analysis the worst case is that the algorithm only stops when $X_i = n$. Starting with $X_i < n$, we consider how X_i evolves over time, and in particular how long it takes before X_i reaches n.

First, if $X_i = 0$ then, for any change in variable value on the next step, we have $X_{i+1} = 1$. Hence

$$\Pr(X_{i+1} = 1 \mid X_i = 0) = 1.$$

Suppose now that $1 \le X_i \le n - 1$. At each step, we choose a clause that is unsatisfied. Since S satisfies the clause, that means that A_i and S disagree on the value of at least one of the variables in this clause. Because the clause has no more than two variables, the probability that we increase the number of matches is at least $1/2$; the probability that we increase the number of matches could be 1 if we are in the case where A_i and S disagree on the value of both variables in this clause. It follows that the probability that we decrease the number of matches is at most $1/2$. Hence, for $1 \le j \le n - 1$,

$$\Pr(X_{i+1} = j + 1 \mid X_i = j) \ge 1/2;$$
$$\Pr(X_{i+1} = j - 1 \mid X_i = j) \le 1/2.$$

The stochastic process $X_0, X_1, X_2, \ldots$ is not necessarily a Markov chain, since the probability that X_i increases could depend on whether A_i and S disagree on one or two variables in the unsatisfied clause the algorithm chooses at that step. This, in turn, might depend on the clauses that have been considered in the past. However, consider the following Markov chain $Y_0, Y_1, Y_2, \ldots$:

$$Y_0 = X_0;$$
$$\Pr(Y_{i+1} = 1 \mid Y_i = 0) = 1;$$
$$\Pr(Y_{i+1} = j + 1 \mid Y_i = j) = 1/2;$$
$$\Pr(Y_{i+1} = j - 1 \mid Y_i = j) = 1/2.$$

The Markov chain $Y_0, Y_1, Y_2, \ldots$ is a pessimistic version of the stochastic process $X_0, X_1, X_2, \ldots$ in that, whereas X_i increases at the next step with probability at least

172

$1/2$, Y_i increases with probability exactly $1/2$. It is therefore clear that the expected time to reach n starting from any point is larger for the Markov chain Y than for the process X, and we use this fact hereafter. (A stronger formal framework for such ideas is developed in Chapter 12.)

This Markov chain models a random walk on an undirected graph G. (We elaborate further on random walks in Section 7.4.) The vertices of G are the integers $0, \ldots, n$ and, for $1 \leq i \leq n - 1$, node i is connected to node $i - 1$ and node $i + 1$. Let h_j be the expected number of steps to reach n when starting from j. For the 2-SAT algorithm, h_j is an upper bound on the expected number of steps to fully match S when starting from a truth assignment that matches S in j locations.

Clearly, $h_n = 0$ and $h_0 = h_1 + 1$, since from h_0 we always move to h_1 in one step. We use linearity of expectations to find an expression for other values of h_j. Let Z_j be a random variable representing the number of steps to reach n from state j. Now consider starting from state j, where $1 \leq j \leq n - 1$. With probability $1/2$, the next state is $j - 1$, and in this case $Z_j = 1 + Z_{j-1}$. With probability $1/2$, the next step is $j + 1$, and in this case $Z_j = 1 + Z_{j+1}$. Hence

$$\mathbf{E}[Z_j] = \mathbf{E}\left[\frac{1}{2}(1 + Z_{j-1}) + \frac{1}{2}(1 + Z_{j+1})\right].$$

But $\mathbf{E}[Z_j] = h_j$ and so, by applying the linearity of expectations, we obtain

$$h_j = \frac{h_{j-1} + 1}{2} + \frac{h_{j+1} + 1}{2} = \frac{h_{j-1}}{2} + \frac{h_{j+1}}{2} + 1.$$

We therefore have the following system of equations:

$$h_n = 0;$$
$$h_j = \frac{h_{j-1}}{2} + \frac{h_{j+1}}{2} + 1, \quad 1 \leq j \leq n - 1;$$
$$h_0 = h_1 + 1.$$

We can show inductively that, for $0 \leq j \leq n - 1$,

$$h_j = h_{j+1} + 2j + 1.$$

It is true when $j = 0$, since $h_1 = h_0 - 1$. For other values of j, we use the equation

$$h_j = \frac{h_{j-1}}{2} + \frac{h_{j+1}}{2} + 1$$

to obtain

$$h_{j+1} = 2h_j - h_{j-1} - 2$$
$$= 2h_j - (h_j + 2(j-1) + 1) - 2$$
$$= h_j - 2j - 1,$$

using the induction hypothesis in the second line. We can conclude that

$$h_0 = h_1 + 1 = h_2 + 1 + 3 = \cdots = \sum_{i=0}^{n-1}(2i + 1) = n^2.$$

173

An alternative approach for solving the system of equations for the h_j is to guess and verify the solution $h_j = n^2 - j^2$. The system has $n + 1$ linearly independent equations and $n + 1$ unknowns, and hence there is a unique solution for each value of n. Therefore, if this solution satisfies the foregoing equations then it must be correct. We have $h_n = 0$. For $1 \leq j \leq n - 1$, we check

$$h_j = \frac{n^2 - (j-1)^2}{2} + \frac{n^2 - (j+1)^2}{2} + 1$$
$$= n^2 - j^2$$

and

$$h_0 = (n^2 - 1) + 1$$
$$= n^2.$$

Thus we have proven the following fact.

Lemma 7.1: *Assume that a 2-SAT formula with n variables has a satisfying assignment and that the 2-SAT algorithm is allowed to run until it finds a satisfying assignment. Then the expected number of steps until the algorithm finds an assignment is at most n^2.*

We now return to the issue of dealing with unsatisfiable formulas by forcing the algorithm to stop after a fixed number of steps.

Theorem 7.2: *The 2-SAT algorithm always returns a correct answer if the formula is unsatisfiable. If the formula is satisfiable, then with probability at least $1 - 2^{-m}$ the algorithm returns a satisfying assignment. Otherwise, it incorrectly returns that the formula is unsatisfiable.*

Proof: It is clear that if there is no satisfying assignment then the algorithm correctly returns that the formula is unsatisfiable. Suppose the formula is satisfiable. Divide the execution of the algorithm into segments of $2n^2$ steps each. Given that no satisfying assignment was found in the first $i - 1$ segments, what is the conditional probability that the algorithm did not find a satisfying assignment in the ith segment? By Lemma 7.1, the expected time to find a satisfying assignment, regardless of its starting position, is bounded by n^2. Let Z be the number of steps from the start of segment i until the algorithm finds a satisfying assignment. Applying Markov's inequality,

$$\Pr(Z > 2n^2) \leq \frac{n^2}{2n^2} = \frac{1}{2}.$$

Thus the probability that the algorithm fails to find a satisfying assignment after m segments is bounded above by $(1/2)^m$. ∎

7.1.2. Application: A Randomized Algorithm for 3-Satisfiability

We now generalize the technique used to develop an algorithm for 2-SAT to obtain a randomized algorithm for 3-SAT. This problem is NP-complete, so it would be rather

---

3-SAT Algorithm:

1. Start with an arbitrary truth assignment.
2. Repeat up to m times, terminating if all clauses are satisfied:
   (a) Choose an arbitrary clause that is not satisfied.
   (b) Choose one of the literals uniformly at random, and change the value of the variable in the current truth assignment.
3. If a valid truth assignment has been found, return it.
4. Otherwise, return that the formula is unsatisfiable.

Algorithm 7.2: 3-SAT algorithm.

surprising if a randomized algorithm could solve the problem in expected time polynomial in n.[3] We present a randomized 3-SAT algorithm that solves 3-SAT in expected time that is exponential in n, but it is much more efficient than the naïve approach of trying all possible truth assignments for the variables.

Let us first consider the performance of a variant of the randomized 2-SAT algorithm when applied to a 3-SAT problem. The basic approach is the same as in the previous section; see Algorithm 7.2. In the algorithm, m is a parameter that controls the probability of success of the algorithm. We focus on bounding the expected time to reach a satisfying assignment (assuming one exists), as the argument of Theorem 7.2 can be extended once such a bound is found.

As in the analysis of the 2-SAT algorithm, assume that the formula is satisfiable and let S be a satisfying assignment. Let the assignment after i steps of the process be A_i, and let X_i be the number of variables in the current assignment A_i that match S. It follows from the same reasoning as for the 2-SAT algorithm that, for $1 \le j \le n - 1$,

$$\Pr(X_{i+1} = j + 1 \mid X_i = j) \ge 1/3;$$
$$\Pr(X_{i+1} = j - 1 \mid X_i = j) \le 2/3.$$

These equations follow because at each step we choose an unsatisfied clause, so A_i and S must disagree on at least one variable in this clause. With probability at least $1/3$, we increase the number of matches between the current truth assignment and S. Again we can obtain an upper bound on the expected number of steps until $X_i = n$ by analyzing a Markov chain $Y_0, Y_1, \ldots$ such that $Y_0 = X_0$ and

$$\Pr(Y_{i+1} = 1 \mid Y_i = 0) = 1,$$
$$\Pr(Y_{i+1} = j + 1 \mid Y_i = j) = 1/3,$$
$$\Pr(Y_{i+1} = j - 1 \mid Y_i = j) = 2/3.$$

In this case, the chain is more likely to go down than up. If we let h_j be the expected number of steps to reach n when starting from j, then the following equations hold

---

[3] Technically, this would not settle the P = NP question, since we would be using a randomized algorithm and not a deterministic algorithm to solve an NP-hard problem. It would, however, have similar far-reaching implications about the ability to solve all NP-complete problems.

for h_j:

$$h_n = 0;$$
$$h_j = \frac{2h_{j-1}}{3} + \frac{h_{j+1}}{3} + 1, \quad 1 \le j \le n - 1;$$
$$h_0 = h_1 + 1.$$

Again, these equations have a unique solution, which is given by

$$h_j = 2^{n+2} - 2^{j+2} - 3(n - j).$$

Alternatively, the solution can be found by using induction to prove the relationship

$$h_j = h_{j+1} + 2^{j+2} - 3.$$

We leave it as an exercise to verify that this solution indeed satisfies the foregoing equations.

The algorithm just described takes $\Theta(2^n)$ steps on average to find a satisfying assignment. This result is not very compelling, since there are only 2^n truth assignments to try! With some insight, however, we can significantly improve the process. There are two key observations.

1. If we choose an initial truth assignment *uniformly at random,* then the number of variables that match S has a binomial distribution with expectation $n/2$. With an exponentially small but nonnegligible probability, the process starts with an initial assignment that matches S in significantly more than $n/2$ variables.
2. Once the algorithm starts, it is more likely to move toward 0 than toward n. The longer we run the process, the more likely it has moved toward 0. Therefore, we are better off restarting the process with many randomly chosen initial assignments and running the process each time for a small number of steps, rather than running the process for many steps on the same initial assignment.

Based on these ideas, we consider the modified procedure of Algorithm 7.3. The modified algorithm has up to $3n$ steps to reach a satisfying assignment starting from a random assignment. If it fails to find a satisfying assignment in $3n$ steps, it restarts the search with a new randomly chosen assignment. We now determine how many times the process needs to restart before it reaches a satisfying assignment.

Let q represent the probability that the modified process reaches S (or some other satisfying assignment) in $3n$ steps starting with a truth assignment chosen uniformly at random. Let q_j be a lower bound on the probability that our modified algorithm reaches S (or some other satisfying assignment) when it starts with a truth assignment that includes exactly j variables that do not agree with S. Consider a particle moving on the integer line, with probability $1/3$ of moving up by one and probability $2/3$ of moving down by one. Notice that

$$\binom{j + 2k}{k} \left(\frac{2}{3}\right)^k \left(\frac{1}{3}\right)^{j+k}$$

is the probability of exactly k moves down and $k + j$ moves up in a sequence of $j + 2k$ moves. It is therefore a lower bound on the probability that the algorithm reaches a

---

Modified 3-SAT Algorithm:

1. Repeat up to m times, terminating if all clauses are satisfied:
    (a) Start with a truth assignment chosen uniformly at random.
    (b) Repeat the following up to $3n$ times, terminating if a satisfying assignment is found:
        i. Choose an arbitrary clause that is not satisfied.
        ii. Choose one of the literals uniformly at random, and change the value of the variable in the current truth assignment.
2. If a valid truth assignment has been found, return it.
3. Otherwise, return that the formula is unsatisfiable.

Algorithm 7.3: Modified 3-SAT algorithm.

satisfying assignment within $j + 2k \leq 3n$ steps, starting with an assignment that has exactly j variables that did not agree with S. That is,

$$q_j \geq \max_{k=0,\dots,j} \binom{j + 2k}{k} \left(\frac{2}{3}\right)^k \left(\frac{1}{3}\right)^{j+k}.$$

In particular, consider the case where $k = j$. In that case we have

$$q_j \geq \binom{3j}{j} \left(\frac{2}{3}\right)^j \left(\frac{1}{3}\right)^{2j}.$$

In order to approximate $\binom{3j}{j}$ we use Stirling's formula, which is similar to the bound of Eqn. (5.5) we have previously proven for factorials. Stirling's formula is tighter, which proves useful for this application. We use the following loose form.

Lemma 7.3 [Stirling's Formula]: *For $m > 0$,*

$$m! = \sqrt{2\pi m} \left(\frac{m}{e}\right)^m (1 \pm o(1)).$$

In particular, for $m > 0$,

$$\sqrt{2\pi m} \left(\frac{m}{e}\right)^m \leq m! \leq 2\sqrt{2\pi m} \left(\frac{m}{e}\right)^m.$$

Hence, when $j > 0$,

$$\binom{3j}{j} = \frac{(3j)!}{j! \, (2j)!}$$

$$\geq \frac{\sqrt{2\pi(3j)}}{4\sqrt{2\pi j}\sqrt{2\pi(2j)}} \left(\frac{3j}{e}\right)^{3j} \left(\frac{e}{2j}\right)^{2j} \left(\frac{e}{j}\right)^j$$

$$= \frac{\sqrt{3}}{8\sqrt{\pi j}} \left(\frac{27}{4}\right)^j$$

$$= \frac{c}{\sqrt{j}} \left(\frac{27}{4}\right)^j$$

177

for a constant $c = \sqrt{3}/8\sqrt{\pi}$. Thus, when $j > 0$,

$$q_j \geq \binom{3j}{j} \left(\frac{2}{3}\right)^j \left(\frac{1}{3}\right)^{2j}$$

$$\geq \frac{c}{\sqrt{j}} \left(\frac{27}{4}\right)^j \left(\frac{2}{3}\right)^j \left(\frac{1}{3}\right)^{2j}$$

$$\geq \frac{c}{\sqrt{j}} \frac{1}{2^j}.$$

Also, $q_0 = 1$.

Having established a lower bound for q_j, we can now derive a lower bound for q, the probability that the process reaches a satisfying assignment in $3n$ steps when starting with a random assignment:

$$q \geq \sum_{j=0}^{n} \Pr(\text{a random assignment has } j \text{ mismatches with } S) \cdot q_j$$

$$\geq \frac{1}{2^n} + \sum_{j=1}^{n} \binom{n}{j} \left(\frac{1}{2}\right)^n \frac{c}{\sqrt{j}} \frac{1}{2^j}$$

$$\geq \frac{c}{\sqrt{n}} \left(\frac{1}{2}\right)^n \sum_{j=0}^{n} \binom{n}{j} \left(\frac{1}{2}\right)^j (1)^{n-j} \qquad (7.3)$$

$$= \frac{c}{\sqrt{n}} \left(\frac{1}{2}\right)^n \left(\frac{3}{2}\right)^n$$

$$= \frac{c}{\sqrt{n}} \left(\frac{3}{4}\right)^n,$$

where in (7.3) we used $\sum_{j=0}^{n} \binom{n}{j} \left(\frac{1}{2}\right)^j (1)^{n-j} = \left(1 + \frac{1}{2}\right)^n$.

Assuming that a satisfying assignment exists, the number of random assignments the process tries before finding a satisfying assignment is a geometric random variable with parameter q. The expected number of assignments tried is $1/q$, and for each assignment the algorithm uses at most $3n$ steps. Thus, the expected number of steps until a solution is found is bounded by $O(n^{3/2}(4/3)^n)$. As in the case of 2-SAT (Theorem 7.2), the modified 3-SAT algorithm (Algorithm 7.3) yields a Monte Carlo algorithm for the 3-SAT problem. If the expected number of steps until a satisfying solution is found is bounded above by a and if m is set to $2ab$, then the probability that no assignment is found when the formula is satisfiable is bounded above by 2^{-b}.

7.2. Classification of States

A first step in analyzing the long-term behavior of a Markov chain is to classify its states. In the case of a finite Markov chain, this is equivalent to analyzing the connectivity structure of the directed graph representing the Markov chain.

Definition 7.2: *State j is* accessible *from state i if, for some integer $n \geq 0$, $P_{i,j}^n > 0$. If two states i and j are accessible from each other, we say that they* communicate *and we write $i \leftrightarrow j$.*

In the graph representation of a chain, $i \leftrightarrow j$ if and only if there are directed paths connecting i to j and j to i.

The communicating relation defines an equivalence relation. That is, the communicating relation is

1. *reflexive* – for any state i, $i \leftrightarrow i$;
2. *symmetric* – if $i \leftrightarrow j$ then $j \leftrightarrow i$; and
3. *transitive* – if $i \leftrightarrow j$ and $j \leftrightarrow k$, then $i \leftrightarrow k$.

Proving this is left as Exercise 7.4. Thus, the communication relation partitions the states into disjoint equivalence classes, which we refer to as *communicating classes*. It might be possible to move from one class to another, but in that case it is impossible to return to the first class.

Definition 7.3: *A Markov chain is* irreducible *if all states belong to one communicating class.*

In other words, a Markov chain is irreducible if, for every pair of states, there is a nonzero probability that the first state can reach the second. We thus have the following lemma.

Lemma 7.4: *A finite Markov chain is irreducible if and only if its graph representation is a strongly connected graph.*

Next we distinguish between transient and recurrent states. Let $r_{i,j}^t$ denote the probability that, starting at state i, the first transition to state j occurs at time t; that is,

$$r_{i,j}^t = \Pr(X_t = j \text{ and, for } 1 \leq s \leq t-1, \ X_s \neq j \mid X_0 = i).$$

Definition 7.4: *A state is* recurrent *if $\sum_{t \geq 1} r_{i,i}^t = 1$, and it is* transient *if $\sum_{t \geq 1} r_{i,i}^t < 1$. A Markov chain is* recurrent *if every state in the chain is recurrent.*

If state i is recurrent then, once the chain visits that state, it will (with probability 1) eventually return to that state. Hence the chain will visit state i over and over again, infinitely often. On the other hand, if state i is transient then, starting at i, the chain will return to i with some fixed probability $p = \sum_{t \geq 1} r_{i,i}^t$. In this case, the number of times the chain visits i when starting at i is given by a geometric random variable. If one state in a communicating class is transient (respectively, recurrent) then all states in that class are transient (respectively, recurrent); proving this is left as Exercise 7.5.

We denote the expected time to return to state i when starting at state i by $h_{i,i} = \sum_{t \geq 1} t \cdot r_{i,i}^t$. Similarly, for any pair of states i and j, we denote by $h_{i,j} = \sum_{t \geq 1} t \cdot r_{i,j}^t$ the expected time to first reach j from state i. It may seem that if a chain is recurrent, so that we visit a state i infinitely often, then $h_{i,i}$ should be finite. This is not the case, which leads us to the following definition.

Definition 7.5: *A recurrent state i is* positive recurrent *if* $h_{i,i} < \infty$. *Otherwise, it is* null recurrent.

To give an example of a Markov chain that has null recurrent states, consider a chain whose states are the positive integers. From state i, the probability of going to state $i + 1$ is $i/(i + 1)$. With probability $1/(i + 1)$, the chain returns to state 1. Starting at state 1, the probability of not having returned to state 1 within the first t steps is thus

$$\prod_{j=1}^{t} \frac{j}{j+1} = \frac{1}{t+1}.$$

Hence the probability of never returning to state 1 from state 1 is 0, and state 1 is recurrent. It follows that

$$r_{1,1}^t = \frac{1}{t(t+1)}.$$

However, the expected number of steps until the first return to state 1 from state 1 is

$$h_{1,1} = \sum_{t=1}^{\infty} t \cdot r_{1,1}^t = \sum_{t=1}^{\infty} \frac{1}{t+1},$$

which is unbounded.

In the foregoing example the Markov chain had an infinite number of states. This is necessary for null recurrent states to exist. The proof of the following important lemma is left as Exercise 7.16.

Lemma 7.5: *In a finite Markov chain:*

1. *at least one state is recurrent; and*
2. *all recurrent states are positive recurrent.*

Finally, for our later study of limiting distributions of Markov chains we will need to define what it means for a state to be aperiodic. As an example of periodicity, consider a random walk whose states are the positive integers. When at state i, with probability $1/2$ the chain moves to $i + 1$ and with probability $1/2$ the chain moves to $i - 1$. If the chain starts at state 0, then it can be at an even-numbered state only after an even number of moves, and it can be at an odd-numbered state only after an odd number of moves. This is an example of periodic behavior.

Definition 7.6: *A state j in a discrete time Markov chain is* periodic *if there exists an integer* $\Delta > 1$ *such that* $\Pr(X_{t+s} = j \mid X_t = j) = 0$ *unless s is divisible by* Δ. *A discrete time Markov chain is* periodic *if any state in the chain is periodic. A state or chain that is not periodic is* aperiodic.

In our example, every state in the Markov chain is periodic because, for every state j, $\Pr(X_{t+s} = j \mid X_t = j) = 0$ unless s is divisible by 2.

We end this section with an important corollary about the behavior of finite Markov chains.

Definition 7.7: *An aperiodic, positive recurrent state is an* ergodic *state. A Markov chain is ergodic if all its states are ergodic.*

Corollary 7.6: *Any finite, irreducible, and aperiodic Markov chain is an ergodic chain.*

Proof: A finite chain has at least one recurrent state by Lemma 7.5, and if the chain is irreducible then all of its states are recurrent. In a finite chain, all recurrent states are positive recurrent by Lemma 7.5 and thus all the states of the chain are positive recurrent and aperiodic. The chain is therefore ergodic. ∎

7.2.1. *Example: The Gambler's Ruin*

When a Markov chain has more than one class of recurrent states, we are often interested in the probability that the process will enter and thus be *absorbed* by a given communicating class.

For example, consider a sequence of independent, fair gambling games between two players. In each round a player wins a dollar with probability $1/2$ or loses a dollar with probability $1/2$. The state of the system at time t is the number of dollars won by player 1. If player 1 has lost money, this number is negative. The initial state is 0.

It is reasonable to assume that there are numbers ℓ_1 and ℓ_2 such that player i cannot lose more than ℓ_i dollars, and thus the game ends when it reaches one of the two states $-\ell_1$ or ℓ_2. At this point, one of the gamblers is ruined; that is, he has lost all his money. To conform with the formalization of a Markov chain, we assume that for each of these two end states there is only one transition out and that it goes back to the same state. This gives us a Markov chain with two absorbing, recurrent states.

What is the probability that player 1 wins ℓ_2 dollars before losing ℓ_1 dollars? If $\ell_2 = \ell_1$, then by symmetry this probability must be $1/2$. We provide a simple argument for the general case using the classification of the states.

Clearly $-\ell_1$ and ℓ_2 are recurrent states. All other states are transient, since there is a nonzero probability of moving from each of these states to either state $-\ell_1$ or state ℓ_2.

Let P_i^t be the probability that, after t steps, the chain is at state i. For $-\ell_1 < i < \ell_2$, state i is transient and so $\lim_{t \to \infty} P_i^t = 0$.

Let q be the probability that the game ends with player 1 winning ℓ_2 dollars, so that the chain was absorbed into state ℓ_2. Then $1 - q$ is the probability the chain was absorbed into state $-\ell_1$. By definition,

$$\lim_{t \to \infty} P_{\ell_2}^t = q.$$

Since each round of the gambling game is fair, the expected gain of player 1 in each step is 0. Let W^t be the gain of player 1 after t steps. Then $\mathbf{E}[W^t] = 0$ for any t by induction. Thus,

$$\mathbf{E}[W^t] = \sum_{i=-\ell_1}^{\ell_2} i P_i^t = 0$$

181

and

$$\lim_{t\to\infty} \mathbf{E}[W^t] = \ell_2 q - \ell_1(1-q)$$
$$= 0.$$

Thus,

$$q = \frac{\ell_1}{\ell_1 + \ell_2}.$$

That is, the probability of winning (or losing) is proportional to the amount of money a player is willing to lose (or win).

Another approach that yields the same answer is to let q_j represent the probability that player 1 wins ℓ_2 dollars before losing ℓ_1 dollars when having won j dollars for $-\ell_1 \le j \le \ell_2$. Clearly, $q_{-\ell_1} = 0$ and $q_{\ell_2} = 1$. For $-\ell_1 < j < \ell_2$, we compute by considering the outcome of the first game:

$$q_j = \frac{q_{j-1}}{2} + \frac{q_{j+1}}{2}.$$

We have $\ell_2 + \ell_1 - 2$ linearly independent equations and $\ell_2 + \ell_1 - 2$ unknowns, so there is a unique solution to this set of equations. It is easy to verify that $q_j = (\ell_1 + j)/(\ell_1 + \ell_2)$ satisfies the given equations.

In Exercise 7.20, we consider the question of what happens if, as is generally the case in real life, one player is at a disadvantage and so is slightly more likely to lose than to win any single game.

7.3. Stationary Distributions

Recall that if $\mathbf{P}$ is the one-step transition probability matrix of a Markov chain and if $\bar{p}(t)$ is the probability distribution of the state of the chain at time t, then

$$\bar{p}(t+1) = \bar{p}(t)\mathbf{P}.$$

Of particular interest are state probability distributions that do not change after a transition.

Definition 7.8: *A stationary distribution (also called an equilibrium distribution) of a Markov chain is a probability distribution $\bar{\pi}$ such that*

$$\bar{\pi} = \bar{\pi}\mathbf{P}.$$

If a chain ever reaches a stationary distribution then it maintains that distribution for all future time, and thus a stationary distribution represents a steady state or an equilibrium in the chain's behavior. Stationary distributions play a key role in analyzing Markov chains. The fundamental theorem of Markov chains characterizes chains that converge to stationary distributions.

We discuss first the case of finite chains and then extend the results to any discrete space chain. Without loss of generality, assume that the finite set of states of the Markov chain is $\{0, 1, \ldots, n\}$.

Theorem 7.7: *Any finite, irreducible, and ergodic Markov chain has the following properties:*

1. *the chain has a unique stationary distribution $\bar{\pi} = (\pi_0, \pi_1, \ldots, \pi_n)$;*
2. *for all j and i, the limit $\lim_{t \to \infty} P_{j,i}^t$ exists and it is independent of j;*
3. *$\pi_i = \lim_{t \to \infty} P_{j,i}^t = 1/h_{i,i}$.*

Under the conditions of this theorem, the stationary distribution $\bar{\pi}$ has two interpretations. First, π_i is the limiting probability that the Markov chain will be in state i infinitely far out in the future, and this probability is independent of the initial state. In other words, if we run the chain long enough, the initial state of the chain is almost forgotten and the probability of being in state i converges to π_i. Second, π_i is the inverse of $h_{i,i} = \sum_{t=1}^{\infty} t \cdot r_{i,i}^t$, the expected number of steps for a chain starting in state i to return to i. This stands to reason; if the average time to return to state i from i is $h_{i,i}$, then we expect to be in state i for $1/h_{i,i}$ of the time and thus, in the limit, we must have $\pi_i = 1/h_{i,i}$.

Proof of Theorem 7.7: We prove the theorem using the following result, which we state without proof. ■

Lemma 7.8: *For any irreducible, ergodic Markov chain and for any state i, the limit $\lim_{t \to \infty} P_{i,i}^t$ exists and*

$$\lim_{t \to \infty} P_{i,i}^t = \frac{1}{h_{i,i}}.$$

This lemma is a corollary of a basic result in renewal theory. We give an informal justification for Lemma 7.8: the expected time between visits to i is $h_{i,i}$, and therefore state i is visited $1/h_{i,i}$ of the time. Thus $\lim_{t \to \infty} P_{i,i}^t$, which represents the probability a state chosen far in the future is at state i when the chain starts at state i, must be $1/h_{i,i}$.

Using the fact that $\lim_{t \to \infty} P_{i,i}^t$ exists, we now show that, for any j and i,

$$\lim_{t \to \infty} P_{j,i}^t = \lim_{t \to \infty} P_{i,i}^t = \frac{1}{h_{i,i}};$$

that is, these limits exist and are independent of the starting state j.

Recall that $r_{j,i}^t$ is the probability that starting at j, the chain first visits i at time t. Since the chain is irreducible we have that $\sum_{t=1}^{\infty} r_{j,i}^t = 1$, and for any $\varepsilon > 0$ there exists (a finite) $t_1 = t_1(\varepsilon)$ such that $\sum_{t=1}^{t_1} r_{j,i}^t \geq 1 - \varepsilon$.

For $j \neq i$, we have

$$P_{j,i}^t = \sum_{k=1}^{t} r_{j,i}^k P_{i,i}^{t-k}.$$

For $t \geq t_1$,

$$\sum_{k=1}^{t_1} r_{j,i}^k P_{i,i}^{t-k} \leq \sum_{k=1}^{t} r_{j,i}^k P_{i,i}^{t-k} = P_{j,i}^t.$$

Using the facts that $\lim_{t\to\infty} P_{i,i}^t$ exists and t_1 is finite, we have

$$
\begin{aligned}
\lim_{t\to\infty} P_{j,i}^t &\geq \lim_{t\to\infty} \sum_{k=1}^{t_1} r_{j,i}^k P_{i,i}^{t-k} \\
&= \sum_{k=1}^{t_1} r_{j,i}^k \lim_{t\to\infty} P_{i,i}^t \\
&= \lim_{t\to\infty} P_{i,i}^t \sum_{k=1}^{t_1} r_{j,i}^k \\
&\geq (1-\varepsilon) \lim_{t\to\infty} P_{i,i}^t.
\end{aligned}
$$

Similarly,

$$
\begin{aligned}
P_{j,i}^t &= \sum_{k=1}^{t} r_{j,i}^k P_{i,i}^{t-k} \\
&\leq \sum_{k=1}^{t_1} r_{j,i}^k P_{i,i}^{t-k} + \varepsilon,
\end{aligned}
$$

from which we can deduce that

$$
\begin{aligned}
\lim_{t\to\infty} P_{j,i}^t &\leq \lim_{t\to\infty} \left(\sum_{k=1}^{t_1} r_{j,i}^k P_{i,i}^{t-k} + \varepsilon \right) \\
&= \sum_{k=1}^{t_1} r_{j,i}^k \lim_{t\to\infty} P_{i,i}^{t-k} + \varepsilon \\
&\leq \lim_{t\to\infty} P_{i,i}^t + \varepsilon.
\end{aligned}
$$

Letting ε approach 0, we have proven that, for any pair i and j,

$$
\lim_{t\to\infty} P_{j,i}^t = \lim_{t\to\infty} P_{i,i}^t = \frac{1}{h_{i,i}}.
$$

Now let

$$
\pi_i = \lim_{t\to\infty} P_{j,i}^t = \frac{1}{h_{i,i}}.
$$

We show that $\bar{\pi} = (\pi_0, \pi_1, \dots)$ forms a stationary distribution.

For every $t \geq 0$, we have $P_{i,i}^t \geq 0$ and thus $\pi_i \geq 0$. For any $t \geq 0$, $\sum_{i=0}^n P_{j,i}^t = 1$ and thus

$$
\lim_{t\to\infty} \sum_{i=0}^n P_{j,i}^t = \sum_{i=0}^n \lim_{t\to\infty} P_{j,i}^t = \sum_{i=0}^n \pi_i = 1,
$$

and $\bar{\pi}$ is a proper distribution. Now,

$$
P_{j,i}^{t+1} = \sum_{k=0}^n P_{j,k}^t P_{k,i}.
$$

Letting $t \to \infty$, we have

$$\pi_i = \sum_{k=0}^{n} \pi_k P_{k,i},$$

proving that $\bar{\pi}$ is a stationary distribution.

Suppose there were another stationary distribution $\bar{\phi}$. Then by the same argument we would have

$$\phi_i = \sum_{k=0}^{n} \phi_k P_{k,i}^t,$$

and taking the limit as $t \to \infty$ yields

$$\phi_i = \sum_{k=0}^{n} \phi_k \pi_i = \pi_i \sum_{k=0}^{n} \phi_k.$$

Since $\sum_{k=0}^{n} \phi_k = 1$ it follows that $\phi_i = \pi_i$ for all i, or $\bar{\phi} = \bar{\pi}$. ∎

It is worth making a few remarks about Theorem 7.7. First, the requirement that the Markov chain be aperiodic is not necessary for the existence of a stationary distribution. In fact, any finite Markov chain has a stationary distribution; but in the case of a periodic state i, the stationary probability π_i is not the limiting probability of being in i but instead just the long-term frequency of visiting state i. Second, any finite chain has at least one component that is recurrent. Once the chain reaches a recurrent component, it cannot leave that component. Thus, the subchain that corresponds to that component is irreducible and recurrent, and the limit theorem applies to any aperiodic recurrent component of the chain.

One way to compute the stationary distribution of a finite Markov chain is to solve the system of linear equations

$$\bar{\pi} \mathbf{P} = \bar{\pi}.$$

This is particularly useful if one is given a specific chain. For example, given the transition matrix

$$\mathbf{P} = \begin{bmatrix} 0 & 1/4 & 0 & 3/4 \\ 1/2 & 0 & 1/3 & 1/6 \\ 1/4 & 1/4 & 1/2 & 0 \\ 0 & 1/2 & 1/4 & 1/4 \end{bmatrix},$$

we have five equations for the four unknowns $\pi_0, \pi_1, \pi_2,$ and π_3 given by $\bar{\pi} \mathbf{P} = \bar{\pi}$ and $\sum_{i=0}^{3} \pi_i = 1$. The equations have a unique solution.

Another useful technique is to study the cut-sets of the Markov chain. For any state i of the chain,

$$\sum_{j=0}^{n} \pi_j P_{j,i} = \pi_i = \pi_i \sum_{j=0}^{n} P_{i,j}$$

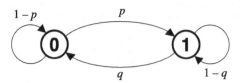

Figure 7.2: A simple Markov chain used to represent bursty behavior.

or

$$\sum_{j\neq i} \pi_j P_{j,i} = \sum_{j\neq i} \pi_i P_{i,j}.$$

That is, in the stationary distribution the probability that a chain leaves a state equals the probability that it enters the state. This observation can be generalized to sets of states as follows.

Theorem 7.9: *Let S be a set of states of a finite, irreducible, aperiodic Markov chain. In the stationary distribution, the probability that the chain leaves the set S equals the probability that it enters S.*

In other words, if C is a cut-set in the graph representation of the chain, then in the stationary distribution the probability of crossing the cut-set in one direction is equal to the probability of crossing the cut-set in the other direction.

A basic but useful Markov chain that serves as an example of cut-sets is given in Figure 7.2. The chain has only two states. From state 0, you move to state 1 with probability p and stay at state 0 with probability $1 - p$. Similarly, from state 1 you move to state 0 with probability q and remain in state 1 with probability $1 - q$. This Markov chain is often used to represent bursty behavior. For example, when bits are corrupted in transmissions they are often corrupted in large blocks, since the errors are often caused by an external phenomenon of some duration. In this setting, being in state 0 after t steps represents that the tth bit was sent successfully, while being in state 1 represents that the bit was corrupted. Blocks of successfully sent bits and corrupted bits both have lengths that follow a geometric distribution. When p and q are small, state changes are rare, and the bursty behavior is modeled.

The transition matrix is

$$\mathbf{P} = \begin{bmatrix} 1 - p & p \\ q & 1 - q \end{bmatrix}.$$

Solving $\bar{\pi}\mathbf{P} = \bar{\pi}$ corresponds to solving the following system of three equations:

$$\pi_0(1 - p) + \pi_1 q = \pi_0;$$
$$\pi_0 p + \pi_1(1 - q) = \pi_1;$$
$$\pi_0 + \pi_1 = 1.$$

The second equation is redundant, and the solution is $\pi_0 = q/(p + q)$ and $\pi_1 = p/(p + q)$. For example, with the natural parameters $p = 0.005$ and $q = 0.1$, in the stationary distribution more than 95% of the bits are received uncorrupted.

Using the cut-set formulation, we have that in the stationary distribution the probability of leaving state 0 must equal the probability of entering state 0, or

$$\pi_0 p = \pi_1 q.$$

Again, now using $\pi_0 + \pi_1 = 1$ yields $\pi_0 = q/(p + q)$ and $\pi_1 = p/(p + q)$.

Finally, for some Markov chains the stationary distribution is easy to compute by means of the following theorem.

Theorem 7.10: *Consider a finite, irreducible, and ergodic Markov chain with transition matrix **P**. If there are nonnegative numbers $\bar{\pi} = (\pi_0, \ldots, \pi_n)$ such that $\sum_{i=0}^{n} \pi_i = 1$ and if, for any pair of states i, j,*

$$\pi_i P_{i,j} = \pi_j P_{j,i},$$

*then $\bar{\pi}$ is the stationary distribution corresponding to **P**.*

Proof: Consider the jth entry of $\bar{\pi}\mathbf{P}$. Using the assumption of the theorem, we find that it equals

$$\sum_{i=0}^{n} \pi_i P_{i,j} = \sum_{i=0}^{n} \pi_j P_{j,i} = \pi_j.$$

Thus $\bar{\pi}$ satisfies $\bar{\pi} = \bar{\pi}\mathbf{P}$. Since $\sum_{i=0}^{n} \pi_i = 1$, it follows from Theorem 7.7 that $\bar{\pi}$ must be the unique stationary distribution of the Markov chain. ∎

Chains that satisfy the condition

$$\pi_i P_{i,j} = \pi_j P_{j,i}$$

are called *time reversible*; Exercise 7.13 helps explain why. You may check that the chain of Figure 7.2 is time reversible.

We turn now to the convergence of Markov chains with countably infinite state spaces. Using essentially the same technique as in the proof of Theorem 7.7, one can prove the next result.

Theorem 7.11: *Any irreducible aperiodic Markov chain belongs to one of the following two categories:*

1. *the chain is ergodic – for any pair of states i and j, the limit $\lim_{t \to \infty} P_{j,i}^t$ exists and is independent of j, and the chain has a unique stationary distribution $\pi_i = \lim_{t \to \infty} P_{j,i}^t > 0$; or*
2. *no state is positive recurrent – for all i and j, $\lim_{t \to \infty} P_{j,i}^t = 0$, and the chain has no stationary distribution.*

Cut-sets and the property of time reversibility can also be used to find the stationary distribution for Markov chains with countably infinite state spaces.

7.3.1. *Example: A Simple Queue*

A *queue* is a line where customers wait for service. We examine a model for a bounded queue where time is divided into steps of equal length. At each time step, exactly one of the following occurs.

- If the queue has fewer than n customers, then with probability λ a new customer joins the queue.
- If the queue is not empty, then with probability μ the head of the line is served and leaves the queue.
- With the remaining probability, the queue is unchanged.

If X_t is the number of customers in the queue at time t, then under the foregoing rules the X_t yield a finite-state Markov chain. Its transition matrix has the following nonzero entries:

$$P_{i,i+1} = \lambda \quad \text{if } i < n;$$
$$P_{i,i-1} = \mu \quad \text{if } i > 0;$$
$$P_{i,i} = \begin{cases} 1 - \lambda & \text{if } i = 0, \\ 1 - \lambda - \mu & \text{if } 1 \le i \le n - 1, \\ 1 - \mu & \text{if } i = n. \end{cases}$$

The Markov chain is irreducible, finite, and aperiodic, so it has a unique stationary distribution $\bar{\pi}$. We use $\bar{\pi} = \bar{\pi}\mathbf{P}$ to write

$$\pi_0 = (1 - \lambda)\pi_0 + \mu\pi_1,$$
$$\pi_i = \lambda\pi_{i-1} + (1 - \lambda - \mu)\pi_i + \mu\pi_{i+1}, \quad 1 \le i \le n - 1,$$
$$\pi_n = \lambda\pi_{n-1} + (1 - \mu)\pi_n.$$

It is easy to verify that

$$\pi_i = \pi_0 \left(\frac{\lambda}{\mu}\right)^i$$

is a solution to the preceding system of equations. Adding the requirement $\sum_{i=0}^{n} \pi_i = 1$, we have

$$\sum_{i=0}^{n} \pi_i = \sum_{i=0}^{n} \pi_0 \left(\frac{\lambda}{\mu}\right)^i = 1$$

or

$$\pi_0 = \frac{1}{\sum_{i=0}^{n}(\lambda/\mu)^i}.$$

For all $0 \le i \le n$,

$$\pi_i = \frac{(\lambda/\mu)^i}{\sum_{i=0}^{n}(\lambda/\mu)^i}. \tag{7.4}$$

Another way to compute the stationary probability in this case is to use cut-sets. For any i, the transitions $i \rightarrow i+1$ and $i+1 \rightarrow i$ constitute a cut-set of the graph representing the Markov chain. Thus, in the stationary distribution, the probability of moving from state i to state $i+1$ must be equal to the probability of moving from state $i+1$ to i, or

$$\lambda \pi_i = \mu \pi_{i+1}.$$

A simple induction now yields

$$\pi_i = \pi_0 \left(\frac{\lambda}{\mu} \right)^i.$$

In the case where there is no upper limit n on the number of customers in a queue, the Markov chain is no longer finite. The Markov chain has a countably infinite state space. Applying Theorem 7.11, the Markov chain has a stationary distribution if and only if the following set of linear equations has a solution with all $\pi_i > 0$:

$$\begin{aligned} \pi_0 &= (1-\lambda)\pi_0 + \mu\pi_1; \\ \pi_i &= \lambda\pi_{i-1} + (1-\lambda-\mu)\pi_i + \mu\pi_{i+1}, \quad i \geq 1. \end{aligned} \tag{7.5}$$

It is easy to verify that

$$\pi_i = \frac{(\lambda/\mu)^i}{\sum_{i=0}^{\infty}(\lambda/\mu)^i} = \left(\frac{\lambda}{\mu} \right)^i \left(1 - \frac{\lambda}{\mu} \right)$$

is a solution of the system of equations (7.5). This naturally generalizes the solution to the case where there is an upper bound n on the number of the customers in the system given in Eqn. (7.4). All of the π_i are greater than 0 if and only if $\lambda < \mu$, which corresponds to the situation when the rate at which customers arrive is lower than the rate at which they are served. If $\lambda > \mu$, then the rate at which customers arrive is higher than the rate at which they depart. Hence there is no stationary distribution, and the queue length will become arbitrarily long. In this case, each state in the Markov chain is transient. The case of $\lambda = \mu$ is more subtle. Again, there is no stationary distribution and the queue length will become arbitrarily long, but now the states are null recurrent. (See the related Exercise 7.17.)

7.4. Random Walks on Undirected Graphs

A random walk on an undirected graph is a special type of Markov chain that is often used in analyzing algorithms. Let $G = (V, E)$ be a finite, undirected, and connected graph.

Definition 7.9: *A random walk on G is a Markov chain defined by the sequence of moves of a particle between vertices of G. In this process, the place of the particle at a given time step is the state of the system. If the particle is at vertex i and if i has $d(i)$ outgoing edges, then the probability that the particle follows the edge (i, j) and moves to a neighbor j is $1/d(i)$.*

189

We have already seen an example of such a walk when we analyzed the randomized 2-SAT algorithm.

For a random walk on an undirected graph, we have a simple criterion for aperiodicity as follows.

Lemma 7.12: *A random walk on an undirected graph G is aperiodic if and only if G is not bipartite.*

Proof: A graph is bipartite if and only if it does not have cycles with an odd number of edges. In an undirected graph, there is always a path of length 2 from a vertex to itself. If the graph is bipartite then the random walk is periodic with period $d = 2$. If the graph is not bipartite then it has an odd cycle, and by traversing that cycle we have an odd-length path from any vertex to itself. It follows that the Markov chain is aperiodic. ■

For the remainder of this section we assume that G is not bipartite. A random walk on a finite, undirected, connected, and non-bipartite graph G satisfies the conditions of Theorem 7.7, and hence the random walk converges to a stationary distribution. We show that this distribution depends only on the degree sequence of the graph.

Theorem 7.13: *A random walk on G converges to a stationary distribution $\bar{\pi}$, where*

$$\pi_v = \frac{d(v)}{2|E|}.$$

Proof: Since $\sum_{v \in V} d(v) = 2|E|$, it follows that

$$\sum_{v \in V} \pi_v = \sum_{v \in V} \frac{d(v)}{2|E|} = 1,$$

and $\bar{\pi}$ is a proper distribution over $v \in V$.

Let $\mathbf{P}$ be the transition probability matrix of the Markov chain. Let $N(v)$ represent the neighbors of v. The relation $\bar{\pi} = \bar{\pi}\mathbf{P}$ is equivalent to

$$\pi_v = \sum_{u \in N(v)} \frac{d(u)}{2|E|} \frac{1}{d(u)} = \frac{d(v)}{2|E|},$$

and the theorem follows. ■

Recall that we have used $h_{u,v}$ to denote the expected time to reach state v when starting at state u. The value $h_{u,v}$ is often referred to as the *hitting time* from u to v, or just the hitting time where the meaning is clear. Another value related to the hitting time is the *commute time* between u and v, given by $h_{u,v} + h_{v,u}$. Unlike the hitting time, the commute time is symmetric; it represents the time to go from u to v and back to u, and this is the same as the time to go from v to u and back to v. Finally, for random walks on graphs, we are also interested in a quantity called the cover time.

Definition 7.10: *The* cover time *of a graph $G = (V, E)$ is the maximum over all vertices $v \in V$ of the expected time to visit all of the nodes in the graph by a random walk starting from v.*

190

We consider here some basic bounds on the commute time and the cover time for standard random walks on a finite, undirected, connected graph $G = (V, E)$.

Lemma 7.14: *If* $(u, v) \in E$, *the commute time* $h_{u,v} + h_{v,u}$ *is at most* $2|E|$.

Proof: Let D be a set of directed edges such that for every edge $(u, v) \in E$ we have the two directed edges $u \to v$ and $v \to u$ in D. We can view the random walk on G as a Markov chain with state space D, where the state of the Markov chain at time t is the directed edge taken by the random walk in its tth transition. The Markov chain has $2|E|$ states and it is easy to verify that it has a uniform stationary distribution. (This is left as Exercise 7.29.) Since the stationary probability of being in state $u \to v$ is $1/2|E|$, once the original random walk traverses the directed edge $u \to v$ the expected time to traverse that directed edge again is $2|E|$. Because the random walk is memoryless, once it reaches vertex v we can "forget" that it reached it through the edge $u \to v$, and therefore the expected time starting at v to reach u and then traverse the edge $u \to v$ back to v is bounded above by $2|E|$. As this is only one of the possible ways to go from v to u and back to v, we have shown that $h_{v,u} + h_{u,v} \leq 2|E|$. ∎

Lemma 7.15: *The cover time of* $G = (V, E)$ *is bounded above by* $2|E|(|V| - 1)$.

Proof: Choose a spanning tree T of G; that is, choose any subset of the edges that gives an acyclic graph connecting all the vertices of G. Starting from any vertex v, there exists a cyclic (Eulerian) tour on the spanning tree in which every edge is traversed once in each direction; for example, such a tour can be found by considering the sequence of vertices passed through by a depth first search. The maximum expected time to go through the vertices in the tour, where the maximum is over the choice of starting vertex, is an upper bound on the cover time. Let $v_0, v_1, \ldots, v_{2|V|-2}$ be the sequence of vertices in the tour starting from $v_0 = v$. Then the expected time to go through all the vertices in sequence order is

$$\sum_{i=0}^{2|V|-3} h_{v_i, v_{i+1}} = \sum_{(x,y)\in T} (h_{x,y} + h_{y,x}) \leq 2|E|(|V| - 1).$$

In words, the commute time for every pair of adjacent vertices in the tree is bounded above by $2|E|$, and there are $|V| - 1$ pairs of adjacent vertices. ∎

The following result is known as Matthews' theorem, which relates the cover time of a graph to the hitting time. Recall that we use $H(n)$ to denote the harmonic number $\sum_{i=1}^{n} 1/i \approx \ln n$.

Lemma 7.16: *The cover time* C_G *of* $G = (V, E)$ *with* n *vertices is bounded by*

$$C_G \leq H(n - 1) \max_{u,v \in V : u \neq v} h_{u,v}.$$

Proof: For convenience let $B = \max_{u,v \in V : u \neq v} h_{u,v}$. Consider a random walk starting from a vertex u. We choose an ordering of the vertices according to a uniform permutation; let $Z_1, Z_2, \ldots, Z_n$ be the ordering. Let T_j be the first time when all of the first j vertices in the order, $Z_1, Z_2, \ldots, Z_j$, have been visited, and let A_j be the last vertex from the set $\{Z_1, \ldots, Z_j\}$ that was visited. Following the spirit of the coupon collector's analysis, we consider the successive time intervals $T_j - T_{j-1}$. If the chain's history is given by $X_1, X_2, \ldots$, then in particular for $j \geq 2$ we consider

$$Y_j = \mathbf{E}[T_j - T_{j-1} \mid Z_1, \ldots, Z_j; X_1, \ldots, X_{T_{j-1}}].$$

The expected time to cover the graph starting from u is

$$\sum_{j=2}^{n} Y_j + \mathbf{E}[T_1].$$

If Z_1 is chosen to be u, which happens with probability $1/n$, then T_1 is 0. Otherwise, $\mathbf{E}[T_1 \mid Z_1] = h_{u,Z_1} \leq B$. Hence $\mathbf{E}[T_1] \leq (1 - 1/n)B$.

For the Y_j, there are two cases to consider. If Z_j is not the last vertex seen from the set $\{Z_1, Z_2, \ldots, Z_j\}$, then Y_j is 0, since $T_j = T_{j-1}$ in that case. If Z_j is the last vertex seen from this set, then, regardless of the rest of the history of the chain, $Y_j \leq B$, since Y_j is the hitting time h_{Z_k,Z_j} for the Z_k that was visited last out of $\{Z_1, Z_2, \ldots, Z_{j-1}\}$. As the Z_j were chosen according to a random permutation, independent of the random walk, we have Z_j is last out of the set $\{Z_1, Z_2, \ldots, Z_j\}$ with probability $1/j$. It follows that

$$\sum_{j=2}^{n} Y_j + \mathbf{E}[T_1] \leq \sum_{j=2}^{n} \frac{1}{j} B + \left(1 - \frac{1}{n}\right) B$$

$$= \left(1 + \sum_{j=2}^{n} \frac{1}{j}\right) B - \frac{1}{n} B$$

$$= H(n-1)B.$$

Since this holds for every starting vertex u, the lemma is proven. ∎

One can similarly obtain lower bounds using the same technique. A natural lower bound is

$$C_G \geq H(n-1) \min_{u,v \in V : u \neq v} h_{u,v}.$$

However, the minimum hitting time can be very small for some graphs, making this bound less useful. In some cases, the lower bound can be made stronger by considering a subset of vertices $V' \subset V$. In this case, the proof can be modified to give

$$C_G \geq H(|V'| - 1) \min_{u,v \in V' : u \neq v} h_{u,v}.$$

The term from the harmonic series is smaller, but the minimum hitting time used in the bound may correspondingly be larger.

7.4.1. Application: An s–t Connectivity Algorithm

Suppose we are given an undirected graph $G = (V, E)$ and two vertices s and t in G. Let $n = |V|$ and $m = |E|$. We want to determine if there is a path connecting s and t. This is easily done in linear time using a standard breadth-first search or depth-first search. Such algorithms, however, require $\Omega(n)$ space.

***s–t* Connectivity Algorithm:**

1. Start a random walk from *s*.
2. If the walk reaches *t* within $2n^3$ steps, return that there is a path. Otherwise, return that there is no path.

Algorithm 7.4: *s–t* Connectivity algorithm.

Here we develop a randomized algorithm that works with only $O(\log n)$ bits of memory. This could be even less than the number of bits required to write the path between *s* and *t*. The algorithm is simple: perform a random walk on *G* for enough steps so that a path from *s* to *t* is likely to be found. We use the cover time result (Lemma 7.16) to bound the number of steps that the random walk has to run. For convenience, assume that the graph *G* has no bipartite connected components, so that the results of Theorem 7.13 apply to any connected component of *G*. (The results can be made to apply to bipartite graphs with some additional technical work.)

Theorem 7.17: *The s–t connectivity algorithm (Algorithm 7.4) returns the correct answer with probability* $1/2$*, and it only errs by returning that there is no path from s to t when there is such a path.*

Proof: If there is no path then the algorithm returns the correct answer. If there is a path, the algorithm errs if it does not find the path within $2n^3$ steps of the walk. The expected time to reach *t* from *s* (if there is a path) is bounded from above by the cover time of their shared component, which by Lemma 7.15 is at most $2nm < n^3$. By Markov's inequality, the probability that a walk takes more than $2n^3$ steps to reach *t* from *s* is at most $1/2$. ∎

The algorithm must keep track of its current position, which takes $O(\log n)$ bits, as well as the number of steps taken in the random walk, which also takes only $O(\log n)$ bits (since we count up only to $2n^3$). As long as there is some mechanism for choosing a random neighbor from each vertex, this is all the memory required.

7.5. Parrondo's Paradox

Parrondo's paradox provides an interesting example of the analysis of Markov chains while also demonstrating a subtlety in dealing with probabilities. The paradox appears to contradict the old saying that two wrongs don't make a right, showing that two losing games can be combined to make a winning game. Because Parrondo's paradox can be analyzed in many different ways, we will go over several approaches to the problem.

First, consider game *A*, in which we repeatedly flip a biased coin (call it coin *a*) that comes up heads with probability $p_a < 1/2$ and tails with probability $1 - p_a$. You win a dollar if the coin comes up heads and lose a dollar if it comes up tails. Clearly, this is a losing game for you. For example, if $p_a = 0.49$, then your expected loss is two cents per game.

In game B, we also repeatedly flip coins, but the coin that is flipped depends on how you have been doing so far in the game. Let w be the number of your wins so far and ℓ the number of your losses. Each round we bet one dollar, so $w - \ell$ represents your winnings; if it is negative, you have lost money. Game B uses two biased coins, coin b and coin c. If your winnings in dollars are a multiple of 3, then you flip coin b, which comes up heads with probability p_b and tails with probability $1 - p_b$. Otherwise, you flip coin c, which comes up heads with probability p_c and tails with probability $1 - p_c$. Again, you win a dollar if the coin comes up heads and lose a dollar if it comes up tails.

This game is more complicated, so let us consider a specific example. Suppose coin b comes up heads with probability $p_b = 0.09$ and tails with probability 0.91 and that coin c comes up heads with probability $p_c = 0.74$ and tails with probability 0.26. At first glance, it might seem that game B is in your favor. If we use coin b for the 1/3 of the time that your winnings are a multiple of 3 and use coin c the other 2/3 of the time, then your probability w of winning is

$$w = \frac{1}{3}\frac{9}{100} + \frac{2}{3}\frac{74}{100} = \frac{157}{300} > \frac{1}{2}.$$

The problem with this line of reasoning is that coin b is not necessarily used 1/3 of the time! To see this intuitively, consider what happens when you first start the game, when your winnings are 0. You use coin b and most likely lose, after which you use coin c and most likely win. You may spend a great deal of time going back and forth between having lost one dollar and breaking even before either winning one dollar or losing two dollars, so you may use coin b more than 1/3 of the time.

In fact, the specific example for game B is a losing game for you. One way to show this is to suppose that we start playing game B when your winnings are 0, continuing until you either lose three dollars or win three dollars. If you are more likely to lose than win in this case, by symmetry you are more likely to lose three dollars than win three dollars whenever your winnings are a multiple of 3. On average, then, you would obviously lose money on the game.

One way to determine if you are more likely to lose than win is to analyze the absorbing states. Consider the Markov chain on the state space consisting of the integers $\{-3, \ldots, 3\}$, where the states represent your winnings. We want to know, when you start at 0, whether or not you are more likely to reach -3 before reaching 3. We can determine this by setting up a system of equations. Let z_i represent the probability you will end up having lost three dollars before having won three dollars when your current winnings are i dollars. We calculate all the probabilities $z_{-3}, z_{-2}, z_{-1}, z_0, z_1, z_2,$ and z_3, although what we are really interested in is z_0. If $z_0 > 1/2$, then we are more likely to lose three dollars than win three dollars starting from 0. Here $z_{-3} = 1$ and $z_3 = 0$; these are boundary conditions. We also have the following equations:

$$z_{-2} = (1 - p_c)z_{-3} + p_c z_{-1},$$
$$z_{-1} = (1 - p_c)z_{-2} + p_c z_0,$$
$$z_0 = (1 - p_b)z_{-1} + p_b z_1,$$
$$z_1 = (1 - p_c)z_0 + p_c z_2,$$
$$z_2 = (1 - p_c)z_1 + p_c z_3.$$

This is a system of five equations with five unknowns, and hence it can be solved easily. The general solution for z_0 is

$$z_0 = \frac{(1 - p_b)(1 - p_c)^2}{(1 - p_b)(1 - p_c)^2 + p_b p_c^2}.$$

For the specific example here, the solution yields $z_0 = 15,379/27,700 \approx 0.555$, showing that one is much more likely to lose than win playing this game over the long run.

Instead of solving these equations directly, there is a simpler way of determining the relative probability of reaching -3 or 3 first. Consider any sequence of moves that starts at 0 and ends at 3 before reaching -3. For example, a possible sequence is

$$s = 0, 1, 2, 1, 2, 1, 0, -1, -2, -1, 0, 1, 2, 1, 2, 3.$$

We create a one-to-one and onto mapping of such sequences with the sequences that start at 0 and end at -3 before reaching 3 by negating every number starting from the last 0 in the sequence. In this example, s maps to $f(s)$, where

$$f(s) = 0, 1, 2, 1, 2, 1, 0, -1, -2, -1, 0, -1, -2, -1, -2, -3.$$

It is simple to check that this is a one-to-one mapping of the relevant sequences.

The following lemma provides a useful relationship between s and $f(s)$.

Lemma 7.18: *For any sequence s of moves that starts at 0 and ends at 3 before reaching -3, we have*

$$\frac{\Pr(s \text{ occurs})}{\Pr(f(s) \text{ occurs})} = \frac{p_b p_c^2}{(1 - p_b)(1 - p_c)^2}.$$

Proof: For any given sequence s satisfying the properties of the lemma, let t_1 be the number of transitions from 0 to 1; t_2, the number of transitions from 0 to -1; t_3, the sum of the number of transitions from -2 to -1, -1 to 0, 1 to 2, and 2 to 3; and t_4, the sum of the number of transitions from 2 to 1, 1 to 0, -1 to -2, and -2 to -3. Then the probability that the sequence s occurs is $p_b^{t_1}(1 - p_b)^{t_2} p_c^{t_3}(1 - p_c)^{t_4}$.

Now consider what happens when we transform s to $f(s)$. We change one transition from 0 to 1 into a transition from 0 to -1. After this point, in s the total number of transitions that move up 1 is two more than the number of transitions that move down 1, since the sequence ends at 3. In $f(s)$, then, the total number of transitions that move down 1 is two more than the number of transitions that move up 1. It follows that the probability that the sequence $f(s)$ occurs is $p_b^{t_1-1}(1 - p_b)^{t_2+1} p_c^{t_3-2}(1 - p_c)^{t_4+2}$. The lemma follows. ∎

By letting S be the set of all sequences of moves that start at 0 and end at 3 before reaching -3, it immediately follows that

$$\frac{\Pr(3 \text{ is reached before } -3)}{\Pr(-3 \text{ is reached before } 3)} = \frac{\sum_{s \in S} \Pr(s \text{ occurs})}{\sum_{s \in S} \Pr(f(s) \text{ occurs})} = \frac{p_b p_c^2}{(1 - p_b)(1 - p_c)^2}.$$

If this ratio is less than 1, then you are more likely to lose than win. In our specific example, this ratio is $12,321/15,379 < 1$.

195

Finally, yet another way to analyze the problem is to use the stationary distribution. Consider the Markov chain on the states $\{0, 1, 2\}$, where here the states represent the remainder when our winnings are divided by 3. (That is, the state keeps track of $w - \ell$ mod 3.) Let π_i be the stationary probability of this chain. The probability that we win a dollar in the stationary distribution, which is the limiting probability that we win a dollar if we play long enough, is then

$$p_b \pi_0 + p_c \pi_1 + p_c \pi_2 = p_b \pi_0 + p_c (1 - \pi_0)$$
$$= p_c - (p_c - p_b)\pi_0.$$

Again, we want to know if this is greater than or less than $1/2$.

The equations for the stationary distribution are easy to write:

$$\pi_0 + \pi_1 + \pi_2 = 1,$$
$$p_b \pi_0 + (1 - p_c)\pi_2 = \pi_1,$$
$$p_c \pi_1 + (1 - p_b)\pi_0 = \pi_2,$$
$$p_c \pi_2 + (1 - p_c)\pi_1 = \pi_0.$$

Indeed, since there are four equations and only three unknowns, one of these equations is actually redundant. The system is easily solved to find

$$\pi_0 = \frac{1 - p_c + p_c^2}{3 - 2p_c - p_b + 2p_b p_c + p_c^2},$$
$$\pi_1 = \frac{p_b p_c - p_c + 1}{3 - 2p_c - p_b + 2p_b p_c + p_c^2},$$
$$\pi_2 = \frac{p_b p_c - p_b + 1}{3 - 2p_c - p_b + 2p_b p_c + p_c^2}.$$

Recall that you lose if the probability of winning in the stationary distribution is less than $1/2$ or, equivalently, if $p_c - (p_c - p_b)\pi_0 < 1/2$. In our specific example, $\pi_0 = 673/1759 \approx 0.3826\ldots$, and

$$p_c - (p_c - p_b)\pi_0 = \frac{86,421}{175,900} < \frac{1}{2}.$$

Again, we find that game B is a losing game in the long run.

We have now completely analyzed game A and game B. Next let us consider what happens when we try to combine these two games. In game C, we repeatedly perform the following bet. We start by flipping a fair coin, call it coin d. If coin d is heads, we proceed as in game A: we flip coin a, and if the coin is heads, you win. If coin d is tails, we then proceed to game B: if your current winnings are a multiple of 3, we flip coin b; otherwise, we flip coin c, and if the coin is heads then you win. It would seem that this must be a losing game for you. After all, game A and game B are both losing games, and this game just flips a coin to decide which of the two games to play.

In fact, game C is exactly like game B, except the probabilities are slightly different. If your winnings are a multiple of 3, then the probability that you win is $p_b^* = \frac{1}{2}p_a + \frac{1}{2}p_b$. Otherwise, the probability that you win is $p_c^* = \frac{1}{2}p_a + \frac{1}{2}p_c$. Using p_b^* and p_c^* in place of p_b and p_c, we can repeat any of the foregoing analyses we used for game B.

For example: if the ratio

$$\frac{p_b^*(p_c^*)^2}{(1 - p_b^*)(1 - p_c^*)^2} < 1,$$

then the game is a losing game for you; if the ratio is larger than 1, it is a winning game. In our specific example the ratio is $438,741/420,959 > 1$, so game C appears to be a winning game.

This seems somewhat odd, so let us recheck by using our other approach of considering the stationary distribution. The game is a losing game if $p_c^* - (p_c^* - p_b^*)\pi_0 < 1/2$ and a winning game if $p_c^* - (p_c^* - p_b^*)\pi_0 > 1/2$, where π_0 is now the stationary distribution for the chain corresponding to game C. In our specific example, $\pi_0 = 30,529/88,597$, and

$$p_c^* - (p_c^* - p_b^*)\pi_0 = \frac{4,456,523}{8,859,700} > \frac{1}{2},$$

so game C again appears to be a winning game.

How can randomly combining two losing games yield a winning game? The key is that game B was a losing game because it had a very specific structure. You were likely to lose the next round in game B if your winnings were divisible by 3, but if you managed to get over that initial barrier you were likely to win the next few games as well. The strength of that barrier made game B a losing game. By combining the games that barrier was weakened, because now when your winnings are divisible by 3 you sometimes get to play game A, which is close to a fair game. Although game A is biased against you, the bias is small, so it becomes easier to overcome that initial barrier. The combined game no longer has the specific structure required to make it a losing game.

You may be concerned that this seems to violate the law of linearity of expectations. If the winnings from a round of game A, B, and C are X_A, X_B, and X_C (respectively), then it seems that

$$E[X_C] = E\left[\frac{1}{2}X_A + \frac{1}{2}X_B\right] = \frac{1}{2}E[X_A] + \frac{1}{2}E[X_B],$$

so if $E[X_A]$ and $E[X_B]$ are negative then $E[X_C]$ should also be negative. The problem is that this equation does not make sense, because we cannot talk about the expected winnings of a round of games B and C without reference to the current winnings. We have described a Markov chain on the states $\{0, 1, 2\}$ for games B and C. Let s represent the current state. We have

$$E[X_C \mid s] = E\left[\frac{1}{2}(X_A + X_B) \mid s\right]$$

$$= \frac{1}{2}E[X_A \mid s] + \frac{1}{2}E[X_B \mid s].$$

Linearity of expectations holds for any given step, but we must condition on the current state. By combining the games we have changed how often the chain spends in each state, allowing the two losing games to become a winning game.

7.6. Exercises

Exercise 7.1: Consider a Markov chain with state space $\{0, 1, 2, 3\}$ and a transition matrix

$$\mathbf{P} = \begin{bmatrix} 0 & 3/10 & 1/10 & 3/5 \\ 1/10 & 1/10 & 7/10 & 1/10 \\ 1/10 & 7/10 & 1/10 & 1/10 \\ 9/10 & 1/10 & 0 & 0 \end{bmatrix},$$

so $P_{0,3} = 3/5$ is the probability of moving from state 0 to state 3.

(a) Find the stationary distribution of the Markov chain.
(b) Find the probability of being in state 3 after 32 steps if the chain begins at state 0.
(c) Find the probability of being in state 3 after 128 steps if the chain begins at a state chosen uniformly at random from the four states.
(d) Suppose that the chain begins in state 0. What is the smallest value of t for which $\max_s |P_{0,s}^t - \pi_s| \le 0.01$? Here $\bar{\pi}$ is the stationary distribution. What is the smallest value of t for which $\max_s |P_{0,s}^t - \pi_s| \le 0.001$?

Exercise 7.2: Consider the two-state Markov chain with the following transition matrix

$$\mathbf{P} = \begin{bmatrix} p & 1-p \\ 1-p & p \end{bmatrix}.$$

Find a simple expression for $P_{0,0}^t$.

Exercise 7.3: Consider a process $X_0, X_1, X_2, \ldots$ with two states, 0 and 1. The process is governed by two matrices, $\mathbf{P}$ and $\mathbf{Q}$. If k is even, the values $P_{i,j}$ give the probability of going from state i to state j on the step from X_k to X_{k+1}. Likewise, if k is odd then the values $Q_{i,j}$ give the probability of going from state i to state j on the step from X_k to X_{k+1}. Explain why this process does not satisfy Definition 7.1 of a (time-homogeneous) Markov chain. Then give a process with a larger state space that is equivalent to this process and satisfies Definition 7.1.

Exercise 7.4: Prove that the communicating relation defines an equivalence relation.

Exercise 7.5: Prove that if one state in a communicating class is transient (respectively, recurrent) then all states in that class are transient (respectively, recurrent).

Exercise 7.6: In studying the 2-SAT algorithm, we considered a 1-dimensional random walk with a completely reflecting boundary at 0. That is, whenever position 0 is reached, with probability 1 the walk moves to position 1 at the next step. Consider now a random walk with a partially reflecting boundary at 0. Whenever position 0 is reached, with probability 1/2 the walk moves to position 1 and with probability 1/2 the walk stays at 0. Everywhere else the random walk moves either up or down 1, each with probability $1/2$. Find the expected number of moves to reach n, starting from position i and using a random walk with a partially reflecting boundary.

Exercise 7.7: Suppose that the 2-SAT Algorithm 7.1 starts with an assignment chosen uniformly at random. How does this affect the expected time until a satisfying assignment is found?

Exercise 7.8: Generalize the randomized algorithm for 3-SAT to k-SAT. What is the expected time of the algorithm as a function of k?

Exercise 7.9: In the analysis of the randomized algorithm for 3-SAT, we made the pessimistic assumption that the current assignment A_i and the truth assignment S differ on just one variable in the clause chosen at each step. Suppose instead that, independently at each step, the two assignments disagree on one variable in the clause with probability p and at least two variables with probability $1 - p$. What is the largest value of p for which you can prove that the expected number of steps before Algorithm 7.2 terminates is polynomial in the number of variables n? Give a proof for this value of p and give an upper bound on the expected number of steps in this case.

Exercise 7.10: A *coloring* of a graph is an assignment of a color to each of its vertices. A graph is k-colorable if there is a coloring of the graph with k colors such that no two adjacent vertices have the same color. Let G be a 3-colorable graph.

(a) Show that there exists a coloring of the graph with two colors such that no triangle is monochromatic. (A triangle of a graph G is a subgraph of G with three vertices, which are all adjacent to each other.)

(b) Consider the following algorithm for coloring the vertices of G with two colors so that no triangle is monochromatic. The algorithm begins with an arbitrary 2-coloring of G. While there are any monochromatic triangles in G, the algorithm chooses one such triangle and changes the color of a randomly chosen vertex of that triangle. Derive an upper bound on the expected number of such recoloring steps before the algorithm finds a 2-coloring with the desired property.

Exercise 7.11: An $n \times n$ matrix $\mathbf{P}$ with entries $P_{i,j}$ is called stochastic if all entries are nonnegative and if the sum of the entries in each row is 1. It is called doubly stochastic if, additionally, the sum of the entries in each column is 1. Show that the uniform distribution is a stationary distribution for any Markov chain represented by a doubly stochastic matrix.

Exercise 7.12: Let X_n be the sum of n independent rolls of a fair die. Show that, for any $k \geq 2$,

$$\lim_{n \to \infty} \Pr(X_n \text{ is divisible by } k) = \frac{1}{k}.$$

199

Exercise 7.13: Consider a finite Markov chain on n states with stationary distribution $\bar{\pi}$ and transition probabilities $P_{i,j}$. Imagine starting the chain at time 0 and running it for m steps, obtaining the sequence of states $X_0, X_1, \ldots, X_m$. Consider the states in reverse order, $X_m, X_{m-1}, \ldots, X_0$.

(a) Argue that given X_{k+1}, the state X_k is independent of $X_{k+2}, X_{k+3}, \ldots, X_m$. Thus the reverse sequence is Markovian.

(b) Argue that for the reverse sequence, the transition probabilities $Q_{i,j}$ are given by

$$Q_{i,j} = \frac{\pi_j P_{j,i}}{\pi_i}.$$

(c) Prove that if the original Markov chain is time reversible, so that $\pi_i P_{i,j} = \pi_j P_{j,i}$, then $Q_{i,j} = P_{i,j}$. That is, the states follow the same transition probabilities whether viewed in forward order or reverse order.

Exercise 7.14: Prove that the Markov chain corresponding to a random walk on an undirected, non-bipartite graph that consists of one component is time reversible.

Exercise 7.15: Let $P_{i,i}^t$ be the probability that a Markov chain returns to state i when started in state i after t steps. Prove that

$$\sum_{t=1}^{\infty} P_{i,i}^t$$

is unbounded if and only if state i is recurrent.

Exercise 7.16: Prove Lemma 7.5.

Exercise 7.17: Consider the following Markov chain, which is similar to the 1-dimensional random walk with a completely reflecting boundary at 0. Whenever position 0 is reached, with probability 1 the walk moves to position 1 at the next step. Otherwise, the walk moves from i to $i+1$ with probability p and from i to $i-1$ with probability $1-p$. Prove that:

(a) if $p < 1/2$, each state is positive recurrent;
(b) if $p = 1/2$, each state is null recurrent;
(c) if $p > 1/2$, each state is transient.

Exercise 7.18: (a) Consider a random walk on the 2-dimensional integer lattice, where each point has four neighbors (up, down, left, and right). Is each state transient, null recurrent, or positive recurrent? Give an argument.
    (b) Answer the problem in (a) for the 3-dimensional integer lattice.

Exercise 7.19: Consider the gambler's ruin problem, where a player plays until she lose ℓ_1 dollars or win ℓ_2 dollars. Prove that the expected number of games played is $\ell_1 \ell_2$.

Exercise 7.20: We have considered the gambler's ruin problem in the case where the game is fair. Consider the case where the game is not fair; instead, the probability of losing a dollar each game is $2/3$ and the probability of winning a dollar each game is $1/3$. Suppose that you start with i dollars and finish either when you reach n or lose it all. Let W_t be the amount you have gained after t rounds of play.

(a) Show that $\mathbf{E}[2^{W_{t+1}}] = \mathbf{E}[2^{W_t}]$.

(b) Use part (a) to determine the probability of finishing with 0 dollars and the probability of finishing with n dollars when starting at position i.

(c) Generalize the preceding argument to the case where the probability of losing is $p > 1/2$. (*Hint:* Try considering $\mathbf{E}[c^{W_t}]$ for some constant c.)

Exercise 7.21: Consider a Markov chain on the states $\{0, 1, \ldots, n\}$, where for $i < n$ we have $P_{i,i+1} = 1/2$ and $P_{i,0} = 1/2$. Also, $P_{n,n} = 1/2$ and $P_{n,0} = 1/2$. This process can be viewed as a random walk on a directed graph with vertices $\{0, 1, \ldots, n\}$, where each vertex has two directed edges: one that returns to 0 and one that moves to the vertex with the next higher number (with a self-loop at vertex n). Find the stationary distribution of this chain. (This example shows that random walks on directed graphs are very different than random walks on undirected graphs.)

Exercise 7.22: A cat and a mouse each independently take a random walk on a connected, undirected, non-bipartite graph G. They start at the same time on different nodes, and each makes one transition at each time step. The cat eats the mouse if they are ever at the same node at some time step. Let n and m denote, respectively, the number of vertices and edges of G. Show an upper bound of $O(m^2 n)$ on the expected time before the cat eats the mouse. (*Hint:* Consider a Markov chain whose states are the ordered pairs (a, b), where a is the position of the cat and b is the position of the mouse.)

Exercise 7.23: One way of spreading information on a network uses a rumor-spreading paradigm. Suppose that there are n hosts currently on the network. Initially, one host begins with a message. Each round, every host that has the message contacts another host chosen independently and uniformly at random from the other $n - 1$ hosts, and sends that host the message. We would like to know how many rounds are necessary before all hosts have received the message with probability 0.9999.

(a) Explain how this problem can be viewed in terms of Markov chains.

(b) Determine a method for computing the probability that j hosts have received the message after round k given that i hosts have received the message after round $k - 1$. (*Hint:* There are various ways of doing this. One approach is to let $P(i, j, c)$ be the probability that j hosts have the message after the first c of the i hosts have made their choices in a round; then find a recurrence for P.)

(c) As a computational exercise, write a program to determine the number of rounds required for a message starting at one host to reach all other hosts with probability 0.9999 when $n = 128$.

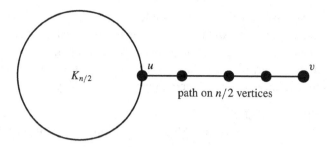

Figure 7.3: Lollipop graph.

Exercise 7.24: The *lollipop* graph on n vertices is a clique on $n/2$ vertices connected to a path on $n/2$ vertices, as shown in Figure 7.3. The node u is a part of both the clique and the path. Let v denote the other end of the path.

(a) Show that the expected covering time of a random walk starting at v is $\Theta(n^2)$.
(b) Show that the expected covering time for a random walk starting at u is $\Theta(n^3)$.

Exercise 7.25: The following is a variation of a simple children's board game. A player starts at position 0. On a player's turn, she rolls a standard six-sided die. If her old position was the positive integer x and her roll is y, then her new position is $x + y$, except in two cases:

- if $x + y$ is divisible by 6 and less than 36, her new position is $x + y - 6$;
- if $x + y$ is greater than 36, the player remains at x.

The game ends when a player reaches the goal position, 36.

(a) Let X_i be a random variable representing the number of rolls needed to get to 36 from position i for $0 \le i \le 35$. Give a set of equations that characterize $\mathbf{E}[X_i]$.
(b) Using a program that can solve systems of linear equations, find $\mathbf{E}[X_i]$ for $0 \le i \le 35$.

Exercise 7.26: Let n equidistant points be marked on a circle. Without loss of generality, we think of the points as being labeled clockwise from 0 to $n - 1$. Initially, a wolf begins at 0 and there is one sheep at each of the remaining $n - 1$ points. The wolf takes a random walk on the circle. For each step, it moves with probability $1/2$ to one neighboring point and with probability $1/2$ to the other neighboring point. At the first visit to a point, the wolf eats a sheep if there is still one there. Which sheep is most likely to be the last eaten?

Exercise 7.27: Suppose that we are given n records, $R_1, R_2, \ldots, R_n$. The records are kept in some order. The cost of accessing the jth record in the order is j. Thus, if we had four records ordered as R_2, R_4, R_3, R_1, then the cost of accessing R_4 would be 2 and the cost of accessing R_1 would be 4.

Suppose further that, at each step, record R_j is accessed with probability p_j, with each step being independent of other steps. If we knew the values of the p_j in advance, we would keep the R_j in decreasing order with respect to p_j. But if we don't know the p_j in advance, we might use the "move to front" heuristic: at each step, put the record that was accessed at the front of the list. We assume that moving the record can be done with no cost and that all other records remain in the same order. For example, if the order was R_2, R_4, R_3, R_1 before R_3 was accessed, then the order at the next step would be R_3, R_2, R_4, R_1.

In this setting, the order of the records can be thought of as the state of a Markov chain. Give the stationary distribution of this chain. Also, let X_k be the cost for accessing the kth requested record. Determine an expression for $\lim_{k \to \infty} \mathbf{E}[X_k]$. Your expression should be easily computable in time that is polynomial in n, given the p_j.

Exercise 7.28: Consider the following variation of the discrete time queue. Time is divided into fixed-length steps. At the beginning of each time step, a customer arrives with probability λ. At the end of each time step, if the queue is nonempty then the customer at the front of the line completes service with probability μ.

(a) Explain how the number of customers in the queue at the beginning of each time step forms a Markov chain, and determine the corresponding transition probabilities.

(b) Explain under what conditions you would expect a stationary distribution $\bar{\pi}$ to exist.

(c) If a stationary distribution exists, then what should be the value of π_0, the probability that no customers are in the queue at the beginning of the time step? (*Hint:* Consider that, in the long run, the rate at which customers enter the queue and the rate at which customers leave the queue must be equal.)

(d) Determine the stationary distribution and explain how it corresponds to your conditions from part (b).

(e) Now consider the variation where we change the order of incoming arrivals and service. That is: at the *beginning* of each time step, if the queue is nonempty then a customer is served with probability μ; and at the *end* of a time step a customer arrives with probability λ. How does this change your answers to parts (a)–(d)?

Exercise 7.29: Prove that the Markov chain from Lemma 7.14 where the states are the $2|E|$ directed edges of the graph has a uniform stationary distribution.

Exercise 7.30: We consider the covering time for the standard random walk on a hypercube with $N = 2^n$ nodes. (See Definition 4.3 if needed to recall the definition of a hypercube.) Let (u, v) be an edge in the hypercube.

(a) Prove that the expected time between traversals of the edge (u, v) from u to v is Nn.

(b) We consider the time between transitions from u to v in a different way. After moving from u to v, the walk must first return to u. When it returns to u, the walk might next move to v, or it might move to another neighbor of u, in which case it must return to u again before moving to v for there to be a transition from u to v.

Use symmetry and the above description to prove the following recurrence:

$$Nn = \sum_{i=1}^{\infty} \frac{1}{n} \left(\frac{n-1}{n} \right)^{i-1} (i(h_{u,v} + 1)) = n(h_{u,v} + 1).$$

(c) Conclude from the above that $h_{u,v} = N - 1$.

(d) Using the result on the hitting time of adjacent vertices and Matthews' theorem, show that the cover time is $O(N \log^2 N)$.

(e) As a much more challenging problem, you can try to prove that the maximum hitting time between any two vertices for the random walk on the hypercube is $O(N)$, and that the cover time is correspondingly $O(N \log N)$.

CHAPTER EIGHT

Continuous Distributions and the Poisson Process

This chapter introduces the general concept of continuous random variables, focusing on two examples of continuous distributions: the uniform distribution and the exponential distribution. We then proceed to study the Poisson process, a continuous time counting process that is related to both the uniform and exponential distributions. We conclude this chapter with basic applications of the Poisson process in queueing theory.

8.1. Continuous Random Variables

8.1.1. *Probability Distributions in $\mathbb{R}$*

The continuous roulette wheel in Figure 8.1 has circumference 1. We spin the wheel, and when it stops, the outcome is the clockwise distance X (computed with infinite precision) from the "0" mark to the arrow.

The sample space Ω of this experiment consists of all real numbers in the range $[0, 1)$. Assume that any point on the circumference of the disk is equally likely to face the arrow when the disk stops. What is the probability p of a given outcome x?

To answer this question, we recall that in Chapter 1 we defined a probability function to be any function that satisfies the following three requirements:

1. $\Pr(\Omega) = 1$;
2. for any event E,

$$0 \le \Pr(E) \le 1;$$

3. for any (finite or enumerable) collection $\mathcal{B}$ of disjoint events,

$$\Pr\left(\bigcup_{E \in \mathcal{B}} E\right) = \sum_{E \in \mathcal{B}} \Pr(E).$$

Let $S(k)$ be a set of k distinct points in the range $[0, 1)$, and let p be the probability that any given point in $[0, 1)$ is the outcome of the roulette experiment. Since the probability

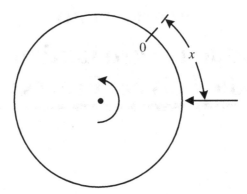

Figure 8.1: A continuous roulette wheel.

of any event is bounded by 1,

$$\Pr(x \in S(k)) = kp \leq 1.$$

We can choose any number k of distinct points in the range $[0, 1)$, so we must have $kp \leq 1$ for any integer k, which implies that $p = 0$. Thus, we observe that in an infinite sample space there may be possible events that have probability 0. Taking the complement of such an event, we observe that in an infinite sample space there can be events with probability 1 that do not correspond to all possible experimental outcomes, and thus there can be events with probability 1 that are, in some sense, not certain!

If the probability of each possible outcome of our experiment is 0, how do we define the probability of larger events with nonzero probability? For probability distributions over $\mathbb{R}$, probabilities are assigned to intervals rather than to individual values.[1]

The probability distribution of a random variable X is given by its *distribution function* $F(x)$, where for any $x \in \mathbb{R}$ we define

$$F(x) = \Pr(X \leq x).$$

We say that a random variable X is *continuous* if its distribution function $F(x)$ is a continuous function of x. We will assume that our random variables are continuous throughout this chapter. In this case, we must have that $\Pr(X = x) = 0$ for any specific value x. This further implies that $\Pr(X \leq x) = \Pr(X < x)$, a fact we make use of freely throughout this chapter.

If there is a function $f(x)$ such that, for all $-\infty < a < \infty$,

$$F(a) = \int_{-\infty}^{a} f(t)\,dt,$$

then $f(x)$ is called the *density function* of $F(x)$, and

$$f(x) = F'(x)$$

where the derivative is well-defined.

---

[1] A formal treatment of nondenumerably infinite probability spaces relies on measure theory and is beyond the scope of this book. We just note here that the probability function needs to be measurable on the set of events. This cannot hold in general for the family of all subsets of the sample space, but it does always hold for the Borel set of intervals.

Because

$$\Pr(x < X \le x + dx) = F(x + dx) - F(x) \approx f(x) \, dx,$$

we can informally think of $f(x) \, dx$ as the "probability" of the infinitesimal interval $(x, x + dx]$. Carrying this analogy forward, in discrete spaces the probability of an event E is the sum of the probabilities of the simple events included in E. The parallel concept in the case of events in $\mathbb{R}$ is the integral of the probability density function over the basic events in E.

For example, the probability of the interval $[a, b)$ is given by the integral

$$\Pr(a \le x < b) = \int_a^b f(x) \, dx,$$

and the expectation and higher moments of a random variable X with density function $f(x)$ are defined by the integrals

$$\mathbf{E}[X^i] = \int_{-\infty}^{\infty} x^i f(x) \, dx.$$

More generally, for any function g,

$$\mathbf{E}[g(X)] = \int_{-\infty}^{\infty} g(x) f(x) \, dx,$$

when this integral exists. The variance of X is given by

$$\mathbf{Var}[X] = \mathbf{E}[(X - \mathbf{E}[X])^2] = \int_{-\infty}^{\infty} (x - \mathbf{E}[X])^2 f(x) \, dx = \mathbf{E}[X^2] - (\mathbf{E}[X])^2.$$

The following lemma gives the continuous analog to Lemma 2.9.

Lemma 8.1: *Let X be a continuous random variable that takes on only nonnegative values. Then*

$$\mathbf{E}[X] = \int_0^{\infty} \Pr(X \ge x) \, dx.$$

Proof: Let $f(x)$ be the density function of X. Then

$$\int_{x=0}^{\infty} \Pr(X \ge x) \, dx = \int_{x=0}^{\infty} \int_{y=x}^{\infty} f(y) \, dy \, dx$$
$$= \int_{y=0}^{\infty} \int_{x=0}^{y} f(y) \, dx \, dy$$
$$= \int_{y=0}^{\infty} y f(y) \, dy$$
$$= \mathbf{E}[X].$$

The interchange of the order of the integrals is justified because the expression being integrated is nonnegative. ∎

207

8.1.2. *Joint Distributions and Conditional Probability*

The notion of a distribution function for a real-valued random variable easily generalizes to multiple random variables.

Definition 8.1: *The* joint distribution function *of X and Y is*

$$F(x, y) = \Pr(X \le x, Y \le y).$$

The variables X and Y have joint density function f if, for all x, y,

$$F(x, y) = \int_{-\infty}^{y} \int_{-\infty}^{x} f(u, v)\, du\, dv.$$

Again, we denote

$$f(x, y) = \frac{\partial^2}{\partial x\, \partial y} F(x, y)$$

when the derivative exists. These definitions are generalized to joint distribution functions over more than two variables in the obvious way.

Given a joint distribution function $F(x, y)$ over X and Y, one may consider the *marginal distribution functions*

$$F_X(x) = \Pr(X \le x), \qquad F_Y(y) = \Pr(Y \le y),$$

and the corresponding marginal density functions $f_X(x)$ and $f_Y(y)$.

Definition 8.2: *The random variables X and Y are* independent *if, for all x and y,*

$$\Pr((X \le x) \cap (Y \le y)) = \Pr(X \le x) \Pr(Y \le y).$$

From the definition, two random variables are independent if and only if their joint distribution function is the product of their marginal distribution functions:

$$F(x, y) = F_X(x) F_Y(y).$$

It follows from taking the derivatives with respect to x and y that, if X and Y are independent, then

$$f(x, y) = f_X(x) f_Y(y),$$

and this condition is sufficient as well.

As an example, let a and b be positive constants, and consider the joint distribution function for two random variables X and Y given by

$$F(x, y) = 1 - e^{-ax} - e^{-by} + e^{-(ax+by)}$$

over the range $x, y \ge 0$. We can compute that

$$F_X(x) = F(x, \infty) = 1 - e^{-ax},$$

and similarly $F_Y(y) = 1 - e^{-by}$. Alternatively, we could compute

$$f(x, y) = abe^{-(ax+by)},$$

208

from which it follows that

$$F_X(z) = \int_{x=0}^{z} \int_{y=0}^{\infty} abe^{-(ax+by)} \, dy \, dx = \int_{x=0}^{z} -ae^{-ax} = 1 - e^{-az}.$$

We obtain

$$F(x, y) = 1 - e^{-ax} - e^{-by} + e^{-(ax+by)} = (1 - e^{-ax})(1 - e^{-by}) = F_X(x)F_Y(y),$$

so X and Y are independent. Alternatively, working with the density functions we verify their independence by

$$f_X(x) = ae^{-ax}, \quad f_Y(y) = be^{-by}, \quad f(x, y) = f_X(x)f_Y(y).$$

Conditional probability for continuous random variables introduces a nontrivial subtlety. The natural definition,

$$\Pr(E \mid F) = \frac{\Pr(E \cap F)}{\Pr(F)},$$

is suitable when $\Pr(F) \neq 0$. For example,

$$\Pr(X \leq 3 \mid Y \leq 6) = \frac{\Pr((X \leq 3) \cap (Y \leq 6))}{\Pr(Y \leq 6)}$$

when $\Pr(Y \leq 6)$ is not zero.

In the discrete case, if $\Pr(F) = 0$ then $\Pr(E \mid F)$ was simply not well-defined. In the continuous case, there are well-defined expressions that condition on events that occur with probability 0. For example, for the joint distribution function $F(x, y) = 1 - e^{-ax} - e^{-by} + e^{-(ax+by)}$ examined previously, it seems reasonable to consider

$$\Pr(X \leq 3 \mid Y = 4),$$

but since $\Pr(Y = 4)$ is an event with probability 0, the definition is not applicable.

If we did apply the definition, it would yield

$$\Pr(X \leq 3 \mid Y = 4) = \frac{\Pr((X \leq 3) \cap (Y = 4))}{\Pr(Y = 4)}.$$

Both the numerator and denominator are zero, suggesting that we should be taking a limit as they both approach zero. The natural choice is

$$\Pr(X \leq 3 \mid Y = 4) = \lim_{\delta \to 0} \Pr(X \leq 3 \mid 4 \leq Y \leq 4 + \delta).$$

This choice leads us to the following definition:

$$\Pr(X \leq x \mid Y = y) = \int_{u=-\infty}^{x} \frac{f(u, y)}{f_Y(y)} \, du.$$

209

To see informally why this is a reasonable choice, consider

$$\lim_{\delta \to 0} \Pr(X \le x \mid y \le Y \le y + \delta)$$

$$= \lim_{\delta \to 0} \frac{\Pr((X \le x) \cap (y \le Y \le y + \delta))}{\Pr(y \le Y \le y + \delta)}$$

$$= \lim_{\delta \to 0} \frac{F(x, y + \delta) - F(x, y)}{F_Y(y + \delta) - F_Y(y)}$$

$$= \lim_{\delta \to 0} \int_{u=-\infty}^{x} \frac{\partial F(u, y + \delta)/\partial x - \partial F(u, y)/\partial x}{F_Y(y + \delta) - F_Y(y)} \, du$$

$$= \int_{u=-\infty}^{x} \lim_{\delta \to 0} \frac{(\partial F(u, y + \delta)/\partial x - \partial F(u, y)/\partial x)/\delta}{(F_Y(y + \delta) - F_Y(y))/\delta} \, du$$

$$= \int_{u=-\infty}^{x} \frac{f(u, y)}{f_Y(y)} \, du.$$

Here we have assumed that we can interchange the limit with the integration and that $f_Y(y) \neq 0$.

The value

$$f_{X|Y}(x, y) = \frac{f(x, y)}{f_Y(y)}$$

is also called a *conditional density function*. We may similarly use

$$f_{Y|X}(x, y) = \frac{f(x, y)}{f_X(x)}.$$

Our definition yields the natural interpretation that, in order to compute $\Pr(X \le x \mid Y = y)$, we integrate the corresponding conditional density function over the appropriate range. You can check that this definition yields the standard definition for $\Pr(X \le x \mid Y \le y)$ through appropriate integration. Similarly, we may compute the conditional expectation

$$\mathbf{E}[X \mid Y = y] = \int_{x=-\infty}^{\infty} x f_{X|Y}(x, y) \, dx$$

using the conditional density function.

For our example, when $F(x, y) = 1 - e^{-ax} - e^{-by} + e^{-(ax+by)}$, it follows that

$$\Pr(X \le 3 \mid Y = 4) = \int_{u=0}^{3} \frac{abe^{-ax+4b}}{be^{-4b}} \, du = 1 - e^{-3a},$$

a result we could also have achieved directly using independence.

8.2. The Uniform Distribution

When a random variable X assumes values in the interval $[a, b]$ such that all subintervals of equal length have equal probability, we say that X has the *uniform distribution* over the interval $[a, b]$ or alternatively that it is uniform over the interval $[a, b]$. We denote such a random variable by $U[a, b]$. We may also talk about uniform distributions over

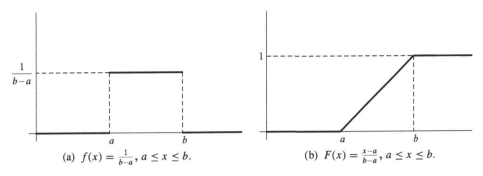

(a) $f(x) = \frac{1}{b-a}$, $a \leq x \leq b$.   (b) $F(x) = \frac{x-a}{b-a}$, $a \leq x \leq b$.

Figure 8.2: The uniform distribution.

the interval $[a, b)$, $(a, b]$, or (a, b). Indeed, since the probability of taking on any specific value is 0 when $b > a$, the distributions are essentially the same.

The probability distribution function of such an X is

$$F(x) = \begin{cases} 0 & \text{if } x \leq a, \\ \frac{x-a}{b-a} & \text{if } a \leq x \leq b, \\ 1 & \text{if } x \geq b, \end{cases}$$

and its density function is

$$f(x) = \begin{cases} 0 & \text{if } x < a, \\ \frac{1}{b-a} & \text{if } a \leq x \leq b, \\ 0 & \text{if } x > b. \end{cases}$$

These are shown in Figure 8.2.

The expectation of X is

$$\mathbf{E}[X] = \int_a^b \frac{x}{b-a}\, dx = \frac{b^2 - a^2}{2(b-a)} = \frac{b+a}{2},$$

and the second moment is

$$\mathbf{E}[X^2] = \int_a^b \frac{x^2}{b-a}\, dx = \frac{b^3 - a^3}{3(b-a)} = \frac{b^2 + ab + a^2}{3}.$$

The variance is computed by

$$\mathbf{Var}[X] = \mathbf{E}[X^2] - (\mathbf{E}[X])^2 = \frac{b^2 + ab + a^2}{3} - \frac{(b+a)^2}{4} = \frac{(b-a)^2}{12}.$$

In our continuous roulette example, the outcome X of the experiment has a uniform distribution over $[0, 1)$. Thus, the expectation of X is $1/2$ and the variance of X is $1/12$.

8.2.1. *Additional Properties of the Uniform Distribution*

Suppose you have a random variable X chosen from a uniform distribution, say over $[0, 1]$, and it is revealed that X is less than or equal to $1/2$. With this information, the conditional distribution of X remains uniform over the smaller interval $[0, 1/2]$.

211

Lemma 8.2: *Let X be a uniform random variable on [a, b]. Then, for c ≤ d,*

$$\Pr(X \le c \mid X \le d) = \frac{c - a}{d - a}.$$

That is, conditioned on the fact that $X \le d$, X is uniform on [a, d].

Proof:

$$\Pr(X \le c \mid X \le d) = \frac{\Pr((X \le c) \cap (X \le d))}{\Pr(X \le d)}$$

$$= \frac{\Pr(X \le c)}{\Pr(X \le d)}$$

$$= \frac{c - a}{d - a}.$$

It follows that X, conditioned on being less than or equal to d, has a distribution function that is exactly that of a uniform random variable on $[a, d]$. ∎

Of course, a similar statement holds if we consider $\Pr(X \le c \mid X \ge d)$; conditioned on $X \ge d$, the resulting distribution is uniform over $[d, b]$.

Another fact about the uniform distribution stems from the intuition that, if n points are uniformly distributed over an interval, we expect them to be roughly equally spaced. We can codify this idea as follows.

Lemma 8.3: *Let $X_1, X_2, \ldots, X_n$ be independent uniform random variables over $[0, 1]$. Let $Y_1, Y_2, \ldots, Y_n$ be the same values as $X_1, X_2, \ldots, X_n$ in increasing sorted order. Then $\mathbf{E}[Y_k] = k/(n + 1)$.*

Proof: Let us first prove the result for Y_1 with an explicit calculation. By definition, $Y_1 = \min(X_1, X_2, \ldots, X_n)$. Now

$$\Pr(Y_1 \ge y) = \Pr(\min(X_1, X_2, \ldots, X_n) \ge y)$$

$$= \Pr((X_1 \ge y) \cap (X_2 \ge y) \cap \cdots \cap (X_n \ge y))$$

$$= \prod_{i=1}^{n} \Pr(X_i \ge y)$$

$$= (1 - y)^n.$$

It follows from Lemma 8.1 that

$$\mathbf{E}[Y_1] = \int_{y=0}^{1} (1 - y)^n \, dy = \frac{1}{n + 1}.$$

Alternatively, one could use $F(y) = 1 - (1 - y)^n$ so that the density function of Y_1 is $f(y) = n(1 - y)^{n-1}$, and hence using integration by parts yields

$$\mathbf{E}[Y_1] = \int_{y=0}^{1} ny(1 - y)^{n-1} \, dy = -y(1 - y)^n \big|_{y=0}^{y=1} + \int_{y=0}^{1} (1 - y)^n \, dy = \frac{1}{n + 1}.$$

This analysis can be extended to find $\mathbf{E}[Y_k]$ with some computation, which we leave as Exercise 8.5. A simpler approach, however, makes use of symmetry. Consider the

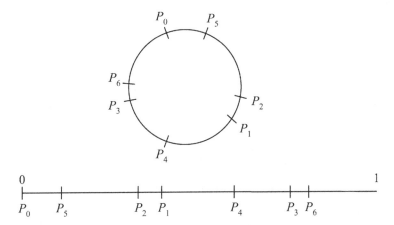

Figure 8.3: A correspondence between random points on a circle and random points on a line.

circle of circumference 1, and place $n + 1$ points $P_0, P_1, \ldots, P_n$ independently and uniformly at random on the circle. This is equivalent to choosing each point by a spin of the continuous roulette wheel of Section 8.1.1. Label the point P_0 as 0, and let X_i be the distance traveling clockwise from P_0 to P_i. The X_i are then independent, uniform random variables from $[0, 1]$. The value Y_k is just the distance to the kth point reached traveling clockwise from P_0. See Figure 8.3.

The distance between Y_k and Y_{k+1} is the length of the arc between the two corresponding adjacent points. By symmetry, however, all of the arcs between adjacent points must have the same expected length. The expected length of each arc is therefore $1/(n + 1)$, since there are $n + 1$ arcs created by the n points and since their total length is 1. By the linearity of expectations, $\mathbf{E}[Y_k]$ is the sum of the expected lengths of the first k arcs, and hence $\mathbf{E}[Y_k] = k/(n + 1)$. ∎

This proof makes use of an interesting one-to-one correspondence between choosing n points independently and uniformly at random from $[0, 1]$ and choosing $n + 1$ points independently and uniformly at random from the boundary of the circle with circumference 1. Such relationships, when they are available, can often greatly simplify an otherwise lengthy analysis. We develop other similar relationships throughout this chapter.

8.3. The Exponential Distribution

Another important continuous distribution is the *exponential distribution*.

Definition 8.3: *An* exponential distribution *with parameter* θ *is given by the following probability distribution function:*

$$F(x) = \begin{cases} 1 - e^{-\theta x} & \text{for } x \geq 0, \\ 0 & \text{otherwise.} \end{cases}$$

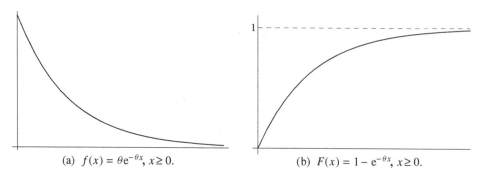

(a) $f(x) = \theta e^{-\theta x}$, $x \geq 0$.　　　　(b) $F(x) = 1 - e^{-\theta x}$, $x \geq 0$.

Figure 8.4: The exponential distribution.

The density function of the exponential distribution is

$$f(x) = \theta e^{-\theta x} \quad \text{for } x \geq 0.$$

See Figure 8.4.

Its first and second moments are

$$\mathbf{E}[X] = \int_0^\infty t\theta e^{-\theta t}\, dt = \frac{1}{\theta},$$

$$\mathbf{E}[X^2] = \int_0^\infty t^2\theta e^{-\theta t}\, dt = \frac{2}{\theta^2}.$$

Hence,

$$\mathbf{Var}[X] = \mathbf{E}[X^2] - (\mathbf{E}[X])^2 = \frac{1}{\theta^2}.$$

8.3.1. *Additional Properties of the Exponential Distribution*

Perhaps the most important property of the exponential distribution is that, like the discrete geometric distribution, it is memoryless.

Lemma 8.4: *For an exponential random variable with parameter θ,*

$$\Pr(X > s + t \mid X > t) = \Pr(X > s).$$

Proof:

$$
\begin{aligned}
\Pr(X > s + t \mid X > t) &= \frac{\Pr(X > s + t)}{\Pr(X > t)} \\
&= \frac{1 - \Pr(X \leq s + t)}{1 - \Pr(X \leq t)} \\
&= \frac{e^{-\theta(s+t)}}{e^{-\theta t}} \\
&= e^{-\theta s} \\
&= \Pr(X > s).
\end{aligned}
$$ ∎

214

The exponential distribution is the only continuous memoryless distribution. It can be viewed as the continuous version of the discrete geometric distribution, which is the only discrete memoryless distribution. The geometric distribution models the time until first success in a sequence of independent identical Bernoulli trials, whereas the exponential distribution models the time until the first event in a memoryless continuous time stochastic process.

The minimum of several exponential random variables also exhibits some interesting properties.

Lemma 8.5: *If $X_1, X_2, \ldots, X_n$ are independent exponentially distributed random variables with parameters $\theta_1, \theta_2, \ldots, \theta_n$, respectively, then $\min(X_1, X_2, \ldots, X_n)$ is exponentially distributed with parameter $\sum_{i=1}^{n} \theta_i$ and*

$$\Pr(\min(X_1, X_2, \ldots, X_n) = X_i) = \frac{\theta_i}{\sum_{i=1}^{n} \theta_i}.$$

Proof: It suffices to prove the statement for two exponential random variables; the general case then follows by induction. Let X_1 and X_2 be independent exponential random variables with parameters θ_1 and θ_2. Then

$$
\begin{aligned}
\Pr(\min(X_1, X_2) > x) &= \Pr((X_1 > x) \cap (X_2 > x)) \\
&= \Pr(X_1 > x) \Pr(X_2 > x) \\
&= e^{-\theta_1 x} e^{-\theta_2 x} \\
&= e^{-(\theta_1 + \theta_2)x}.
\end{aligned}
$$

Hence the minimum has an exponential distribution with parameter $\theta_1 + \theta_2$.

Moreover, let $f(x_1, x_2)$ be the joint distribution of (X_1, X_2). Since the variables are independent, we have $f(x_1, x_2) = \theta_1 e^{-\theta_1 x_1} \theta_2 e^{-\theta_2 x_2}$. Hence

$$
\begin{aligned}
\Pr(X_1 < X_2) &= \int_{x_2=0}^{\infty} \int_{x_1=0}^{x_2} f(x_1, x_2) \, dx_1 \, dx_2 \\
&= \int_{x_2=0}^{\infty} \theta_2 e^{-\theta_2 x_2} \left(\int_{x_1=0}^{x_2} \theta_1 e^{-\theta_1 x_1} \, dx_1 \right) dx_2 \\
&= \int_{x_2=0}^{\infty} \theta_2 e^{-\theta_2 x_2} (1 - e^{-\theta_1 x_2}) \, dx_2 \\
&= \int_{x_2=0}^{\infty} (\theta_2 e^{-\theta_2 x_2} - \theta_2 e^{-(\theta_1 + \theta_2)x_2}) \, dx_2 \\
&= 1 - \frac{\theta_2}{\theta_1 + \theta_2} \\
&= \frac{\theta_1}{\theta_1 + \theta_2}.
\end{aligned}
$$
∎

For example, suppose that an airline ticket counter has n service agents, where the time that agent i takes per customer has an exponential distribution with parameter θ_i. You stand at the head of the line at time T_0, and all of the n agents are busy. What is the average time you wait for an agent?

Because service times are exponentially distributed, it does not matter for how long each agent has been helping another customer before time T_0; the remaining time for each customer is still exponentially distributed. This is a feature of the memoryless property of the exponential distribution. Lemma 8.5 therefore applies. The time until the first agent becomes free is exponentially distributed with parameter $\sum_{i=1}^{n} \theta_i$, so the expected waiting time is $1/\sum_{i=1}^{n} \theta_i$. Indeed, you can even determine the probability that each agent is the first to become free; the jth agent is first with probability $\theta_j/\sum_{i=1}^{n} \theta_i$.

8.3.2.* *Example: Balls and Bins with Feedback*

As an application of the exponential distribution, we consider an interesting variation of our standard balls-and-bins model. In this problem we have only two bins, and balls arrive one by one. Initially both bins have at least one ball. Suppose that, if bin 1 has x balls and bin 2 has y balls, then the probability that bin 1 obtains the next ball is $x/(x + y)$ while the probability that bin 2 obtains the next ball is $y/(x + y)$. This system has feedback: the more balls a bin has, the more balls it is likely to obtain in the future. An equivalent problem is given in Exercise 1.6. You may wish to check (by induction) that, if both bins start with one ball and there are n total balls, then the number of balls in bin 1 is uniformly distributed in the range $[1, n - 1]$.

Suppose instead that we strengthen the feedback in the following way. If bin 1 has x balls and bin 2 has y balls, then the probability that bin 1 obtains the next ball is $x^p/(x^p + y^p)$ and the probability that bin 2 obtains the next ball is $y^p/(x^p + y^p)$ for some $p > 1$. For example, when $p = 2$, if bin 1 has three balls and bin 2 has four balls, then the probability that the next ball goes into bin 1 is only $9/25 < 3/7$. Setting $p > 1$ strengthens the advantage of the bin with more balls.

This model has been suggested to describe economic situations that result in monopoly. For example, suppose there are two operating systems, Lindows and Winux. Users will tend to purchase machines with the same operating system that other users have in order to maintain compatibility. This effect might be nonlinear in the number of users of each system; this is modeled by the parameter p.

We now show a remarkable result: as long as $p > 1$, there is some point at which one bin obtains all the rest of the balls thrown. In the economic setting, this is a very strong form of monopoly; the other competitor simply stops obtaining new customers.

Theorem 8.6: *Under any starting conditions, if $p > 1$ then with probability 1 there exists a number c such that one of the two bins gets no more than c balls.*

Note the careful wording of the theorem. We are not saying that there is some fixed c (perhaps dependent on the initial conditions) such that one bin gets no more than c balls. (If we meant this, we would say that there exists a number c such that, with probability 1, one bin gets no more than c balls.) Instead, we are saying that, with probability 1, at some point (which we do not know ahead of time) one bin stops receiving balls.

Proof: For convenience, assume that both bins start with one ball; this does not affect the result.

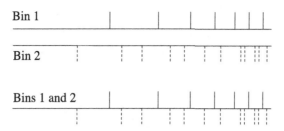

Figure 8.5: In the setup where the time between ball arrivals is exponentially distributed, each bin can be considered separately; an outcome of the original process is obtained by simply combining the timelines of the two bins.

We start by considering a very closely related process. Consider two bins that start with one ball at time 0. Balls arrive at each of the bins. If bin 1 obtains its zth ball at time t then it obtains its next ball at a time $t + T_z$, where T_z is a random variable exponentially distributed with parameter z^p. Similarly, if bin 2 obtains its zth ball at time t then it obtains its next ball at a time $t + U_z$, where U_z is also a random variable exponentially distributed with parameter z^p. All values of T_z and U_z are independent. Each bin can be considered independently in this setup; what happens at one bin does not affect the other.

Although this process may not seem related to the original problem, we now claim that it mimics it exactly. Consider the point at which a ball arrives, leaving x balls in bin 1 and y balls in bin 2. By the memoryless nature of the exponential distribution, it does not matter which bin the most recently arrived ball has landed in; the time for the next ball to land in bin 1 is exponentially distributed with mean x^{-p} and the time for the next ball to land in bin 2 is exponentially distributed with mean y^{-p}. Moreover, by Lemma 8.5, the next ball lands in bin 1 with probability $x^p/(x^p + y^p)$ and in bin 2 with probability $y^p/(x^p + y^p)$. Therefore, this setup mimics exactly what happens in the original problem. See Figure 8.5.

Let us define the *saturation time* F_1 for bin 1 by $F_1 = \sum_{j=1}^{\infty} T_j$, and similarly $F_2 = \sum_{j=1}^{\infty} U_j$. The saturation time represents the first time in which the total number of balls received by a bin is unbounded. It is not clear that saturation times are well-defined random variables: What if the sum does not converge, and thus its value is infinity? It is here that we make use of the fact that $p > 1$. We have

$$\mathbf{E}[F_1] = \mathbf{E}\left[\sum_{j=1}^{\infty} T_j\right] = \sum_{j=1}^{\infty} \mathbf{E}[T_j] = \sum_{j=1}^{\infty} \frac{1}{j^p}.$$

Here we used linearity of expectations for a countably infinite summation of random variables, which holds if $\sum_{j=1}^{\infty} \mathbf{E}[|T_j|]$ converges. (Chapter 2 discusses the applicability of the linearity of expectations to countably infinite summations; see in particular Exercise 2.29.) It suffices to show that $\sum_{j=1}^{\infty} 1/j^p$ converges to a finite number whenever $p > 1$. This follows from bounding the summation by the appropriate integral:

$$\sum_{j=1}^{\infty} \frac{1}{j^p} \leq 1 + \int_{u=1}^{\infty} \frac{1}{u^p}\, du = 1 + \frac{1}{p-1}.$$

Indeed, all of the integral moments converge to a finite number. It follows that both F_1 and F_2 are, with probability 1, finite and hence well-defined.

Furthermore, F_1 and F_2 are distinct with probability 1. To see this, suppose that the values for all of the random variables T_z and U_z are given except for T_1. Then, for F_1 to equal F_2, it must be the case that

$$T_1 = \sum_{j=1}^{\infty} U_j - \sum_{j=2}^{\infty} T_j.$$

But the probability that T_1 takes on any specific value is 0, just as the probability that our roulette wheel takes on any specific value is 0. Hence, $F_1 \neq F_2$ with probability 1.

Suppose that $F_1 < F_2$. Then we must have for some n that

$$\sum_{j=1}^{n} U_j < F_1 < \sum_{j=1}^{n+1} U_j.$$

This implies that, for *any* sufficiently large number m,

$$\sum_{j=1}^{n} U_j < \sum_{i=1}^{m} T_i < \sum_{j=1}^{n+1} U_j,$$

which means that bin 1 has obtained m balls before bin 2 has obtained its $(n+1)$th ball. Since our new process corresponds exactly to the original balls-and-bins process, this is also what happens in the original process. But this means that, once bin 2 has n balls, it does not receive any others; they all go to bin 1. The argument is the same if $F_2 < F_1$. Hence, with probability 1, there exists some n such that one bin obtains no more than n balls. ∎

When p is close to 1 or when the bins start with a large and nearly equal number of balls, it can take a long time before one bin dominates enough to obtain such a monopoly. On the other hand, monopoly happens quickly when p is much greater than 1 (such as $p = 2$) and the bins start with just one ball each. You are asked to simulate this process in Exercise 8.25.

8.4. The Poisson Process

The Poisson process is an important counting process that is related to both the uniform and the exponential distribution. Consider a sequence of random events, such as arrivals of customers to a queue or emissions of alpha particles from a radioactive material. Let $N(t)$ denote the number of events in the interval $[0, t]$. The process $\{N(t), t \geq 0\}$ is a *stochastic counting process*.

Definition 8.4: *A Poisson process* with *parameter (or rate)* λ *is a stochastic counting process* $\{N(t), t \geq 0\}$ *such that the following statements hold.*

1. $N(0) = 0$.
2. *The process has independent and stationary increments. That is, for any $t, s > 0$, the distribution of $N(t + s) - N(s)$ is identical to the distribution of $N(t)$, and for any*

two disjoint intervals $[t_1, t_2]$ *and* $[t_3, t_4]$, *the distribution of* $N(t_2) - N(t_1)$ *is independent of the distribution of* $N(t_4) - N(t_3)$.

3. $\lim_{t \to 0} \Pr(N(t) = 1)/t = \lambda$. *That is, the probability of a single event in a short interval* t *tends to* λt.

4. $\lim_{t \to 0} \Pr(N(t) \geq 2)/t = 0$. *That is, the probability of more than one event in a short interval* t *tends to zero.*

The surprising fact is that this set of broad, relatively natural conditions defines a unique process. In particular, the number of events in a given time interval follows the Poisson distribution defined in Section 5.3.

Theorem 8.7: *Let* $\{N(t) \mid t \geq 0\}$ *be a Poisson process with parameter* λ. *For any* $t, s \geq 0$ *and any integer* $n \geq 0$,

$$P_n(t) = \Pr(N(t + s) - N(s) = n) = e^{-\lambda t} \frac{(\lambda t)^n}{n!}.$$

Proof: We first observe that $P_n(t)$ is well-defined since, by the second property of Definition 8.4, the distribution of $N(t + s) - N(s)$ depends only on t and is independent of s.

To compute $P_0(t)$, we note that the number of events in the intervals $[0, t]$ and $(t, t + h]$ are independent random variables and therefore

$$P_0(t + h) = P_0(t)P_0(h).$$

We now write

$$
\begin{aligned}
\frac{P_0(t + h) - P_0(t)}{h} &= P_0(t)\frac{P_0(h) - 1}{h} \\
&= P_0(t)\frac{1 - \Pr(N(h) = 1) - \Pr(N(h) \geq 2) - 1}{h} \\
&= P_0(t)\frac{-\Pr(N(h) = 1) - \Pr(N(h) \geq 2)}{h}.
\end{aligned}
$$

Taking the limit as $h \to 0$ and applying properties 2–4 of Definition 8.4, we obtain

$$
\begin{aligned}
P_0'(t) &= \lim_{h \to 0} \frac{P_0(t + h) - P_0(t)}{h} \\
&= \lim_{h \to 0} P_0(t)\frac{-\Pr(N(h) = 1) - \Pr(N(h) \geq 2)}{h} \\
&= -\lambda P_0(t).
\end{aligned}
$$

To solve

$$P_0'(t) = -\lambda P_0(t),$$

we rewrite it as

$$\frac{P_0'(t)}{P_0(t)} = -\lambda.$$

Integrating with respect to t gives

$$\ln P_0(t) = -\lambda t + C,$$

or

$$P_0(t) = e^{-\lambda t + C}.$$

Since $P_0(0) = 1$, we conclude that

$$P_0(t) = e^{-\lambda t}. \tag{8.1}$$

For $n \geq 1$, we write

$$P_n(t + h) = \sum_{k=0}^{n} P_{n-k}(t) P_k(h)$$

$$= P_n(t) P_0(h) + P_{n-1}(t) P_1(h) + \sum_{k=2}^{n} P_{n-k}(t) \Pr(N(h) = k).$$

Computing the first derivative of $P_n(t)$ yields

$$P_n'(t) = \lim_{h \to 0} \frac{P_n(t + h) - P_n(t)}{h}$$

$$= \lim_{h \to 0} \frac{1}{h} \left(P_n(t)(P_0(h) - 1) + P_{n-1}(t) P_1(h) + \sum_{k=2}^{n} P_{n-k}(t) \Pr(N(h) = k) \right)$$

$$= -\lambda P_n(t) + \lambda P_{n-1}(t),$$

where we use the facts that

$$\lim_{h \to 0} \frac{P_1(h)}{h} = \lambda$$

(by properties 2 and 3) and

$$0 \leq \lim_{h \to 0} \frac{1}{h} \sum_{k=2}^{n} P_{n-k}(t) \Pr(N(h) = k) \leq \lim_{h \to 0} \frac{\Pr(N(h) \geq 2)}{h} = 0$$

(by property 4), so

$$\lim_{h \to 0} \frac{1}{h} \sum_{k=2}^{n} P_{n-k}(t) \Pr(N(h) = k) = 0.$$

To solve

$$P_n'(t) = -\lambda P_n(t) + \lambda P_{n-1}(t)$$

we write

$$e^{\lambda t}(P_n'(t) + \lambda P_n(t)) = e^{\lambda t} \lambda P_{n-1}(t),$$

which gives

$$\frac{d}{dt}(e^{\lambda t} P_n(t)) = \lambda e^{\lambda t} P_{n-1}(t). \tag{8.2}$$

Using Eqn. (8.1) then yields

$$\frac{d}{dt}(e^{\lambda t} P_1(t)) = \lambda e^{\lambda t} P_0(t) = \lambda,$$

implying

$$P_1(t) = (\lambda t + c)e^{-\lambda t}.$$

Since $P_1(0) = 0$, we conclude that

$$P_1(t) = \lambda t e^{-\lambda t}. \tag{8.3}$$

We continue by induction on n to prove that, for all $n \geq 0$,

$$P_n(t) = e^{-\lambda t} \frac{(\lambda t)^n}{n!}.$$

Using Eqn. (8.2) and the induction hypothesis, we have

$$\frac{d}{dt}(e^{\lambda t} P_n(t)) = \lambda e^{\lambda t} P_{n-1}(t) = \frac{\lambda^n t^{n-1}}{(n-1)!}.$$

Integrating and using the fact that $P_n(0) = 0$ gives the result. ∎

The parameter λ is also called the *rate* of the Poisson process, since (as we have proved) the number of events during any time period of length t is a Poisson random variable with expectation λt.

The reverse is also true. That is, we could equivalently have defined the Poisson process as a process with Poisson arrivals, as follows.

Theorem 8.8: *Let $\{N(t) \mid t \geq 0\}$ be a stochastic process such that:*

1. *$N(0) = 0$;*
2. *the process has independent increments (i.e., the number of events in disjoint time intervals are independent events); and*
3. *the number of events in an interval of length t has a Poisson distribution with mean λt.*

Then $\{N(t) \mid t \geq 0\}$ is a Poisson process with rate λ.

Proof: The process clearly satisfies conditions 1 and 2 of Definition 8.4. To prove condition 3, we have

$$\lim_{t \to 0} \frac{\Pr(N(t) = 1)}{t} = \lim_{t \to 0} \frac{e^{-\lambda t} \lambda t}{t} = \lambda.$$

Condition 4 follows from

$$\lim_{t \to 0} \frac{\Pr(N(t) \geq 2)}{t} = \sum_{k \geq 2} \frac{e^{-\lambda t} (\lambda t)^k}{k! t} = 0.$$

∎

8.4.1. *Interarrival Distribution*

Let X_1 be the time of the first event of the Poisson process, and let X_n be the interval of time between the $(n-1)$th and the nth event. The X_n are generally referred to as *interarrival times*, since they represent the time between arrivals of events. Here, we show that all of the X_n have the same distribution and that this distribution is exponential.

We begin by deriving the distribution of X_1.

Theorem 8.9: X_1 *has an exponential distribution with parameter* λ.

Proof:

$$\Pr(X_1 > t) = \Pr(N(t) = 0) = e^{-\lambda t}.$$

Thus,

$$F(X_1) = 1 - \Pr(X_1 > t) = 1 - e^{-\lambda t}. \qquad \blacksquare$$

Using the fact that the Poisson process has independent and stationary increments, we can prove the following stronger result.

Theorem 8.10: *The random variables* X_i, $i = 1, 2, \ldots$, *are independent, identically distributed, exponential random variables with parameter* λ.

Proof: The distribution of X_i is given by

$$\Pr(X_i > t_i \mid (X_0 = t_0) \cap (X_1 = t_1) \cap \cdots \cap (X_{i-1} = t_{i-1}))$$

$$= \Pr\left(N\left(\sum_{k=0}^{i} t_k\right) - N\left(\sum_{k=0}^{i-1} t_k\right) = 0\right)$$

$$= e^{-\lambda t_i}.$$

Thus, the distribution of X_i is exponential with parameter λ, and it is independent of other interarrival values. $\qquad \blacksquare$

Theorem 8.10 states that, if we have a Poisson arrival process, then the interarrival times are identically distributed exponential random variables. In fact, it is easy to check that the reverse is also true (this is left as Exercise 8.17).

Theorem 8.11: *Let* $\{N(t) \mid t \geq 0\}$ *be a stochastic process such that*:

1. $N(0) = 0$; *and*
2. *the interarrival times are independent, identically distributed, exponential random variables with parameter* λ.

Then $\{N(t) \mid t \geq 0\}$ *is a Poisson process with rate* λ.

8.4.2. Combining and Splitting Poisson Processes

The correspondence between Poisson processes and exponentially distributed interarrival times is quite useful in proving facts about the behavior of Poisson processes. One immediate fact is that Poisson processes combine in a natural way. We say that two Poisson processes $N_1(t)$ and $N_2(t)$ are *independent* if and only if the values $N_1(x)$ and $N_2(y)$ are independent for any x and y. Let $N_1(t) + N_2(t)$ denote the process that counts the number of events corresponding to both of the processes $N_1(t)$ and $N_2(t)$. We show that, if $N_1(t)$ and $N_2(t)$ are independent Poisson processes, then they combine to form a Poisson process $N_1(t) + N_2(t)$.

Theorem 8.12: *Let $N_1(t)$ and $N_2(t)$ be independent Poisson processes with parameters λ_1 and λ_2, respectively. Then $N_1(t) + N_2(t)$ is a Poisson process with parameter $\lambda_1 + \lambda_2$, and each event of the process $N_1(t) + N_2(t)$ arises from the process $N_1(t)$ with probability $\lambda_1/(\lambda_1 + \lambda_2)$.*

Proof: Clearly $N_1(0) + N_2(0) = 0$, and since the two processes are independent and each has independent increments, the sum of the two processes also has independent increments. The number of arrivals $N_1(t) + N_2(t)$ is a sum of two independent Poisson random variables, which (as we saw in Lemma 5.2) has a Poisson distribution with parameter $\lambda_1 + \lambda_2$. Thus, by Theorem 8.8, $N_1(t) + N_2(t)$ is a Poisson process with rate $\lambda_1 + \lambda_2$.

By Theorem 8.9, the interarrival time for $N_1(t) + N_2(t)$ is exponentially distributed with parameter $\lambda_1 + \lambda_2$, and by Lemma 8.5 an event in $N_1(t) + N_2(t)$ comes from the process $N_1(t)$ with probability $\lambda_1/(\lambda_1 + \lambda_2)$. ∎

The theorem extends to more than two processes by induction.

It is interesting to note that Poisson processes can be split as well as combined. If we split a Poisson process with rate λ by labeling each event as being either type 1 with probability p or type 2 with probability $(1 - p)$, then it seems that we should get two Poisson processes with rates λp and $\lambda(1 - p)$. In fact, we can say something even stronger: the two processes will be independent.

Theorem 8.13: *Suppose that we have a Poisson process $N(t)$ with rate λ. Each event is independently labeled as being type 1 with probability p or type 2 with probability $1 - p$. Then the type-1 events form a Poisson process $N_1(t)$ of rate λp, the type-2 events form a Poisson process $N_2(t)$ of rate $\lambda(1 - p)$, and the two Poisson processes are independent.*

Proof: We first show that the type-1 events in fact form a Poisson process. Clearly $N_1(t) = 0$, and since the process $N(t)$ has independent increments, so does the process $N_1(t)$. Next we show that $N_1(t)$ has a Poisson distribution:

$$
\begin{aligned}
\Pr(N_1(t) = k) &= \sum_{j=k}^{\infty} \Pr(N_1(t) = k \mid N(t) = j)\, \Pr(N(t) = j) \\
&= \sum_{j=k}^{\infty} \binom{j}{k} p^k (1 - p)^{j-k} \frac{e^{-\lambda t}(\lambda t)^j}{j!} \\
&= \frac{e^{-\lambda pt}(\lambda pt)^k}{k!} \sum_{j=k}^{\infty} \frac{e^{-\lambda t(1-p)}(\lambda t(1 - p))^{j-k}}{(j - k)!} \\
&= \frac{e^{-\lambda pt}(\lambda pt)^k}{k!}.
\end{aligned}
$$

Thus, by Theorem 8.8, $N_1(t)$ is a Poisson process with rate λp.

To show independence, we need to show that $N_1(t)$ and $N_2(u)$ are independent for any t and u. In fact, it suffices to show that $N_1(t)$ and $N_2(t)$ are independent for any t;

we can then show that $N_1(t)$ and $N_2(u)$ are independent for any t and u by taking advantage of the fact that Poisson processes have independent and stationary increments (see Exercise 8.18). We have:

$$
\begin{aligned}
\Pr((N_1(t) = m) \cap (N_2(t) = n)) &= \Pr((N(t) = m + n) \cap (N_2(t) = n)) \\
&= \frac{e^{-\lambda t}(\lambda t)^{m+n}}{(m+n)!} \binom{m+n}{n} p^m (1-p)^n \\
&= \frac{e^{-\lambda t}(\lambda t)^{m+n}}{m!\,n!} p^m (1-p)^n \\
&= \frac{e^{-\lambda tp}(\lambda tp)^m}{m!} \frac{e^{-\lambda t(1-p)}(\lambda t(1-p))^n}{n!} \\
&= \Pr(N_1(t) = m) \Pr(N_2(t) = n). \qquad \blacksquare
\end{aligned}
$$

8.4.3. *Conditional Arrival Time Distribution*

We have used the fact that a Poisson process has independent increments to show that the distribution of the interarrival times is exponential. Another application of this assumption is the following: If we condition on exactly one event occurring in an interval, then the actual time at which that event occurs is uniformly distributed over that interval. To see this, consider a Poisson process where $N(t) = 1$, and consider the time X_1 of the single event that falls in the interval $(0, t]$:

$$
\begin{aligned}
\Pr(X_1 < s \mid N(t) = 1) &= \frac{\Pr((X_1 < s) \cap (N(t) = 1))}{\Pr(N(t) = 1)} \\
&= \frac{\Pr((N(s) = 1) \cap (N(t) - N(s) = 0))}{\Pr(N(t) = 1)} \\
&= \frac{(\lambda s e^{-\lambda s}) e^{-\lambda(t-s)}}{\lambda t e^{-\lambda t}} \\
&= \frac{s}{t}.
\end{aligned}
$$

Here we have used the independence of $N(s)$ and $N(t) - N(s)$.

To generalize this to the case of $N(t) = n$, we use the concept of order statistics. Let $X_1, \ldots, X_n$ be n independent observations of a random variable. The *order statistics* of $X_1, \ldots, X_n$ consists of the n observations in (increasing) sorted order. For example, if X_1, X_2, X_3, X_4 are independent random variables generated by taking a number chosen uniformly on $[0, 1]$ and rounding to two decimal places, we might have $X_1 = 0.47$, $X_2 = 0.33$, $X_3 = 0.93$, and $X_4 = 0.26$. The corresponding order statistics, where $Y_{(i)}$ is used to refer to the ith smallest, would be $Y_{(1)} = 0.26$, $Y_{(2)} = 0.33$, $Y_{(3)} = 0.47$, and $Y_{(4)} = 0.93$.

Theorem 8.14: *Given that $N(t) = n$, the n arrival times have the same distribution as the order statistics of n independent random variables with uniform distribution over $[0, t]$.*

Proof: We first compute the distribution of the order statistics of n independent observations $X_1, X_2, \ldots, X_n$ drawn from a uniform distribution in $[0, t]$. Let $Y_{(1)}, \ldots, Y_{(n)}$ denote the order statistics.

We want an expression for

$$\Pr(Y_{(1)} \leq s_1, \; Y_{(2)} \leq s_2, \ldots, \; Y_{(n)} \leq s_n).$$

Let $\mathcal{E}$ be the event that

$$Y_{(1)} \leq s_1, \; Y_{(2)} \leq s_2, \ldots, \; Y_{(n)} \leq s_n.$$

For any permutation $i_1, i_2, \ldots, i_n$ of the numbers from 1 to n, let $\mathcal{E}_{i_1, i_2, \ldots, i_n}$ be the event that

$$X_{i_1} \leq s_1, \; X_{i_1} \leq X_{i_2} \leq s_2, \ldots, \; X_{i_{n-1}} \leq X_{i_n} \leq s_n.$$

The events $\mathcal{E}_{i_1, i_2, \ldots, i_n}$ are disjoint, except for the cases where $X_{i_j} = X_{i_{j+1}}$ for some j. Since two uniform random variables are equal with probability 0, the total probability of such events is 0 and can be ignored. By symmetry, all events $\mathcal{E}_{i_1, i_2, \ldots, i_n}$ have the same probability. Also,

$$\mathcal{E} = \bigcup \mathcal{E}_{i_1, i_2, \ldots, i_n},$$

where the union is over all permutations. It follows that

$$\Pr(Y_{(1)} \leq s_1, Y_{(2)} \leq s_2, \ldots, Y_{(n)} \leq s_n)$$
$$= \sum \Pr(X_{i_1} \leq s_1, \; X_{i_1} \leq X_{i_2} \leq s_2, \ldots, X_{i_{n-1}} \leq X_{i_n} \leq s_n)$$
$$= n! \; \Pr(X_1 \leq s_1, X_1 \leq X_2 \leq s_2, \ldots, \; X_{n-1} \leq X_n \leq s_n),$$

where the sum in the second line is over all $n!$ permutations. If we now think of u_i as representing the value taken on by X_i, then

$$\Pr(X_1 \leq s_1, X_1 \leq X_2 \leq s_2, \ldots, \; X_{n-1} \leq X_n \leq s_n)$$
$$= \int_{u_1=0}^{s_1} \int_{u_2=u_1}^{s_2} \cdots \int_{u_n=u_{n-1}}^{s_n} \left(\frac{1}{t}\right)^n du_n \cdots du_1,$$

where we use the fact that the density function of a uniform random variable on $[0, t]$ is $f(t) = 1/t$. This gives

$$\Pr(Y_{(1)} \leq s_1, Y_{(2)} \leq s_2, \ldots, \; Y_{(n)} \leq s_n) = \frac{n!}{t^n} \int_{u_1=0}^{s_1} \int_{u_2=u_1}^{s_2} \cdots \int_{u_n=u_{n-1}}^{s_n} du_n \cdots du_1.$$

We now consider the distribution of the arrival times for a Poisson process, conditioned on $N(t) = n$. Let $S_1, \ldots, S_{n+1}$ be the first $n + 1$ arrival times. Also, let $T_1 = S_1$ and $T_i = S_i - S_{i-1}$ be the length of the interarrival intervals. By Theorem 8.10, we know that (a) without the condition $N(t) = n$, the distributions of the random variables $T_1, \ldots, T_n$ are independent, and (b) for each i, T_i has an exponential distribution with parameter λ. Recalling that the density function of the exponential distribution is $\lambda e^{-\lambda t}$,

we have

$$\Pr(S_1 \le s_1, S_2 \le s_2, \ldots, S_n \le s_n, N(t) = n)$$

$$= \Pr\left(T_1 \le s_1, T_2 \le s_2 - T_1, \ldots, T_n \le s_n - \sum_{i=1}^{n-1} T_i, T_{n+1} > t - \sum_{i=1}^{n} T_i\right)$$

$$= \int_{t_1=0}^{s_1} \int_{t_2=0}^{s_2-t_1} \cdots \int_{t_n=0}^{s_n - \sum_{i=1}^{n-1} t_i} \int_{t_{n+1}=t-\sum_{i=1}^{n} t_i}^{\infty} \lambda^{n+1} e^{-\lambda(\sum_{i=1}^{n+1} t_i)} \, dt_{n+1} \cdots dt_1.$$

Integrating with respect to t_{n+1} then yields

$$\int_{t_{n+1}=t-\sum_{i=1}^{n} t_i}^{\infty} \lambda^{n+1} e^{-\lambda(\sum_{i=1}^{n+1} t_i)} \, dt_{n+1} = -\lambda^n \left[e^{-\lambda \sum_{i=1}^{n+1} t_i} \right]_{t_{n+1}=t-\sum_{i=1}^{n} t_i}^{\infty}$$

$$= \lambda^n e^{-\lambda t}.$$

Thus,

$$\Pr(S_1 \le s_1, S_2 \le s_2, \ldots, S_n \le s_n, N(t) = n)$$

$$= \lambda^n e^{-\lambda t} \int_{t_1=0}^{s_1} \int_{t_2=0}^{s_2-t_1} \cdots \int_{t_n=0}^{s_n - \sum_{i=1}^{n-1} t_i} dt_n \cdots dt_1$$

$$= \lambda^n e^{-\lambda t} \int_{u_1=0}^{s_1} \int_{u_2=u_1}^{s_2} \cdots \int_{u_n=u_{n-1}}^{s_n} du_n \cdots du_1,$$

where the last equation is obtained by substituting $u_i = \sum_{j=1}^{i} t_i$.

Since

$$\Pr(N(t) = n) = e^{-\lambda t} \frac{(\lambda t)^n}{n!}$$

and because the number of events in an interval of length t has a Poisson distribution with parameter λt, the conditional probability computation gives

$$\Pr(S_1 \le s_1, S_2 \le s_2, \ldots, S_n \le s_n \mid N(t) = n)$$

$$= \frac{\Pr(S_1 \le s_1, S_2 \le s_2, \ldots, S_n \le s_n, N(t) = n)}{\Pr(N(t) = n)}$$

$$= \frac{n!}{t^n} \int_{u_1=0}^{s_1} \int_{u_2=u_1}^{s_2} \cdots \int_{u_n=u_{n-1}}^{s_n} du_n \cdots du_1.$$

This is exactly the distribution function of the order statistics, proving the theorem. ∎

8.5. Continuous Time Markov Processes

In Chapter 7 we studied discrete time and discrete space Markov chains. With the introduction of continuous random variables, we can now study the continuous time analogue of Markov chains, where the process spends a random interval of time in a state before moving to the next one. To distinguish between the discrete and continuous processes, when dealing with continuous time we speak of *Markov processes*.

Definition 8.5: *A continuous time random process* $\{X_t \mid t \geq 0\}$ *is* Markovian (*or is called a* Markov *process*) *if, for all* $s, t \geq 0$:

$$\Pr(X(s + t) = x \mid X(u),\ 0 \leq u \leq t) = \Pr(X(s + t) = x \mid X(t)),$$

and this probability is independent of the time t.[2]

The definition says that distribution of the state of the system at time $X(s + t)$, conditioned on the history up to time t, depends only on the state $X(t)$ and is independent of the particular history that led the process to state $X(t)$.

Restricting our discussion to discrete space, continuous time Markov processes, there is another equivalent way of formulating such processes that is more convenient for analysis. Recall that a discrete time Markov chain is determined by a transition matrix $\mathbf{P} = (P_{i,j})$, where $P_{i,j}$ is the probability of a transition from state i to state j in one step. A continuous time Markov process can be expressed as a combination of two random processes as follows.

1. A transition matrix $\mathbf{P} = (p_{i,j})$, where $p_{i,j}$ is the probability that the next state is j given that the current state is i. (We use lowercase letters here for the transition probabilities in order to distinguish them from the transition probabilities for corresponding discrete time processes.) The matrix $\mathbf{P}$ is the transition matrix for what is called the *embedded* or *skeleton* Markov chain of the corresponding Markov process.
2. A vector of parameters $(\theta_1, \theta_2, \ldots)$ such that the distribution of time that the process spends in state i before moving to the next step is exponential with parameter θ_i. The distribution of time spent at a given state must be exponential in order to satisfy the memoryless requirement of the Markov process.

A formal treatment of continuous time Markov processes is more involved than their discrete counterparts, and a full discussion is beyond the scope of this book. We limit our discussion to the question of computing the *stationary distribution* (also called *equilibrium distribution*) for discrete space, continuous time processes, assuming that a stationary distribution exists. As for the discrete time case, the value π_i in a stationary distribution $\bar{\pi}$ gives the limiting probability that the Markov process will be in state i infinitely far out in the future, regardless of the initial state. That is, if we let $P_{j,i}(t)$ be the probability of being in state i at time t when starting from state j at time 0, then

$$\lim_{t \to \infty} P_{j,i}(t) = \pi_i.$$

Similarly, π_i gives the long-term proportion of the time the process is in state i. Furthermore, if the initial state j is chosen from the stationary distribution, then the probability of being in state i at time t is π_i for all t.

---

[2] Technically, as with the discrete time Markov chains, this is a time-homogeneous Markov process; this will be the only type we study in this book.

To determine the stationary distribution, consider the derivative $P'_{j,i}(t)$:

$$P'_{j,i}(t) = \lim_{h \to 0} \frac{P_{j,i}(t+h) - P_{j,i}(t)}{h}$$

$$= \lim_{h \to 0} \frac{\sum_k P_{j,k}(t) P_{k,i}(h) - P_{j,i}(t)}{h}$$

$$= \lim_{h \to 0} \left(\sum_{k \neq i} \frac{P_{k,i}(h)}{h} P_{j,k}(t) - \frac{1 - P_{i,i}(h)}{h} P_{j,i}(t) \right).$$

Since the distribution of time spent at state k is exponential with parameter θ_k, we can use the properties of the Poisson process to observe that, as h tends to zero, the limiting probability of a transition out of state k in an interval of length h is $h\theta_k$, and the limiting probability of more than one transition is 0. Thus,

$$\lim_{h \to 0} \frac{P_{k,i}(h)}{h} = \theta_k p_{k,i}.$$

Similarly, $1 - P_{i,i}(h)$ is the probability that a transition occurs over the interval of time h, and the transition is not from state i back to itself. Thus,

$$\lim_{h \to 0} \frac{1 - P_{i,i}(h)}{h} = \theta_i (1 - p_{i,i}).$$

We now assume that we can interchange the limit and the summation; we emphasize that this interchange is not always justified for countably infinite spaces. Subject to this assumption,

$$\lim_{h \to 0} \left(\sum_{k \neq i} \frac{P_{k,i}(h)}{h} P_{j,k}(t) - \frac{1 - P_{i,i}(h)}{h} P_{j,i}(t) \right)$$

$$= \sum_{k \neq i} \theta_k p_{k,i} P_{j,k}(t) - P_{j,i}(t)(\theta_i - \theta_i p_{i,i})$$

$$= \sum_k \theta_k p_{k,i} P_{j,k}(t) - \theta_i P_{j,i}(t).$$

Taking the limit as $t \to \infty$, we have

$$\lim_{t \to \infty} P'_{j,i}(t) = \lim_{t \to \infty} \sum_k \theta_k p_{k,i} P_{j,k}(t) - \theta_i P_{i,i}(t) = \sum_k \theta_k p_{k,i} \pi_k - \theta_i \pi_i.$$

If the process has a stationary distribution, it must be that

$$\lim_{t \to \infty} P'_{j,i}(t) = 0.$$

Otherwise, $P_{j,i}(t)$ would not converge to a stationary value. Hence, in the stationary distribution $\bar{\pi}$ we have the following *rate equations*:

$$\pi_i \theta_i = \sum_k \pi_k \theta_k p_{k,i}. \tag{8.4}$$

This set of equations has a nice interpretation. The expression on the left, $\pi_i \theta_i$, is the rate at which transitions occur out of state i. The expression on the right, $\sum_k \pi_k \theta_k p_{k,i}$, is the rate at which transitions occur into state i. (A transition that goes from state i back to state i is counted both as a transition into and as a transition out of state i.) At the stationary distribution, these rates must be equal, so that the long-term rates of transitions into and out of the state are equal. This equalization of rates into and out of every state provides a simple, intuitive way to find stationary distributions for continuous Markovian processes. This observation can be generalized to sets of states, showing that a result similar to the cut-set equations of Theorem 7.9 for discrete time Markov chains can be formulated for continuous time Markov processes.

If the exponential distributions governing the time spent in all of the states have the same parameter, so that all the θ_i are equal, then Eqn. (8.4) becomes

$$\pi_i = \sum_k \pi_k p_{k,i}.$$

This corresponds to

$$\bar{\pi} = \bar{\pi}\mathbf{P},$$

where $\mathbf{P}$ is the transition matrix of the embedded Markov chain. We can conclude that the stationary distribution of the continuous time process is the same as the stationary distribution of the embedded Markov chain in this case.

8.6. Example: Markovian Queues

Queues appear in many basic applications in computer science. In operating systems, schedulers can hold tasks in a queue until the processor or other required resources are available. In parallel or distributed programming, threads can queue for a critical section that allows access to only one thread at a time. In networks, packets are queued while waiting to be forwarded by a router. Even before computer systems were prevalent, queues were widely studied to understand the performance of telephone networks, where similar scheduling issues arise. In this section we analyze some of the most basic queueing models, which use Poisson processes to model the stochastic process of customers arriving at a queue and exponentially distributed random variables to model the time required for service.

In what follows, we refer to queue models using the standard notation $Y/Z/n$, where Y represents the distribution of the incoming stream of customers, Z represents the service time distribution, and n represents the number of servers. The standard notation for a Markovian or memoryless distribution is M. Thus, $M/M/n$ stands for a queue model with customers arriving according to a Poisson process and served by n servers having identical and independent exponentially distributed service times. Other queueing models include the $M/M/\infty$ model, where there are an infinite number of servers, and the $M/G/1$ model, where the G indicates that the service time can be any arbitrary general distribution.

A queue must also have a rule for determining the order in which customers are served. Unless otherwise specified, we assume that a queue follows the First In First Out (FIFO) rule, where customers are served in order of their arrival.

8.6.1. *M/M/1 Queue in Equilibrium*

Assume that customers arrive to a queue according to a Poisson process with parameter λ, and assume they are served by one server. The service times for the customers are independent and exponentially distributed with parameter μ.

Let $M(t)$ be the number of customers in the queue at time t. Since both the arrival process and the service time have memoryless distributions, the process $\{M(t) \mid t \geq 0\}$ defines a continuous time Markov process. We consider the stationary distribution for this process.

Let

$$P_k(t) = \Pr(M(t) = k)$$

denote the probability that the queue has k customers at time t. We use the fact that, in the limit as h approaches 0, the probability of an arrival (respectively, a departure) over a time interval is λh (respectively, μh). Thus,

$$
\begin{aligned}
\frac{dP_0(t)}{dt} &= \lim_{h \to 0} \frac{P_0(t+h) - P_0(t)}{h} \\
&= \lim_{h \to 0} \frac{P_0(t)(1 - \lambda h) + P_1(t)\mu h - P_0(t)}{h} \\
&= -\lambda P_0(t) + \mu P_1(t),
\end{aligned}
\tag{8.5}
$$

and for $k \geq 1$,

$$
\begin{aligned}
\frac{dP_k(t)}{dt} &= \lim_{h \to 0} \frac{P_k(t+h) - P_k(t)}{h} \\
&= \lim_{h \to 0} \frac{P_k(t)(1 - \lambda h - \mu h) + P_{k-1}(t)\lambda h + P_{k+1}(t)\mu h - P_k(t)}{h} \\
&= -(\lambda + \mu)P_k(t) + \lambda P_{k-1}(t) + \mu P_{k+1}(t).
\end{aligned}
\tag{8.6}
$$

In equilibrium,

$$\frac{dP_k(t)}{dt} = 0 \text{ for } k = 0, 1, 2, \ldots.$$

If the system converges to a stationary distribution[3] $\bar{\pi}$, then applying Eqn. (8.5) yields

$$\mu \pi_1 = \lambda \pi_0.$$

This equation has a simple interpretation in terms of rates. In equilibrium, the rate into the state where there are no customers in the queue is $\mu \pi_1$; the rate out is $\lambda \pi_0$. These two rates must be equal. If we write this as $\pi_1 = \pi_0(\lambda/\mu)$, then Eqn. (8.6) and a simple induction give

$$\pi_k = \pi_{k-1}\left(\frac{\lambda}{\mu}\right) = \pi_0 \left(\frac{\lambda}{\mu}\right)^k.$$

---

[3] Again, the proof that the system indeed converges relies on renewal theory and is beyond the scope of this book.

Since $\sum_{k \geq 0} \pi_k = 1$, we must have

$$\pi_0 \sum_{k \geq 0} \left(\frac{\lambda}{\mu} \right)^k = 1. \tag{8.7}$$

Assuming that $\lambda < \mu$, it follows that

$$\pi_0 = 1 - \frac{\lambda}{\mu} \quad \text{and} \quad \pi_k = \left(1 - \frac{\lambda}{\mu} \right) \left(\frac{\lambda}{\mu} \right)^k.$$

If $\lambda > \mu$, then the summation in Eqn. (8.7) does not converge and, in fact, the system does not reach a stationary distribution. This is intuitively clear; if the rate of arrival of new customers is larger than the rate of service completions, then the system cannot reach a stationary distribution. If $\lambda = \mu$, the system also cannot reach an equilibrium distribution, as discussed in Exercise 8.23.

To compute the expected number of customers in the system in equilibrium, which we denote by L, we write

$$
\begin{aligned}
L &= \sum_{k=0}^{\infty} k \pi_k \\
&= \frac{\lambda}{\mu} \sum_{k=1}^{\infty} k \left(1 - \frac{\lambda}{\mu} \right) \left(\frac{\lambda}{\mu} \right)^{k-1} \\
&= \frac{\lambda}{\mu} \frac{1}{1 - \lambda/\mu} \\
&= \frac{\lambda}{\mu - \lambda},
\end{aligned}
$$

where in the third equation we used the fact that the sum is the expectation of a geometric random variable with parameter $1 - \lambda/\mu$.

It is interesting that we have nowhere used the fact that the service rule was to serve the customer that had been waiting the longest. Indeed, since all service times are exponentially distributed and since the exponential distribution is memoryless, all customers appear equivalent to the queue in terms of the distribution of the service time required until they leave, regardless of how long they have already been served. Thus, our equations for the equilibrium distribution and the expected number of customers in the system hold for any service rule that serves some customer whenever at least one customer is in the queue.

Next we compute the expected time a customer spends in the system when the system is in equilibrium, denoted by W, assuming a FIFO queue. Let $L(k)$ denote the event that a new customer finds k customers in the queue. We can write

$$W = \sum_{k=0}^{\infty} \mathbf{E}[W \mid L(k)] \Pr(L(k)).$$

Since the service times are independent, memoryless, and have expectation $1/\mu$, it follows that

$$\mathbf{E}[W \mid L(k)] = (k+1)\frac{1}{\mu}.$$

To compute $\Pr(L(k))$, we observe that if the system is in equilibrium then the rate of transitions out of state k is $\pi_k\theta_k$, where $\theta_0 = \lambda$ and $\theta_k = \lambda + \mu$ for $k \geq 1$. Applying Lemma 8.5, the probability that the next transition from state k is caused by the arrival of a new customer is λ/θ_k. Therefore, the rate at which customers arrive and find k customers already in the queue is

$$\pi_k\theta_k\frac{\lambda}{\theta_k} = \pi_k\lambda.$$

Since the total rate of new arrivals to the system is λ, we conclude that the probability that a new arrival finds k customers in the system is

$$\Pr(L(k)) = \frac{\pi_k\lambda}{\lambda} = \pi_k.$$

This is an example of the PASTA principle, which states that Poisson Arrivals See Time Averages. That is, if a Markov process with Poisson arrivals has a stationary distribution and if the fraction of time the system is in state k is π_k, then π_k is also the proportion of arrivals that find the system in state k when they arrive. The PASTA principle, which is due to the independence and memoryless properties of the Poisson process, is a useful tool that often simplifies analysis. A proof of the PASTA principle for more general situations is beyond the scope of this book.

We can now compute

$$\begin{aligned}
W &= \sum_{k=0}^{\infty} \mathbf{E}[W \mid L(k)] \Pr(L(k)) \\
&= \sum_{k=0}^{\infty} \frac{k+1}{\mu}\pi_k \\
&= \frac{1}{\mu}\left(1 + \sum_{k=0}^{\infty} k\pi_k\right) \\
&= \frac{1}{\mu}(1 + L) \\
&= \frac{1}{\mu}\left(1 + \frac{\lambda}{\mu - \lambda}\right) \\
&= \frac{1}{\mu - \lambda} \\
&= \frac{L}{\lambda}.
\end{aligned}$$

The relationship $L = \lambda W$ is known as Little's result, and it holds not only for $M/M/1$ queues but for any stable queueing system. The proof of this fundamental result is beyond the scope of this book.

Although the $M/M/1$ queue represents a very simple process, it can be useful for studying more complicated processes. For example, suppose that we have several types of customers entering a queue, with each type arriving according to a Poisson process, and that all customers have exponentially distributed service times of mean μ. Since Poisson processes combine, the arrival process to the queue is Poisson, and this can be modeled as an $M/M/1$ queue. Similarly, suppose that we have a single Poisson arrival process, and we establish a separate queue for each type of customer. If each arriving customer is of type i with some fixed probability p_i, then the Poisson process splits into independent Poisson processes for each type of customer, and hence the queue for each type is an $M/M/1$ queue. This type of splitting might occur, for example, if we use separate processors for different types of jobs in a computer network.

8.6.2. $M/M/1/K$ Queue in Equilibrium

An $M/M/1/K$ queue is an $M/M/1$ queue with bounded queue size. If a customer arrives while the queue already has K customers, then this customer leaves the system instead of joining the queue. Models with bounded queue size are useful for applications such as network routers, where packets that arrive once the packet buffer is full must be dropped.

The system is entirely similar to the previous example. In equilibrium we have

$$\pi_k = \begin{cases} \pi_0(\lambda/\mu)^k & \text{for } k \leq K, \\ 0 & \text{for } k > K, \end{cases}$$

and

$$\pi_0 = \frac{1}{\sum_{k=0}^{K}(\lambda/\mu)^k}.$$

These equations define a proper probability distribution for any $\lambda, \mu > 0$, and we no longer require that $\lambda < \mu$.

8.6.3. The Number of Customers in an $M/M/\infty$ Queue

Suppose new users join a peer-to-peer network according to a Poisson process with rate λ. The length of time a user stays connected to the network has exponential distribution with parameter μ. Assume that, at time 0, no users were connected to the network. Let $M(t)$ be the number of connected users at time t. What is the distribution of $M(t)$?

We can view this process as a Markovian queue with an unlimited number of servers. A customer starts being served the moment she joins the system and leaves when she is done. We demonstrate two ways of analyzing this process. We first use the rate equations (8.4) to compute the stationary distribution for the process. The second approach is more complex, but it yields more information: we explicitly compute the distribution of the number of customers in the system at time t and then consider the limit as t goes to infinity.

To write the rate equations of the process, we observe that if (at a given time) there are $k \geq 0$ customers in the system, then the next event can be either termination of service of one of the k current customers or the arrival of a new customer. Thus, the time to the first event is the minimum of $k + 1$ independent exponentially distributed random variables; k of these variables have parameter μ, and one has parameter λ. Applying Lemma 8.5 shows that, when there are k customers in the system, the time to the first event has an exponential distribution with parameter $k\mu + \lambda$. Furthermore, the lemma implies that, given that an event occurs, the probability that the event is an arrival of a new customer is

$$p_{k,k+1} = \frac{\lambda}{\lambda + k\mu},$$

and when $k \geq 1$ the probability that the event is the departure of a customer is

$$p_{k,k-1} = \frac{k\mu}{\lambda + k\mu}.$$

Plugging these values into (8.4), we have that the stationary distribution $\bar{\pi}$ satisfies

$$\pi_0 \lambda = \pi_1 \mu$$

and, for $k \geq 1$,

$$\pi_k(\lambda + k\mu) = \pi_{k-1}\lambda + \pi_{k+1}(k+1)\mu. \tag{8.8}$$

We rewrite (8.8) as

$$\pi_{k+1}(k+1)\mu = \pi_k(\lambda + k\mu) - \pi_{k-1}\lambda$$
$$= \pi_k\lambda + \pi_k k\mu - \pi_{k-1}\lambda.$$

A simple induction yields that

$$\pi_k k\mu = \pi_{k-1}\lambda,$$

and therefore

$$\pi_{k+1} = \frac{\lambda}{\mu(k+1)}\pi_k.$$

Now, again a simple induction yields

$$\pi_k = \pi_0 \left(\frac{\lambda}{\mu}\right)^k \frac{1}{k!},$$

and therefore

$$1 = \sum_{k=0}^{\infty} \pi_0 \left(\frac{\lambda}{\mu}\right)^k \frac{1}{k!} = \pi_0 e^{\lambda/\mu}.$$

We conclude that $\pi_0 = e^{-\lambda/\mu}$ and, more generally,

$$\pi_k = \frac{e^{-\lambda/\mu}(\lambda/\mu)^k}{k!},$$

so that the equilibrium distribution is the discrete Poisson distribution with parameter λ/μ.

We now proceed with our second approach: computing the distribution of the number of customers in the system at time t, denoted by $M(t)$, and then considering the limit of $M(t)$ as t goes to infinity. Let $N(t)$ be the total number of users that have joined the network in the interval $[0, t]$. Since $N(t)$ has a Poisson distribution, we can condition on this value and write

$$\Pr(M(t) = j) = \sum_{n=0}^{\infty} \Pr(M(t) = j \mid N(t) = n) e^{-\lambda t} \frac{(\lambda t)^n}{n!}. \tag{8.9}$$

If a user joins the network at time x, then the probability that she is still connected at time t is $e^{-\mu(t-x)}$. From Section 8.4.3, we know that the arrival time of an arbitrary user is uniform on $[0, t]$. Thus, the probability that an arbitrary user is still connected at time t is given by

$$p = \int_0^t e^{-\mu(t-x)} \frac{dx}{t} = \frac{1}{\mu t}(1 - e^{-\mu t}).$$

Because the events for different users are independent, for $j \le n$ we have

$$\Pr(M(t) = j \mid N(t) = n) = \binom{n}{j} p^j (1 - p)^{n-j}.$$

Plugging this value into Eqn. (8.9), we find that

$$\Pr(M(t) = j) = \sum_{n=j}^{\infty} \binom{n}{j} p^j (1 - p)^{n-j} e^{-\lambda t} \frac{(\lambda t)^n}{n!}$$

$$= e^{-\lambda t} \frac{(\lambda t p)^j}{j!} \sum_{n=j}^{\infty} \frac{(\lambda t (1 - p))^{n-j}}{(n - j)!}$$

$$= e^{-\lambda t} \frac{(\lambda t p)^j}{j!} \sum_{m=0}^{\infty} \frac{(\lambda t (1 - p))^m}{m!}$$

$$= e^{-\lambda t} \frac{(\lambda t p)^j}{j!} e^{\lambda t (1-p)}$$

$$= e^{-\lambda t p} \frac{(\lambda t p)^j}{j!}.$$

Thus, the number of users at time t has a Poisson distribution with parameter $\lambda t p$. Since

$$\lim_{t \to \infty} \lambda t p = \lim_{t \to \infty} \lambda t \frac{1}{\mu t}(1 - e^{-\mu t}) = \frac{\lambda}{\mu},$$

it follows that, in the limit, the number of customers has a Poisson distribution with parameter λ/μ, matching our previous calculation.

8.7. Exercises

Exercise 8.1: Let X and Y be independent, uniform random variables on $[0, 1]$. Find the density function and distribution function for $X + Y$.

Exercise 8.2: Let X and Y be independent, exponentially distributed random variables with parameter 1. Find the density function and distribution function for $X + Y$.

Exercise 8.3: Let X be a uniform random variable on $[0, 1]$. Determine $\Pr(X \le 1/2 \mid 1/4 \le X \le 3/4)$ and $\Pr(X \le 1/4 \mid (X \le 1/3) \cup (X \ge 2/3))$.

Exercise 8.4: We agree to try to meet between 12 and 1 for lunch at our favorite sandwich shop. Because of our busy schedules, neither of us is sure when we'll arrive; we assume that, for each of us, our arrival time is uniformly distributed over the hour. So that neither of us has to wait too long, we agree that we will each wait exactly 15 minutes for the other to arrive, and then leave. What is the probability we actually meet each other for lunch?

Exercise 8.5: In Lemma 8.3, we found the expectation of the smallest of n independent uniform random variables over $[0, 1]$ by directly computing the probability that it was larger than y for $0 \le y \le 1$. Perform a similar calculation to find the probability that the kth smallest of the n random variables is larger than y, and use this to show that its expected value is $k/(n + 1)$.

Exercise 8.6: Let $X_1, X_2, \ldots, X_n$ be independent exponential random variables with parameter 1. Find the expected value of the kth largest of the n random variables.

Exercise 8.7: Consider a complete graph on n vertices. Each edge is assigned a weight chosen independently and uniformly at random from the real interval $[0, 1]$. Show that the expected weight of the minimum spanning tree of this graph is at least $1 - 1/\left(1 + \binom{n}{2}\right)$. Find a similar bound when each edge is independently assigned a weight from an exponential distribution with parameter 1.

Exercise 8.8: Consider a complete graph on n vertices. Each edge is assigned a weight chosen independently and uniformly at random from the real interval $[0, 1]$. We propose the following greedy method for finding a small-weight Hamiltonian cycle in the graph. At each step, there is a head vertex. Initially the head is vertex 1. At each step, we find the edge of least weight between the current head vertex and a new vertex that has never been the head. We add this edge to the cycle and set the head vertex to the new vertex. After $n - 1$ steps, we have a Hamiltonian path, which we complete to make a Hamiltonian cycle by adding the edge from the last head vertex back to vertex 1. What is the expected weight of the Hamiltonian cycle found by this greedy approach? Also, find the expectation when each edge is independently assigned a weight from an exponential distribution with parameter 1.

Exercise 8.9: You would like to write a simulation that uses exponentially distributed random variables. Your system has a random number generator that produces

236

independent, uniformly distributed numbers from the real interval $(0, 1)$. Give a procedure that transforms a uniform random number as given to an exponentially distributed random variable with parameter λ.

Exercise 8.10: Let n points be placed uniformly at random on the boundary of a circle of circumference 1. These n points divide the circle into n arcs. Let Z_i for $1 \le Z_i \le n$ be the length of these arcs in some arbitrary order.

(a) Prove that all Z_i are at most $c \ln n/(n - 1)$ with probability at least $1 - 1/n^{c-1}$.
(b) Prove that, for sufficiently large n, there exists a constant c' such that at least one Z_i is at least $c' \ln n$ with probability at least $1/2$. (*Hint:* Use the second moment method.)
(c) Prove that all Z_i are at least $1/2n^2$ with probability at least $1/2$.
(d) Prove that, for sufficiently large n, there exists a constant c' such that at least one Z_i is at most c'/n^2 with probability at least $1/2$. (*Hint:* Use the second moment method.)
(e) Explain how these results relate to the following problem: $X_1, X_2, \ldots, X_{n-1}$ are values chosen independently and uniformly at random from the real interval $[0, 1]$. We let $Y_1, Y_2, \ldots, Y_{n-1}$ represent these values in increasing sorted order, and we also define $Y_0 = 0$ and $Y_n = 1$. The points Y_i break the unit interval into n segments. What can we say about the shortest and longest of these segments?

Exercise 8.11: Bucket sort is a simple sorting algorithm discussed in Section 5.2.2.

(a) Explain how to implement Bucket sort so that its expected running time is $O(n)$ when the n elements to be sorted are independent, uniform random numbers that are chosen from $[0, 1]$.
(b) We now consider how to implement Bucket sort when the elements to be sorted are not necessarily uniform over an interval. Specifically, suppose the elements to be sorted are numbers of the form $X + Y$, where (for each element) X and Y are independent, uniform random numbers chosen from $[0, 1]$. How can you modify the buckets so that Bucket sort still has expected running time $O(n)$? What if the elements to be sorted were numbers of the form $\max(X, Y)$ instead of $X + Y$?

Exercise 8.12: Let n points be placed uniformly at random on the boundary of a circle of circumference 1. These n points divide the circle into n arcs. Let Z_i for $1 \le Z_i \le n$ be the length of these arcs in some arbitrary order, and let X be the number of Z_i that are at least $1/n$. Find $\mathbf{E}[X]$ and $\mathbf{Var}[X]$.

Exercise 8.13: A digital camera needs two batteries. You buy a pack of n batteries, labeled 1 to n. Initially, you install batteries 1 and 2. Whenever a battery is drained, you immediately replace the drained battery with the lowest numbered unused battery. Assume that each battery lasts for an amount of time that is exponentially distributed with mean μ before being drained, independent of all other batteries. Eventually, all the batteries but one will be drained.

(a) Find the probability that the battery numbered i is the one that is not eventually drained.

(b) Find the expected time your camera will be able to run with this pack of batteries.

Exercise 8.14: Let $X_1, X_2, \ldots$ be exponential random variables with parameter 1.

(a) Argue that $X_1 + X_2$ is not an exponential random variable.

(b) Let N be a geometric random variable with parameter p. Prove that $\sum_{i=1}^{N} X_i$ is exponentially distributed with parameter p.

Exercise 8.15: **(a)** Let $X_1, X_2, \ldots$ be a sequence of independent exponential random variables, each with mean 1. Given a positive real number k, let N be defined by

$$N = \min \left\{ n : \sum_{i=1}^{n} X_i > k \right\}.$$

That is, N is the smallest number for which the sum of the first N of the X_i is larger than k. Determine $\mathbf{E}[N]$.

(b) Let $X_1, X_2, \ldots$ be a sequence of independent uniform random variables on the interval $(0, 1)$. Given a positive real number k with $0 < k < 1$, let N be defined by

$$N = \min \left\{ n : \prod_{i=1}^{n} X_i < k \right\}.$$

That is, N is the smallest number for which the product of the first N of the X_i is smaller than k. Determine $\mathbf{E}[N]$. (*Hint:* You may find Exercise 8.9 helpful.)

Exercise 8.16: There are n tasks that are given to n processors. Each task has two phases, and the time for each phase is given by an exponentially distributed random variable with parameter 1. The times for all phases and for all tasks are independent. We say that a task is half-done if it has finished one of its two phases.

(a) Derive an expression for the probability that there are k tasks that are half-done at the instant when exactly one task becomes completely done.

(b) Derive an expression for the expected time until exactly one task becomes completely done.

(c) Explain how this problem is related to the birthday paradox.

Exercise 8.17: Prove Theorem 8.11.

Exercise 8.18: Complete the proof of Theorem 8.13 by showing formally that, if $N_1(t)$ and $N_2(t)$ are independent, then so are $N_1(t)$ and $N_2(u)$ for any $t, u > 0$.

Exercise 8.19: You are waiting at a bus stop to catch a bus across town. There are actually n different bus lines you can take, each following a different route. Which bus you decide to take will depend on which bus gets to the bus stop first. As long as you are waiting, the time you have to wait for a bus on the ith line is exponentially distributed with mean μ_i minutes. Once you get on a bus on the ith line, it will take you t_i minutes to get across town.

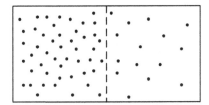

Figure 8.6: The Ehrenfest model.

Design an algorithm for deciding – when a bus arrives – whether or not you should get on the bus, assuming your goal is to minimize the expected time to cross town. (*Hint:* You want to determine the set of buses that you want to take as soon as they arrive. There are 2^n possible sets, which is far too large for an efficient algorithm. Argue that you need only consider a small number of these sets.)

Exercise 8.20: Given a discrete space, continuous time Markov process $X(t)$, we can derive a discrete time Markov chain $Z(t)$ by considering the states the process visits. That is, let $Z(0) = X(0)$, let $Z(1)$ be the state that process $X(t)$ first moves to after time $t = 0$, let $Z(2)$ be the next state process $X(t)$ moves to, and so on. (If the Markov process $X(t)$ makes a transition from state i to state i, which can occur when $p_{i,i} \neq 0$ in the associated transition matrix, then the Markov chain $Z(t)$ should also make a transition from state i to state i.)

(a) Suppose that, in the process $X(t)$, the time spent in state i is exponentially distributed with parameter $\theta_i = \theta$ (which is the same for all i). Further suppose that the process $X(t)$ has a stationary distribution. Show that the Markov chain $Z(t)$ has the same stationary distribution.

(b) Give an example showing that, if the θ_i are not all equal, then the stationary distributions for $X(t)$ and $Z(t)$ may differ.

Exercise 8.21: The *Ehrenfest* model is a basic model used in physics. There are n particles moving randomly in a container. We consider the number of particles in the left and right halves of the container. A particle in one half of the container moves to the other half after an amount of time that is exponentially distributed with parameter 1, independently of all other particles. See Figure 8.6.

(a) Find the stationary distribution of this process.

(b) What state has the highest probability in the stationary distribution? Can you suggest an explanation for this?

Exercise 8.22: The following type of geometric random graph arises in the analysis of dynamic wireless and sensor networks. We have n points uniformly distributed in a square S of area n. Each point is connected to its k closest points in the square. Denote this random graph by $G_{n,k}$. We show that there is a constant $c > 0$ such that if $k = c \log n$ then with probability at least $1 - 1/n$ the graph $G_{n,k}$ is connected. Consider tessellating (tiling with smaller squares) the square S with $n/(b \log n)$ squares of area $b \log n$ each, for some constant b; we assume that $b \log n$ divides n for convenience.

(a) Choose constants b and c_1 such that with sufficiently high probability, every square has at least 1 point, and at most $c_1 \log n$ points.

(b) Conclude that with $c \geq 25c_1$, the graph is connected with probability at least $1 - 1/n$.

Exercise 8.23: We can obtain a discrete time Markov chain from the $M/M/1$ queueing process in the manner described in Exercise 8.20. The discrete time chain tracks the number of customers in the queue. It is useful to allow departure events to occur with rate λ at the queue even when it is empty; this does not affect the queue behavior, but it gives transitions from state 0 to state 0 in the corresponding Markov chain.

(a) Describe the possible transitions of this discrete-time chain and give their probabilities.

(b) Show that the stationary distribution of this chain when $\lambda < \mu$ is the same as for the $M/M/1$ process.

(c) Show that, in the case $\lambda = \mu$, there is no valid stationary distribution for the Markov chain.

Exercise 8.24: In a *tandem* queue, customers arrive to an $M/M/1$ queue according to a Poisson process of rate λ with service times independent and exponentially distributed with parameter μ_1. After completing service at this first queue, the customers proceed immediately to a second queue, also being served by a single server, where service times are independent and exponentially distributed with parameter μ_2. Find the stationary distribution of this system. (*Hint:* Try to generalize the form of the stationary distribution for a single queue.)

Exercise 8.25: Write a program to simulate the model of balls and bins with feedback.

(a) Start your simulation with 51 balls in bin 1 and 49 balls in bin 2, using $p = 2$. Run your program 100 times, having it stop each time one bin has 60% of the balls. On average, how many balls are in the bins when the program stops? How often does bin 1 have the majority?

(b) Perform the same experiment as in part (a) but start with 52 balls in bin 1 and 48 balls in bin 2. How much does this change your answers?

(c) Perform the same experiment as in part (a) but start with 102 balls in bin 1 and 98 balls in bin 2. How much does this change your answers?

(d) Perform the same experiment as in part (a), but now use $p = 1.5$. How much does this change your answers?

Exercise 8.26: We consider here one approach for studying a FIFO queue with a constant service time of duration 1 and Poisson arrivals with parameter $\lambda < 1$. We replace the constant service time by k exponentially distributed service stages, each of mean duration $1/k$. A customer must pass through all k stages before leaving the queue, and once one customer begins going through the k stages, no other customer can receive service until that customer finishes.

(a) Derive Chernoff bounds for the probability that the total time taken in k exponentially distributed stages, each of mean $1/k$, deviates significantly from 1.

(b) Derive a set of equations that define the stationary distribution for this situation. (*Hint:* Try letting π_j be the limiting probability of having j stages of service left to be served the queue. Each waiting customer requires k stages; the one being served requires between 1 and k stages.) You should not try to solve these equations to give a closed form for π_j.

(c) Use these equations to *numerically* determine the average number of customers in the queue in equilibrium, say for $\lambda = 0.8$ and for $k = 10, 20, 30, 40$, and 50. Discuss whether your results seem to be converging as k increases, and compare the expected number of customers to an $M/M/1$ queue with arrival rate $\lambda < 1$ and expected service time $\mu = 1$.

Exercise 8.27: Write a simulation for a bank of n $M/M/1$ FIFO queues, each with Poisson arrivals of rate $\lambda < 1$ per second and each with service times exponentially distributed with mean 1 second. Your simulation should run for t seconds and return the average amount of time spent in the system per customer who completed service. You should present results for your simulations for $n = 100$ and for $t = 10{,}000$ seconds with $\lambda = 0.5, 0.8, 0.9$, and 0.99.

A natural way to write the simulation that we now describe is to keep a *priority queue* of events. Such a queue stores the times of all pending events, such as the next time a customer will arrive or the next time a customer will finish service at a queue. A priority queue can answer queries of the form, "What is the next event?" Priority queues are often implemented as heaps, for example.

When a customer bound for queue k arrives, the arrival time for the next customer to queue k must then be calculated and entered in the priority queue. If queue k is empty, the time that the arriving customer will complete service should be put in the priority queue. If queue k is not empty, the customer is put at the tail of the queue. If a queue is not empty after completing service for a customer, then the time that the next customer (at the head of the queue) will complete service should be calculated and put in the priority queue. You will have to track each customer's arrival time and completion time.

You may find ways to simplify this general scheme. For example, instead of considering a separate arrival process for each queue, you can combine them into a single arrival process based on what we know from Section 8.4.2. Explain whatever simplifications you use.

You may wish to use Exercise 8.9 to help construct exponentially distributed random variables for your simulation.

Modify your simulation so that, instead of service times being exponentially distributed with mean 1 second, they are always exactly 1 second. Again present results for your simulation for $n = 100$ and for $t = 10{,}000$ seconds with $\lambda = 0.5, 0.8, 0.9$, and 0.99. Do customers complete more quickly with exponentially distributed service times or constant service times?

241

CHAPTER NINE

The Normal Distribution

The normal (or Gaussian) distribution plays a central role in probability theory and statistics. Empirically, many real-world observable quantities, such as height, weight, grades, and measurement error, are often well approximated by the normal distribution. Furthermore, the central limit theorem states that under very general conditions the distribution of the average of a large number of independent random variables converges to the normal distribution.

In this chapter we introduce the basic properties of univariate and multivariate normal random variables, prove the central limit theorem, compute maximum likelihood estimates for the parameters of the normal distribution, and demonstrate the application of the Expectation Maximization (EM) algorithm to the analysis of a mixture of Gaussian distributions.[1]

9.1. The Normal Distribution

9.1.1. *The Standard Normal Distribution*

The *standard normal distribution*, denoted $N(0, 1)$, is the basic building block of all univariate and multivariate normal distributions. We say a standard normal random variable Z comes from $N(0, 1)$, or just say that Z is a standard normal random variable, where the meaning is clear. The standard normal distribution is a continuous distribution over the real numbers, with density function

$$\phi(z) = \frac{1}{\sqrt{2\pi}} e^{-z^2/2},$$

and distribution function

$$\Phi(z) = \frac{1}{\sqrt{2\pi}} \int_{-\infty}^{z} e^{-x^2/2} dx.$$

---

[1] Following the conventions of the different communities we use the term normal distribution in the context of probability theory and the term Gaussian distribution in the context of machine learning.

Because (see Exercise 9.1)

$$\int_{-\infty}^{\infty} \frac{1}{\sqrt{2\pi}} e^{-x^2/2} dx = 1,$$

the density function defines a proper probability distribution.

While the distribution function $\Phi(z)$ is well-defined for any z, it does not have a closed form expression. The actual values of the standard normal distribution can be computed numerically, as seen in Table 9.1. The distribution is related to what is known as the error function in statistics, which is commonly denoted by

$$\text{erf}(z) = \frac{2}{\sqrt{\pi}} \int_0^z e^{-x^2} dx,$$

and it is straightforward to check that

$$\Phi(z) = \frac{1}{2} + \frac{1}{2}\text{erf}\left(\frac{z}{\sqrt{2}}\right).$$

Since the density of a standard normal random variable Z is symmetric with respect to $z = 0$, it follows that $\mathbf{E}[Z] = 0$. The variance of Z can be found by using integration by parts (where the parts used below are $u = x$ and $dv = xe^{-x^2/2}dx$):

$$\mathbf{Var}[Z] = \mathbf{E}[Z^2] = \frac{1}{\sqrt{2\pi}} \int_{-\infty}^{\infty} x^2 e^{-x^2/2} dx$$

$$= \frac{1}{\sqrt{2\pi}} \int_{-\infty}^{\infty} (x)\left(xe^{-x^2/2}\right) dx$$

$$= -\frac{1}{\sqrt{2\pi}} xe^{-x^2/2}\big|_{-\infty}^{\infty} + \frac{1}{\sqrt{2\pi}} \int_{-\infty}^{\infty} e^{-x^2/2} dx = 1.$$

In the last equality, the first term is 0, and we have already observed that the second term equals 1.

9.1.2. *The General Univariate Normal Distribution*

The univariate (or single-variable) normal distribution is characterized by two parameters μ and σ, corresponding to the mean and the standard deviation, and is denoted by $N(\mu, \sigma^2)$. Notice that we use the variance rather than the standard deviation in how we denote the normal distribution, for reasons that will become clear later. As before, we may say that X is a normal random variable (with parameters μ and σ) to denote that X is a random variable with a normal distribution.

The density function of a normal random variable X from $N(\mu, \sigma^2)$ is

$$f_X(x) = \frac{1}{\sqrt{2\pi}\sigma} e^{-((x-\mu)/\sigma)^2/2},$$

243

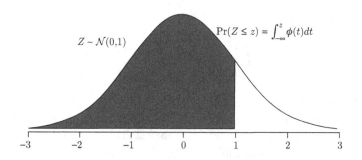

**Table of Distribution Function Φ
of the standard normal $N(0, 1)$ distribution**

z	0.00	0.01	0.02	0.03	0.04	0.05	0.06	0.07	0.08	0.09
0.0	0.5000	0.5040	0.5080	0.5120	0.5160	0.5199	0.5239	0.5279	0.5319	0.5359
0.1	0.5398	0.5438	0.5478	0.5517	0.5557	0.5596	0.5636	0.5675	0.5714	0.5753
0.2	0.5793	0.5832	0.5871	0.5910	0.5948	0.5987	0.6026	0.6064	0.6103	0.6141
0.3	0.6179	0.6217	0.6255	0.6293	0.6331	0.6368	0.6406	0.6443	0.6480	0.6517
0.4	0.6554	0.6591	0.6628	0.6664	0.6700	0.6736	0.6772	0.6808	0.6844	0.6879
0.5	0.6915	0.6950	0.6985	0.7019	0.7054	0.7088	0.7123	0.7157	0.7190	0.7224
0.6	0.7257	0.7291	0.7324	0.7357	0.7389	0.7422	0.7454	0.7486	0.7517	0.7549
0.7	0.7580	0.7611	0.7642	0.7673	0.7704	0.7734	0.7764	0.7794	0.7823	0.7852
0.8	0.7881	0.7910	0.7939	0.7967	0.7995	0.8023	0.8051	0.8078	0.8106	0.8133
0.9	0.8159	0.8186	0.8212	0.8238	0.8264	0.8289	0.8315	0.8340	0.8365	0.8389
1.0	0.8413	0.8438	0.8461	0.8485	0.8508	0.8531	0.8554	0.8577	0.8599	0.8621
1.1	0.8643	0.8665	0.8686	0.8708	0.8729	0.8749	0.8770	0.8790	0.8810	0.8830
1.2	0.8849	0.8869	0.8888	0.8907	0.8925	0.8944	0.8962	0.8980	0.8997	0.9015
1.3	0.9032	0.9049	0.9066	0.9082	0.9099	0.9115	0.9131	0.9147	0.9162	0.9177
1.4	0.9192	0.9207	0.9222	0.9236	0.9251	0.9265	0.9279	0.9292	0.9306	0.9319
1.5	0.9332	0.9345	0.9357	0.9370	0.9382	0.9394	0.9406	0.9418	0.9429	0.9441
1.6	0.9452	0.9463	0.9474	0.9484	0.9495	0.9505	0.9515	0.9525	0.9535	0.9545
1.7	0.9554	0.9564	0.9573	0.9582	0.9591	0.9599	0.9608	0.9616	0.9625	0.9633
1.8	0.9641	0.9649	0.9656	0.9664	0.9671	0.9678	0.9686	0.9693	0.9699	0.9706
1.9	0.9713	0.9719	0.9726	0.9732	0.9738	0.9744	0.9750	0.9756	0.9761	0.9767
2.0	0.9772	0.9778	0.9783	0.9788	0.9793	0.9798	0.9803	0.9808	0.9812	0.9817
2.1	0.9821	0.9826	0.9830	0.9834	0.9838	0.9842	0.9846	0.9850	0.9854	0.9857
2.2	0.9861	0.9864	0.9868	0.9871	0.9875	0.9878	0.9881	0.9884	0.9887	0.9890
2.3	0.9893	0.9896	0.9898	0.9901	0.9904	0.9906	0.9909	0.9911	0.9913	0.9916
2.4	0.9918	0.9920	0.9922	0.9925	0.9927	0.9929	0.9931	0.9932	0.9934	0.9936
2.5	0.9938	0.9940	0.9941	0.9943	0.9945	0.9946	0.9948	0.9949	0.9951	0.9952
2.6	0.9953	0.9955	0.9956	0.9957	0.9959	0.9960	0.9961	0.9962	0.9963	0.9964
2.7	0.9965	0.9966	0.9967	0.9968	0.9969	0.9970	0.9971	0.9972	0.9973	0.9974
2.8	0.9974	0.9975	0.9976	0.9977	0.9977	0.9978	0.9979	0.9979	0.9980	0.9981
2.9	0.9981	0.9982	0.9982	0.9983	0.9984	0.9984	0.9985	0.9985	0.9986	0.9986
3.0	0.9987	0.9987	0.9987	0.9988	0.9988	0.9989	0.9989	0.9989	0.9990	0.9990
3.1	0.9990	0.9991	0.9991	0.9991	0.9992	0.9992	0.9992	0.9992	0.9993	0.9993

Table 9.1: Standard normal distribution table. For $z < 0$ use $\Phi(z) = 1 - \Phi(-z)$.

and its distribution function is

$$F_X(x) = \frac{1}{\sqrt{2\pi}\sigma} \int_{-\infty}^{x} e^{-((t-\mu)/\sigma)^2/2} dt.$$

These expressions generalize the corresponding expressions for standard normal random variables, where $\mu = 0$ and $\sigma = 1$.

Indeed, let X be a normal random variable with parameters μ and σ, and let $Z = (X - \mu)/\sigma$. Then

$$\Pr(Z \leq z) = \Pr(X \leq \sigma z + \mu) = \frac{1}{\sqrt{2\pi}\,\sigma} \int_{-\infty}^{\sigma z + \mu} e^{-((t-\mu)/\sigma)^2/2} dt.$$

Substituting $x = (t - \mu)/\sigma$ and using $dt = \sigma\,dx$, we find the density of the standard normal distribution,

$$\Pr(Z \leq z) = \frac{1}{\sqrt{2\pi}} \int_{-\infty}^{z} e^{-x^2/2} dx = \Phi(z).$$

We see that the normal distribution X is a linear transformation of the standard normal distribution. That is, if X is a normal random variable with parameters μ and σ, then $Z = (X - \mu)/\sigma$ is a standard normal random variable (with mean 0 and variance 1), and similarly, if Z is a standard normal random variable, then $X = \sigma Z + \mu$ is a normal random variable with parameters μ and σ. We have shown the following.

Lemma 9.1: *A random variable has a normal distribution if and only if it is a linear transformation of a standard normal random variable.*

Since a random variable X from the distribution $N(\mu, \sigma^2)$ has the same distribution as $\sigma Z + \mu$, we have that $\mathbf{E}[X] = \mu$ and $\mathbf{Var}[X] = \sigma^2$, so μ and σ are indeed the mean and standard deviation.

Example: Signal Detection

Assume that we have a transmitter that is sending a bit via the encoding $S \in \{-1, +1\}$, and the communication channel adds noise Y to the signal, where Y is a normal random variable with mean 0 and standard deviation σ. The receiver decodes by taking the sign of the received signal, $R = \mathrm{sgn}(S + Y)$. (Here sgn is the sign function, where $\mathrm{sgn}(x) = 1$ if $x > 0$, $\mathrm{sgn}(x) = -1$ if $x < 0$, and by convention $\mathrm{sgn}(0) = 0$.) We find the probability that the decoded message is different from the original message, that is the probability that $R \neq S$.

The probability of an error when $S = 1$ is the probability that $Y \leq -1$:

$$\Pr(Y \leq -1) = \Pr\left(\frac{Y - \mu}{\sigma} \leq \frac{-1 - \mu}{\sigma}\right) = \Phi\left(-\frac{1}{\sigma}\right).$$

Similarly, the probability of an error when $S = -1$ is the probability that $Y \geq 1$:

$$\Pr(Y \geq 1) = 1 - \Pr\left(\frac{Y - \mu}{\sigma} \leq \frac{1 - \mu}{\sigma}\right) = 1 - \Phi\left(\frac{1}{\sigma}\right).$$

By the symmetry of the normal distribution around its mean, $\Phi\left(-\frac{1}{\sigma}\right) = 1 - \Phi\left(\frac{1}{\sigma}\right)$, and the total error probability is $2\left(1 - \Phi\left(\frac{1}{\sigma}\right)\right)$.

We can use Table 9.1 to determine the error probabilities (up to four decimal places). For $\sigma = 0.5, 1, 2$, we find $\Phi(2) = 0.9772$, $\Phi(1) = 0.8413$, and $\Phi(0.50) = 0.6915$. The error probabilities are therefore $0.0456, 0.3174$, and 0.6170, respectively.

9.1.3. *The Moment Generating Function*

We next compute the moment generating function of normal random variable X from $N(\mu, \sigma^2)$. In what follows, let $z = (x - \mu)/\sigma$, and note $\sigma\,dz = dx$.

$$
\begin{aligned}
M_X(t) &= \mathbf{E}[e^{tX}] \\
&= \frac{1}{\sqrt{2\pi}\,\sigma} \int_{x=-\infty}^{\infty} e^{tx} e^{-(x-\mu)^2/(2\sigma^2)}\,dx \\
&= \frac{1}{\sqrt{2\pi}\,\sigma} \int_{z=-\infty}^{\infty} e^{t\sigma z + t\mu} e^{-z^2/2}\,\sigma\,dz \\
&= \frac{1}{\sqrt{2\pi}} e^{\mu t} \int_{z=-\infty}^{\infty} e^{-(z-t\sigma)^2/2 + (t\sigma)^2/2}\,dz \\
&= \left(e^{t^2\sigma^2/2 + \mu t} \right) \frac{1}{\sqrt{2\pi}} \int_{z=-\infty}^{\infty} e^{-(z-t\sigma)^2/2}\,dz \\
&= e^{t^2\sigma^2/2 + \mu t}.
\end{aligned}
$$

Here in the last equality we used the fact that

$$
\frac{1}{\sqrt{2\pi}} \int_{-\infty}^{\infty} e^{-(z-t\sigma)^2/2}\,dz = 1;
$$

to see this, note that

$$
\frac{1}{\sqrt{2\pi}} \int_{-\infty}^{x} e^{-(z-t\sigma)^2/2}\,dz
$$

is the distribution function of a normal random variable with mean $t\sigma$ and standard deviation 1, and hence when x goes to infinity the integral is 1.

We can use the moment generating function to verify our computation of the expectation and variance of the normal distribution from Section 9.1.2.

$$
M_X'(t) = (\mu + t\sigma^2) e^{t^2\sigma^2/2 + \mu t}
$$

and

$$
M_X''(t) = (\mu + t\sigma^2)^2 e^{t^2\sigma^2/2 + \mu t} + \sigma^2 e^{t^2\sigma^2/2 + \mu t}.
$$

Thus, $\mathbf{E}[X] = M'(0) = \mu$, $\mathbf{E}[X^2] = M''(0) = \mu^2 + \sigma^2$, and $\mathbf{Var}[X] = \mathbf{E}[X^2] - (\mathbf{E}[X])^2 = \sigma^2$.

Another important property of the normal distribution is that a linear combination of normal random variables has a normal distribution:

Theorem 9.2: *Let X and Y be independent random variables with distributions $N(\mu_1, \sigma_1^2)$ and $N(\mu_2, \sigma_2^2)$, respectively. Then $X + Y$ is distributed according to the normal distribution $N(\mu_1 + \mu_2, \sigma_1^2 + \sigma_2^2)$.*

Proof: The moment generating function of a sum of independent random variables is the product of their moment generating functions (Theorem 4.3). Thus,

$$
M_{X+Y}(t) = M_Y(t) M_Y(t) = e^{t^2\sigma_1^2/2 + \mu_1 t} e^{t^2\sigma_2^2/2 + \mu_2 t} = e^{t^2(\sigma_1^2 + \sigma_2^2)/2 + (\mu_1 + \mu_2)t}.
$$

The rightmost expression is the moment generating function of a normal distribution. Theorem 4.2 implies that $X + Y$ has a normal distribution with the corresponding parameters. ∎

Using the moment generating function we can also obtain a large deviation bound for a normal random variable.

Theorem 9.3: *Let X have distribution $N(\mu, \sigma^2)$, then*

$$\Pr\left(\left|\frac{X - \mu}{\sigma}\right| \geq a\right) \leq 2e^{-a^2/2}.$$

Proof: Let $Z = (X - \mu)/\sigma$, so Z has distribution $N(0, 1)$. Using the general technique presented in Section 4.2, for any $t > 0$,

$$\Pr(Z \geq a) = \Pr(e^{tZ} \geq e^{ta})$$
$$\leq \frac{\mathbf{E}[e^{tZ}]}{e^{ta}}$$
$$\leq e^{t^2/2 - ta}$$
$$\leq e^{-a^2/2},$$

where in the last inequality we set $t = a$. The case $Z \leq a$ similarly yields the same bound, proving the claim. ∎

9.2.* Limit of the Binomial Distribution

A function similar to the density of the normal distribution appeared first (around 1738) in the De Moivre–Laplace approximation of the binomial distribution. De Moivre used it to approximate the number of heads in a sequence of coin tosses, Laplace extended the result to a sequence of Bernoulli trials. We present this result here since it gives insight into the density function of the normal distribution and to the central limit theorem presented in the next section.

Theorem 9.4: *For a constant p with $0 < p < 1$ and $q = 1 - p$, for $k = np \pm O(\sqrt{npq})$,*

$$\lim_{n \to \infty} \binom{n}{k} p^k (1 - p)^{n-k} = \frac{1}{\sqrt{2\pi npq}} e^{-(k-np)^2/(2npq)}.$$

Proof: Applying Stirling's formula (Lemma 7.3),

$$\lim_{n \to \infty} n! = \sqrt{2\pi n} \left(\frac{n}{e}\right)^n (1 \pm o(1)),$$

247

we have

$$\binom{n}{k}p^k(1-p)^{n-k} = \frac{n!}{k!(n-k)!}p^k(1-p)^{n-k}$$

$$= \frac{\sqrt{2\pi n}}{\sqrt{2\pi k}\sqrt{2\pi(n-k)}}\frac{e^k e^{n-k} n^n}{e^n k^k (n-k)^{n-k}}p^k(1-p)^{n-k}(1\pm o(1))$$

$$= \frac{1}{\sqrt{2\pi n \frac{k}{n}\frac{n-k}{n}}}\left(\frac{k}{np}\right)^{-k}\left(\frac{n-k}{nq}\right)^{-(n-k)}(1\pm o(1)).$$

For $k = np \pm O(\sqrt{npq})$,

$$\lim_{n\to\infty}\frac{1}{\sqrt{2\pi n \frac{k}{n}\frac{n-k}{n}}} = \frac{1}{\sqrt{2\pi npq}}.$$

Let $t = (k - np)/\sqrt{npq} = O(1)$. Then $k = np + t\sqrt{npq}$, and $n - k = nq - t\sqrt{npq}$. Thus

$$\left(\frac{k}{np}\right)^{-k}\left(\frac{n-k}{nq}\right)^{-(n-k)} = \left(1 + \frac{t\sqrt{q}}{\sqrt{np}}\right)^{-k}\left(1 - \frac{t\sqrt{p}}{\sqrt{nq}}\right)^{-(n-k)}.$$

Using the Taylor series expansion

$$\ln(1 + x) = x - \frac{x^2}{2} + O(x^3),$$

we have

$$\ln\left[\left(\frac{k}{np}\right)^{-k}\left(\frac{n-k}{nq}\right)^{-(k-n)}\right]$$

$$= \ln\left[\left(1 + \frac{t\sqrt{q}}{\sqrt{np}}\right)^{-k}\left(1 - \frac{t\sqrt{p}}{\sqrt{nq}}\right)^{-(n-k)}\right]$$

$$= -(np + t\sqrt{npq})\left(\frac{t\sqrt{q}}{\sqrt{np}} - \frac{t^2 q}{2np}\right) - (nq - t\sqrt{npq})\left(-\frac{t\sqrt{p}}{\sqrt{nq}} - \frac{t^2 p}{2nq}\right) + O\left(\frac{t^3}{\sqrt{n}}\right)$$

$$= \left(-t\sqrt{npq} + \frac{t^2 q}{2} - t^2 q\right) + \left(t\sqrt{npq} + \frac{t^2 p}{2} - t^2 p\right) + O\left(\frac{t^3}{\sqrt{n}}\right)$$

$$= -\frac{t^2}{2} + O\left(\frac{t^3}{\sqrt{n}}\right).$$

Thus,

$$\lim_{n\to\infty}\left(\frac{k}{np}\right)^{-k}\left(\frac{n-k}{nq}\right)^{-(k-n)} = e^{-t^2/2}.$$

Combining the two limits we obtain

$$\lim_{n\to\infty}\binom{n}{k}p^k(1-p)^{n-k} = \frac{1}{\sqrt{2\pi npq}}e^{-t^2/2} = \frac{1}{\sqrt{2\pi npq}}e^{-(k-np)^2/(2npq)}. \qquad \blacksquare$$

Theorem 9.4 estimates a discrete probability; it does not define a density function. However, as $n \to \infty$, it implies the following estimate which is a simple version of the central limit theorem for a sum of independent Bernoulli random variables:

$$\lim_{n \to \infty} \Pr\left(a \le \frac{k - np}{\sqrt{npq}} \le b\right) = \sum_{k=np-a\sqrt{npq}}^{np+b\sqrt{npq}} \frac{1}{\sqrt{2\pi npq}} e^{-(k-np)^2/(2npq)}$$

$$\approx \int_{k=np-a\sqrt{npq}}^{np+b\sqrt{npq}} \frac{1}{\sqrt{2\pi npq}} e^{-(k-np)^2/(2npq)} dk$$

$$\approx \frac{1}{\sqrt{2\pi}} \int_a^b e^{-t^2/2} dt,$$

where we have approximated the sum by an integral and again used the substitution $t = (k - np)/\sqrt{npq}$.

9.3. The Central Limit Theorem

The central limit theorem is one of the most fundamental results in probability theory, giving the theoretical foundation for many statistical analysis techniques. The theorem states that, under various mild conditions, the distribution of the average of a large number of independent random variables converges to the normal distribution, regardless of the distribution of each of the random variables. The convergence is *in distribution*.

Definition 9.1: *A sequence of distributions $F_1, F_2, \ldots$ converges in distribution to a distribution F, denoted $F_n \xrightarrow{D} F$, if for any $a \in \mathbb{R}$ at which F is continuous,*

$$\lim_{n \to \infty} F_n(a) = F(a).$$

Convergence in distribution is a relatively weak notion of convergence. In particular, it does not guarantee a uniform bound on the rate of convergence of $F_n(a)$ for different values of a.

We prove here a basic version of the central limit theorem for the average of independent, identically distributed, random variables with finite mean and variance.

Theorem 9.5 [The Central Limit Theorem]: *Let $X_1, \ldots, X_n$ be n independent, identically distributed random variables with mean μ and variance σ^2. Let $\bar{X}_n = \frac{1}{n} \sum_{i=1}^n X_i$. Then for any a and b,*

$$\lim_{n \to \infty} \Pr\left(a \le \frac{\bar{X}_n - \mu}{\sigma/\sqrt{n}} \le b\right) \xrightarrow{D} \Phi(b) - \Phi(a).$$

That is, the average $\bar{X}_n$ converges in distribution to a normal distribution with the appropriate mean and variance. Our proof of the central limit theorem uses the following result, which we quote without proof.

Theorem 9.6 [Lévy's Continuuity Theorem]: *Let $Y_1, Y_2, \ldots$ be a sequence of random variables with Y_i having distribution F_i and moment generating functions M_i. Let Y be a random variable with distribution F and moment generating function M. If $\lim_{n \to \infty} M_n(t) = M(t)$ for all t, then $F_n \xrightarrow{D} F$ for all t for which $F(t)$ is continuous.*

Proof of the Central Limit Theorem: Let $Z_i = (X_i - \mu)/\sigma$. Then $Z_1, Z_2, \ldots$ are independent, identically distributed, random variables with expectation $\mathbf{E}[Z_i] = 0$, variance $\mathbf{Var}[Z_i] = 1$, and

$$\frac{\bar{X}_n - \mu}{\sigma/\sqrt{n}} = \frac{\sqrt{n}}{n} \sum_{i=1}^{n} \frac{X_i - \mu}{\sigma} = \frac{\sum_{i=1}^{n} Z_i}{\sqrt{n}}.$$

To apply Theorem 9.6 we show that the moment generating functions for the random variables $Y_n = \sum_{i=1}^{n} Z_i/\sqrt{n}$ converge to the moment generating function of the standard normal distribution. That is, we need to show that

$$\lim_{n \to \infty} \mathbf{E}\left[e^{t \sum_{i=1}^{n} Z_i/\sqrt{n}}\right] = e^{t^2/2}$$

for all t.

Let $M(t) = \mathbf{E}[e^{tZ_i}]$ be the moment generation function of Z_i, so the moment generating function of $Z_i/\sqrt{n}$ is

$$\mathbf{E}\left[e^{tZ_i/\sqrt{n}}\right] = M\left(\frac{t}{\sqrt{n}}\right).$$

Since the Z_i are independent and identically distributed,

$$\mathbf{E}\left[e^{t \sum_{i=1}^{n} Z_i/\sqrt{n}}\right] = \left(M\left(\frac{t}{\sqrt{n}}\right)\right)^n.$$

Let $L(t) = \ln M(t)$. Since $M(0) = 1$, we have $L(0) = 0$, and $L'(0) = \frac{M'(0)}{M(0)} = \mathbf{E}[Z_i] = 0$. We also can compute the second derivative:

$$L''(0) = \frac{M(0)M''(0) - (M'(0))^2}{(M(0))^2} = \mathbf{E}[Z_i^2] = 1.$$

We need to show that $(M(t/\sqrt{n}))^n \to e^{t^2/2}$, or equivalently $nL(t/\sqrt{n}) \to t^2/2$. Applying L'Hôpital's rule (twice), we have

$$\begin{aligned}
\lim_{n \to \infty} \frac{L(t/\sqrt{n})}{n^{-1}} &= \lim_{n \to \infty} \frac{-L'(t/\sqrt{n})n^{-3/2}t}{-2n^{-2}} \\
&= \lim_{n \to \infty} \frac{L'(t/\sqrt{n})t}{2n^{-1/2}} \\
&= \lim_{n \to \infty} \frac{-L''(t/\sqrt{n})n^{-3/2}t^2}{-2n^{-3/2}} \\
&= \lim_{n \to \infty} L''(t/\sqrt{n})\frac{t^2}{2} \\
&= \frac{t^2}{2}.
\end{aligned}$$

∎

The central limit theorem can be proven under a variety of conditions. For example, in the following version of the theorem that we do not provide a proof for, the random variables are not required to be identically distributed.

Theorem 9.7: *Let $X_1, \ldots, X_n$ be n independent random variables with $\mathrm{E}[X_i] = \mu_i$ and $\mathrm{Var}[X_i] = \sigma_i^2$. Assume that:*

1. For some value M, $\Pr(|X_i| < M) = 1$ for all i; and
2. $\lim_{n \to \infty} \sum_{i=1}^{n} \sigma_i^2 = \infty$.

Then

$$\Pr\left(a \le \frac{\sum_{i=1}^{n}(X_i - \mu_i)}{\sqrt{\sum_{i=1}^{n} \sigma_i^2}} \le b \right) \xrightarrow{D} \Phi(b) - \Phi(a).$$

While the central limit theorem only gives convergence in distribution, under somewhat more stringent conditions one can prove a uniform convergence result.

Theorem 9.8 [Berry–Esséen Theorem]: *Let $X_1, \ldots, X_n$ be n independent, identically distributed random variables with finite mean μ and variance σ^2. Let $\rho = E[|X_i - \mu|^3]$ and $\bar{X}_n = \frac{1}{n} \sum_{i=1}^{n} X_i$. Then there is a constant C such that for any a*

$$\left| \Pr\left(\frac{\bar{X}_n - \mu}{\sigma/\sqrt{n}} \le a \right) - \Phi(a) \right| \le C \frac{\rho}{\sigma^3 \sqrt{n}}.$$

Example: Public Opinion Poll

Suppose that we want to estimate the support for the Yellow party. We poll n people to determine if they support the party or not. We assume the n people can be considered independent, uniform samples. If we assume further that n is sufficiently large to justify approximating the results using a normal distribution as suggested by the central limit theorem, what is the minimum number of samples needed to guarantee an estimate of the true fraction of supporters p within an error of at most 0.05 with a 0.95 confidence interval? Recall from Definition 4.2 that a $1 - \gamma$ confidence interval for a parameter p is an interval $[\tilde{p} - \delta, \tilde{p} + \delta]$ such that

$$\Pr(p \in [\tilde{p} - \delta, \tilde{p} + \delta]) \ge 1 - \gamma.$$

Let $X_i = 1$ if the ith polled person supports the party and $X_i = 0$ otherwise. The fraction of support observed in the sample is given by

$$\bar{X}_n = \frac{1}{n} \sum_{i=1}^{n} X_i.$$

Let $\delta = 0.05$ be our target error.

Clearly $\mathrm{E}[\bar{X}_n] = p$ and $\mathrm{Var}[\bar{X}_n] = \frac{1}{n} p(1 - p)$. Under our assumption that

$$Z_n = \frac{\bar{X}_n - \mathrm{E}[\bar{X}_n]}{\sqrt{\mathrm{Var}[\bar{X}_n]}} = \frac{\sqrt{n}(\bar{X}_n - p)}{\sqrt{p(1 - p)}}$$

251

is distributed as a standard normal distribution, we need to compute the minimum n such that

$$\Pr(|\bar{X}_n - p| \geq \delta) = \Pr\left(\frac{\sqrt{n}(\bar{X}_n - p)}{\sqrt{p(1-p)}} > \frac{\sqrt{n}\delta}{\sqrt{p(1-p)}}\right)$$

$$+ \Pr\left(\frac{\sqrt{n}(\bar{X}_n - p)}{\sqrt{p(1-p)}} < -\frac{\sqrt{n}\delta}{\sqrt{p(1-p)}}\right)$$

$$= 2\left(1 - \Phi\left(\frac{\sqrt{n}\delta}{\sqrt{p(1-p)}}\right)\right) \leq 0.05.$$

Thus, we are looking for the minimum n such that

$$\Phi\left(\frac{\sqrt{n}\delta}{\sqrt{p(1-p)}}\right) \geq 0.975 = \Phi(1.96).$$

Solving

$$\frac{\delta\sqrt{n}}{\sqrt{p(1-p)}} \geq 1.96,$$

we obtain

$$n \geq \left(\frac{1.96\sqrt{p(1-p)}}{\delta}\right)^2.$$

Using the fact that $p(1-p) \leq 1/4$, we find $n \geq 385$ suffices.

9.4.* Multivariate Normal Distributions

Assume that we want to study the relationship between the heights of parents and their children. More concretely, consider families with at least one daughter and one son, and for each such family let (x_1, x_2, x_3, x_4) be the heights of the mother, father, first daughter, and first son, respectively. We know that each component in this vector can be approximated by a univariate normal distribution, but what is the joint distribution of the four variables? It turns out that for many natural phenomena, such as this one, the joint distribution is well approximated by a *multivariate normal distribution*.

We saw in Lemma 9.1 that a univariate normal variable is always a linear transformation of a standard normal random variable. Similarly, the multivariate normal distribution is a linear transformation of a number of independent, standard normal random variables.

Let $X = (X_1, \ldots, X_n)^T$ denote a vector of n independent, standard normal random variables. Let $\bar{x} = (x_1, \ldots, x_n)^T$ be a vector of real values. We define

$$\Pr(X \leq \bar{x}) = \Pr(X_1 \leq x_1, X_2 \leq x_2, \ldots, X_n \leq x_n).$$

The joint cumulative distribution function for X is given as follows, where $\bar{w} = (w_1, \ldots, w_n)^T$:

$$\Pr(X \le \bar{x}) = \prod_{i=1}^{n} \left(\frac{1}{\sqrt{2\pi}} \int_{w_i=-\infty}^{x_i} e^{-w_i^2/2} dw_i \right)$$

$$= \frac{1}{(2\pi)^{n/2}} \int_{w_1=-\infty}^{x_1} \cdots \int_{w_n=-\infty}^{x_n} e^{-\bar{w}^T \bar{w}/2} dw_1 \, dw_2 \cdots dw_n.$$

Consider now a random variable vector $Y = (Y_1, \ldots, Y_m)^T$ obtained by a linear transformation on the vector X:

$$Y_1 = a_{11}X_1 + a_{12}X_2 + \cdots + a_{1n}X_n + \mu_1;$$
$$Y_2 = a_{21}X_1 + a_{22}X_2 + \cdots + a_{2n}X_n + \mu_2;$$

$$\cdots$$

$$Y_m = a_{m1}X_1 + a_{m2}X_2 + \cdots + a_{mn}X_n + \mu_m.$$

Let $\mathbf{A}$ denote the matrix of coefficients a_{ij}, and $\bar{\mu} = (\mu_1, \ldots, \mu_m)^T$. Then we can write

$$Y = \mathbf{A}X + \bar{\mu}.$$

The Y_is each have a normal distribution, specifically Y_i has distribution $N(\mu_i, \sum_{j=1}^{n} a_{ij}^2)$. However, the Y_is are *not* independent. In particular,

$$\mathbf{Cov}(Y_i, Y_j) = \sum_{k=1}^{n} a_{i,k} a_{j,k}.$$

(This is left as Exercise 9.3.)

The *covariance matrix* for Y is given by

$$\mathbf{\Sigma} = \mathbf{AA}^T = \begin{pmatrix} \mathbf{Var}[Y_1] & \mathbf{Cov}(Y_1, Y_i) & \ldots & \mathbf{Cov}(Y_i, Y_n) \\ \mathbf{Cov}(Y_1, Y_2) & \mathbf{Var}[Y_2] & \ldots & \mathbf{Cov}(Y_2, Y_n) \\ \cdots & \cdots & \cdots & \cdots \\ \cdots & \cdots & \cdots & \cdots \\ \mathbf{Cov}(Y_m, Y_1) & \mathbf{Cov}(Y_m, Y_2) & \ldots & \mathbf{Var}[Y_m] \end{pmatrix} = \mathbf{E}[(Y - \bar{\mu})(Y - \bar{\mu})^T].$$

If $\mathbf{A}$ has a full rank, then $X = \mathbf{A}^{-1}(Y - \bar{\mu})$, and we can derive a density function for the joint distribution.

$$\Pr(Y \le \bar{y}) = \Pr(Y - \bar{\mu} \le \bar{y} - \bar{\mu})$$
$$= \Pr(\mathbf{A}X \le \bar{y} - \bar{\mu})$$
$$= \Pr(X \le \mathbf{A}^{-1}(\bar{y} - \bar{\mu}))$$
$$= \frac{1}{(2\pi)^{n/2}} \int_{\bar{w} \le \mathbf{A}^{-1}(\bar{y}-\bar{\mu})} e^{-\bar{w}^T \bar{w}/2} dw_1 \cdots dw_n.$$

Changing the integration variables to $\bar{z} = A\bar{w} + \bar{\mu}$ we have

$$\Pr(Y \le \bar{y}) = \frac{1}{\sqrt{(2\pi)^n |\mathbf{AA}^T|}} \int_{-\infty}^{y_1} \cdots \int_{-\infty}^{y_n} e^{-(\bar{z}-\bar{\mu})^T (\mathbf{A}^{-1})^T \mathbf{A}^{-1}(\bar{z}-\bar{\mu})/2} dz_1 \cdots dz_n.$$

Here $|\mathbf{A}\mathbf{A}^T|$ denotes the determinant of $\mathbf{A}\mathbf{A}^T$, a term which arises under the multivariate change of variables.

Applying $(\mathbf{A}^{-1})^T\mathbf{A}^{-1} = (\mathbf{A}^T)^{-1}\mathbf{A}^{-1} = (\mathbf{A}\mathbf{A}^T)^{-1} = \mathbf{\Sigma}^{-1}$, we can write the distribution function of Y as

$$\Pr(Y \leq \bar{y}) = \frac{1}{\sqrt{(2\pi)^n|\mathbf{\Sigma}|}} \int_{-\infty}^{y_1} \cdots \int_{-\infty}^{y_n} e^{-(\bar{z}-\bar{\mu})^T\mathbf{\Sigma}^{-1}(\bar{z}-\bar{\mu})/2} dz_1 \cdots dz_n \quad (9.1)$$

where, again,

$$\mathbf{\Sigma} = \mathbf{A}\mathbf{A}^T = \mathbf{E}[(Y-\bar{\mu})(Y-\bar{\mu})^T].$$

In general we have the following definition.

Definition 9.2: *A vector $Y = (Y_1, \ldots, Y_n)^T$ has a* multivariate normal distribution, *denoted $Y \sim N(\bar{\mu}, \mathbf{\Sigma})$, if and only if there is an $n \times k$ matrix $\mathbf{A}$, a vector $X = (X_1, \ldots, X_k)^T$ of k independent standard normal random variables, and a vector $\bar{\mu} = (\mu_1, \ldots, \mu_n)^T$, such that*

$$Y = \mathbf{A}X + \bar{\mu}.$$

If $\mathbf{\Sigma} = \mathbf{A}\mathbf{A}^T = \mathbf{E}[(Y-\bar{\mu})(Y-\bar{\mu})^T]$ has full rank, then the density of Y is

$$\frac{1}{\sqrt{(2\pi)^n|\mathbf{\Sigma}|}} e^{-\frac{1}{2}(Y-\bar{\mu})^T\mathbf{\Sigma}^{-1}(Y-\bar{\mu})}.$$

If $\mathbf{\Sigma}$ is not invertible then the joint distribution has no density function.[2]

Note that sometimes instead of saying that random variables have a multivariate normal distribution, one says that they are jointly normal.

The corollary below follows readily, keeping in mind that a multivariate random variable is a vector of random variables.

Corollary 9.9: *Any linear combination of mutually independent multivariate normal random variables of equal dimension has a multivariate normal distribution.*

The special case of the bivariate normal density, with just two random variables, has a simpler expression, using the correlation coefficient between the two random variables.

Definition 9.3: *The* correlation coefficient *between random variables X and Y is*

$$\rho_{XY} = \frac{\mathbf{Cov}(X, Y)}{\sigma_X \sigma_Y}.$$

As noted in Exercise 9.4, the correlation coefficient is always in $[-1, 1]$.

If $(X, Y)^T$ has a bivariate normal distribution,

$$\begin{pmatrix} X \\ Y \end{pmatrix} \sim N\left(\begin{pmatrix} \mu_X \\ \mu_Y \end{pmatrix}, \begin{pmatrix} \sigma_X & \rho_{XY}\sigma_X\sigma_Y \\ \rho_{XY}\sigma_X\sigma_Y & \sigma_Y \end{pmatrix} \right),$$

---

[2] In some settings multivariate normal distributions are defined so that $\mathbf{\Sigma}$ is required to be a symmetric positive definite matrix and therefore invertible, but there are also settings where it is sensible to have $\mathbf{\Sigma}$ not invertible, and therefore a distribution with no density function.

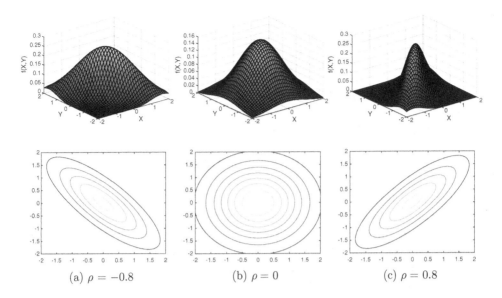

(a) $\rho = -0.8$ (b) $\rho = 0$ (c) $\rho = 0.8$

Figure 9.1: Bivariate Normal density function $f(X, Y)$ (top) and the contour of the function at increasing values of $f(X, Y)$ (bottom), with $\mu_X = \mu_Y = 0$, $\sigma_X = \sigma_Y = 1$, and $\rho = -0.8, 0, 0.8$.

then for any $|\rho_{XY}| < 1$ (and $\sigma_X, \sigma_Y > 0$) the joint density function of X and Y is given by

$$\frac{1}{2\pi \sigma_X \sigma_Y \sqrt{1 - \rho_{XY}^2}} e^{-\left((X-\mu_X)^2/(2\sigma_X^2)+(Y-\mu_Y)^2/(2\sigma_Y^2)-\rho_{XY}(X-\mu_X)(Y-\mu_Y)/(\sigma_X\sigma_Y)\right)/(1-\rho_{XY})}.$$

(9.2)

Examples of bivariate normal distributions are shown in Figure 9.1.

9.4.1. *Properties of the Multivariate Normal Distribution*

We outline several important properties of the multivariate normal distribution that make it particularly amendable to analysis. The proofs are left as Exercise 9.10.

Theorem 9.10: *Assume that X is an $n \times 1$ vector distributed as $N(\bar{\mu}, \Sigma)$. Let*

$$X = \begin{pmatrix} X_1 \\ X_2 \end{pmatrix} \quad and \quad \bar{\mu} = \begin{pmatrix} \bar{\mu}_1 \\ \bar{\mu}_2 \end{pmatrix},$$

where X_1 and X_2 are $k \times 1$ and $(n - k) \times 1$ vectors respectively, and $\bar{\mu}_1$ and $\bar{\mu}_2$ are the expectation vectors of X_1 and X_2 respectively. Similarly, let

$$\Sigma = \begin{pmatrix} \Sigma_{11} & \Sigma_{12} \\ \Sigma_{12} & \Sigma_{22} \end{pmatrix},$$

where Σ_{11} is the $k \times k$ correlation matrix of X_1, Σ_{22} is the $(n - k) \times (n - k)$ correlation matrix of X_2, Σ_{12} is the corresponding $(n - k) \times k$ matrix, and Σ_{21} is the corresponding $k \times (n - k)$ matrix.

255

(1) *The marginal distributions of X_i, $i = 1, 2$, are $N(\bar{\mu}_i, \Sigma_{ii})$.*

(2) *The distribution of X_i conditioned on $X_j = \bar{x}_j$ is $N(\bar{\mu}_{i|j}, \Sigma_{i|j})$ where*

$$\bar{\mu}_{i|j} = \bar{\mu}_i + \Sigma_{ij}\Sigma_{jj}^{-1}(\bar{x}_j - \bar{\mu}_j) \quad and \quad \Sigma_{i|j} = \Sigma_{jj} - \Sigma_{ij}^T\Sigma_{ii}^{-1}\Sigma_{ij}.$$

(3) *X_1 and X_2 are independent if and only if the matrix $\Sigma_{12} = 0$ (i.e. all its entries are 0).*

9.5. Application: Generating Normally Distributed Random Values

One natural question is how to produce random values that follow a normal distribution. More specifically, given random values distributed uniformly in $(0, 1)$, which is a useful and standard primitive operation to assume that we have available, can we generate random values that follow a normal distribution? As we have seen, it suffices to generate random values with a standard normal distribution. These values can then be scaled to follow a normal distribution with mean μ and variance σ^2.

The standard approach to convert a random variable X uniformly distributed in $(0, 1)$ to a random variable Z with cumulative distribution function $F(Z)$ is to set $Z = F^{-1}(X)$. That is, for $X = x$ we set $Z = z$ where $F(z) = x$. Indeed

$$\Pr(Z \le z) = \Pr(F^{-1}(X) \le F^{-1}(x)) = \Pr(F(Z) \le F(z)) = \Pr(X \le F(z)) = F(z).$$

This method cannot be readily used for the normal distribution because the cumulative distribution function $\Phi(X)$ does not have a closed form, and therefore we cannot directly compute $\Phi^{-1}(X)$, although there are various means to approximate $\Phi^{-1}(X)$ accurately at some expense in computation or memory.

One simple approach to approximating a standard normal random variable, suggested by the central limit theorem, is to generate $U_1, U_2, \ldots, U_{12}$, with the U_i independent and uniform on $(0, 1)$, and compute

$$X = \left(\sum_{i=1}^{12} U_i\right) - 6.$$

In this case X is obviously not distributed as a standard normal; in particular, it can only take on values in the range $(-6, 6)$. It is, however, a surprisingly good approximation, as shown further in Exercise 9.6. You should note that X has both expectation 0 and variance 1.

It turns out, however, that a standard normal random variable can be generated exactly using random numbers from $(0, 1)$, with some additional mathematical operations. In fact, there are two natural related ways to do this. Both rely on the same approach: instead of generating just one value, we produce two.

To start, consider the joint cumulative distribution for two independent standard normal random variables X and Y:

$$F(x', y') = \int_{-\infty}^{y'} \int_{-\infty}^{x'} \frac{1}{2\pi} e^{-(x^2+y^2)/2} dx\, dy. \tag{9.3}$$

256

The $x^2 + y^2$ term in the double integral actually helps us; it allows us to naturally move the problem into polar coordinates.

We can think of X and Y as being plotted as a pair (X, Y) on the two-dimensional plane. Then we let $R^2 = X^2 + Y^2$, where R is the radius of the circle centered at the origin that the point (X, Y) lies on, and similarly let $\Theta = \tan^{-1} \frac{Y}{X}$ be the angle the point makes with the x-axis. Thus

$$X = R \cos \Theta, \quad Y = R \sin \Theta.$$

We use a change of variables in Eqn. (9.3) above; with $x = r \cos \theta$ and $y = r \sin \theta$, we have

$$F(r', \theta') = \int_0^{\theta'} \int_0^{r'} \frac{1}{2\pi} e^{-r^2/2} r \, dr \, d\theta.$$

Here we have used that under this change of variables, $dx \, dy = r \, dr \, d\theta$. More formally, from multivariable calculus, the Jacobian for the transformation is

$$\frac{\partial(x, y)}{\partial(r, \theta)} = \begin{vmatrix} \dfrac{\partial x}{\partial r} & \dfrac{\partial x}{\partial \theta} \\ \dfrac{\partial y}{\partial r} & \dfrac{\partial y}{\partial \theta} \end{vmatrix} = \begin{vmatrix} \cos \theta & -r \sin \theta \\ \sin \theta & -r \cos \theta \end{vmatrix} = r(\cos^2 \theta + \sin^2 \theta) = r.$$

Hence the additional factor of r when we change variables. This expression integrates nicely to

$$F(r', \theta') = \frac{\theta'}{2\pi} \left(1 - e^{-(r')^2/2}\right).$$

In particular, notice that $F(r', \theta') = G(r')H(\theta')$ where $H(\theta') = \frac{\theta'}{2\pi}$ and $G(r') = 1 - e^{-(r')^2/2}$. This means that the radius R and the angle Θ determined by X and Y are independent random variables.

But now, thinking in the other direction, we can directly generate R and Θ to obtain our independent standard normal random variables X and Y. We can see from the form of $H(\theta')$ that the angle Θ is uniformly distributed over $[0, 2\pi]$; this also follows naturally from symmetry considerations. Hence, given a uniform random variable U on $(0, 1)$, we can take $\Theta = 2\pi U$. For R, we have

$$\Pr(R \geq r') = e^{-(r')^2/2},$$

while for a uniform $(0, 1)$ random variable V,

$$\Pr(V \geq v) = 1 - v.$$

Setting the right-hand sides equal, we find $r' = \sqrt{-2 \ln(1 - v)}$. Hence, we can take $R = \sqrt{-2 \ln(1 - V)}$ to obtain a suitably distributed radius R. Since $1 - V$ and V both have uniform $(0, 1)$ distributions, equivalently we can take $R = \sqrt{-2 \ln V}$ instead. To conclude, given two uniform $(0, 1)$ random variables U and V, we can take

$$X = \sqrt{-2 \ln V} \cos(2\pi U), \quad Y = \sqrt{-2 \ln V} \sin(2\pi U)$$

to obtain two independent standard normal random variables. This is commonly referred to as the Box–Muller transform.

A common variation avoids using the sine and cosine functions. Let U' and V' be independent and uniform on $(0, 1)$, and let $U = 2U' - 1$ and $V = 2V' - 1$, so that U and V are independent and uniform on $(-1, 1)$. If $S = U^2 + V^2 \geq 1$, we throw these values away and start over again. Otherwise, generate

$$X = U\sqrt{\frac{-2\ln S}{S}}, \quad Y = V\sqrt{\frac{-2\ln S}{S}}.$$

The result is that X and Y are independent standard normal random variables. Think of the point (U, V) in the xy-plane, and note that $U/\sqrt{S}$ and $V/\sqrt{S}$ play the role of $\cos \Theta$ and $\sin \Theta$ in the Box–Muller transform; note here that the corresponding Θ is independent of the value of S itself. Also, S is uniformly distributed over $[0, 1)$, because (U, V) is uniform over the circle of radius 1 centered at $(0, 0)$, and hence

$$\Pr(S \leq s) = \Pr(U^2 + V^2 \leq s)$$

is the probabilility that a random point in the unit circle lies within a circle of radius $\sqrt{s}$ around the origin. But this probability is just

$$\Pr(S \leq s) = \Pr(U^2 + V^2 \leq s) = \frac{\pi s}{\pi} = s,$$

so S has a uniform distribution. Hence $\sqrt{-2\ln S}$ takes the role of $\sqrt{-2\ln V}$ in the Box–Muller transform. (As S takes on the value 0 with probability 0, we can equivalently think of S as uniform on $(0, 1)$.)

9.6. Maximum Likelihood Point Estimates

Normal distributions are often used to model observed data. We see a sample of data points, such as the heights of individuals, and then we try to fit a normal distribution to that data. How do we characterize and find the best fit? This is similar in some ways to the question of the confidence interval. We have seen in Chapter 4 and in this chapter that when obtaining a sample by polling for a yes–no question, the natural estimate is to take the fraction of responders that answer "yes" and use that as our guess for the fraction of the population that would answer yes to the question. We could also find probabilistic guarantees that this fraction was within some interval of the true answer, under assumptions about the independence of our samples.

Here we also consider the question of finding the best parameter for a distribution given a collection of data points, but more generally. Our goal is to find the best representative value for the parameter. *Maximum likelihood (ML) estimators* give such a value.[3]

---

[3] Here we follow a classical statistics approach, where the ML estimator assumes no prior knowledge on the parameter and just reports the value that maximizes the probability or the density of the observed data, as described in Definition 9.4. In contrast, the Bayesian statistics approach starts with a prior distribution on the space of possible parameter choices and computes a *maximum a posteriori estimation*, which is the value of the parameter conditioned on the observed data. The two estimators give the same value when the prior distribution is uniform on the range of the parameter, as discussed further in Exercise 9.13.

Definition 9.4:

1. Let $P_X(x, \theta)$ be the probability function of a discrete random variable X that depends on a parameter θ. Let $x_1, \ldots, x_n$ be n independent observations of X. The Maximum Likelihood (ML) estimator of θ is

$$\arg\max_{\theta} \prod_{i=1}^{n} P_X(x_i, \theta).$$

2. Let $f_X(x, \theta)$ be the density function of a continuous random variable X that depends on a parameter θ. Let $x_1, \ldots, x_n$ be n independent observations of X. The Maximum Likelihood (ML) estimator of θ is

$$\arg\max_{\theta} \prod_{i=1}^{n} f_X(x_i, \theta).$$

Note that θ in Definition 9.4 can correspond to a single parameter (such as for the exponential distribution) or a vector of parameters (such as the mean and variance for the normal distribution).

As a simple example consider a sequence of n independent, identically distributed, Bernoulli experiments with k successes. What is the maximum likelihood estimate for the probability of success p? Intuitively, it seems that it should be the fraction of flips that came up heads. We prove this intuition holds.

For a success probability of p, the probability of obtaining k heads is

$$f(p) = \binom{n}{k} p^k (1-p)^{n-k}.$$

We therefore need to compute

$$\arg\max_{p} f(p) = \arg\max_{p} \binom{n}{k} p^k (1-p)^{n-k}.$$

Computing the first derivative of $f(p)$ yields

$$f'(p) = k\binom{n}{k} p^{k-1}(1-p)^{n-k} - (n-k)\binom{n}{k} p^k (1-p)^{n-k-1}.$$

We see that $f'(p) = 0$ when $p = k/n$. A further check shows that k/n provides the local maximum, not a local minimum. It follows that the maximum likelihood value is the fraction of successes, matching our intuition.

We turn now to computing an ML estimator for the expectation and the variance of the normal distribution. In the case of continuous random variables it is often easier to maximize the logarithm of the likelihood function, which is referred to as the log-likelihood function, $\sum_{i=1}^{n} \ln(f_X(x_i, \theta))$. This is equivalent to maximizing the likelihood function, since

$$\arg\max_{\theta} \prod_{i=1}^{n} f_X(x_i, \theta) = \arg\max_{\theta} \sum_{i=1}^{n} \ln(f_X(x_i, \theta)).$$

259

Let $x_1, \ldots, x_n$ be n independent observations from a normal distribution with unknown expectation and variance. The ML estimate is given by

$$\arg\max_{(\mu,\sigma)} \prod_{i=1}^{n} \frac{1}{\sqrt{2\pi}\sigma} e^{-(x_i-\mu)^2/(2\sigma^2)} = \arg\max_{(\mu,\sigma)} \frac{1}{(2\pi\sigma^2)^{n/2}} e^{-\sum_{i=1}^{n}(x_i-\mu)^2/(2\sigma^2)}$$

$$= \arg\min_{(\mu,\sigma)} \left[\frac{n}{2}\log(2\pi\sigma^2) + \frac{\sum_{i=1}^{n}(x_i-\mu)^2}{2\sigma^2} \right],$$

where here we restrict $\sigma > 0$.

Let $M_n = \frac{1}{n}\sum_{i=1}^{n} x_i$ and $S_n^2 = \frac{1}{n}\sum_{i=1}^{n}(x_i - M_n)^2$, and observe that

$$\sum_{i=1}^{n}(x_i - \mu)^2 = \sum_{i=1}^{n}((x_i - M_n) + (M_n - \mu))^2$$

$$= \sum_{i=1}^{n}(x_i - M_n)^2 + n(M_n - \mu)^2 + 2\sum_{i=1}^{n}(x_i - M_n)(M_n - \mu)$$

$$= nS_n^2 + n(M_n - \mu)^2 + 2(M_n - \mu)\sum_{i=1}^{n}(x_i - M_n)$$

$$= nS_n^2 + n(M_n - \mu)^2.$$

Thus we need to compute

$$\arg\min_{\mu,\sigma} \left[\frac{n}{2}\log(2\pi\sigma^2) + \frac{nS_n^2}{2\sigma^2} + \frac{n(M_n - \mu)^2}{2\sigma^2} \right].$$

For any value of $\sigma > 0$ the argument above is minimized when $\mu = M_n$. Hence it suffices to minimize

$$f(\sigma) = \frac{n}{2}\log(2\pi\sigma^2) + \frac{nS_n^2}{2\sigma^2}.$$

We find

$$f'(\sigma) = -\frac{n}{2}\frac{2\pi}{2\pi\sigma^2} + \frac{nS_n^2}{2(\sigma^2)^2} = \frac{n}{2\sigma^2}\left(\frac{S_n^2}{\sigma^2} - 1 \right).$$

The derivative is 0 when $\sigma^2 = S_n^2$. We therefore find that $\mu = M_n$, $\sigma^2 = S_n^2$ provide the maximum likelihood estimates of the parameters.

The estimator of a parameter is itself a random variable that is a function of the observed data. It seems reasonable that its expectation would be equal to the value it estimates, but this is not always the case.

Definition 9.5: *Let Θ_n be a function of n observations $X_1, \ldots, X_n$ that depend on a parameter θ.*

- Θ_n *is an* unbiased estimator *for a parameter θ if*

$$\mathbf{E}[\Theta_n] = \theta.$$

260

- Θ_n *is an* asymptotically unbiased estimator *for a parameter* θ *if*

$$\lim_{n \to \infty} \mathbf{E}[\Theta_n] = \theta.$$

For example, for samples X_i taken from any distribution with finite expectation, the estimator $M_n = \frac{1}{n} \sum_{i=1}^{n} X_i$ gives an unbiased estimate for the expectation. However, the ML estimate for the variance of a normal distribution we found above, $S_n^2 = \frac{1}{n} \sum_{i=1}^{n} (X_i - M_n)^2$, is not an unbiased estimator for the variance. Since the X_i are independent and identically distributed, let $\mathbf{E}[X] = \mathbf{E}[X_i]$, and note that for $i \neq j$, $\mathbf{E}[X_i X_j] = (\mathbf{E}[X])^2$. Then,

$$\begin{aligned}
\mathbf{E}[S_n^2] &= \frac{1}{n} \sum_{i=1}^{n} \left(\mathbf{E}[X_i^2] - 2\mathbf{E}[M_n X_i] + \mathbf{E}[(M_n)^2] \right) \\
&= \mathbf{E}[X^2] - \mathbf{E}\left[(M_n)^2 \right] \\
&= \mathbf{E}[X^2] - \frac{1}{n^2} \left(\mathbf{E}\left[\sum_{i=1}^{n} X_i^2 \right] + \sum_{i \neq j} \mathbf{E}\left[X_i X_j \right] \right) \\
&= \frac{n-1}{n} (\mathbf{E}[X^2] - (\mathbf{E}[X])^2) \\
&= \frac{n-1}{n} \sigma^2.
\end{aligned}$$

Thus, the ML estimator for the variance of the normal distribution is only asymptotically unbiased. However, $\frac{n}{n-1} S_n^2$ is an unbiased estimator for σ^2.

Indeed, in statistical analysis, when sampling one generally uses

$$\frac{n}{n-1} S_n^2 = \frac{1}{n-1} \sum_{i=1}^{n} (x_i - M_n)^2$$

as the estimate of the variance because it is unbiased. This quantity is called the *sample variance*, while

$$\frac{1}{n} \sum_{i=1}^{n} (x_i - M_n)^2$$

is called the *population variance*. The population variance is the correct formula for the variance when you have the entire population.

9.7. Application: EM Algorithm For a Mixture of Gaussians

Assume that $\bar{x} = x_1, \ldots, x_n$ is a sample of the heights of n students chosen independently and uniformly at random. All we know about the students is their height; we do not know whether each student is male or female. Assume that the height distribution of females follows a normal distribution $N(\mu_1, \sigma_1)$ and the height of males follows a normal distribution $N(\mu_2, \sigma_2)$. Let γ be the fraction of female students and $1 - \gamma$ the fraction of male students; we assume in what follows that γ is not known in advance. We also assume the student population is large enough that we do not worry about the distinction of sampling with replacement or without replacement; concretely, we sample without replacement, but we treat γ as a fixed parameter throughout the sampling.

The density function of each observation in the sample is

$$D(x_i, \gamma, \mu_1, \mu_2, \sigma_1, \sigma_2) = \gamma \frac{1}{\sqrt{2\pi\sigma_1^2}} e^{-(x_i-\mu_1)^2/(2\sigma_1^2)} + (1-\gamma)\frac{1}{\sqrt{2\pi\sigma_2^2}} e^{-(x_i-\mu_2)^2/(2\sigma_2^2)}.$$

To estimate the parameters of the two normal distributions for the sample $\bar{x}$ we want to compute a maximum likelihood estimator for the vector $(\gamma, \mu_1, \mu_2, \sigma_1, \sigma_2)$. The likelihood function is

$$L(\bar{x}, \gamma, \mu_1, \mu_2, \sigma_1, \sigma_2) = \prod_{i=1}^{n}\left(\gamma \frac{1}{\sqrt{2\pi\sigma_1^2}} e^{-(x_i-\mu_1)^2/(2\sigma_1^2)} + (1-\gamma)\frac{1}{\sqrt{2\pi\sigma_2^2}} e^{-(x_i-\mu_2)^2/(2\sigma_2^2)}\right)$$

and our goal is to find the maximum likelihood vector

$$\left(\gamma^{ML}, \mu_1^{ML}, \mu_2^{ML}, \sigma_1^{ML}, \sigma_2^{ML}\right) = \arg \max_{(\gamma,\mu_1,\mu_2,\sigma_1,\sigma_2)} L(\bar{x}, \gamma, \mu_1, \mu_2, \sigma_1, \sigma_2).$$

This problem is a simple example of an important task in statistical data analysis – estimating the parameters of a mixture of distributions. The intuitive difficulty behind solving this problem is that it is not clear which distribution each observation belongs to; if we knew which students were male and which were female, we could separate them and solve for each distribution separately. Natural approaches for the problem would simultaneously assign each observation to one of the distributions, or at least provide a probability for each observation for which distribution it came from, while also estimating the parameters of these distributions. The two distributions will overlap, making it hard to disentangle which data points correspond to each distribution. Intuitively, the more overlap, the harder it is to find the most likely parameters.

The *Expectation–Maximization (EM)* algorithm is a simple iterative heuristic for estimating the maximum likelihood of a distribution that depends on unobserved variables, such as the assignments of each observation to the distributions that generated it. We describe and analyze here the EM algorithm for the problem of learning the parameters of a mixture of two univariate Gaussian distributions. Extensions of the algorithm to multivariate Gaussians and to more than two distributions are discussed in Exercises 9.11 and 9.12. The EM algorithm is also used in many other contexts.

The EM algorithm starts with arbitrary values for the parameters $\mu_1, \mu_2, \sigma_1^2, \sigma_2^2$. We say more about the initialization below. Each iteration of the algorithm starts with an **E**xpectation step followed by a **M**aximization step. The expectation step computes, for each sample point x_i, the probabilities $p_1(x_i)$ and $p_2(x_i)$ that x_i was generated by the first or second distribution, respectively, conditioned on the current estimates of the parameters of the two distributions. Here $p_2(x_i) = 1 - p_1(x_i)$, but for a larger number of distributions one would compute all of these conditional probabilities. This step provides a probabilistic assignment of samples to distributions. The maximization step then computes a new ML estimate for the parameters $\mu_1, \mu_2, \sigma_1^2, \sigma_2^2$ based on this assignment (see Algorithm 9.1). The ML estimate generalizes the ML estimate we used for a single Gaussian in Section 9.6.

EM Algorithm for Mixture of Two Gaussian Distributions

Input: n samples $x_1, \ldots, x_n$.
Output: ML-estimate $(\mu_1, \mu_2, \sigma_1^2, \sigma_2^2, \gamma)$

1. Start with arbitrary values for $\mu_1, \mu_2, \sigma_1^2, \sigma_2^2$, and with $\gamma = 1/2$.
2. For $j = 1, 2$ let $f(x, \mu_j, \sigma_j) = \frac{1}{\sqrt{2\pi\sigma_j^2}} e^{-(x-\mu_j)^2/(2\sigma_j^2)}$.
3. Repeat until convergence
   (or no significant improvement in $L(\bar{x}, \gamma, \mu_1, \mu_2, \sigma_1, \sigma_2)$):
   (a) For $i = 1$ to n
      i. $p_1(x_i) = \frac{\gamma f(x_i, \mu_1\sigma_1)}{\gamma f(x_i, \mu_1\sigma_1) + (1-\gamma)f(x_i, \mu_2, \sigma_2)}$
      ii. $p_2(x_i) = 1 - p_1(x_i)$
   (b) For $j = 1, 2$
      i. $\mu_i = \frac{\sum_{i=1}^{n} p_j(x_i)x_i}{\sum_{i=1}^{n} p_j(x_i)}$
      ii. $\sigma_j^2 = \frac{\sum_{i=1}^{n} p_j(x_i)(x_i - \mu_j)^2}{\sum_{i=1}^{n} p_j(x_i)}$
   (c) $\gamma = \frac{1}{n} \sum_{i=1}^{n} p_1(x_i)$.

Algorithm 9.1: EM Algorithm for a Mixture of Two Gaussians.

In practice the initialization can affect the running time. One approach would be to choose two random observation values as the initial means, and calculate the initial variance σ_1^2 by assuming all observations came from a single Gaussian with mean μ_1 (and similarly for σ_2^2). An initial value of $\gamma = 1/2$ is natural as it corresponds to each point coming with equal probability from each distribution. More complex methods for initialization can be used.

The following theorem shows that the likelihood function is nondecreasing throughout the execution of the algorithm. Thus, the EM algorithm always terminates at a local maximum. The algorithm is not guaranteed to find the maximum likelihood estimate, which is a global maximum. Nevertheless, the algorithm gives good results in practice.

Theorem 9.11: *Let $\gamma^t, \mu_1^t, \mu_2^t, \sigma_1^t, \sigma_2^t$ be the estimated parameters at the end of the tth iteration of the EM algorithm for a mixture of two Gaussians, with the initial values corresponding to $t = 0$. Then for all $t \geq 0$,*

$$L(\bar{x}, \gamma^{t+1}, \mu_1^{t+1}, \mu_2^{t+1}, \sigma_1^{t+1}, \sigma_2^{t+1}) \geq L(\bar{x}, \gamma^t, \mu_1^t, \mu_2^t, \sigma_1^t, \sigma_2^t).$$

Proof: The proof has two parts. We first show that, given values $\mu_1^t, \mu_2^t, \sigma_1^t, \sigma_2^t$, the algorithm's choice of γ^{t+1} maximizes the likelihood, so that

$$\gamma^{t+1} = \arg\max_{\gamma} L(\bar{x}, \gamma, \mu_1^t, \mu_2^t, \sigma_1^t, \sigma_2^t).$$

In particular, this implies

$$L(\bar{x}, \gamma^{t+1}, \mu_1^t, \mu_2^t, \sigma_1^t, \sigma_2^t) \geq L(\bar{x}, \gamma^t, \mu_1^t, \mu_2^t, \sigma_1^t, \sigma_2^t).$$

Next we show that, given γ^{t+1},

$$(\mu_1^{t+1}, \mu_2^{t+1}, \sigma_1^{t+1}, \sigma_2^{t+1}) = \arg\max_{(\mu_1, \mu_2, \sigma_1, \sigma_2)} L(\bar{x}, \gamma^{t+1}, \mu_1, \mu_2, \sigma_1, \sigma_2).$$

263

Thus

$$L\left(\bar{x}, \gamma^{t+1}, \mu_1^{t+1}, \mu_2^{t+1}, \sigma_1^{t+1}, \sigma_2^{t+1}\right) \geq L\left(\bar{x}, \gamma^{t+1}, \mu_1^t, \mu_2^t, \sigma_1^t, \sigma_2^t\right).$$

Let $f(x, \mu_j, \sigma_j) = \frac{1}{\sqrt{2\pi\sigma_j^2}} e^{-(x-\mu_j)^2/(2\sigma_j^2)}$, and let

$$L(\bar{x}, \gamma, \mu_1, \mu_2, \sigma_1, \sigma_2) = \prod_{i=1}^{n} \left(\gamma f(x_i, \mu_1, \sigma_1) + (1-\gamma)f(x_i, \mu_2, \sigma_2)\right).$$

Taking the derivative of $L(\bar{x}, \gamma, \mu_1, \mu_2, \sigma_1, \sigma_2)$ with respect to γ we have

$$\frac{\partial L}{\partial \gamma} = \sum_{i=1}^{n} \left[\prod_{j \neq i} \left(\gamma f(x_j, \mu_1, \sigma_1) + (1-\gamma)f(x_j, \mu_2, \sigma_2)\right) f(x_i, \mu_1, \sigma_1) - f(x_i, \mu_2, \sigma_2)\right) \right]$$

$$= L(\bar{x}, \gamma, \mu_1, \mu_2, \sigma_1, \sigma_2) \sum_{i=1}^{n} \frac{f(x_i, \mu_1, \sigma_1) - f(x_i, \mu_2, \sigma_2)}{\gamma f(x_i, \mu_1, \sigma_1) + (1-\gamma)f(x_i, \mu_2, \sigma_2)}.$$

The likelihood function is never 0. So, when the derivative is 0,

$$\sum_{i=1}^{n} \frac{f(x_i, \mu_1, \sigma_1)}{\gamma f(x_i, \mu_1, \sigma_1) + (1-\gamma)f(x_i, \mu_2, \sigma_2)}$$

$$= \sum_{i=1}^{n} \frac{f(x_i, \mu_2, \sigma_2)}{\gamma f(x_i, \mu_1, \sigma_1) + (1-\gamma)f(x_i, \mu_2, \sigma_2)} = \lambda.$$

Now

$$\lambda = \gamma\lambda + (1-\gamma)\lambda$$

$$= \sum_{i=1}^{n} \frac{\gamma f(x_i, \mu_1, \sigma_1)}{\gamma f(x_i, \mu_1, \sigma_1) + (1-\gamma)f(x_i, \mu_2, \sigma_2)}$$

$$+ \sum_{i=1}^{n} \frac{(1-\gamma)f(x_i, \mu_2, \sigma_2)}{\gamma f(x_i, \mu_1, \sigma_1) + (1-\gamma)f(x_i, \mu_2, \sigma_2)}$$

$$= n.$$

Since $\lambda = n$,

$$n = \sum_{i=1}^{n} \frac{f(x_i, \mu_1, \sigma_1)}{\gamma f(x_i, \mu_1, \sigma_1) + (1-\gamma)f(x_i, \mu_2, \sigma_2)},$$

and hence

$$\gamma = \frac{1}{n} \sum_{i=1}^{n} \frac{\gamma f(x_i, \mu_1, \sigma_1)}{\gamma f(x_i, \mu_1, \sigma_1) + (1-\gamma)f(x_i, \mu_2, \sigma_2)} = \frac{1}{n} \sum_{i=1}^{n} p_1(x_i).$$

Thus, the choice of probabilities $p_1(x_i)$ in each iteration maximizes the likelihood function with respect to γ.

Next we show that

$$\left(\mu_1^{t+1}, \mu_2^{t+1}, \sigma_1^{t+1}, \sigma_2^{t+1}\right) = \arg \max_{(\mu_1, \mu_2, \sigma_1, \sigma_2)} L(\bar{x}, \gamma^{t+1}, \mu_1, \mu_2, \sigma_1, \sigma_2)$$

$$= \arg \max_{(\mu_1, \mu_2, \sigma_1, \sigma_2)} \prod_{i=1}^{n} (\gamma f(x_i, \mu_1, \sigma_1) + (1 - \gamma) f(x_i, \mu_2, \sigma_2)).$$

Taking the derivative with respect to μ_1 we have

$$\frac{\partial L}{\partial \mu_1} = \sum_{i=1}^{n} \frac{2\gamma (x_i - \mu_1)}{2\sigma_1^2} f(x_i, \mu_i, \sigma_1) \prod_{j \neq i} (\gamma f(x_i, \mu_1, \sigma_1) + (1 - \gamma) f(x_i, \mu_2, \sigma_2))$$

$$= -\sum_{i=1}^{n} \frac{2p_1(x_i)(x_i - \mu_1)}{2\sigma_1^2} L(\bar{x}, \gamma^{t+1}, \mu_1, \mu_2, \sigma_1, \sigma_2).$$

When the derivative is 0, independent of the choice of μ_2, σ_1, and σ_2, we have

$$\sum_{i=1}^{n} \frac{2p_1(x_i)(x_i - \mu_1)}{2\sigma_1^2} = 0,$$

or

$$\mu_1 = \frac{\sum_{i=1}^{n} p_1(x_i) x_i}{\sum_{i=1}^{n} p_1(x_i)}.$$

Similar computations show the choices used in the algorithm for μ_1, μ_2, σ_1, and σ_2 all individually maximize the likelihood function over that iteration given γ^{t+1} and regardless of the values of the other parameters. We conclude

$$L\left(\bar{x}, \gamma^{t+1}, \mu_1^{t+1}, \mu_2^{t+1}, \sigma_1^{t+1}, \sigma_2^{t+1}\right) \geq L\left(\bar{x}, \gamma^{t+1}, \mu_1^t, \mu_2^t, \sigma_1^t, \sigma_2^t\right). \qquad \blacksquare$$

9.8. Exercises

Exercise 9.1: Prove that for any μ and $\sigma > 0$,

$$\int_{-\infty}^{\infty} \frac{1}{\sqrt{2\pi}\sigma} e^{-(x-\mu)^2/(2\sigma^2)} dx = 1.$$

Hint: As a lemma, use a transformation to polar coordinates to prove that

$$\int_{-\infty}^{\infty} \int_{-\infty}^{\infty} e^{-(u^2+v^2)/(2\sigma^2)} du \, dv = 2\pi\sigma^2.$$

Exercise 9.2: Let X be a standard normal random variable. Prove that $\mathbf{E}[X^n] = 0$ for odd $n \geq 1$, and $\mathbf{E}[X^n] \geq 1$ for even $n \geq 2$. (*Hint:* you can use integration by parts to derive an expression for $\mathbf{E}[X^n]$ in terms of $\mathbf{E}[X^{n-2}]$.)

Exercise 9.3: Recall that in discussing multivariate normal distributions we considered random variables

$$Y_1 = a_{11}X_1 + a_{12}X_2 + \cdots + a_{1n}X_n + \mu_1;$$
$$Y_2 = a_{21}X_1 + a_{22}X_2 + \cdots + a_{2n}X_n + \mu_2;$$
$$\cdots$$
$$Y_m = a_{m1}X_1 + a_{m2}X_2 + \cdots + a_{mn}X_n + \mu_m.$$

Here the a_{ij} and μ_i are constants, and the X_i are independent standard normal random variables. Prove that

$$\mathbf{Cov}(Y_i, Y_j) = \sum_{k=1}^{n} a_{i,k}a_{j,k}.$$

Exercise 9.4: Let $\rho_{XY} = \frac{\mathrm{Cov}(X,Y)}{\sigma_X \sigma_Y}$ be the correlation coefficient of X and Y.

(a) Prove that for any two random variables X and Y, $|\rho_{XY}| \leq 1$.
(b) Prove that if X and Y are independent then $\rho_{XY} = 0$.
(c) Give an example of two random variables X and Y that are not independent but $\rho_{XY} = 0$.

Exercise 9.5: Prove that for the bivariate normal distribution the right hand side of Eqn. (9.1) and the expression given in (9.2) are equal.

Exercise 9.6: Let

$$X = \left(\sum_{i=1}^{12} U_i \right) - 6,$$

where the U_i are independent and uniform on $(0, 1)$. Let Y be a random variable from $N(0, 1)$. Using a computer program or other tools, find as good an approximation as you can to $\max_z |\Pr(X \leq z) - \Pr(Y \leq z)|$. If you can, try to ensure that your approximation is an upper bound.

Exercise 9.7: Write a program that generates independent uniform $(0, 1)$ random variables U and V, and compute

$$X = \sqrt{-2 \ln V} \cos(2\pi U), \quad Y = \sqrt{-2 \ln V} \sin(2\pi U)$$

to obtain two values according to the Box–Muller method. Repeat this experiment 100,000 times, and plot the corresponding distribution function for the 200,000 samples. Also, determine how many sampled values x satisfy $|x| \leq k$ for $k = 1, 2, 3, 4$. Do your results seem reasonable? Explain.

Exercise 9.8: Write a program that generates independent uniform $(0, 1)$ random variables U and V, and repeats this process until finding a pair such that $S = U^2 + V^2 < 1$.

Then compute

$$X = U\sqrt{\frac{-2\ln S}{S}}, \quad Y = V\sqrt{\frac{-2\ln S}{S}}$$

to obtain two values. Repeat this experiment 100,000 times, and plot the corresponding distribution function for the 200,000 samples. Also, determine how many sampled values x satisfy $|x| \le k$ for $k = 1, 2, 3, 4$. Do your results seem reasonable? Explain.

Exercise 9.9: Suppose that X is normally distributed with expectation 1 and standard deviation 0.25, Y is normally distributed with expectation 1.5 and standard deviation 0.4, and X and Y have correlation coefficient 0.4. Calculate the following probabilities:

(a) $\Pr(X + Y \ge 2)$;
(b) $\Pr(X + Y \ge 3)$;
(c) $\Pr(Y \le X)$;
(d) Perform the same calculations above but with correlation coefficient 0.6;
(e) How do these probabilities seem to change as the correlation ceofficient increases? Explain.

Exercise 9.10: In this exercise we prove Theorem 9.10.

(a) Prove that the marginal distribution of X_1 is $N(\mu_1, \Sigma_{11})$.
(b) Use $f(X_1|X_2) = \frac{f(X_1, X_2)}{f(X_2)}$ to prove that the distribution of X_1 conditioned on $X_2 = \bar{x}_2$ is $N(\bar{\mu}_{1|2}, \Sigma_{1|2})$ where

$$\bar{\mu}_{1|2} = \bar{\mu}_1 + \Sigma_{12}\Sigma_{22}^{-1}(\bar{x}_2 - \bar{\mu}_2) \quad \text{and} \quad \Sigma_{1|2} = \Sigma_{22} - \Sigma_{12}^{T}\Sigma_{11}^{-1}\Sigma_{12}.$$

(This is relatively easy to show for the bivariate distribution, more challenging for a higher dimension multivariate distribution.)
(c) Show that when $\Sigma_{12} = 0$ the joint density function of X_1 and X_2 can be written as a product of the marginal densities of X_1 and X_2, proving that the two random variables are independent.

Exercise 9.11: Assume that $(x_1, y_i), \ldots, (x_n, y_n)$ are n independent samples from a mixture of two bivariate normal distributions. Write and analyze an EM algorithm for computing a maximum likelihood estimate of the parameters of the mixed distribution.

Exercise 9.12: Assume that $x_1, \ldots, x_n$ are n independent samples from a mixture of three normal distributions. Write and analyze an EM algorithm for computing a maximum likelihood estimate of the parameters of the mixed distribution.

Exercise 9.13: We briefly consider the setting of maximum a posterior estimation. For convenience, assume that we are working over discrete spaces. Let $P_X(x, \theta)$ be the probability function of a discrete random variable X that depends on a parameter θ. Let $x_1, \ldots, x_n$ be n independent observations of X. We think now in terms of the following setting: the parameter Θ was chosen according to some initial distribution, and we wish

267

to find the value θ that maximizes

$$\Pr(\Theta = \theta \mid X_1 = x_1, X_2 = x_2, \ldots, X_n = x_n),$$

where the X_i correspond to random variables whose values are that of the observed data. That is, we seek the θ value that is most likely given our observations.

(a) Argue that

$$\begin{aligned}
&\Pr(\Theta = \theta \mid X_1 = x_1, X_2 = x_2, \ldots, X_n = x_n) \\
&= \frac{\Pr(X_1 = x_1, X_2 = x_2, \ldots, X_n = x_n \mid \Theta = \theta)\Pr(\Theta = \theta)}{\Pr(X_1 = x_1, X_2 = x_2, \ldots, X_n = x_n)},
\end{aligned}$$

where here $\Pr(\Theta = \theta)$ is the distribution governing the initial choice of θ.

(b) Suppose that $\Pr(\Theta = \theta)$ is uniform over all possible values. Then explain why maximizing $\Pr(\Theta = \theta \mid X_1 = x_1, X_2 = x_2, \ldots, X_n = x_n)$ yields the same result as maximizing $\Pr(X_1 = x_1, X_2 = x_2, \ldots, X_n = x_n \mid \Theta = \theta)$.

(c) Modify the above argument to hold for settings where the observations X and the parameter Θ are governed by continuous probability distributions.

Exercise 9.14: Let X be a standard normal random variable, and let $Y = XZ$, where Z is a random variable independent of X that takes on the value 1 with probability $1/2$ and the value -1 with probability $1/2$.

(a) Show that Y is also a standard normal random variable.

(b) Explain why X and Y are not independent.

(c) Provide a reasoning that shows that X and Y are not jointly normal.

(d) Calculate the correlation coefficient of X and Y.

Exercise 9.15: The *standard Cauchy distribution* has density function

$$f(x) = \frac{1}{\pi(1 + x^2)}.$$

(a) Show that the standard Cauchy distribution is actually a probability distribution.

(b) Find the distribution function for the standard Cauchy distribution.

(c) Show that the standard Cauchy distribution does not have a finite expectation.

(d) Let X and Y be independent standard normal random variables. Show that the distribution of X/Y is the standard Cauchy distribution.

CHAPTER TEN

Entropy, Randomness, and Information

Suppose that we have two biased coins. One comes up heads with probability 3/4, and the other comes up heads with probability 7/8. Which coin produces more randomness per flip? In this chapter, we introduce the *entropy* function as a universal measure of randomness. In particular, we show that the number of independent unbiased random bits that can be extracted from a sequence of biased coin flips corresponds to the entropy of the coin. Entropy also plays a fundamental role in information and communication. To demonstrate this role, we examine some basic results in compression and coding and see how they relate to entropy. The main result we prove is Shannon's coding theorem for the binary symmetric channel, one of the fundamental results of the field of information theory. Our proof of Shannon's theorem uses several ideas that we have developed in previous chapters, including Chernoff bounds, Markov's inequality, and the probabilistic method.

10.1. The Entropy Function

The *entropy* of a random variable is a function of its distribution that, as we shall see, gives a measure of the randomness of the distribution.

Definition 10.1:

1. The entropy *in bits of a discrete random variable X is given by*

$$H(X) = -\sum_x \Pr(X = x) \log_2 \Pr(X = x),$$

where the summation is over all values x in the range of X. Equivalently, we may write

$$H(X) = \mathbf{E}\left[\log_2 \frac{1}{\Pr(X)}\right].$$

2. The binary entropy function *H(p) for a random variable that assumes only two possible outcomes, one of which occurs with probability p, is*

$$H(p) = -p \log_2 p - (1 - p) \log_2(1 - p).$$

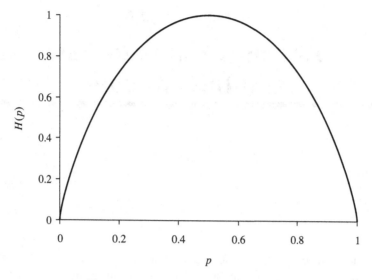

Figure 10.1: The binary entropy function.

We define $H(0) = H(1) = 0$, so the binary entropy function is continuous in the interval $[0, 1]$. The function is drawn in Figure 10.1.

For our two biased coins, the entropy of the coin that comes up heads with probability $3/4$ is

$$H\left(\frac{3}{4}\right) = -\frac{3}{4}\log_2\frac{3}{4} - \frac{1}{4}\log_2\frac{1}{4} = 2 - \frac{3}{4}\log_2 3 \approx 0.8113,$$

while the entropy of the coin that comes up heads with probability $7/8$ is

$$H\left(\frac{7}{8}\right) = -\frac{7}{8}\log_2\frac{7}{8} - \frac{1}{8}\log_2\frac{1}{8} = 3 - \frac{7}{8}\log_2 7 \approx 0.5436.$$

Hence the coin that comes up heads with probability $3/4$ has a larger entropy.

Taking the derivative of $H(p)$,

$$\frac{dH(p)}{dp} = -\log_2 p + \log_2(1 - p) = \log_2\frac{1 - p}{p},$$

we see that $H(p)$ is maximized when $p = 1/2$ and that $H(1/2) = 1$ bit. One way of interpreting this statement is to say: each time we flip a two-sided coin, we get out at most 1 bit worth of randomness, and we obtain exactly 1 bit of randomness when the coin is fair. Although this seems quite clear, it is not yet clear in what sense $H(3/4) = 2 - \frac{3}{4}\log_2 3$ means that we obtain $H(3/4)$ random bits each time we flip a coin that lands heads with probability $3/4$. We clarify this later in the chapter.

As another example, the entropy of a standard six-sided die that comes up on each side with probability $1/6$ has entropy $\log_2 6$. In general, a random variable that has n equally likely outcomes has entropy

$$-\sum_{i=1}^{n}\frac{1}{n}\log_2\frac{1}{n} = \log_2 n.$$

The entropy of an eight-sided die is therefore 3 bits. This result should seem quite natural; if the faces of the die were numbered from 0 to 7 written in binary, then the outcome of the die roll would give a sequence of 3 bits uniform over the set $\{0, 1\}^3$, which is equivalent to 3 bits generated independently and uniformly at random.

It is worth emphasizing that the entropy of a random variable X depends not on the values that X can take but only on the probability distribution of X over those values. The entropy of an eight-sided die does not depend on what numbers are on the faces of the die; it only matters that all eight sides are equally likely to come up. This property does not hold for the expectation or variance of X, but it does makes sense for a measure of randomness. To measure the randomness in a die, we should not care about what numbers are on the faces but only about how often the die comes up on each side.

Often in this chapter we consider the entropy of a sequence of independent random variables, such as the entropy of a sequence of independent coin flips. For such situations, the following lemma allows us to consider the entropy of each random variable to find the entropy of the sequence.

Lemma 10.1: *Let X_1 and X_2 be independent random variables, and let $Y = (X_1, X_2)$. Then*

$$H(Y) = H(X_1) + H(X_2).$$

Of course, the lemma is trivially extended by induction to the case where Y is any finite sequence of independent random variables.

Proof: In what follows, the summations are to be taken over all possible values that can be assumed by X_1 and X_2. The result follows by using the independence of X_1 and X_2 to simplify the expression:

$$H(Y) = -\sum_{x_1, x_2} \Pr((X_1, X_2) = (x_1, x_2)) \log_2 \Pr((X_1, X_2) = (x_1, x_2))$$

$$= -\sum_{x_1, x_2} \Pr(X_1 = x_1) \Pr(X_2 = x_2) \log_2 (\Pr(X_1 = x_1) \Pr(X_2 = x_2))$$

$$= -\sum_{x_1, x_2} \Pr(X_1 = x_1) \Pr(X_2 = x_2)(\log_2 \Pr(X_1 = x_1) + \log_2 \Pr(X_2 = x_2))$$

$$= -\sum_{x_1} \sum_{x_2} \Pr(X_2 = x_2) \Pr(X_1 = x_1) \log_2 \Pr(X_1 = x_1)$$
$$\quad - \sum_{x_2} \sum_{x_1} \Pr(X_1 = x_1) \Pr(X_2 = x_2) \log_2 \Pr(X_2 = x_2)$$

$$= -\left(\sum_{x_1} \Pr(X_1 = x_1) \log_2 \Pr(X_1 = x_1) \right) \left(\sum_{x_2} \Pr(X_2 = x_2) \right)$$
$$\quad - \left(\sum_{x_2} \Pr(X_2 = x_2) \log_2 \Pr(X_2 = x_2) \right) \left(\sum_{x_1} \Pr(X_1 = x_1) \right)$$

$$= -\sum_{x_1} \Pr(X_1 = x_1) \log_2 \Pr(X_1 = x_1) - \sum_{x_2} \Pr(X_2 = x_2) \log_2 \Pr(X_2 = x_2)$$

$$= H(X_1) + H(X_2). \qquad \blacksquare$$

10.2. Entropy and Binomial Coefficients

As a prelude to showing the various applications of entropy, we first demonstrate how it naturally arises in a purely combinatorial context.

Lemma 10.2: *Suppose that nq is an integer in the range $[0, n]$. Then*

$$\frac{2^{nH(q)}}{n+1} \leq \binom{n}{nq} \leq 2^{nH(q)}.$$

Proof: The statement is trivial if $q = 0$ or $q = 1$, so assume that $0 < q < 1$. To prove the upper bound, notice that by the binomial theorem we have

$$\binom{n}{nq} q^{qn}(1-q)^{(1-q)n} \leq \sum_{k=0}^{n} \binom{n}{k} q^k (1-q)^{n-k} \leq (q + (1-q))^n = 1.$$

Hence,

$$\binom{n}{nq} \leq q^{-qn}(1-q)^{-(1-q)n} = 2^{-qn \log_2 q} 2^{-(1-q)n \log_2(1-q)} = 2^{nH(q)}.$$

For the lower bound, we know that $\binom{n}{nq} q^{qn}(1-q)^{(1-q)n}$ is one term of the expression $\sum_{k=0}^{n} \binom{n}{k} q^k (1-q)^{n-k}$. We show that it is the *largest* term. Consider the difference between two consecutive terms as follows:

$$\binom{n}{k} q^k (1-q)^{n-k} - \binom{n}{k+1} q^{k+1}(1-q)^{n-k-1}$$

$$= \binom{n}{k} q^k (1-q)^{n-k} \left(1 - \frac{n-k}{k+1} \frac{q}{1-q}\right).$$

This difference is nonnegative whenever

$$1 - \frac{n-k}{k+1} \frac{q}{1-q} \geq 0$$

or (equivalently, after some algebra) whenever

$$k \geq qn - 1 + q.$$

The terms are therefore increasing up to $k = qn$ and decreasing after that point. Thus $k = qn$ gives the largest term in the summation.

Since the summation has $n + 1$ terms and since $\binom{n}{nq} q^{qn}(1-q)^{(1-q)n}$ is the largest term, we have

$$\binom{n}{nq} q^{qn}(1-q)^{(1-q)n} \geq \frac{1}{n+1}$$

or

$$\binom{n}{nq} \geq \frac{q^{-qn}(1-q)^{-(1-q)n}}{n+1} = \frac{2^{nH(q)}}{n+1}. \qquad \blacksquare$$

We often use the following slightly more specific corollary.

Corollary 10.3: *When* $0 \leq q \leq 1/2$,

$$\binom{n}{\lfloor nq \rfloor} \leq 2^{nH(q)}; \tag{10.1}$$

similarly, when $1/2 \leq q \leq 1$,

$$\binom{n}{\lceil nq \rceil} \leq 2^{nH(q)}. \tag{10.2}$$

For $1/2 \leq q \leq 1$,

$$\frac{2^{nH(q)}}{n+1} \leq \binom{n}{\lfloor nq \rfloor}; \tag{10.3}$$

similarly, when $0 \leq q \leq 1/2$,

$$\frac{2^{nH(q)}}{n+1} \leq \binom{n}{\lceil nq \rceil}. \tag{10.4}$$

Proof: We first prove Eqn. (10.1); the proof of Eqn. (10.2) is entirely similar. When $0 \leq q \leq 1/2$,

$$\binom{n}{\lfloor nq \rfloor} q^{qn}(1-q)^{(1-q)n} \leq \binom{n}{\lfloor nq \rfloor} q^{\lfloor qn \rfloor}(1-q)^{n-\lfloor qn \rfloor} \leq \sum_{k=0}^{n} \binom{n}{k} q^k (1-q)^{n-k} = 1,$$

from which we can proceed exactly as in Lemma 10.2.

Eqn. (10.3) holds because, when $q \geq 1/2$, Lemma 10.2 gives

$$\binom{n}{\lfloor nq \rfloor} \geq \frac{2^{nH(\lfloor nq \rfloor/n)}}{n+1} \geq \frac{2^{nH(q)}}{n+1};$$

Eqn. (10.4) is derived similarly. ∎

Although these bounds are loose, they are sufficient for our purposes. The relation between the combinatorial coefficients and the entropy function arises repeatedly in the proofs of this chapter when we consider a sequence of biased coin tosses, where the coin lands heads with probability $p > 1/2$. Applying the Chernoff bound, we know that, for sufficiently large n, the number of heads will almost always be close to np. Thus the sequence will almost always be one of roughly $\binom{n}{np} \approx 2^{nH(p)}$ sequences, where the approximation follows from Lemma 10.2. Moreover, each such sequence occurs with probability roughly

$$p^{np}(1-p)^{n(1-p)} \approx 2^{-nH(p)}.$$

Hence, when we consider the outcome of n flips with a biased coin, we can essentially restrict ourselves to the roughly $2^{nH(p)}$ outcomes that occur with roughly equal probability.

10.3. Entropy: A Measure of Randomness

One way of interpreting the entropy of a random variable is as a measure of how many unbiased, independent bits can be extracted, on average, from one instantiation of the random variable. We consider this question in the context of a biased coin, showing that, for sufficiently large n, the expected number of bits that can be extracted from n flips of a coin that comes up heads with probability $p > 1/2$ is essentially $nH(p)$. In other words, on average, one can generate approximately $H(p)$ independent bits from each flip of a coin with entropy $H(p)$. This result can be generalized to other random variables, but we focus on the specific case of biased coins here (and throughout this chapter) to keep the arguments more transparent.

We begin with a definition that clarifies what we mean by extracting random bits.

Definition 10.2: *Let $|y|$ be the number of bits in a sequence of bits y. An extraction function Ext takes as input the value of a random variable X and outputs a sequence of bits y such that*

$$\Pr(\text{Ext}(X) = y \mid |y| = k) = 1/2^k$$

whenever $\Pr(|y| = k) > 0.$

In the case of a biased coin, the input X is the outcome of n flips of our biased coin. The number of bits in the output is not fixed but instead can depend on the input. If the extraction function outputs k bits, we can think of these bits as having been generated independently and uniformly at random, since each sequence of k bits is equally likely to appear. Also, there is nothing in the definition that requires that the extraction function be efficient to compute. We do not concern ourselves with efficiency here, although we do consider an efficient extraction algorithm in Exercise 10.12.

As a first step toward proving our results about extracting unbiased bits from biased coins, we consider the problem of extracting random bits from a uniformly distributed integer random variable. For example, let X be an integer chosen uniformly at random from $\{0, \ldots, 7\}$, and let Y be the sequence of 3 bits obtained when we write X as a binary number. If $X = 0$ then $Y = 000$, and if $X = 7$ then $Y = 111$. It is easy to check that every sequence of 3 bits is equally likely to arise, so we have a trivial extraction function Ext by associating any input X with the corresponding output Y.

Things are slightly harder when X is uniform over $\{0, \ldots, 11\}$. If $X \leq 7$, then we can again let Y be the sequence of 3 bits obtained when we write X in binary. This leaves the case $X \in \{8, 9, 10, 11\}$. We can associate each of these four possibilities with a distinct sequence of 2 bits, for example, by letting Y be the sequence of 2 bits obtained from writing $X - 8$ as a binary number. Thus, if $X = 8$ then $Y = 00$, and if $X = 11$ then

Input	0	1	2	3	4	5	6	7
Output	000	001	010	011	100	101	110	111

Input	0	1	2	3	4	5	6	7	8	9	10	11
Output	000	001	010	011	100	101	110	111	00	01	10	11

Figure 10.2: Extraction functions for numbers that are chosen uniformly at random from $\{0, \ldots, 7\}$ and $\{0, \ldots, 11\}$.

$Y = 11$. The entire extraction function is shown in Figure 10.2. Every 3-bit sequence arises with the same probability $1/12$, and every 2-bit sequence arises with the same probability $1/12$, so Definition 10.2 is satisfied.

We generalize from these examples to the following theorem.

Theorem 10.4: *Suppose that the value of a random variable X is chosen uniformly at random from the integers $\{0, \ldots, m-1\}$, so that $H(X) = \log_2 m$. Then there is an extraction function for X that outputs on average at least $\lfloor \log_2 m \rfloor - 1 = \lfloor H(X) \rfloor - 1$ independent and unbiased bits.*

Proof: If $m > 1$ is a power of 2, then the extraction function can simply output the bit representation of the input X using $\log_2 m$ bits. (If $m = 1$, then it outputs nothing or, equivalently, an empty sequence.) All output sequences have $\log_2 m$ bits, and all sequences of $\log_2 m$ bits are equally likely to appear, so this satisfies Definition 10.2. If m is not a power of 2, then matters become more complicated. We describe the extraction function recursively. (A nonrecursive description is given in Exercise 10.8.) Let $\alpha = \lfloor \log_2 m \rfloor$. If $X \le 2^\alpha - 1$, then the function outputs the α-bit binary representation of X; all sequences of α bits are equally likely to be output in this case. If $X \ge 2^\alpha$, then $X - 2^\alpha$ is uniformly distributed in the set $\{0, \ldots, m - 2^\alpha - 1\}$, which is smaller than the set $\{0, \ldots, m\}$. The extraction function can then recursively produce the output from the extraction function for the variable $X - 2^\alpha$.

The recursive extraction function maintains the property that, for every k, each of the 2^k sequences of k bits is output with the same probability. We claim by induction that the expected number of unbiased, independent bits produced by this extraction function is at least $\lfloor \log_2 m \rfloor - 1$. The cases where m is a power of 2 are trivial. Otherwise, by induction, the number of bits Y in the output satisfies

$$\mathbf{E}[Y] \ge \frac{2^\alpha}{m}\alpha + \frac{m - 2^\alpha}{m}(\lfloor \log_2(m - 2^\alpha) \rfloor - 1)$$

$$= \alpha - \frac{m - 2^\alpha}{m}(\alpha - \lfloor \log_2(m - 2^\alpha) \rfloor + 1).$$

275

Suppose $\lfloor \log_2(m - 2^\alpha) \rfloor = \beta$, where $0 \leq \beta \leq \alpha - 1$. Then $(m - 2^\alpha)/m$ is maximized when m is as large as possible, which corresponds to $m = 2^\alpha + 2^{\beta+1} - 1$. Hence

$$\mathbf{E}[Y] \geq \alpha - \frac{2^{\beta+1} - 1}{2^\alpha + 2^{\beta+1} - 1}(\alpha - \beta + 1)$$

$$\geq \alpha - \frac{1}{2^{\alpha-\beta-1} + 1}(\alpha - \beta + 1)$$

$$\geq \alpha - 1,$$

where we use $2^\alpha + 2^{\beta+1} - 1 \geq (2^{\beta+1} - 1)(2^{\alpha-\beta-1} + 1)$ for the second line, and $x/(2^{x-2} + 1) \leq 1$ for integers $x \geq 2$ for the third line.

This completes the induction. ∎

We use Theorem 10.4 in our proof of the main result of this section.

Theorem 10.5: *Consider a coin that comes up heads with probability $p > 1/2$. For any constant $\delta > 0$ and for n sufficiently large:*

1. *there exists an extraction function* Ext *that outputs, on an input sequence of n independent flips, an average of at least $(1 - \delta)nH(p)$ independent random bits; and*
2. *the average number of bits output by any extraction function* Ext *on an input sequence of n independent flips is at most $nH(p)$.*

Proof: We begin by describing an extraction function that generates, on average, at least $(1 - \delta)nH(p)$ random bits from n flips of the biased coin. We saw before that, in the case of a biased coin, the outcome of n flips is most likely to be one of roughly $2^{nH(p)}$ sequences, each occurring with probability roughly $2^{-nH(p)}$. If we actually had a uniform distribution of this type, we could use the extraction function that we have just described for numbers chosen uniformly at random to obtain on average almost $nH(p)$ uniform random bits. In what follows, we handle the technical details that arise because the distribution is not exactly uniform.

There are $\binom{n}{j}$ possible sequences with exactly j heads, and each of them has the same probability of occurring, $p^j(1 - p)^{n-j}$. For each value of j, $0 \leq j \leq n$, we map each of the $\binom{n}{j}$ sequences with j heads to a unique integer in the set $\{0, \ldots, \binom{n}{j} - 1\}$. When j heads come up, we map the sequence to the corresponding number. Conditioned on there being j heads, this number is uniform on the integers $\{0, \ldots, \binom{n}{j} - 1\}$, and hence we can apply the extraction function of Theorem 10.4 designed for this case. Let Z be a random variable representing the number of heads flipped, and let B be the random variable representing the number of bits our extraction function produces. Then

$$\mathbf{E}[B] = \sum_{k=0}^{n} \Pr(Z = k)\mathbf{E}[B \mid Z = k]$$

and, by Theorem 10.4,

$$\mathbf{E}[B \mid Z = k] \geq \left\lfloor \log_2 \binom{n}{k} \right\rfloor - 1.$$

Let $\varepsilon < \min(p - 1/2, 1 - p)$ represent a constant to be determined. We compute a lower bound for $\mathbf{E}[B]$ by considering only values of k with $n(p - \varepsilon) \leq k \leq n(p + \varepsilon)$.

For every such k,

$$\binom{n}{k} \geq \binom{n}{\lfloor n(p+\varepsilon)\rfloor} \geq \frac{2^{nH(p+\varepsilon)}}{n+1},$$

where the last inequality follows from Corollary 10.3. Hence

$$\mathbf{E}[B] \geq \sum_{k=\lfloor n(p-\varepsilon)\rfloor}^{\lceil n(p+\varepsilon)\rceil} \Pr(Z=k)\mathbf{E}[B \mid Z=k]$$

$$\geq \sum_{k=\lfloor n(p-\varepsilon)\rfloor}^{\lceil n(p+\varepsilon)\rceil} \Pr(Z=k)\left(\left\lfloor \log_2\binom{n}{k}\right\rfloor - 1\right)$$

$$\geq \left(\log_2 \frac{2^{nH(p+\varepsilon)}}{n+1} - 2\right)\sum_{k=\lfloor n(p-\varepsilon)\rfloor}^{\lceil n(p+\varepsilon)\rceil} \Pr(Z=k)$$

$$\geq (nH(p+\varepsilon) - \log_2(n+1) - 2)\Pr(|Z-np| \leq \varepsilon n).$$

Now $\mathbf{E}[Z] = np$, and $\Pr(|Z-np| > \varepsilon n)$ can be bounded by using the Chernoff bound of Eqn. (4.6), giving

$$\Pr(|Z-np| > \varepsilon n) \leq 2e^{-n\varepsilon^2/3p}.$$

Hence

$$\mathbf{E}[B] \geq (nH(p+\varepsilon) - \log_2(n+1) - 2)(1 - 2e^{-n\varepsilon^2/3p}).$$

We conclude that, for any constant $\delta > 0$, we can have

$$\mathbf{E}[B] \geq (1-\delta)nH(p)$$

by choosing ε sufficiently small and n sufficiently large. For example, for sufficiently small ε,

$$nH(p+\varepsilon) \geq (1-\delta/3)nH(p),$$

and when $n > (3p/\varepsilon^2)\ln(6/\delta)$ we have

$$1 - 2e^{-n\varepsilon^2/3p} \geq 1 - \delta/3.$$

Hence, with these choices,

$$\mathbf{E}[B] \geq ((1-\delta/3)nH(p) - \log_2(n+1) - 2)(1 - \delta/3).$$

As long as we now also choose n sufficiently large that $(\delta/3)nH(p)$ is greater than $\log_2(n+1) + 2$, we have

$$\mathbf{E}[B] \geq ((1-2\delta/3)nH(p))(1-\delta/3) \geq (1-\delta)nH(p),$$

proving there exists an extraction function that can extract $(1-\delta)nH(p)$ independent and uniform bits on average from n flips of the biased coin.

We now show that no extraction function can obtain more than $nH(p)$ bits on average. The proof relies on the following basic fact: If an input sequence x occurs with probability q, then the corresponding output sequence $\text{Ext}(x)$ can have at most

$|\text{Ext}(x)| \leq \log_2(1/q)$ bits. This is because all sequences with $|\text{Ext}(x)|$ bits would have probability at least q, so

$$2^{|\text{Ext}(x)|}q \leq 1,$$

giving the desired bound on $\text{Ext}(x)$. Given any extraction function, if B is a random variable representing the number of bits our extraction function produces on input X, then

$$\mathbf{E}[B] = \sum_x \Pr(X = x)|\text{Ext}(x)|$$

$$\leq \sum_x \Pr(X = x) \log_2 \frac{1}{\Pr(X = x)}$$

$$= \mathbf{E}\left[\log_2 \frac{1}{\Pr(X)}\right]$$

$$= H(X). \qquad \blacksquare$$

Another natural question to ask is how we can generate biased bits from an unbiased coin. This question is partially answered in Exercise 10.11.

10.4. Compression

A second way of interpreting the entropy value comes from compression. Again suppose we have a coin that comes up heads with probability $p > 1/2$ and that we flip it n times, keeping track of which flips are heads and which flips are tails. We could represent every outcome by using one bit per flip, with 0 representing heads and 1 representing tails, and use a total of n bits. If we take advantage of the fact that the coin is biased, we can do better on average. For example, suppose that $p = 3/4$. For a pair of consecutive flips, we use 0 to represent that both flips were heads, 10 to represent that the first flip was heads and the second tails, 110 to represent that the first flip was tails and the second heads, and 111 to represent that both flips were tails. Then the average number of bits we use per pair of flips is

$$1 \cdot \frac{9}{16} + 2 \cdot \frac{3}{16} + 3 \cdot \frac{3}{16} + 3 \cdot \frac{1}{16} = \frac{27}{16} < 2.$$

Hence, on average, we can use less than the 1 bit per flip of the standard scheme by breaking a sequence of n flips into pairs and representing each pair in the manner shown. This is an example of *compression*.

It is worth emphasizing that the representation that we used here has a special property: if we write the representation of a sequence of flips, it can be uniquely decoded simply by parsing it from left to right. For example, the sequence

$$011110$$

corresponds to two heads, followed by two tails, followed by a heads and a tails. There is no ambiguity, because no other sequence of flips could produce this output.

Our representation has this property because no bit sequence we use to represent a pair of flips is the prefix of another bit sequence used in the representation. Representations with this property are called *prefix codes,* which are discussed further in Exercise 10.15.

Compression continues to be a subject of considerable study. When storing or transmitting information, saving bits usually corresponds to saving resources, so finding ways to reduce the number of used bits by taking advantage of the data's structure is often worthwhile.

We consider here the special case of compressing the outcome of a sequence of biased coin flips. For a biased coin with entropy $H(p)$, we show (a) that the outcome of n flips of the coin can be represented by approximately $nH(p)$ bits on average and (b) that approximately $nH(p)$ bits on average are necessary. In particular, any representation of the outcome of n flips of a fair coin essentially requires n bits. The entropy is therefore a measure of the average number of bits generated by each coin flip after compression. This argument can be generalized to any discrete random variable X, so that n independent, identically distributed random variables $X_1, X_2, \ldots, X_n$ with the same distribution X can be represented using approximately $nH(X)$ bits on average. In the setting of compression, entropy can be viewed as measuring the amount of information in the input sequence. The larger the entropy of the sequence, the more bits are needed in order to represent it.

We begin with a definition that clarifies what we mean by compression in this context.

Definition 10.3: *A compression function Com takes as input a sequence of n coin flips, given as an element of $\{H, T\}^n$, and outputs a sequence of bits such that each input sequence of n flips yields a distinct output sequence.*

Definition 10.3 is rather weak, but it will prove sufficient for our purposes. Usually, compression functions must satisfy stronger requirements; for example, we may require a prefix code to simplify decoding. Using this weaker definition makes our lower-bound proof stronger. Also, though we are not concerned here with the efficiency of compressing and decompressing procedures, there are very efficient compression schemes that perform nearly optimally in many situations. We will consider an efficient compression scheme in Exercise 10.17.

The following theorem formalizes the relationship between the entropy of a biased coin and compression.

Theorem 10.6: *Consider a coin that comes up heads with probability $p > 1/2$. For any constant $\delta > 0$, when n is sufficiently large:*

1. *there exists a compression function Com such that the expected number of bits output by Com on an input sequence of n independent coin flips is at most $(1 + \delta)nH(p)$; and*

2. *the expected number of bits output by any compression function on an input sequence of n independent coin flips is at least $(1 - \delta)nH(p)$.*

Theorem 10.6 is quite similar to Theorem 10.5. The lower bound on the expected number of bits output by any compression function is slightly weaker. In fact, we could raise this lower bound to $nH(p)$ if we insisted that the code be a prefix code – so that no output is the prefix of any other – but we do not prove this here. The compression function we design to prove an upper bound on the expected number of output bits does yield a prefix code. Our construction of this compression function follows roughly the same intuition as Theorem 10.5. We know that, with high probability, the outcome from the n flips will be one of roughly $2^{nH(p)}$ sequences with roughly np heads. We can use about $nH(p)$ bits to represent each one of these sequences, yielding the existence of an appropriate compression function.

Proof of Theorem 10.6: We first show that there exists a compression function as guaranteed by the theorem. Let $\varepsilon > 0$ be a suitably small constant with $p - \varepsilon > 1/2$. Let X be the number of heads in n flips of the coin. The first bit output by the compression function we use as a flag. We set it to 0 if there are at least $n(p - \varepsilon)$ heads in the sequence and to 1 otherwise. When the first bit is a 1, the compression function uses the expensive default scheme, using 1 bit for each of the n flips. This requires that $n + 1$ total bits be output; however, by the Chernoff bound of Eqn. (4.5), the probability that this case happens is bounded by

$$\Pr(X < n(p - \varepsilon)) \leq e^{-n\varepsilon^2/2p}.$$

Now let us consider the case where there are at least $n(p - \varepsilon)$ heads. The number of coin-flip sequences of this form is

$$\sum_{j=\lceil n(p-\varepsilon)\rceil}^{n} \binom{n}{j} \leq \sum_{j=\lceil n(p-\varepsilon)\rceil}^{n} \binom{n}{\lceil n(p-\varepsilon)\rceil} \leq \frac{n}{2} 2^{nH(p-\varepsilon)}.$$

The first inequality arises because the binomial terms are decreasing as long as $j > n/2$, and the second is a consequence of Corollary 10.3. For each such sequence of coin flips, the compression function can assign a unique sequence of exactly $\lfloor nH(p - \varepsilon) + \log_2 n \rfloor$ bits to represent it, since

$$2^{\lfloor nH(p-\varepsilon)+\log_2 n\rfloor} \geq \frac{n}{2} 2^{nH(p-\varepsilon)}.$$

Including the flag bit, it therefore takes at most $nH(p - \varepsilon) + \log_2 n + 1$ bits to represent the sequences of coin flips with this many heads.

Totaling these results, we find that the expected number of bits required by the compression function is at most

$$e^{-n\varepsilon^2/2p}(n + 1) + (1 - e^{-n\varepsilon^2/2p})(nH(p - \varepsilon) + \log_2 n + 1) \leq (1 + \delta)nH(p),$$

where the inequality holds by first taking ε sufficiently small and then taking n sufficiently large in a manner similar to that of Theorem 10.5.

We now show the lower bound. To begin, recall that the probability that a specific sequence with k heads is flipped is $p^k(1 - p)^{n-k}$. Because $p > 1/2$, if sequence S_1 has more heads than another sequence S_2, then S_1 is more likely to appear than S_2. Also, we have the following lemma.

Lemma 10.7: *If sequence S_1 is more likely than S_2, then the compression function that minimizes the expected number of bits in the output assigns a bit sequence to S_2 that is at least as long as S_1.*

Proof: Suppose that a compression function assigns a bit sequence to S_2 that is shorter than the bit sequence it assigns to S_1. We can improve the expected number of bits output by the compression function by switching the output sequences associated with S_1 and S_2, and therefore this compression function is not optimal. ∎

Hence sequences with more heads should get shorter strings from an optimal compression function.

We also make use of the following simple fact. If the compression function assigns distinct sequences of bits to represent each of s coin-flip sequences, then one of the output bit sequences for the s input sequences must have length at least $\log_2 s - 1$ bits. This is because there are at most $1 + 2 + 4 + \cdots + 2^b = 2^{b+1} - 1$ distinct bit sequences with up to b bits, so if each of s sequences of coin flips is assigned a bit sequence of at most b bits, then we must have $2^{b+1} > s$ and hence $b > \log_2 s - 1$.

Fix a suitably small $\varepsilon > 0$ and count the number of input sequences that have $\lfloor (p + \varepsilon)n \rfloor$ heads. There are $\binom{n}{\lfloor (p+\varepsilon)n \rfloor}$ sequences with $\lfloor (p + \varepsilon)n \rfloor$ heads and, by Corollary 10.3,

$$\binom{n}{\lfloor (p + \varepsilon)n \rfloor} \geq \frac{2^{nH(p+\varepsilon)}}{n + 1}.$$

Hence any compression function must output at least $\log_2(2^{nH(p+\varepsilon)}/(n + 1)) - 1 = nH(p + \varepsilon) - \log_2(n + 1) - 1$ bits on at least one of the sequences of coin flips with $\lfloor (p + \varepsilon)n \rfloor$ heads. The compression function that minimizes the expected output length must therefore use at least this many bits to represent any sequence with fewer heads, by Lemma 10.7.

By the Chernoff bound of Eqn. (4.2), the number of heads X satisfies

$$\Pr(X \geq \lfloor n(p + \varepsilon) \rfloor) \leq \Pr(X \geq n(p + \varepsilon - 1/n)) \leq e^{-n(\varepsilon - 1/n)^2/3p} \leq e^{-n\varepsilon^2/12p}$$

as long as n is sufficiently large (specifically, $n > 2/\varepsilon$). We thus obtain, with probability at least $1 - e^{-n\varepsilon^2/12p}$, an input sequence with fewer than $\lfloor n(p + \varepsilon) \rfloor$ heads, and by our previous reasoning the compression function that minimizes the expected output length must still output at least $nH(p + \varepsilon) - \log_2(n + 1) - 1$ bits in this case. The expected number of output bits is therefore at least

$$(1 - e^{-n\varepsilon^2/12p})(nH(p + \varepsilon) - \log_2(n + 1) - 1).$$

This can be made to be at least $(1 - \delta)nH(p)$ by first taking ε to be sufficiently small and then taking n to be sufficiently large. ∎

10.5.* Coding: Shannon's Theorem

We have seen how compression can reduce the expected number of bits required to represent data by changing the representation of the data. Coding also changes the representation of the data. Instead of reducing the number of bits required to represent the data, however, coding adds redundancy in order to protect the data against loss or errors.

In coding theory, we model the information being passed from a sender to a receiver through a *channel*. The channel may introduce noise, distorting the value of some of the bits during the transmission. The channel can be a wired connection, a wireless connection, or a storage network. For example, if I store data on a recordable medium and later try to read it back, then I am both the sender and the receiver, and the storage medium acts as the channel. In this section, we focus on one specific type of channel.

Definition 10.4: *The input to a* binary symmetric channel *with parameter p is a sequence of bits $x_1, x_2, \ldots$, and the output is a sequence of bits $y_1, y_2, \ldots$, such that $\Pr(x_i = y_i) = 1 - p$ independently for each i. Informally, each bit sent is flipped to the wrong value independently with probability p.*

To get useful information out of the channel, we may introduce redundancy to help protect against the introduction of errors. As an extreme example, suppose the sender wants to send the receiver a single bit of information over a binary symmetric channel. To protect against the possibility of error, the sender and receiver agree to repeat the bit n times. If $p < 1/2$, a natural decoding scheme for the receiver is to look at the n bits received and decide that the value that was received more frequently is the bit value the sender intended. The larger n is, the more likely the receiver determines the correct bit; by repeating the bit enough times, the probability of error can be made arbitrarily small. This example is considered more extensively in Exercise 10.18.

Coding theory studies the trade-off between the amount of redundancy required and the probability of a decoding error over various types of channels. For the binary symmetric channel, simply repeating bits may not be the best use of redundancy. Instead we consider more general *encoding functions*.

Definition 10.5: *A (k, n) encoding function Enc: $\{0,1\}^k \rightarrow \{0,1\}^n$ takes as input a sequence of k bits and outputs a sequence of n bits. A (k, n) decoding function Dec: $\{0,1\}^n \rightarrow \{0,1\}^k$ takes as input a sequence of n bits and outputs a sequence of k bits.*

With coding, the sender takes a k-bit message and encodes it into a block of $n \geq k$ bits via the encoding function. These bits are then sent over the channel. The receiver examines the n bits received and attempts to determine the original k-bit message using the decoding function.

Given a binary channel with parameter p and a target encoding length of n, we wish to determine the largest value of k so that there exist (k, n) encoding and decoding functions with the property that, for any input sequence of k bits, with suitably large probability the receiver decodes the correct input from the corresponding n-bit encoding sequence after it has been distorted by the channel.

Let $m \in \{0,1\}^k$ be the message to be sent and Enc(m) the sequence of bits sent over the channel. Let the random variable X denote the sequence of received bits. We require that Dec(X) = m with probability at least $1 - \gamma$ for all possible messages m and a prechosen constant γ. If there were no noise, then we could send the original k bits over the channel. The noise reduces the information that the receiver can extract from each bit sent, and so the sender can reliably send messages of only about $k = n(1 - H(p))$ bits within each block of n bits. This result is known as Shannon's theorem, which we prove in the following form.

Theorem 10.8: *For a binary symmetric channel with parameter $p < 1/2$ and for any constants $\delta, \gamma > 0$, when n is sufficiently large:*

1. *for any $k \leq n(1 - H(p) - \delta)$, there exist (k, n) encoding and decoding functions such that the probability the receiver fails to obtain the correct message is at most γ for every possible k-bit input message; and*
2. *there are no (k, n) encoding and decoding functions with $k \geq n(1 - H(p) + \delta)$ such that the probability of decoding correctly is at least γ for a k-bit input message chosen uniformly at random.*

Proof: We first prove the existence of suitable (k, n) encoding and decoding functions when $k \leq n(1 - H(p) - \delta)$ by using the probabilistic method. In the end, we want our encoding and decoding functions to have error probability at most γ on *every* possible input. We begin with a weaker result, showing that there exist appropriate coding functions when the input is chosen uniformly at random from all k-bit inputs.

The encoding function assigns to each of the 2^k strings an n-bit *codeword* chosen independently and uniformly at random from the space of all n-bit sequences. Label these codewords $X_0, X_1, \ldots, X_{2^k-1}$. The encoding function simply outputs the codeword assigned to the k-bit message using a large lookup table containing an entry for each k-bit string. (You may be concerned that two codewords may turn out to be the same; the probability of this is very small and is handled in the analysis that follows.)

To describe the decoding function, we provide a decoding algorithm based on the lookup table for the encoding function, which we may assume the receiver possesses. The decoding algorithm makes use of the fact that the receiver expects the channel to make roughly pn errors. The receiver therefore looks for a codeword that differs from the n bits received in between $(p - \varepsilon)n$ and $(p + \varepsilon)n$ places for some suitably small constant $\varepsilon > 0$. If just one codeword has this property, then the receiver will assume that this was the codeword sent and will recover the message accordingly. If more than one codeword has this property, the decoding algorithm fails. The decoding algorithm described here requires exponential time and space. As in the rest of this chapter, we are not now concerned with efficiency issues.

The corresponding (k, n) decoding function can be obtained from the algorithm by simply running through all possible n-bit sequences. Whenever a sequence decodes properly with the foregoing algorithm, the output of the decoding function for that sequence is set to the k-bit sequence associated with the corresponding codeword. Whenever the algorithm fails, the output for the sequence can be any arbitrary sequence of k bits. For the decoding function to fail, at least one of the two following events must occur:

- the channel does not make between $(p - \varepsilon)n$ and $(p + \varepsilon)n$ errors; or
- when a codeword is sent, the received sequence differs from some other codeword in between $(p - \varepsilon)n$ and $(p + \varepsilon)n$ places.

283

The path of the proof is now clear. A Chernoff bound can be used to show that, with high probability, the channel does not make too few or too many errors. Conditioning on the number of errors being neither too few nor too many, the question becomes how large k can be while ensuring that, with the required probability, the received sequence does not differ from multiple codewords in between $(p - \varepsilon)n$ and $(p + \varepsilon)n$ places.

Now that we have described the encoding and decoding functions, we establish the notation to be used in the analysis. Let R be the received sequence of bits. For sequences s_1 and s_2 of n bits, we write $\Delta(s_1, s_2)$ for the number of positions where these sequences differ. This value $\Delta(s_1, s_2)$ is referred to as the *Hamming distance* between the two strings. We say that the pair (s_1, s_2) has *weight*

$$w(s_1, s_2) = p^{\Delta(s_1, s_2)}(1 - p)^{n - \Delta(s_1, s_2)}.$$

The weight corresponds to the probability that s_2 is received when s_1 is sent over the channel. We introduce random variables $S_0, S_1, \ldots, S_{2^{k-1}}$ and $W_0, W_1, \ldots, W_{2^{k-1}}$ defined as follows. The set S_i is the set of all received sequences that decode to X_i. The value W_i is given by

$$W_i = \sum_{r \notin S_i} w(X_i, r).$$

The S_i and W_i are random variables that depend only on the random choices of $X_0, X_1, \ldots, X_{2^{k-1}}$. The variable W_i represents the probability that, when X_i is sent, the received sequence R does not lie in S_i and hence is decoded incorrectly. It is also helpful to express W_i in the following way: letting $I_{i,s}$ be an indicator random variable that is 1 if $s \notin S_i$ and 0 otherwise, we can write

$$W_i = \sum_r I_{i,r} w(X_i, r).$$

We start by bounding $\mathbf{E}[W_i]$. By symmetry, $\mathbf{E}[W_i]$ is the same for all i, so we bound $\mathbf{E}[W_0]$. Now

$$\mathbf{E}[W_0] = \mathbf{E}\left[\sum_r I_{0,r} w(X_0, r)\right]$$
$$= \sum_r \mathbf{E}[w(X_0, r) I_{0,r}].$$

We split the sum into two parts. Let $T_1 = \{s : |\Delta(X_0, s) - pn| > \varepsilon n\}$ and $T_2 = \{s : |\Delta(X_0, s) - pn| \leq \varepsilon n\}$, where $\varepsilon > 0$ is some constant to be determined. Then

$$\sum_r \mathbf{E}[w(X_0, r) I_{0,r}] = \sum_{r \in T_1} \mathbf{E}[w(X_0, r) I_{0,r}] + \sum_{r \in T_2} \mathbf{E}[w(X_0, r) I_{0,r}],$$

and we bound each term.

284

We first bound

$$\sum_{r \in T_1} \mathbf{E}[w(X_0, r)I_{0,r}] \le \sum_{r \in T_1} w(X_0, r)$$

$$= \sum_{r:|\Delta(X_0,r)-pn|>\varepsilon n} p^{\Delta(X_0,r)}(1-p)^{n-\Delta(X_0,r)}$$

$$= \Pr(|\Delta(X_0, R) - np| > \varepsilon n).$$

That is, to bound the first term, we simply bound the probability that the receiver fails to decode correctly and the number of errors is not in the range $[(p - \varepsilon)n, (p + \varepsilon)n]$ by the probability that the number of errors is not in this range. Equivalently, we obtain our bound by assuming that, whenever there are too many or too few errors introduced by the channel, we fail to decode correctly. This probability is very small, as we can see by using the Chernoff bound of Eqn. (4.6):

$$\Pr(|\Delta(X_0, R) - np| > \varepsilon n) \le 2e^{-\varepsilon^2 n/3p}.$$

For any $\varepsilon > 0$, we can choose n sufficiently large so that this probability, and hence $\sum_{r \in T_1} \mathbf{E}[w(X_0, r)I_{0,r}]$, is less than $\gamma/2$.

We now find an upper bound for $\sum_{r \in T_2} \mathbf{E}[w(X_0, r)I_{0,r}]$. For every $r \in T_2$, the decoding algorithm will be successful when r is received unless r differs from some other codeword X_i in between $(p - \varepsilon)n$ and $(p + \varepsilon)n$ places. Hence $I_{0,r}$ will be 1 only if such an X_i exists, and thus for any values of X_0 and $r \in T_2$ we have

$$\mathbf{E}[w(X_0, r)I_{0,r}]$$
$$= w(X_0, r) \Pr(\text{for some } X_i \text{ with } 1 \le i \le 2^k - 1, |\Delta(X_i, r) - pn| \le \varepsilon n).$$

It follows that if we obtain an upper bound

$$\Pr(\text{for some } X_i \text{ with } 1 \le i \le 2^k - 1, |\Delta(X_i, r) - pn| \le \varepsilon n) \le \gamma/2$$

for any values of X_0 and $r \in T_2$, then

$$\sum_{r \in T_2} \mathbf{E}[w(X_0, r)I_{0,r}] \le \sum_{r \in T_2} w(X_0, r)\frac{\gamma}{2} \le \frac{\gamma}{2}.$$

To obtain this upper bound, we recall that the other codewords $X_1, X_2, \ldots, X_{2^{k-1}}$ are chosen independently and uniformly at random. The probability that any other specific codeword X_i, $i > 0$, differs from any given string r of length n in between $(p - \varepsilon)n$ and $(p + \varepsilon)n$ places is therefore at most

$$\sum_{j=\lceil n(p-\varepsilon)\rceil}^{\lfloor n(p+\varepsilon)\rfloor} \frac{\binom{n}{j}}{2^n} \le n\frac{\binom{n}{\lfloor n(p+\varepsilon)\rfloor}}{2^n}.$$

Here we have bounded the summation by n times its largest term; $\binom{n}{j}$ is largest when $j = \lfloor n(p + \varepsilon) \rfloor$ over the range of j in the summation, as long as ε is chosen so that $p + \varepsilon < 1/2$.

285

Using Corollary 10.3,

$$\frac{\binom{n}{\lfloor n(p+\varepsilon)\rfloor}}{2^n} \leq \frac{2^{H(p+\varepsilon)n}}{2^n}$$
$$= 2^{-n(1-H(p+\varepsilon))}.$$

Hence the probability that any specific X_i matches a string r on a number of bits so as to cause a decoding failure is at most $n2^{-n(1-H(p+\varepsilon))}$. By a union bound, the probability that any of the $2^k - 1$ other codewords cause a decoding failure when X_0 is sent is at most

$$n2^{-n(1-H(p+\varepsilon))}(2^k - 1) \leq n2^{n(H(p+\varepsilon)-H(p)-\delta)},$$

where we have used the fact that $k \leq n(1 - H(p) - \delta)$. By choosing ε small enough so that $H(p + \varepsilon) - H(p) - \delta$ is negative and then choosing n sufficiently large, we can make this term as small as desired, and in particular we can make it less than $\gamma/2$.

By summing the bounds over the two sets T_1 and T_2, which correspond to the two types of error in the decoding algorithm, we find that $\mathbf{E}[W_0] \leq \gamma$.

We can bootstrap this result to show that there exists a specific code such that, if the k-bit message to be sent is chosen uniformly at random, then the code fails with probability γ. We use the linearity of expectations and the probabilistic method. We have that

$$\sum_{j=0}^{2^k-1} \mathbf{E}[W_j] = \mathbf{E}\left[\sum_{j=0}^{2^k-1} W_j\right] \leq 2^k\gamma,$$

where again the expectation is over the random choices of the codewords $X_0, X_1, \ldots, X_{2^k-1}$. By the probabilistic method, there must exist a specific set of codewords $x_0, x_1, \ldots, x_{2^k-1}$ such that

$$\sum_{j=0}^{2^k-1} W_j \leq 2^k\gamma.$$

When a k-bit message to be sent is chosen uniformly at random, the probability of error is

$$\frac{1}{2^k}\sum_{j=0}^{2^k-1} W_j \leq \gamma$$

for this set of codewords, proving the claim.

We now prove the stronger statement in the theorem: we can choose the codewords so that the probability of failure for each individual codeword is bounded above by γ. Notice that this is not implied by the previous analysis, which simply shows that the *average* probability of failure over the codewords is bounded above by γ.

We have shown that there exists a set of codewords $x_0, x_1, \ldots, x_{2^k-1}$ for which

$$\sum_{j=0}^{2^k-1} W_j \le 2^k \gamma.$$

Without loss of generality, let us assume that the x_i are sorted in increasing order of W_i. Suppose that we remove the half of the codewords that have the largest values W_i; that is, we remove the codewords that have the highest probability of yielding an error when being sent. We claim that each x_i, $i < 2^{k-1}$, must satisfy $W_i \le 2\gamma$. Otherwise we would have

$$\sum_{j=2^{k-1}}^{2^k-1} W_j > 2^{k-1}(2\gamma) = 2^k \gamma,$$

a contradiction. (We used similar reasoning in the proof of Markov's inequality in Section 3.1.)

We can set up new encoding and decoding functions on all $(k-1)$-bit strings using just these 2^{k-1} codewords, and now the error probability for every codeword is simultaneously at most 2γ. Hence we have shown that, when $k - 1 \le n(1 - H(p) - \delta)$, there exists a code such that the probability that the receiver fails to obtain the correct message is at most 2γ for any message that is sent. Since δ and γ were arbitrary constants, we see that this implies the first half of the theorem.

Having completed the first half of the theorem, we now move to the second half: for any constants $\delta, \gamma > 0$ and for n sufficiently large, there do not exist (k, n) encoding and decoding functions with $k \ge n(1 - H(p) + \delta)$ such that the probability of decoding correctly is at least γ for a k-bit input message chosen uniformly at random.

Before giving the proof, let us first consider some helpful intuition. We know that the number of errors introduced by the channel is, with high probability, between $\lceil (p - \varepsilon)n \rceil$ and $\lfloor (p + \varepsilon)n \rfloor$ for a suitable constant $\varepsilon > 0$. Suppose that we try to set up the decoding function so that each codeword is decoded properly whenever the number of errors is between $(p - \varepsilon)n$ and $(p + \varepsilon)n$. Then each codeword is associated with

$$\sum_{k=\lceil n(p-\varepsilon) \rceil}^{\lfloor n(p+\varepsilon) \rfloor} \binom{n}{k} \ge \binom{n}{\lceil np \rceil} \ge \frac{2^{nH(p)}}{n+1}$$

bit sequences by the decoding function; the last inequality follows from Corollary 10.3. But there are 2^k different codewords, and

$$2^k \frac{2^{nH(p)}}{n+1} \ge 2^{n(1-H(p)+\delta)} \frac{2^{nH(p)}}{n+1} > 2^n$$

when n is sufficiently large. Since there are only 2^n possible bit sequences that can be received, we cannot create a decoding function that always decodes properly whenever the number of errors is between $(p - \varepsilon)n$ and $(p + \varepsilon)n$.

We now need to extend the argument for *any* encoding and decoding functions. This argument is more complex, since we cannot assume that the decoding function necessarily tries to decode properly whenever the number of errors is between $(p - \varepsilon)n$ and $(p + \varepsilon)n$, even though this would seem to be the best strategy to pursue.

Given any fixed encoding function with codewords $x_0, x_1, \ldots, x_{2^k-1}$ and any fixed decoding function, let z be the probability of successful decoding. Define S_i to be the set of all received sequences that decode to x_i. Then

$$
\begin{aligned}
z &= \sum_{i=0}^{2^k-1} \sum_{s \in S_i} \Pr((x_i \text{ is sent}) \cap (R = s)) \\
&= \sum_{i=0}^{2^k-1} \sum_{s \in S_i} \Pr(x_i \text{ is sent}) \Pr(R = s \mid x_i \text{ is sent}) \\
&= \frac{1}{2^k} \sum_{i=0}^{2^k-1} \sum_{s \in S_i} \Pr(R = s \mid x_i \text{ is sent}) \\
&= \frac{1}{2^k} \sum_{i=0}^{2^k-1} \sum_{s \in S_i} w(x_i, s).
\end{aligned}
$$

The second line follows from the definition of conditional probability. The third line uses the fact that the message sent and hence the codeword sent is chosen uniformly at random from all codewords. The fourth line is just the definition of the weight function.

To bound this last line, we again split the summation $\sum_{i=0}^{2^k-1} \sum_{s \in S_i} w(x_i, s)$ into two parts. Let $S_{i,1} = \{s \in S_i : |\Delta(x_i, s) - pn| > \varepsilon n\}$ and $S_{i,2} = \{s \in S_i : |\Delta(x_i, s) - pn| \leq \varepsilon n\}$, where again $\varepsilon > 0$ is some constant to be determined. Then

$$
\sum_{s \in S_i} w(x_i, s) = \sum_{s \in S_{i,1}} w(x_i, s) + \sum_{s \in S_{i,2}} w(x_i, s).
$$

Now

$$
\sum_{s \in S_{i,1}} w(x_i, s) \leq \sum_{s : |\Delta(x_i, s) - pn| > \varepsilon n} w(x_i, s),
$$

which can be bounded using Chernoff bounds. The summation on the right is simply the probability that the number of errors introduced by the channel is not between $(p - \varepsilon)n$ and $(p + \varepsilon)n$, which we know from previous arguments is at most $2e^{-\varepsilon^2 n / 3p}$. This bound is equivalent to assuming that decoding is successful even if there are too many or too few errors introduced by the channel; since the probability of too many or too few errors is small, this assumption still yields a good bound.

To bound $\sum_{s \in S_{i,2}} w(x_i, s)$, we note that $w(x_i, s)$ is decreasing in $\Delta(x_i, s)$. Hence, for $s \in S_{i,2}$,

$$w(x_i, s) \leq p^{(p-\varepsilon)n}(1 - p)^{(1-p+\varepsilon)n}$$

$$= p^{pn}(1 - p)^{(1-p)n} \left(\frac{1-p}{p}\right)^{\varepsilon n}$$

$$= 2^{-H(p)n} \left(\frac{1-p}{p}\right)^{\varepsilon n}.$$

Therefore,

$$\sum_{s \in S_{i,2}} w(x_i, s) \leq \sum_{s \in S_{i,2}} 2^{-H(p)n} \left(\frac{1-p}{p}\right)^{\varepsilon n}$$

$$= 2^{-H(p)n} \left(\frac{1-p}{p}\right)^{\varepsilon n} |S_{i,2}|.$$

We continue with

$$z = \frac{1}{2^k} \sum_{i=0}^{2^k-1} \sum_{s \in S_i} w(x_i, s)$$

$$= \frac{1}{2^k} \sum_{i=0}^{2^k-1} \left(\sum_{s \in S_{i,1}} w(x_i, s) + \sum_{s \in S_{i,2}} w(x_i, s) \right)$$

$$\leq \frac{1}{2^k} \sum_{i=0}^{2^k-1} \left(2e^{-\varepsilon^2 n/3p} + 2^{-H(p)n} \left(\frac{1-p}{p}\right)^{\varepsilon n} |S_{i,2}| \right)$$

$$= 2e^{-\varepsilon^2 n/3p} + \frac{1}{2^k} 2^{-H(p)n} \left(\frac{1-p}{p}\right)^{\varepsilon n} \sum_{i=0}^{2^k-1} |S_{i,2}|$$

$$\leq 2e^{-\varepsilon^2 n/3p} + \frac{1}{2^k} 2^{-H(p)n} \left(\frac{1-p}{p}\right)^{\varepsilon n} 2^n.$$

In this last line, we have used the important fact that the sets of bit sequences S_i and hence all the $S_{i,2}$ are disjoint, so their total size is at most 2^n. This is where the fact that we are using a decoding function comes into play, allowing us to establish a useful bound.

To conclude,

$$z \leq 2e^{-\varepsilon^2 n/3p} + 2^{n-(1-H(p)+\delta)n-H(p)n} \left(\frac{1-p}{p}\right)^{\varepsilon n}$$

$$= 2e^{-\varepsilon^2 n/3p} + \left(\left(\frac{1-p}{p}\right)^{\varepsilon} 2^{-\delta} \right)^n.$$

As long as we choose ε sufficiently small that

$$\left(\frac{1-p}{p}\right)^{\varepsilon} 2^{-\delta} < 1,$$

then, when n is sufficiently large, $z < \gamma$, which proves Theorem 10.8. ∎

Shannon's theorem demonstrates the existence of codes that transmit arbitrarily closely to the capacity of the binary symmetric channel over long enough blocks. It does not give explicit codes, nor does it say that such codes can be encoded and decoded efficiently. It took decades after Shannon's original work before practical codes with near-optimal performance were found.

10.6. Exercises

Exercise 10.1: **(a)** Let $S = \sum_{k=1}^{10} 1/k^2$. Consider a random variable X such that $\Pr(X = k) = 1/Sk^2$ for integers $k = 1, \ldots, 10$. Find $H(X)$.

(b) Let $S = \sum_{k=1}^{10} 1/k^3$. Consider a random variable X such that $\Pr(X = k) = 1/Sk^3$ for integers $k = 1, \ldots, 10$. Find $H(X)$.

(c) Consider $S_\alpha = \sum_{k=1}^{10} 1/k^\alpha$, where $\alpha > 1$ is a constant. Consider random variables X_α such that $\Pr(X_\alpha = k) = 1/S_\alpha k^\alpha$ for integers $k = 1, \ldots, 10$. Give an intuitive explanation explaining whether $H(X_\alpha)$ is increasing or decreasing with α and why.

Exercise 10.2: Consider an n-sided die, where the ith face comes up with probability p_i. Show that the entropy of a die roll is maximized when each face comes up with equal probability $1/n$.

Exercise 10.3: **(a)** A fair coin is repeatedly flipped until the first heads occurs. Let X be the number of flips required. Find $H(X)$.

(b) Your friend flips a fair coin repeatedly until the first heads occurs. You want to determine how many flips were required. You are allowed to ask a series of yes–no questions of the following form: you give your friend a set of integers, and your friend answers "yes" if the number of flips is in that set and "no" otherwise. Describe a strategy so that the expected number of questions you must ask before determining the number of flips is $H(X)$.

(c) Give an intuitive explanation of why you cannot come up with a strategy that would allow you to ask fewer than $H(X)$ questions on average.

Exercise 10.4: **(a)** Show that

$$S = \sum_{k=2}^{\infty} \frac{1}{k \ln^2 k}$$

is finite.

(b) Consider the integer-valued discrete random variable X given by

$$\Pr(X = k) = \frac{1}{Sk \ln^2 k}, \quad k \geq 2.$$

Show that $H(X)$ is unbounded.

Exercise 10.5: Suppose p is chosen uniformly at random from the real interval $[0, 1]$. Calculate $\mathbf{E}[H(p)]$.

Exercise 10.6: The *conditional entropy* $H(Y \mid X)$ is defined by

$$H(Y \mid X) = \sum_{x,y} \Pr((X = x) \cap (Y = y)) \log_2 \Pr(Y = y \mid X = x).$$

If $Z = (X, Y)$, show that

$$H(Z) = H(X) + H(Y \mid X).$$

Exercise 10.7: One form of Stirling's formula is

$$\sqrt{2\pi n} \left(\frac{n}{e}\right)^n < n! < \sqrt{2\pi n} \left(\frac{n}{e}\right)^n e^{1/(12n)}.$$

Using this, prove

$$\binom{n}{qn} \geq \frac{2^{nH(q)}}{2\sqrt{n}},$$

which is a tighter bound than that of Lemma 10.2.

Exercise 10.8: We have shown in Theorem 10.5 that we can use a recursive procedure to extract, on average, at least $\lfloor \log_2 m \rfloor - 1$ independent, unbiased bits from a number X chosen uniformly at random from $S = \{0, \ldots, m - 1\}$. Consider the following extraction function: let $\alpha = \lfloor \log_2 m \rfloor$, and write

$$m = \beta_\alpha 2^\alpha + \beta_{\alpha-1} 2^{\alpha-1} + \cdots + \beta_0 2^0,$$

where each β_i is either 0 or 1.

Let k be the number of values of i for which β_i equals 1. Then we split S into k disjoint subsets in the following manner: there is one set for each value of β_i that equals 1, and the set for this i has 2^i elements. The assignment of S to sets can be arbitrary, as long as the resulting sets are disjoint. To get an extraction function, we map the elements of the subset with 2^i elements in a one-to-one manner with the 2^i binary strings of length i.

Show that this mapping is equivalent to the recursive extraction procedure given in Theorem 10.5 in that both produce i bits with the same probability for all i.

Exercise 10.9: We have shown that we can extract, on average, at least $\lfloor \log_2 m \rfloor - 1$ independent, unbiased bits from a number chosen uniformly at random from

291

$\{0, \ldots, m-1\}$. It follows that if we have k numbers chosen independently and uniformly at random from $\{0, \ldots, m-1\}$ then we can extract, on average, at least $k\lfloor \log_2 m \rfloor - k$ independent, unbiased bits from them. Give a better procedure that extracts, on average, at least $k\lfloor \log_2 m \rfloor - 1$ independent, unbiased bits from these numbers.

Exercise 10.10: Suppose that we have a means of generating independent, fair coin flips.

(a) Give an algorithm using the coin to generate a number uniformly from $\{0, 1, \ldots, n-1\}$, where n is a power of 2, using exactly $\log_2 n$ flips.

(b) Argue that, if n is *not* a power of 2, then no algorithm can generate a number uniformly from $\{0, 1, \ldots, n-1\}$ using exactly k coin flips for any fixed k.

(c) Argue that, if n is not a power of 2, then no algorithm can generate a number uniformly from $\{0, 1, \ldots, n-1\}$ using *at most* k coin flips for any fixed k.

(d) Give an algorithm using the coin to generate a number uniformly from $\{0, 1, \ldots, n-1\}$, even when n is not a power of 2, using at most $2\lceil \log_2 n \rceil$ *expected* flips.

Exercise 10.11: Suppose that we have a means of generating independent, fair coin flips.

(a) Give an algorithm using the fair coin that simulates flipping a biased coin that comes up heads with probability p. The expected number of flips your algorithm uses should be at most 2. (*Hint:* Think of p written as a decimal in binary, and use the fair coin to generate binary decimal digits.)

(b) Give an algorithm using the coin to generate a number uniformly from $\{0, 1, \ldots, n-1\}$. The expected number of flips your algorithm uses should be at most $\lceil \log_2 n \rceil + 2$.

Exercise 10.12: Here is an extraction algorithm $\mathcal{A}$ whose input is a sequence $X = x_1, x_2, \ldots, x_n$ of n independent flips of a coin that comes up heads with probability $p > 1/2$. Break the sequence into $\lfloor n/2 \rfloor$ pairs, $a_i = (x_{2i-1}, x_{2i})$ for $i = 1, \ldots, \lfloor n/2 \rfloor$. Consider the pairs in order. If $y_i = $ (heads, tails) then output a 0; if $a_i = $ (tails, heads) then output a 1; otherwise, move on to the next pair.

(a) Show that the bits extracted are independent and unbiased.

(b) Show that the expected number of extracted bits is $\lfloor n/2 \rfloor 2p(1-p) \approx np(1-p)$.

(c) We can derive another set of flips $Y = y_1, y_2, \ldots$ from the sequence X as follows. Start with $j, k = 1$. Repeat the following operations until $j = \lfloor n/2 \rfloor$: If $a_j = $ (heads, heads), set y_k to heads and increment j and k; if $a_j = $ (tails, tails), set y_k to tails and increment j and k; otherwise, increment j. See Figure 10.3 for an example.

The intuition here is that we take some of the randomness that $\mathcal{A}$ was unable to use effectively and re-use it. Show that the bits produced by running $\mathcal{A}$ on Y

X	H H T T H T H H H T H H H T T T H T T T
Y	H T H H T T
Z	H H T H T H T H T H

Y	H T H H T T	Z	H H T H T H T H T H
	H T		H
	T H H		H T T T T

Figure 10.3: After running $\mathcal{A}$ on the input sequence X, we can derive further sequences Y and Z; after running $\mathcal{A}$ on each of Y and Z, we can derive further sequences from them; and so on.

are independent and unbiased, and further argue that they are independent of those produced from running $\mathcal{A}$ on X.

(d) We can derive a second set of flips $Z = z_1, z_2, \ldots, z_{\lfloor n/2 \rfloor}$ from the sequence X as follows: let z_i be heads if $a_i =$ (heads, heads) or (tails, tails), and let z_i be tails otherwise. See Figure 10.3 for an example. Show that the bits produced by running $\mathcal{A}$ on Z are independent and unbiased, and further argue that they are independent of those produced from running $\mathcal{A}$ on X and Y.

(e) After we derive and run $\mathcal{A}$ on Y and Z, we can recursively derive two further sequences from each of these sequences in the same way, run $\mathcal{A}$ on those, and so on. See Figure 10.3 for an example. Let $A(p)$ be the average number of bits extracted for each flip (with probability p of coming up heads) in the sequence X, in the limit as the length of the sequence X goes to infinity. Argue that $A(p)$ satisfies the recurrence

$$A(p) = p(1 - p) + \frac{1}{2}(p^2 + q^2) A\left(\frac{p^2}{p^2 + q^2}\right) + \frac{1}{2}A(p^2 + (1 - p)^2).$$

(f) Show that the entropy function $H(p)$ satisfies this recurrence for $A(p)$.

(g) Implement the recursive extraction procedure explained in part (e). Run it 1000 times on sequences of 1024 bits generated by a coin that comes up heads with probability $p = 0.7$. Give the distribution of the number of flips extracted over the 1000 runs and discuss how close your results are to $1024 \cdot H(0.7)$.

Exercise 10.13: Suppose that, instead of a biased coin, we have a biased six-sided die with entropy $h > 0$. Modify our extraction function for the case of biased coins so that it extracts, on average, almost h random bits per roll from a sequence of die rolls. Prove formally that your extraction function works by modifying Theorem 10.5 appropriately.

Exercise 10.14: Suppose that, instead of a biased coin, we have a biased six-sided die with entropy $h > 0$. Modify our compression function for the case of biased coins so that it compresses a sequence of n die rolls to almost nh bits on average. Prove formally that your compression function works by modifying Theorem 10.6 appropriately.

Exercise 10.15: We wish to compress a sequence of independent, identically distributed random variables $X_1, X_2, \ldots$. Each X_j takes on one of n values. We map the ith value to a codeword, which is a sequence of ℓ_i bits. We wish these codewords to have the property that no codeword is the prefix of any other codeword.

(a) Explain how this property can be used to easily decompress the string created by the compression algorithm when reading the bits sequentially.
(b) Prove that the ℓ_i must satisfy

$$\sum_{i=1}^{n} 2^{-\ell_i} \le 1.$$

This is known as the Kraft inequality.

Exercise 10.16: We wish to compress a sequence of independent, identically distributed random variables $X_1, X_2, \ldots$. Each X_j takes on one of n values. The ith value occurs with probability p_i, where $p_1 \ge p_2 \ge \cdots \ge p_n$. The result is compressed as follows. Set

$$T_i = \sum_{j=1}^{i-1} p_j,$$

and let the ith codeword be the first $\lceil \log_2(1/p_i) \rceil$ bits of T_i. Start with an empty string, and consider the X_j in order. If X_j takes on the ith value, append the ith codeword to the end of the string.

(a) Show that no codeword is the prefix of any other codeword.
(b) Let z be the average number of bits appended for each random variable X_j. Show that

$$H(X) \le z \le H(X) + 1.$$

Exercise 10.17: *Arithmetic coding* is a standard compression method. In the case where the string to be compressed is a sequence of biased coin flips, it can be described as follows. Suppose that we have a sequence of bits $X = (X_1, X_2, \ldots, X_n)$, where each X_i is independently 0 with probability p and 1 with probability $1 - p$. The sequences can be ordered lexicographically, so for $x = (x_1, x_2, \ldots, x_n)$ and $y = (y_1, y_2, \ldots, y_n)$ we say $x < y$ if $x_i = 0$ and $y_i = 1$ in the first coordinate i such that $x_i \ne y_i$. If z_x is the number of zeroes in the string x, then define $p(x) = p^{z_x}(1-p)^{n-z_x}$ and $q(x) = \sum_{y<x} p(y)$.

(a) Suppose we are given $X = (X_1, X_2, \ldots, X_n)$ sequentially. Explain how to compute $q(X)$ in time $O(n)$. (You may assume that any operation on real numbers takes constant time.)
(b) Argue that the intervals $[q(x), q(x) + p(x))$ are disjoint subintervals of $[0, 1)$.
(c) Given (a) and (b), the sequence X can be represented by any point in the interval $[q(X), q(X) + p(X))$. Show that we can choose a codeword in $[q(X), q(X) +$

$p(X))$ with $\lceil \log_2(1/p(X)) \rceil + 1$ binary decimal digits to represent X in such a way that no codeword is the prefix of any other codeword.

(d) Given a codeword chosen as in (c), explain how to decompress it to determine the corresponding sequence $(X_1, X_2, \ldots, X_n)$.

(e) Using a Chernoff bound, argue that $\log_2(1/p(X))$ is close to $nH(p)$ with high probability. Hence this approach yields an effective compression scheme.

Exercise 10.18: Alice wants to send Bob the result of a fair coin flip over a binary symmetric channel that flips each bit with probability $p < 1/2$. To avoid errors in transmission, she encodes heads as a sequence of $2k + 1$ zeroes and tails as a sequence of $2k + 1$ ones.

(a) Consider the case where $k = 1$, so heads is encoded as 000 and tails as 111. For each of the eight possible sequences of 3 bits that can be received, determine the probability that Alice flipped a heads conditioned on Bob receiving that sequence.

(b) Bob decodes by examining the 3 bits. If two or three of the bits are 0, then Bob decides the corresponding coin flip was a heads. Prove that this rule minimizes the probability of error for each flip.

(c) Argue that, for general k, Bob minimized the probability of error by deciding the flip was heads if at least $k + 1$ of the bits are 0.

(d) Give a formula for the probability that Bob makes an error that holds for general k. Evaluate the formula for $p = 0.1$ and k ranging from 1 to 6.

(e) Give a bound on the probability computed in part (d) using Chernoff bounds.

Exercise 10.19: Consider the following channel. The sender can send a symbol from the set $\{0, 1, 2, 3, 4\}$. The channel introduces errors; when the symbol k is sent, the recipient receives $k + 1 \bmod 5$ with probability $1/2$ and receives $k - 1 \bmod 5$ with probability $1/2$. The errors are mutually independent when multiple symbols are sent.

Let us define encoding and decoding functions for this channel. A (j, n) encoding function Enc maps a number in $\{0, 1, \ldots, j - 1\}$ into sequences from $\{0, 1, 2, 3, 4\}^n$, and a (j, n) decoding function Dec maps sequences from $\{0, 1, 2, 3, 4\}^n$ back into $\{0, 1, \ldots, j - 1\}$. Notice that this definition is slightly different than the one we used for bit sequences over the binary symmetric channel.

There are $(1, 1)$ encoding and decoding functions with zero probability of error. The encoding function maps 0 to 0 and 1 to 1. When a 0 is sent, the receiver will receive either a 1 or 4, so the decoding function maps 1 and 4 back to 0. When a 1 is sent, the receiver will receiver either a 2 or 0, so the decoding function maps 2 and 0 back to 1. This guarantees that no error is made. Hence at least one bit can be sent without error per channel use.

(a) Show that there are $(5, 2)$ encoding and decoding functions with zero probability of error. Argue that this means more than one bit of information can be sent per use of the channel.

(b) Show that if there are (j, n) encoding and decoding functions with zero probability of error, then $n \geq \log_2 j/(\log_2 5 - 1)$.

Exercise 10.20: A *binary erasure channel* transfers a sequence of n bits. Each bit either arrives successfully without error or fails to arrive successfully and is replaced by a '?' symbol, denoting that it is not known if that bit is a 0 or a 1. Failures occur independently with probability p. We can define (k, n) encoding and decoding functions for the binary erasure channel in a similar manner as for the binary symmetric channel, except here the decoding function Dec: $\{0, 1, ?\}^n \to \{0, 1\}^k$ must handle sequences with the '?' symbol.

Prove that, for any $p > 0$ and any constants $\delta, \gamma > 0$, if n is sufficiently large then there exist (k, n) encoding and decoding functions with $k \le n(1 - p - \delta)$ such that the probability that the receiver fails to obtain the correct message is at most γ for every possible k-bit input message.

Exercise 10.21: In proving Shannon's theorem, we used the following decoding method: Look for a codeword that differs from the received sequence of bits in between $(p - \varepsilon)n$ and $(p + \varepsilon)n$ places, for an appropriate choice of ε; if there is only one such codeword, the decoder concludes that that codeword was the one sent. Suppose instead that the decoder looks for the codeword that differs from the received sequence in the smallest number of bits (breaking ties arbitrarily), and concludes that that codeword was the one sent. Show how to modify the proof of Shannon's theorem for this decoding technique to obtain a similar result.

CHAPTER ELEVEN

The Monte Carlo Method

The *Monte Carlo method* refers to a collection of tools for estimating values through sampling and simulation. Monte Carlo techniques are used extensively in almost all areas of physical sciences and engineering. In this chapter, we first present the basic idea of estimating a value through sampling, using a simple experiment that gives an estimate of the value of the constant π. Estimating through sampling is often more complex than this simple example suggests. We demonstrate the potential difficulties that can arise in devising an efficient sampling procedure by considering how to appropriately sample in order to estimate the number of satisfying assignments of a disjunctive normal form (DNF) Boolean formula.

We then move to more general considerations, demonstrating a general reduction from almost uniform sampling to approximate counting of combinatorial objects. This leads us to consider how to obtain almost uniform samples. One method is the Markov chain Monte Carlo (MCMC) technique, introduced in the last section of this chapter.

11.1. The Monte Carlo Method

Consider the following approach for estimating the value of the constant π. Let (X, Y) be a point chosen uniformly at random in a 2×2 square centered at the origin $(0, 0)$. This is equivalent to choosing X and Y independently from a uniform distribution on $[-1, 1]$. The circle of radius 1 centered at $(0, 0)$ lies inside this square and has area π. If we let

$$Z = \begin{cases} 1 & \text{if } \sqrt{X^2 + Y^2} \le 1, \\ 0 & \text{otherwise,} \end{cases}$$

then – because the point was chosen uniformly from the 2×2 square – the probability that $Z = 1$ is exactly the ratio of the area of the circle to the area of the square. See Figure 11.1. Hence

$$\Pr(Z = 1) = \frac{\pi}{4}.$$

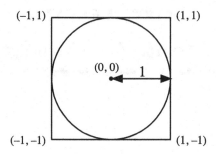

Figure 11.1: A point chosen uniformly at random in the square has probability $\pi/4$ of landing in the circle.

Assume that we run this experiment m times (with X and Y chosen independently among the runs), with Z_i being the value of Z at the ith run. If $W = \sum_{i=1}^{m} Z_i$, then

$$\mathbf{E}[W] = \mathbf{E}\left[\sum_{i=1}^{m} Z_i\right] = \sum_{i=1}^{m} \mathbf{E}[Z_i] = \frac{m\pi}{4},$$

and hence $W' = (4/m)W$ is a natural estimate for π. Applying the Chernoff bound of Eqn. (4.6), we compute

$$\Pr(|W' - \pi| \geq \varepsilon\pi) = \Pr\left(\left|W - \frac{m\pi}{4}\right| \geq \frac{\varepsilon m\pi}{4}\right)$$
$$= \Pr(|W - \mathbf{E}[W]| \geq \varepsilon\mathbf{E}[W])$$
$$\leq 2e^{-m\pi\varepsilon^2/12}.$$

Therefore, by using a sufficiently large number of samples we can obtain, with high probability, as tight an approximation of π as we wish.

This method for approximating π is an example of a more general class of approximation algorithms that we now characterize.

Definition 11.1: *A randomized algorithm gives an (ε, δ)-approximation for the value V if the output X of the algorithm satisfies*

$$\Pr(|X - V| \leq \varepsilon V) \geq 1 - \delta.$$

Our method for estimating π gives an (ε, δ)-approximation, as long as $\varepsilon < 1$ and we choose m large enough to make

$$2e^{-m\pi\varepsilon^2/12} \leq \delta.$$

Algebraic manipulation yields that choosing

$$m \geq \frac{12\ln(2/\delta)}{\pi\varepsilon^2}$$

is sufficient.

We may generalize the idea behind our technique for estimating π to provide a relation between the number of samples and the quality of the approximation. We use the following simple application of the Chernoff bound throughout this chapter.

298

Theorem 11.1: *Let $X_1, \ldots, X_m$ be independent and identically distributed indicator random variables, with $\mu = \mathbf{E}[X_i]$. If $m \geq (3\ln(2/\delta))/\varepsilon^2\mu$, then*

$$\Pr\left(\left|\frac{1}{m}\sum_{i=1}^{m}X_i - \mu\right| \geq \varepsilon\mu\right) \leq \delta.$$

That is, m samples provide an (ε, δ)-approximation for μ.

The proof is left as Exercise 11.1.

More generally, we will want an algorithm that approximates not just a single value but instead takes as input a problem instance and approximates the solution value for that problem. Here we are considering problems that map inputs x to values $V(x)$. For example, given an input graph, we might want to know an approximation to the number of independent sets in the graph.

You might ask why we should settle for an approximation; perhaps we should aim for an exact answer. In the case of π, we cannot obtain an exact answer because π is an irrational number. Another reason for seeking an approximation is that, as we shall see shortly, there are problems for which the existence of an algorithm that gives an exact answer would imply that P = NP, and hence it is unlikely that such an algorithm will be found. This, however, does not preclude the possibility of an efficient approximation algorithm.

Definition 11.2: *A fully polynomial randomized approximation scheme (FPRAS) for a problem is a randomized algorithm for which, given an input x and any parameters ε and δ with $0 < \varepsilon, \delta < 1$, the algorithm outputs an (ε, δ)-approximation to $V(x)$ in time that is polynomial in $1/\varepsilon$, $\ln\delta^{-1}$, and the size of the input x.*

Exercise 11.3 considers a seemingly weaker but actually equivalent definition of an FPRAS that avoids the parameter δ.

The Monte Carlo method essentially consists of the approach we have outlined here to obtain an efficient approximation for a value V. We require an efficient process that generates a sequence of independent and identically distributed random samples $X_1, X_2, \ldots, X_n$ such that $\mathbf{E}[X_i] = V$. We then take enough samples to get an (ε, δ)-approximation to V. Generating a good sequence of samples is often a nontrivial task and is a major focus of the Monte Carlo method.

The Monte Carlo method is also sometimes called *Monte Carlo simulation*. As an example, suppose we want to estimate the expected price of a stock sometime in the future. We may develop a model where the price $p(Y_1, \ldots, Y_k)$ of the stock at that time depends on random variables $Y_1, Y_2, \ldots, Y_k$. If we can repeatedly generate independent random vectors $(y_1, y_2, \ldots, y_k)$ from the joint distribution of the Y_i, then we can repeatedly generate independent random variables $X_1, X_2, \ldots$, where

$$X_i = p(Y_1, \ldots, Y_k).$$

We can then use the X_i to estimate the expected future price $\mathbf{E}[p(Y_1, \ldots, Y_k)]$ with the Monte Carlo method. That is, by simulating the possible future outcomes of the Y_i many times, we can estimate the desired expectation.

11.2. Application: The DNF Counting Problem

As an example of an estimation problem that requires a nontrivial sampling technique, we consider the problem of counting the number of satisfying assignments of a Boolean formula in *disjunctive normal form* (DNF). A DNF formula is a disjunction (OR) of clauses $C_1 \vee C_2 \vee \cdots \vee C_t$, where each clause is a conjunction (AND) of literals. For example, the following is a DNF formula:

$$(x_1 \wedge \overline{x_2} \wedge x_3) \vee (x_2 \wedge x_4) \vee (\overline{x_1} \wedge x_3 \wedge x_4).$$

Recall from Section 6.2.2 that, in a standard satisfiability problem, the input formula is a conjunction (AND) of a set of clauses, and each clause is the disjunction (OR) of literals. This is commonly called *conjunctive normal form* (CNF). While determining the satisfiability of a formula in CNF form is difficult, determining the satisfiability of a formula in DNF form is simple. Since a satisfying assignment for a DNF formula needs to satisfy only one clause, it is easy to find a satisfying assignment or prove that it is not satisfiable.

How hard is it to exactly count the number of satisfying assignments of a DNF formula? Given any CNF formula H, we can apply de Morgan's laws to obtain a DNF formula for $\bar{H}$, the negation of the formula H, with the same number of variables and clauses as the original CNF formula. The formula H has a satisfying assignment if and only if there is some assignment for the variables that does not satisfy $\bar{H}$. Thus, H has a satisfying assignment if and only if the number of satisfying assignments of $\bar{H}$ is strictly less than 2^n, the total number of possible assignments for n Boolean variables. We conclude that counting the number of satisfying assignments of a DNF formula is at least as hard as solving the NP-complete problem SAT.

There is a complexity class associated with the problem of counting solutions to problems in NP, denoted by $\sharp P$ and pronounced "sharp-P". Formally, a problem is in the class $\sharp P$ if there is a polynomial time, nondeterministic Turing machine such that, for any input I, the number of accepting computations equals the number of different solutions associated with the input I. Counting the number of satisfying assignments of a DNF formula is actually $\sharp P$-complete; that is, this problem is as hard as any other problem in this class. Other complete problems for the class $\sharp P$ include counting the number of Hamiltonian cycles in a graph and counting the number of perfect matchings in a bipartite graph.

It is unlikely that there is a polynomial time algorithm that computes the exact number of solutions of a $\sharp P$-complete problem, as at the very least such an algorithm would imply that P = NP. It is therefore interesting to find an FPRAS for the number of satisfying assignments of a DNF formula.

11.2.1. *The Naïve Approach*

We start by trying to generalize the approach that we used to approximate π, and we demonstrate why it is unsuitable in general. We then show how to improve our sampling technique in order to solve the problem.

DNF Counting Algorithm I:

Input: A DNF formula F with n variables.

Output: $Y =$ an approximation of $c(F)$.

1. $X \leftarrow 0$.
2. For $k = 1$ to m, do:
   (a) Generate a random assignment for the n variables, chosen uniformly at random from all 2^n possible assignments.
   (b) If the random assignment satisfies F, then $X \leftarrow X + 1$.
3. Return $Y \leftarrow (X/m)2^n$.

Algorithm 11.1: DNF counting algorithm I.

Let $c(F)$ be the number of satisfying assignments of a DNF formula F. Here we assume that $c(F) > 0$, since it is easy to check whether $c(F) = 0$ before running our sampling algorithm. In Section 11.1 we approximated π by generating points uniformly at random from the 2×2 square and checking to see if they were in the target: a circle of radius 1. We try a similar approach in Algorithm 11.1: we generate assignments uniformly at random for the n variables and then see if the resulting assignment is in the target of satisfying assignments for F.

Let X_k be 1 if the kth iteration in the algorithm generated a satisfying assignment and 0 otherwise. Then $X = \sum_{k=1}^{m} X_k$, where the X_k are independent 0–1 random variables that each take the value 1 with probability $c(F)/2^n$. Hence, by linearity of expectations,

$$\mathbf{E}[Y] = \frac{\mathbf{E}[X]2^n}{m} = c(F).$$

Applying Theorem 11.1, we see that X/m gives an (ε, δ)-approximation of $c(F)/2^n$, and hence that Y gives an (ε, δ)-approximation of $c(F)$, when

$$m \geq \frac{3 \cdot 2^n \ln(2/\delta)}{\varepsilon^2 c(F)}.$$

If $c(F) \geq 2^n/\alpha(n)$ for some polynomial α, then the foregoing analysis tells us we only need a number of samples m that is polynomial in n, $1/\varepsilon$, and $\ln(1/\delta)$. We cannot, however, exclude the possibility that $c(F)$ is much less than 2^n. In particular, $c(F)$ might be polynomial in n. Since our analysis requires a number of samples m that is proportional to $2^n/c(F)$, our analysis does not yield that the run time of the algorithm is always polynomial in the problem size.

This is not simply an artifact of the analysis. We provide a rough sketch of an argument that is elaborated on in Exercise 11.4. If the number of satisfying assignments is polynomial in n and if at each step we sample uniformly at random from all 2^n possible assignments, then with high probability we must sample an exponential number of assignments before finding the first satisfying assignment. We can conclude, for example, that we cannot distinguish between instances with n, n^2, and n^3 satisfying assignments without considering exponentially many random assignments, since with high probability we would obtain zero satisfying assignments in all three cases.

The problem with this sampling approach is that the set of satisfying assignments might not be sufficiently dense in the set of all assignments. This is an additional requirement of our sampling technique that was not explicit before. In the phrasing of Theorem 11.1, the value μ that we are attempting to approximate needs to be sufficiently large that sampling is efficient.

To obtain an FPRAS for this problem, we need to devise a better sampling scheme that avoids wasting so many steps on assignments that do not satisfy the formula. We need to construct a sample space that includes all the satisfying assignments of F and, moreover, has the property that these assignments are sufficiently dense in the sample space to allow for efficient sampling.

11.2.2. *A Fully Polynomial Randomized Scheme for DNF Counting*

We now revise our sampling procedure to obtain an FPRAS. Let $F = C_1 \vee C_2 \vee \cdots \vee C_t$, and assume without loss of generality that no clause includes a variable and its negation. (If there is such a clause, it is not satisfiable and we can eliminate it from the formula.) A satisfying assignment of F needs to satisfy at least one of the clauses $C_1, \ldots, C_t$. Each clause is a conjunction of literals, so there is only one assignment of the variables appearing in the clause that satisfies the clause. All other variables can have arbitrary values. For example, for the clause $(x_1 \wedge \overline{x_2} \wedge x_3)$ to be satisfied, x_1 and x_3 must be set to True and x_2 must be set to False.

It follows that if clause C_i has ℓ_i literals then there are exactly $2^{n-\ell_i}$ satisfying assignments for C_i. Let SC_i denote the set of assignments that satisfy clause i, and let

$$U = \{(i, a) \mid 1 \leq i \leq t \text{ and } a \in SC_i\}.$$

Notice that we know the size of U, since

$$\sum_{i=1}^{t} |SC_i| = |U|,$$

and we can compute $|SC_i|$.

The value that we want to estimate is given by

$$c(F) = \left| \bigcup_{i=1}^{t} SC_i \right|.$$

Here $c(F) \leq |U|$, since an assignment can satisfy more than one clause and thus appear in more than one pair in U.

To estimate $c(F)$, we define a subset S of U with size $c(F)$. We construct this set by selecting, for each satisfying assignment of F, exactly one pair in U that has this assignment; specifically, we can use the pair with the smallest clause index number, giving

$$S = \{(i, a) \mid 1 \leq i \leq t, a \in SC_i, a \notin SC_j \text{ for } j < i\}.$$

DNF Counting Algorithm II:

Input: A DNF formula F with n variables.

Output: Y = an approximation of $c(F)$.

1. $X \leftarrow 0$.
2. For $k = 1$ to m, do:
   (a) With probability $|SC_i| / \sum_{i=1}^{t} |SC_i|$ choose, uniformly at random, an assignment $a \in SC_i$.
   (b) If a is not in any SC_j, $j < i$, then $X \leftarrow X + 1$.
3. Return $Y \leftarrow (X/m) \sum_{i=1}^{t} |SC_i|$.

Algorithm 11.2: DNF counting algorithm II.

Since we know the size of U, we can estimate the size of S by estimating the ratio $|S|/|U|$. We can estimate this ratio efficiently if we sample uniformly at random from U using our previous approach, choosing pairs uniformly at random from U and counting how often they are in S. We can avoid the problem we encountered when simply sampling assignments at random, because S is relatively dense in U. Specifically, since each assignment can satisfy at most t different clauses, $|S|/|U| \geq 1/t$.

The only question left is how to sample uniformly from U. Suppose that we first choose the first coordinate, i. Because the ith clause has $|SC_i|$ satisfying assignments, we should choose i with probability proportional to $|SC_i|$. Specifically, we should choose i with probability

$$\frac{|SC_i|}{\sum_{i=1}^{t} |SC_i|} = \frac{|SC_i|}{|U|}.$$

We then can choose a satisfying assignment uniformly at random from SC_i. This is easy to do; we choose the value True or False independently and uniformly at random for each literal not in clause i. Then the probability that we choose the pair (i, a) is

$$\Pr((i, a) \text{ is chosen}) = \Pr(i \text{ is chosen}) \cdot \Pr(a \text{ is chosen} \mid i \text{ is chosen})$$
$$= \frac{|SC_i|}{|U|} \frac{1}{|SC_i|}$$
$$= \frac{1}{|U|},$$

giving a uniform distribution.

These observations are implemented in Algorithm 11.2.

Theorem 11.2: *DNF counting algorithm II is a fully polynomial randomized approximation scheme (FPRAS) for the DNF counting problem when $m = \lceil (3t/\varepsilon^2) \ln(2/\delta) \rceil$.*

Proof: Step 2(a) of the algorithm chooses an element of U uniformly at random. The probability that this element belongs to S is at least $1/t$. Fix any $\varepsilon > 0$ and $\delta > 0$, and let

$$m = \left\lceil \frac{3t}{\varepsilon^2} \ln \frac{2}{\delta} \right\rceil.$$

Then m is polynomial in t, ε, and $\ln(1/\delta)$, and the processing time of each sample is polynomial in t. By Theorem 11.1, with this number of samples, X/m gives an (ε, δ)-approximation of $c(F)/|U|$ and hence Y gives an (ε, δ)-approximation of $c(F)$. ∎

11.3. From Approximate Sampling to Approximate Counting

The example of DNF formulas demonstrates that there is a fundamental connection between being able to sample from an appropriate space and being able to count the number of objects with some property in that space. In this section we present the outline of a general reduction that shows that, if you can sample almost uniformly a solution to a "self-reducible" combinatorial problem, then you can construct a randomized algorithm that approximately counts the number of solutions to that problem. We demonstrate this technique for the problem of counting the number of independent sets in a graph. In the next chapter, we also consider the problem of counting the number of proper colorings in a graph, applying this technique there as well.

We first need to formulate the concept of approximate uniform sampling. In this setting we are given a problem instance in the form of an input x, and there is an underlying finite sample space $\Omega(x)$ associated with the input.

Definition 11.3: *Let w be the (random) output of a sampling algorithm for a finite sample space Ω. The sampling algorithm generates an ε-uniform sample of Ω if, for any subset S of Ω,*

$$\left| \Pr(w \in S) - \frac{|S|}{|\Omega|} \right| \le \varepsilon.$$

A sampling algorithm is a fully polynomial almost uniform sampler (FPAUS) for a problem if, given an input x and a parameter $\varepsilon > 0$, it generates an ε-uniform sample of $\Omega(x)$ and runs in time that is polynomial in $\ln \varepsilon^{-1}$ and the size of the input x.

In the next chapter, we introduce the notion of *total variation distance*, which allows for an equivalent definition of an ε-uniform sample.

As an example, an FPAUS for independent sets would take as input a graph $G = (V, E)$ and a parameter ε. The sample space would be all independent sets in the graph. The output would be an ε-uniform sample of the independent sets, and the time to produce such a sample would be polynomial in the size of the graph and $\ln \varepsilon^{-1}$. In fact, in the reduction that follows we only need the running time to be polynomial in ε^{-1}, but we use the standard definition given in Definition 11.3.

Our goal is to show that, given an FPAUS for independent sets, we can construct an FPRAS for counting the number of independent sets. Assume that the input G has m edges, and let $e_1, \ldots, e_m$ be an arbitrary ordering of the edges. Let E_i be the set of the first i edges in E and let $G_i = (V, E_i)$. Note that $G = G_m$ and that G_{i-1} is obtained from G_i by removing a single edge.

We let $\Omega(G_i)$ denote the set of independent sets in G_i. The number of independent sets in G can then be expressed as

$$|\Omega(G)| = \frac{|\Omega(G_m)|}{|\Omega(G_{m-1})|} \times \frac{|\Omega(G_{m-1})|}{|\Omega(G_{m-2})|} \times \frac{|\Omega(G_{m-2})|}{|\Omega(G_{m-3})|} \times \cdots \times \frac{|\Omega(G_1)|}{|\Omega(G_0)|} \times |\Omega(G_0)|.$$

Since G_0 has no edges, every subset of V is an independent set and $\Omega(G_0) = 2^n$. In order to estimate $|\Omega(G)|$, we need good estimates for the ratios

$$r_i = \frac{|\Omega(G_i)|}{|\Omega(G_{i-1})|}, \quad i = 1, \ldots, m.$$

More formally, we will develop estimates $\tilde{r}_i$ for the ratios r_i, and then our estimate for the number of independent sets in G will be

$$2^n \prod_{i=1}^{m} \tilde{r}_i,$$

while the true number is

$$|\Omega(G)| = 2^n \prod_{i=1}^{m} r_i.$$

To evaluate the error in our estimate, we need to bound the ratio

$$R = \prod_{i=1}^{m} \frac{\tilde{r}_i}{r_i}.$$

Specifically, to have an (ε, δ)-approximation, we want $\Pr(|R - 1| \leq \varepsilon) \geq 1 - \delta$. We will make use of the following lemma.

Lemma 11.3: *Suppose that for all i, $1 \leq i \leq m$, $\tilde{r}_i$ is an $(\varepsilon/2m, \delta/m)$-approximation for r_i. Then*

$$\Pr(|R - 1| \leq \varepsilon) \geq 1 - \delta.$$

Proof: For each $1 \leq i \leq m$, we have

$$\Pr\left(|\tilde{r}_i - r_i| \leq \frac{\varepsilon}{2m} r_i\right) \geq 1 - \frac{\delta}{m}.$$

Equivalently,

$$\Pr\left(|\tilde{r}_i - r_i| > \frac{\varepsilon}{2m} r_i\right) < \frac{\delta}{m}.$$

By the union bound, the probability that $|\tilde{r}_i - r_i| > (\varepsilon/2m)r_i$ for any i is at most δ; therefore, $|\tilde{r}_i - r_i| \leq (\varepsilon/2m)r_i$ for all i with probability at least $1 - \delta$. Equivalently,

$$1 - \frac{\varepsilon}{2m} \leq \frac{\tilde{r}_i}{r_i} \leq 1 + \frac{\varepsilon}{2m}$$

305

Estimating r_i:

Input: Graphs $G_{i-1} = (V, E_{i-1})$ and $G_i = (V, E_i)$.

Output: $\tilde{r}_i =$ an approximation of r_i.

1. $X \leftarrow 0$.
2. Repeat for $M = \lceil 1296m^2\varepsilon^{-2}\ln(2m/\delta) \rceil$ independent trials:
   (a) Generate an $(\varepsilon/6m)$-uniform sample from $\Omega(G_{i-1})$.
   (b) If the sample is an independent set in G_i, let $X \leftarrow X + 1$.
3. Return $\tilde{r}_i \leftarrow X/M$.

Algorithm 11.3: Estimating r_i.

holds for all i with probability at least $1 - \delta$. When these bounds hold for all i, we can combine them to obtain

$$1 - \varepsilon \le \left(1 - \frac{\varepsilon}{2m}\right)^m \le \prod_{i=1}^{m} \frac{\tilde{r}_i}{r_i} \le \left(1 + \frac{\varepsilon}{2m}\right)^m \le 1 + \varepsilon,$$

giving the lemma. ∎

Hence all we need is a method for obtaining an $(\varepsilon/2m, \delta/m)$-approximation for the r_i. We estimate each of these ratios by a Monte Carlo algorithm that uses the FPAUS for sampling independent sets. To estimate r_i, we sample independent sets in G_{i-1} and compute the fraction of these sets that are also independent sets in G_i, as described in Algorithm 11.3. The constants in the procedure were chosen to facilitate the proof of Lemma 11.4.

Lemma 11.4: *When $m \ge 1$ and $0 < \varepsilon \le 1$, the procedure for estimating r_i yields an $(\varepsilon/2m, \delta/m)$-approximation for r_i.*

Proof: We first show that r_i is not too small, avoiding the problem that we found in Section 11.2.1. Suppose that G_{i-1} and G_i differ in that edge (u, v) is present in G_i but not in G_{i-1}. An independent set in G_i is also an independent set in G_{i-1}, so

$$\Omega(G_i) \subseteq \Omega(G_{i-1}).$$

An independent set in $\Omega(G_{i-1}) \setminus \Omega(G_i)$ contains both u and v. To bound the size of the set $\Omega(G_{i-1}) \setminus \Omega(G_i)$, we associate each $I \in \Omega(G_{i-1}) \setminus \Omega(G_i)$ with an independent set $I \setminus \{v\} \in \Omega(G_i)$. In this mapping an independent set $I' \in \Omega(G_i)$ is associated with no more than one independent set $I' \cup \{v\} \in \Omega(G_{i-1}) \setminus \Omega(G_i)$, and thus $|\Omega(G_{i-1}) \setminus \Omega(G_i)| \le |\Omega(G_i)|$. It follows that

$$r_i = \frac{|\Omega(G_i)|}{|\Omega(G_{i-1})|} = \frac{|\Omega(G_i)|}{|\Omega(G_i)| + |\Omega(G_{i-1}) \setminus \Omega(G_i)|} \ge \frac{1}{2}.$$

Now consider our M samples, and let $X_k = 1$ if the kth sample is in $\Omega(G_i)$ and 0 otherwise. Because our samples are generated by an $(\varepsilon/6m)$-uniform sampler, by Definition 11.3 each X_i must satisfy

$$\left| \Pr(X_k = 1) - \frac{|\Omega(G_i)|}{|\Omega(G_{i-1})|} \right| \leq \frac{\varepsilon}{6m}.$$

Since the X_k are indicator random variables, it follows that

$$\left| \mathbf{E}[X_k] - \frac{|\Omega(G_i)|}{|\Omega(G_{i-1})|} \right| \leq \frac{\varepsilon}{6m}$$

and further, by linearity of expectations,

$$\left| \mathbf{E}\left[\frac{\sum_{k=1}^{M} X_k}{M} \right] - \frac{|\Omega(G_i)|}{|\Omega(G_{i-1})|} \right| \leq \frac{\varepsilon}{6m}.$$

We therefore have

$$|\mathbf{E}[\tilde{r}_i] - r_i| = \left| \mathbf{E}\left[\frac{\sum_{i=k}^{M} X_k}{M} \right] - \frac{|\Omega(G_i)|}{|\Omega(G_{i-1})|} \right|$$

$$\leq \frac{\varepsilon}{6m}.$$

We now complete the lemma by combining (a) the fact just shown that $\mathbf{E}[\tilde{r}_i]$ is close to r_i and (b) the fact that $\tilde{r}_i$ will be close to $\mathbf{E}[\tilde{r}_i]$ for a sufficiently large number of samples. Using $r_i \geq 1/2$, we have

$$\mathbf{E}[\tilde{r}_i] \geq r_i - \frac{\varepsilon}{6m} \geq \frac{1}{2} - \frac{\varepsilon}{6m} \geq \frac{1}{3}.$$

Applying Theorem 11.1 yields that, if the number of samples M satisfies

$$M \geq \frac{3\ln(2m/\delta)}{(\varepsilon/12m)^2(1/3)} = 1296m^2\varepsilon^{-2}\ln\frac{2m}{\delta},$$

then

$$\Pr\left(\left| \frac{\tilde{r}_i}{\mathbf{E}[\tilde{r}_i]} - 1 \right| \geq \frac{\varepsilon}{12m} \right) = \Pr\left(|\tilde{r}_i - \mathbf{E}[\tilde{r}_i]| \geq \frac{\varepsilon}{12m}\mathbf{E}[\tilde{r}_i] \right) \leq \frac{\delta}{m}.$$

Equivalently, with probability $1 - \delta/m$,

$$1 - \frac{\varepsilon}{12m} \leq \frac{\tilde{r}_i}{\mathbf{E}[\tilde{r}_i]} \leq 1 + \frac{\varepsilon}{12m}. \tag{11.1}$$

As $|\mathbf{E}[\tilde{r}_i] - r_i| \leq \varepsilon/6m$, we have that

$$1 - \frac{\varepsilon}{6mr_i} \leq \frac{\mathbf{E}[\tilde{r}_i]}{r_i} \leq 1 + \frac{\varepsilon}{6mr_i}.$$

Using that $r_i \geq 1/2$ then yields

$$1 - \frac{\varepsilon}{3m} \leq \frac{\mathbf{E}[\tilde{r}_i]}{r_i} \leq 1 + \frac{\varepsilon}{3m}. \tag{11.2}$$

307

Combining Eqns. (11.1) and (11.2), it follows that, with probability $1 - \delta/m$,

$$1 - \frac{\varepsilon}{2m} \le \left(1 - \frac{\varepsilon}{3m}\right)\left(1 - \frac{\varepsilon}{12m}\right) \le \frac{\tilde{r}_i}{r_i} \le \left(1 + \frac{\varepsilon}{3m}\right)\left(1 + \frac{\varepsilon}{12m}\right) \le 1 + \frac{\varepsilon}{2m}.$$

This gives the desired $(\varepsilon/2m, \delta/m)$-approximation. ∎

The number of samples M is polynomial in m, ε, and $\ln \delta^{-1}$, and the time for each sample is polynomial in the size of the graph and $\ln \varepsilon^{-1}$. We therefore have the following theorem.

Theorem 11.5: *Given a fully polynomial almost uniform sampler (FPAUS) for independent sets in any graph, we can construct a fully polynomial randomized approximation scheme (FPRAS) for the number of independent sets in a graph G.*

In fact, this theorem is more often used in the following form.

Theorem 11.6: *Given a fully polynomial almost uniform sampler (FPAUS) for independent sets in any graph with maximum degree at most Δ, we can construct a fully polynomial randomized approximation scheme (FPRAS) for the number of independent sets in a graph G with maximum degree at most Δ.*

This version of the theorem follows from our previous argument, since our graphs G_i are subgraphs of the initial graph G. Hence, if we start with a graph of maximum degree at most Δ, then our FPAUS need only work on graphs with maximum degree at most Δ. In the next chapter, we will see how to create an FPAUS for graphs with maximum degree 4.

This technique can be applied to a broad range of combinatorial counting problems. For example, in Chapter 12 we consider its application to finding proper colorings of a graph G. The only requirement is that we can construct a sequence of refinements of the problem, starting with an instance that is easy to count (the number of independent sets in a graph with no edges, in our example) and ending with the actual counting problem, and such that the ratio between the counts in successive instances is at most polynomial in the size of the problem.

11.4. The Markov Chain Monte Carlo Method

The Monte Carlo method is based on sampling. It is often difficult to generate a random sample with the required probability distribution. For example, we saw in the previous section that we can count the number of independent sets in a graph if we can generate an almost uniform sample from the set of independent sets. But how can we generate an almost uniform sample?

The Markov chain Monte Carlo (MCMC) method provides a very general approach to sampling from a desired probability distribution. The basic idea is to define an ergodic Markov chain whose set of states is the sample space and whose stationary distribution is the required sampling distribution. Let $X_0, X_1, \ldots, X_n$ be a run of the chain. The Markov chain converges to the stationary distribution from any starting state X_0

and so, after a sufficiently large number of steps r, the distribution of the state X_r will be close to the stationary distribution, so it can be used as a sample. Similarly, repeating this argument with X_r as the starting point, we can use X_{2r} as a sample, and so on. We can therefore use the sequence of states $X_r, X_{2r}, X_{3r}, \ldots$ as almost independent samples from the stationary distribution of the Markov chain. The efficiency of this approach depends on (a) how large r must be to ensure a suitably good sample and (b) how much computation is required for each step of the Markov chain. In this section, we focus on finding efficient Markov chains with the appropriate stationary distribution and ignore the issue of how large r needs to be. *Coupling*, which is one method for determining the relationship between the value of r and the quality of the sample, is discussed in the next chapter.

In the simplest case, the goal is to construct a Markov chain with a stationary distribution that is uniform over the state space Ω. The first step is to design a set of moves that ensures the state space is irreducible under the Markov chain. Let us call the set of states reachable in one step from a state x (but excluding x) the *neighbors* of x, denoted by $N(x)$. We adopt the restriction that if $y \in N(x)$ then also $x \in N(y)$. Generally $N(x)$ will be a small set, so that performing each move is simple computationally.

We again use the setting of independent sets in a graph $G = (V, E)$ as an example. The state space is all of the independent sets of G. A natural neighborhood framework is to say that states x and y, which are independent sets, are neighbors if they differ in just one vertex. That is, x can be obtained from y by adding or deleting just one vertex. This neighbor relationship guarantees that the state space is irreducible, since all independent sets can reach (respectively, can be reached from) the empty independent set by a sequence of vertex deletions (respectively, vertex additions).

Once the neighborhoods are established, we need to establish transition probabilities. One natural approach to try would be performing a random walk on the graph of the state space. This might not lead to a uniform distribution, however. We saw in Theorem 7.13 that, in the stationary distribution of a random walk, the probability of a vertex is proportional to the degree of the vertex. Nothing in our previous discussion requires all states to have the same number of neighbors, which is equivalent to all vertices in the graph of the state space having the same degree.

The following lemma shows that, if we modify the random walk by giving each vertex an appropriate self-loop probability, then we can obtain a uniform stationary distribution.

Lemma 11.7: *For a finite state space Ω and neighborhood structure $\{N(X) \mid x \in \Omega\}$, let $N = \max_{x \in \Omega} |N(x)|$. Let M be any number such that $M \geq N$. Consider a Markov chain where*

$$P_{x,y} = \begin{cases} 1/M & \text{if } x \neq y \text{ and } y \in N(x), \\ 0 & \text{if } x \neq y \text{ and } y \notin N(x), \\ 1 - N(x)/M & \text{if } x = y. \end{cases}$$

If this chain is irreducible and aperiodic, then the stationary distribution is the uniform distribution.

Proof: We show that the chain is time reversible and then apply Theorem 7.10. For any $x \neq y$, if $\pi_x = \pi_y$ then

$$\pi_x P_{x,y} = \pi_y P_{y,x},$$

since $P_{x,y} = P_{y,x} = 1/M$. It follows that the uniform distribution $\pi_x = 1/|\Omega|$ is the stationary distribution. ∎

Consider now the following simple Markov chain, whose states are independent sets in a graph $G = (V, E)$.

1. X_0 is an arbitrary independent set in G.
2. To compute X_{i+1}:
    (a) choose a vertex v uniformly at random from V;
    (b) if $v \in X_i$ then $X_{i+1} = X_i \setminus \{v\}$;
    (c) if $v \notin X_i$ and if adding v to X_i still gives an independent set, then $X_{i+1} = X_i \cup \{v\}$;
    (d) otherwise, $X_{i+1} = X_i$.

This chain has the property that the neighbors of a state X_i are all independent sets that differ from X_i in just one vertex. Since every state can reach and is reachable from the empty set, the chain is irreducible. Assuming that G has at least one edge (u, v), then the state $\{v\}$ has a self-loop ($P_{v,v} > 0$), and the chain is aperiodic. Further, when $y \neq x$, it follows that $P_{x,y} = 1/|V|$ or 0. Lemma 11.7 therefore applies, and the stationary distribution is the uniform distribution.

11.4.1. The Metropolis Algorithm

We have seen how to construct chains with a uniform stationary distribution. In some cases, however, we may want to sample from a chain with a nonuniform stationary distribution. The *Metropolis algorithm* refers to a general construction that transforms any irreducible Markov chain on a state space Ω to a time-reversible Markov chain with a required stationary distribution. The approach generalizes the idea we used before to create chains with uniform stationary distributions: add self-loop probabilities to states in order to obtain the desired stationary distribution.

Let us again assume that we have designed an irreducible state space for our Markov chain; now we want to construct a Markov chain on this state space with a stationary distribution $\pi_x = b(x)/B$, where for all $x \in \Omega$ we have $b(x) > 0$ and such that $B = \sum_{x \in \Omega} b(x)$ is finite. As we see in the following lemma (which generalizes Lemma 11.7), we only need the ratios between the required probabilities; the sum B can be unknown.

Lemma 11.8: *For a finite state space Ω and neighborhood structure $\{N(X) \mid x \in \Omega\}$, let $N = \max_{x \in \Omega} |N(x)|$. Let M be any number such that $M \geq N$. For all $x \in \Omega$, let $\pi_x > 0$ be the desired probability of state x in the stationary distribution. Consider a Markov* *chain where*

$$P_{x,y} = \begin{cases} (1/M)\min(1, \pi_y/\pi_x) & \textit{if } x \neq y \textit{ and } y \in N(x), \\ 0 & \textit{if } x \neq y \textit{ and } y \notin N(x), \\ 1 - \sum_{y \neq x} P_{x,y} & \textit{if } x = y. \end{cases}$$

Then, if this chain is irreducible and aperiodic, the stationary distribution is given by the probabilities π_x.

Proof: As in the proof of Lemma 11.7, we show that the chain is time reversible and apply Theorem 7.10. For any $x \neq y$, if $\pi_x \leq \pi_y$ then $P_{x,y} = 1$ and $P_{y,x} = \pi_x/\pi_y$. It follows that $\pi_x P_{x,y} = \pi_y P_{y,x}$. Similarly, if $\pi_x > \pi_y$ then $P_{x,y} = \pi_y/\pi_x$ and $P_{y,x} = 1$, and it follows that $\pi_x P_{x,y} = \pi_y P_{y,x}$. By Theorem 7.10, the stationary distribution is given by the values π_x. ∎

As an example of how to apply Lemma 11.8, let us consider how to modify our previous Markov chains on independent sets. Let us suppose that now we want to create a Markov chain where, in the stationary distribution, each independent set I has probability proportional to $\lambda^{|I|}$ for some constant parameter $\lambda > 0$. That is, $\pi_x = \lambda^{|I_x|}/B$, where I_x is the independent set corresponding to state x and where $B = \sum_x \lambda^{|I_x|}$. When $\lambda = 1$, this is the uniform distribution; when $\lambda > 1$, larger independent sets have a larger probability than smaller independent sets; and when $\lambda < 1$, larger independent sets have a smaller probability than smaller independent sets.

Consider now the following variation on the previous Markov chain for independent sets in a graph $G = (V, E)$.

1. X_0 is an arbitrary independent set in G.
2. To compute X_{i+1}:
   (a) choose a vertex v uniformly at random from V;
   (b) if $v \in X_i$, set $X_{i+1} = X_i \setminus \{v\}$ with probability $\min(1, 1/\lambda)$;
   (c) if $v \notin X_i$ and if adding v to X_i still gives an independent set, then put $X_{i+1} = X_i \cup \{v\}$ with probability $\min(1, \lambda)$;
   (d) otherwise, set $X_{i+1} = X_i$.

We now follow a two-step approach. We first propose a move by choosing a vertex v to add or delete, where each vertex is chosen with probability $1/M$; here $M = |V|$. This proposal is then accepted with probability $\min(1, \pi_y/\pi_x)$, where x is the current state and y is the proposed state to which the chain will move. Here, π_y/π_x is λ if the chain attempts to add a vertex and is $1/\lambda$ if the chain attempts to delete a vertex. This two-step approach is the hallmark of the Metropolis algorithm: each neighbor is selected with probability $1/M$, and then it is accepted with probability $\min(1, \pi_y/\pi_x)$. Using this two-step approach, we naturally obtain that the transition probability $P_{x,y}$ is

$$P_{x,y} = \frac{1}{M} \min\left(1, \frac{\pi_y}{\pi_x}\right),$$

so Lemma 11.8 applies.

It is important that, in designing this Markov chain, we never needed to know $B = \sum_x \lambda^{|I_x|}$. A graph with n vertices can have exponentially many independent sets, and calculating this sum directly would be too expensive computationally for many graphs. Our Markov chain gives the correct stationary distribution by using the ratios π_y/π_x, which are much easier to deal with.

11.5. Exercises

Exercise 11.1: Formally prove Theorem 11.1.

Exercise 11.2: Another method for approximating π using Monte Carlo techniques is based on Buffon's needle experiment. Research and explain Buffon's needle experiment, and further explain how it can be used to obtain an approximation for π.

Exercise 11.3: Show that the following alternative definition is equivalent to the definition of an FPRAS given in the chapter: A *fully polynomial randomized approximation scheme (FPRAS)* for a problem is a randomized algorithm for which, given an input x and any parameter ε with $0 < \varepsilon < 1$, the algorithm outputs an $(\varepsilon, 1/4)$-approximation in time that is polynomial in $1/\varepsilon$ and the size of the input x. (*Hint:* To boost the probability of success from $3/4$ to $1 - \delta$, consider the *median* of several *independent* runs of the algorithm. Why is the median a better choice than the mean?)

Exercise 11.4: Suppose we have a class of instances of the DNF satisfiability problem, each with $\alpha(n)$ satisfying truth assignments for some polynomial α. Suppose we apply the naïve approach of sampling assignments and checking whether they satisfy the formula. Show that, after sampling $2^{n/2}$ assignments, the probability of finding even a single satisfying assignment for a given instance is exponentially small in n.

Exercise 11.5: **(a)** Let $S_1, S_2, \ldots, S_m$ be subsets of a finite universe U. We know $|S_i|$ for $1 \le i \le m$. We wish to obtain an (ε, δ)-approximation to the size of the set

$$S = \bigcup_{i=1}^{m} S_i.$$

We have available a procedure that can, in one step, choose an element uniformly at random from a set S_i. Also, given an element $x \in U$, we can determine the number of sets S_i for which $x \in S_i$. We call this number $c(x)$.

Define p_i to be

$$p_i = \frac{|S_i|}{\sum_{j=1}^{m} |S_j|}.$$

The jth trial consists of the following steps. We choose a set S_j, where the probability of each set S_i being chosen is p_i, and then we choose an element x_j uniformly at random from S_j. In each trial the random choices are independent of all other trials. After t

trials, we estimate $|S|$ by

$$\left(\frac{1}{t} \sum_{j=1}^{t} \frac{1}{c(x_j)} \right) \left(\sum_{i=1}^{m} |S_i| \right).$$

Determine – as a function of m, ε, and δ – the number of trials needed to obtain an (ε, δ)-approximation to $|S|$.

(b) Explain how to use your results from part (a) to obtain an alternative approximation algorithm for counting the number of solutions to a DNF formula.

Exercise 11.6: The problem of counting the number of solutions to a knapsack instance can be defined as follows: Given items with sizes $a_1, a_2, \ldots, a_n > 0$ and an integer $b > 0$, find the number of vectors $(x_1, x_2, \ldots, x_n) \in \{0, 1\}^n$ such that $\sum_{i=1}^{n} a_i x_i \leq b$. The number b can be thought of as the size of a knapsack, and the x_i denote whether or not each item is put into the knapsack. Counting solutions corresponds to counting the number of different sets of items that can be placed in the knapsack without exceeding its capacity.

(a) A naïve way of counting the number of solutions to this problem is to repeatedly choose $(x_1, x_2, \ldots, x_n) \in \{0, 1\}^n$ uniformly at random, and return the 2^n times the fraction of samples that yield valid solutions. Argue why this is not a good strategy in general; in particular, argue that it will work poorly when each a_i is 1 and $b = \sqrt{n}$.

(b) Consider a Markov chain $X_0, X_1, \ldots$ on vectors $(x_1, x_2, \ldots, x_n) \in \{0, 1\}^n$. Suppose X_j is $(x_1, x_2, \ldots, x_n)$. At each step, the Markov chain chooses $i \in [1, n]$ uniformly at random. If $x_i = 1$, then X_{j+1} is obtained from X_j by setting x_i to 0. If $x_i = 0$, then X_{j+1} is obtained from X_j by setting x_i to 1 if doing so maintains the restriction $\sum_{i=1}^{n} a_i x_i \leq b$. Otherwise, $X_{j+1} = X_j$.

Argue that this Markov chain has a uniform stationary distribution whenever $\sum_{i=1}^{n} a_i > b$. Be sure to argue that the chain is irreducible and aperiodic.

(c) Argue that, if we have an FPAUS for the knapsack problem, then we can derive an FPRAS for the problem. To set the problem up properly, assume without loss of generality that $a_1 \leq a_2 \leq \cdots \leq a_n$. Let $b_0 = 0$ and $b_i = \sum_{j=1}^{i} a_j$. Let $\Omega(b_i)$ be the set of vectors $(x_1, x_2, \ldots, x_n) \in \{0, 1\}^n$ that satisfy $\sum_{i=1}^{n} a_i x_i \leq b_i$. Let k be the smallest integer such that $b_k \geq b$. Consider the equation

$$|\Omega(b)| = \frac{|\Omega(b)|}{|\Omega(b_{k-1})|} \times \frac{|\Omega(b_{k-1})|}{|\Omega(b_{k-2})|} \times \cdots \times \frac{|\Omega(b_1)|}{|\Omega(b_0)|} \times |\Omega(b_0)|.$$

You will need to argue that $|\Omega(b_{i-1})|/|\Omega(b_i)|$ is not too small. Specifically, argue that $|\Omega(b_i)| \leq (n+1)|\Omega(b_{i-1})|$.

Exercise 11.7: An alternative definition for an ε-uniform sample of Ω is as follows: A sampling algorithm generates an ε-uniform sample w if, for all $x \in \Omega$,

$$\frac{|\Pr(w = x) - 1/|\Omega||}{1/|\Omega|} \leq \varepsilon.$$

Show that an ε-uniform sample under this definition yields an ε-uniform sample as given in Definition 11.3

Exercise 11.8: Let $S = \sum_{i=1}^{\infty} i^{-2} = \pi^2/6$. Design a Markov chain based on the Metropolis algorithm on the positive integers such that, in the stationary distribution, $\pi_i = 1/Si^2$. The neighbors of any integer $i > 1$ for your chain should be only $i - 1$ and $i + 1$, and the only neighbor of 1 should be the integer 2.

Exercise 11.9: Recall the Bubblesort algorithm of Exercise 2.22. Suppose we have n cards labeled 1 through n. The order of the cards X can be the state of a Markov chain. Let $f(X)$ be the number of Bubblesort moves necessary to put the cards in increasing sorted order. Design a Markov chain based on the Metropolis algorithm such that, in the stationary distribution, the probability of an order X is proportional to $\lambda^{f(X)}$ for a given constant $\lambda > 0$. Pairs of states of the chain are connected if they correspond to pairs of orderings that can be obtained by interchanging at most two adjacent cards.

Exercise 11.10: A Δ-coloring C of an undirected graph $G = (V, E)$ is an assignment labeling each vertex with a number, representing a color, from the set $\{1, 2, \ldots, \Delta\}$. An edge (u, v) is *improper* if both u and v are assigned the same color. Let $I(C)$ be the number of improper edges of a coloring C. Design a Markov chain based on the Metropolis algorithm such that, in the stationary distribution, the probability of a coloring C is proportional to $\lambda^{I(C)}$ for a given constant $\lambda > 0$. Pairs of states of the chain are connected if they correspond to pairs of colorings that differ in just one vertex.

Exercise 11.11: In Section 11.4.1 we constructed a Markov chain on the independent sets of a graph where, in the stationary distribution, $\pi_x = \lambda^{|I_x|}/B$. Here I_x is the independent set corresponding to state x and $B = \sum_x \lambda^{|I_x|}$. Using a similar approach, construct a Markov chain on the independent sets of a graph *excluding the empty set*, where $\pi_x = |I_x|/B$ for a constant B. Because the chain excludes the empty set, you should first design a neighborhood structure that ensures the state space is connected.

Exercise 11.12: The following generalization of the Metropolis algorithm is due to Hastings. Suppose that we have a Markov chain on a state space Ω given by the transition matrix $\mathbf{Q}$ and that we want to construct a Markov chain on this state space with a stationary distribution $\pi_x = b(x)/B$, where for all $x \in \Omega$, $b(x) > 0$ and $B = \sum_{x \in \Omega} b(x)$ is finite. Define a new Markov chain as follows. When $X_n = x$, generate a random variable Y with $\Pr(Y = y) = Q_{x,y}$. Notice that Y can be generated by simulating one step of the original Markov chain. Set X_{n+1} to Y with probability

$$\min\left(\frac{\pi_y Q_{y,x}}{\pi_x Q_{x,y}}, 1\right),$$

and otherwise set X_{n+1} to X_n. Argue that, if this chain is aperiodic and irreducible, then it is also time reversible and has a stationary distribution given by the π_x.

Exercise 11.13: Suppose we have a program that takes as input a number x on the real interval $[0, 1]$ and outputs $f(x)$ for some bounded function f taking on values in the range $[1, b]$. We want to estimate

$$\int_{x=0}^{1} f(x)\,dx.$$

Assume that we have a random number generator that can generate independent uniform random variables $X_1, X_2, \ldots$. Show that

$$\sum_{i=1}^{m} \frac{f(X_i)}{m}$$

gives an (ε, δ)-approximation for the integral for a suitable value of m.

11.6. An Exploratory Assignment on Minimum Spanning Trees

Consider a complete, undirected graph with $\binom{n}{2}$ edges. Each edge has a weight, which is a real number chosen uniformly at random on $[0, 1]$.

Your goal is to estimate how the expected weight of the minimum spanning tree grows as a function of n for such graphs. This will require implementing a minimum spanning tree algorithm as well as procedures that generate the appropriate random graphs. (You should check to see what sorts of random number generators are available on your system and determine how to seed them – say, with a value from the machine's clock.)

Depending on the algorithm you use and your implementation, you may find that your program uses too much memory when n is large. To reduce memory when n is large, we suggest the following approach. In this setting, the minimum spanning tree is extremely unlikely to use any edge of weight greater than $k(n)$ for some function $k(n)$. We can first estimate $k(n)$ by using repeated runs for small values of n and then throw away edges of weight larger than $k(n)$ when n is large. If you use this approach, be sure to explain why throwing away edges in this manner will not lead to a situation where the program finds a spanning tree that is not actually minimal.

Run your program for $n = 16, 32, 64, 128, 256, 512, 1024, 2048, 4096, 8192$, and larger values, if your program runs fast enough. Run your program at least five times for each value of n and take the average. (Make sure you re-seed the random number generator appropriately!) You should present a table listing the average tree size for the values of n that your program runs successfully. What seems to be happening to the average size of the minimum spanning tree as n grows?

In addition, you should write one or two pages discussing your experiments in more depth. The discussion should reflect what you have learned from this assignment and might address the following topics.

- What minimum spanning tree algorithm did you use, and why?
- What is the running time of your algorithm?

315

- If you chose to throw away edges, how did you determine $k(n)$, and how effective was this approach?
- Can you give a rough explanation for your results? (The limiting behavior as n grows large can be proven rigorously, but it is very difficult; you need not attempt to prove any exact result.)
- Did you have any interesting experiences with the random number generator? Do you trust it?

CHAPTER TWELVE[*]

Coupling of Markov Chains

In our study of discrete time Markov chains in Chapter 7, we found that ergodic Markov chains converge to a stationary distribution. However, we did not determine how *quickly* they converge, which is important in a number of algorithmic applications, such as sampling using the Markov chain Monte Carlo technique. In this chapter, we introduce the concept of coupling, a powerful method for bounding the rate of convergence of Markov chains. We demonstrate the coupling method in several applications, including card-shuffling problems, random walks, and Markov chain Monte Carlo sampling of independent sets and vertex coloring.

12.1. Variation Distance and Mixing Time

Consider the following method for shuffling n cards. At each step, a card is chosen independently and uniformly at random and put on the top of the deck. We can think of the shuffling process as a Markov chain, where the state is the current order of the cards. You can check that the Markov chain is finite, irreducible, and aperiodic, and hence it has a stationary distribution.

Let x be a state of the chain, and let $N(x)$ be the set of states that can reach x in one step. Here $|N(x)| = n$, since the top card in x could have been in n different places in the previous step. If π_y is the probability associated with state y in the stationary distribution, then for any state x we have

$$\pi_x = \frac{1}{n} \sum_{y \in N(x)} \pi_y.$$

The uniform distribution satisfies these equations, and hence the unique stationary distribution is uniform over all possible permutations.

We know that the stationary distribution is the limiting distribution of the Markov chain as the number of steps grows to infinity. If we could run the chain "forever", then in the limit we would obtain a state that was uniformly distributed. In practice,

317

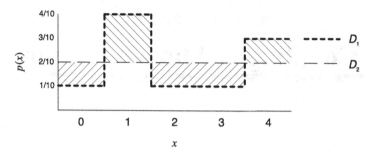

Figure 12.1: Example of variation distance. The areas shaded by upward diagonal lines correspond to values x where $D_1(x) < D_2(x)$; the areas shaded by downward diagonal lines correspond to values x where $D_1(x) > D_2(x)$. The total area shaded by upward diagonal lines must equal the total area shaded by downward diagonal lines, and the variation distance equals one of these two areas.

we run the chain for a finite number of steps. If we want to use this Markov chain to shuffle the deck, how many steps are necessary before we obtain a shuffle that is close to uniformly distributed?

To quantify what we mean by "close to uniform", we must introduce a distance measure.

Definition 12.1: *The* variation distance *between two distributions D_1 and D_2 on a countable state space S is given by*

$$\|D_1 - D_2\| = \frac{1}{2} \sum_{x \in S} |D_1(x) - D_2(x)|.$$

A pictorial example of the variation distance is given in Figure 12.1.

The factor $1/2$ in the definition of variation distance guarantees that the variation distance is between 0 and 1. It also allows the following useful alternative characterization.

Lemma 12.1: *For any $A \subseteq S$, let $D_i(A) = \sum_{x \in A} D_i(x)$ for $i = 1, 2$. Then*

$$\|D_1 - D_2\| = \max_{A \subseteq S} |D_1(A) - D_2(A)|.$$

A careful examination of Figure 12.1 helps make the proof of this lemma transparent.

Proof: Let $S^+ \subseteq S$ be the set of states such that $D_1(x) \geq D_2(x)$, and let $S^- \subseteq S$ be the set of states such that $D_2(x) > D_1(x)$.

Clearly,

$$\max_{A \subseteq S} D_1(A) - D_2(A) = D_1(S^+) - D_2(S^+)$$

and

$$\max_{A \subseteq S} D_2(A) - D_1(A) = D_2(S^-) - D_1(S^-).$$

But since $D_1(S) = D_2(S) = 1$, we have

$$D_1(S^+) + D_1(S^-) = D_2(S^+) + D_2(S^-) = 1,$$

which implies that

$$D_1(S^+) - D_2(S^+) = D_2(S^-) - D_1(S^-).$$

Hence

$$\max_{A \subseteq S} |D_1(A) - D_2(A)| = |D_1(S^+) - D_2(S^+)| = |D_1(S^-) - D_2(S^-)|.$$

Finally, since

$$|D_1(S^+) - D_2(S^+)| + |D_1(S^-) - D_2(S^-)| = \sum_{x \in S} |D_1(x) - D_2(x)| = 2\|D_1 - D_2\|,$$

we have

$$\max_{A \subseteq S} |D_1(A) - D_2(A)| = \|D_1 - D_2\|,$$

completing the proof. ∎

As an application of Lemma 12.1, suppose that we run our shuffling Markov chain until the variation distance between the distribution of the chain and the uniform distribution is less than ε. This is a strong notion of close to uniform, because every permutation of the cards must have probability at most $1/n! + \varepsilon$. In fact the bound on the variation distance gives an even stronger statement: For any subset $A \subseteq S$, the probability that the final permutation is from the set A is at most $\pi(A) + \varepsilon$. For example, suppose someone is trying to make the top card in the deck an ace. If the variation distance from the distribution to the uniform distribution is less than ε, we can safely say that probability that an ace is the first card in the deck is at most ε greater than if we had a perfect shuffle.

As another example, suppose we take a 52-card deck and shuffle all the cards – but leave the ace of spades on top. In this case, the variation distance between the resulting distribution D_1 and the uniform distribution D_2 could be bounded by considering the set B of states where the ace of spades is on the top of the deck:

$$\|D_1 - D_2\| = \max_{A \subseteq S} |D_1(A) - D_2(A)| \geq |D_1(B) - D_2(B)| = 1 - \frac{1}{52} = \frac{51}{52}.$$

The definition of variation distance coincides with the definition of an ε-uniform sample (given in Definition 11.3). A sampling algorithm returns an ε-uniform sample on Ω if and only if the variation distance between its output distribution D and the uniform distribution U satisfies

$$\|D - U\| \leq \varepsilon.$$

Bounding the variation distance between the uniform distribution and the distribution of the state of a Markov chain after some number of steps can therefore be a useful way of proving the existence of efficient ε-uniform samplers, which (as we showed in Chapter 11) can in turn lead to efficient approximate counting algorithms.

We now consider how to bound this variation distance after t steps. In what follows, we assume that the Markov chains under consideration are ergodic discrete space and discrete time chains with well-defined stationary distributions. The following definitions will be useful.

Definition 12.2: *Let $\bar{\pi}$ be the stationary distribution of an ergodic Markov chain with state space S. Let p_x^t represent the distribution of the state of the chain starting at state x after t steps. We define*

$$\Delta_x(t) = \| p_x^t - \bar{\pi} \|; \qquad \Delta(t) = \max_{x \in S} \Delta_x(t).$$

That is, $\Delta_x(t)$ is the variation distance between the stationary distribution and p_x^t, and $\Delta(t)$ is the maximum of these values over all states x.
  We also define

$$\tau_x(\varepsilon) = \min\{t : \Delta_x(t) \le \varepsilon\}; \qquad \tau(\varepsilon) = \max_{x \in S} \tau_x(\varepsilon).$$

That is, $\tau_x(\varepsilon)$ is the first step t at which the variation distance between p_x^t and the stationary distribution is less than ε, and $\tau(\varepsilon)$ is the maximum of these values over all states x.

When $\tau(\varepsilon)$ is considered as a function of ε, it is generally called the *mixing time* of the Markov chain. A chain is called *rapidly mixing* if $\tau(\varepsilon)$ is polynomial in $\log(1/\varepsilon)$ and the size of the problem. The size of the problem depends on the context; in the shuffling example, the size would be the number of cards.

12.2. Coupling

Coupling of Markov chains is a general technique for bounding the mixing time of a Markov chain.

Definition 12.3: *A coupling of a Markov chain M_t with state space S is a Markov chain $Z_t = (X_t, Y_t)$ on the state space $S \times S$ such that:*

$$\Pr(X_{t+1} = x' \mid Z_t = (x, y)) = \Pr(M_{t+1} = x' \mid M_t = x);$$
$$\Pr(Y_{t+1} = y' \mid Z_t = (x, y)) = \Pr(M_{t+1} = y' \mid M_t = y).$$

That is, a coupling consists of two copies of the Markov chain M running simultaneously. These two copies are not literal copies; the two chains are not necessarily in the same state, nor do they necessarily make the same move. Instead, we mean that each copy behaves exactly like the original Markov chain in terms of its transition probabilities. One obvious way to obtain a coupling is simply to take two independent runs of the Markov chain. As we shall see, such a coupling is generally not very useful for our purposes.

  Instead, we are interested in couplings that (a) bring the two copies of the chain to the same state and then (b) keep them in the same state by having the two chains make identical moves once they are in the same state. When the two copies of the chain reach the same state, they are said to have *coupled*. The following lemma motivates why we seek couplings that couple.

Lemma 12.2 [Coupling Lemma]: *Let $Z_t = (X_t, Y_t)$ be a coupling for a Markov chain M on a state space S. Suppose that there exists a T such that, for every $x, y \in S$,*

$$\Pr(X_T \neq Y_T \mid X_0 = x, Y_0 = y) \leq \varepsilon.$$

Then

$$\tau(\varepsilon) \leq T.$$

That is, for any initial state, the variation distance between the distribution of the state of the chain after T steps and the stationary distribution is at most ε.

Proof: Consider the coupling when Y_0 is chosen according to the stationary distribution and X_0 takes on any arbitrary value. For the given T and ε and for any $A \subseteq S$,

$$
\begin{aligned}
\Pr(X_T \in A) &\geq \Pr((X_T = Y_T) \cap (Y_T \in A)) \\
&= 1 - \Pr((X_T \neq Y_T) \cup (Y_T \notin A)) \\
&\geq (1 - \Pr(Y_T \notin A)) - \Pr(X_T \neq Y_T) \\
&\geq \Pr(Y_T \in A) - \varepsilon \\
&= \pi(A) - \varepsilon.
\end{aligned}
$$

Here the third line follows from the union bound. For the fourth line, we used the fact that $\Pr(X_T \neq Y_T) \leq \varepsilon$ for any initial states X_0 and Y_0; in particular, this holds when Y_0 is chosen according to the stationary distribution. For the last line, we used that $\Pr(Y_T \in A) = \pi(A)$, since Y_T is also distributed according to the stationary distribution. The same argument for the set $S - A$ shows that $\Pr(X_T \notin A) \geq \pi(S - A) - \varepsilon$, or $\Pr(X_T \in A) \leq \pi(A) + \varepsilon$.

It follows that

$$\max_{x,A} |p_x^T(A) - \pi(A)| \leq \varepsilon,$$

so by Lemma 12.1 the variation distance from the stationary distribution after the chain runs for T steps is bounded above by ε. ∎

12.2.1. *Example: Shuffling Cards*

To apply the coupling lemma effectively to the card-shuffling Markov chain, we must choose an appropriate coupling. Given two copies X_t and Y_t of the chain in different states, one possibility for the coupling is to choose a position j uniformly at random from 1 to n and simultaneously move to the top the jth card from the top in both chains. This is a valid coupling, because each chain individually acts as the original shuffling Markov chain. Although this coupling is natural, it does not appear immediately useful. Since the chains start in different states, the jth cards from the top in the two chains will usually be different. Moving these two different cards to the top does not seem to bring the two copies of the chain toward the same state.

A more useful coupling is to choose a position j uniformly at random from 1 to n and then obtain X_{t+1} from X_t by moving the jth card to the top. Denote the value of this card by C. To obtain Y_{t+1} from Y_t, move the card with value C to the top. The coupling is again valid, because in both chains the probability a specific card is moved to the top at each step is $1/n$. With this coupling, it is easy to see by induction that, once a card C is moved to the top, it is always in the same position in both copies of the chain. Hence, the two copies are sure to become coupled once every card has been moved to the top at least once.

Now our coupling problem for the shuffling Markov chain looks like a coupon collector's problem; to bound the number of steps until the chains couple, we simply bound how many times cards must be chosen uniformly at random before every card is chosen at least once. We know that when the Markov chain runs for $n \ln n + cn$ steps, the probability that a specific card has not been moved to the top at least once is at most

$$\left(1 - \frac{1}{n}\right)^{n \ln n + cn} \leq e^{-(\ln n + c)} = \frac{e^{-c}}{n},$$

and thus (by the union bound) the probability that any card has not been moved to the top at least once is at most e^{-c}. Hence, after only $n \ln n + n \ln(1/\varepsilon) = n \ln(n/\varepsilon)$ steps, the probability that the chains have not coupled is at most ε. The coupling lemma allows us to conclude that the variation distance between the uniform distribution and the distribution of the state of the chain after $n \ln(n/\varepsilon)$ steps is bounded above by ε.

12.2.2. *Example: Random Walks on the Hypercube*

Recall from Section 4.6.1 that an n-dimensional hypercube, or n-cube, consists of $N = 2^n$ nodes numbered from 0 to $N - 1$. Let $\bar{x} = (x_1, \ldots, x_n)$ be the binary representation of x. Nodes x and y are connected by an edge if and only if $\bar{x}$ and $\bar{y}$ differ in exactly one bit.

We consider the following Markov chain defined on the n-cube. At each step, choose a coordinate i uniformly at random from $[1, n]$. The new state x' is obtained from the current state x by keeping all coordinates of $\bar{x}$ the same, except possibly for x_i. The coordinate x_i is set to 0 with probability $1/2$ and to 1 with probability $1/2$. This Markov chain is exactly the random walk on the hypercube, except that with probability $1/2$ the chain stays at the same vertex instead of moving to a new one, which removes the potential problem of periodicity. It follows easily that the stationary distribution of the chain is uniform over the vertices of the hypercube.

We bound the mixing time $\tau(\varepsilon)$ of this Markov chain by using the obvious coupling between two copies X_t and Y_t of the Markov chain: at each step, we have both chains make the same move. With this coupling, the two copies of the chain will surely agree on the ith coordinate, once the ith coordinate has been chosen for a move of the Markov chain. Hence the chains will have coupled after all n coordinates have each been chosen at least once.

The mixing time can therefore be bounded by bounding the number of steps until each coordinate has been chosen at least once by the Markov chain. This again reduces to the coupon collector's problem, just as in the case of the shuffling chain. By the same argument, the probability is less than ε that after $n \ln(n\varepsilon^{-1})$ steps the chains have not coupled, and hence by the coupling lemma the mixing time satisfies

$$\tau(\varepsilon) \leq n \ln(n\varepsilon^{-1}).$$

12.2.3. *Example: Independent Sets of Fixed Size*

We consider a Markov chain whose states are all independent sets of size exactly k in a graph $G = (V, E)$. Because we restrict ourselves to independent sets of a fixed size, we need a different Markov chain than the chain for all independent sets developed in Section 11.4. A move is made from the independent set X_t by choosing a vertex $v \in X_t$ uniformly at random and a vertex $w \in V$ uniformly at random. The move $m(v, w, X_t)$ can be described as follows: if $w \notin X_t$ and $(X_t - \{v\}) \cup \{w\}$ is an independent set, then $X_{t+1} = (X_t - \{v\}) \cup \{w\}$; otherwise, $X_{t+1} = X_t$. Let n be the number of vertices in the graph and let Δ be the maximum degree of any vertex. We show here that this chain is rapidly mixing whenever $k \leq n/(3\Delta + 3)$. We leave the task of showing that the Markov chain is ergodic and has a uniform stationary distribution as Exercise 12.11, and assume this in the following argument.

We consider a coupling on $Z_t = (X_t, Y_t)$. Our coupling will require an arbitrary perfect matching M between the vertices of $X_t - Y_t$ and $Y_t - X_t$ at each step; for example, we may label the vertices 1 to n and match the elements of $X_t - Y_t$ in sorted order via a one-to-one mapping with the elements of $Y_t - X_t$ in sorted order. For our coupling, we first choose a transition for the chain X_t by choosing $v \in X_t$ and $w \in V$ uniformly at random and then perform the move $m(v, w, X_t)$. Clearly, the copy of the chain X_t follows the original Markov chain faithfully as required by Definition 12.3. For the transition of Y_t, if $v \in Y_t$ then we use the same pair of vertices v and w and perform the move $m(v, w, Y_t)$; if $v \notin Y_t$, we perform the move $m(M(v), w, Y_t)$ (where $M(v)$ denotes the vertex matched to v). The copy of the chain Y_t also follows the original Markov chain faithfully, since each pair of vertices with $v \in Y_t$ and $w \in V$ is chosen with probability $1/kn$.

An alternative way of establishing the coupling is as follows. We again choose $v \in X_t$ and $w \in V$ uniformly at random and then perform the move $m(v, w, X_t)$ in the chain X_t. If $v \in Y_t$, we perform the move $m(v, w, Y_t)$ in the chain Y_t; otherwise, we choose uniformly at random a vertex $v' \in Y_t - X_t$ and perform the move $m(v', w, Y_t)$ in the chain Y_t. We see in Exercise 12.10 that this also satisfies Definition 12.3.

Let $d_t = |X_t - Y_t|$ measure the difference between the two independent sets after t steps. Clearly d_t can change by at most 1 at each step. We show that d_t is more likely to decrease than increase, and we use this fact to establish an upper bound on the probability that $d_t > 0$ for sufficiently large t.

Suppose that $d_t > 0$. In order for $d_{t+1} = d_t + 1$, it must be that at time t the vertex v is chosen from $X_t \cap Y_t$, and w is chosen so that there is a transition in exactly one of the chains. Thus, w must be either a vertex or a neighbor of a vertex in the set $(X_t - Y_t) \cup (Y_t - X_t)$. It follows that

$$\Pr(d_{t+1} = d_t + 1 \mid d_t > 0) \leq \frac{k - d_t}{k} \frac{2d_t(\Delta + 1)}{n}.$$

Similarly, in order for $d_{t+1} = d_t - 1$, it is sufficient that at time t we have $v \notin Y_t$ and w neither a vertex nor a neighbor of a vertex in the set $X_t \cup Y_t - \{v, v'\}$. Note that $|X_t \cup Y_t| = k + d_t$. Therefore,

$$\Pr(d_{t+1} = d_t - 1 \mid d_t > 0) \geq \frac{d_t}{k} \frac{n - (k + d_t - 2)(\Delta + 1)}{n}.$$

We thus have, for $d_t > 0$,

$$\begin{aligned}
\mathbf{E}[d_{t+1} \mid d_t] &= d_t + \Pr(d_{t+1} = d_t + 1) - \Pr(d_{t+1} = d_t - 1) \\
&\leq d_t + \frac{k - d_t}{k} \frac{2d_t(\Delta + 1)}{n} - \frac{d_t}{k} \frac{n - (k + d_t - 2)(\Delta + 1)}{n} \\
&= d_t \left(1 - \frac{n - (3k - d_t - 2)(\Delta + 1)}{kn} \right) \\
&\leq d_t \left(1 - \frac{n - (3k - 3)(\Delta + 1)}{kn} \right).
\end{aligned}$$

Once $d_t = 0$, the two chains follow the same path and so $\mathbf{E}[d_{t+1} \mid d_t = 0] = 0$.

Using the conditional expectation equality, we have

$$\mathbf{E}[d_{t+1}] = \mathbf{E}[\mathbf{E}[d_{t+1} \mid d_t]] \leq \mathbf{E}[d_t] \left(1 - \frac{n - (3k - 3)(\Delta + 1)}{kn} \right).$$

By induction, we find that

$$\mathbf{E}[d_t] \leq d_0 \left(1 - \frac{n - (3k - 3)(\Delta + 1)}{kn} \right)^t.$$

Since $d_0 \leq k$ and since d_t is a nonnegative integer, it follows that

$$\Pr(d_t \geq 1) \leq \mathbf{E}[d_t] \leq k \left(1 - \frac{n - (3k - 3)(\Delta + 1)}{kn} \right)^t \leq k e^{-t(n - (3k - 3)(\Delta + 1))/(kn)}.$$

A consequence of this result is that the variation distance converges to zero whenever $k \leq n/(3\Delta + 3)$, and in this case

$$\tau(\varepsilon) \leq \frac{kn \ln(k\varepsilon^{-1})}{n - (3k - 3)(\Delta + 1)}.$$

We thus find that $\tau(\varepsilon)$ is polynomial in n and $\ln(1/\varepsilon)$, implying that the chain is rapidly mixing, whenever $k \leq n/(3\Delta + 3)$.

We can actually improve upon this result. In Exercise 12.12 we use a slightly more sophisticated coupling to obtain a bound that holds for any $k \leq n/(2\Delta + 2)$.

12.3. Application: Variation Distance Is Nonincreasing

We know that an ergodic Markov chain eventually converges to its stationary distribution. In fact, the variation distance between the state of a Markov chain and its stationary distribution is nonincreasing in time. To show this, we start with an interesting lemma that gives another useful property of the variation distance.

Lemma 12.3: *Given distributions σ_X and σ_Y on a state space S, let $Z = (X, Y)$ be a random variable on $S \times S$, where X is distributed according to σ_X and Y is distributed according to σ_Y. Then*

$$\Pr(X \neq Y) \geq \|\sigma_X - \sigma_Y\|. \tag{12.1}$$

Moreover, there exists a joint distribution $Z = (X, Y)$, where X is distributed according to σ_X and Y is distributed according to σ_Y, for which equality holds.

Again, examining a specific example (such as in Figure 12.1) helps us understand the following proof.

Proof: For each $s \in S$, we have

$$\Pr(X = Y = x) \leq \min(\Pr(X = x), \Pr(Y = x)).$$

Hence

$$\Pr(X = Y) \leq \sum_{x \in S} \min(\Pr(X = x), \Pr(Y = x)),$$

and therefore

$$\Pr(X \neq Y) \geq 1 - \sum_{x \in S} \min(\Pr(X = x), \Pr(Y = x))$$
$$= \sum_{x \in S} \left(\Pr(X = x) - \min(\Pr(X = x), \Pr(Y = x)) \right).$$

Hence we are done if we can show

$$\|\sigma_X - \sigma_Y\| = \sum_{x \in S} \left(\Pr(X = x) - \min(\Pr(X = x), \Pr(Y = x)) \right). \tag{12.2}$$

But $\Pr(X = x) - \min(\Pr(X = x), \Pr(Y = x)) = 0$ when $\sigma_X(x) < \sigma_Y(x)$, and when $\sigma_X(x) \geq \sigma_Y(x)$ it is

$$\Pr(X = x) - \Pr(Y = x) = \sigma_X(x) - \sigma_Y(x).$$

If we let S^+ be the set of all states for which $\sigma_X(x) \geq \sigma_Y(x)$, then the right-hand side of Eqn. (12.2) is equal to $\sigma_X(S^+) - \sigma_Y(S^+)$, which equals $\|\sigma_X - \sigma_Y\|$ from the argument in Lemma 12.1. This gives the first part of the lemma.

Equality holds in Eqn. (12.1) if we take a joint distribution where $X = Y$ as much as possible. Specifically, let $m(x) = \min(\Pr(X = x), \Pr(Y = x))$. If $\sum_x m(x) = 1$, then X and Y have the same distribution and we are done. Otherwise, let $Z = (X, Y)$ be defined by

$$\Pr(X = x, Y = y) = \begin{cases} m(x) & \text{if } x = y; \\ \dfrac{(\sigma_X(x) - m(x))(\sigma_Y(y) - m(y))}{1 - \sum_z m(z)} & \text{otherwise.} \end{cases}$$

The idea behind this choice of Z is to first match X and Y as much as possible and then force X and Y to behave independently if they do not match.

For this choice of Z,

$$\Pr(X = Y) = \sum_x m(x) = 1 - \|\sigma_X - \sigma_Y\|.$$

It remains to show that, for this choice of Z, $\Pr(X = x) = \sigma_X(x)$; the same argument will hold for $\Pr(Y = y)$. If $m(x) = \sigma_X(x)$ then $\Pr(X = x, Y = x) = m(x)$ and $\Pr(X = x, Y = y) = 0$ when $x \neq y$, so $\Pr(X = x) = \sigma_X(x)$. If $m(x) = \sigma_Y(x)$, then

$$\Pr(X = x) = \sum_y \Pr(X = x, Y = y)$$

$$= m(x) + \sum_{y \neq x} \frac{(\sigma_X(x) - m(x))(\sigma_Y(y) - m(y))}{1 - \sum_z m(z)}$$

$$= m(x) + \frac{(\sigma_X(x) - m(x)) \sum_{y \neq x} (\sigma_Y(y) - m(y))}{1 - \sum_z m(z)}$$

$$= m(x) + \frac{(\sigma_X(x) - m(x))\left(1 - \sigma_Y(x) - \left(\sum_z m(z) - m(x)\right)\right)}{1 - \sum_z m(z)}$$

$$= m(x) + (\sigma_X(x) - m(x))$$

$$= \sigma_X(x),$$

completing the proof. ∎

Recall that $\Delta(t) = \max_x \Delta_x(t)$, where $\Delta_x(t)$ is the variation distance between the stationary distribution and the distribution of the state of the Markov chain after t steps when starting at state x. Using Lemma 12.3, we can prove that $\Delta(t)$ is nonincreasing over time.

Theorem 12.4: *For any ergodic Markov chain M_t, $\Delta(T + 1) \leq \Delta(T)$.*

Proof: Let x be any given state, and let y be a state chosen from the stationary distribution. Then

$$\Delta_x(T) = \|p_x^T - p_y^T\|.$$

Indeed, if X_T is distributed according to p_x^T and if Y_T is distributed according to p_y^T, then by Lemma 12.3 there exists a random variable $Z_T = (X_T, Y_T)$ with $\Pr(X_T \neq Y_T) = \Delta_x(T)$. From this state Z_T, consider any one-step coupling for the Markov chain that takes $Z_T = (X_T, Y_T)$ to $Z_{T+1} = (X_{T+1}, Y_{T+1})$ in such a way that, whenever $X_T = Y_T$, the coupling makes the same move, so that $X_{T+1} = Y_{T+1}$. Now X_{T+1} is distributed according to p_x^{T+1} and Y_{T+1} is distributed according to p_y^{T+1}, which is the stationary distribution. Hence, by Lemma 12.3,

$$\Delta_x(T) = \Pr(X_T \neq Y_T)$$

$$\geq \Pr(X_{T+1} \neq Y_{T+1})$$

$$\geq \|p_x^{T+1} - p_y^{T+1}\|$$

$$= \Delta_x(T + 1).$$

The second line follows from the first because the one-step coupling assures $X_{T+1} = Y_{T+1}$ whenever $X_T = Y_T$. The result follows since the foregoing relations hold for every state x. ∎

12.4. Geometric Convergence

The following general result, derived from a trivial coupling, is useful for bounding the mixing time of some Markov chains.

Theorem 12.5: *Let* **P** *be the transition matrix for a finite, irreducible, aperiodic Markov chain. Let* m_j *be the smallest entry in the jth column of the matrix, and let* $m = \sum_j m_j$. *Then, for all x and t,*

$$\| p_x^t - \pi \| \leq (1 - m)^t.$$

Proof: If the minimum entry in column j is m_j, then in one step the chain reaches state j with probability at least m_j from every state. Hence we can design a coupling where the two copies of the chain both move to state j together with probability at least m_j in every step. Since this holds for all j, at each step the two chains can be made to couple with probability at least m. Hence the probability they have not coupled after m steps is at most $(1 - m)^t$, yielding the theorem via the coupling lemma. ∎

Theorem 12.5 is not immediately helpful if there is a zero entry in each column, in which case $m = 0$. In Exercise 12.6, we consider how to make it useful for any finite, irreducible, aperiodic Markov chain. Theorem 12.5 shows that, under very general conditions, Markov chains converge quickly to their stationary distributions, with the variation distance converging geometrically in the number of steps.

A more general related result is the following. Suppose that we can obtain an upper bound on $\tau(c)$ for some constant $c < 1/2$. For example, such a bound might be found by a coupling. This is sufficient to bootstrap a bound for $\tau(\varepsilon)$ for any $\varepsilon > 0$.

Theorem 12.6: *Let* **P** *be the transition matrix for a finite, irreducible, aperiodic Markov chain* M_t *with* $\tau(c) \leq T$ *for some* $c < 1/2$. *Then, for this Markov chain,* $\tau(\varepsilon) \leq \lceil \ln \varepsilon / \ln(2c) \rceil T$.

Proof: Consider any two initial states $X_0 = x$ and $Y_0 = y$. By the definition of $\tau(c)$, we have $\| p_x^T - \pi \| \leq c$ and $\| p_y^T - \pi \| \leq c$. It follows that $\| p_x^T - p_y^T \| \leq 2c$ and hence, by Lemma 12.3, there exists a random variable $Z_{T,x,y} = (X_T, Y_T)$ with X_T distributed according to p_x^T and Y_T distributed according to p_y^T such that $\Pr(X_T \neq Y_T) \leq 2c$.

Now consider the Markov chain M_t' given by the transition matrix $\mathbf{P}^T$, which corresponds to a chain that takes T steps of M_t for each of its steps; the $Z_{T,x,y}$ give a coupling for this new chain. That is, given two copies of the chain M_t' in the paired state (x, y), we can let the next paired state be given by the distribution $Z_{T,x,y}$, which guarantees that the probability the two states have not coupled in one step is at most $2c$. The probability that this coupling of the chain M_t' has not coupled over k steps is then at most $(2c)^k$ by induction. By the coupling lemma, M_t' is within variation distance ε of its stationary distribution after k steps if

$$(2c)^k \leq \varepsilon.$$

It follows that, after at most $\lceil \ln \varepsilon / \ln(2c) \rceil$ steps, M'_t is within variation distance ε of its stationary distribution. But M'_t and M_t have the same stationary distribution, and each step of M'_t corresponds to T steps of M_t. Therefore,

$$\tau(\varepsilon) \leq \left\lceil \frac{\ln \varepsilon}{\ln(2c)} \right\rceil T$$

for the Markov chain M_t. ∎

12.5. Application: Approximately Sampling Proper Colorings

A *vertex coloring* of a graph gives each vertex v a color from a set C, which we can assume without loss of generality is the set $\{1, 2, \ldots, c\}$. In a *proper coloring,* the two endpoints of every edge are colored by two different colors. Any graph with maximum degree Δ can be colored properly with $\Delta + 1$ colors by the following procedure: choose an arbitrary ordering of the vertices, and color them one at a time, labeling each vertex with a color not already used by any of its neighbors.

Here we are interested in sampling almost uniformly at random a proper coloring of a graph. We present a Markov chain Monte Carlo (MCMC) process that generates such a sample and then use a coupling technique to show that it is rapidly mixing. In the terminology of Chapter 11, this gives an FPAUS for proper colorings. Applying the general reduction from approximate counting to almost uniform sampling, as in Theorem 11.5, we can use the FPAUS for sampling proper colorings to obtain an FPRAS for the number of proper colorings. The details of this reduction are left as part of Exercise 12.15.

To begin, we present a straightforward coupling that allows us to approximately sample colorings efficiently when there are $c > 4\Delta + 1$ colors. We then show how to improve the coupling to reduce the number of colors necessary to $2\Delta + 1$.

Our Markov chain on proper colorings is the simplest one possible. At each step, choose a vertex v uniformly at random and a color ℓ uniformly at random. Recolor vertex v with color ℓ if the new coloring is proper (that is, v does not have a neighbor colored ℓ), and otherwise let the state of the chain be unchanged. This finite Markov chain is aperiodic because it has nonzero probability of staying in the same state. When $c \geq \Delta + 2$, it is also irreducible. To see how from any state X we can reach any other state Y, consider an arbitrary ordering of the vertices. Recolor the vertices in X to match Y in this order. If there is a conflict at any step, it must arise because a vertex v that needs to be colored is blocked by some other vertex v' later in the ordering. But v' can be recolored to some other nonconflicting color, since $c \geq \Delta + 2$, allowing the process to continue. Hence, when $c \geq \Delta + 2$, the Markov chain has a stationary distribution. The fact that this stationary distribution is uniform over all proper colorings can be verified by applying Lemma 11.7.

When there are $4\Delta + 1$ colors, we use a trivial coupling on the pair of chains (X_t, Y_t): choose the same vertex and color on both chains at each step.

Theorem 12.7: *For any graph with n vertices and maximum degree Δ, the mixing time of the graph-coloring Markov chain satisfies*

$$\tau(\varepsilon) \leq \left\lceil \frac{nc}{c - 4\Delta} \ln\left(\frac{n}{\varepsilon}\right) \right\rceil,$$

provided that $c \geq 4\Delta + 1$.

Proof: Let D_t be the set of vertices that have different colors in the two chains at time t, and let $d_t = |D_t|$. At each step in which $d_t > 0$, either d_t remains at the same value or d_t increases or decreases by at most 1. We show that d_t is actually more likely to decrease than increase; then we use this fact to bound the probability that d_t is nonzero for sufficiently large t.

Consider any vertex v that is colored differently in the two chains. Since the degree of v is at most Δ, there are at least $c - 2\Delta$ colors that do not appear on the neighbors of v in either of the two chains. If the vertex is recolored to one of these $c - 2\Delta$ colors, it will have the same color in both chains. Hence

$$\Pr(d_{t+1} = d_t - 1 \mid d_t > 0) \geq \frac{d_t}{n} \frac{c - 2\Delta}{c}.$$

Now consider any vertex v that is colored the same in both chains. For v to be colored differently at the next step, it must have some neighbor w that is differently colored in the two chains; in that case, it is possible that trying to recolor v using a color that the neighbor w has in one of the two chains will recolor the vertex v in one chain but not the other. Every vertex colored differently in the two chains can affect at most Δ neighbors in this way. Hence, when $d_t > 0$,

$$\Pr(d_{t+1} = d_t + 1 \mid d_t > 0) \leq \frac{\Delta d_t}{n} \frac{2}{c}.$$

We find that

$$\begin{aligned}
\mathbf{E}[d_{t+1} \mid d_t] &= d_t + \Pr(d_{t+1} = d_t + 1) - \Pr(d_{t+1} = d_t - 1) \\
&\leq d_t + \frac{\Delta d_t}{n} \frac{2}{c} - \frac{d_t}{n} \frac{c - 2\Delta}{c} \\
&= d_t \left(1 - \frac{c - 4\Delta}{nc}\right),
\end{aligned}$$

which also holds if $d_t = 0$.

Using the conditional expectation equality, we have

$$\mathbf{E}[d_{t+1}] = \mathbf{E}[\mathbf{E}[d_{t+1} \mid d_t]] \leq \mathbf{E}[d_t]\left(1 - \frac{c - 4\Delta}{nc}\right).$$

By induction, we find

$$\mathbf{E}[d_t] \leq d_0 \left(1 - \frac{c - 4\Delta}{nc}\right)^t.$$

329

Since $d_0 \leq n$ and since d_t is a nonnegative integer, it follows that

$$\Pr(d_t \geq 1) \leq \mathbf{E}[d_t] \leq n \left(1 - \frac{c - 4\Delta}{nc} \right)^t \leq ne^{-t(c-4\Delta)/nc}.$$

Hence the variation distance is at most ε after

$$t = \left\lceil \frac{nc}{c - 4\Delta} \ln \left(\frac{n}{\varepsilon} \right) \right\rceil$$

steps. ∎

Assuming that each step of the Markov chain can be accomplished efficiently in time that is polynomial in n, Theorem 12.7 gives an FPAUS for proper colorings.

Theorem 12.7 is rather wasteful. For example, when bounding the probability that d_t decreases, we used the loose bound $c - 2\Delta$. The number of colors that decrease d_t could be much higher if some of the vertices around v have the same color in both chains. By being a bit more careful and slightly more clever with the coupling, we can improve Theorem 12.7 to hold for any $c \geq 2\Delta + 1$.

Theorem 12.8: *Given an n-vertex graph with maximum degree Δ, the mixing time of the graph-coloring Markov chain satisfies*

$$\tau(\varepsilon) \leq \left\lceil \frac{nc}{c - 2\Delta} \ln \left(\frac{n}{\varepsilon} \right) \right\rceil,$$

provided that $c \geq 2\Delta + 1$.

Proof: As before, let D_t be the set of vertices that have different colors in the two chains at time t, with $|D_t| = d_t$. Let A_t be the set of vertices that have the same color in the two chains at time t. For a vertex v in A_t, let $d'(v)$ be the number of vertices adjacent to v that are in D_t; similarly, for a vertex w in D_t, let $d'(w)$ be the number of vertices adjacent to w that are in A_t. Note that

$$\sum_{v \in A_t} d'(v) = \sum_{w \in D_t} d'(w),$$

since the two sums both count the number of edges connecting vertices in A_t to vertices in D_t. Denote this summation by m'.

Consider the following coupling: if a vertex $v \in D_t$ is chosen to be recolored, we simply choose the same color in both chains. That is, when v is in D_t, we are using the same coupling we used before. The vertex v will have the same color whenever the color chosen is different from any color on any of the neighbors of v in both copies of the chain. There are $c - 2\Delta + d'(v)$ such colors; notice that this is a tighter bound than we used in the proof of Theorem 12.7. Hence the probability that $d_{t+1} = d_t - 1$ when $d_t > 0$ is at least

$$\frac{1}{n} \sum_{v \in D_t} \frac{c - 2\Delta + d'(v)}{c} = \frac{1}{cn}((c - 2\Delta)d_t + m').$$

Assume now that the vertex to be recolored is $v \in A_t$. In this case we change the coupling slightly. Recall that, in the previous coupling, recoloring a vertex $v \in A_t$ results in v becoming differently colored in the two chains if the randomly chosen color appears

330

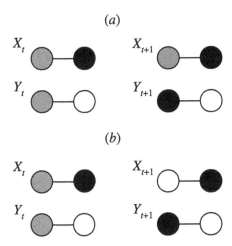

Figure 12.2: (*a*), original coupling; (*b*), improved coupling. In the original coupling of part (*a*), the gray vertex has the same color in both chains and has a neighbor with different colors in the two chains, one black and one white. If an attempt is made to recolor the gray vertex black, then the move will succeed in one chain but not the other, increasing d_t. Similarly, if an attempt is made to recolor the gray vertex white, then the move will succeed in one chain but not the other, giving a second move that increases d_t. In the improved coupling of part (*b*), if the gray vertex is recolored white in X_t then the gray vertex is recolored black in Y_t and vice versa, giving just one move that increases d_t.

on a neighbor of v in one chain but not the other. For example: if v is colored green, and a neighbor w is colored red in one chain and blue in the other, and no other neighbor of v is colored red or blue in either chain, then attempting to color v either red or blue will cause v to be recolored in one chain but not the other. Hence there are two potential choices for v's color that increase d_t.

In this specific case where just one vertex w neighboring v has different colors in the two chains, we could improve the coupling as follows: when we try to recolor v blue in the first chain, we try to recolor it red in the second chain; and when we try to recolor it red in the first chain, we try to recolor it blue in the second chain. Now v either changes color in both chains or stays the same in both chains. By changing the coupling, we have collapsed two potentially bad moves that increase d_t into just one bad move. See Figure 12.2 for an example.

More generally, if there are $d'(v)$ differently colored vertices around v then we can couple the colors so that at most $d'(v)$ color choices cause d_t to increase, instead of up to $2d'(v)$ choices in the original coupling. Concretely, let $S_1(v)$ be the set of colors on neighbors of v in the first chain but not the second, and similarly let $S_2(v)$ be the set of colors on neighbors of v in the second chain but not the first. Couple pairs of colors $c_1 \in S_1(v)$ and $c_2 \in S_2(v)$ as much as possible, so that when c_1 is chosen in one chain c_2 is chosen in the other. Then the total number of ways to color v that increases d_t is at most $\max(|S_1(v)|, |S_2(v)|) \le d'(v)$.

As a result, the probability that $d_{t+1} = d_t + 1$ when $d_t > 0$ is at most

$$\frac{1}{n} \sum_{v \in A_t} \frac{d'(v)}{c} = \frac{m'}{cn}.$$

331

We therefore find that

$$\mathbf{E}[d_{t+1} \mid d_t] \le d_t \left(1 - \frac{c - 2\Delta}{nc} \right).$$

Following the same reasoning as in the proof of Theorem 12.7, we have

$$\Pr(d_t \ge 1) \le \mathbf{E}[d_t] \le n \left(1 - \frac{c - 2\Delta}{nc} \right)^t \le n e^{-t(c-2\Delta)/nc},$$

and the variation distance is at most ε after

$$t = \left\lceil \frac{nc}{c - 2\Delta} \ln \left(\frac{n}{\varepsilon} \right) \right\rceil$$

steps. ∎

Hence we can use the Markov chain for proper colorings to give us an FPAUS whenever $c > 2\Delta$.

12.6. Path Coupling

In Section 11.3 we showed that, if we can obtain an FPAUS for independent sets for graphs of degree at most Δ, then we can approximately count the number of independent sets in such graphs. Here we present a Markov chain on independent sets, together with a coupling argument, to prove that the chain gives such an FPAUS when $\Delta \le 4$. The coupling argument uses a further technique, *path coupling*. We demonstrate this technique specifically for the Markov chain sampling independent sets in a graph, although with appropriate definitions the approach can be generalized to other problems.

Interestingly, it is very difficult to prove that the simple Markov chain for sampling independent sets given in Section 11.4, which removes or attempts to add a random vertex to the current independent set at each step, mixes quickly. Instead, we consider here a different Markov chain that simplifies the analysis. We assume without loss of generality that the graph consists of a single connected component. At each step, the Markov chain chooses an *edge* (u, v) in the graph uniformly at random. If X_t is the independent set at time t, then the move proceeds as follows.

- With probability $1/3$, set $X_{t+1} = X_t - \{u, v\}$. (This move removes u and v, if they are in the set.)
- With probability $1/3$, let $Y = (X_t - \{u\}) \cup \{v\}$. If Y is an independent set, then $X_{t+1} = Y$; otherwise, $X_{t+1} = X_t$. (This move tries to remove u if it is in the set and then add v.)
- With probability $1/3$, let $Y = (X_t - \{v\}) \cup \{u\}$. If Y is an independent set, then $X_{t+1} = Y$; otherwise, $X_{t+1} = X_t$. (This move tries to remove v if it is in the set and then add u.)

It is easy to verify that the chain has a stationary distribution that is uniform on all independent sets. We now use the path coupling argument to bound the mixing time of the chain.

The idea of path coupling is to start with a coupling for pairs of states (X_t, Y_t) that differ in just one vertex. This coupling is then extended to a general coupling over all pairs of states. When it applies, path coupling is very powerful, because it is often much easier to analyze the situation where the two states differ in a small way (here, in just one vertex) than to analyze all possible pairs of states.

Consider a graph $G = (V, E)$. We say that a vertex is *bad* if it is an element of X_t or Y_t but not both; otherwise, the vertex is *good*. Let $d_t = |X_t - Y_t| + |Y_t - X_t|$, so that d_t counts the number of bad vertices. Assume that X_t and Y_t differ in exactly one vertex (i.e., $d_t = 1$). We apply a simple coupling, performing the same move in both states, and show that under this coupling $\mathbf{E}[d_{t+1} \mid d_t] \leq d_t$ when $d_t = 1$ or, equivalently, that $\mathbf{E}[d_{t+1} - d_t \mid d_t = 1] \leq 0$.

Without loss of generality, let $X_t = I$ and $Y_t = I \cup \{x\}$. A change in d_t can occur only when a move involves a neighbor of x. Thus, in analyzing this coupling, we can restrict our discussion to moves in which the chosen random edge is adjacent to a neighbor of x. Let $\delta_z = 1$ if the vertex $z \neq x$ goes from good to bad between step t and step $t + 1$. Similarly, let $\delta_x = -1$ if the vertex x goes from bad to good between step t and step $t + 1$. By linearity of expectations,

$$\mathbf{E}[d_{t+1} - d_t \mid d_t = 1] = \mathbf{E}\left[\sum_w \delta_w \mid d_t = 1\right] = \sum_w \mathbf{E}[\delta_w \mid d_t = 1].$$

As we shall see, in the summation we need only consider those w that are equal to x, a neighbor of x, or a neighbor of a neighbor of x, since these are the only vertices that can change from good to bad or bad to good in one step of the chain. We shall demonstrate how to balance the moves in such a way that it becomes clear that $\mathbf{E}[d_{t+1} - d_t \mid d_t = 1] \leq 0$ as long as $\Delta \leq 4$.

Assume that x has k neighbors, and let y be one of these neighbors. For each vertex y that is a neighbor of x, we consider all of the moves that choose an edge adjacent to y. The subsequent analysis makes use of the restriction $\Delta \leq 4$. There are three cases, as shown in Figure 12.3.

1. Suppose that y has two or more neighbors in the independent set $I = X_t$. Then no move that involves y can increase the number of bad vertices, and hence d_{t+1} cannot be larger than d_t as a result of any such move.
2. Suppose that y has no neighbors in I. Then d_t can increase by 1 if the edge (y, z_i) (where $1 \leq i \leq 3$) is chosen and an attempt is made to add y and remove z_i. These moves are successful on X_t but not on Y_t, and hence $\delta_y = 1$ with probability at most $3 \cdot 1/3|E| = 1/|E|$. No other move involving y increases d_t.

   The possible gain from δ_y is balanced by moves that decrease δ_x. Any of the three possible moves on the edge (x, y) match the vertex x, so that $\delta_x = -1$, and no other bad vertices are created. Hence $\delta_x = -1$ with probability at least $1/|E|$. We see that

333

(1) (2) (3)

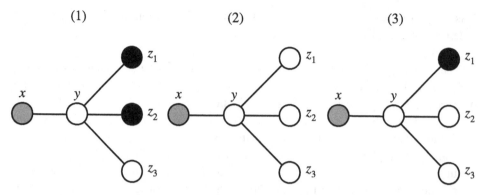

Figure 12.3: Three cases for the independent set Markov chain. Vertices colored black are in both independent sets of the coupling. Vertex x is colored gray, to represent that it is a member of the independent set of one chain in the coupling but not the other.

the total effect of all of these moves on $\sum_w \mathbf{E}[\delta_w \mid d_t = 1]$ is

$$1 \cdot \frac{1}{|E|} - 1 \cdot \frac{1}{|E|} = 0,$$

so that the moves from this case do not increase $\mathbf{E}[d_{t+1} - d_t \mid d_t = 1]$.

3. Suppose that y has one neighbor in I. If the edge (x, y) is chosen, then two moves can give $\delta_x = -1$: the move that removes both x and y, or the move that removes y and adds x. The third move, which tries to add y and remove x, fails in both chains because y has a neighbor in I. Hence $\delta_x = -1$ with probability at least $\frac{2}{3}(1/|E|)$.

Let z be the neighbor of y in I. Both y and z can become bad in one step if the edge (y, z) is chosen and an attempt is made to add y and remove z. This move is successful on X_t but not on Y_t, causing d_t to increase by 2 since δ_y and δ_z both equal 1. No other move increases d_t. Hence the probability that the number of bad vertices is increased in this case is $1/3|E|$, and the increase is by 2. Again, the total effect of all of these moves on $\sum_w \mathbf{E}[\delta_w \mid d_t = 1]$ is

$$2 \cdot \frac{1}{3|E|} - 1 \cdot \frac{2}{3} \frac{1}{|E|} = 0,$$

so that the moves from this case do not increase $\mathbf{E}[d_{t+1} - d_t \mid d_t = 1]$.

The case analysis shows that if we consider moves that involve a specific neighbor y, they balance so that every move that increases $d_{t+1} - d_t$ is matched by corresponding moves that decrease $d_{t+1} - d_t$. Summing over all vertices, we can conclude that

$$\mathbf{E}[d_{t+1} - d_t \mid d_t = 1] = \mathbf{E}\left[\sum_w \delta_w \mid d_t = 1\right] = \sum_w \mathbf{E}[\delta_w \mid d_t = 1] \le 0.$$

We now use an appropriate coupling to argue that $\mathbf{E}[d_{t+1} \mid d_t] \le d_t$ for any pair of states (X_t, Y_t). The statement is trivial if $d_t = 0$, and we have just shown it to be true if $d_t = 1$. If $d_t > 1$, then create a chain of states $Z_0, Z_1, \ldots, Z_{d_t}$ as follows: $Z_0 = X_t$, and each successive Z_i is obtained from Z_{i-1} by either removing a vertex from $X_t - Y_t$ or adding a vertex from $Y_t - X_t$. This can be done, for example, by first removing all vertices in $X_t - Y_t$ one by one and then adding vertices from $Y_t - X_t$ one by one. Our coupling now arises as follows. When a move is made in $X_t = Z_0$, the coupling for the case when $d_t = 1$ gives a corresponding move for the state Z_1. This move in Z_1 can similarly be coupled with a move in state Z_2, and so on, until the move in Z_{d_t-1} yields a move for $Z_{d_t} = Y_t$. Let Z_i' be the state after the move is made from state Z_i, and let

$$\Delta(Z_{i-1}', Z_i') = |Z_{i-1}' - Z_i'| + |Z_i' - Z_{i-1}'|.$$

Note that $Z_0' = X_{t+1}$ and $Z_{d_t}' = Y_{t+1}$. We have shown that $\mathbf{E}[d_{t+1} - d_t \mid d_t = 1] \leq 0$, so we can conclude that

$$\mathbf{E}[\Delta(Z_{i-1}', Z_i')] \leq 1;$$

that is, because the two states Z_{i-1} and Z_i differ in just one vertex, the expected number of vertices in which they differ after one step is at most 1. Using the triangle inequality for sets,

$$|A - B| \leq |A - C| + |C - B|,$$

we obtain

$$|X_{t+1} - Y_{t+1}| + |Y_{t+1} - X_{t+1}| \leq \sum_{i=1}^{d_t} (|Z_{i-1}' - Z_i'| + |Z_i' - Z_{i-1}'|)$$

or

$$d_{t+1} = |X_{t+1} - Y_{t+1}| + |Y_{t+1} - X_{t+1}| \leq \sum_{i=1}^{d_t} \Delta(Z_{i-1}', Z_i').$$

Hence,

$$\mathbf{E}[d_{t+1} \mid d_t] \leq \mathbf{E}\left[\sum_{i=1}^{d_t} \Delta(Z_{i-1}', Z_i') \right]$$

$$= \sum_{i=1}^{d_t} \mathbf{E}[\Delta(Z_{i-1}', Z_i')]$$

$$\leq d_t.$$

In previous examples we were able to prove a strict inequality of the form

$$\mathbf{E}[d_{t+1} \mid d_t] \leq \beta d_t$$

for some $\beta < 1$, and we used this strict inequality to bound the mixing time. However, the weaker condition $\mathbf{E}[d_{t+1} \mid d_t] \leq d_t$ that we have here is sufficient for rapid mixing, as we shall see in Exercise 12.7. Thus, the Markov chain gives an FPAUS for independent sets in graphs when the maximum degree is at most 4; as we showed in Section 11.3, this can be used to obtain an FPRAS for this problem.

335

12.7. Exercises

Exercise 12.1: Write a program that takes as input two positive integers n_1 and n_2 and two real numbers p_1, p_2 with $0 \le p_1, p_2 \le 1$. The output of your program should be the variation distance between the binomial random variables $B(n_1, p_1)$ and $B(n_2, p_2)$, rounded to the nearest thousandth. Use your program to compute the variation distance between the following pairs of distributions: $B(20, 0.5)$ and $B(20, 0.49)$; $B(20, 0.5)$ and $B(21, 0.5)$; and $B(21, 0.5)$ and $B(21, 0.49)$.

Exercise 12.2: Consider the Markov chain for shuffling n cards, where at each step a card is chosen uniformly at random and moved to the top. Suppose that, instead of running the chain for a fixed number of steps, we stop the chain at the first step where every card has been moved to the top at least once. Show that, at this stopping time, the state of the chain is uniformly distributed on the $n!$ possible permutations of the cards.

Exercise 12.3: Consider the Markov chain for shuffling n cards, where at each step a card is chosen uniformly at random and moved to the top. Show that, if the chain is run for only $(1 - \varepsilon)n \ln n$ steps for some constant $\varepsilon > 0$, then the variation distance is $1 - o(1)$.

Exercise 12.4: **(a)** Consider the Markov chain given by the transition matrix

$$\mathbf{P} = \begin{bmatrix} 1/2 & 0 & 1/2 & 0 & 0 \\ 0 & 1/2 & 1/2 & 0 & 0 \\ 1/4 & 1/4 & 0 & 1/4 & 1/4 \\ 0 & 0 & 1/2 & 1/2 & 0 \\ 0 & 0 & 1/2 & 0 & 1/2 \end{bmatrix}.$$

Explain why Theorem 12.5 is not useful when applied directly to $\mathbf{P}$. Then apply Theorem 12.5 to the Markov chain with transition matrix $\mathbf{P}^2$, and explain the implications for the convergence of the original Markov chain to its stationary distribution.

(b) Consider the Markov chain given by the transition matrix

$$\mathbf{P} = \begin{bmatrix} 1/2 & 0 & 1/2 & 0 & 0 \\ 0 & 1/2 & 1/2 & 0 & 0 \\ 1/5 & 1/5 & 1/5 & 1/5 & 1/5 \\ 0 & 0 & 1/2 & 1/2 & 0 \\ 0 & 0 & 1/2 & 0 & 1/2 \end{bmatrix}.$$

Apply Theorem 12.5 to $\mathbf{P}$. Then apply Theorem 12.5 to the Markov chain with transition matrix $\mathbf{P}^2$, and explain the implications for the convergence of the original Markov chain to its stationary distribution. Which application gives better bounds on the variation distance?

Exercise 12.5: Suppose I repeatedly roll a standard six-sided die and obtain a sequence of independent random variables $X_1, X_2, \ldots$, where X_i is the outcome of the ith roll.

336

Let

$$Y_j = \sum_{i=1}^{j} X_i \bmod 10$$

be the sum of the first j rolls considered modulo 10. The sequence Y_j forms a Markov chain. Determine its stationary distribution, and determine a bound on $\tau(\varepsilon)$ for this chain. (*Hint:* One approach is to use the method of Exercise 12.4.)

Exercise 12.6: Theorem 12.5 is useful only if there exists a nonzero entry in at least one column of the transition matrix $\mathbf{P}$ of the Markov chain. Argue that for any finite, aperiodic, irreducible Markov chain, there exists a time T such that every entry of $\mathbf{P}^T$ is nonzero. Explain how this can be used in conjunction with Theorem 12.5.

Exercise 12.7: A technique we use repeatedly in the chapter is to define a distance function d_t that represent the distance between the two states of our coupling after t steps, and then show that when $d_t > 0$ there exists a $\beta < 1$ such that

$$\mathbf{E}[d_{t+1} \mid d_t] \le \beta d_t.$$

(a) Under this condition, give an upper bound for $\tau(\varepsilon)$ in terms of β and d^*, where d^* is the maximum distance over all possible pairs of initial states for the coupling.
(b) Suppose that instead we have

$$\mathbf{E}[d_{t+1} \mid d_t] \le d_t.$$

Suppose we have the additional conditions that d_{t+1} is one of $d_t, d_t - 1$, or $d_t + 1$ and that $\Pr(d_t \ne d_{t+1}) \ge \gamma$. Give an upper bound for $\tau(\varepsilon)$ in terms of ε, d^*, and γ. Your answer should by polynomial in d^* and $1/\gamma$. (*Hint:* Think of d_t as being similar to a random walk on the line.)
(c) Using (a) and (b), show that the mixing time of the coloring chain of Section 12.5 is polynomial in the number of vertices in the graph and $\ln(1/\varepsilon)$, even when the number of colors is only 2Δ.
(d) By extending the argument of part (b), show that the mixing time of the Markov chain for independent sets given in Section 12.6 is polynomial in the number of vertices in the graph and $\ln(1/\varepsilon)$.

Exercise 12.8: Consider the random walk on a non-bipartite, connected graph on n vertices, where each vertex has the same degree $d > n/2$, $d < n$. Show that

$$\tau(\varepsilon) \le \frac{\ln \varepsilon}{\ln(1 - (2d - n)/d)}.$$

Exercise 12.9: Consider a Markov chain on n points $[0, n-1]$ lying in order on a circle. At each step, the chain stays at the current point with probability $1/2$ or moves to the next point in the clockwise direction with probability $1/2$. Find the stationary distribution and show that, for any $\varepsilon > 0$, the mixing time $\tau(\varepsilon)$ is $O(n^2 \ln(1/\varepsilon))$.

Exercise 12.10: In Section 12.2.3, we suggested the following coupling $Z_t = (X_t, Y_t)$. First choose a transition for the chain X_t, with $v \in X_t$ and $w \in V$. If $v \in Y_t$, use the same vertices v and w for the transition of the chain Y_t; otherwise, choose uniformly at random a vertex $v' \in Y_t - X_t$ and then perform the transition in the chain Y_t with the pair v' and w. Show that this is a valid coupling that satisfies Definition 12.3.

Exercise 12.11: Show that the Markov chain for sampling all independent sets of size exactly $k \leq n/(3\Delta + 3)$ in a graph with n nodes and maximum degree Δ, as defined in Section 12.2.3, is ergodic and has a uniform stationary distribution.

Exercise 12.12: We wish to improve the coupling technique used in Section 12.2.3 in order to obtain a better bound. The improvement here is related to the technique used to prove Theorem 12.8. As with the coupling in Section 12.2.3, if an attempt is made to move $v \in X_t - Y_t$ to a vertex w then the same attempt is made with the matched vertex in the other chain. If, however, an attempt is made to move a vertex $v \in X_t \cap Y_t$ in both chains, we no longer attempt to make the same move.

(a) Assume there exists a set S_1 of exactly $d_t(\Delta + 1)$ distinct vertices that are members of or neighbors of vertices in $X_t - Y_t$ and, likewise, a set S_2 of exactly $d_t(\Delta + 1)$ distinct vertices that are members of or neighbors of vertices in $Y_t - X_t$; assume further that S_2 and S_1 are disjoint. Suppose that we match up the vertices in S_1 and S_2 in a one-to-one fashion. Argue that the moves can be coupled so that, when one chain attempts and fails to move v to a vertex in S_1 in one chain, it also attempts and fails to move v to the matching vertex in S_2 in the other chain. Similarly, argue that the moves can be coupled so that, when one chain attempts and succeeds in moving v to a vertex in S_1 in one chain, it also attempts and succeeds in moving v to the matching vertex in S_2 in the other chain. Show that the coupling gives

$$\Pr(d_{t+1} = d_t + 1) \leq \frac{k - d_t}{k} \frac{d_t(\Delta + 1)}{n}.$$

(b) In the general case, S_1 and S_2 are not necessarily disjoint or of equal size. Show that in this case, by pairing up failing moves as much as possible, the number of choices for w that can increase d_t is $\max(|S_1|, |S_2|) \leq d_t(\Delta + 1)$. Then argue that

$$\Pr(d_{t+1} = d_t + 1) \leq \frac{k - d_t}{k} \frac{d_t(\Delta + 1)}{n}$$

holds in all cases.

(c) Use this coupling to obtain a polynomial bound on $\tau(\varepsilon)$ that holds for any $k \leq n/(2\Delta + 2)$.

Exercise 12.13: Consider a Markov chain with state space S and a stationary distribution $\bar{\pi}$, and recall the definitions of p_x^t and $\Delta(t)$ from Definition 12.2. For any nonnegative integer t let

$$\bar{\Delta}(t) = \max_{x, y \in S} \| p_x^t - p_y^t \|.$$

Assume also that the Markov chain has a stationary distribution.

(a) Prove $\bar{\Delta}(s+t) \le \bar{\Delta}(s)\bar{\Delta}(t)$ for any positive integers s and t.

(b) Prove $\Delta(s+t) \le \Delta(s)\bar{\Delta}(t)$ for any positive integers s and t.

(c) Prove

$$\Delta(t) \le \bar{\Delta}(t) \le 2\Delta(t)$$

for any positive integer t.

Exercise 12.14: Consider the following variation on shuffling for a deck of n cards. At each step, two specific cards are chosen uniformly at random from the deck, and their positions are exchanged. (It is possible both choices give the same card, in which case no change occurs.)

(a) Argue that the following is an equivalent process: at each step, a specific card is chosen uniformly at random from the deck, and a position from $[1, n]$ is chosen uniformly at random; then the card at position i exchanges positions with the specific card chosen.

(b) Consider the coupling where the two choices of card and position are the same for both copies of the chain. Let X_t be the number of cards whose positions are different in the two copies of the chain. Show that X_t is nonincreasing over time.

(c) Show that

$$\Pr(X_{t+1} \le X_t - 1 \mid X_t > 0) \ge \left(\frac{X_t}{n}\right)^2.$$

(d) Argue that the expected time until X_t is 0 is $O(n^2)$, regardless of the starting state of the two chains.

Exercise 12.15: Modify the arguments of Lemma 11.3 and Lemma 11.4 to show that, if we have an FPAUS for proper colorings for any $c \ge \Delta + 2$, then we also have an FPRAS for this value of c.

Exercise 12.16: Consider the following simple Markov chain whose states are independent sets in a graph $G = (V, E)$. To compute X_{i+1} from X_i:

- choose a vertex v uniformly at random from V, and flip a fair coin;
- if the flip is heads and $v \in X_i$, then $X_{i+1} = X_i \setminus \{v\}$;
- if the flip is heads and $v \notin X_i$, then $X_{i+1} = X_i$;
- if the flip is tails, $v \notin X_i$, and adding v to X_i still gives an independent set, then $X_{i+1} = X_i \cup \{v\}$;
- if the flip is tails and $v \in X_i$, then $X_{i+1} = X_i$.

(a) Show that the stationary distribution of this chain is uniform over all independent sets.

(b) We consider this Markov chain specifically on cycles and line graphs. For a line graph with n vertices, the vertices are labeled 1 to n, and there is an edge from 1 to 2, 2 to 3, ..., $n - 1$ to n. A cycle graph on n vertices is the same with the addition of an edge from n to 1.

Devise a coupling (X_t, Y_t) for this Markov chain such that, on line graphs and cycle graphs, if $d_t = |X_t - Y_t| + |Y_t - X_t|$ is the number of vertices on which the two independent sets disagree, then at each step the coupling is at least as likely to reduce d_t as to increase d_t.

(c) With the coupling from part (b), argue that you can use this chain to obtain an FPAUS for independent sets on a cycle graph or line graph. You may want to use Exercise 12.7.

(d) For the special cases of line graphs and cycle graphs, we can derive exact formulas for the number of independent sets. Derive exact formulas for these cases and prove that your formulas are correct. (*Hint:* You may want to express your results in terms of Fibonacci numbers.)

Exercise 12.17: For integers a and b, an $a \times b$ *grid* is a graph whose vertices are all ordered pairs of integers (x, y) with $0 \leq x < a$ and $0 \leq y < b$. The edges of the graph connect all pairs of distinct vertices (x, y) and (x', y') such that $|x - x'| + |y - y'| = 1$. That is, every vertex is connected to the neighbors up, down, left, and right of it, where vertices on the boundary are connected to the relevant points only. Consider the following problems on the graph given by the 10×10 grid.

(a) Implement an FPAUS to generate an ε-uniform proper 10-coloring of the graph, where ε is given as an input. Discuss how many steps your Markov chain runs for, what your starting state is, and any other relevant details.

(b) Using your FPAUS as a subroutine, implement an FPRAS to generate an (ε, δ)-approximation to the number of proper 10-colorings of the graph. Test your code by running it to obtain a $(0.1, 0.001)$-approximation. (*Note:* This may take a significant amount of time to run.) Discuss the ordering you choose on the edges, how many samples are required at each step, how many steps of the Markov chain you perform in total throughout the process, and any other relevant details.

Exercise 12.18: In Section 12.2.3 we considered the following Markov chain on independent sets: a move is made from the independent set X_t by choosing a vertex $v \in X_t$ uniformly at random and picking a vertex w uniformly at random from the graph. If $X_t - \{v\} + \{w\}$ is an independent set, then $X_{t+1} = X_t - \{v\} + \{w\}$; otherwise, $X_{t+1} = X_t$. We have shown that the chain converges quickly to its stationary distribution via bounding $\tau(\varepsilon)$ by an expression that is polynomial in n and $\ln(1/\varepsilon)$ whenever $k \leq n/(2\Delta + 2)$. Use the idea of path coupling to simplify the proof.

Exercise 12.19: In Section 12.5, we considered a simple Markov chain for coloring. Suppose that we can apply the path coupling technique. (You do not need to show this.) In this case, we can just consider the case where $d_t = 1$. Give a simpler argument that, when $d_t = 1$ and $c > 2\Delta$, $\mathbf{E}[d_{t+1} \mid d_t] \leq \beta d_t$ for some $\beta < 1$. Also show that, when $d_t = 1$ and $c = 2\Delta$, $\mathbf{E}[d_{t+1} \mid d_t] \leq d_t$.

CHAPTER THIRTEEN

Martingales

Martingales are sequences of random variables satisfying certain conditions that arise in numerous applications, such as random walks and gambling problems. We focus here on three useful analysis tools related to martingales: the martingale stopping theorem, Wald's inequality, and the Azuma–Hoeffding inequality. The martingale stopping theorem and Wald's equation are important tools for computing the expectation of compound stochastic processes. The Azuma–Hoeffding inequality is a powerful technique for deriving Chernoff-like tail bounds on the values of functions of dependent random variables. We conclude this chapter with applications of the Azuma–Hoeffding inequality to problems in pattern matching, balls and bins, and random graphs.

13.1. Martingales

Definition 13.1: *A sequence of random variables $Z_0, Z_1, \ldots$ is a* martingale *with respect to the sequence $X_0, X_1, \ldots$ if, for all $n \geq 0$, the following conditions hold:*

- *Z_n is a function of $X_0, X_1, \ldots, X_n$;*
- *$\mathbf{E}[|Z_n|] < \infty$;*
- *$\mathbf{E}[Z_{n+1} \mid X_0, \ldots, X_n] = Z_n$.*

A sequence of random variables $Z_0, Z_1, \ldots$ is called a martingale when it is a martingale with respect to itself. That is, $\mathbf{E}[|Z_n|] < \infty$, and $\mathbf{E}[Z_{n+1} \mid Z_0, \ldots, Z_n] = Z_n$.

A martingale can have a finite or a countably infinite number of elements. The indexing of the martingale sequence does not need to start at 0. In fact, in many applications it is more convenient to start it at 1. When we say that $Z_0, Z_1, \ldots$ is a martingale with respect to $X_1, X_2, \ldots$, then we may consider X_0 to be a constant that is omitted.

For example, consider a gambler who plays a sequence of fair games. Let X_i be the amount the gambler wins on the ith game (X_i is negative if the gambler loses), and let Z_i be the gambler's total winnings at the end of the ith game. Because each game is fair, $\mathbf{E}[X_i] = 0$ and

$$\mathbf{E}[Z_{i+1} \mid X_1, X_2, \ldots, X_i] = Z_i + \mathbf{E}[X_{i+1}] = Z_i.$$

Thus, $Z_1, Z_2, \ldots, Z_n$ is a martingale with respect to the sequence $X_1, X_2, \ldots, X_n$. Interestingly, the sequence is a martingale regardless of the amount bet on each game, even if these amounts are dependent upon previous results.

A *Doob martingale* refers to a martingale constructed using the following general approach. Let $X_0, X_1, \ldots, X_n$ be a sequence of random variables, and let Y be a random variable with $\mathbf{E}[|Y|] < \infty$. (Generally, Y will depend on $X_0, \ldots, X_n$.) Then

$$Z_i = \mathbf{E}[Y \mid X_0, \ldots, X_i], \quad i = 0, 1, \ldots, n,$$

gives a martingale with respect to $X_0, X_1, \ldots, X_n$, since

$$\begin{aligned}
\mathbf{E}[Z_{i+1} \mid X_0, \ldots, X_i] &= \mathbf{E}[\mathbf{E}[Y \mid X_0, \ldots, X_{i+1}] \mid X_0, \ldots, X_i] \\
&= \mathbf{E}[Y \mid X_0, \ldots, X_i] \\
&= Z_i.
\end{aligned}$$

Here we have used the fact that $\mathbf{E}[Y \mid X_0, \ldots, X_{i+1}]$ is itself a random variable and that Definition 2.7 for conditional expectation yields

$$\mathbf{E}[V \mid W] = \mathbf{E}[\mathbf{E}[V \mid U, W] \mid W].$$

In most applications we start the Doob martingale with $Z_0 = \mathbf{E}[Y]$, which corresponds to X_0 being a trivial random variable that is independent of Y. To understand the concept of the Doob martingale, assume that we want to predict the value of the random variable Y and that the value of Y is a function of the values of the random variables $X_1, \ldots, X_n$. The sequence $Z_0, Z_1, \ldots, Z_n$ represents a sequence of refined estimates of the value of Y, gradually using more information on the values of the random variables $X_1, X_2, \ldots, X_n$. The first element, Z_0, is just the expectation of Y. Element Z_i is the expected value of Y when the values of $X_1, \ldots, X_i$ are known, and if Y is fully determined by $X_1, \ldots, X_n$ then $Z_n = Y$.

We now consider two examples of Doob martingales that arise in evaluating the properties of random graphs. Let G be a random graph from $G_{n,p}$. Label the $m = \binom{n}{2}$ possible edge slots in some arbitrary order, and let

$$X_j = \begin{cases} 1 & \text{if there is an edge in the } j\text{th edge slot,} \\ 0 & \text{otherwise.} \end{cases}$$

Consider any finite-valued function F defined over graphs; for example, let $F(G)$ be the size of the largest independent set in G. Now let $Z_0 = \mathbf{E}[F(G)]$ and

$$Z_i = \mathbf{E}[F(G) \mid X_1, \ldots, X_i], \quad i = 1, \ldots, m.$$

The sequence $Z_0, Z_1, \ldots, Z_m$ is a Doob martingale that represents the conditional expectations of $F(G)$ as we reveal whether each edge is in the graph, one edge at a time. This process of revealing edges gives a martingale that is commonly called the *edge exposure martingale*.

Similarly, instead of revealing edges one at a time, we could reveal the set of edges connected to a given vertex, one vertex at a time. Fix an arbitrary numbering of the vertices 1 through n, and let G_i be the subgraph of G induced by the first i vertices. Then, setting $Z_0 = \mathbf{E}[F(G)]$ and

$$Z_i = \mathbf{E}[F(G) \mid G_1, \ldots, G_i], \quad i = 1, \ldots, n,$$

gives a Doob martingale that is commonly called the *vertex exposure martingale*.

13.2. Stopping Times

Returning to the gambler who participates in a sequence of fair gambling rounds, we saw in the previous section that $Z_1, Z_2, \ldots$ is a martingale, where Z_i is the gambler's winnings after the ith game. If the player decides (before starting to play) to quit after exactly k games, what are the gambler's expected winnings?

Lemma 13.1: *If the sequence $Z_0, Z_1, \ldots, Z_n$ is a martingale with respect to $X_0, X_1, \ldots, X_n$, then*

$$\mathbf{E}[Z_n] = \mathbf{E}[Z_0].$$

Proof: Since $Z_0, Z_1, \ldots$ is a martingale with respect to $X_0, X_1, \ldots, X_n$, it follows that

$$Z_i = \mathbf{E}[Z_{i+1} \mid X_0, \ldots, X_i].$$

Taking the expectation of both sides and using the definition of conditional expectation, we have

$$\mathbf{E}[Z_{i+1}] = \mathbf{E}[\mathbf{E}[Z_{i+1} \mid X_0, \ldots, X_i]] = \mathbf{E}[Z_i].$$

Repeating this argument yields

$$\mathbf{E}[Z_n] = \mathbf{E}[Z_0]. \qquad \blacksquare$$

Thus, if the number of games played is initially fixed then the expected gain from the sequence of games is zero. Suppose now that the number of games played is not fixed. For example, the gambler could choose to play a random number of games. An even more complex (and realistic) situation arises when the gambler's decision to quit playing is based on the outcome of the games already played. For example, the gambler could decide to keep playing until his winnings total at least a hundred dollars. The following notion proves quite powerful.

Definition 13.2: *A nonnegative integer-valued random variable T is a* stopping time *for the sequence $\{Z_i, i \geq 0\}$ if the probability of the event $T = n$ is independent of the variables $\{Z_{n+j} \mid Z_1, \ldots, Z_n, j \geq 1\}$ (i.e. the variables $Z_{n+1}, Z_{n+2}, \ldots$ conditioned on the values of $Z_1, \ldots, Z_n$).*[1]

---

[1] More formally, in the discrete case we define a "filtration" $\mathcal{F}_0, \mathcal{F}_1, \ldots$ such that the distribution of Z_0 is fully defined by events in $\mathcal{F}_0$, and the joint distribution of $Z_0, \ldots, Z_n$ is fully defined by events in $\mathcal{F}_n$. The event $T = n$ is a stopping time if it is an event in $\mathcal{F}_n$.

A stopping time corresponds to a strategy for determining when to stop a sequence based only on the outcomes seen so far. For example, the first time the gambler wins five games in a row is a stopping time, since this can be determined by looking at the outcomes of the games played. Similarly, the first time the gambler has won at least a hundred dollars is also a stopping time. Letting T be the *last* time the gambler wins five games in a row, however, would not be a stopping time, since determining whether $T = n$ cannot be done without knowing $Z_{n+1}, Z_{n+2}, \ldots$.

In order to fully utilize the martingale property, we need to characterize conditions on the stopping time T that maintain the property $\mathbf{E}[Z_T] = \mathbf{E}[Z_0] = 0$. It would seem, if the game is fair, that $\mathbf{E}[Z_T] = 0$ should always hold. But consider the case where the gambler's stopping time is the first T such that $Z_T > B$, where B is a fixed constant greater than 0. In this case, the expected gain when the gambler quits playing is greater than 0. The subtle problem with this stopping time is that it might not be finite, so the gambler may never finish playing. The *martingale stopping theorem* shows that, under certain conditions and in particular when the stopping time is bounded or has bounded expectation, the expected value of the martingale at the stopping time is equal to $\mathbf{E}[Z_0]$. We state a version of the martingale stopping theorem (sometimes called the optional stopping theorem) without proof.

Theorem 13.2 [Martingale Stopping Theorem]: *If $Z_0, Z_1, \ldots$ is a martingale with respect to $X_1, X_2, \ldots$ and if T is a stopping time for $X_1, X_2, \ldots$, then*

$$\mathbf{E}[Z_T] = \mathbf{E}[Z_0]$$

whenever one of the following holds:

- *the Z_i are bounded, so there is a constant c such that, for all i, $|Z_i| \leq c$;*
- *T is bounded;*
- *$\mathbf{E}[T] < \infty$, and there is a constant c such that $\mathbf{E}[|Z_{i+1} - Z_i| \mid X_1, \ldots, X_i] < c$.*

We use the martingale stopping theorem to derive a simple solution to the gambler's ruin problem introduced in Section 7.2.1. Consider a sequence of independent, fair gambling games. In each round, a player wins a dollar with probability $1/2$ or loses a dollar with probability $1/2$. Let $Z_0 = 0$, let X_i be the amount won on the ith game, and let Z_i be the total won by the player after i games (again, X_i and Z_i are negative if the player loses money). Assume that the player quits the game when she either loses ℓ_1 dollars or wins ℓ_2 dollars. What is the probability that the player wins ℓ_2 dollars before losing ℓ_1 dollars?

Let the time T be the first time the player has either won ℓ_2 or lost ℓ_1. Then T is a stopping time for $X_1, X_2, \ldots$. The sequence $Z_0, Z_1, \ldots$ is a martingale and, since the values of the Z_i are clearly bounded, we can apply the martingale stopping theorem. We therefore have

$$\mathbf{E}[Z_T] = 0.$$

Let q be the probability that the gambler quits playing after winning ℓ_2 dollars. Then

$$\mathbf{E}[Z_T] = \ell_2 q - \ell_1(1 - q) = 0,$$

giving

$$q = \frac{\ell_1}{\ell_1 + \ell_2},$$

matching the result found in Section 7.2.1.

13.2.1. *Example: A Ballot Theorem*

The following ballot theorem is another application of the martingale stopping theorem. Suppose that two candidates run for an election. Candidate A obtains a votes, and candidate B obtains $b < a$ votes. The votes are counted in a random order, chosen uniformly at random from all permutations on the $a + b$ votes. We show that the probability that candidate A is always ahead in the count is $(a - b)/(a + b)$. Although this can be determined combinatorially, we provide an elegant martingale argument.

Let $n = a + b$ be the total number of votes, and let S_k be the number of votes by which candidate A is leading after k votes are counted (S_k can be negative). Then $S_n = a - b$. For $0 \leq k \leq n - 1$, define

$$X_k = \frac{S_{n-k}}{n - k}.$$

We first show that the sequence $X_0, X_1, \ldots, X_{n-1}$ forms a martingale. Note that the sequence $X_0, X_1, \ldots, X_n$ relates to the counting process in a backward order; X_0 is a function of S_n, X_{n-1} is a function of S_1, and so on. Consider

$$\mathbf{E}[X_k \mid X_0, \ldots, X_{k-1}].$$

Conditioning on $X_0, \ldots, X_{k-1}$ is equivalent to conditioning on $S_n, S_{n-1}, \ldots, S_{n-k+1}$, which in turn is equivalent to conditioning on the values of the count when counting the last $k - 1$ votes.

Conditioning on S_{n-k+1}, the number of votes that candidate A had after counting the first $n - k + 1$ votes is

$$\frac{n - k + 1 + S_{n-k+1}}{2},$$

and the number of votes that candidate B had is

$$\frac{n - k + 1 - S_{n-k+1}}{2}.$$

The $(n - k + 1)$th vote in the count is a random vote from among these first $n - k + 1$ votes. Also, S_{n-k} is equal to $S_{n-k+1} + 1$ if the $(n - k + 1)$th vote was for candidate B and equal to $S_{n-k+1} - 1$ if that vote was for candidate A. Thus, for $k \geq 1$,

$$\mathbf{E}[S_{n-k} \mid S_{n-k+1}] = (S_{n-k+1} + 1)\frac{n - k + 1 - S_{n-k+1}}{2(n - k + 1)}$$

$$+ (S_{n-k+1} - 1)\frac{n - k + 1 + S_{n-k+1}}{2(n - k + 1)}$$

$$= S_{n-k+1}\frac{n - k}{n - k + 1}.$$

345

Therefore,

$$\mathbf{E}[X_k \mid X_0, \ldots, X_{k-1}] = \mathbf{E}\left[\frac{S_{n-k}}{n-k} \mid S_n, \ldots, S_{n-k+1}\right]$$

$$= \frac{S_{n-k+1}}{n-k+1}$$

$$= X_{k-1},$$

showing that the sequence $X_0, X_1, \ldots, X_{n-1}$ is a martingale.

Define T to be the minimum k such that $X_k = 0$ if such a k exists, and $T = n - 1$ otherwise. Then T is a bounded stopping time, satisfying the requirements of the martingale stopping theorem, and

$$\mathbf{E}[X_T] = \mathbf{E}[X_0] = \frac{\mathbf{E}[S_n]}{n} = \frac{a-b}{a+b}.$$

We now consider two cases.

Case 1: Candidate A leads throughout the count. In this case, all S_{n-k} (and therefore all X_k) are positive for $0 \le k \le n - 1$, $T = n - 1$, and

$$X_T = X_{n-1} = S_1 = 1.$$

That $S_1 = 1$ follows because candidate A must receive the first vote in the count to be ahead throughout the count.

Case 2: Candidate A does not lead throughout the count. In that case we claim that for some $k < n - 1$, $X_k = 0$. Candidate A clearly has more votes at the end. If candidate B ever leads, then there must be some intermediate point k where S_k (and therefore X_k) is 0. In this case, $T = k < n - 1$ and $X_T = 0$.

Observe that

$$\mathbf{E}[X_T] = \frac{a-b}{a+b} = 1 \cdot \Pr(\text{Case 1}) + 0 \cdot \Pr(\text{Case 2}),$$

and thus the probability of Case 1, in which candidate A leads throughout the count, is $(a - b)/(a + b)$.

13.3. Wald's Equation

An important corollary of the martingale stopping theorem is known as Wald's equation. Wald's equation deals with the expectation of the sum of independent random variables in the case where the number of random variables being summed is itself a random variable.

Theorem 13.3 [Wald's Equation]: *Let $X_1, X_2, \ldots$ be nonnegative, independent, identically distributed random variables with distribution X. Let T be a stopping time for* *this sequence. If T and X have bounded expectation, then*

$$\mathbf{E}\left[\sum_{i=1}^{T} X_i\right] = \mathbf{E}[T] \cdot \mathbf{E}[X].$$

In fact, Wald's equation holds more generally; there are different proofs of the equality that do not require the random variables $X_1, X_2, \ldots$ to be nonnegative.

Proof: For $i \geq 1$, let

$$Z_i = \sum_{j=1}^{i} (X_j - \mathbf{E}[X]).$$

The sequence $Z_1, Z_2, \ldots$ is a martingale with respect to $X_1, X_2, \ldots$, and $\mathbf{E}[Z_1] = 0$.
  Now, $\mathbf{E}[T] < \infty$ and

$$\mathbf{E}[|Z_{i+1} - Z_i| \mid X_1, \ldots, X_i] = \mathbf{E}[|X_{i+1} - \mathbf{E}[X]|] \leq 2\mathbf{E}[X].$$

Hence we can apply the martingale stopping theorem to compute

$$\mathbf{E}[Z_T] = \mathbf{E}[Z_1] = 0.$$

We now find

$$\mathbf{E}[Z_T] = \mathbf{E}\left[\sum_{j=1}^{T}(X_j - \mathbf{E}[X])\right]$$

$$= \mathbf{E}\left[\left(\sum_{j=1}^{T} X_j\right) - T\mathbf{E}[X]\right]$$

$$= \mathbf{E}\left[\sum_{j=1}^{T} X_j\right] - \mathbf{E}[T] \cdot \mathbf{E}[X]$$

$$= 0,$$

which gives the result. ∎

In the case of a sequence of independent random variables, we have an equivalent, simpler definition of stopping time that is easier to apply.

Definition 13.3: *Let $Z_0, Z_1, \ldots$ be a sequence of independent random variables. A nonnegative, integer-valued random variable T is a* stopping time *for the sequence if the event $T = n$ is independent of $Z_{n+1}, Z_{n+2}, \ldots.$.*

As a simple example, consider a gambling game in which a player first rolls one standard die. If the outcome of the roll is X then she rolls X new standard dice and her gain Z is the sum of the outcomes of the X dice. What is the expected gain of this game?

For $1 \leq i \leq X$, let Y_i be the outcome of the ith die in the second round. Then

$$\mathbf{E}[Z] = \mathbf{E}\left[\sum_{i=1}^{X} Y_i\right].$$

By Definition 13.3, X is a stopping time, and hence by Wald's equality we obtain

$$\mathbf{E}[Z] = \mathbf{E}[X] \cdot \mathbf{E}[Y_i] = \left(\frac{7}{2}\right)^2 = \frac{49}{4}.$$

Wald's equation can arise in the analysis of Las Vegas algorithms, which always give the right answer but have variable running times, as we saw for the randomized algorithm for the median described in Section 3.5. In a Las Vegas algorithm we often repeatedly perform some randomized subroutine that may or may not return the right answer. We then use some deterministic checking subroutine to determine whether or not the answer is correct; if it is correct then the Las Vegas algorithm terminates with the correct answer, and otherwise the randomized subroutine is run again. If N is the number of trials until a correct answer is found and if X_i is the running time for the two subroutines on the ith trial, then – as long as the X_i are independent and identically distributed with distribution X – Wald's equation gives that the expected running time for the algorithm is

$$\mathbf{E}\left[\sum_{i=1}^{N} X_i\right] = \mathbf{E}[N] \cdot \mathbf{E}[X].$$

An example of this approach is given in Exercise 13.13.

As another example, consider a set of n servers communicating through a shared channel. Time is divided into discrete slots. At each time slot, any server that needs to send a packet can transmit it through the channel. If exactly one packet is sent at that time, the transmission is successfully completed. If more than one packet is sent, then none are successful (and the senders detect the failure). Packets are stored in the server's buffer until they are successfully transmitted. Servers follow the following simple protocol: at each time slot, if the server's buffer is not empty then with probability $1/n$ it attempts to send the first packet in its buffer. Assume that servers have an infinite sequence of packets in their buffers. What is the expected number of time slots used until each server successfully sends at least one packet?

Let N be the number of packets successfully sent until each server has successfully sent at least one packet. Let t_i be the time slot in which the ith successfully transmitted packet is sent, starting from time $t_0 = 0$, and let $r_i = t_i - t_{i-1}$. Then T, the number of time slots until each server successfully sends at least one packet, is given by

$$T = \sum_{i=1}^{N} r_i.$$

You may check that N is independent of the r_i, and N is bounded in expectation; hence N is a stopping time for the sequence of r_i.

348

The probability that a packet is successfully sent in a given time slot is

$$p = \binom{n}{1}\left(\frac{1}{n}\right)\left(1 - \frac{1}{n}\right)^{n-1} \approx e^{-1}.$$

The r_i each have a geometric distribution with parameter p, so $\mathbf{E}[r_i] = 1/p \approx e$.

Given that a packet was successfully sent at a given time slot, the sender of that packet is uniformly distributed among the n servers, independent of previous steps. Using our analysis of the expectation of the coupon collector's problem from Chapter 2, we deduce that $\mathbf{E}[N] = nH(n) = n \ln n + O(n)$. We now use Wald's equality to compute

$$\mathbf{E}[T] = \mathbf{E}\left[\sum_{i=1}^{N} r_i\right]$$
$$= \mathbf{E}[N] \cdot \mathbf{E}[r_i]$$
$$= \frac{nH(n)}{p},$$

which is about $en \ln n$.

13.4. Tail Inequalities for Martingales

Perhaps the most useful property of martingales for the analysis of algorithms is that Chernoff-like tail inequalities can apply, even when the underlying random variables are not independent. The main results in this area are Azuma's inequality and Hoeffding's inequality. They are quite similar, so they are often together referred to as the Azuma–Hoeffding inequality.

Theorem 13.4 [Azuma–Hoeffding Inequality]: *Let $X_0, \ldots, X_n$ be a martingale such that*

$$|X_k - X_{k-1}| \le c_k.$$

Then, for all $t \ge 1$ and any $\lambda > 0$,

$$\Pr(|X_t - X_0| \ge \lambda) \le 2e^{-\lambda^2/(2\sum_{k=1}^{t} c_k^2)}.$$

Proof: The proof follows the same format as that for Chernoff bounds (Section 4.2). We first derive an upper bound for $\mathbf{E}[e^{\alpha(X_t-X_0)}]$. Toward that end, we define

$$Y_i = X_i - X_{i-1}, \quad i = 1, \ldots, t.$$

Note that $|Y_i| \le c_i$ and, since $X_0, X_1, \ldots$ is a martingale,

$$\mathbf{E}[Y_i \mid X_0, X_1, \ldots, X_{i-1}] = \mathbf{E}[X_i - X_{i-1} \mid X_0, X_1, \ldots, X_{i-1}]$$
$$= \mathbf{E}[X_i \mid X_0, X_1, \ldots, X_{i-1}] - X_{i-1} = 0.$$

Now consider

$$\mathbf{E}[e^{\alpha Y_i} \mid X_0, X_1, \ldots, X_{i-1}].$$

349

Writing

$$Y_i = -c_i \frac{1 - Y_i/c_i}{2} + c_i \frac{1 + Y_i/c_i}{2}$$

and using the convexity of $e^{\alpha Y_i}$, we have that

$$e^{\alpha Y_i} \leq \frac{1 - Y_i/c_i}{2} e^{-\alpha c_i} + \frac{1 + Y_i/c_i}{2} e^{\alpha c_i}$$

$$= \frac{e^{\alpha c_i} + e^{-\alpha c_i}}{2} + \frac{Y_i}{2c_i}(e^{\alpha c_i} - e^{-\alpha c_i}).$$

Since $\mathbf{E}[Y_i \mid X_0, X_1, \ldots, X_{i-1}] = 0$, we have

$$\mathbf{E}[e^{\alpha Y_i} \mid X_0, X_1, \ldots, X_{i-1}] \leq \mathbf{E}\left[\frac{e^{\alpha c_i} + e^{-\alpha c_i}}{2} + \frac{Y_i}{2c_i}(e^{\alpha c_i} - e^{-\alpha c_i}) \mid X_0, X_1, \ldots, X_{i-1}\right]$$

$$= \frac{e^{\alpha c_i} + e^{-\alpha c_i}}{2}$$

$$\leq e^{(\alpha c_i)^2/2}.$$

Here we have used the Taylor series expansion of e^x to find

$$\frac{e^{\alpha c_i} + e^{-\alpha c_i}}{2} \leq e^{(\alpha c_i)^2/2},$$

in a manner similar to the proof of Theorem 4.7. It follows that

$$\mathbf{E}\left[e^{\alpha(X_t - X_0)}\right] = \mathbf{E}\left[\prod_{i=1}^{t} e^{\alpha Y_i}\right]$$

$$= \mathbf{E}\left[\prod_{i=1}^{t-1} e^{\alpha Y_i}\right] \mathbf{E}[e^{\alpha Y_t} \mid X_0, X_1, \ldots, X_{t-1}]$$

$$\leq \mathbf{E}\left[\prod_{i=1}^{t-1} e^{\alpha Y_i}\right] e^{(\alpha c_t)^2/2}$$

$$\leq e^{\alpha^2 \sum_{k=1}^{t} c_k^2/2}.$$

Hence,

$$\Pr(X_t - X_0 \geq \lambda) = \Pr(e^{\alpha(X_t - X_0)} \geq e^{\alpha \lambda})$$

$$\leq \frac{\mathbf{E}[e^{\alpha(X_t - X_0)}]}{e^{\alpha \lambda}}$$

$$\leq e^{\alpha^2 \sum_{k=1}^{t} c_k^2/2 - \alpha \lambda}$$

$$\leq e^{-\lambda^2/(2 \sum_{k=1}^{t} c_k^2)},$$

where the last inequality comes from choosing $\alpha = \lambda / \sum_{k=1}^{t} c_k^2$. A similar argument gives the bound for $\Pr(X_t - X_0 \leq -\lambda)$, as can be seen for example by replacing X_i everywhere by $-X_i$, giving the theorem. ∎

The following corollary is often easier to apply.

Corollary 13.5: *Let $X_0, X_1, \ldots$ be a martingale such that, for all $k \geq 1$,*

$$|X_k - X_{k-1}| \leq c.$$

Then, for all $t \geq 0$ and $\lambda > 0$,

$$\Pr\left(|X_t - X_0| \geq \lambda c \sqrt{t}\right) \leq 2e^{-\lambda^2/2}.$$

We now present a more general form of the Azuma–Hoeffding inequality that yields slightly tighter bounds in our applications.

Theorem 13.6 [Azuma–Hoeffding Inequality]: *Let $X_0, \ldots, X_n$ be a martingale such that*

$$B_k \leq X_k - X_{k-1} \leq B_k + d_k$$

for some constants d_k and for some random variables B_k that may be functions of $X_0, X_1, \ldots, X_{k-1}$. Then, for all $t \geq 0$ and any $\lambda > 0$,

$$\Pr(|X_t - X_0| \geq \lambda) \leq 2e^{-2\lambda^2/(\sum_{k=1}^{t} d_k^2)}.$$

This version of the inequality generalizes the requirement of a bound on $|X_k - X_{k-1}|$. The key is the gap d_k between the lower and upper bounds for $X_k - X_{k-1}$. Notice that, when we have the bound $|X_k - X_{k-1}| \leq c_k$, this result is equivalent to Theorem 13.4 using $B_k = -c_k$ with a gap $d_k = 2c_k$. The proof is similar to that for Theorem 13.4 and is left as Exercise 13.7.

13.5. Applications of the Azuma–Hoeffding Inequality

13.5.1. *General Formalization*

Before giving several applications of the Azuma–Hoeffding inequality, we describe a useful general technique. Let us say that a function

$$f(\bar{X}) = f(X_1, X_2, \ldots, X_n)$$

satisfies a *Lipschitz condition* with bound c if, for any i and for any set of values $x_1, \ldots, x_n$ and y_i,

$$|f(x_1, x_2, \ldots, x_{i-1}, x_i, x_{i+1}, \ldots, x_n) - f(x_1, x_2, \ldots, x_{i-1}, y_i, x_{i+1}, \ldots, x_n)| \leq c.$$

That is, changing the value of any single coordinate can change the function value by at most c.

Let

$$Z_0 = \mathbf{E}[f(X_1, X_2, \ldots, X_n)]$$

and

$$Z_k = \mathbf{E}[f(X_1, X_2, \ldots, X_n) \mid X_1, X_2, \ldots, X_k].$$

351

The sequence $Z_0, Z_1, \ldots$ is a Doob martingale, and if the X_k are independent random variables then we claim that there exist random variables B_k, depending only on $Z_0, \ldots, Z_{k-1}$, with $B_k \leq Z_k - Z_{k-1} \leq B_k + c$. The gap between the lower and upper bounds on $Z_k - Z_{k-1}$ is then at most c, so the Azuma–Hoeffding inequality of Theorem 13.6 applies. This variation on the Azuma-Hoeffding inequality is often referred to as McDiarmid's inequality, which we now formalize.

Theorem 13.7 [McDiarmid's Inequality]: *Let f be a function on n variables that satisfies the above Lipschitz condition with bound c. Let $X_1, \ldots, X_n$ be independent random variables such that $f(X_1, \ldots, X_n)$ is in the domain of f. Then*

$$\Pr(|f(X_1, \ldots, X_n) - \mathbf{E}[f(X_1, \ldots, X_n)] \geq \lambda) \leq 2e^{-2\lambda^2/(nc^2)}.$$

Proof: We prove this for the case of discrete random variables (although the result holds more generally). To ease the notation, we use S_k as shorthand for $X_1, X_2, \ldots, X_k$, so that we write

$$\mathbf{E}[f(\bar{X}) \mid S_k]$$

for

$$\mathbf{E}[f(\bar{X}) \mid X_1, X_2, \ldots, X_k].$$

Also, let us abuse notation and define

$$f_k(\bar{X}, x) = f(X_1, \ldots, X_{k-1}, x, X_{k+1}, \ldots, X_n).$$

That is, $f_k(\bar{X}, x)$ is $f(\bar{X})$ with the value x in the kth coordinate. We shall likewise write

$$f_k(\bar{z}, x) = f(z_1, \ldots, z_{k-1}, x, z_{k+1}, \ldots, z_n).$$

Given this notation, we have

$$Z_k - Z_{k-1} = \mathbf{E}[f(\bar{X}) \mid S_k] - \mathbf{E}[f(\bar{X}) \mid S_{k-1}].$$

Hence $Z_k - Z_{k-1}$ is bounded above by

$$\sup_x \mathbf{E}[f(\bar{X}) \mid S_{k-1}, X_k = x] - \mathbf{E}[f(\bar{X}) \mid S_{k-1}]$$

and bounded below by

$$\inf_y \mathbf{E}[f(\bar{X}) \mid S_{k-1}, X_k = y] - \mathbf{E}[f(\bar{X}) \mid S_{k-1}].$$

(If we are dealing with random variables that can take on only a finite number of values, we could use max and min in place of sup and inf.) Therefore, letting

$$B_k = \inf_y \mathbf{E}[f(\bar{X}) \mid S_{k-1}, X_k = y] - \mathbf{E}[f(\bar{X}) \mid S_{k-1}],$$

if we can bound

$$\sup_x \mathbf{E}[f(\bar{X}) \mid S_{k-1}, X_k = x] - \inf_y \mathbf{E}[f(\bar{X}) \mid S_{k-1}, X_k = y] \leq c$$

then we will have appropriately bounded the gap $Z_k - Z_{k-1}$. Now

$$\sup_x \mathbf{E}[f(\bar{X}) \mid S_{k-1}, X_k = x] - \inf_y \mathbf{E}[f(\bar{X}) \mid S_{k-1}, X_k = y]$$

$$= \sup_{x,y} \left(\mathbf{E}[f(\bar{X}) \mid S_{k-1}, X_k = x] - \mathbf{E}[f(\bar{X}) \mid S_{k-1}, X_k = y] \right)$$

$$= \sup_{x,y} \mathbf{E}[f_k(\bar{X}, x) - f_k(\bar{X}, y) \mid S_{k-1}].$$

Because the X_i are independent, the probability of any specific set of values for X_{k+1} through X_n does not depend on the values of $X_1, \ldots, X_k$. Hence, for any values $x, y, z_1, \ldots, z_{k-1}$ we have that

$$\mathbf{E}[f_k(\bar{X}, x) - f_k(\bar{X}, y) \mid X_1 = z_1, \ldots, X_{k-1} = z_{k-1}]$$

is equal to

$$\sum_{z_{k+1}, \ldots, z_n} \Pr((X_{k+1} = z_{k+1}) \cap \cdots \cap (X_n = z_n)) \cdot (f_k(\bar{z}, x) - f_k(\bar{z}, y)).$$

But

$$f_k(\bar{z}, x) - f_k(\bar{z}, y) \le c,$$

and hence

$$\mathbf{E}[f_k(\bar{X}, x) - f_k(\bar{X}, y) \mid S_{k-1}] \le c,$$

giving the required bound, so that we may apply Theorem 12.6 to conclude the proof. ∎

The requirement that the X_i be independent random variables is essential to applying this general framework. Finding a counterexample when the X_i are not independent is left as Exercise 13.21.

13.5.2. *Application: Pattern Matching*

In many scenarios, including examining DNA structure, a goal is to find interesting patterns in a sequence of characters. In this context, the phrase "interesting patterns" often refers to strings that occur more often than one would expect if the characters were simply generated randomly. This notion of "interesting" is reasonable if the number of occurrences of a string is concentrated around its expectation in the random model. We show concentration using the Azuma–Hoeffding inequality for a simple random model.

Let $X = (X_1, \ldots, X_n)$ be a sequence of characters chosen independently and uniformly at random from an alphabet Σ, where $s = |\Sigma|$. Let $B = (b_1, \ldots, b_k)$ be a fixed string of k characters from Σ. Let F be the number of occurrences of the fixed string B in the random string X. Clearly,

$$\mathbf{E}[F] = (n - k + 1) \left(\frac{1}{s} \right)^k.$$

We use a Doob martingale and the Azuma–Hoeffding inequality to show that, if k is relatively small with respect to n, then the number of occurrences of B in X is highly concentrated around its mean.

Let

$$Z_0 = \mathbf{E}[F],$$

and for $1 \le i \le n$ let

$$Z_i = \mathbf{E}[F \mid X_1, \ldots, X_i].$$

The sequence $Z_0, \ldots, Z_n$ is a Doob martingale, and

$$Z_n = F.$$

Since each character in the string X can participate in no more than k possible matches, for any $0 \le i \le n$ we have

$$|Z_{i+1} - Z_i| \le k.$$

In other words, the value of X_{i+1} can affect the value of F by at most k in either direction, since X_{i+1} participates in no more than k possible matches. Hence the difference

$$|\mathbf{E}[F \mid X_1, \ldots, X_{i+1}] - \mathbf{E}[F \mid X_1, \ldots, X_i]| = |Z_{i+1} - Z_i|$$

must be at most k. Applying Theorem 13.4 yields

$$\Pr(|F - \mathbf{E}[F]| \ge \varepsilon) \le 2e^{-\varepsilon^2/2nk^2},$$

or (from Corollary 13.5)

$$\Pr\left(|F - \mathbf{E}[F]| \ge \lambda k \sqrt{n}\right) \le 2e^{-\lambda^2/2}.$$

We can obtain slightly better bounds by applying the general framework of Theorem 13.6. Let $F = f(X_1, X_2, \ldots, X_n)$. Then, by our preceding argument, changing the value of any single X_i can change the value of F by at most k, and hence the function satisfies the Lipschitz condition with bound k. Theorem 13.6 then applies to give

$$\Pr(|F - \mathbf{E}[F]| \ge \varepsilon) \le 2e^{-2\varepsilon^2/nk^2},$$

improving the value in the exponent by a factor of 4.

13.5.3. Application: Balls and Bins

Suppose that we are throwing m balls independently and uniformly at random into n bins. Let X_i be the random variable representing the bin into which the ith ball falls.

Let F be the number of empty bins after the m balls are thrown. Then the sequence

$$Z_i = \mathbf{E}[F \mid X_1, \ldots, X_i]$$

is a Doob martingale. We claim that $F = f(X_1, X_2, \ldots, X_m)$ satisfies the Lipschitz condition with bound 1. Consider how F changes from the placement of the ith ball. If the ith ball lands in a bin on its own, then changing X_i so that the ith ball lands in a bin with some other ball will increase F by 1. Similarly, if the ith ball lands in a bin with other balls, then changing X_i so that the ith ball lands in an otherwise empty bin decreases F by 1. In all other cases, changing X_i leaves F the same. We therefore obtain

$$\Pr(|F - \mathbf{E}[F]| \geq \varepsilon) \leq 2e^{-2\varepsilon^2/m}$$

by the Azuma–Hoeffding inequality of Theorem 13.6. We could also apply Theorem 13.4 with $|Z_{i+1} - Z_i| \leq 1$, but this gives a slightly weaker result. Here

$$\mathbf{E}[F] = n \left(1 - \frac{1}{n}\right)^m,$$

but we could obtain the concentration result without knowing $\mathbf{E}[F]$.

This result can be improved by taking more care in bounding the gap between the bounds on $Z_{i+1} - Z_i$. This is considered in Exercise 13.20.

13.5.4. *Application: Chromatic Number*

Given a random graph G in $G_{n,p}$, the *chromatic number* $\chi(G)$ is the minimum number of colors needed in order to color all vertices of the graph so that no adjacent vertices have the same color. We use the vertex exposure martingale defined in Section 13.1 to obtain a concentration result for $\chi(G)$.

Let G_i be the random subgraph of G induced by the set of vertices $1, \ldots, i$, let $Z_0 = \mathbf{E}[\chi(G)]$, and let

$$Z_i = \mathbf{E}[\chi(G) \mid G_1, \ldots, G_i].$$

Since a vertex uses no more than one new color, again we have that the gap between Z_i and Z_{i-1} is at most 1, so we can apply the general framework of the Azuma–Hoeffding inequality from Theorem 13.6. We conclude that

$$\Pr\left(|\chi(G) - \mathbf{E}[\chi(G)]| \geq \lambda\sqrt{n}\right) \leq 2e^{-2\lambda^2}.$$

This result holds even without knowing $\mathbf{E}[\chi(G)]$.

13.6. Exercises

Exercise 13.1: Show that, if $Z_0, Z_1, \ldots, Z_n$ is a martingale with respect to $X_0, X_1, \ldots, X_n$, then it is also a martingale with respect to itself.

Exercise 13.2: Let $X_0, X_1, \ldots$ be a sequence of random variables, and let $S_i = \sum_{j=1}^{i} X_j$. Show that if $S_0, S_1, \ldots$ is a martingale with respect to $X_0, X_1, \ldots$, then for all $i \neq j$, $\mathbf{E}[X_i X_j] = 0$.

Exercise 13.3: Let $X_0 = 0$ and for $j \geq 0$ let X_{j+1} be chosen uniformly over the real interval $[X_j, 1]$. Show that, for $k \geq 0$, the sequence

$$Y_k = 2^k(1 - X_k)$$

is a martingale.

Exercise 13.4: Let $X_1, X_2, \ldots$ be independent and identically distributed random variables with expectation 0 and variance $\sigma^2 < \infty$. Let

$$Z_n = \left(\sum_{i=1}^{n} X_i \right)^2 - n\sigma^2.$$

Show that $Z_1, Z_2, \ldots$ is a martingale.

Exercise 13.5: Consider the gambler's ruin problem, where a player plays a sequence of independent games, either winning one dollar with probability $1/2$ or losing one dollar with probability $1/2$. The player continues until either losing ℓ_1 dollars or winning ℓ_2 dollars. Let X_n be 1 if the player wins the nth game and -1 otherwise. Let $Z_n = \left(\sum_{i=1}^{n} X_i \right)^2 - n$.

(a) Show that $Z_1, Z_2, \ldots$ is a martingale.
(b) Let T be the stopping time when the player finishes playing. Determine $\mathbf{E}[Z_T]$.
(c) Calculate $\mathbf{E}[T]$. (*Hint:* You can use what you already know about the probability that the player wins.)

Exercise 13.6: Consider the gambler's ruin problem, where now the independent games are such that the player either wins one dollar with probability $p < 1/2$ or loses one dollar with probability $1 - p$. As in Exercise 13.5, the player continues until either losing ℓ_1 dollars or winning ℓ_2 dollars. Let X_n be 1 if the player wins the nth game and -1 otherwise, and let Z_n be the player's total winnings after n games.

(a) Show that

$$A_n = \left(\frac{1-p}{p} \right)^{Z_n}$$

is a martingale with mean 1.
(b) Determine the probability that the player wins ℓ_2 dollars before losing ℓ_1 dollars.
(c) Show that

$$B_n = Z_n - (2p - 1)n$$

is a martingale with mean 0.
(d) Let T be the stopping time when the player finishes playing. Determine $\mathbf{E}[Z_T]$, and use it to determine $\mathbf{E}[T]$. (*Hint:* You can use what you already know about the probability that the player wins.)

Exercise 13.7: Prove Theorem 13.6. [*Hint:* Use Lemma 4.13.]

Exercise 13.8: In the bin-packing problem, we are given items with sizes $a_1, a_2, \ldots, a_n$ with $0 \le a_i \le 1$ for $1 \le i \le n$. The goal is to pack them into the minimum number of bins, with each bin being able to hold any collection of items whose total sizes sum to at most 1. Suppose that each of the a_i is chosen independently according to some distribution (which might be different for each i). Let P be the number of bins required in the best packing of the resulting items. Prove that

$$\Pr(|P - \mathbf{E}[P]| \geq \lambda) \leq 2e^{-2\lambda^2/n}.$$

Exercise 13.9: Consider an n-cube with $N = 2^n$ nodes. Let S be a nonempty set of vertices on the cube, and let x be a vertex chosen uniformly at random among all vertices of the cube. Let $D(x, S)$ be the minimum number of coordinates in which x and y differ over all points $y \in S$. Give a bound on

$$\Pr(|D(x, S) - \mathbf{E}[D(x, S)]| > \lambda).$$

Exercise 13.10: In Chapter 4 we developed a tail bound for the sum of $\{0, 1\}$ random variables. We can use martingales to generalize this result for the sum of any random variables whose range lies in $[0, 1]$. Let $X_1, X_2, \ldots, X_n$ be independent random variables such that $\Pr(0 \leq X_i \leq 1) = 1$. If $S_n = \sum_{i=1}^n X_i$, show that

$$\Pr(|S_n - \mathbf{E}[S_n]| \geq \lambda) \leq 2e^{-2\lambda^2/n}.$$

Exercise 13.11: A parking-lot attendant has mixed up n keys for n cars. The n car owners arrive together. The attendant gives each owner a key according to a permutation chosen uniformly at random from all permutations. If an owner receives the key to his car, he takes it and leaves; otherwise, he returns the key to the attendant. The attendant now repeats the process with the remaining keys and car owners. This continues until all owners receive the keys to their cars.

Let R be the number of rounds until all car owners receive the keys to their cars. We want to compute $\mathbf{E}[R]$. Let X_i be the number of owners who receive their car keys in the ith round. Prove that

$$Y_i = \sum_{j=1}^i (X_j - \mathbf{E}[X_j \mid X_1, \ldots, X_{j-1}])$$

is a martingale. Use the martingale stopping theorem to compute $\mathbf{E}[R]$.

Exercise 13.12: Alice and Bob play each other in a checkers tournament, where the first player to win four games wins the match. The players are evenly matched, so the probability that each player wins each game is $1/2$, independent of all other games. The number of minutes for each game is uniformly distributed over the integers in the range $[30, 60]$, again independent of other games. What is the expected time they spend playing the match?

Exercise 13.13: Consider the following extremely inefficient algorithm for sorting n numbers in increasing order. Start by choosing one of the n numbers uniformly at random, and placing it first. Then choose one of the remaining $n - 1$ numbers uniformly at random, and place it second. If the second number is smaller than the first, start over again from the beginning. Otherwise, next choose one of the remaining $n - 2$ numbers uniformly at random, place it third, and so on. The algorithm starts over from the beginning whenever it finds that the kth item placed is smaller than the $(k - 1)$th item. Determine the expected number of times the algorithm tries to place a number, assuming that the input consists of n distinct numbers.

Exercise 13.14: Suppose that you are arranging a chain of n dominos so that, once you are done, you can have them all fall sequentially in a pleasing manner by knocking down the lead domino. Each time you try to place a domino in the chain, there is some chance that it falls, taking down all of the other dominos you have already carefully placed. In that case, you must start all over again from the very first domino.

(a) Let us call each time you try to place a domino a *trial*. Each trial succeeds with probability p. Using Wald's equation, find the expected number of trials necessary before your arrangement is ready. Calculate this number of trials for $n = 100$ and $p = 0.1$.

(b) Suppose instead that you can break your arrangement into k components, each of size n/k, in such a way so that once a component is complete, it will not fall when you place further dominos. For example: if you have 10 components of size 10, then once the first component of 10 dominos are placed successfully they will not fall; misplacing a domino later might take down another component, but the first will remain ready. Find the expected number of trials necessary before your arrangement is ready in this case. Calculate the number of trials for $n = 100$, $k = 10$, and $p = 0.1$, and compare with your answer from part (a).

Exercise 13.15: **(a)** Let $X_1, X_2, \ldots$ be a sequence of independent exponential random variables, each with mean 1. Given a positive real number k, let N be defined by

$$N = \min\left\{n : \sum_{i=1}^{n} X_i > k\right\}.$$

That is, N is the smallest number for which the sum of the first N of the X_i is larger than k. Use Wald's inequality to determine $\mathbf{E}[N]$.

(b) Let $X_1, X_2, \ldots$ be a sequence of independent uniform random variables on the interval $(0, 1)$. Given a positive real number k with $0 < k < 1$, let N be defined by

$$N = \min\left\{n : \prod_{i=1}^{n} X_i < k\right\}.$$

That is, N is the smallest number for which the product of the first N of the X_i is smaller than k. Determine $\mathbf{E}[N]$. (*Hint:* You may find Exercise 8.9 helpful.)

Exercise 13.16: A *subsequence* of a string s is any string that can be obtained by deleting characters from s. Consider two strings x and y of length n, where each character in each string is independently a 0 with probability $1/2$ and a 1 with probability $1/2$. We consider the *longest common subsequence* of the two strings.

(a) Show that the expected length of the longest common subsequence is greater than $c_1 n$ and less than $c_2 n$ for constants $c_1 > 1/2$ and $c_2 < 1$ when n is sufficiently large.

358

(Any constants c_1 and c_2 will do; as a challenge, you may attempt to find the best constants c_1 and c_2 that you can.)

(b) Use a martingale inequality to show that the length of the longest common subsequence is highly concentrated around its mean.

Exercise 13.17: Given a bag with r red balls and g green balls, suppose that we uniformly sample n balls from the bin without replacement. Set up an appropriate martingale and use it to show that the number of red balls in the sample is tightly concentrated around $nr/(r+g)$.

Exercise 13.18: We showed in Chapter 5 that the fraction of entries that are 0 in a Bloom filter is concentrated around

$$p' = \left(1 - \frac{1}{n}\right)^{km},$$

where m is the number of data items, k is the number of hash functions, and n is the size of the Bloom filter in bits. Derive a similar concentration result using a martingale inequality.

Exercise 13.19: Consider a random graph from $G_{n,N}$, where $N = cn$ for some constant $c > 0$. Let X be the number of isolated vertices (i.e., vertices of degree 0).

(a) Determine $\mathbf{E}[X]$.

(b) Show that

$$\Pr\left(|X - \mathbf{E}[X]| \geq 2\lambda\sqrt{cn}\right) \leq 2e^{-\lambda^2/2}.$$

(*Hint:* Use a martingale that reveals the locations of the edges in the graph, one at a time.)

Exercise 13.20: We improve our bound from the Azuma–Hoeffding inequality for the problem where m balls are thrown into n bins. We let F be the number of empty bins after the m balls are thrown and X_i the bin in which the ith ball lands. We define $Z_0 = \mathbf{E}[F]$ and $Z_i = \mathbf{E}[F \mid X_1, \ldots, X_i]$.

(a) Let A_i denote the number of bins that are empty after the ith ball is thrown. Show that in this case

$$Z_{i-1} = A_{i-1}\left(1 - \frac{1}{n}\right)^{m-i+1}.$$

(b) Show that, if the ith ball lands in a bin that is empty when it is thrown, then

$$Z_i = (A_{i-1} - 1)\left(1 - \frac{1}{n}\right)^{m-i}.$$

(c) Show that, if the ith ball lands in a bin that is not empty when it is thrown, then

$$Z_i = A_{i-1}\left(1 - \frac{1}{n}\right)^{m-i}.$$

(d) Show that the Azuma–Hoeffding inequality of Theorem 13.6 applies with $d_i = (1 - 1/n)^{m-i}$.

(e) Using part (d), prove that

$$\Pr(|F - \mathbf{E}[F]| \geq \lambda) \leq 2e^{-\lambda^2(2n-1)/(n^2-(\mathbf{E}[F])^2)}.$$

Exercise 13.21: Let $f(X_1, X_2, \ldots, X_n)$ satisfy the Lipschitz condition so that, for any i and any values $x_1, \ldots, x_n$ and y_i,

$$|f(x_1, x_2, \ldots, x_{i-1}, x_i, x_{i+1}, \ldots, x_n) - f(x_1, x_2, \ldots, x_{i-1}, y_i, x_{i+1}, \ldots, x_n)| \leq c.$$

We set

$$Z_0 = \mathbf{E}[f(X_1, X_2, \ldots, X_n)]$$

and

$$Z_i = \mathbf{E}[f(X_1, X_2, \ldots, X_n) \mid X_1, X_2, \ldots, X_i].$$

Give an example to show that, if the X_i are not independent, then it is possible that $|Z_i - Z_{i-1}| > c$.

CHAPTER FOURTEEN
Sample Complexity, VC Dimension, and Rademacher Complexity

Sampling is a powerful technique at the core of statistical data analysis and machine learning. Using a finite, often small, set of observations, we attempt to estimate properties of an entire sample space. How good are estimates obtained from a sample? Any rigorous application of sampling requires an understanding of the *sample complexity* of the problem – the minimum size sample needed to obtain the required results. In this chapter we focus on the sample complexity of two important applications of sampling: range detection and probability estimation. Here a range is just a subset of the underlying space. Our goal is to use one set of samples to detect a set of ranges or estimate the probabilities of a set of ranges, where the set of possible ranges is large, in fact possibly infinite. For detection, we mean that we want the sample to intersect with each range in the set, while for probability estimation, we want the fraction of points in the sample that intersect with each range in the set to approximate the probability associated with that range.

As an example, consider a sample $x_1, \ldots, x_m$ of m independent observations from an unknown distribution $\mathcal{D}$, where the values for our samples are in $\mathbb{R}$. Given an interval $[a, b]$, if the probability of the interval is at least ϵ, i.e., $\Pr(x \in [a, b]) \geq \epsilon$, then the probability that a sample of size $m = \frac{1}{\epsilon} \ln \frac{1}{\delta}$ intersects (or, in this context, detects) the interval $[a, b]$ is at least $1 - (1 - \epsilon)^m \geq 1 - \delta$. Given a set of k intervals, each of which has probability at least ϵ, we can apply a union bound to show that the probability that a sample of size $m' = \frac{1}{\epsilon} \ln \frac{k}{\delta}$ intersects each of the k intervals is at least $1 - k(1 - \epsilon)^{m'} \geq 1 - \delta$.

In many applications we need a sample that intersects with *every* interval that has probability at least ϵ, and there can be an infinite number of such intervals. What sample size guarantees that? We cannot use a simple union bound to answer this question, as our above analysis does not make sense when k is infinite. However, if there are many such intervals, there can be significant overlap between them. For example, consider samples chosen uniformly over $[0, 1]$ with $\epsilon = 1/10$; there are infinitely many intervals $[a, b]$ of length at least $1/10$, but the largest number of disjoint intervals of size at least $1/10$ is ten. A sample point may intersect with many intervals, and thus a small sample may be sufficient.

Indeed, the technique we will develop in this chapter will show that for any distribution $\mathcal{D}$, a sample of size $\Omega(\frac{1}{\epsilon} \ln \frac{1}{\delta})$, with probability at least $1 - \delta$, intersects all intervals of probability at least ϵ. Similarly, we will show that a sample of size $\Omega(\frac{1}{\epsilon^2} \ln \frac{1}{\delta})$, with probability at least $1 - \delta$, simultaneously estimates the probabilities of all intervals, where each probability is estimated within an additive error bounded by ϵ.

The above example shows that the set of intervals on a line corresponds to a set of ranges that is easy to sample. In this chapter we develop general methods for evaluating the sample complexity of sets of ranges. We will see an example of sets of ranges with significantly larger sample complexity than the intervals example, and even sets of ranges with infinite sample complexity for either detection or probability estimation. We also present applications of the theory to rigorous machine learning and data mining analysis.

14.1. The Learning Setting

The study of sample complexity was motivated by statistical machine learning. To motivate our discussion of these concepts, we show how the task of learning a binary classification can be framed as either a detection or a probability estimation problem.

As a starting example, suppose that we know that a publisher uses a certain rule when determining whether to review or reject a book based on the submitted manuscript. The rule is a conjunction over certain Boolean variables (or their negations); for example, there could be a Boolean variable for whether the manuscript is over 100 pages, for whether the topic was of wide interest, for whether the author had suitable experience, and so on. As outsiders, we might not know the rule, and the question is whether we can learn the rule after seeing enough examples.

A second example involves learning the range of temperatures in which some electronic equipment is functioning correctly. We test the equipment at various temperatures: some are too low and some are too high, but in between there is an interval of temperatures in which the equipment is functioning correctly. The question is to determine an appropriate range of temperatures where the equipment functions.

Here is a general model for this sort of problem; we formalize these definitions later. We have a universe U of objects that we wish to classify, and let $c : U \to \{-1, 1\}$ be the correct, unknown classification. Usually $c(x) = 1$ corresponds to x being a "positive" example, and $c(x) = -1$ corresponds to x being a "negative" example. The correct classification also can be thought of as the subset of the universe corresponding to the positive examples.

The learning algorithm receives a training set $(x_1, c(x_1)), \ldots, (x_m, c(x_m))$, where $x_i \in U$ is chosen according to an unknown distribution $\mathcal{D}$, and $c(x_i)$ is the correct classification of x_i. The algorithm also receives a collection $\mathcal{C}$ of hypotheses, or possible classifications, to choose from. This collection of hypotheses can be referred to as the concept class. The output of the algorithm is a classification $h \in \mathcal{C}$. In the context of binary classification, every $h \in \mathcal{C}$ is also a function $h : U \to \{-1, 1\}$. Equivalently, each hypothesis is itself a subset of the universe, corresponding to the elements x with

$h(x) = 1$. The correctness of the chosen classification is evaluated with respect to its error in classifying new objects chosen according to the distribution $\mathcal{D}$.

In our first example, $\mathcal{C}$ is the collection of all possible conjunctions of subsets of the Boolean variables or their negations. That is, each $h \in \mathcal{C}$ corresponds to a Boolean formula given by a conjunction of variables; $h(x)$ is 1 if the Boolean expression evaluates to true on x, and -1 if it evaluates to false. In the second example, $\mathcal{C}$ is the set of all intervals in $\mathbb{R}$, so that for each $h \in \mathcal{C}$, $h(x) = 1$ if x is a point in the corresponding interval and $h(x) = -1$ otherwise.

Assume first that the correct classification c is included in the collection $\mathcal{C}$ of possible classifications. For any other $h \in \mathcal{C}$ let

$$\Delta(c, h) = \{x \in U \mid c(x) \neq h(x)\}$$

be the set of objects that are not classified correctly by classification h. The probability of a set $\Delta(c, h)$ is the probability that the distribution $\mathcal{D}$ generates an object in $\Delta(c, h)$. If our training set intersects with every set $\Delta(c, h)$ that has probability at least ϵ, then the learning algorithm can eliminate any classification $h \in \mathcal{C}$ that has error at least ϵ on input from $\mathcal{D}$. Thus, a sample (training set) that with probability $1 - \delta$ detects (or intersects with) all sets $\{\Delta(c, h) \mid \Pr_{\mathcal{D}}(\Delta(c, h)) \geq \epsilon, h \in C\}$ guarantees that such an algorithm outputs with probability $1 - \delta$ a classification that errs with probability bounded by ϵ.

A more realistic scenario is that no classification in $\mathcal{C}$ is perfectly correct. In that case, we require the algorithm to return a classification in $\mathcal{C}$ with an error probability that is no more than ϵ larger (with respect to $\mathcal{D}$) than any classification in $\mathcal{C}$. If our training set approximates all sets $\{\Delta(c, h) \mid h \in \mathcal{C}\}$ to within an additive error $\epsilon/2$, then the learning algorithm has sufficient information to eliminate any $h \in \mathcal{C}$ with error which is at least ϵ larger than the error of the best hypothesis in $\mathcal{C}$.

Finally, we note a major difference between the two examples above. Since the number of possible conjunctions over a bounded number of variables or their complements is bounded, the set of possible classifications in the first example is finite, and we can use standard techniques (union bound and Chernoff bound) to bound the size of the required sample (training set), though the bound may be loose. In the second example, the size of the concept class is not bounded and we need more advanced techniques to obtain a bound on the sample complexity. We present here two major techniques to evaluate the sample complexity, VC dimension and Rademacher complexity.

14.2. VC Dimension

We begin with the formal definitions, using the setting of intervals on a line to help explain them, and then consider other examples.

The Vapnik–Chervonenkis (VC) dimension is defined on range spaces.

Definition 14.1: *A range space is a pair $(X, \mathcal{R})$ where:*

1. X is a (finite or infinite) set of points;
2. $\mathcal{R}$ is a family of subsets of X, called ranges.

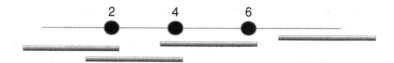

Figure 14.1: Let $\mathcal{R}$ be the collection of all closed intervals in $\mathbb{R}$. Any 2 points can be shattered, but there is no interval that separates $\{2, 6\}$ from $\{4\}$. The VC dimension of $(\mathbb{R}, \mathcal{R})$ is therefore 2.

If for example $X = \mathbb{R}$ is the set of real numbers, then $\mathcal{R}$ could be the family of all closed intervals $[a, b]$ in $\mathbb{R}$.

Given a set $S \subseteq X$, one can obtain a subset of S by intersecting it with a range $R \in \mathcal{R}$. The *projection* of $\mathcal{R}$ on S corresponds to the collection of all subsets that can be obtained in this way.

Definition 14.2: *Let $(X, \mathcal{R})$ be a range space and let $S \subseteq X$. The* projection *of $\mathcal{R}$ on S is*

$$\mathcal{R}_S = \{R \cap S \mid R \in \mathcal{R}\}.$$

For example, let $X = \mathbb{R}$ and $\mathcal{R}$ be the set of all closed intervals. Consider $S = \{2, 4\}$. The intersection of S with the interval $[0, 1]$ gives the empty set; the intersection of S with the interval $[1, 3]$ is $\{2\}$; the intersection of S with the interval $[3, 5]$ is $\{4\}$; and the intersection of S with the interval $[1, 5]$ is $\{2, 4\}$. Hence the projection of $\mathcal{R}$ on S is the set of all possible subsets of S in this case, and indeed the same is true for any set of two distinct points.

Consider now a set $S = \{2, 4, 6\}$. You should convince yourself that the projection of $\mathcal{R}$ on S includes seven of the eight subsets of S, but not $\{2, 6\}$. This is because an interval containing 2 and 6 must also contain 4. More generally, the projection of $\mathcal{R}$ on any set S of three distinct points would contain only seven of the eight possible subsets of S.

We measure the complexity of a range space $(X, \mathcal{R})$ by considering the largest subset S of X such that all subsets of S are contained in the projection of $\mathcal{R}$ on S.

Definition 14.3: *Let $(X, \mathcal{R})$ be a range space. A set $S \subseteq X$ is* shattered *by $\mathcal{R}$ if $|\mathcal{R}_S| = 2^{|S|}$. The* Vapnik–Chervonenkis (VC) dimension *of a range space $(X, \mathcal{R})$ is the maximum cardinality of a set $S \subseteq X$ that is shattered by $\mathcal{R}$. If there are arbitrarily large finite sets that are shattered by $\mathcal{R}$, then the VC dimension is infinite.*

We have shown that any set of two points is shattered by closed intervals on the real number line, but that any set of three points is not. Of course, that argument also shows that no larger set of points is shattered by closed intervals. Therefore, the VC dimension of that range space is 2. Our example shows that a range space with an infinite set of points and an infinite number of ranges can have a bounded VC dimension. (See Figure 14.1.)

An important subtlety in the definition is that the VC dimension of a range space is d if there is *some* set of cardinality d that is shattered by $\mathcal{R}$. It does not imply that all sets of cardinality d are shattered by $\mathcal{R}$. On the other hand, to show that the VC dimension

Figure 14.2: Let $\mathcal{R}$ be the collection of all half-space partitions on $\mathbb{R}^2$. Any three points can be shattered, but there is no half-space partition that separates the two white points from the two black points. Thus, the VC dimension of $(\mathbb{R}^2, \mathcal{R})$ is 3.

is not $d + 1$ or larger, one must show that *all* sets of cardinality larger than d are not shattered by $\mathcal{R}$.

14.2.1. *Additional Examples of VC Dimension*

We consider some other simple examples of VC dimension.

Linear half-spaces

Let $X = \mathbb{R}^2$ and let $\mathcal{R}$ be the set of all half-spaces defined by a linear partition of the plane. That is, we consider all possible lines $ax + by = c$ in the plane, and $\mathcal{R}$ consists of all half-spaces $ax + by \geq c$. The VC dimenstion in this case is at least 3, since any set of three points that do not lie on a line can be shattered. On the other hand, no set of four points can be shattered. To see this, we need to consider several cases. First, if any three points lie on a line they cannot be shattered, as we cannot separate the middle point from the other two by any half-space. Hence we may assume no three points lie on a line; this is often referred to as the points being in "general position". Second, if one point lies within the convex hull defined by the other three points, no half-space can separate that point from the other three. Finally, if the four points define a convex hull, then there is no half-space that separates two non-neighboring points from the other two. (See Figure 14.2.)

While harder to visualize, if $X = \mathbb{R}^d$ and $\mathcal{R}$ corresponds to all half-spaces in d dimensions, the VC dimension is $d + 1$. (See Exercise 14.7.)

Convex sets

Let $X = \mathbb{R}^2$ and let $\mathcal{R}$ be the family of all closed convex sets on the plane. We show that this range space has infinite VC dimension by showing that for every n there exists a set of size n that can be shattered. Let $S_n = \{x_1, \ldots, x_n\}$ be a set of n points on the boundary of a circle. Any subset $Y \subseteq S_n, Y \neq \emptyset$ defines a convex set that does not include any point in $S_n \setminus Y$, and hence Y is included in the projection of $\mathcal{R}$ on S_n. The empty set is easily seen to be in the projection as well. Hence, for any number of points n, the set S_n is shattered and the VC dimension is therefore infinite. (See Figure 14.3.)

Monotone Boolean conjunctions

Let $y_1, y_2, \ldots, y_n$ be n Boolean variables, and let MC_n be the collection of functions defined by conjunctions of subsets of the non-negated variables y_i. Let $X = \{0, 1\}^n$

Figure 14.3: Let $\mathcal{R}$ be the set of all convex bodies in $\mathbb{R}^2$. Any partition of the set of points on the circle can be defined by a convex body. Therefore, the VC dimension of $(\mathbb{R}^2, \mathcal{R})$ is infinite.

correspond to all possible truth assignments of the n variables in the natural way. For each function $f \in MC_n$ let $R_f = \{\bar{a} \in X \ : \ f(\bar{a}) = 1\}$ be the set of inputs that satisfy f, and let $\mathcal{R} = \{R_f \mid f \in MC_n\}$. Consider the set $S \subseteq X$ of n points:

$$(0, 1, 1, \ldots, 1)$$
$$(1, 0, 1, \ldots, 1)$$
$$(1, 1, 0, \ldots, 1)$$
$$\vdots$$
$$(1, 1, 1, \ldots, 0).$$

We claim that each subset of S is equal to $S \cap R_f$ for some R_f. For example, the complete set S corresponds to $S \cap R_f$ for the trivial function that is always 1, i.e., $f(\bar{a}) = 1$. More generally, the subset of S that has all points except those with a 0 in coordinates $i_1, i_2, \ldots, i_j$ is equal to $S \cap R_f$ for $f(\bar{a}) = y_{i_1} \wedge y_{i_2} \wedge \cdots \wedge y_{i_j}$. This set can therefore be shattered by $\mathcal{R}$ and the VC dimension is at least n. The VC dimension cannot be larger than n since $|\mathcal{R}| = |MC_n| = 2^n$, and hence there can be at most 2^n distinct intersections of the form $S \cap R_f$. If the VC dimension was larger than n, at least 2^{n+1} different intersections would be needed.

14.2.2. Growth Function

The combinatorial significance of the concept of the VC dimension is that it gives a bound on the number of different ranges in the projection of the range space on a smaller set of points. In particular, when a range space with finite VC dimension $d \geq 2$ is projected on a set of n points, the number of different ranges in the projection is bounded by a polynomial in n with maximum degree d.

To prove this property we define the *growth function*

$$\mathcal{G}(d, n) = \sum_{i=0}^{d} \binom{n}{i}.$$

For $n = d$, we have $\mathcal{G}(d, n) = 2^d$, and for $n > d \geq 2$, we have

$$\mathcal{G}(d, n) \leq \sum_{i=0}^{d} \frac{n^i}{i!} \leq n^d.$$

The growth function is related to the VC dimension through the following theorem.

Theorem 14.1 [Sauer–Shelah]: *Let $(X, \mathcal{R})$ be a range space with $|X| = n$ and VC dimension d. Then $|\mathcal{R}| \leq \mathcal{G}(d, n)$.*

Proof: We prove the claim by induction on d, and for each d by induction on n. As the base case, the claim clearly holds for $d = 0$ or $n = 0$, as in both of these cases $G(d, n) = 1$, with the only possible $\mathcal{R}$ being the family containing only the empty set.

Assume that the claim holds for $d - 1$ and $n - 1$, and for d and $n - 1$. We may therefore assume $|X| = n > 0$. For some $x \in X$, consider two range spaces on $X \setminus \{x\}$:

$$\mathcal{R}_1 = \{R \setminus \{x\} \mid R \in \mathcal{R}\}$$

and

$$\mathcal{R}_2 = \{R \setminus \{x\} \mid R \cup \{x\} \in \mathcal{R} \text{ and } R \setminus \{x\} \in \mathcal{R}\}.$$

We first observe that $|\mathcal{R}| = |\mathcal{R}_1| + |\mathcal{R}_2|$. Indeed, each set $R \in \mathcal{R}$ is mapped to a set $R \setminus \{x\} \in \mathcal{R}_1$, but if both $R \cup \{x\}$ and $R \setminus \{x\}$ are in $\mathcal{R}$, then both sets are mapped to the same set $R \setminus \{x\} \in \mathcal{R}_1$. By including that set again in $\mathcal{R}_2$, we have $|\mathcal{R}| = |\mathcal{R}_1| + |\mathcal{R}_2|$.

Now $(X \setminus \{x\}, \mathcal{R}_1)$ is a range space on $n - 1$ items, and its VC dimension is bounded above by d, the VC dimension of $(X, \mathcal{R})$. To see this, assume that $\mathcal{R}_1$ shatters a set S of size $d + 1$ in $X \setminus \{x\}$. Then S is also shattered by $\mathcal{R}$, as for any $R \in \mathcal{R}_1$, there is a corresponding R' in $\mathcal{R}$ that is either R or $R \cup \{x\}$, and in either case the projection of $\mathcal{R}$ on S contains $S \cap R' = S \cap R$. But then $\mathcal{R}$ would shatter the set S, contradicting the assumption that $(X, \mathcal{R})$ has VC dimension d.

Similarly, $(X \setminus \{x\}, \mathcal{R}_2)$ is a range space on $n - 1$ items, and its VC dimension is bounded above by $d - 1$. To see this, assume that $\mathcal{R}_2$ shatters a set S of size d in $X \setminus \{x\}$. Then consider the set $S \cup \{x\}$ in $\mathcal{R}$. For any $R \in \mathcal{R}_2$, both R and $R \cup \{x\}$ are in $\mathcal{R}$, and hence one can obtain both $(S \cup \{x\}) \cap R = S \cap R$ and $(S \cup \{x\}) \cap (R \cup \{x\}) = S \cup \{x\}$ in the projection of $\mathcal{R}$ on S. But then $\mathcal{R}$ would shatter the set $S \cup \{x\}$, contradicting the assumption that $(X, \mathcal{R})$ has VC dimension d.

Applying the induction hypothesis we get

$$|\mathcal{R}| = |\mathcal{R}_1| + |\mathcal{R}_2| \leq \mathcal{G}(d, n - 1) + \mathcal{G}(d - 1, n - 1)$$

$$\leq \sum_{i=0}^{d} \binom{n-1}{i} + \sum_{i=0}^{d-1} \binom{n-1}{i}$$

$$= 1 + \sum_{i=0}^{d-1} \left(\binom{n-1}{i+1} + \binom{n-1}{i} \right)$$

$$= \sum_{i=0}^{d} \binom{n}{i} = \mathcal{G}(d, n). \qquad \blacksquare$$

14.2.3. *VC dimension component bounds*

We can sometimes bound the VC dimension of a complex range space as a function of the VC dimension of its simpler components.

The projection of a range space $(X, \mathcal{R})$ on a set $Y \subseteq X$ defines a range space $(Y, \mathcal{R}_Y)$ with $\mathcal{R}_Y = \{R \cap Y \mid R \in \mathcal{R}\}$. We have the following corollary of Theorem 14.1.

Corollary 14.2: *Let $(X, \mathcal{R})$ be a range space with VC dimension d, and let $Y \subseteq X$. Then*

$$|\mathcal{R}_Y| \leq \mathcal{G}(d, |Y|).$$

We also require the following technical lemma.

Lemma 14.3: *If $y \geq x \ln x \geq e$, then $\frac{2y}{\ln y} \geq x$.*

Proof: For $y = x \ln x$ we have $\ln y = \ln x + \ln \ln x \leq 2 \ln x$. Thus

$$\frac{2y}{\ln y} \geq \frac{2x \ln x}{2 \ln x} = x.$$

Differentiating $f(y) = \frac{\ln y}{2y}$ we find that $f(y)$ is monotonically decreasing when $y \geq x \ln x \geq e$, and hence $\frac{2y}{\ln y}$ is monotonically increasing on the same interval, proving the lemma. ∎

We are now ready for the following theorem.

Theorem 14.4: *Let $(X, \mathcal{R}^1), \ldots, (X, \mathcal{R}^k)$ be k range spaces, each with VC dimension at most d. Let $f : (\mathcal{R}^1, \ldots, \mathcal{R}^k) \to 2^X$ be a mapping of k-tuples $(r_1, \ldots, r_k) \in (\mathcal{R}^1, \ldots, \mathcal{R}^k)$ to subsets of X, and let*

$$\mathcal{R}^f = \{f(r_1, \ldots, r_k) \mid r_1 \in \mathcal{R}^1, \ldots, r_k \in \mathcal{R}^k\}.$$

The VC dimension of the range space $(X, \mathcal{R}^f)$ is $O(kd \ln(kd))$.

Proof: Let the VC dimension of $(X, \mathcal{R}^f)$ be at least t, so there is a set $Y \subseteq X$ shattered by $\mathcal{R}^f$ with $t = |Y|$. Since the VC dimension of $(X, \mathcal{R}^i)$, $1 \leq i \leq k$, is at most d, by Corollary 14.2, $|\mathcal{R}_Y^i| \leq \mathcal{G}(d, t) \leq t^d$. Thus, the number of subsets in the projection of $\mathcal{R}^f$ on Y is bounded by

$$|\mathcal{R}_Y^f| \leq |\mathcal{R}_Y^1| \times \cdots \times |\mathcal{R}_Y^k| \leq t^{dk}.$$

Since $\mathcal{R}_Y^f$ shatters Y, $|\mathcal{R}_Y^f| \geq 2^t$. Hence $t^{dk} \geq 2^t$. Let us assume that $y \geq x \ln x$ for $y = t$ and $x = \frac{2(dk+1)}{\ln 2}$ and derive a contradiction. Applying Lemma 14.3,

$$\frac{2y}{\ln y} = \frac{2t}{\ln t} \geq \frac{2(dk + 1)}{\ln 2}.$$

It follows that

$$t \geq (dk + 1) \log_2 t,$$

so $2^t \geq t^{dk+1} > t^{kd}$. Hence if $t \geq x \ln x$, which is $\Omega(dk \ln(dk))$, we have a contradiction. It follows that t must be $O(kd \ln(kd))$. ∎

The following stronger result below is proven in Exercise 14.10.

Theorem 14.5: *Let $(X, \mathcal{R}^1), \ldots, (X, \mathcal{R}^k)$ be k range spaces each with VC dimensions at most d. Let $f : (\mathcal{R}^1, \ldots, \mathcal{R}^k) \to 2^X$ be a mapping of k-tuples $(r_1, \ldots, r_k) \in (\mathcal{R}^1, \ldots, \mathcal{R}^k)$ to subsets of X, and let*

$$\mathcal{R}^f = \{f(r_1, \ldots, r_k) \mid r_1 \in \mathcal{R}^1, \ldots, r_k \in \mathcal{R}^k\}.$$

The VC dimension of the range space $(X, \mathcal{R}^f)$ is $O(kd \ln k)$.

This yields the following corollary.

Corollary 14.6: *Let $(X, \mathcal{R}^1)$ and $(X, \mathcal{R}^2)$ be two range spaces, each with VC dimension at most d. Let*

$$\mathcal{R}^\cup = \{r_1 \cup r_2 \mid r_1 \in \mathcal{R}^1 \text{ and } r_2 \in \mathcal{R}^2\},$$

and

$$\mathcal{R}^\cap = \{r_1 \cap r_2 \mid r_1 \in \mathcal{R}^1 \text{ and } r_2 \in \mathcal{R}^2\}.$$

The VC dimensions of the range spaces $(X, \mathcal{R}^\cup)$ and $(X, \mathcal{R}^\cap)$ are $O(d)$.

14.2.4. ϵ-nets and ϵ-samples

The applications of VC dimension to sampling, including to the types of learning problems mentioned at the beginning of the chapter, can be formulated in terms of objects called ϵ-nets and ϵ-samples.

As a combinatorial object, an ϵ-net for a subset $A \subseteq X$ of a range space is a subset $N \subseteq A$ of points that intersects with all ranges in the range space that are not too small with respect to A, in that the range contains an ϵ-fraction of A. The object is called a net because it "catches," or intersects, every range of sufficient size.

Definition 14.4 [combinatorial definition]: *Let $(X, \mathcal{R})$ be a range space, and let $A \subseteq X$ be a finite subset of X. A set $N \subseteq A$ is a combinatorial ϵ-net for A if N has a nonempty intersection with every set $R \in \mathcal{R}$ such that $|R \cap A| \geq \epsilon |A|$.*

However, ϵ-nets can also be defined more generally with respect to a distribution $\mathcal{D}$ on the point set X. The combinatorial definition above corresponds to a setting where the distribution $\mathcal{D}$ is uniform over the set A. The more general form below is more useful for many algorithmic applications. In what follows, recall that $\Pr_\mathcal{D}(R)$ for a set R is the probability that a point chosen according to $\mathcal{D}$ is in R.

Definition 14.5: *Let $(X, \mathcal{R})$ be a range space, and let $\mathcal{D}$ be a probability distribution on X. A set $N \subseteq X$ is an ϵ-net for X with respect to $\mathcal{D}$ if for any set $R \in \mathcal{R}$ such that $\Pr_\mathcal{D}(R) \geq \epsilon$, the set R contains at least one point from N, i.e.,*

$$\forall R \in \mathcal{R}, \ \Pr_\mathcal{D}(R) \geq \epsilon \Rightarrow R \cap N \neq \emptyset.$$

An ϵ-sample (also called an ϵ-approximation) provides even stronger guarantees than an ϵ-net. It not only intersects every suitably large range, but also ensures that every range has roughly the right relative frequency within the sample.

Definition 14.6: *Let $(X, \mathcal{R})$ be a range space, and let $\mathcal{D}$ be a probability distribution on X. A set $S \subseteq X$ is an ϵ-sample for X with respect to $\mathcal{D}$ if for all sets $R \in \mathcal{R}$,*

$$\left| \Pr_{\mathcal{D}}(R) - \frac{|S \cap R|}{|S|} \right| \leq \epsilon.$$

Again, by fixing the distribution $\mathcal{D}$ to be uniform over a finite set $A \subseteq X$, we obtain the combinatorial version of this concept.

Definition 14.7 [combinatorial definition]: *Let $(X, \mathcal{R})$ be a range space, and let $A \subseteq X$ be a finite subset of X. A set $N \subseteq A$ is a combinatorial ϵ-sample for A if for all sets $R \in \mathcal{R}$,*

$$\left| \frac{|A \cap R|}{|A|} - \frac{|N \cap R|}{|N|} \right| \leq \epsilon.$$

In what follows, we may say ϵ-net and ϵ-sample in place of the more exact terms combinatorial ϵ-net and combinatorial ϵ-sample when the meaning should be clear from context.

Our goal is to obtain ϵ-nets and ϵ-samples through sampling. We say that a set S is a sample of size m from a distribution $\mathcal{D}$ if the m elements of S were chosen independently with distribution $\mathcal{D}$.

Definition 14.8: *A range space $(X, \mathcal{R})$ has the uniform convergence property if for every $\epsilon, \delta > 0$ there is a sample size $m = m(\epsilon, \delta)$ such that for every distribution $\mathcal{D}$ over X, if S is a random sample from $\mathcal{D}$ of size m then, with probability at least $1 - \delta$, S is an ϵ-sample for X with respect to $\mathcal{D}$.*

In the following sections we show that the minimum sample size that contains an ϵ-net or an ϵ-sample for a range space can be bounded in terms of the VC dimension of the range space, independent of the numbers of its points or ranges. In particular, we will show that a range space has the uniform convergence property if and only if its VC dimension is finite. These results show that the VC dimension is a concrete, useful measure of the complexity of a range space.

14.3. The ϵ-net Theorem

As a first step, we use a standard union bound argument to obtain bounds on the size of a combinatorial ϵ-net via the probabilistic method.

Theorem 14.7: *Let $(X, \mathcal{R})$ be a range space with VC dimension $d \geq 2$ and let $A \subseteq X$ have size $|A| = n$. Then there exists a combinatorial ϵ-net N for A of size at most $\lceil \frac{d \ln n}{\epsilon} \rceil$.*

Proof: Consider the projection of the range space $\mathcal{R}$ on A; denote this by $\mathcal{R}'$. By Theorem 14.1, the size of $\mathcal{R}'$ is at most $\mathcal{G}(d, n) \leq n^d$.

Suppose we take a sample of $k = \lceil \frac{d \ln n}{\epsilon} \rceil$ points of A independently and uniformly at random. For each set $R \in \mathcal{R}$ such that $|R \cap A| \geq \epsilon |A|$, there is a corresponding set $R' \in \mathcal{R}'$. The probability that our sample misses a given set R' is $(1 - \epsilon)^k$, and there are

370

at most n^d possible sets R' to consider. Applying a union bound, the probability that the sample misses at least one such R' is at most

$$n^d (1 - \epsilon)^k < n^d e^{-d \ln n} = 1.$$

Since the probability that a random sample of size $k = \lceil \frac{d \ln n}{\epsilon} \rceil$ misses at least one set R' is strictly less than 1, by the probabilistic method there is a set of that size that misses no set $R' \in \mathcal{R}'$, and is therefore an ϵ-net for A. ∎

We can, however, in general do much better than the bound of Theorem 14.7. Our goal is to show that with high probability we can obtain an ϵ-net from a random sample of elements where the size of the sample does not depend on n, *as long as the VC dimension is finite*. This may appear somewhat surprising; while $O(1/\epsilon)$ points on average are needed to hit any particular range, it is not clear how to hit all of them without some dependence on n. Essentially, we are finding that the union bound of Theorem 14.7 is too weak an approach in this setting, and that the VC dimension provides a means to avoid it.

The following theorem, whose proof takes a somewhat unusual path that we sometimes refer to as "double sampling", provides our main results on ϵ-nets. The theorem holds for our more general notion of ϵ-nets, not just combinatorial ϵ-nets.

Theorem 14.8: *Let $(X, \mathcal{R})$ be a range space with VC dimension d and let $\mathcal{D}$ be a probability distribution on X. For any $0 < \delta, \epsilon \le 1/2$, there is an*

$$m = O\left(\frac{d}{\epsilon} \ln \frac{d}{\epsilon} + \frac{1}{\epsilon} \ln \frac{1}{\delta} \right)$$

such that a random sample from $\mathcal{D}$ of size greater than or equal to m is an ϵ-net for X with probability at least $1 - \delta$.

In particular, Theorem 14.8 implies that there exists an ϵ-net of size $O(\frac{d}{\epsilon} \ln \frac{d}{\epsilon})$.

Proof: Let M be a set of m independent samples from X according to $\mathcal{D}$, and let E_1 be the event that M is not an ϵ-net for X with respect to the distribution $\mathcal{D}$, i.e.,

$$E_1 = \{ \exists R \in \mathcal{R} \mid \Pr_{\mathcal{D}}(R) \ge \epsilon \text{ and } |R \cap M| = 0 \}.$$

We want to show that $\Pr(E_1) \le \delta$ for a suitable m. Notice that for any particular R, since $\Pr_{\mathcal{D}}(R) \ge \epsilon$, the expected size of $|R \cap M|$ would be at least ϵm, and hence it seems natural that $\Pr(E_1)$ is small. However, as the union bound argument of Theorem 14.7 is too weak to provide this strong a bound, we use an indirect means to bound $\Pr(E_1)$.

To do this, we choose a second set T of m independent samples from X according to $\mathcal{D}$ and define E_2 to be the event that some range R with $\Pr_{\mathcal{D}}(R) \ge \epsilon$ has an empty intersection with M but a reasonably large intersection with T:

$$E_2 = \{ \exists R \in \mathcal{R} \mid \Pr_{\mathcal{D}}(R) \ge \epsilon \text{ and } |R \cap M| = 0 \text{ and } |R \cap T| \ge \epsilon m/2 \}.$$

Since T is a random sample and $\Pr_{\mathcal{D}}(R) \ge \epsilon$, the event $|R \cap T| \ge \epsilon m/2$ should occur with nontrivial probability and therefore the events E_1 and E_2 should have similar probability. The following lemma formalizes this intuition:

Lemma 14.9: *For $m \geq 8/\epsilon$,*

$$\Pr(E_2) \leq \Pr(E_1) \leq 2\Pr(E_2).$$

Proof: As the event E_2 is included in the event E_1, we have $\Pr(E_2) \leq \Pr(E_1)$. For the second inequality, note that if event E_1 holds, there is some particular R' so that $|R' \cap M| = 0$ and $\Pr_{\mathcal{D}}(R') \geq \epsilon$. We use the definition of conditional probability to obtain

$$\frac{\Pr(E_2)}{\Pr(E_1)} = \frac{\Pr(E_1 \cap E_2)}{\Pr(E_1)} = \Pr(E_2 \mid E_1) \geq \Pr(|T \cap R'| \geq \epsilon m/2).$$

Now for a fixed range R' and a random sample T the random variable $|T \cap R'|$ has a binomial distribution $B(m, \Pr_{\mathcal{D}}(R'))$. Since $\Pr_{\mathcal{D}}(R') \geq \epsilon$, by applying the Chernoff bound (Theorem 4.5), we have for $m \geq 8/\epsilon$,

$$\Pr(|T \cap R'| < \epsilon m/2) \leq e^{-\epsilon m/8} < 1/2.$$

Thus,

$$\frac{\Pr(E_2)}{\Pr(E_1)} = \Pr(E_2 \mid E_1) \geq \Pr(|T \cap R'| \geq \epsilon m/2) \geq 1/2,$$

giving $\Pr(E_1) \leq 2\Pr(E_2)$ as desired. ∎

The lemma above gives us an approach to showing that $\Pr(E_1)$ is small. The intuition is as follows: since M and T are both random samples of size m, it would be very surprising to have $|M \cap R| = 0$ but $|T \cap R|$ be large for some R. If we think of first sampling the m items that form M and then sampling the m items that form T, we must have somehow been very unlucky to have all the samples that intersect R come in the second set of m samples, and none in the first.

Formally, we bound the probability of E_2 by the probability of a larger event E_2':

$$E_2' = \{\exists R \in \mathcal{R} \mid |R \cap M| = 0 \text{ and } |R \cap T| \geq \epsilon m/2\}.$$

The event E_2' excludes the condition that $\Pr_{\mathcal{D}}(R) \geq \epsilon$; in some sense, that has been replaced by the condition on the size of $|R \cap T|$. The event E_2' now depends only on the elements in $M \cup T$.

Lemma 14.10: *It holds that*

$$\Pr(E_1) \leq 2\Pr(E_2) \leq 2\Pr(E_2') \leq 2(2m)^d 2^{-\epsilon m/2}.$$

Proof: Since M and T are random samples, we can assume that we first choose a set of $2m$ elements and then partition it randomly into two equal size sets M and T.

For a fixed $R \in \mathcal{R}$ and $k = \epsilon m/2$, let

$$E_R = \{|R \cap M| = 0 \text{ and } |R \cap T| \geq k\}.$$

To bound the probability of E_R we note that this event implies that $M \cup T$ has at least k elements of R, but all these elements were placed in T by the random partition. That is, of the $\binom{2m}{m}$ possible partitions of $M \cup T$, we chose one of the $\binom{2m-k}{m}$ partitions where no element of R is in M.

Hence

$$
\begin{aligned}
\Pr(E_R) &\leq \Pr(|M \cap R| = 0 \mid |R \cap (M \cup T)| \geq k) \\
&= \frac{\binom{2m-k}{m}}{\binom{2m}{m}} \\
&= \frac{(2m-k)!\,m!}{(2m)!\,(m-k)!} \\
&= \frac{m(m-1)\cdots(m-k+1)}{(2m)(2m-1)\cdots(2m-k+1)} \\
&\leq 2^{-\epsilon m/2}.
\end{aligned}
$$

Our bound on $\Pr(E_R)$ does not depend on the choice of the set $T \cup M$, only on its random partition into T and M. By Theorem 14.1 the projection of $\mathcal{R}$ on $M \cup T$ has no more than $(2m)^d$ ranges. Thus,

$$
\Pr(E_2') \leq (2m)^d 2^{-\epsilon m/2}. \qquad \blacksquare
$$

To complete the proof of Theorem 14.8 we show that for

$$
m \geq \frac{8d}{\epsilon} \ln \frac{16d}{\epsilon} + \frac{4}{\epsilon} \ln \frac{2}{\delta},
$$

we have

$$
\Pr(E_1) \leq 2\Pr(E_2') \leq 2(2m)^d 2^{-\epsilon m/2} \leq \delta.
$$

Equivalently, we require

$$
\epsilon m/2 \geq \ln(2/\delta) + d \ln(2m).
$$

Clearly it holds that $\epsilon m/4 \geq \ln(2/\delta)$, since $m > \frac{4}{\epsilon} \ln \frac{2}{\delta}$. It therefore suffices to show that $\epsilon m/4 \geq d \ln(2m)$ to complete the proof.

Applying Lemma 14.3 with $y = 2m \geq \frac{16d}{\epsilon} \ln \frac{16d}{\epsilon}$ and $x = \frac{16d}{\epsilon}$, we have

$$
\frac{4m}{\ln(2m)} \geq \frac{16d}{\epsilon},
$$

so

$$
\frac{\epsilon m}{4} \geq d \ln(2m)
$$

as required. $\qquad \blacksquare$

The above theorem gives a near tight bound, as shown by the following theorem (see Exercise 14.13 for a proof).

Theorem 14.11: *A random sample of a range space with VC dimension d that, with probability at least $1 - \delta$, is an ϵ-net must have size $\Omega(\frac{d}{\epsilon})$.*

14.4. Application: PAC Learning

Probably Approximately Correct (PAC) Learning provides a framework for mathematical analysis of computational learning from examples. PAC characterizes the complexity of a learning problem in terms of the number of examples and computation needed to provide answers that are approximately correct, in that they are approximately correct with good probability, on as yet unseen examples. We use the model of PAC learning to demonstrate an application of VC dimension to learning theory. However, we note that the VC dimension technique applies to a broader setting of statistical machine learning.

We turn now to a formal definition of PAC learning. We assume a set of items X and a probability distribution $\mathcal{D}$ defined on X. We work here in the setting of binary classifications, where a *concept* (or *classification*) can be treated as a subset $C \subseteq X$; all items in C are said to have a positive classification and all items in $X \setminus C$ are said to have a negative classification. Equivalently, a classification can be treated as a function $c(x)$ that is 1 if $x \in C$ and -1 if $x \notin C$. We use both notions of a classification interchangeably, where the meaning is clear. The *concept class* $\mathcal{C}$ is the set of all possible classifications defined by the problem.

The learning algorithm calls a function ORACLE that produces a pair $(x, c(x))$, where x is distributed according to $\mathcal{D}$, and $c(x)$ is 1 if $x \in C$ and -1 otherwise. We assume that successive calls to ORACLE are independent. For clarity, we may write ORACLE$(C, \mathcal{D})$ to specify the concept and distribution under consideration. We also assume that the classification problem is *realizable*, i.e. there is a classification $h \in C$ that conforms with our input distribution. Formally,

$$\exists h \in C \text{ such that } \Pr_{\mathcal{D}}(h(x) \neq c(x)) = 0.$$

We now define what it means for a concept to be learnable.

Definition 14.9 [PAC Learning]: *A concept class $\mathcal{C}$ over input set X is PAC learnable[1] if there is an algorithm L, with access to a function ORACLE$(C, \mathcal{D})$, that satisfies the following properties: for every correct concept $C \in \mathcal{C}$, every distribution $\mathcal{D}$ on X, and every $0 < \epsilon, \delta \leq 1/2$, the number of calls that the algorithm L makes to the function ORACLE$(C, \mathcal{D})$ is polynomial in ϵ^{-1} and δ^{-1}, and with probability at least $1 - \delta$ the algorithm L outputs a hypothesis h such that $\Pr_{\mathcal{D}}(h(x) \neq c(x)) \leq \epsilon$.*

We first prove that any finite concept class is PAC learnable.

Theorem 14.12: *Any finite concept class $\mathcal{C}$ can be PAC learned with $m = \frac{1}{\epsilon}(\ln |\mathcal{C}| + \ln \frac{1}{\delta})$ samples.*

Proof: Let $c^* \in \mathcal{C}$ be the correct classification. A hypothesis h is said to be "bad" if $\Pr_{\mathcal{D}}(h(x) \neq c^*(x)) \geq \epsilon$. The probability that any particular bad hypothesis is consistent

---

[1] PAC learning is mainly concerned with the computational complexity of learning. In particular, a concept class $\mathcal{C}$ is *efficiently PAC learnable* if the algorithm runs in time polynomial in the size of the problem, $1/\epsilon$ and $1/\delta$. Such an algorithm uses at most polynomially many samples. Here we are only interested in the sample complexity of the learning process; however, we note that the computational complexity of the learning algorithm is not necessarily polynomial in the sample size.

with m random samples is bounded above by $(1 - \epsilon)^m$, and hence the probability that any bad hypothesis is consistent with m random samples is bounded above by

$$|\mathcal{C}|(1 - \epsilon)^m \le \delta.$$

The result follows. ∎

We can also apply the PAC learning framework to infinite concept classes. Let us consider learning an interval $[a, b] \in \mathbb{R}$. The concept class here is the collection of all closed intervals in $\mathbb{R}$:

$$\mathcal{C} = \{[x, y] \mid x \le y\} \cup \emptyset.$$

Notice that we also include a trivial concept that corresponds to the empty interval.

Let $c^* \in \mathcal{C}$ be the concept to be learned, and h be the hypothesis returned by our algorithm. The training set is a collection of n points drawn from a distribution $\mathcal{D}$ on $\mathbb{R}$, where each point in the interval $[a, b]$ is a positive example and each point outside the interval is a negative example. If none of the sample points are positive examples, then our algorithm returns the trivial hypothesis, where $h(x) = -1$ everywhere. If any of the sample points are positive examples, then let c and d respectively be the smallest and largest values of positive examples. Our algorithm then returns the interval $[c, d]$ as its hypothesis. (If there is only one positive example, the algorithm will return an interval of the form $[c, c]$.) By design, our algorithm can only make an error on an input x if $x \in [a, b]$; our algorithm will not make an error outside this interval, because it always returns -1 for points $x \notin [a, b]$.

We now determine the probability that our algorithm returns a bad hypothesis. Let us first consider the case where $\Pr_{\mathcal{D}}(x \in [a, b]) \le \epsilon$. Because our algorithm can only return an incorrect answer on points in the interval $[a, b]$, our algorithm always returns a hypothesis with a probability of error at most ϵ in this case, and hence never returns a bad hypothesis.

Now let us consider when $\Pr_{\mathcal{D}}(x \in [a, b]) > \epsilon$. In this case, let $a' \ge a$ be the smallest value such that $\Pr_{\mathcal{D}}([a, a']) \ge \epsilon/2$. Similarly, let $b' \le b$ be the largest value such that $\Pr_{\mathcal{D}}([b', b]) \ge \epsilon/2$. Here $a' \le b'$ since $\Pr_{\mathcal{D}}(x \in [a, b]) > \epsilon$. For convenience, we assume $a' < b'$; the case $a' = b'$ can be handled similarly. (If $a' = b'$, then the point a' has nonzero probability of being selected, and we can divide up that probability among the intervals $[a, a']$ and $[b', b]$ so the probability of each is at least $\epsilon/2$.) For our algorithm to return a bad hypothesis with error at least ϵ, it must be the case that no sample points fell either in the interval $[a, a']$ or the interval $[b', b]$, or both. Otherwise, our algorithm would return a range $[c, d]$ that covers $[a', b']$, and correspondingly the probability our hypothesis would be incorrect on a new input chosen from $\mathcal{D}$ would be at most ϵ.

The probability that a training set of n points does not have any examples from either $[a, a']$ or $[b, b']$ is bounded above by

$$2\left(1 - \frac{\epsilon}{2}\right)^n \le 2e^{-\epsilon n/2}.$$

Hence choosing $n \ge 2\ln(2/\delta)/\epsilon$ samples guarantees that the probability of choosing a bad hypothesis is bounded above by δ, and therefore this concept class is PAC learnable.

375

While the above example of learning intervals demonstrates an infinite concept class that is PAC learnable, the approach to this problem of considering intervals around the maximum and minimum sampled points appears ad hoc. The idea behind this approach, however, can be generalized. Observe that a concept class C over input set X defines a range space (X, C). We show that the number of examples required to PAC learn a concept class is the same as the number of samples needed to construct an ϵ-net for a range space of VC dimension equal to the VC dimension of the range space defined by the concept class.

Theorem 14.13: *Let C be a concept class that defines a range space with VC dimension d. For any $0 < \delta, \epsilon \le 1/2$, there is an*

$$m = O\left(\frac{d}{\epsilon} \ln \frac{d}{\epsilon} + \frac{1}{\epsilon} \ln \frac{1}{\delta}\right)$$

such that C is PAC learnable with m samples.

Proof: Let X be the ground set of inputs and assume that $c \in C$ is the correct classification. For any $c' \in C, c' \neq c$ let $\Delta(c', c) = \{x \mid c(x) \neq c'(x)\}$, where $c(x)$ and $c'(x)$ are the labeling functions for c and c' respectively. Let $\Delta(c) = \{\Delta(c', c) \mid c' \in C\}$. That is, $\Delta(c)$ is a collection of all the possible sets of points of disagreement with the correct classification. The symmetric difference range space with respect to C and c is $(X, \Delta(c))$. We prove the following lemma about the symmetric difference range space.

Lemma 14.14: *The VC dimension of $(X, \Delta(c))$ is equal to the VC dimension of (X, C).*

Proof: For any set $S \subseteq X$ we define a bijection from the projection of (X, C) on S, denoted by C_S, to the projection of $(X, \Delta(c))$ on S, denoted by $\Delta(c)_S$. The bijection maps each element $c' \cap S \in C_S$ to $\Delta(c' \cap S, c \cap S) \in \Delta(c)_S$. To show this is a bijection, we first consider two elements $c', c'' \in C$ with $c' \cap S \neq c'' \cap S$, and show that $\Delta(c' \cap S, c \cap S) \neq \Delta(c'' \cap S, c \cap S)$. If $c' \cap S \neq c'' \cap S$, then there is an element $y \in S$ such that $c'(y) \neq c''(y)$. Without loss of generality, assume that $c'(y) \neq c(y)$ but $c''(y) = c(y)$. In that case $y \in \Delta(c' \cap S, c) \cap S$ but $y \notin \Delta(c'' \cap S, c \cap S)$. Similarly, if for two elements $c', c'' \in C$ there is an element $y \in S$ such that $\Delta(c' \cap S, c \cap S) \neq \Delta(c'' \cap S, c \cap S)$, then there is an element $y \in S$ such that $c'(y) \neq c''(y)$, so $c' \cap S \neq c'' \cap S$, proving the bijection.

Thus, for any $S \subseteq X$, $|C_S| = |\Delta(c)_S|$, and S is shattered by C if and only if it is shattered by $\Delta(c)$. The two range spaces therefore have the same VC dimension. ∎

Since the range space $(X, \Delta(c))$ has a VC dimension d, by Theorem 14.8 there is an

$$m = O\left(\frac{d}{\epsilon} \ln \frac{d}{\epsilon} + \frac{1}{\epsilon} \ln \frac{1}{\delta}\right)$$

so that any sample of size m or larger is, with probability at least $1 - \delta$, an ϵ-net for that range space, and therefore has a nonempty intersection with every set $\Delta(c', c)$ that has probability at least ϵ. Thus, with probability at least $1 - \delta$, our training set allows the algorithm to exclude any hypothesis with error probability at least ϵ. ∎

We saw in Section 14.2.1 that the VC dimension of the collection of closed intervals on $\mathbb{R}$ is 2. Applying Theorem 14.13 to the problem of learning an interval on the line gives an alternative proof to the result we saw in Section 14.4 that this range space can be learned with $O(\frac{1}{\epsilon} \ln \frac{1}{\delta})$ samples.

14.5. The ϵ-sample Theorem

Recall that an ϵ-sample for a range space $(X, \mathcal{R})$ maintains the relative probability weight of all sets $R \in \mathcal{R}$ within a tolerance of ϵ (Definition 14.6), while an ϵ-net just includes at least one element from each range with total probability at least ϵ. Surprisingly, adding just another $O(1/\epsilon)$ factor to the sample size gives an ϵ-sample, again with probability at least $1 - \delta$. The proof of this result uses the same "double sampling" method as in the proof of the ϵ-net theorem, albeit with a somewhat more complicated argument.

Theorem 14.15: *Let $(X, \mathcal{R})$ be a range space with VC dimension d and let $\mathcal{D}$ be a probability distribution on X. For any $0 < \epsilon, \delta < 1/2$, there is an*

$$m = O\left(\frac{d}{\epsilon^2} \ln \frac{d}{\epsilon} + \frac{1}{\epsilon^2} \ln \frac{1}{\delta}\right)$$

such that a random sample from $\mathcal{D}$ of size greater than or equal to m is an ϵ-sample for X with probability at least $1 - \delta$.

Proof: Let M be a set of m independent samples from X according to $\mathcal{D}$, and let E_1 be the event that M is not an ϵ-sample for X with respect to the distribution $\mathcal{D}$, i.e.

$$E_1 = \left\{ \exists R \in \mathcal{R} \mid \left| \mathrm{Pr}_{\mathcal{D}}(R) - \frac{|M \cap R|}{|M|} \right| > \epsilon \right\}.$$

We want to show that $\mathrm{Pr}(E_1) \leq \delta$ for a suitable m. We choose a second set T of m independent samples from X according to $\mathcal{D}$, and define E_2 to be the event that some range R is not well approximated by M but is reasonably well approximated by T:

$$E_2 = \left\{ \exists R \in \mathcal{R} \mid \left| \frac{|R \cap M|}{|M|} - \mathrm{Pr}_{\mathcal{D}}(R) \right| > \epsilon \text{ and } \left| \frac{|R \cap T|}{|T|} - \mathrm{Pr}_{\mathcal{D}}(R) \right| \leq \frac{\epsilon}{2} \right\}.$$

Lemma 14.16:

$$\mathrm{Pr}(E_2) \leq \mathrm{Pr}(E_1) \leq 2 \mathrm{Pr}(E_2).$$

Proof: Clearly the event E_2 is included in the event E_1, thus $\mathrm{Pr}(E_2) \leq \mathrm{Pr}(E_1)$. For the second inequality we again use conditional probability. If E_1 holds, there is some particular R' so that $\left| \frac{|R' \cap M|}{|M|} - \mathrm{Pr}_{\mathcal{D}}(R') \right| > \epsilon$. Therefore,

$$\frac{\mathrm{Pr}(E_2)}{\mathrm{Pr}(E_1)} = \frac{\mathrm{Pr}(E_1 \cap E_2)}{\mathrm{Pr}(E_1)} = \mathrm{Pr}(E_2 \mid E_1) \geq \mathrm{Pr}\left(\left| \frac{|R' \cap T|}{|T|} - \mathrm{Pr}_{\mathcal{D}}(R') \right| \leq \frac{\epsilon}{2} \right).$$

Now for a fixed range R' and a random sample T, the random variable $|T \cap R'|$ has a binomial distribution $B(m, \mathrm{Pr}_{\mathcal{D}}(R'))$, and applying the Chernoff bound (Theorem 4.5)

377

we have

$$\Pr(||T \cap R'| - m\Pr_{\mathcal{D}}(R')| > \epsilon m/2) \leq 2e^{-\epsilon m/12} < 1/2$$

for $m \geq 24/\epsilon$. We conclude

$$\frac{\Pr(E_2)}{\Pr(E_1)} = \Pr(E_2 \mid E_1) \geq \Pr\left(\left|\frac{|R' \cap T|}{|T|} - \Pr_{\mathcal{D}}(R')\right| \leq \frac{\epsilon}{2}\right) \geq 1/2. \qquad \blacksquare$$

Next we bound the probability of E_2 by the probability of a larger event E_2':

$$E_2' = \left\{\exists R \in \mathcal{R} \mid ||R \cap T| - |R \cap M|| \geq \frac{\epsilon}{2}m\right\}.$$

To see that $E_2 \subseteq E_2'$, assume that a set R satisfies the conditions of E_2, i.e.

$$||R \cap M| - m\Pr_{\mathcal{D}}(R)| \geq \epsilon m,$$

and

$$||R \cap T| - m\Pr_{\mathcal{D}}(R)| \leq \epsilon m/2.$$

In that case

$$||R \cap M| - m\Pr_{\mathcal{D}}(R)| - ||R \cap T| - m\Pr_{\mathcal{D}}(R)| \geq \epsilon m/2,$$

and by the reverse triangle inequality[2]

$$||R \cap T| - |R \cap M|| \geq ||R \cap M| - m\Pr_{\mathcal{D}}(R)| - ||R \cap T| - m\Pr_{\mathcal{D}}(R)| \geq \epsilon m/2.$$

The event E_2' depends only on the elements in $M \cup T$.

Lemma 14.17:

$$\Pr(E_2) \leq \Pr(E_2') \leq (2m)^d e^{-\epsilon^2 m/8}.$$

Proof: Since M and T are random samples, we can assume that we first choose a random sample of $2m$ elements $Z = z_1, \ldots, z_{2m}$ and then partition it randomly into two sets of size m each. Since Z is a random sample, any partition that is independent of the actual values of the elements generates two random samples. We will use the following partition: for each pair of sampled items z_{2i-1} and z_{2i}, $i = 1, \ldots, m$, with probability $1/2$ (independent of other choices) we place z_{2i-1} in T and z_{2i} in M, otherwise we place z_{2i-1} in M and z_{2i} in T.

For a fixed $R \in \mathcal{R}$, let E_R be the event $\{||R \cap T| - |R \cap M|| \geq \frac{\epsilon}{2}m\}$. To bound the probability of E_R we consider the contribution of the assignment of each pair z_{2i-1}, z_{2i} to the value of $||R \cap T| - |R \cap M||$. If the two items are both in R or the two items are both not in R, the contribution of the pair is 0. If one item is in R and the other is not in R then the contribution of the pair is 1 with probability $1/2$ and -1 with probability

---

[2] The reverse triangle inequality is simply $|x - y| \geq ||x| - |y||$, which follows easily from the triangle inequality.

1/2. There are no more than m such pairs, so from the Chernoff bound in Theorem 4.7 we can conclude

$$\Pr(E_R) \leq e^{-\epsilon^2 m/8}.$$

By Theorem 14.1 the projection of $\mathcal{R}$ on Z has no more than $(2m)^d$ ranges. Thus, by the union bound we have

$$\Pr(E_2') \leq (2m)^d e^{-\epsilon^2 m/8}. \qquad\blacksquare$$

To complete the proof of Theorem 14.15 we show that for

$$m \geq \frac{32d}{\epsilon^2} \ln \frac{64d}{\epsilon^2} + \frac{16}{\epsilon^2} \ln \frac{2}{\delta}$$

we have

$$\Pr(E_1) \leq 2 \Pr(E_2') \leq 2(2m)^d e^{-\epsilon^2 m/8} \leq \delta.$$

We remark that this value of m satisfies

$$m = O\left(\frac{d}{\epsilon^2} \ln \frac{d}{\epsilon} + \frac{1}{\epsilon^2} \ln \frac{1}{\delta} \right)$$

as given in the statement of the theorem; although our explicit bound has a $\ln \frac{64d}{\epsilon^2}$, that term is $O(\ln \frac{d}{\epsilon})$. Equivalently, we require

$$\epsilon^2 m/8 \geq \ln(2/\delta) + d \ln(2m).$$

Clearly it holds that $\epsilon^2 m/16 \geq \ln(2/\delta)$, since $m > \frac{16}{\epsilon^2} \ln \frac{2}{\delta}$. It therefore suffices to show that $\epsilon^2 m/16 \geq d \ln(2m)$ to complete the proof.

Applying Lemma 14.3 with $y = 2m \geq \frac{64d}{\epsilon^2} \ln \frac{64d}{\epsilon^2}$ and $x = \frac{64d}{\epsilon^2}$, we have

$$\frac{4m}{\ln(2m)} \geq \frac{64d}{\epsilon^2},$$

so

$$\frac{\epsilon^2 m}{16} \geq d \ln(2m)$$

as required. $\qquad\blacksquare$

Since an ϵ-sample is also an ϵ-net, the lower bound on the sample complexity of ϵ-nets in Theorem 14.11 holds for ϵ-samples. Together with the upper bound of Theorem 14.15, this gives:

Theorem 14.18: *A range space has the uniform convergence property if and only if its VC dimension is finite.*

14.5.1. *Application: Agnostic Learning*

In our discussion of PAC learning in Section 14.4, we assumed that the algorithm is given a concept class $\mathcal{C}$ that includes the correct classification c. That is, there is a classification that is correct on all items in X, and in particular conforms with all examples in the training set. This assumption does not hold in most applications. First, the training set may have some errors. Second, we may not know any concept class that is guaranteed to include the correct classification and is also simple to represent and compute. In this section we extend our discussion of PAC learning to the case in which the concept class does not necessarily include a perfectly correct classification, which is referred to as the *unrealizable* case or *agnostic* learning. Since the concept class may not have a correct or even close to correct classification, the goal of the the algorithm in this case is to select a classification $c' \in C$ with an error that is no more than ϵ larger than that of any other classification in C. Formally, let c be the correct classification (which may not be in C). We require the output classification c' to satisfy the following inequality:

$$\Pr_D(c'(x) \neq c(x)) \leq \inf_{h \in C} \Pr_D(h(x) \neq c(x)) + \epsilon.$$

Recall from Section 14.4 that the symmetric difference range space with respect to the concept class C and the correct classification c is $(X, \Delta(c))$. If the examples in the training set define an $\epsilon/2$-sample for that range space then the algorithm has sufficiently many examples to estimate the error probability of each $c' \in C$ to within an additive error $\epsilon/2$, and thus can select a classification that satisfies the above requirement.[3] Applying Theorem 14.15, agnostic learning of a concept class with VC dimension d requires $O\left(\min\left(|X|, \frac{d}{\epsilon^2} \ln \frac{d}{\epsilon^2} + \frac{1}{\epsilon^2} \ln \frac{1}{\delta}\right)\right)$ samples.

Finally, we state a general characterization of concept classes that are agnostic PAC learnable.

Theorem 14.19: *The following three conditions are equivalent:*

1. A concept class C over a domain X is agnostic PAC learnable.
2. The range space (X, C) has the uniform convergence property.
3. The range space (X, C) has a finite VC dimension.

14.5.2. Application: Data Mining

Data mining involves extracting useful information from raw data. In some cases, such as anomaly detection, one is interested in rare events. Finding such rare events may require a complete analysis of the entire data set that is expensive in both computational time and memory requirements. In other cases, however, the goal of data mining is to detect major patterns or trends in data and ignore random fluctuations. In such settings, analyzing a properly selected sample of the data instead of the entire data set can give an excellent approximation at a fraction of the cost. The crucial question here is how large the sample should be to give a reliable estimate. We give here two examples where using ϵ-samples can provide an answer to this question.

---

[3] Recall that we are only concerned here with the sampling complexity of the problem. Depending on the particular concept class, the computation cost may not be practically feasible.

Example: Estimating dense neighborhoods

Assume that we are given a large set of n points in the plane and we need to answer a sequence of queries of the form "what fraction of the points are at distance at most r from point (x, y)?", for arbitrary values of (x, y) and r. Estimates of this kind are used by businesses to determine where to locate new stores or other resources. For example, if points represent home locations for customers, query locations (x, y) might represent possible locations for a bank to place an automated teller machine, in which case quick estimates of how many customers are near the location would be useful for planning purposes.

We can answer each query by scanning the entire set of n points. Alternatively, we can define a range space $(\mathbb{R}^2, \mathcal{R})$, where $\mathcal{R}$ includes, for each pair $(x, y) \in \mathbb{R}^2$ and $r \in \mathbb{R}^+$, the set of all the points inside the disk of radius r centered at (x, y). Since the VC dimension of the set of all disks on the plane is 3 (see Exercise 14.6), we can sample a random set of $m = O\left(\frac{1}{\epsilon^2} \ln \frac{1}{\epsilon} + \frac{1}{\epsilon^2} \ln \frac{1}{\delta}\right)$ points and give fast approximate answers to all the queries by scanning only the sample.

Generating a random sample may require an initial scan of all the n points, but we need to execute it only once. The ϵ-sample theorem guarantees that with probability at least $1 - \delta$, the answers to *all* of the queries are within ϵ of the correct value. Furthermore, since the ϵ-sample estimates all possible disks, we could also use it for other purposes, such as approximately identifying the k densest disks.

Example: Mining frequent itemsets

Consider a supermarket that wants to design discounts for customers based on buying a collection of items. In this case, the supermarket is interested not only in what are the most frequent items purchased, but also in what sets of items are most frequently bought together. This problem arises in many settings, and is commonly referred to as the problem of mining frequent itemsets. Formally, we can describe the problem as follows: we are given a set of items $\mathcal{I}$ and a collection of transactions $\mathcal{T}$, where a transaction is a subset of $\mathcal{I}$. We are interested in sets of items that appear in many transactions, where what is meant by many transactions can depend on the setting. We might use a threshold, or a percentage of transactions.

Mining frequent itemsets is challenging to accomplish efficiently, both because the number of customer transactions is usually large, and because it takes significant memory to store all possible frequent itemsets. Even if one limits the problem to itemsets of size up to k, there are $\binom{|\mathcal{I}|}{k}$ possible itemsets, which grows large even for small k. All known exact solutions to this problem require either several passes over the data or significant storage or both to store candidate frequent itemsets and their counts. On the other hand, solving the problem on a relatively small sample can give effective results much more efficiently.

A natural goal would be to make sure we find all sufficiently frequent itemsets and discard all sufficiently infrequent itemsets. There might be some itemsets that are ambiguously in between the thresholds we set for frequent and infrequent itemsets, and that could therefore be characterized either way. Suppose that we want to correctly characterize all sets with frequency greater than θ as frequent and all sets with frequency less than $\theta - \epsilon$ as infrequent; sets with frequency $[\theta - \epsilon, \theta]$ would be in the ambiguous range. How many transactions do we need to sample?

Our goal is to approximate the true frequency of each set within an additive error of $\epsilon/2$. Then we can treat all sets with frequency at least $\theta - \epsilon/2$ as frequent itemsets and all sets with frequency less than $\theta - \epsilon/2$ as infrequent itemsets, ensuring that we correctly characterize sets with frequency greater than θ and sets with frequency less than $\theta - \epsilon$.

If all transactions have size at most ℓ, then there are $O(|\mathcal{I}|^\ell)$ different itemsets that could be frequent. Applying a Chernoff bound and a union bound would require a sample of size $\Omega\left(\frac{\theta}{\epsilon^2}\left(\ell \ln |\mathcal{I}| + \ln \frac{1}{\delta}\right)\right)$. In practice, $\ell << |\mathcal{I}|$. In such a case an ϵ-sample can give a significantly better bound. (Although, strictly speaking, here we need an $(\epsilon/2)$-sample.)

For each subset $s \subseteq \mathcal{I}$, let $T(s) = \{t \in \mathcal{T} \text{ and } s \subseteq t\}$ denote the collection of all transactions in the data set that include s. Let $\mathcal{R} = \{T(s) \mid s \subseteq \mathcal{I}\}$, and consider the range space $(\mathcal{T}, \mathcal{R})$. We would like to bound the VC dimension of this range space by a parameter that can be evaluated in one pass over the data (say when the data is first loaded to the system). We first observe that the VC dimension is bounded by ℓ, the maximum size of any transaction in the data set. Indeed, a transaction of size q has 2^q subsets and is therefore included in no more than 2^q ranges. Since no transaction can belong to more than 2^ℓ ranges, no set of more than ℓ transactions can be shattered. Thus, by Theorem 14.15, with probability at least $1 - \delta$, a sample of size

$$O\left(\frac{\ell}{\epsilon^2} \ln \frac{\ell}{\epsilon} + \frac{1}{\epsilon^2} \ln \frac{1}{\delta}\right) \tag{14.1}$$

can guarantee that all itemsets are accurately determined to within $\epsilon/2$ of their true proportion with probability at least $1 - \delta$, and thus is sufficient for identifying all the frequent itemsets. A better bound is proven in Exercise 14.12.

14.6. Rademacher Complexity

Rademacher complexity is an alternative approach for computing sample complexity. Unlike the VC-dimension based bounds, which were distribution independent, the Rademacher complexity bounds depend on the training set distribution, and thus can give better bounds for specific input distributions. Furthermore, the Rademacher complexity can, in principle, be estimated from the training set, allowing for strong bounds derived from a sample itself. Another advantage of Rademacher complexity is that it can be applied to the estimation of any function, not just 0–1 classification functions. (There are, to be clear, generalizations of VC dimensions to non-binary function.)

To motivate the definition of Rademacher averages, let us start with the binary classification setting we used in section 14.1 and then generalize. We have a training set $(x_1, c(x_1)), \ldots, (x_m, c(x_m))$ where $x_i \in U$ and $c(x_i) \in \{-1, 1\}$, and a set of possible hypotheses $h \in \mathcal{C}$ where each h is a function from the universe U to $\{-1, 1\}$. The *training error* of a hypothesis on the training set is the fraction of samples where the hypothesis disagrees with the given classification. Formally,

$$\hat{err}(h) = \frac{1}{m}|\{i : h(x_i) \neq c(x_i), 1 \leq i \leq m\}|.$$

Now we make use of the fact that, because $h(x_i)$ and $c(x_i)$ take on values in $\{-1, 1\}$,

$$\frac{1 - c(x_i)h(x_i)}{2} = \begin{cases} 0 & \text{if } c(x_i) = h(x_i), \\ 1 & \text{if } c(x_i) \neq h(x_i). \end{cases}$$

Hence we can write

$$\hat{err}(h) = \frac{1}{m}\sum_{i=1}^{m}\frac{1 - c(x_i)h(x_i)}{2}$$

$$= \frac{1}{2} - \frac{1}{2m}\sum_{i=1}^{m}c(x_i)h(x_i).$$

The expression $\frac{1}{m}\sum_{i=1}^{m}c(x_i)h(x_i)$ represents the correlation between c and h; if c and h always agree, the value of the expression is 1, and if they alway disagree, the value is -1. The hypothesis that minimizes the training error is the hypothesis that maximizes the correlation.

Now, given a collection of sample points x_i, $1 \leq i \leq m$, we consider how well our class of possible hypotheses C can align with all possible classifications of these sample points. To consider all possible classifications, we use the *Rademacher variables*: m independent random variables, $\sigma = (\sigma_1, \ldots, \sigma_m)$, with $\Pr(\sigma_i = -1) = \Pr(\sigma_i = 1) = 1/2$. The hypothesis that aligns best with fixed values of the Rademacher variables σ is then the one that maximizes the value

$$\frac{1}{m}\sum_{i=1}^{m}\sigma_i h(x_i),$$

and our training error is

$$\frac{1}{2} - \max_{h \in C}\frac{1}{2m}\sum_{i=1}^{m}\sigma_i h(x_i).$$

To consider all possible sample points, we consider the expectation over all possible outcomes for σ, or

$$\mathbf{E}_\sigma \max_{h \in C}\frac{1}{m}\sum_{i=1}^{m}\sigma_i h(x_i). \tag{14.2}$$

This expression corresponds intuitively to how expressive our class of hypotheses C is. For example, if C consisted of just a single hypothesis h, the expectation would be 0, as $h(x_i) = \sigma_i$ with probability $1/2$ for any randomly chosen σ. On the other hand, if C shatters the set $\{x_1, x_2, \ldots, x_m\}$, then the expectation would be 1, as there would be some $h \in C$ so that $h(x_i) = \sigma_i$ for all i for each possible randomly chosen σ. In this particular setting, the expectation is always between 0 and 1, and intuitively a higher number corresponds to a more expressive set of hypotheses.

To move to a more general definition of Rademacher averages, instead of thinking of sets of hypotheses, we consider a set of real-valued functions $\mathcal{F}$, where the inputs to the function are defined according to a probability space with distribution $\mathcal{D}$. Hence, for $f \in \mathcal{F}$, when we refer to $\mathbf{E}[f]$, this would correspond to $\mathbf{E}[f(Z)]$ where Z is a random variable with distribution $\mathcal{D}$. We generalize the expectation (14.2) as follows.

Definition 14.10: *The* empirical Rademacher average *of a set of functions $\mathcal{F}$ with respect to a sample $S = \{z_1, \ldots, z_m\}$, is defined as*

$$\tilde{R}_m(\mathcal{F}, S) = \mathbf{E}_\sigma \left[\sup_{f \in \mathcal{F}} \frac{1}{m} \sum_{i=1}^{m} \sigma_i f(z_i) \right],$$

where the expectation is taken over the distribution of the Rademacher variables $\sigma = (\sigma_1, \ldots, \sigma_m)$.

We remark that we use sup instead of max since we are dealing with a family of real-valued functions, so the maximum technically may not exist.

For a fixed assignment of values to the Rademacher variables the value of $\sup_{f \in \mathcal{F}} \frac{1}{m} \sum_{i=1}^{m} \sigma_i f(z_i)$ represents the best correlation between any function in $\mathcal{F}$ and the vector $(\sigma_1, \ldots, \sigma_m)$, generalizing the correlation for binary classifications. The empirical Rademacher average therefore measures how well one can correlate random partitions of the sample with some function in the set $\mathcal{F}$, which provides a measure of how expressive the set is. We therefore use the terms empirical Rademacher average and empirical Rademacher complexity interchangeably (both terms are used in the literature).

Now let us look at the empirical Rademacher average in a different way. For large m, an average $\frac{1}{m} \sum_{i=1}^{m} f(z_i)$ over a random sample $S = \{z_1, \ldots, z_m\}$, should provide a good approximation to $\mathbf{E}[f]$. Multiplying by the Rademacher variables, the expression $\frac{1}{m} \sum_{i=1}^{m} \sigma_i f(z_i)$ corresponds to splitting the sample S into two subsamples, corresponding to the values of i where $\sigma_i = 1$ and the values of i where $\sigma_i = -1$. If S is a random sample then the expression is similar to the difference between the average of the two random subsamples, and hence the expectation

$$\mathbf{E}_\sigma \left[\frac{1}{m} \sum_{i=1}^{m} \sigma_i f(z_i) \right],$$

should be small. Finally, the empirical Rademacher complexity

$$\tilde{R}_m(\mathcal{F}, S) = \mathbf{E}_\sigma \left[\sup_{f \in \mathcal{F}} \frac{1}{m} \sum_{i=1}^{m} \sigma_i f(z_i) \right]$$

considers the supremum of this expectation over all functions in $\mathcal{F}$. Intuitively, if the empirical Rademacher average with respect to a sample of size m is small, then we expect m to be sufficiently large for a sample to provide a good estimate for all functions in $\mathcal{F}$. We formulate and prove this intuition in Theorem 14.20.

To remove the dependency on a particular sample we can take an expectation over the distribution of all samples S of size m, where the samples are taken from the distribution $\mathcal{D}$.

Definition 14.11: *The* Rademacher average *of $\mathcal{F}$ is defined as*

$$R_m(\mathcal{F}) = \mathbf{E}_S[\tilde{R}_m(\mathcal{F}, S)] = \mathbf{E}_S\mathbf{E}_\sigma\left[\sup_{f\in\mathcal{F}} \frac{1}{m}\sum_{i=1}^{m}\sigma_i f(z_i)\right],$$

where the expectation over S corresponds to samples of size m from a given distribution $\mathcal{D}$.

We similarly use the terms Rademacher average and Rademacher complexity interchangeably.

14.6.1. *Rademacher Complexity and Sample Error*

A key property of the Rademacher complexity of a set of functions $\mathcal{F}$ is that it bounds the expected maximum error in estimating the mean of any function $f \in \mathcal{F}$ using a sample.

Let $\mathbf{E}_\mathcal{D}[f(z)]$ be the true mean of f with respect to distribution $\mathcal{D}$. The estimate of $\mathbf{E}_\mathcal{D}[f(z)]$ using the sample $S = \{z_1, \ldots, z_m\}$ is $\frac{1}{m}\sum_{i=1}^{m} f(z_i)$. The expected maximum error, averaged over all samples of size m from $\mathcal{D}$, is given by

$$\mathbf{E}_S\left[\sup_{f\in\mathcal{F}}\left(\mathbf{E}_\mathcal{D}[f(z)] - \frac{1}{m}\sum_{i=1}^{m} f(z_i)\right)\right].$$

The following theorem bounds this error in terms of the Rademacher complexity of $\mathcal{F}$.

Theorem 14.20:

$$\mathbf{E}_S\left[\sup_{f\in\mathcal{F}}\left(\mathbf{E}_\mathcal{D}[f(z)] - \frac{1}{m}\sum_{i=1}^{m} f(z_i)\right)\right] \leq 2R_m(\mathcal{F}).$$

Proof: Pick a second sample $S' = \{z_1', \ldots, z_m'\}$.

$$\mathbf{E}_S\left[\sup_{f\in\mathcal{F}}\left(\mathbf{E}_\mathcal{D}[f(z)] - \frac{1}{m}\sum_{i=1}^{m} f(z_i)\right)\right]$$

$$= \mathbf{E}_S\left[\sup_{f\in\mathcal{F}}\left(\mathbf{E}_{S'}\frac{1}{m}\sum_{i=1}^{m} f(z_i') - \frac{1}{m}\sum_{i=1}^{m} f(z_i)\right)\right]$$

$$\leq \mathbf{E}_{S,S'}\left[\sup_{f\in\mathcal{F}}\left(\frac{1}{m}\sum_{i=1}^{m} f(z_i') - \frac{1}{m}\sum_{i=1}^{m} f(z_i)\right)\right]$$

$$= \mathbf{E}_{S,S',\sigma}\left[\sup_{f\in\mathcal{F}}\left(\frac{1}{m}\sum_{i=1}^{m}\sigma_i(f(z_i) - f(z_i'))\right)\right]$$

$$\leq \mathbf{E}_{S,\sigma}\left[\sup_{f\in\mathcal{F}}\frac{1}{m}\sum_{i=1}^{m}\sigma_i f(z_i)\right] + \mathbf{E}_{S',\sigma}\left[\sup_{f\in\mathcal{F}}\frac{1}{m}\sum_{i=1}^{m}\sigma_i f(z_i')\right]$$

$$= 2R_m(\mathcal{F}).$$

The first equality holds because the expectation from the sample S' is the expectation of f. The first inequality, in which the order of the expectation with respect to S' with the operation $\sup_{f \in \mathcal{F}}$ is interchanged, follows from Jensen's inequaliy (Theorem 2.4), and the fact that supremum is a convex function. For the second equality, we use the fact that multiplying $f(z_i) - f(z_i')$ by a Rademacher variable σ_i does not change the expectation of the sum. If $\sigma_i = 1$ there is clearly no change, and if $\sigma_i = -1$ this is equivalent to switching z_i and z_i' between the two samples, which does not change the expectation. For the second inequality, we use that σ_i and $-\sigma_i$ have the same distribution, so we can change the sign to simplify the expression. ∎

Next we show that for bounded functions the Rademacher complexity is well approximated by the empirical Rademacher complexity, and the estimation error is well approximated by twice the Rademacher complexity, thereby obtaining a probabilistic bound on the estimation error of any bounded function in $\mathcal{F}$ from a sample.

Theorem 14.21: *Let $\mathcal{F}$ be a set of functions such that for any $f \in \mathcal{F}$ and for any two values x and y in the domain of f, $|f(x) - f(y)| \le c$ for some constant c. Let $R_m(\mathcal{F})$ be the Rademacher complexity, and $\tilde{R}_m(\mathcal{F}, S)$ the empirical Rademacher complexity of the set $\mathcal{F}$, with respect to a random sample $S = \{z_1, \ldots, z_m\}$ of size m from a distribution $\mathcal{D}$.*

(1) For any $\epsilon \in (0, 1)$,

$$\Pr(|\tilde{R}_m(\mathcal{F}, S) - R_m(\mathcal{F})|) \ge \epsilon) \le 2e^{-2m\epsilon^2/c^2}.$$

(2) For all $f \in \mathcal{F}$ and $\epsilon \in (0, 1)$,

$$\Pr\left(\mathbf{E}_{\mathcal{D}}[f(z)] - \frac{1}{m} \sum_{i=1}^{m} f(z_i) \ge 2\tilde{R}_m(\mathcal{F}, S) + 3\epsilon \right) \le 2e^{-2m\epsilon^2/c^2}.$$

Proof: To prove the first part of the theorem we observe that $\tilde{R}_m(\mathcal{F}, S)$ is a function of m random variables, $z_1, \ldots, z_m$, and any change in one of these variables can change the value of $\tilde{R}_m(\mathcal{F}, S)$ by no more than c/m. Since $\mathbf{E}_S[\tilde{R}_m(\mathcal{F}, S)] = R_m(\mathcal{F})$ we can apply Theorem 13.7 to obtain

$$\Pr(|\tilde{R}_m(\mathcal{F}, S) - R_m(\mathcal{F})| \ge \epsilon) \le 2e^{-2m\epsilon^2/c^2}.$$

To prove the second part, we observe that $\mathbf{E}_{\mathcal{D}}[f(z)] - \frac{1}{m} \sum_{i=1}^{m} f(z_i)$ is a function of $z_1, \ldots, z_m$, and a change in one of the z_i changes the value of that function by no more than c/m. Applying a one-sided form of Theorem 13.7 we have

$$\Pr\left(\left(\mathbf{E}_{\mathcal{D}}[f(z)] - \frac{1}{m} \sum_{i=1}^{m} f(z_i) \right) - \mathbf{E}_S\left[\mathbf{E}_{\mathcal{D}}[f(z)] - \frac{1}{m} \sum_{i=1}^{m} f(z_i) \right] \ge \epsilon \right) \le e^{-2m\epsilon^2/c^2}.$$

We now apply the bound in Theorem 14.20,

$$\mathbf{E}_S\left[\mathbf{E}_{\mathcal{D}}[f(z)] - \frac{1}{m} \sum_{i=1}^{m} f(z_i) \right] \le 2R_m(\mathcal{F}),$$

to obtain,

$$\Pr\left(\mathbf{E}_{\mathcal{D}}[f(z)] - \frac{1}{m}\sum_{i=1}^{m} f(z_i) \geq 2R_m(\mathcal{F}) + \epsilon\right) \leq e^{-2m\epsilon^2/c^2}. \tag{14.3}$$

From the first part of the theorem we know that $R_m(\mathcal{F}) \leq \tilde{R}_m(\mathcal{F}, S) + \epsilon$ with probability at least $1 - e^{-2m\epsilon^2/c^2}$. Combining this with Eqn. (14.3), we have the second part of the theorem,

$$\Pr\left(\mathbf{E}_{\mathcal{D}}[f(z)] - \frac{1}{m}\sum_{i=1}^{m} f(z_i) \geq 2\tilde{R}_m(\mathcal{F}, S) + 3\epsilon\right) \leq 2e^{-2m\epsilon^2/c^2}. \qquad \blacksquare$$

14.6.2. Estimating the Rademacher Complexity

While the Rademacher complexity can, in principle, be computed from a sample, in practice it is often hard to compute the expected supremum over a large (or even infinite) set of functions. Massart's theorem provides a bound that is often easy to compute for finite sets of functions.

Theorem 14.22 [Massart's theorem]: *Assume that $|\mathcal{F}|$ is finite. Let $S = \{z_1, \ldots, z_m\}$ be a sample, and let*

$$B = \max_{f \in \mathcal{F}} \left(\sum_{i=1}^{m} f^2(z_i)\right)^{\frac{1}{2}}$$

then

$$\tilde{R}_m(\mathcal{F}, S) \leq \frac{B\sqrt{2\ln|\mathcal{F}|}}{m}.$$

Proof: For any $s > 0$,

$$e^{sm\tilde{R}_m(\mathcal{F},S)} = e^{s\mathbf{E}_\sigma\left[\sup_{f\in\mathcal{F}}\sum_{i=1}^{m}\sigma_i f(z_i)\right]},$$

where the expectation is taken over the assignments of the Rademacher variables $\sigma = (\sigma_1, \ldots, \sigma_m)$.

By Jensen's inequality (Theorem 2.4),

$$e^{s\mathbf{E}_\sigma\left[\sup_{f\in\mathcal{F}}\sum_{i=1}^{m}\sigma_i f(z_i)\right]} \leq \mathbf{E}_\sigma\left[e^{s\sup_{f\in\mathcal{F}}\sum_{i=1}^{m}\sigma_i f(z_i)}\right]$$

$$= \mathbf{E}_\sigma\left[\sup_{f\in\mathcal{F}}\left(e^{\sum_{i=1}^{m} s\sigma_i f(z_i)}\right)\right]$$

$$\leq \sum_{f\in\mathcal{F}}\mathbf{E}_\sigma\left[\left(e^{\sum_{i=1}^{m} s\sigma_i f(z_i)}\right)\right]$$

$$= \sum_{f\in\mathcal{F}}\mathbf{E}_\sigma\left[\prod_{i=1}^{m} e^{s\sigma_i f(z_i)}\right]$$

$$= \sum_{f\in\mathcal{F}}\prod_{i=1}^{m}\mathbf{E}_\sigma\left[e^{s\sigma_i f(z_i)}\right].$$

387

Here the first line follows from Jensen's inequality, and the second line is just a rearrangement of terms. The third line bounds the supremum by a summation, which is possible since all the terms are positive. The fourth line changes the sum in the exponent to a product, and the last line arises from the independence of the sample values.

Since $\mathbf{E}[\sigma_i f(z_i)] = 0$ and $-f(z_i) \le \sigma_i f(z_i) \le f(z_i)$, we can apply Hoeffding's Lemma (Lemma 4.13) to obtain

$$\mathbf{E}\left[e^{s\sigma_i f(z_i)}\right] \le e^{s^2(2f(z_i))^2/8} = e^{s^2 f(z_i)^2/2}.$$

Thus,

$$e^{sm\tilde{R}_m(\mathcal{F},S)} = e^{s\mathbf{E}[\sup_{f\in\mathcal{F}}\sum_{i=1}^{m}\sigma_i f(z_i)]}$$

$$\le \sum_{f\in\mathcal{F}}\prod_{i=1}^{m} e^{s^2 f(z_i)^2/2}$$

$$= \sum_{f\in\mathcal{F}} e^{s^2/2\sum_{i=1}^{m} f(z_i)^2}$$

$$\le |\mathcal{F}|e^{(s^2 B^2)/2}.$$

Hence, for any $s > 0$,

$$\tilde{R}_m(\mathcal{F}, S) \le \frac{1}{m}\left(\frac{\ln|\mathcal{F}|}{s} + \frac{sB^2}{2}\right).$$

Setting $s = \frac{\sqrt{2\ln|\mathcal{F}|}}{B}$ yields

$$\tilde{R}_m(\mathcal{F}, S) \le \frac{B\sqrt{2\ln|\mathcal{F}|}}{m}. \qquad \blacksquare$$

14.6.3. Application: Agnostic Learning of a Binary Classification

Let C be a binary concept class defined on a domain X, and let $\mathcal{D}$ be a probability distribution on X. For each $x \in X$ let $c(x)$ be the correct classification of x. For each hypothesis $h \in C$ we define a function $f_h(x)$ by

$$f_h(x) = \begin{cases} 1 & \text{if } h(x) = c(x) \\ -1 & \text{otherwise.} \end{cases}$$

Let $\mathcal{F} = \{f_h \mid h \in C\}$. Our goal is to find $h' \in C$ such that with probability at least $1 - \delta$

$$\mathbf{E}[f_{h'}] \ge \sup_{f_h \in \mathcal{F}} \mathbf{E}[f_h] - \epsilon.$$

Let S be a sample of size m. We apply Theorem 14.22 to bound the empirical Rademacher average $\mathcal{F}$ with respect to S. Since the functions in $\mathcal{F}$ take on only the values -1 and 1,

$$B = \max_{f\in\mathcal{F}}\left(\sum_{i=1}^{m} f^2(z_i)\right)^{\frac{1}{2}} = \sqrt{m},$$

and for a finite $\mathcal{F}$

$$\tilde{R}_m(\mathcal{F}, S) \leq \sqrt{\frac{2 \ln |\mathcal{F}|}{m}}.$$

Next we express this bound in terms of the VC dimension of the concept class C. Each function $f_h \in \mathcal{F}$ corresponds to a hypothesis $h \in C$. Let d be the VC dimension of C. The projection of the range space (X, C) on a sample of size m has no more than m^d different sets, as we know from Theorem 14.1. Thus, the set of different functions we need to consider is bounded by m^d, and hence

$$\tilde{R}_m(\mathcal{F}, S) \leq \sqrt{\frac{2d \ln m}{m}}.$$

The bound on $\tilde{R}_m(\mathcal{F}, S)$ in conjunction with Theorem 14.21 can be used to obtain an alternative bound on the sample complexity of agnostic learning, similar to the bound found in Section 14.5.1. The details are considered in Exercise 14.15. However, for specific distributions, the projection of (X, C) on the training set can be significantly smaller, yielding a smaller Rademacher complexity and smaller sample complexity.

14.7. Exercises

Exercise 14.1: Consider a range space (X, C) where $X = \{1, 2, \ldots, n\}$ and C is the set of all subsets of X of size k for some $k < n$. What is the VC dimension of C?

Exercise 14.2: Consider a range space $(\mathbb{R}^2, C)$ of all axis-aligned rectangles in $\mathbb{R}^2$. That is, $c \in C$ if for some $x_0 < x_1$ and $y_0 < y_1$, $c = \{(x, y) \in \mathbb{R}^2 \mid x_0 \leq x \leq x_1 \text{ and } y_0 \leq y \leq y_1\}$.

(a) Show that the VC dimension of $(\mathbb{R}^2, C)$ is equal to 4. You should show both a set of four points that can be shattered, and show that no larger set can be shattered.
(b) Construct and analyze a PAC learning algorithm for the concept class of all axis-aligned rectangles in $\mathbb{R}^2$.

Exercise 14.3: Consider a range space $(\mathbb{R}^2, C)$ of all axis-aligned squares in $\mathbb{R}^2$. Show that the VC dimension of $(\mathbb{R}^2, C)$ is equal to 3.

Exercise 14.4: Consider a range space $(\mathbb{R}^2, C)$ of all squares (that need not be axis-aligned) in $\mathbb{R}^2$. Show that the VC dimension of $(\mathbb{R}^2, C)$ is equal to 5.

Exercise 14.5: Consider a range space $(\mathbb{R}^3, C)$ of all axis-aligned rectangular boxes in $\mathbb{R}^3$. Find the VC dimension of $(\mathbb{R}^3, C)$; you should show both the largest number of points that can be shattered, and show that no larger set can be shattered.

Exercise 14.6: Prove that the VC dimension of the collection of all closed disks on the plane is 3.

Exercise 14.7: Prove that the VC dimension of the range space $(\mathbb{R}^d, \mathcal{R})$, where $\mathcal{R}$ is the set of all half-spaces in $\mathbb{R}^d$, is at least $d + 1$, by showing that the set consisting of the origin $(0, 0, \ldots, 0)$ and the d unit points $(1, 0, 0, \ldots, 0), (0, 1, 0, \ldots, 0), \ldots, (0, 0, \ldots, 1)$ is shattered by $\mathcal{R}$.

Exercise 14.8: Let $S = (X, R)$ and $S' = (X, R')$ be two range spaces. Prove that if $R' \subseteq R$ then the VC dimension of S' is no larger than the VC dimension of S.

Exercise 14.9: Show that for $n \geq 2d$ and $d \geq 1$ the growth function satisfies

$$\mathcal{G}(d, n) = \sum_{i=0}^{d} \binom{n}{i} \leq 2 \left(\frac{ne}{d} \right)^d.$$

Exercise 14.10: Use the bound of Exercise 14.9 to improve the result of Theorem 14.4 to show the VC dimension of the range space $(X, \mathcal{R}^f)$ is $O(kd \ln k)$.

Exercise 14.11: Use the bound of Exercise 14.9 to improve the result of Theorem 14.8 to show that there is an

$$m = O \left(\frac{d}{\epsilon} \ln \frac{1}{\epsilon} + \frac{1}{\epsilon} \ln \frac{1}{\delta} \right)$$

such that a random sample from $\mathcal{D}$ of size greater than or equal to m suffices to obtain the required ϵ-net with probability at least $1 - \delta$. (*Hint:* Use Lemma 14.3 with $x = O(\frac{1}{\epsilon})$ and $y = \frac{2m}{d}$.)

Exercise 14.12: **(a)** Improve the result in Eqn. (14.1) by showing that the VC dimension of the frequent-itemsets range space is bounded by the maximum number q such that the data set has q different transactions all of size at least q.
　(b) Show how to compute an upper bound on the number q defined in (a) in one pass over the data.

Exercise 14.13: Prove Theorem 14.11 using the following hints. Let (X, R) be a range space with VC dimension d. Let $Y = \{y_1, \ldots, y_d\} \subseteq X$ be a set of d elements that is shattered by R. Define a probability distribution $\mathcal{D}$ on R as follows: $\Pr(y_1) = 1 - 16\epsilon$, $\Pr(y_2) = \Pr(y_3) = \cdots = \Pr(y_d) = 16\epsilon/(d - 1)$, and all other elements have probability 0. Consider a sample of size $m = (d - 1)/(64\epsilon)$. Show that with probability at least $1/2$ the sample does not include at least half of the elements in $\{y_2, \ldots, y_d\}$. Conclude that with probability $\delta \geq 1/2$ the output classification has error at least ϵ.

Exercise 14.14: Given a set of functions $\mathcal{F}$ and constants $a, b \in \mathbb{R}$, consider the set of functions

$$\mathcal{F}_{a,b} = \{af + b \mid f \in \mathcal{F}\}.$$

Let $R_m()$ and $\tilde{R}_m()$ denote the Rademacher complexity and the empirical Rademacher complexity, respectively. Prove that

(a) $\tilde{R}_m(\mathcal{F}_{a,b}, S) = |a|\tilde{R}_m(\mathcal{F}, S)$,
(b) $R_m(\mathcal{F}_{a,b}) = |a|R_m(\mathcal{F})$.

Exercise 14.15: We apply Theorem 14.21 to compute a bound on the sample complexity of agnostic learning a binary classification. Assume a concept class with VC dimension d and a sample size m.

(a) Find a sample size m_1 such that the Empirical Rademacher Average of the corresponding set of functions is at most $\epsilon/4$.
(b) Use Theorem 14.21 to find a sample size m such that with probability at least $1 - \delta$ the expectation of all the functions are estimated within error ϵ.
(c) Compare your bound to the result obtained in Section 14.5.1.

CHAPTER FIFTEEN

Pairwise Independence and Universal Hash Functions

In this chapter we introduce and apply a limited notion of independence, known as k-wise independence, focusing in particular on the important case of pairwise independence. Applying limited dependence can allow us to reduce the amount of randomness used by a randomized algorithm, in some cases enabling us to convert a randomized algorithm into an efficient deterministic one. Limited dependence is also used in the design of universal and strongly universal families of hash functions, giving space- and time-efficient data structures. We consider why universal hash functions are effective in practice and show how they lead to simple perfect hash schemes. Finally, we apply these ideas to the design of effective and practical approximation algorithms for finding frequent objects in data streams, generalizing the Bloom filter data structure introduced in Chapter 5.

15.1. Pairwise Independence

Recall that in Chapter 2 we defined a set of events $E_1, E_2, \ldots, E_n$ to be mutually independent if, for any subset $I \subseteq [1, n]$,

$$\Pr\left(\bigcap_{i \in I} E_i\right) = \prod_{i \in I} \Pr(E_i).$$

Similarly, we defined a set of random variables $X_1, X_2, \ldots, X_n$ to be mutually independent if, for any subset $I \subseteq [1, n]$ and any values x_i, $i \in I$,

$$\Pr\left(\bigcap_{i \in I}(X_i = x_i)\right) = \prod_{i \in I} \Pr(X_i = x_i).$$

Mutual independence is often too much to ask for. Here, we examine a more limited notion of independence that proves useful in many contexts: k-wise independence.

Definition 15.1:

1. A set of events $E_1, E_2, \ldots, E_n$ is k-wise independent if, for any subset $I \subseteq [1, n]$ with $|I| \leq k$,

$$\Pr\left(\bigcap_{i \in I} E_i\right) = \prod_{i \in I} \Pr(E_i).$$

2. A set of random variables $X_1, X_2, \ldots, X_n$ is k-wise independent if, for any subset $I \subseteq [1, n]$ with $|I| \leq k$ and for any values x_i, $i \in I$,

$$\Pr\left(\bigcap_{i \in I} (X_i = x_i)\right) = \prod_{i \in I} \Pr(X_i = x_i).$$

3. The random variables $X_1, X_2, \ldots, X_n$ are said to be pairwise independent if they are 2-wise independent. That is, for any pair i, j and any values a, b,

$$\Pr((X_i = a) \cap (X_j = b)) = \Pr(X_i = a)\Pr(X_j = b).$$

15.1.1. *Example: A Construction of Pairwise Independent Bits*

A random bit is uniform if it assumes the values 0 and 1 with equal probability. Here we show how to derive $m = 2^b - 1$ uniform pairwise independent bits from b independent, uniform random bits $X_1, \ldots, X_b$.

Enumerate the $2^b - 1$ nonempty subsets of $\{1, 2, \ldots, b\}$ in some order, and let S_j be the jth subset in this ordering. Set

$$Y_j = \bigoplus_{i \in S_j} X_i,$$

where $\oplus$ is the exclusive-or operation. Equivalently, we could write this as

$$Y_j = \sum_{i \in S_j} X_i \bmod 2.$$

Lemma 15.1: *The Y_j are pairwise independent uniform bits.*

Proof: We first show that, for any nonempty set S_j, the random bit

$$Y_j = \bigoplus_{i \in S_j} X_i$$

is uniform. This follows easily using the principle of deferred decisions (see Section 1.3). Let z be the largest element of S. Then

$$Y_j = \left(\bigoplus_{i \in S_j - \{z\}} X_i\right) \oplus X_z.$$

Suppose we reveal the values for X_i for all $i \in S_j - \{z\}$. Then it is clear that the value of X_z determines the value of Y_j and that Y_j will take on the values 0 and 1 with equal probability.

Now consider any two variables Y_k and Y_ℓ with their corresponding sets S_k and S_ℓ. Without loss of generality, let z be an element of S_ℓ that is not in S_k and consider, for any values $c, d \in \{0, 1\}$,

$$\Pr(Y_\ell = d \mid Y_k = c).$$

We claim, again by the principle of deferred decisions, that this probability is $1/2$. For suppose that we reveal the values for X_i for all i in $(S_k \cup S_\ell) - \{z\}$. Even though this determines the value of Y_k, the value of X_z will determine Y_ℓ. The conditioning on the value of Y_k therefore does not change that Y_ℓ is equally likely to be 0 or 1. Hence

$$\Pr((Y_k = c) \cap (Y_\ell = d)) = \Pr(Y_\ell = d \mid Y_k = c)\Pr(Y_k = c)$$
$$= 1/4.$$

Since this holds for any values of $c, d \in \{0, 1\}$, we have proven pairwise independence. ∎

15.1.2. Application: Derandomizing an Algorithm for Large Cuts

In Chapter 6, we examined a simple randomized algorithm for finding a large cut in an undirected graph $G = (V, E)$: the algorithm places each vertex on one side of the cut independently with probability $1/2$. The expected value of a cut generated this way is $m/2$, where m is the number of edges in the graph. We also showed (in Section 6.3) that this algorithm could be derandomized effectively using conditional expectations.

Here we present another way to derandomize this algorithm, using pairwise independence. This argument exemplifies the approach of derandomization using k-wise independence.

Suppose that we have a collection $Y_1, Y_2, \ldots, Y_n$ of pairwise independent bits, where $n = |V|$ is the number of vertices in the graph. We define our cut by putting all vertices i with $Y_i = 0$ on one side of the cut and all vertices i with $Y_i = 1$ on the other side of the cut. We show that, in this case, the expected number of edges that crosses the cut remains $m/2$. That is, we do not require complete independence to analyze the expectation; pairwise independence suffices.

Recall the argument of Section 6.2.1: number the edges from 1 to m, and let $Z_i = 1$ if the ith edge crosses the cut and $Z_i = 0$ otherwise. Then $Z = \sum_{i=1}^{m} Z_i$ is the number of edges crossing the cut, and

$$E[Z] = E\left[\sum_{i=1}^{m} Z_i\right] = \sum_{i=1}^{m} E[Z_i].$$

Let a and b be the two vertices adjacent to the ith edge. Then

$$\Pr(Z_i = 1) = \Pr(Y_a \neq Y_b) = 1/2,$$

where we have used the pairwise independence of Y_a and Y_b. Hence $\mathbf{E}[Z_i] = 1/2$, and it follows that $\mathbf{E}[Z] = m/2$.

Now let our n pairwise independent bits $Y_1, \ldots, Y_n$ be generated from b independent, uniform random bits $X_1, X_2, \ldots, X_b$ in the manner of Lemma 15.1 (here $b = \lceil \log_2(n + 1) \rceil$). Then $\mathbf{E}[Z] = m/2$ for the resulting cut, where the sample space is just all the possible choices for the initial b random bits. By the probabilistic method (specifically, Lemma 6.2), there is some setting of the b bits that gives a cut with value at least $m/2$. We can try all possible 2^b settings for the bits to find such a cut. Since 2^b is $O(n)$ and since, for each cut, the number of crossing edges can easily be calculated in $O(m)$ time, it follows that we can find a cut with at least $m/2$ crossing edges deterministically in $O(mn)$ time.

Although this approach does not appear to be as efficient as the derandomization of Section 6.3, one redeeming feature of the scheme is that it is trivial to parallelize. If we have sufficiently many processors available, then each of the $\Omega(n)$ possibilities for the random bits $X_1, X_2, \ldots, X_b$ can be assigned to a single processor, with each possibility giving a cut. The parallelization reduces the running time by a factor of $\Omega(n)$ using $O(n)$ processors. In fact, using $O(mn)$ processors, we can assign a processor for each combination of a specific edge with a specific sequence of random bits and then determine, in constant time, whether the edge crosses the cut for that setting of the random bits. After that, only $O(\log n)$ time is necessary to collect the results and find the large cut.

15.1.3. *Example: Constructing Pairwise Independent Values Modulo a Prime*

We consider another construction that provides pairwise independent values $Y_0, Y_1, \ldots, Y_{p-1}$ that are uniform over the values $\{0, 1, \ldots, p - 1\}$ for a prime p. Our construction requires only two independent, uniform values X_1 and X_2 over $\{0, 1, \ldots, p - 1\}$, from which we derive

$$Y_i = X_1 + iX_2 \bmod p \quad \text{for } i = 0, \ldots, p - 1.$$

Lemma 15.2: *The variables $Y_0, Y_1, \ldots, Y_{p-1}$ are pairwise independent uniform random variables over $\{0, 1, \ldots, p - 1\}$.*

Proof: It is clear that each Y_i is uniform over $\{0, 1, \ldots, p - 1\}$, again by applying the principle of deferred decisions. Given X_2, the p distinct possible values for X_1 give p distinct possible values for Y_i modulo p, each of which is equally likely.

Now consider any two variables Y_i and Y_j. We wish to show that, for any $a, b \in \{0, 1, \ldots, p - 1\}$,

$$\Pr((Y_i = a) \cap (Y_j = b)) = \frac{1}{p^2},$$

which implies pairwise independence. The event $Y_i = a$ and $Y_j = b$ is equivalent to

$$X_1 + iX_2 = a \bmod p \quad \text{and} \quad X_1 + jX_2 = b \bmod p.$$

This is a system of two equations and two unknowns with just one solution:

$$X_2 = \frac{b-a}{j-i} \bmod p \quad \text{and} \quad X_1 = a - \frac{i(b-a)}{j-i} \bmod p.$$

Since X_1 and X_2 are independent and uniform over $\{0, 1, \ldots, p-1\}$, the result follows. ∎

This proof can be extended to the following useful result: given $2n$ independent, uniform random bits, one can construct up to 2^n pairwise independent and uniform strings of n bits. The extension requires knowledge of finite fields, so we only sketch the result here. The setup and proof are exactly the same as for Lemma 15.2 except that, instead of working modulo p, we perform all arithmetic in a fixed finite field with 2^n elements (such as the field $GF(2^n)$ of all polynomials with coefficients in $GF(2)$ modulo some irreducible polynomial of degree n). That is, we assume a fixed one-to-one mapping f from strings of n bits, which can also be thought of as numbers in $\{0, 1, \ldots, 2^n - 1\}$, to field elements. We let

$$Y_i = f^{-1}(f(X_1) + f(i) \cdot f(X_2)),$$

where X_1 and X_2 are chosen independently and uniformly over $\{0, 1, \ldots, 2^n - 1\}$, i runs over the values $\{0, 1, \ldots, 2^n - 1\}$, and the addition and multiplication are performed over the field. The Y_i are then pairwise independent.

15.2. Chebyshev's Inequality for Pairwise Independent Variables

Pairwise independence is much weaker than mutual independence. For example, we can use Chernoff bounds to evaluate the tail distribution of a sum of independent random variables, but we cannot directly apply a Chernoff bound if the X_i are only pairwise independent. However, pairwise independence is strong enough to allow for easy calculation of the variance of the sum, which allows for a useful application of Chebyshev's inequality.

Theorem 15.3: *Let $X = \sum_{i=1}^{n} X_i$, where the X_i are pairwise independent random variables. Then*

$$\mathbf{Var}[X] = \sum_{i=1}^{n} \mathbf{Var}[X_i].$$

Proof: We saw in Chapter 3 that

$$\mathbf{Var}\left[\sum_{i=1}^{n} X_i\right] = \sum_{i=1}^{n} \mathbf{Var}[X_i] + 2\sum_{i<j} \mathbf{Cov}(X_i, X_j),$$

where

$$\mathbf{Cov}(X_i, X_j) = \mathbf{E}[(X_i - \mathbf{E}[X_i])(X_j - \mathbf{E}[X_j])] = \mathbf{E}[X_iX_j] - \mathbf{E}[X_i]\mathbf{E}[X_j].$$

Since $X_i, X_2, \ldots, X_n$ are pairwise independent, it is clear (by the same argument as in Theorem 3.3) that for any $i \neq j$ we have

$$\mathbf{E}[X_i X_j] - \mathbf{E}[X_i]\mathbf{E}[X_j] = 0.$$

Therefore,

$$\mathbf{Var}[X] = \sum_{i=1}^{n} \mathbf{Var}[X_i].$$
∎

Applying Chebyshev's inequality to the sum of pairwise independent variables yields the following.

Corollary 15.4: *Let $X = \sum_{i=1}^{n} X_i$, where the X_i are pairwise independent random variables. Then*

$$\Pr(|X - \mathbf{E}[X]| \geq a) \leq \frac{\mathbf{Var}[X]}{a^2} = \frac{\sum_{i=1}^{n} \mathbf{Var}[X_i]}{a^2}.$$

15.2.1. *Application: Sampling Using Fewer Random Bits*

We apply Chebyshev's inequality for pairwise independent random variables to obtain a good approximation through sampling. This uses less randomness than the natural approach based on Chernoff bounds.

Suppose that we have a function $f : \{0, 1\}^n \to [0, 1]$ mapping n-bit vectors into real numbers. Let $\bar{f} = \left(\sum_{x \in \{0,1\}^n} f(x) \right)/2^n$ be the average value of f. We want to compute a $1 - \delta$ confidence interval for $\bar{f}$. That is, we wish to find an interval $[\tilde{f} - \varepsilon, \tilde{f} + \varepsilon]$ such that

$$\Pr(\bar{f} \in [\tilde{f} - \varepsilon, \tilde{f} + \varepsilon]) \geq 1 - \delta.$$

As a concrete example, suppose that we have an integrable function $g : [0, 1] \to [0, 1]$ and that the derivative of g exists with $|g'(x)| \leq C$ for some fixed constant C over the entire interval $(0, 1)$. We are interested in $\int_{x=0}^{1} g(x)\, dx$. There may be no direct way to compute this integral exactly, but through sampling we can obtain a good estimate. If X is a uniform random variable on $[0, 1]$, then $\mathbf{E}[g(X)] = \int_{x=0}^{1} g(x)\, dx$ by the definition of the expectation of a continuous random variable. By taking the average of multiple independent samples, we can approximate the integral. If our source of randomness generates only random bits instead of random real numbers, then we might approximate the integral as follows. For a string of bits $x \in \{0, 1\}^n$, we may interpret x as a real number $\tilde{x} \in [0, 1]$ by considering it as a decimal in binary; for example, 11001 would correspond to $0.11001 = 25/32$. Let $f(x)$ denote the value of the function g at the decimal value $\tilde{x}$. Then, for any integer i with $0 \leq i \leq 2^n - 1$, for $y \in [i/2^n, (i+1)/2^n)$ we have

$$f\left(\frac{i}{2^n}\right) - \frac{C}{2^n} \leq g(y) \leq f\left(\frac{i}{2^n}\right) + \frac{C}{2^n}.$$

397

It follows that

$$\frac{1}{2^n} \sum_{x \in \{0,1\}^n} \left(f(x) - \frac{C}{2^n} \right) \leq \int_{x=0}^{1} g(x)dx \leq \frac{1}{2^n} \sum_{x \in \{0,1\}^n} \left(f(x) + \frac{C}{2^n} \right).$$

By taking n sufficiently large, we can guarantee that $\bar{f} = \left(\sum_{x \in \{0,1\}^n} f(x) \right)/2^n$ differs from the integral of g by at most a constant γ. In this case, a confidence interval $[\bar{f} - \varepsilon, \bar{f} + \varepsilon]$ for $\bar{f}$ would yield a confidence interval $[\tilde{g} - \varepsilon - \gamma, \tilde{g} + \varepsilon + \gamma]$ for the integral of g.

We could handle the problem of finding a confidence interval for the average value $\bar{f}$ by using independent samples and applying a Chernoff bound. That is, suppose that we sample uniformly with replacement random points in $\{0, 1\}^n$, evaluate f at all of these points, and take the average of our samples. This is similar to the parameter estimation of Section 4.2.3. Theorem 15.5 is an immediate consequence of the following Chernoff bound, which can be derived using Exercises 4.13 and 4.19. If $Z_1, Z_2, \ldots, Z_m$ are independent, identically distributed, real-valued random variables with mean μ that take on one of a finite possible set of values in the range $[0, 1]$, then

$$\Pr \left(\left| \sum_{i=1}^{m} Z_i - m\mu \right| \geq \varepsilon m \right) \leq 2e^{-2m\varepsilon^2}.$$

Theorem 15.5: Let $f : \{0, 1\}^n \to [0, 1]$ and $\bar{f} = \left(\sum_{x \in \{0,1\}^n} f(x) \right)/2^n$. Let $X_1, \ldots, X_m$ be chosen independently and uniformly at random from $\{0, 1\}^n$. If $m > \ln(2/\delta)/2\varepsilon^2$, then

$$\Pr \left(\left| \frac{1}{m} \sum_{i=1}^{m} f(X_i) - \bar{f} \right| \geq \varepsilon \right) \leq \delta.$$

Although the exact choice of m depends on the Chernoff bound used, in general this straightforward approach requires $\Omega(\ln(1/\delta)/\varepsilon^2)$ samples to achieve the desired bounds.

A possible problem with this approach is that it requires a large number of random bits to be available. Each sample of f requires n independent bits, so applying Theorem 15.5 means that we need at least $\Omega(n \ln(1/\delta)/\varepsilon^2)$ independent, uniform random bits to obtain an approximation that has additive error at most ε with probability at least $1 - \delta$.

A related problem arises when we need to record how the samples were obtained, so that the work can be reproduced and verified at a later time. In this case, we also need to store the random bits used for archival purposes. In this case, using fewer random bits would lessen the storage requirements.

We can use pairwise independent samples to obtain a similar approximation using less randomness. Let $X_1, \ldots, X_m$ be pairwise independent points chosen from $\{0, 1\}^n$, and let $Y = \left(\sum_{i=1}^{m} f(X_i) \right)/m$. Then $\mathbf{E}[Y] = \bar{f}$, and we can apply Chebyshev's inequality to obtain

$$\Pr(|Y - \bar{f}| \geq \varepsilon) \leq \frac{\mathbf{Var}[Y]}{\varepsilon^2}$$
$$= \frac{\mathbf{Var}\left[\left(\sum_{i=1}^{m} f(X_i)\right)/m\right]}{\varepsilon^2}$$
$$= \frac{\sum_{i=1}^{m} \mathbf{Var}[f(X_i)]}{m^2 \varepsilon^2}$$
$$\leq \frac{m}{m^2 \varepsilon^2} = \frac{1}{m \varepsilon^2},$$

since $\mathbf{Var}[f(X_i)] \leq \mathbf{E}[(f(X_i))^2] \leq 1$. We therefore find $\Pr(|Y - \bar{f}| \geq \varepsilon) \leq \delta$ when $m = 1/\delta\varepsilon^2$. (In fact, one can prove that $\mathbf{Var}[f(X_i)] \leq 1/4$, giving a slightly better bound; this is left as Exercise 15.4.)

Using pairwise independent samples requires more samples: $\Theta(1/\delta\varepsilon^2)$ instead of the $\Theta(\ln(1/\delta)/\varepsilon^2)$ samples when they are independent. But recall from Section 15.1.3 that we can obtain up to 2^n pairwise independent samples with just $2n$ uniform independent bits. Hence, as long as $1/\delta\varepsilon^2 < 2^n$, just $2n$ random bits suffice; this is much less than the number required when using completely independent samples. Usually ε and δ are fixed constants independent of n, and this type of estimation is quite efficient in terms of both the number of random bits used and the computational cost.

15.3. Universal Families of Hash Functions

Up to this point, when studying hash functions we modeled them as being completely random in the sense that, for any collection of items $x_1, x_2, \ldots, x_k$, the hash values $h(x_1), h(x_2), \ldots, h(x_k)$ were considered uniform and independent over the range of the hash function. This was the framework we used to analyze hashing as a balls-and-bins problem in Chapter 5. The assumption of a completely random hash function simplifies the analysis for a theoretical study of hashing. In practice, however, completely random hash functions are too expensive to compute and store, so the model does not fully reflect reality.

Two approaches are commonly used to implement practical hash functions. In many cases, heuristic or ad hoc functions designed to appear random are used. Although these functions may work suitably for some applications, they generally do not have any associated provable guarantees, making their use potentially risky. Another approach is to use hash functions for which there are some provable guarantees. We trade away the strong statements one can make about completely random hash functions for weaker statements with hash functions that are efficient to store and compute.

We consider one of the computationally simplest classes of hash functions that provide useful provable performance guarantees: universal families of hash functions. These functions are widely used in practice.

Definition 15.2: *Let U be a universe with $|U| \geq n$ and let $V = \{0, 1, \ldots, n - 1\}$. A family of hash functions $\mathcal{H}$ from U to V is said to be k-universal if, for any elements*

$x_1, x_2, \ldots, x_k$ *and for a hash function h chosen uniformly at random from $\mathcal{H}$, we have*

$$\Pr(h(x_1) = h(x_2) = \cdots = h(x_k)) \leq \frac{1}{n^{k-1}}.$$

A family of hash functions $\mathcal{H}$ from U to V is said to be strongly k-universal *if, for any elements $x_1, x_2, \ldots, x_k$, any values $y_1, y_2, \ldots, y_k \in \{0, 1, \ldots, n - 1\}$, and a hash function h chosen uniformly at random from $\mathcal{H}$, we have*

$$\Pr((h(x_1) = y_1) \cap (h(x_2) = y_2) \cap \cdots \cap (h(x_k) = y_k)) = \frac{1}{n^k}.$$

We will primarily be interested in 2-universal and strongly 2-universal families of hash functions. When we choose a hash function from a family of 2-universal hash functions, the probability that any two elements x_1 and x_2 have the same hash value is at most $1/n$. In this respect, a hash function chosen from a 2-universal family acts like a random hash function. It does not follow, however, that for 2-universal families the probability of any three values x_1, x_2, and x_3 having the same hash value is at most $1/n^2$, as would be the case if the hash values of x_1, x_2, and x_3 were mutually independent.

When a family is strongly 2-universal and we choose a hash function from that family, the values $h(x_1)$ and $h(x_2)$ are pairwise independent, since the probability that they take on any specific pair of values is $1/n^2$. Because of this, hash functions chosen from a strongly 2-universal family are also known as *pairwise independent* hash functions. More generally, if a family is strongly k-universal and we choose a hash function from that family, then the values $h(x_1), h(x_2), \ldots, h(x_k)$ are k-wise independent. Notice that a strongly k-universal hash function is also k-universal.

To gain some insight into the behavior of universal families of hash functions, let us revisit a problem we considered in the balls-and-bins framework of Chapter 5. We saw in Section 5.2 that, when n items are hashed into n bins by a completely random hash function, the maximum load is $\Theta(\log n/ \log \log n)$ with high probability. We now consider what bounds can be obtained on the maximum load when n items are hashed into n bins using a hash function chosen from a 2-universal family.

First, consider the more general case where we have m items labeled $x_1, x_2, \ldots, x_m$. For $1 \leq i < j \leq m$, let $X_{ij} = 1$ if items x_i and x_j land in the same bin. Let $X = \sum_{1 \leq i < j \leq m} X_{ij}$ be the total number of collisions between pairs of items. By the linearity of expectations,

$$\mathbf{E}[X] = \mathbf{E}\left[\sum_{1 \leq i < j \leq m} X_{ij} \right] = \sum_{1 \leq i < j \leq m} \mathbf{E}[X_{ij}].$$

Since our hash function is chosen from a 2-universal family, it follows that

$$\mathbf{E}[X_{ij}] = \Pr(h(x_i) = h(x_j)) \leq \frac{1}{n}$$

and hence

$$\mathbf{E}[X] \leq \binom{m}{2} \frac{1}{n} < \frac{m^2}{2n}. \tag{15.1}$$

Markov's inequality then yields

$$\Pr\left(X \ge \frac{m^2}{n}\right) \le \Pr(X \ge 2\mathbf{E}[X]) \le \frac{1}{2}.$$

If we now suppose that the maximum number of items in a bin is Y, then the number of collisions X must be at least $\binom{Y}{2}$. Therefore,

$$\Pr\left(\binom{Y}{2} \ge \frac{m^2}{n}\right) \le \Pr\left(X \ge \frac{m^2}{n}\right) \le \frac{1}{2},$$

which implies that

$$\Pr\left(Y - 1 \ge m\sqrt{2/n}\right) \le \frac{1}{2}.$$

In particular, in the case where $m = n$, the maximum load is at most $1 + \sqrt{2n}$ with probability at least $1/2$.

This result is much weaker than the one for perfectly random hash functions, but it is extremely general in that it holds for any 2-universal family of hash functions. The result will prove useful for designing perfect hash functions, as we describe in Section 15.3.3.

15.3.1. *Example: A 2-Universal Family of Hash Functions*

Let the universe U be the set $\{0, 1, 2, \ldots, m - 1\}$ and let the range of our hash function be $V = \{0, 1, 2, \ldots, n - 1\}$, with $m \ge n$. Consider the family of hash functions obtained by choosing a prime $p \ge m$, letting

$$h_{a,b}(x) = ((ax + b) \bmod p) \bmod n$$

and then taking the family

$$\mathcal{H} = \{h_{a,b} \mid 1 \le a \le p - 1, 0 \le b \le p - 1\}.$$

Notice that a cannot here take on the value 0.

Lemma 15.6: $\mathcal{H}$ *is 2-universal.*

Proof: We count the number of functions in $\mathcal{H}$ for which two distinct elements x_1 and x_2 from U collide.

First we note that, for any $x_1 \ne x_2$,

$$ax_1 + b \ne ax_2 + b \bmod p.$$

This follows because $ax_1 + b = ax_2 + b \bmod p$ implies that $a(x_1 - x_2) = 0 \bmod p$, yet here both a and $(x_1 - x_2)$ are nonzero modulo p.

In fact, for every pair of values (u, v) such that $u \ne v$ and $0 \le u, v \le p - 1$, there exists exactly one pair of values (a, b) for which $ax_1 + b = u \bmod p$ and $ax_2 + b = v$

401

mod p. This pair of equations has two unknowns, and its unique solution is given by:

$$a = \frac{v - u}{x_2 - x_1} \bmod p,$$
$$b = u - ax_1 \bmod p.$$

Since there is exactly one hash function for each pair (a, b), it follows that there is exactly one hash function in $\mathcal{H}$ for which

$$ax_1 + b = u \bmod p \quad \text{and} \quad ax_2 + b = v \bmod p.$$

Therefore, in order to bound the probability that $h_{a,b}(x_1) = h_{a,b}(x_2)$ when $h_{a,b}$ is chosen uniformly at random from $\mathcal{H}$, it suffices to count the number of pairs (u, v), $0 \leq u, v \leq p - 1$, for which $u \neq v$ but $u = v \bmod n$. For each choice of u there are at most $\lceil p/n \rceil - 1$ possible appropriate values for v, giving at most $p(\lceil p/n \rceil - 1) \leq p(p - 1)/n$ pairs. Each pair corresponds to one of $p(p - 1)$ hash functions, so

$$\Pr(h_{a,b}(x_1) = h_{a,b}(x_2)) \leq \frac{p(p - 1)/n}{p(p - 1)} = \frac{1}{n},$$

proving that $\mathcal{H}$ is 2-universal. ∎

15.3.2. *Example: A Strongly 2-Universal Family of Hash Functions*

We can apply ideas similar to those used to construct the 2-universal family of hash functions in Lemma 15.6 to construct strongly 2-universal families of hash functions. To start, suppose that both our universe U and the range V of the hash function are $\{0, 1, 2, \ldots, p - 1\}$ for some prime p. Now let

$$h_{a,b}(x) = (ax + b) \bmod p,$$

and consider the family

$$\mathcal{H} = \{h_{a,b} \mid 0 \leq a, b \leq p - 1\}.$$

Notice that here a can take on the value 0, in contrast with the family of hash functions used in Lemma 15.6.

Lemma 15.7: $\mathcal{H}$ *is strongly 2-universal.*

Proof: This is entirely similar to the proof of Lemma 15.2. For any two elements x_1 and x_2 in U and any two values y_1 and y_2 in V, we need to show that

$$\Pr((h_{a,b}(x_1) = y_1) \cap (h_{a,b}(x_2) = y_2)) = \frac{1}{p^2}.$$

The condition that both $h_{a,b}(x_1) = y_1$ and $h_{a,b}(x_2) = y_2$ yields two equations modulo p with two unknowns, the values for a and b: $ax_1 + b = y_1 \bmod p$ and $ax_2 + b = y_2 \bmod p$. This system of two equations and two unknowns has just one solution:

$$a = \frac{y_2 - y_1}{x_2 - x_1} \bmod p,$$
$$b = y_1 - ax_1 \bmod p.$$

Hence only one choice of the pair (a, b) out of the p^2 possibilities results in x_1 and x_2 hashing to y_1 and y_2, proving that

$$\Pr((h_{a,b}(x_1) = y_1) \cap (h_{a,b}(x_2) = y_2)) = \frac{1}{p^2},$$

as required. ∎

Although this gives a strongly 2-universal hash family, the restriction that the universe U and the range V be the same makes the result almost useless; usually we want to hash a large universe into a much smaller range. We can extend the construction in a natural way that allows much larger universes. Let $V = \{0, 1, 2, \ldots, p - 1\}$, but now let $U = \{0, 1, 2, \ldots, p^k - 1\}$ for some integer k and prime p. We can interpret an element u in the universe U as a vector $\bar{u} = (u_0, u_1, \ldots, u_{k-1})$, where $0 \le u_i \le p - 1$ for $0 \le i \le k - 1$ and where $\sum_{i=0}^{k-1} u_i p^i = u$. In fact, this gives a one-to-one mapping between vectors of this form and elements of U.

For any vector $\bar{a} = (a_0, a_1, \ldots, a_{k-1})$ with $0 \le a_i \le p - 1$, $0 \le i \le k - 1$, and for any value b with $0 \le b \le p - 1$, let

$$h_{\bar{a},b}(u) = \left(\sum_{i=0}^{k-1} a_i u_i + b \right) \bmod p,$$

and consider the family

$$\mathcal{H} = \{h_{\bar{a},b} \mid 0 \le a_i, b \le p - 1 \text{ for all } 0 \le i \le k - 1\}.$$

Lemma 15.8: $\mathcal{H}$ *is strongly 2-universal.*

Proof: We follow the proof of Lemma 15.7. For any two elements u_1 and u_2 with corresponding vectors $\bar{u}_i = (u_{i,0}, u_{i,1}, \ldots, u_{i,k-1})$ and for any two values y_1 and y_2 in V, we need to show that

$$\Pr((h_{\bar{a},b}(u_1) = y_1) \cap (h_{\bar{a},b}(u_2) = y_2)) = \frac{1}{p^2}.$$

Since u_1 and u_2 are different, they must differ in at least one coordinate. Without loss of generality let $u_{1,0} \ne u_{2,0}$. For any given values of $a_1, a_2, \ldots, a_{k-1}$, the condition that $h_{\bar{a},b}(u_1) = y_1$ and $h_{\bar{a},b}(u_2) = y_2$ is equivalent to:

$$a_0 u_{1,0} + b = \left(y_1 - \sum_{j=1}^{k-1} a_j u_{1,j} \right) \bmod p$$

$$a_0 u_{2,0} + b = \left(y_1 - \sum_{j=1}^{k-1} a_j u_{2,j} \right) \bmod p.$$

For any given values of $a_1, a_2, \ldots, a_{k-1}$, this gives a system with two equations and two unknowns (namely, a_0 and b), which – as in Lemma 15.8 – has exactly one solution. Hence, for every $a_1, a_2, \ldots, a_{k-1}$, only one choice of the pair (a_0, b) out of the p^2

possibilities results in u_1 and u_2 hashing to y_1 and y_2, proving that

$$\Pr((h_{\bar{a},b}(u_1) = y_1) \cap (h_{\bar{a},b}(u_2) = y_2)) = \frac{1}{p^2},$$

as required. ∎

Although we have described both the 2-universal and the strongly 2-universal hash families in terms of arithmetic modulo a prime number, we could extend these techniques to work over general finite fields – in particular, fields with 2^n elements represented by sequences of n bits. The extension requires knowledge of finite fields, so we just sketch the result here. The setup and proof are exactly the same as for Lemma 15.8 except that, instead of working modulo p, we perform all arithmetic in a fixed finite field with 2^n elements. We assume a fixed one-to-one mapping f from strings of n bits, which can also be thought of as numbers in $\{0, 1, \ldots, 2^n - 1\}$, to field elements. We let

$$h_{\bar{a},b}(u) = f^{-1}\left(\sum_{i=0}^{k-1} f(a_i) \cdot f(u_i) + f(b)\right),$$

where the a_i and b are chosen independently and uniformly over $\{0, 1, \ldots, 2^n - 1\}$ and where the addition and multiplication are performed over the field. This gives a strongly 2-universal hash function with a range of size 2^n.

15.3.3. Application: Perfect Hashing

Perfect hashing is an efficient data structure for storing a *static dictionary*. In a static dictionary, items are permanently stored in a table. Once the items are stored, the table is used only for search operations: a search for an item gives the location of the item in the table or returns that the item is not in the table.

Suppose that a set S of m items is hashed into a table of n bins, using a hash function from a 2-universal family and chain hashing. In chain hashing (see Section 5.5.1), items hashed to the same bin are kept in a linked list. The number of operations for looking up an item x is proportional to the number of items in x's bin. We have the following simple bound.

Lemma 15.9: *Assume that m elements are hashed into an n-bin chain hashing table by using a hash function h chosen uniformly at random from a 2-universal family. For an arbitrary element x, let X be the number of items at the bin $h(x)$. Then*

$$E[X] \leq \begin{cases} m/n & \text{if } x \notin S, \\ 1 + (m-1)/n & \text{if } x \in S. \end{cases}$$

Proof: Let $X_i = 1$ if the ith element of S (under some arbitrary ordering) is in the same bin as x and 0 otherwise. Because the hash function is chosen from a 2-universal family, it follows that

$$\Pr(X_i = 1) \leq 1/n.$$

Then the first result follows from

$$E[X] = E\left[\sum_{i=1}^{m} X_i\right] = \sum_{i=1}^{m} E[X_i] \leq \frac{m}{n},$$

where we have used the universality of the hash function to conclude that $E[X_i] \leq 1/n$. Similarly, if x is an element of S then (without loss of generality) let it be the first element of S. Hence $X_1 = 1$, and again

$$\Pr(X_i = 1) \leq 1/n$$

when $i \neq 1$. Therefore,

$$E[X] = E\left[\sum_{i=1}^{m} X_i\right] = 1 + \sum_{i=2}^{m} E[X_i] \leq 1 + \frac{m-1}{n}.$$

∎

Lemma 15.9 shows that the average performance of hashing when using a hash function from a 2-universal family is good, since the time to look through a bin of any item is bounded by a small number. For instance, if $m = n$ then, when searching the hash table for x, the expected number of items other than x that must be examined is at most 1. However, this does not give us a bound on the worst-case time of a lookup. Some bin may contain $\sqrt{n}$ elements or more, and a search for one of these elements requires a much longer lookup time.

This motivates the idea of *perfect hashing*. Given a set S, we would like to construct a hash table that gives excellent worst-case performance. Specifically, by perfect hashing we mean that only a constant number of operations are required to find an item in a hash table (or to determine that it isn't there).

We first show that perfect hashing is easy if we are given sufficient space for the hash table and a suitable 2-universal family of hash functions.

Lemma 15.10: *If $h \in \mathcal{H}$ is chosen uniformly at random from a 2-universal family of hash functions mapping the universe U to $[0, n-1]$ then, for any set $S \subset U$ of size m, the probability of h being perfect is at least $1/2$ when $n \geq m^2$.*

Proof: Let $s_1, s_2, \ldots, s_m$ be the m items of S. Let X_{ij} be 1 if the $h(s_i) = h(s_j)$ and 0 otherwise. Let $X = \sum_{1 \leq i < j \leq m} X_{ij}$. Then, as we saw in Eqn. (15.1), the expected number of collisions when using a 2-universal hash function is

$$E[X] = E\left[\sum_{1 \leq i < j \leq m} X_{ij}\right] = \sum_{1 \leq i < j \leq m} E[X_{ij}] \leq \binom{m}{2}\frac{1}{n} < \frac{m^2}{2n}.$$

Markov's inequality then yields

$$\Pr\left(X \geq \frac{m^2}{n}\right) \leq \Pr(X \geq 2E[X]) \leq \frac{1}{2}.$$

Hence, when $n \geq m^2$, we find $X < 1$ with probability at least $1/2$. This implies that a randomly chosen hash function is perfect with probability at least $1/2$. ∎

To find a perfect hash function when $n \geq m^2$, we may simply try hash functions chosen uniformly at random from the 2-universal family until we find one with no collisions. This gives a Las Vegas algorithm. On average we need to try at most two hash functions.

We would like to have perfect hashing without requiring space for $\Omega(m^2)$ bins to store the set of m items. We can use a two-level scheme that accomplishes perfect hashing using only $O(m)$ bins. First, we hash the set into a hash table with m bins using a hash function from a 2-universal family. Some of these bins will have collisions. For each such bin, we provide a second hash function from an appropriate 2-universal family and an entirely separate second hash table. If the bin has $k > 1$ items in it then we use k^2 bins in the secondary hash table. We have already shown in Lemma 15.10 that with k^2 bins we can find a hash function from a 2-universal family that will give no collisions. It remains to show that, by carefully choosing the first hash function, we can guarantee that the total space used by the algorithm is only $O(m)$.

Theorem 15.11: *The two-level approach gives a perfect hashing scheme for m items using $O(m)$ bins.*

Proof: As we showed in Lemma 15.10, the number of collisions X in the first stage satisfies

$$\Pr\left(X \geq \frac{m^2}{n}\right) \leq \Pr(X \geq 2\mathbf{E}[X]) \leq \frac{1}{2}.$$

When $n = m$, this implies that the probability of having more than m collisions is at most $1/2$. Using the probabilistic method, there exists a choice of hash function from the 2-universal family in the first stage that gives at most m collisions. In fact, such a hash function can be found efficiently by trying hash functions chosen uniformly at random from the 2-universal family, giving a Las Vegas algorithm. We may therefore assume that we have found a hash function for the first stage that gives at most m collisions.

Let c_i be the number of items in the ith bin. Then there are $\binom{c_i}{2}$ collisions between items in the ith bin, so

$$\sum_{i=1}^{m} \binom{c_i}{2} \leq m.$$

For each bin with $c_i > 1$ items, we find a second hash function that gives no collisions using space c_i^2. Again, for each bin, this hash function can be found using a Las Vegas algorithm. The total number of bins used is then bounded above by

$$m + \sum_{i=1}^{m} c_i^2 \leq m + 2\sum_{i=1}^{m} \binom{c_i}{2} + \sum_{i=1}^{m} c_i \leq m + 2m + m = 4m.$$

Hence, the total number of bins used is only $O(m)$. ∎

15.4. Application: Finding Heavy Hitters in Data Streams

A router forwards packets through a network. At the end of the day, a natural question for a network administrator to ask is whether the number of bytes traveling from a source s to a destination d that have passed through the router is larger than a predetermined threshold value. We call such a source–destination pair a *heavy hitter*.

When designing an algorithm for finding heavy hitters, we must keep in mind the restrictions of the router. Routers have very little memory and so cannot keep a count for each possible pair s and d, since there are simply too many such pairs. Also, routers must forward packets quickly, so the router must perform only a small number of computational operations for each packet. We present a randomized data structure that is appropriate even with these limitations. The data structure requires a *threshold* q; all source–destination pairs that are responsible for at least q total bytes are considered heavy hitters. Usually q is some fixed percentage, such as 1%, of the total expected daily traffic. At the end of the day, the data structure gives a list of possible heavy hitters. All true heavy hitters (responsible for at least q bytes) are listed, but some other pairs may also appear in the list. Two other input constants, ε and δ, are used to control what extraneous pairs might be put in the list of heavy hitters. Suppose that Q represents the total number of bytes over the course of the day. Our data structure has the guarantee that any source–destination pair that constitutes less than $q - \varepsilon Q$ bytes of traffic is listed with probability at most δ. In other words, all heavy hitters are listed; all pairs that are sufficiently far from being a heavy hitter are listed with probability at most δ; pairs that are close to heavy hitters may or may not be listed.

This router example is typical of many situations where one wants to keep a succinct summary of a large data stream. In most *data stream models,* large amounts of data arrive sequentially in small blocks, and each block must be processed before the next block arrives. In the setting of network routers, each block is generally a packet. The amount of data being handled is often so large and the time between arrivals is so small that algorithms and data structures that use only a small amount of memory and computation per block are required.

We can use a variation of a Bloom filter, discussed in Section 5.5.3, to solve this problem. Unlike our solution there, which assumed the availability of completely random hash functions, here we obtain strong, provable bounds using only a family of 2-universal hash functions. This is important, because efficiency in the router setting demands the use of only very simple hash functions that are easy to compute, yet at the same time we want provable performance guarantees.

We refer to our data structure as a *count-min filter.* The count-min filter processes a sequential stream of pairs $X_1, X_2, \ldots$ of the form $X_t = (i_t, c_t)$, where i_t is an item and $c_t > 0$ is an integer count increment. In our routing setting, i_t would be the pair of source–destination addresses of a packet and c_t would be the number of bytes in the packet. Let

$$\text{Count}(i, T) = \sum_{t: i_t = i, 1 \leq t \leq T} c_t.$$

That is, $\text{Count}(i, T)$ is the total count associated with an item i up to time T. In the routing setting, $\text{Count}(i, T)$ would be the total number of bytes associated with packets with an address pair i up to time T. The count-min filter keeps a running approximation of $\text{Count}(i, T)$ for all items i and all times T in such a way that it can track heavy hitters.

A count-min filter consists of m counters. We assume henceforth that our counters have sufficiently many bits that we do not need to worry about overflow; in many practical situations, 32-bit counters will suffice and are convenient for implementation. A count-min filter uses k hash functions. We split the counters into k disjoint groups $G_1, G_2, \ldots, G_k$ of size m/k. For convenience, we assume in what follows that k divides m evenly. We label the counters by $C_{a,j}$, where $1 \leq a \leq k$ and $0 \leq j \leq m/k - 1$, so that $C_{a,j}$ corresponds to the jth counter in the ath group. That is, we can think of our counters as being organized in a 2-dimensional array, with m/k counters per row and k columns. Our hash functions should map items from the universe into counters, so we have hash functions H_a for $1 \leq a \leq k$, where $H_a : U \to [0, m/k - 1]$. That is, each of the k hash functions takes an item from the universe and maps it into a number $[0, m/k - 1]$. Equivalently, we can think of each hash function as taking an item i and mapping it to the counter $C_{a,H_a(i)}$. The H_a should be chosen independently and uniformly at random from a 2-universal hash family.

We use our counters to keep track of an approximation of $\text{Count}(i, T)$. Initially, all the counters are set to 0. To process a pair (i_t, c_t), we compute $H_a(i_t)$ for each a with $1 \leq a \leq k$ and increment $C_{a,H_a(i_t)}$ by c_t. Let $C_{a,j}(T)$ be the value of the counter $C_{a,j}$ after processing X_1 through X_T. We claim that, for any item, the smallest counter associated with that item is an upper bound on its count, and with bounded probability the smallest counter associated with that item is off by no more than ε times the total count of all the pairs (i_t, c_t) processed up to that point. Specifically, we have the following theorem.

Theorem 15.12: *For any i in the universe U and for any sequence $(i_1, c_1), \ldots, (i_T, c_T)$,*

$$\min_{j=H_a(i), 1 \leq a \leq k} C_{a,j}(T) \geq \text{Count}(i, T).$$

Furthermore, with probability $1 - (k/m\varepsilon)^k$ over the choice of hash functions,

$$\min_{j=H_a(i), 1 \leq a \leq k} C_{a,j}(T) \leq \text{Count}(i, T) + \varepsilon \sum_{t=1}^{T} c_t.$$

Proof: The first bound,

$$\min_{j=H_a(i), 1 \leq a \leq k} C_{a,j}(T) \geq \text{Count}(i, T),$$

is trivial. Each counter $C_{a,j}$ with $j = H_a(i)$ is incremented by c_t when the pair (i, c_t) is seen in the stream. It follows that the value of each such counter is at least $\text{Count}(i, T)$ at any time T.

For the second bound, consider any specific i and T. We first consider the specific counter $C_{1,H_1(i)}$ and then use symmetry. We know that the value of this counter is at least $\text{Count}(i, T)$ after the first T pairs. Let the random variable Z_1 be the amount the counter is incremented owing to items other than i. Let X_t be a random variable that is

1 if $i_t \neq i$ and $H_1(i_t) = H_1(i)$; X_t is 0 otherwise. Then

$$Z_1 = \sum_{\substack{t:1 \leq t \leq T, i_t \neq i \\ H_1(i_t) = H_1(i)}} c_t = \sum_{t=1}^{T} X_t c_t.$$

Because H_1 is chosen from a 2-universal family, for any $i_t \neq i$ we have

$$\Pr(H_1(i_t) = H_1(i)) \leq \frac{k}{m}$$

and hence

$$\mathbf{E}[X_t] \leq \frac{k}{m}.$$

It follows that

$$\mathbf{E}[Z_1] = \mathbf{E}\left[\sum_{t=1}^{T} X_t c_t\right] = \sum_{t=1}^{T} c_t \mathbf{E}[X_t] \leq \frac{k}{m} \sum_{t=1}^{T} c_t.$$

By Markov's inequality,

$$\Pr\left(Z_1 \geq \varepsilon \sum_{t=1}^{T} c_t\right) \leq \frac{k/m}{\varepsilon} = \frac{k}{m\varepsilon}. \tag{15.2}$$

Let $Z_2, Z_3, \ldots, Z_k$ be corresponding random variables for each of the other hash functions. By symmetry, all of the Z_i satisfy the probabilistic bound of Eqn. (15.2). Moreover, the Z_i are independent, since the hash functions are chosen independently from the family of hash functions. Hence

$$\Pr\left(\min_{j=1}^{k} Z_j \geq \varepsilon \sum_{t=1}^{T} c_t\right) = \prod_{j=1}^{k} \Pr\left(Z_j \geq \varepsilon \sum_{t=1}^{T} c_t\right) \tag{15.3}$$

$$\leq \left(\frac{k}{m\varepsilon}\right)^k. \tag{15.4}$$

∎

It is easy to check using calculus that $(k/m\varepsilon)^k$ is minimized when $k = m\varepsilon/e$, in which case

$$\left(\frac{k}{m\varepsilon}\right)^k = e^{-m\varepsilon/e}.$$

Of course, k needs to be chosen so that k and m/k are integers, but this does not substantially affect the probability bounds.

We can use a count-min filter to track heavy hitters in the routing setting as follows. When a pair (i_T, c_T) arrives, we update the count-min filter. If the minimum hash value associated with i_T is at least the threshold q for heavy hitters, then we put the item into a list of potential heavy hitters. We do not concern ourselves with the details of performing operations on this list, but note that it can be organized to allow updates and searches in time logarithmic in its size by using standard balanced search-tree data structures; alternatively, it could be organized in a large array or a hash table.

Recall that we use Q to represent the total traffic at the end of the day.

Corollary 15.13: *Suppose that we use a count-min filter with $k = \lceil \ln \frac{1}{\delta} \rceil$ hash functions, $m = \lceil \ln \frac{1}{\delta} \rceil \cdot \lceil \frac{e}{\varepsilon} \rceil$ counters, and a threshold q. Then all heavy hitters are put on the list, and any source–destination pair that corresponds to fewer than $q - \varepsilon Q$ bytes is put on the list with probability at most δ.*

Proof: Since counts increase over time, we can simply consider the situation at the end of the day. By Theorem 15.12, the count-min filter will ensure that all true heavy hitters are put on the list, since the smallest counter value for a true heavy hitter will be at least q. Further, by Theorem 15.12, the smallest counter value for any source–destination pair that corresponds to fewer than $q - \varepsilon Q$ bytes reaches q with probability at most

$$\left(\frac{k}{m\varepsilon} \right)^k \le e^{-\ln(1/\delta)} = \delta. \qquad \blacksquare$$

The count-min filter is very efficient in terms of using only limited randomness in its hash functions, only $O\left(\frac{1}{\varepsilon} \ln \frac{1}{\delta}\right)$ counters, and only $O\left(\ln \frac{1}{\delta}\right)$ computations to process each item. (Additional computation and space might be required to handle the list of potential heavy hitters, depending on its representation.)

Before ending our discussion of the count-min filter, we describe a simple improvement known as *conservative update* that often works well in practice, although it is difficult to analyze. When a pair (i_t, c_t) arrives, our original count-min filter adds c_t to each counter $C_{a,j}$ that the item i hashes to, thereby guaranteeing that

$$\min_{j=H_a(i), 1 \le a \le k} C_{a,j}(T) \ge \text{Count}(i, T)$$

holds for all i and T. In fact, this can often be guaranteed without adding c_t to each counter. Consider the state after the $(t - 1)$th pair has been processed. Suppose that, inductively, up to that point we have, for all i,

$$\min_{j=H_a(i), 1 \le a \le k} C_{a,j}(t - 1) \ge \text{Count}(i, t - 1).$$

Then, when (i_t, c_t) arrives, we need to ensure that

$$C_{a,j}(t) \ge \text{Count}(i_t, t)$$

for all counters, where $j = H_a(i_t)$, $a \le 1 \le k$. But

$$\text{Count}(i_t, t) = \text{Count}(i_t, t - 1) + c_t \le \min_{j=H_a(i_t), 1 \le a \le k} C_{a,j}(t - 1) + c_t.$$

Hence we can look at the minimum counter value v obtained from the k counters that i_t hashes to, add c_t to that value, and increase to $v + c_t$ any counter that is smaller than $v + c_t$. An example is given in Figure 15.1. An item arrives with a count of 3; at the time of arrival, the smallest counter associated with the item has value 4. It follows that the count for this item is at most 7, so we can update all associated counters to ensure they are all at least 7. In general, if all the counters i_t hashes to are equal, conservative

$(i,3)$

3	8	5	1
4	8	3	2
3	0	5	9

3	8	5	1
7	8	3	2
3	0	7	9

Figure 15.1: An item comes in, and 3 is to be added to the count. The initial state is on the left; the shaded counters need to be updated. Using conservative update, the minimum counter value 4 determines that all corresponding counters need to be pushed up to at least $4 + 3 = 7$. The resulting state after the update is shown on the right.

update is equivalent to just adding c_t to each counter. When the i_t are not all equal, the conservative update improvement adds less to some of the counters, which will tend to reduce the errors that the filter produces.

15.5. Exercises

Exercise 15.1: A fair coin is flipped n times. Let X_{ij}, with $1 \le i < j \le n$, be 1 if the ith and jth flip landed on the same side; let $X_{ij} = 0$ otherwise. Show that the X_{ij} are pairwise independent but not independent.

Exercise 15.2: (a) Let X and Y be numbers that are chosen independently and uniformly at random from $\{0, 1, \ldots, n\}$. Let Z be their sum modulo $n + 1$. Show that X, Y, and Z are pairwise independent but not independent.

(b) Extend this example to give a collection of random variables that are k-wise independent but not $(k + 1)$-wise independent.

Exercise 15.3: For any family of hash functions from a finite set U to a finite set V, show that, when h is chosen at random from that family of hash functions, there exists a pair of elements x and y such that

$$\Pr(h(x) = h(y)) \ge \frac{1}{|V|} - \frac{1}{|U|}.$$

This result should not depend on how the function h is chosen from the family.

Exercise 15.4: Show that, for any discrete random variable X that takes on values in the range $[0, 1]$, $\mathbf{Var}[X] \le 1/4$.

Exercise 15.5: Suppose we have a randomized algorithm Test for testing whether a string appears in a language L that works as follows. Given an input x, the algorithm Test chooses a random integer r uniformly from the set $S = \{0, 1, \ldots, p - 1\}$ for some prime p. If x is in the language, then Test$(x, r) = 1$ for at least half of the possible values of r. A value of r such that Test$(x, r) = 1$ is called a *witness* for x. If x is not in the language, then Test$(x, r) = 0$ always.

411

If we run the algorithm Test twice on an input $x \in L$ by choosing two numbers r_1 and r_2 independently and uniformly from S and evaluating $\text{Test}(x, r_1)$ and $\text{Test}(x, r_2)$, then we find a witness with probability at least $3/4$. Argue that we can obtain a witness with probability at least $1 - 1/t$ using the same amount of randomness by letting $s_i = r_1 i + r_2 \mod p$ and evaluating $\text{Test}(x, s_i)$ for values $0 \le i \le t < p$.

Exercise 15.6: Our analysis of Bucket sort in Section 5.2.2 assumed that n elements were chosen independently and uniformly at random from the range $[0, 2^k)$. Suppose instead that n elements are chosen uniformly from the range $[0, 2^k)$ in such a way that they are only pairwise independent. Show that, under these conditions, Bucket sort still requires linear expected time.

Exercise 15.7: **(a)** We have shown that the maximum load when n items are hashed into n bins using a hash function chosen from a 2-universal family of hash functions is at most $1 + \sqrt{2n}$ with probability at least $1/2$. Generalize this argument to k-universal hash functions. That is, find a value such that the probability that the maximum load is larger than that value is at most $1/2$.

(b) In Lemma 5.1 we showed that, under the standard balls-and-bins model, the maximum load when n balls are thrown independently and uniformly at random into n bins is at most $3 \ln n / \ln \ln n$ with probability $1 - 1/n$. Find the smallest value of k such that the maximum load is at most $3 \ln n / \ln \ln n$ with probability at least $1/2$ when choosing a hash function from a k-universal family.

Exercise 15.8: We can generalize the problem of finding a large cut to finding a large k-cut. A k-cut is a partition of the vertices into k disjoint sets, and the value of a cut is the weight of all edges crossing from one of the k sets to another. In Section 15.1.2 we considered 2-cuts when all edges had the same weight 1, and we showed how to derandomize the standard randomized algorithm using collections of n pairwise independent bits. Explain how this derandomization could be generalized to obtain a polynomial time algorithm for 3-cuts, and give the running time for your algorithm. (*Hint:* You may want to use a hash function of the type found in Section 15.3.2.)

Exercise 15.9: Suppose we are given m vectors $\bar{v}_1, \bar{v}_2, \dots, \bar{v}_m \in \{0, 1\}^\ell$ such that any k of the m vectors are linearly independent modulo 2. Let $\bar{v}_i = (v_{i,1}, v_{i,2}, \dots, v_{i,\ell})$. Let $\bar{u}$ be chosen uniformly at random from $\{0, 1\}^\ell$, and let $X_i = \sum_{j=1}^{\ell} v_{i,j} u_j \mod 2$. Show that the X_i are uniform, k-wise independent bits.

Exercise 15.10: We examine a specific way in which 2-universal hash functions differ from completely random hash functions. Let $S = \{0, 1, 2, \dots, k\}$, and consider a hash function h with range $\{0, 1, 2, \dots, p - 1\}$ for some prime p much larger than k. Consider the values $h(0), h(1), \dots, h(k)$. If h is a completely random hash function, then the probability that $h(0)$ is smaller than any of the other values is roughly $1/(k + 1)$. (There may be a tie for the smallest value, so the probability that any $h(i)$ is the unique smallest value is slightly less than $1/(k + 1)$.) Now consider a hash function h chosen uniformly from the family

$$\mathcal{H} = \{h_{a,b} \mid 0 \le a, b \le p - 1\}$$

of Section 15.3.2. Estimate the probability that $h(0)$ is smaller than $h(1), \ldots, h(k)$ by randomly choosing 10,000 hash functions from h and computing $h(x)$ for all $x \in S$. Run this experiment for $k = 32$ and $k = 128$, using primes $p = 5{,}023{,}309$ and $p = 10{,}570{,}849$. Is your estimate close to $1/(k + 1)$?

Exercise 15.11: In a multi-set, each element can appear multiple times. Suppose that we have two multi-sets, S_1 and S_2, consisting of positive integers. We want to test if the two sets are the "same" – that is, if each item appears the same number of times in each set. One way of doing this is to sort both sets and then compare the sets in sorted order. This takes $O(n \log n)$ time if each multi-set contains n elements.

(a) Consider the following algorithm. Hash each element of S_1 into a hash table with cn counters; the counters are initially 0, and the ith counter is incremented each time the hash value of an element is i. Using another table of the same size and using the same hash function, do the same for S_2. If the ith counter in the first table matches the ith counter in the second table for all i, report that the sets are the same, and otherwise report that the sets are different.

Analyze the running time and error probability of this algorithm, assuming that the hash function is chosen from a 2-universal family. Explain how this algorithm can be extended to a Monte Carlo algorithm, and analyze the trade-off between its running time and its error probability.

(b) We can also design a Las Vegas algorithm for this problem. Now each entry in the hash table corresponds to a linked list of counters. Each entry holds a list of the number of occurrences of each element that hashes to that location; this list can be kept in sorted order. Again, we create a hash table for S_1 and a hash table for S_2, and we test after hashing if the resulting tables are equal.

Argue that this algorithm requires only linear expected time using only linear space.

Exercise 15.12: In Section 15.3.1 we showed that the family

$$\mathcal{H} = \{h_{a,b} \mid 1 \le a \le p - 1, \; 0 \le b \le p - 1\}$$

is 2-universal when $p \ge n$, where

$$h_{a,b}(x) = ((ax + b) \bmod p) \bmod n.$$

Consider now the hash functions

$$h_a(x) = (ax \bmod p) \bmod n$$

and the family

$$\mathcal{H}' = \{h_a \mid 1 \le a \le p - 1\}.$$

413

Give an example to show that $\mathcal{H}'$ is not 2-universal. Then prove that $\mathcal{H}'$ is almost 2-universal in the following sense: for any $x, y \in \{0, 1, 2, \ldots, p - 1\}$, if h is chosen uniformly at random from $\mathcal{H}'$ then

$$\Pr(h(x) = h(y)) \leq \frac{2}{n}.$$

Exercise 15.13: In describing count-min filters, we assumed that the data stream consisted of pairs of the form (i_t, c_t), where i_t was an item and $c_t > 0$ an integer count increment. Suppose that one were also allowed to decrement the count for an item, so that the stream could include pairs of the form (i_t, c_t) with $c_t < 0$. We could require that the total count for an item i,

$$\text{Count}(i, T) = \sum_{t:i_t=i, 1 \leq t \leq T} c_t,$$

always be positive.

Explain how you could modify or otherwise use count-min filters to find heavy hitters in this situation.

CHAPTER SIXTEEN

Power Laws and Related Distributions

In this chapter, we explore some additional basic probability distributions that arise in a number of computer science applications. One family of distributions we focus on are called *power law* distributions. An interesting aspect of these distributions is that, unlike many of the distributions we have seen, the variance of the distribution can be extremely large – with some natural choices of parameters, the variance is infinite. As a result, certain methods we usually rely on in probabilistic arguments, such as concentration of the sum of random variables, may not apply.

Power laws and related distributions may initially appear surprising or unusual, but in fact they are quite natural, and arise easily from a number of basic models. We examine some of these models in the course of the chapter. Power laws may contrast sharply with other distributions we have seen, such as Gaussian distributions, which also appear quite frequently in real-world settings, but both types of distributions have their uses and their place.

As some groundwork, suppose we want to consider the average height of women in the United States. We could take a random sample of women, and we would expect that a fairly small number of samples would quickly lead to a good estimate. (The U.S. Census Bureau publishes data on height distribution; currently, the average woman's height is somewhere between 5' 4" and 5' 5", although the range depends on the age group you are considering.) This is because heights fall in a narrow range, with the number of people of a certain height falling very quickly as you move away from the average – very few women are more than 7 feet tall. On the other hand, suppose we wanted to find the average number of times a word appears in all the books printed in the United States in a year. Some common words, such as "the", "of", and "an", appear remarkably frequently, while most words would only appear at most a handful of times. In fact, the distribution of words in literature has been studied in some detail, and has been found to roughly follow a power law distribution. We consider later some proposed arguments for why that might naturally be the case.

Many other phenomena share this property that the corresponding distribution is not well concentrated around its mean, such as the sizes of cities, the strength of

415

earthquakes, and the distribution of wealth among families. For many such examples, a power law distribution provides a plausible model for the distribution.

16.1. Power Law Distributions: Basic Definitions and Properties

Before defining a power law distribution, it may help to give an example. A *Pareto distribution* with parameters $\alpha > 0$ and minimum value $m > 0$ satisfies

$$\Pr(X \geq x) = \left(\frac{x}{m}\right)^{-\alpha}.$$

Here the minimum value m appropriately satisfies $\Pr(X \geq m) = 1$. The value α is sometimes called the *tail index*. Correspondingly, the density function for the Pareto distribution is

$$f(x) = \alpha m^{\alpha} x^{-\alpha-1}.$$

Let us try to examine the moments of this random variable. The mean $\mathbf{E}[X]$ is given by

$$
\begin{aligned}
\mathbf{E}[X] &= \int_{x=m}^{\infty} x f(x) dx \\
&= \int_{x=m}^{\infty} x(\alpha m^{\alpha} x^{-\alpha-1}) dx \\
&= \alpha m^{\alpha} \int_{x=m}^{\infty} x^{-\alpha} dx.
\end{aligned}
$$

We already notice something unusual; the mean is not finite when $\alpha \leq 1$, as the integral in the expression above diverges. For $\alpha > 1$, we can complete the calculation to find the mean is given by

$$\mathbf{E}[X] = \frac{\alpha m}{\alpha - 1}.$$

If we look at the jth moment $\mathbf{E}[X^j]$, we have

$$
\begin{aligned}
\mathbf{E}[X^j] &= \int_{x=m}^{\infty} x^j f(x) dx \\
&= \int_{x=m}^{\infty} x^j (\alpha m^{\alpha} x^{-\alpha-1}) dx \\
&= \alpha m^{\alpha} \int_{x=m}^{\infty} x^{j-1-\alpha} dx.
\end{aligned}
$$

The jth moment is not finite when $\alpha \leq j$; for $\alpha > j$, we have

$$\mathbf{E}[X^j] = \frac{\alpha m^j}{\alpha - j}.$$

So, for example, when $\alpha \leq 2$, the second moment is infinite. Correspondingly, the variance is infinite when $1 < \alpha \leq 2$; for $\alpha \leq 1$ since both the first and second moments are infinite the variance is not well-defined.

416

More generally, we say that a nonnegative random variable X is said to have a *power law distribution* if

$$\Pr(X \geq x) \sim cx^{-\alpha}$$

for constants $c > 0$ and $\alpha > 0$. Here $f(x) \sim g(x)$ represents that the limit of the ratio of $f(x)$ and $g(x)$ converges to 1 as x grows large. Roughly speaking, a power law distribution asymptotically behaves like a Pareto distribution. It is worth noting that the term is sometimes used slightly differently in other contexts. For example, sometimes people use power law distribution interchangeably with Pareto distribution, and refer to what we have called a power law distribution as an *asymptotic power law distribution*. Also, sometimes people use $\alpha + 1$ in the definition where we have used α. (This convention yields that the density function, rather than the complementary cumulative distribution function, has parameter α.) Finally, sometimes one allows the ratio to converge not to 1, but to some slowly growing function.

A power law is best visualized on what is called a *log–log plot*, where both axes are presented using logarithmic scales. On a log–log plot the relationship $y = ax^b$ is shown by presenting $\ln y = b \ln x + \ln a$, so that the polynomial relationship appears as a straight line whose slope depends on the exponent b. (Here we use a natural logarithm for our log–log plot, but we could use any base for the logarithm and still obtain a straight line.) For a Pareto distribution with parameters $\alpha > 0$ and $m > 0$, a log–log plot of $\bar{F}(x) = \Pr(X \geq x)$ (which we recall is called the complementary cumulative distribution function) therefore follows a straight line:

$$\ln \bar{F}(x) = -\alpha \ln x + \alpha \ln m.$$

More generally, if X has a power law distribution, then in a log–log plot of the complementary cumulative distribution function, asymptotically the behavior will be a straight line. This provides a simple empirical test for whether a random variable may behave according to a power law given an appropriate sample; while a nearly straight line does not guarantee a power law distribution, if the results are far from a straight line, a power law is unlikely. (It is important to emphasize that the "straight-line" test on a log–log plot is sometimes used to infer that a sample arises from a distribution that follows a power law, but because many other distributions produce nearly linear outcomes on a log–log plot, one must take more care to test for power laws.) On a log–log plot the density function for the Pareto distribution also is a straight line:

$$\ln f(x) = (-\alpha - 1) \ln x + \alpha \ln m + \ln \alpha.$$

Similarly, asymptotically the density function for a power law will approach a straight line.

Thus far we have focused on the mathematical definitions for continuous power law distributions. But we could also consider discrete variations. For example, the *zeta distribution* with parameter $s > 1$ is defined for all positive integer values according to

$$\Pr(X = k) = \frac{k^{-s}}{\zeta(s)},$$

where the Riemann zeta function $\zeta(s)$ is given by $\zeta(s) = \sum_{j=1}^{\infty} j^{-s}$. The fact that $\Pr(X = k)$ is proportional to k^{-s} is the natural discrete analogue for a power law distribution.

16.2. Power Laws in Language

16.2.1. *Zipf's Law and Other Examples*

It has long been observed that the distribution of word frequencies appears to follow a power law. That is, the frequency of the kth most frequent word in a language is roughly proportional to k^{-s} for some exponent s, so the frequency distribution is well modeled by a (discrete) power law. In terms of probability, this means that if you choose a word uniformly at random from a collection of texts, the kth most frequent word will be chosen with probability roughly proportional to k^{-s}. Equivalently, the rank of the frequency of a randomly chosen word is well modeled by a zeta distribution. For several languages, the value of s is close to 1.

This empirical observation is commonly referred to as Zipf's law, as the linguist George Zipf popularized it in the first half of the twentieth century, although it appears to have been noticed by others before Zipf. One sometimes also sees reference to the Zipf–Mandelbrot law, which offers the generalization that the frequency of the kth most frequent word in a language is roughly proportional to $(k + q)^{-s}$ for some exponent s and some constant q. Also, while one usually hears Zipf's law in reference to languages, sometimes Zipf's law is used to refer to other natural occurences where the frequency of ranked items of a collection of objects follows a power law distribution.

Is there a mathematical framework that might explain the power law behavior of languages? Below, we consider multiple models that lead to power laws, and might apply. (However, we encourage healthy skepticism regarding whether any particular simple mathematical model offers a complete or compelling explanation for Zipf's law.)

Before continuing, it is worth noting that historically power laws have been observed in a variety of fields in the natural and social sciences, not merely in languages. Perhaps the earliest references appear in the work by Vilfredo Pareto, whose name we have seen in the context of the Pareto distribution; he introduced this distribution around 1897 to describe the distribution of income. Over a century ago the German physicist Felix Auerbach first suggested that city sizes appear to follow a power law distribution, although Zipf is often credited with this finding as well. Alfred Lotka in the 1920s found in examining the number of articles produced by chemists that the distribution followed a power law; the finding that publication frequency follows a power law is commonly called Lotka's Law. The Richter scale for measuring the magnitude of an earthquake is based on the Gutenberg–Richter law, which says that the relationship between the frequency of earthquakes and their magnitude follows a power law. The historical record shows that several natural occurrences of power laws have been known for a long time; it is therefore not especially surprising that power laws would also naturally occur in several places in computer science and engineering.

16.2.2. *Languages via Optimization*

One argument for power laws arising in the context of word frequencies arises naturally under a framework where the goal is to maximize the efficiency of the language in a specific sense. Consider a language consisting of n words. Let the cost of using the kth most frequent word of the language be C_k. For example, if we think of English text, the cost of a word might be thought of as the number of letters plus the additional cost of a space. This is the cost to write the word, and (at least roughly) might correspond to the cost of speaking it.

If the alphabet Σ has size d, then we have d^j possible words of length j. We would naturally assign more frequent words to shorter strings to reduce the cost. With such an assignment, the words with frequency ranks $1 + (d^j - 1)/(d - 1)$ to $(d^{j+1} - 1)/(d - 1)$ have j letters. As a simplification, the length of the kth most frequent word would be approximately $\log_d k$, and hence a natural cost function has $C_k \sim \log_d k$. For convenience, let us take $C_k = \log_d k$ in what follows.

Now suppose that we had the power to design the frequencies of words in our language in order to maximize the ratio between the average amount of information obtained for each word written and the corresponding average cost. This seems like a natural goal. We first need to quantify what we mean by information. The natural choice to use here is entropy. (See Chapter 10.) That is, we now think of each word used as being selected randomly according to a probability distribution, and the probability that the kth most frequent word in the language is chosen is p_k. Then the average information given per word is the entropy $H = -\sum_{k=1}^{n} p_k \log_2 p_k$, and the average cost per word is $C = \sum_{k=1}^{n} p_k C_k$. The question is how would the p_k be chosen to maximize the ratio $R = H/C$. It is slightly easier to look at the equivalent problem of minimizing the ratio $A = C/H$.

Taking derivatives, we find

$$\frac{dA}{dp_k} = \frac{C_k H + C \log_2(e p_k)}{H^2}.$$

Hence all the derivatives are 0 (and A is in fact minimized) when

$$p_k = 2^{-HC_k/C}/e = 2^{-RC_k}/e.$$

Using $C_k = \log_d k$, we find

$$p_k = 2^{-R\log_d k}/e = k^{-R\log_d 2}/e.$$

That is, regardless of what the optimal value R turns out to be, the corresponding p_k fall according to a power law distribution.

16.2.3. *Monkeys Typing Randomly*

The optimization argument appears quite compelling. However, another argument shows that power law word frequency distributions can arise even without an underlying optimization.

Consider the following experiment. A monkey types randomly on a keyboard with d characters and a space bar. A space is hit with probability q; all other characters are hit with equal probability $(1 - q)/d$. A space is used to separate words. We consider the frequency distribution of words.

It is clear that as the monkey types, each word with j characters occurs with probability

$$q_j = \left(\frac{1 - q}{d}\right)^j q,$$

and there are d^j words of length j. (We allow the empty word of length 0 for convenience.) The words of longer length are less likely and hence occur lower in the rank order of word frequency. In particular, the words with frequency ranks $1 + (d^j - 1)/(d - 1)$ to $(d^{j+1} - 1)/(d - 1)$ have j letters. Hence, the word with frequency rank $k = d^j$ has length $j = \log_d k$ and occurs with probability

$$p_k = \left(\frac{1 - q}{d}\right)^{\log_d k} q = k^{\log_d(1-q)-1} q.$$

For $k \neq d^j$, as in Section 16.2.2 it is reasonable to use as an approximation that the length of the kth most frequent word is $\log_d k$, in which case $p_k \approx k^{\log_d(1-q)-1} q$, and the power law behavior is apparent.[1]

The power law associated with word frequency, although it naturally arises from optimization, does not seem to actually require it. This result serves as something of a warning; there are multiple ways that power law distributions can arise. Indeed, we next turn to one of the most frequently used models that leads to power law distributions, preferential attachment.

16.3. Preferential Attachment

To describe preferential attachment, let us work with a very simple model of the World Wide Web. The World Wide Web conists of web pages and directed hyperlinks from one page to another. The World Wide Web can naturally be thought of as a graph, with pages corresponding to vertices and hyperlinks corresponding to directed edges. The graph grows and changes as pages and links are added to the Web.

Our model of the Web's growth will be very basic; our goal is not detailed accuracy, but a high-level understanding of what might be happening. Let us start with two pages, each linking to the other; the starting configuration does not make a substantial difference, so this configuration is chosen for convenience. At each time step, a new page appears, with just a single link. (One could try to be more accurate by having multiple links or a distribution on links, but having a single link per page simplifies our

---

[1] The attentive reader might note that technically the result above does not quite match a power law as we have defined it; the appropriate limit does not tend to 1 but is bounded above and below by a constant, because instead of a steady decrease in the frequency with the rank there are discrete jumps. That is, instead of taking a power law to be defined by $\Pr(X \geq x) \sim cx^{-\alpha}$, we instead have a case here where $\Pr(X \geq x)$ is $\Theta(x^{-\alpha})$. This is a minor point; small amounts of noise in the frequency of how individual letters are chosen would lead to a smoother behavior. Also, in some settings, random variables where $\Pr(X \geq x)$ is $\Theta(x^{-\alpha})$ are referred to as power laws.

analysis and yields the important insights.) How should we model what page the new link points to?

The idea behind preferential attachment is that new links will tend to attach to popular pages. In the case of the Web graph, new links tend to go to pages that already have links. We can model this by thinking of the new page as copying a random link, with some probability. Specifically, with probability $\gamma < 1$, the link for the new page points to a page chosen uniformly at random, but with probability $1 - \gamma$, the new page copies a random link, so that the new page points to an existing page chosen proportionally to the indegree of that page. We point out that our preferential attachment model of the World Wide Web is a Markov chain, as we do not care about the history of how links attached when a new link is added. We only care about the number of links directed into each page.

Let us start with a not entirely rigorous argument that provides the intuition for how this model behaves. Let $X_j(t)$ (or just X_j where the meaning is clear) be the number of pages with indegree j when there are t pages in the system. Then for $j \geq 1$ the probability that X_j increases is just

$$\gamma X_{j-1}(t)/t + (1 - \gamma)(j - 1)X_{j-1}(t)/t;$$

the first term is the probability a new link is chosen at random and chooses a page with indegree $j - 1$, and the second term is the probability that a new link is chosen proportionally to the indegrees and chooses a page with indegree $j - 1$. Similarly, the probability that X_j decreases is

$$\gamma X_j(t)/t + (1 - \gamma)j X_j(t)/t.$$

Let us write $\Delta(X_j(t))$ for $X_j(t + 1) - X_j(t)$. Then we can write

$$\mathbf{E}[\Delta(X_j(t)) \mid X_{j-1}(t), X_j(t)] = \frac{\gamma X_{j-1}(t)}{t} + \frac{(1 - \gamma)(j - 1)X_{j-1}(t)}{t}$$
$$- \frac{\gamma X_j(t)}{t} - \frac{(1 - \gamma)j X_j(t)}{t}. \tag{16.1}$$

The case of X_0 must be treated specially, since each new page introduces a new vertex of indegree 0. Hence

$$\mathbf{E}[\Delta(X_0(t)) \mid X_0(t)] = 1 - \frac{\gamma X_0(t)}{t}. \tag{16.2}$$

While not required for our analysis, it is worth observing that for any value k, the vector of values $(X_0(t), X_1(t), \ldots, X_k(t))$ is also a Markov chain.

Now as t grows large, we would suspect that pages of indegree j will constitute a fraction c_j of the total pages. Suppose that in the limit as t grows large $X_j(t) = c_j \cdot t$, with high probability. What values of c_j are consistent with this family of equations? With these assumptions, we can solve for the appropriate c_j, successively starting from c_0. In this case, $\mathbf{E}[\Delta(X_0(t)) \mid X_0(t)] = c_0$, because on average X_0 must increase by c_0 per new page in order for $X_0(t)$ to grow like $c_0 t$. Hence, Eqn. (16.2) becomes

$$c_0 = 1 - \gamma c_0,$$

so $c_0 = \frac{1}{1+\gamma}$. More generally, we find using Eqn. (16.1) that

$$c_j = \gamma c_{j-1} + (1 - \gamma)(j - 1)c_{j-1} - \gamma c_j - (1 - \gamma)jc_j. \qquad (16.3)$$

This gives the following recurrence for c_j.

$$c_j = c_{j-1}\frac{(\gamma + (j - 1)(1 - \gamma))}{(1 + \gamma + j(1 - \gamma))}. \qquad (16.4)$$

This is enough for us to find the values for c_j explicitly. If we focus on the asymptotics, we find that for large j

$$\frac{c_j}{c_{j-1}} = 1 - \frac{2 - \gamma}{1 + \gamma + j(1 - \gamma)} \sim 1 - \left(\frac{2 - \gamma}{1 - \gamma}\right)\left(\frac{1}{j}\right).$$

Asymptotically, for the above to hold we have $c_j \sim j^{-\frac{2-\gamma}{1-\gamma}}$, giving a power law. To see this, we observe that $c_j \sim j^{-\frac{2-\gamma}{1-\gamma}}$ implies

$$\frac{c_j}{c_{j-1}} \sim \left(\frac{j - 1}{j}\right)^{\frac{2-\gamma}{1-\gamma}} \sim 1 - \left(\frac{2 - \gamma}{1 - \gamma}\right)\left(\frac{1}{j}\right).$$

16.3.1. *A Formal Version*

We can formalize the above argument for preferential attachment by using martingales. We first show that it is enough to find the expectations of the degrees for the preferential attachment process, as the number of vertices of each degree can be placed in the framework of a Doob martingale, allowing us to utilize Azuma–Hoeffding tail bounds. We then formalize how to compute the corresponding expectations.

Consider the preferential attachment process described previously, until there are T pages overall. To be clear, we start with two pages, pointing at each other. We let Z_i refer to the random variables corresponding to the choices made when there are i pages in the system to determine the page linked to by the $(i + 1)$st page. Let $X_{j,t}$ be a random variable corresponding to the number of pages of degree j when there are t pages. Further, for $t \geq 2$, let $Y_{j,t} = \mathbf{E}[X_{j,T} \mid Z_2, Z_3, \ldots, Z_{t-1}]$.

Lemma 16.1: *Then*

$$\Pr(|X_{j,T} - \mathbf{E}[X_{j,T}]| \geq \lambda) \leq 2e^{-\lambda^2/(8T)}.$$

Proof: As mentioned, we show that the $Y_{j,t}$ form a Doob martingale with

$$|Y_{j,t} - Y_{j,t+1}| \leq 2;$$

then the result follows immediately from Theorem 13.6. (We could replace the T by $T - 2$ in the denominator, as there are only $T - 2$ time steps, but this notation is easier.) The sequence is clearly a Doob martingale, obtained by revealing the choices at each step. To bound the difference $|Y_{j,t} - Y_{j,t+1}|$, we claim that the choice corresponding to Z_t affects the number of vertices with degree j at the end of the process by at most 2. Specifically, if a vertex v_1 is chosen to receive a link at the tth step, and we instead consider what would have happened if another vertex v_2 had been chosen, the only vertex degrees affected are those of v_1 and v_2. To see this, consider the evolution of graphs G_1 and G_2 arising after choosing v_1 or v_2, respectively, at the tth step. If the next step creates a link to a random vertex (the same random vertex in both graphs, as the Z_{t+1} would be the same), the degree of every vertex besides v_1 and v_2 remains the same in G_1 and G_2. Similarly, consider if the next step creates a link by copying a random link; that is, Z_{t+1} says to copy the link created at the ℓth step of the process for some ℓ. If $\ell \neq t$, then again the degree of every vertex besides v_1 and v_2 clearly remains the same in G_1 and G_2, since the same vertex receives a new link. If $\ell = t$, then v_1 obtains an extra link in G_1 and v_2 obtains an extra link in G_2; however, this only affects the degrees of vertices v_1 and v_2, so the bound on $|Y_{j,t} - Y_{j,t+1}|$ still holds. ∎

It remains to determine the expectations $\mathbf{E}[X_{j,T}]$. We start with $\mathbf{E}[X_{0,t}]$.

Lemma 16.2: *For $t \geq 2$.*

$$\frac{1}{1+\gamma} - \frac{2}{t} \leq \frac{\mathbf{E}[X_{0,t}]}{t} \leq \frac{1}{1+\gamma}.$$

Proof: It follows from Eqn. (16.2), Theorem 2.7, and the linearity of expectations that

$$\mathbf{E}[X_{0,t+1}] = \mathbf{E}[X_{0,t}] + 1 - \frac{\gamma \mathbf{E}[X_{0,t}]}{t} = 1 + \left(1 - \frac{\gamma}{t}\right)\mathbf{E}[X_{0,t}]. \tag{16.5}$$

Because we started with two pages pointing to each other for convenience, we have the initial condition $\mathbf{E}[X_{0,2}] = 0$.

For $t \geq 2$, let

$$\delta(t) = \frac{1}{1+\gamma}t - \mathbf{E}[X_{0,t}].$$

From Eqn. (16.5), it is easy to calculate $\delta(2) = \frac{2}{1+\gamma}$ and $\delta(3) = \frac{2-\gamma}{1+\gamma}$. More generally,

$$\delta(t+1) - \delta(t) = \mathbf{E}[X_{0,t}] - \mathbf{E}[X_{0,t+1}] + \frac{1}{1+\gamma}$$

$$= -1 + \frac{\gamma \mathbf{E}[X_{0,t}]}{t} + \frac{1}{1+\gamma}$$

$$= -\frac{\gamma \delta(t)}{t}.$$

It follows that $\delta(t)$ is decreasing in t, but is always greater than 0. The lemma follows, since $\delta(t) < 2$. ∎

More generally, we have the following:

Lemma 16.3: *Let c_j be the constants given by Eqn. (16.3). For any constant j, there is a constant B_j such that for $t \geq 2$*

$$\left|\frac{\mathbf{E}[X_{j,t}]}{t} - c_j\right| \leq \frac{B_j}{t}.$$

423

Before beginning the proof, we outline the reasoning behind it. The idea is that if $\mathbf{E}[X_{j,t}]$ is too far from $c_j t$, at the next step there will be a push to reduce the difference. If $\mathbf{E}[X_{j,t}]$ becomes too large, then it becomes more likely that at the next step a vertex with degree j will gain a link to it and become a vertex of degree $j + 1$, reducing the difference between $\mathbf{E}[X_{j,t}]$ and $c_j t$. Similarly, if $\mathbf{E}[X_{j,t}]$ becomes too small, then it is less likely that a vertex with degree j will gain a link and the difference is similarly reduced. The complication is that $X_{j,t+1}$ also depends on $\mathbf{E}[X_{j-1,t}]$, which may itself be deviating from $c_{j-1} t$, and therefore may also serve to push $\mathbf{E}[X_{j,t}]$ from $c_j t$. Inductively, however, those deviations are small, and as such their effect is overcome by the initial effect that pushes $\mathbf{E}[X_{j,t}]$ to $c_j t$.

Proof: We know the statement is true for $j = 0$, and we prove it by induction for larger j, by also performing an induction on the time t. For $j \geq 0$ and $t \geq 2$, let

$$\delta_j(t) = c_j t - \mathbf{E}[X_{j,t}],$$

where c_j is given by Eqn. (16.3). From Eqn. (16.1), we have for $j \geq 1$

$$\mathbf{E}[X_{j,t+1}] = \mathbf{E}[X_{j,t}] + \frac{\gamma + (1-\gamma)(j-1)}{t}\mathbf{E}[X_{j-1,t}] - \frac{\gamma + (1-\gamma)j}{t}\mathbf{E}[X_{j,t}]. \quad (16.6)$$

Using Eqn. (16.6), we find for $j \geq 1$

$$\delta_j(t+1) = c_j(t+1) - \mathbf{E}[X_{j,t+1}]$$

$$= c_j t + c_j - \mathbf{E}[X_{j,t}] - \frac{\gamma + (1-\gamma)(j-1)}{t}\mathbf{E}[X_{j-1,t}] + \frac{\gamma + (1-\gamma)j}{t}\mathbf{E}[X_{j,t}]$$

$$= c_j + \delta_j(t) - \frac{\gamma + (1-\gamma)(j-1)}{t}\mathbf{E}[X_{j-1,t}] + \frac{\gamma + (1-\gamma)j}{t}\mathbf{E}[X_{j,t}]$$

$$= c_j + \delta_j(t) - \frac{\gamma + (1-\gamma)(j-1)}{t}(c_{j-1}t - \delta_{j-1}(t))$$

$$\quad + \frac{\gamma + (1-\gamma)j}{t}(c_j t - \delta_j(t))$$

$$= \delta_j(t) + \frac{\gamma + (1-\gamma)(j-1)}{t}\delta_{j-1}(t) - \frac{\gamma + (1-\gamma)j}{t}\delta_j(t).$$

Suppose inductively that $|\delta_{j-1}(t)| \leq B_{j-1}$. Now for $t \leq \gamma + (1-\gamma)j$ we can find a constant B_j so that $|\delta_{j-1}(t)| \leq B_j$, since this is only over a constant number of steps. Let us also suppose that $B_j \geq B_{j-1}$; if not, we could simply increase B_j to this value. For $t > \gamma + (1-\gamma)j$, the right-hand side above has absolute value bounded by

$$\left| \left(1 - \frac{\gamma + (1-\gamma)j}{t}\right)\delta_j(t) + \frac{\gamma + (1-\gamma)(j-1)}{t}\delta_{j-1}(t) \right|.$$

As $t > \gamma + (1-\gamma)j$ implies $\frac{\gamma + (1-\gamma)j}{t} < 1$, this expression is bounded above by

$$\left(1 - \frac{\gamma + (1-\gamma)j}{t}\right)B_j + \frac{\gamma + (1-\gamma)(j-1)}{t}B_{j-1} \leq B_j$$

where here we have inductively assumed $\delta_j(t) \leq B_j$, and the right-hand side then follows from $\frac{\gamma + (1-\gamma)j}{t} \geq \frac{\gamma + (1-\gamma)(j-1)}{t}$ and $B_j \geq B_{j-1}$.

As a result we have $|\delta_j(t+1)| \leq B_j$ and by induction the lemma follows. ∎

To summarize, we have shown that under appropriate initial conditions for the preferential attachment model for the World Wide Web with high probability the fraction of pages with j other pages linking to that page converges to c_j, where the c_j follow a power law given by $c_j \sim j^{-\frac{2-\gamma}{1-\gamma}}$. Here $1 - \gamma$ is the probability a link for a new page is chosen by copying an existing link.

Although we have presented preferential attachment as a potential model for the Web graph, our analysis applies generally to preferential attachment models. In fact, the idea of preferential attachment arose much earlier than the World Wide Web; in 1925, Yule used a similar analysis to explain the distribution of species among genera of plants, which had been shown empirically to satisfy a power law distribution. Another development of how preferential attachment leads to a power law was given by Simon in 1955. While Simon was a bit too early to provide a model for the graph arising from the World Wide Web, he suggested several potential applications of this type of preferential attachment model: distributions of word frequencies in documents, distributions of numbers of papers published by scientists, distribution of cities by population, distribution of incomes, and distribution of species among genera.

16.4. Using the Power Law in Algorithm Analysis

In some cases, algorithms can be designed to take advantage of or analyzed taking advantage of the fact that the object being studied is related to a power law. One prototypical example involves listing or counting triangles in graphs. Counting triangles often proves important in network analysis; the number of triangles is related to the clustering coefficient of a graph, which measures the tendency of vertices in a graph to cluster together. For example, in social networks, where vertices represent people and edges represent friendships, the closing of a triangle represents two people with a mutual friend becoming friends themselves.

Let us work in the simple setting of undirected graphs with no self-loops or multiple parallel edges between vertices, and with n vertices and m edges. Counting and listing triangles can naturally be done in $\Theta(n^3)$ time by checking all possible triples of vertices. Counting can be done faster via matrix multiplication; if A is the adjacency matrix of the graph, then the diagonal of A^3 is related to the number of triangles in the graph. Specifically, the ith diagonal entry is equal to twice the number of triangles in which the ith vertex is contained. Hence one can divide the sum of the diagonal entries by six to obtain the total number of triangles in the graph. Since matrix multiplication can be done in time $o(n^3)$, this approach is faster than checking all possible triples.

For sparse graphs, we can do even better. We provide an algorithm that can count and list triangles in $O(m^{3/2})$ time, which is optimal in that there can be $\Omega(m^{3/2})$ triangles in a graph. We then show that the running time of the algorithm can be improved, under the assumption that the degree sequence of the graph is governed by a power law.

Theorem 16.4: *The Triangle Listing Algorithm runs in $O(m^{3/2})$ time (assuming $m \geq n$).*

Triangle Listing Algorithm:

Input: An undirected graph $G = (V, E)$ with no self-loops or multiple edges between vertices, in adjacency list form.

Output: A listing of all triangles in the graph.

Main routine:

1. Sort the vertices by degree, from smallest to largest; let $d(v)$ be the degree of v, and $N(v)$ be the set of neighbors of v.
2. Let $d^*(v)$ be v's position in the sorted order, with ties broken arbitrarily.
3. Create an array of n lists, where $A[v]$ is a list associated with v. Initially all lists are empty.
4. For each vertex v, in decreasing order of $d^*(v)$:
   (a) For each $u \in N(v)$ with $d^*(u) < d^*(v)$:
      i. for each $w \in A[u] \cap A[v]$ output the triangle $\{u, v, w\}$;
      ii. add v to the list $A[u]$.

Algorithm 16.1: Triangle Listing.

Proof: We first show that all triangles are listed exactly once. Consider a triangle $\{x, y, z\}$ with $d^*(x) > d^*(y) > d^*(z)$. Let us say a vertex v is processed when we reach it as we go through the vertices in decreasing order of the d^* values. Then vertex x is processed before vertices y and z. The triangle is listed precisely when vertex y is processed, since vertex x was added to $A[y]$ and $A[z]$ when x was processed, and when y is processed we have that $z \in N(y)$ and $d^*(z) < d^*(y)$, so the triangle will be output. Moreover, this will be the only time this triangle is output, since when vertex x is processed neither y nor z is in $A[x]$, and when vertex z is processed both $d^*(x)$ and $d^*(y)$ are greater than $d^*(z)$.

To bound the running time, we first see that calculating the vertex degrees is $O(m)$ and the initial sorting step is $O(n \log n)$, and these are each $O(m^{3/2})$. We claim that for each of the $O(m)$ edges, corresponding to the step "For each $u \in N(v)$", we do at most $O(\sqrt{m})$ work to calculate the intersection of $A[u]$ and $A[v]$. Because $A[u]$ and $A[v]$ are in sorted order with vertices ordered by d^* as they are added to the list, the intersection can be computed in time proportional to the maximum list size. But for any vertex x, $A[x]$ contains only vertices with degree at least as large as x's degree. If x's degree was larger than $2\sqrt{m}$, then all of x's neighbors in $A[x]$ would also have degree larger than $2\sqrt{m}$, which would yield at least $(2\sqrt{m})^2/2 = 2m$ edges in the graph. (We divide by 2 as each edge might be counted twice.) This contradicts that there are only m edges in the graph, so every list $A[x]$ has size at most $O(\sqrt{m})$, and the total running time is bounded by $O(m^{3/2})$. ∎

Now let us consider this algorithm in the setting where the graph has a degree distribution that is governed by a power law. There are various ways one could define the degree distribution being governed by a power law, but for our purposes here it will suffice to say that we assume we have a graph where the number of vertices of degree at least j is at most $cnj^{-\alpha}$ for some constants c and α. Notice that if the number of vertices of degree exactly j is at most $c_2 nj^{-\beta}$ for some constants c_2 and β, then this condition is satisfied, with $\alpha = \beta - 1$. Such an assumption could hold with high probability for a random graph produced by, for example, a preferential attachment model.

Theorem 16.5: *The Triangle Listing Algorithm runs in $O(mn^{1/(1+\alpha)})$ time if the number of vertices of degree at least j is at most $cnj^{-\alpha}$ for some constants c and α.*

Theorem 16.5 offers an improved bound over Theorem 16.4 when $\alpha > 1$. Notice that such power law graphs are sparse, so in this case $m = O(n)$; hence the running time could also be expressed as $O(n^{(2+\alpha)/(1+\alpha)})$.

Proof: We again bound the work to calculate the intersections of $A[u]$ and $A[v]$. For any vertex x, $|A[x]| \leq d(x)$, since only neighbors of x are on the list $A[x]$. Also, $A[x]$ only contains vertices with degree at least $d(x)$. Hence $|A[x]| \leq \min(d(x), cn(d(x))^{-\alpha})$. Equalizing terms in the minimization, we find $|A[x]| \leq (cn)^{1/(1+\alpha)}$. The theorem follows. ∎

16.5. Other Related Distributions

While power law distributions can often provide a natural model, there are other distributions with similar behaviors that may provide better models in some situations. Indeed, there can be controversy as to what is the best model in various situations, and because the tail of a power law distribution corresponds to relatively rare events, the choice of model can have significant implications regarding the importance of these rare events. It could be important to have a good model, for example, of exactly how rarely very strong earthquakes will occur. Here we examine some distributions that are often suggested as alternatives to a power law distribution.

16.5.1. *Lognormal Distributions*

A non-negative random variable X has a lognormal distribution if the random variable $Y = \ln X$ has a normal (or Gaussian) distribution. Recall from Chapter 9 that the normal distribution Y is given by the density function

$$g(y) = \frac{1}{\sqrt{2\pi}\sigma} e^{-(y-\mu)^2/2\sigma^2}$$

where μ is the mean, σ is the standard deviation (σ^2 is the variance), and the range is $-\infty < y < \infty$. The density function $f(x)$ for a lognormal random variable X is simply $g(\ln x)/x$, over the range $0 < x < \infty$. The x in the denominator arises because

$$f(x)\,dx = g(y)\,dy$$

for $y = \ln x$, which gives $dy = dx/x$.

427

The density function for a lognormal distribution X therefore satisfies

$$f(x) = \frac{1}{\sqrt{2\pi}\sigma x} e^{-(\ln x - \mu)^2/2\sigma^2}$$

and the complementary cumulative distribution function for a lognormal distribution is given by

$$\Pr(X \geq x) = \int_{z=x}^{\infty} \frac{1}{\sqrt{2\pi}\sigma z} e^{-(\ln z - \mu)^2/2\sigma^2} dz.$$

We say that X has parameters μ and σ^2 when the associated normal distribution Y has mean μ and variance σ^2, where the meaning is clear. The lognormal distribution is skewed, with mean $e^{\mu + \frac{1}{2}\sigma^2}$, median e^{μ}, and mode $e^{\mu - \sigma^2}$. (Proving these values is left as Exercise 16.13.) A lognormal distribution has finite mean and variance, in contrast with power law distributions, which as we have seen can have infinite mean and variance under some parameters.

An interesting property of lognormal distributions is that the *product* of independent lognormal distributions is again lognormal. This follows from the fact that normal distributions have the property that the sum of two independent normal random variables Y_1 and Y_2 with μ_1 and μ_2 and variances σ_1^2 and σ_2^2 respectively is a normal random variable with mean $\mu_1 + \mu_2$ and variance $\sigma_1^2 + \sigma_2^2$.

Although it has finite moments, the lognormal distribution is extremely similar in "shape" to a power law distribution, in the following sense: if X has a lognormal distribution, then in a log–log plot of the complementary cumulative distribution function or the density function of X, the plot can appear to be close to linear for much of the distribution, depending on the variance of the corresponding normal distribution. If the variance is large, the log–log plot may appear linear for several orders of magnitude.

To see this, let us look at the logarithm of the density function, which is slightly easier to work with than the complementary cumulative distribution function. We have

$$\ln f(x) = -\ln x - \ln \sqrt{2\pi}\sigma - \frac{(\ln x - \mu)^2}{2\sigma^2}. \tag{16.7}$$

If σ is large, then the quadratic term in Eqn. (16.7) will be small for a large range of x values, so $\ln f(x)$ appears almost linear in $\ln x$ over a large range. Recall that checking for linearity over a log–log plot is the first test (albeit an "eyeball" test) one uses to check if a distribution is a power law; the lognormal distribution shows why the linearity test is generally not enough to allow one to conclude that a sampled distribution follows a power law.

16.5.2. *Power Law with Exponential Cutoff*

The power law with exponential cutoff refers to a distribution where the density function is of the form

$$f(x) \sim x^{-\alpha} e^{-\lambda x}$$

for some $\alpha, \lambda > 0$. The idea behind using such a distribution is that, similar to a lognormal distribution, it can roughly follow a power law distribution for much of the body of the distribution when λ is small, but for sufficiently large values of x the exponential term will dominate. The exponential cutoff can model power laws that eventually must end because of resource limitations. For example, the distribution of wealth may be better fit to a power law with an exponential cutoff rather than a power law; eventually, there are limits to the money to be had, and as such the exponential cutoff may better model the tail of the distribution.

16.6. Exercises

Exercise 16.1: (a) Pareto distributions are often said to be "scale invariant" in the following sense. If X is a random variable that follows a Pareto distribution and has density $f(x)$, then the rescaled random variable having density $g(x) = f(cx)$ has density proportional to $f(x)$. Prove this statement.

(b) An implication of scale invariance is that if we measure our random variable in different units, it remains a Pareto distribution. For example, if we think wealth follows a Pareto distribution and we rescale to measure wealth in millions of dollars instead of dollars, we still have a Pareto distribution. Show that, under such a rescaling (where $g(x) = f(cx)$), a Pareto distribution remains a straight line on a log–log plot, and is just shifted up or down.

Exercise 16.2: Suppose that the time to finish a project in hours is given by a Pareto distribution with parameter $\alpha = 2$ and a minimum time of one hour. What is the expected time to complete the project? Now suppose that the project is not completed after three hours. If the time to complete the project is given by the initial Pareto distribution conditioned on the completion time being at least three hours, what is the expected *remaining* time until the completion of the project? How does this compare with the original expected time to complete the project?

Exercise 16.3: Consider a random variable X that has a Pareto distribution with parameters $\alpha > 0$ and minimum value m. Determine for $x \geq y \geq m$ the conditional distribution

$$\Pr(X \geq x \mid X \geq y).$$

Exercise 16.4: Suppose that the time to finish a project in hours is given by a Pareto distribution with parameter α and a minimum time of one hour. Pareto distributions can have the property that the longer the project goes without completing, the longer it is expected to take to complete. That is, if X is the time the project finishes, we are concerned with

$$f(y) = \mathbf{E}[X - y \mid X \geq y].$$

Show that f is an increasing function when $\alpha > 1$.

429

Exercise 16.5: In section 9.6, we discussed maximizing the log-likelihood function in order to find a maximum likelihood estimate of a parameter. Suppose we have n samples from a Pareto distribution, $x_1, x_2, \ldots, x_n$, where the minimum value is known to be 1 but the parameter α is unknown.

(a) What is the log-likelihood function in terms of the parameter α and the sample values $x_1, x_2, \ldots, x_n$?
(b) What is the maximum likelihood estimator for α?

Exercise 16.6: Power law distributions are often described anecdotally by phrases such as "20% of the population has 80% of the income." If one assumes a Pareto distribution, this phrase determines a parameter α. What value of α corresponds to this phrase? Your argument should explain why your result is independent of the minimum value m.

Exercise 16.7: Consider the standard random walk $X_0, X_1, X_2, \ldots$ on the integers that starts at 0 and moves from X_i to $X_i + 1$ with probability $1/2$ at each step and from X_i to $X_i - 1$ with probability $1/2$ at each step. We are interested in the first return time to 0. Note that this time must be even. Let f_t be the probability that the first time the walk returns to 0 is at time $2t$. Let u_t be the probability the walk is at 0 at time $2t$.

(a) Prove that $u_t = \binom{2t}{t} 2^{-2t}$.
(b) Consider the probability $\Pr(X_1 > 0, X_2 > 0, \ldots, X_{2t-1} > 0 \mid X_{2t} = 0)$. Show that this probability is $\frac{1}{2t-1}$. (*Hint*: this can be done using the Ballot Theorem from Section 13.2.1.)
(c) Prove that $f_t = \frac{u_t}{2t-1}$.
(d) Using Stirling's formula, show that f_t follows a power law.

Exercise 16.8: Consider the monkey typing randomly experiment with an alphabet of two letters that are hit with differing probabilities: "a" occurs with probability q, "b" occurs with probability q^2, and a space occurs with probability $1 - q - q^2$. (Here q satisfies $1 - q - q^2 > 0$.)

(a) Show that every word the monkey can type occurs with probability $q^j(1 - q - q^2)$ for some integer j.
(b) Let us say a word has pseudo-rank j if it occurs with probability $q^j(1 - q - q^2)$. Show that the number of words with pseudo-rank j is the $(j + 1)$st Fibonacci number F_{j+1} (where here we start with $F_0 = 0$ and $F_1 = 1$).
(c) Use facts about the Fibonacci numbers, such as $\sum_{i=1}^{k} F_k = F_{k+2} - 1$, and $F_k \approx \phi^k/\sqrt{5}$ for large k where $\phi = \frac{1+\sqrt{5}}{2}$, to show that the frequency of the jth most frequent word behaves (roughly) like a power law, following a similar approach to that used to analyze the setting of the monkeys typing randomly experiment with equal character probabilities.

Exercise 16.9: Write a program to simulate the monkeys typing randomly experiment of Section 16.2.3. Your simulation should consider the following two scenarios.

- You have an alphabet of 8 letters and space; the space is chosen with probability 0.2, and the other letters are chosen with equal probability.
- You have an alphabet of 8 letters and space; the space is chosen with probability 0.2, and the probability for each of the other letters is chosen uniformly at random, with the constraint that the sum of their probabilities is 0.8.

For each scenario, generate 1 million words, and track the frequency for each word that appears. Recall that the empty word should be treated as a word, and you will have many fewer than 1 million distinct words to track.

(a) In practice, you should be able to represent each word seen in an experiment using at most 256 bits (at least most of the time). Explain why this is the case.

(b) Plot the distribution of word frequencies for each scenario on a log–log plot. The x-axis should be the rank of the word in terms of its frequency, and the y-axis should be the frequency. Do the two plots differ?

(c) Do your plots appear to follow a power law? Explain.

Exercise 16.10: Write a program to simulate the preferential attachment process, starting with four pages linked together as a cycle on four vertices, adding pages each with one outlink until there are 1 million pages, and using $\gamma = 0.5$ as the probability a link is to a page chosen uniformly at random and $1 - \gamma = 0.5$ as the probabiliy a link is copied from existing links. Draw a plot of the degree distribution, showing the number of vertices of each degree on a log–log plot. Also draw a plot showing the complimentary cumulative degree distribution – that is, the number of vertices with degree at least k for every value of k – on a log–log plot. Does the degree distribution appear to follow a power law? Explain.

Exercise 16.11: Write a program to simulate the preferential attachement process as in the prevous problem, but now start with four pages with each page pointing to the other three, and add pages each with three outlinks until there are 1 million pages. Again draw the plots of the degree distribution and the complimentary cumulative degree distribution. How do these plots differ from those in the previous problem? Does the degree distribution appear to follow a power law?

Exercise 16.12: Derive the expressions for the mean and variance of a power law distribution with an exponential cutoff with parameters α and λ. (You may assume α is a positive integer.)

Exercise 16.13: Derive the expressions for the mean, median, and mode of a lognormal distribution with parameters μ and σ^2. Recall the mean is $e^{\mu + \frac{1}{2}\sigma^2}$, the median is e^{μ}, and the mode is $e^{\mu - \sigma^2}$.

Exercise 16.14: Consider the count-min filter from Section 15.4. We show that the bounds on its performance can be improved if the distribution of item counts follows a power law distribution. Suppose we have a collection of N items, where the total count associated with the ℓth most frequent item is given by $f_\ell = c/\ell^z$ for a constant $z > 1$ and

431

a value c. (You may assume all the f_ℓ are suitably rounded integers for convenience.) As described in Section 15.4, we assume we have k disjoint groups of counters, each with m/k counters. We use the minimum counter $C_{a,j}$ that an item hashes to as an estimate for its count.

(a) Show that the tail of the total count for all items after removing the $b \geq 1$ most frequent items is bounded by

$$\sum_{i=b+1}^{N} f_i \leq \frac{cb^{1-z}}{z-1} \leq Fb^{1-z},$$

where $F = \sum_{i=1}^{N} f_i$.

(b) Consider now an element i with total count f_i, and let us consider a single group of counters. Show that the probability that i collides with any of the $m/(3k)$ items with the largest count (besides possibly itself) is at most $1/3$.

(c) Show that, conditioned on the event $\mathcal{E}$ that i does not collide with any of the $m/(3k)$ items with the largest count, the expected count for the counter $C_{a,j}$ that i hashes to is bounded by

$$\mathbf{E}[C_{a,j} \mid \mathcal{E}] \leq f_i + F\frac{(m/3k)^{1-z}}{(m/k)}.$$

(d) Let $\gamma = 3\frac{(m/3k)^{1-z}}{m/k}$. Prove that $C_{a,j} \leq f_i + \gamma F$ with probability at least $1/3$.

(e) Explain why the above implies that the count-min filter produces an estimate for f_i that is at most $f_i + \gamma F$ with probability at least $1 - (2/3)^k$.

(f) Suppose we want to find all items with a count of at least q; when an item is hashed into the count-min filter, it is put on a list if its minimum counter is at least q. Prove that we can construct a count-min filter with $O(\lceil \ln \frac{1}{\delta} \rceil)$ hash functions and $O(\lceil \ln \frac{1}{\delta} \rceil \lceil \epsilon^{-1/z} \rceil)$ counters so that all items with count at least q are put on the list, and any item that has a count of less than $q - \epsilon F$ is put on the list with probability at most δ. (This improves the result of Corollary 15.13 for this type of skewed distribution of item counts.)

CHAPTER SEVENTEEN

Balanced Allocations and Cuckoo Hashing

In this chapter, we examine simple and powerful variants of the classic balls-and-bins paradigm, where each ball may have a choice of a small number of bins where it can be placed. In our first setting, often referred to as balanced allocations, the balls have choices, and a choice of where a ball is to be placed must be made once and for all when the ball enters the system. In our second setting, referred to as cuckoo hashing, balls may move to another choice after their initial placement under some circumstances.

17.1. The Power of Two Choices

Suppose that we sequentially place n balls into n bins by putting each ball into a bin chosen independently and uniformly at random. We studied this classic balls-and-bins problem in Chapter 5. There we showed that, at the end of the process, the most balls in any bin – the maximum load – is $\Theta(\ln n/\ln \ln n)$ with high probability.

In a variant of the process, each ball comes with d possible destination bins, each chosen independently and uniformly at random, and is placed in the least full bin among the d possible locations at the time of the placement. The original balls-and-bins process corresponds to the case where $d = 1$. Surprisingly, even when $d = 2$, the behavior is completely different: when the process terminates, the maximum load is $\ln \ln n/\ln 2 + O(1)$ with high probability. Thus, an apparently minor change in the random allocation process results in an exponential decrease in the maximum load. We may then ask what happens if each ball has three choices; perhaps the resulting load is then $O(\ln \ln \ln n)$. We shall consider the general case of d choices per ball and show that, when $d \geq 2$, with high probability the maximum load is $\ln \ln n/\ln d + \Theta(1)$. Although having more than two choices does reduce the maximum load, for any constant d the reduction changes it by only a constant factor, so it remains $\Theta(\ln \ln n)$ for a constant d.

17.1.1. *The Upper Bound*

Theorem 17.1: *Suppose that n balls are sequentially placed into n bins in the following manner. For each ball, $d \geq 2$ bins are chosen independently and uniformly at* *random (with replacement). Each ball is placed in the least full of the d bins at the time of the placement, with ties broken randomly. After all the balls are placed, the maximum load of any bin is at most* $\ln \ln n / \ln d + O(1)$ *with probability* $1 - o(1/n)$.

The proof is rather technical, so before beginning we informally sketch the main points. In order to bound the maximum load, we need to approximately bound the number of bins with i balls for all values of i. In fact, for any given i, instead of trying to bound the number of bins with load *exactly* i, it will be easier to bound the number of bins with load *at least* i. The argument proceeds via what is, for the most part, a straightforward induction. We wish to find a sequence of values β_i such that the number of bins with load at least i is bounded above by β_i with high probability.

Suppose that we knew that, over the entire course of the process, the number of bins with load at least i was bounded above by β_i. Let us consider how we would determine an appropriate inductive bound for β_{i+1} that holds with high probability. Define the *height* of a ball to be one more than the number of balls already in the bin in which the ball is placed. That is, if we think of balls as being stacked in the bin by order of arrival, the height of a ball is its position in the stack. The number of balls of height at least $i + 1$ gives an upper bound for the number of bins with at least $i + 1$ balls.

A ball will have height at least $i + 1$ only if each of its d choices for a bin has load at least i. If there are indeed at most β_i bins with load at least i at all times, then the probability that each choice yields a bin with load at least i is at most β_i/n. Therefore, the probability that a ball has height at least $i + 1$ is at most $(\beta_i/n)^d$. We can use a Chernoff bound to conclude that, with high probability, the number of balls of height at least $i + 1$ will be at most $2n(\beta_i/n)^d$. That is, if everything works as sketched, then

$$\frac{\beta_{i+1}}{n} \le 2 \left(\frac{\beta_i}{n} \right)^d.$$

We examine this recursion carefully in the analysis and show that β_j becomes $O(\ln n)$ when $j = \ln \ln n / \ln d + O(1)$. At this point, we must be a bit more careful in our analysis because Chernoff bounds will no longer be sufficiently useful, but the result is easy to finish from there.

The proof is technically challenging primarily because one must handle the conditioning appropriately. In bounding β_{i+1}, we assumed that we had a bound on β_i. This assumption must be treated as a conditioning in the formal argument, which requires some care.

We shall use the following notation: the state at time t refers to the state of the system immediately after the tth ball is placed. The variable $h(t)$ denotes the height of the tth ball, and $\nu_i(t)$ and $\mu_i(t)$ refer (respectively) to the number of bins with load at least i and the number of balls with height at least i at time t. We use ν_i and μ_i for $\nu_i(n)$ and $\mu_i(n)$ when the meaning is clear. An obvious but important fact, of which we make frequent use in the proof, is that $\nu_i(t) \le \mu_i(t)$, since every bin with load at least i must contain at least one ball with height at least i.

Before beginning, we make note of two simple lemmas. First, we utilize a specific Chernoff bound for binomial random variables, easily derived from Eqn. (4.2) by letting $\delta = 1$.

Lemma 17.2:

$$\Pr(B(n, p) \geq 2np) \leq e^{-np/3}. \tag{17.1}$$

The following lemma will help us cope with dependent random variables in the main proof.

Lemma 17.3: *Let $X_1, X_2, \ldots, X_n$ be a sequence of random variables in an arbitrary domain, and let $Y_1, Y_2, \ldots, Y_n$ be a sequence of binary random variables with the property that $Y_i = Y_i(X_1, \ldots, X_i)$. If*

$$\Pr(Y_i = 1 \mid X_1, \ldots, X_{i-1}) \leq p,$$

then

$$\Pr\left(\sum_{i=1}^{n} Y_i > k\right) \leq \Pr(B(n, p) > k).$$

Proof: If we consider the Y_i one at a time, then each Y_i is less likely to take on the value 1 than an independent Bernoulli trial with success probability p, regardless of the values of the X_i. The result then follows by a simple induction. ∎

We now begin the main proof.

Proof of Theorem 17.1: Following the earlier sketch, we shall construct values β_i such that, with high probability, $v_i(n) \leq \beta_i$ for all i. Let $\beta_4 = n/4$, and let $\beta_{i+1} = 2\beta_i^d/n^{d-1}$ for $4 \leq i < i^*$, where i^* is to be determined. We let $\mathcal{E}_i$ be the event that $v_i(n) \leq \beta_i$. Note that $\mathcal{E}_4$ holds with probability 1; there cannot be more than $n/4$ bins with at least 4 balls when there are only n balls. We now show that, with high probability, if $\mathcal{E}_i$ holds then $\mathcal{E}_{i+1}$ holds for $4 \leq i < i^*$.

Fix a value of i in the given range. Let Y_t be a binary random variable such that

$$Y_t = 1 \text{ if and only if } h(t) \geq i + 1 \text{ and } v_i(t - 1) \leq \beta_i.$$

That is, Y_t is 1 if the height of the tth ball is at least $i + 1$ and if, at time $t - 1$, there are at most β_i bins with load at least i. The requirement that Y_t be 1 only if there are at most β_i bins with load at least i may seem a bit odd; however, it makes handling the conditioning much easier.

Specifically, let ω_j represent the bins selected by the jth ball. Then

$$\Pr(Y_t = 1 \mid \omega_1, \ldots, \omega_{t-1}) \leq \frac{\beta_i^d}{n^d}.$$

That is, given the choices made by the first $t - 1$ balls, the probability that Y_t is 1 is bounded by $(\beta_i/n)^d$. This is because, in order for Y_t to be 1, there must be at most β_i bins with load at least i; and when this condition holds, the d choices of bins for the tth ball all have load at least i with probability $(\beta_i/n)^d$. If we did not force Y_t to be 0 if there are more than β_i bins with load at least i, then we would not be able to bound this conditional probability in this way.

Let $p_i = \beta_i^d/n^d$. Then, from Lemma 17.3, we can conclude that

$$\Pr\left(\sum_{t=1}^{n} Y_t > k\right) \leq \Pr(B(n, p_i) > k).$$

This holds independently of any of the events $\mathcal{E}_i$, owing to our careful definition of Y_t. (Had we not included the condition that $Y_t = 1$ only if $v_i(t-1) \leq \beta_i$, the inequality would not necessarily hold.)

Conditioned on $\mathcal{E}_i$, we have $\sum_{t=1}^{n} Y_t = \mu_{i+1}$. Since $v_{i+1} \leq \mu_{i+1}$, we have

$$\Pr(v_{i+1} > k \mid \mathcal{E}_i) \leq \Pr(\mu_{i+1} > k \mid \mathcal{E}_i)$$
$$= \Pr\left(\sum_{t=1}^{n} Y_t > k \mid \mathcal{E}_i\right)$$
$$\leq \frac{\Pr\left(\sum_{t=1}^{n} Y_t > k\right)}{\Pr(\mathcal{E}_i)}$$
$$\leq \frac{\Pr(B(n, p_i) > k)}{\Pr(\mathcal{E}_i)}.$$

We bound the tail of the binomial distribution by using the Chernoff bound of Lemma 17.2. Letting $k = \beta_{i+1} = 2np_i$ in the previous equations yields

$$\Pr(v_{i+1} > \beta_{i+1} \mid \mathcal{E}_i) \leq \frac{\Pr(B(n, p_i) > 2np_i)}{\Pr(\mathcal{E}_i)} \leq \frac{1}{e^{p_i n/3}\,\Pr(\mathcal{E}_i)},$$

which gives

$$\Pr(\neg\mathcal{E}_{i+1} \mid \mathcal{E}_i) \leq \frac{1}{n^2\,\Pr(\mathcal{E}_i)} \tag{17.2}$$

whenever $p_i n \geq 6 \ln n$.

We now remove the conditioning by using the fact that

$$\Pr(\neg\mathcal{E}_{i+1}) = \Pr(\neg\mathcal{E}_{i+1} \mid \mathcal{E}_i)\,\Pr(\mathcal{E}_i) + \Pr(\neg\mathcal{E}_{i+1} \mid \neg\mathcal{E}_i)\,\Pr(\neg\mathcal{E}_i)$$
$$\leq \Pr(\neg\mathcal{E}_{i+1} \mid \mathcal{E}_i)\,\Pr(\mathcal{E}_i) + \Pr(\neg\mathcal{E}_i); \tag{17.3}$$

then, by Eqns. (17.2) and (17.3),

$$\Pr(\neg\mathcal{E}_{i+1}) \leq \Pr(\neg\mathcal{E}_i) + \frac{1}{n^2} \tag{17.4}$$

as long as $p_i n \geq 6 \ln n$.

Hence, whenever $p_i n \geq 6 \ln n$ and $\mathcal{E}_i$ holds with high probability, then so does $\mathcal{E}_{i+1}$. To conclude we need two more steps. First, we need to show that $p_i n < 6 \ln n$ when i is approximately $\ln \ln n / \ln d$, since this is our desired bound on the maximum load. Second, we must carefully handle the case where $p_i n < 6 \ln n$ separately, since the Chernoff bound is no longer strong enough to give appropriate bounds once p_i is this small.

Let i^* be the smallest value of i such that $p_i = \beta_i^d/n^d < 6\ln n/n$. We show that i^* is $\ln\ln n/\ln d + O(1)$. To do this, we prove inductively the bound

$$\beta_{i+4} = \frac{n}{2^{2d^i - \sum_{j=0}^{i-1} d^j}}.$$

This holds true when $i = 0$, and the induction argument follows:

$$\beta_{(i+1)+4} = \frac{2\beta_{i+4}^d}{n^{d-1}}$$

$$= \frac{2\left(\dfrac{n}{2^{2d^i - \sum_{j=0}^{i-1} d^j}}\right)^d}{n^{d-1}}$$

$$= \frac{n}{2^{2d^{i+1} - \sum_{j=0}^{i} d^j}}.$$

The first line is the definition of β_i; the second follows from the induction hypothesis. It follows that $\beta_{i+4} \leq n/2^{d^i}$ and hence that i^* is $\ln\ln n/\ln d + O(1)$. By inductively applying Eqn. (17.4), we find that

$$\Pr(\neg\mathcal{E}_{i^*}) \leq \frac{i^*}{n^2}.$$

We now handle the case where $p_i n < 6\ln n$. We have

$$\Pr(v_{i^*+1} > 18\ln n \mid \mathcal{E}_{i^*}) \leq \Pr(\mu_{i^*+1} > 18\ln n \mid \mathcal{E}_{i^*})$$
$$\leq \frac{\Pr(B(n, 6\ln n/n) \geq 18\ln n)}{\Pr(\mathcal{E}_{i^*})}$$
$$\leq \frac{1}{n^2\,\Pr(\mathcal{E}_{i^*})},$$

where the last inequality again follows from the Chernoff bound. Removing the conditioning as before then yields

$$\Pr(v_{i^*+1} > 18\ln n) \leq \Pr(\neg\mathcal{E}_{i^*}) + \frac{1}{n^2} \leq \frac{i^*+1}{n^2}. \tag{17.5}$$

To wrap up, we note that

$$\Pr(v_{i^*+3} \geq 1) \leq \Pr(\mu_{i^*+3} \geq 1) \leq \Pr(\mu_{i^*+2} \geq 2)$$

and bound the latter quantity as follows:

$$\Pr(\mu_{i^*+2} \geq 2 \mid v_{i^*+1} \leq 18\ln n) \leq \frac{\Pr(B(n, (18\ln n/n)^d) \geq 2)}{\Pr(v_{i^*+1} \leq 18\ln n)}$$
$$\leq \frac{\binom{n}{2}(18\ln n/n)^{2d}}{\Pr(v_{i^*+1} \leq 18\ln n)}.$$

Here the last inequality comes from applying the crude union bound; there are $\binom{n}{2}$ ways of choosing two balls, and for each pair the probability that both balls have height at least $i^* + 2$ is at most $(18\ln n/n)^{2d}$.

Removing the conditioning as before and then using Eqn. (17.5) yields

$$\Pr(\nu_{i^*+3} \geq 1) \leq \Pr(\mu_{i^*+2} \geq 2)$$
$$\leq \Pr(\mu_{i^*+2} \geq 2 \mid \nu_{i^*+1} \leq 18 \ln n) \Pr(\nu_{i^*+1} \leq 18 \ln n)$$
$$+ \Pr(\nu_{i^*+1} > 18 \ln n)$$
$$\leq \frac{(18 \ln n)^{2d}}{n^{2d-2}} + \frac{i^* + 1}{n^2},$$

showing that $\Pr(\nu_{i^*+3} \geq 1)$ is $o(1/n)$ for $d \geq 2$ and hence that the probability the maximum bin load is more than $i^* + 3 = \ln \ln n / \ln d + O(1)$ is $o(1/n)$. ∎

Breaking ties randomly is convenient for the proof, but in practice any natural tie-breaking scheme will suffice. For example, in Exercise 17.1 we show that if the bins are numbered from 1 to n then breaking ties in favor of the smaller-numbered bin is sufficient.

As an interesting variation, suppose that we split the n bins into two groups of equal size. Think of half of the bins as being on the left and the other half on the right. Each ball now chooses one bin independently and uniformly at random from each half. Again, each ball is placed in the least loaded of the two bins – but now, if there is a tie, the ball is placed in the bin on the left half. Surprisingly, by splitting the bins and breaking ties in this fashion, we can obtain a slightly better bound on the maximum load: $\ln \ln n / (2 \ln((1 + \sqrt{5})/2)) + O(1)$. One can generalize this approach by splitting the bins into d ordered equal-sized groups; in case of a tie for the least-loaded bin, the bin in the lowest-ranked group obtains the ball. This variation is the subject of Exercise 17.13.

17.2. Two Choices: The Lower Bound

In this section we demonstrate that the result of Theorem 17.1 is essentially tight by proving a corresponding lower bound.

Theorem 17.4: *Suppose that n balls are sequentially placed into n bins in the following manner. For each ball, $d \geq 2$ bins are chosen independently and uniformly at random (with replacement). Each ball is placed in the least full of the d bins at the time of the placement, with ties broken randomly. After all the balls are placed, the maximum load of any bin is at least $\ln \ln n / \ln d - O(1)$ with probability $1 - o(1/n)$.*

The proof is similar in spirit to the upper bound, but there are some key differences. As with the upper bound, we wish to find a sequence of values γ_i such that the number of bins with load at least i is bounded below by γ_i with high probability. In deriving the upper bound, we used the number of balls with height at least i as an upper bound on the number of bins with height at least i. We cannot do this in proving a lower bound, however. Instead, we find a lower bound on the number of balls with height exactly i and then use this as a lower bound on the number of bins with height at least i.

In a similar vein, for the proof of the upper bound we used that the number of bins with at least i balls at time n was at least $\nu_i(t)$ for any time $t \leq n$. This is not helpful now that we are proving a lower bound; we need a lower bound on $v_i(t)$, not an upper bound, to determine the probability that the tth ball has height $i + 1$. To cope with this, we determine a lower bound γ_i on the number of bins with load at least i that exist at time $n(1 - 1/2^i)$ and then bound the number of balls of height $i + 1$ that arise over the interval $(n(1 - 1/2^i), n(1 - 1/2^{i+1})]$. This guarantees that appropriate lower bounds hold when we need them in the induction, as we shall clarify in the proof.

We state the lemmas that we need, which are similar to those for the upper bound.

Lemma 17.5:

$$\Pr(B(n, p) \le np/2) \le e^{-np/8}. \tag{17.6}$$

Lemma 17.6: *Let $X_1, X_2, \ldots, X_n$ be a sequence of random variables in an arbitrary domain, and let $Y_1, Y_2, \ldots, Y_n$ be a sequence of binary random variables with the property that $Y_i = Y_i(X_1, \ldots, X_i)$. If*

$$\Pr(Y_i = 1 \mid X_1, \ldots, X_{i-1}) \ge p,$$

then

$$\Pr\left(\sum_{i=1}^{n} Y_i > k\right) \ge \Pr(B(n, p) > k).$$

Proof of Theorem 17.4: Let $\mathcal{F}_i$ be the event that $v_i(n(1 - 1/2^i)) \ge \gamma_i$, where γ_i is given by:

$$\gamma_0 = n;$$

$$\gamma_{i+1} = \frac{n}{2^{i+3}} \left(\frac{\gamma_i}{n}\right)^d.$$

Clearly $\mathcal{F}_0$ holds with probability 1. We now show inductively that successive $\mathcal{F}_i$ hold with sufficiently high probability to obtain the desired lower bound.

We want to compute

$$\Pr(\neg \mathcal{F}_{i+1} \mid \mathcal{F}_i).$$

With this in mind, for t in the range $R = [n(1 - 1/2^i), n(1 - 1/2^{i+1})]$, define the binary random variable by

$$Z_t = 1 \text{ if and only if } h(t) = i + 1 \text{ or } v_{i+1}(t - 1) \ge \gamma_{i+1}.$$

Hence Z_t is always 1 if $v_{i+1}(t - 1) \ge \gamma_{i+1}$.

The probability that the tth ball has height exactly $i + 1$ is

$$\left(\frac{v_i(t - 1)}{n}\right)^d - \left(\frac{v_{i+1}(t - 1)}{n}\right)^d.$$

The first term is the probability that all the d bins chosen by the tth ball have load at least i. This is necessary for the height of the tth ball to have height exactly $i + 1$. However, we must subtract out the probability that all d choices have at least $i + 1$ balls, because in this case the height of the ball will be larger than $i + 1$.

Again letting ω_j represent the bins selected by the jth ball, we conclude that

$$\Pr(Z_t = 1 \mid \omega_1, \ldots, \omega_{t-1}, \mathcal{F}_i) \geq \left(\frac{\gamma_i}{n}\right)^d - \left(\frac{\gamma_{i+1}}{n}\right)^d.$$

This is because Z_t is automatically 1 if $v_{i+1}(t - 1) \geq \gamma_{i+1}$; hence we can consider the probability in the case where $v_{i+1}(t - 1) \leq \gamma_{i+1}$. Also, conditioned on $\mathcal{F}_i$, we have $v_i(t - 1) \geq \gamma_i$.

From the definition of the γ_i we can further conclude that

$$\Pr(Z_t = 1 \mid \omega_1, \ldots, \omega_{t-1}, \mathcal{F}_i) \geq \left(\frac{\gamma_i}{n}\right)^d - \left(\frac{\gamma_{i+1}}{n}\right)^d \geq \frac{1}{2}\left(\frac{\gamma_i}{n}\right)^d.$$

Let $p_i = \frac{1}{2}(\gamma_i/n)^d$.

Applying Lemma 14.6 yields

$$\Pr\left(\sum_{t \in R} Z_t < k \mid \mathcal{F}_i\right) \leq \Pr\left(B\left(\frac{n}{2^{i+1}}, p_i\right) < k\right).$$

Now our choice of γ_i nicely satisfies

$$\gamma_{i+1} = \frac{1}{2}\frac{n}{2^{i+1}}p_i.$$

By the Chernoff bound,

$$\Pr\left(B\left(\frac{n}{2^{i+1}}, p_i\right) < \gamma_{i+1}\right) \leq e^{-np_i/(8 \cdot 2^{i+1})},$$

which is $o(1/n^2)$ provided that $p_i n/2^{i+1} \geq 17 \ln n$. Let i^* be a lower bound on the largest integer for which this holds. We subsequently show that i^* can be chosen to be $\ln \ln n/\ln d - O(1)$; for now let us assume that this is the case. Then, for $i \leq i^*$, we have shown that

$$\Pr\left(\sum_{t \in R} Z_t < \gamma_{i+1} \mid \mathcal{F}_i\right) \leq \Pr\left(B\left(\frac{n}{2^{i+1}}, p_i\right) < \gamma_{i+1}\right) = o\left(\frac{1}{n^2}\right).$$

Further, by definition we have that $\sum_{t \in R} Z_t < \gamma_{i+1}$ implies $\neg\mathcal{F}_{i+1}$. Hence, for $i \leq i^*$,

$$\Pr(\neg\mathcal{F}_{i+1} \mid \mathcal{F}_i) \leq \Pr\left(\sum_{t \in R} Z_t < \gamma_{i+1} \mid \mathcal{F}_i\right) = o\left(\frac{1}{n^2}\right).$$

Therefore, for sufficiently large n,

$$\begin{aligned}
\Pr(\mathcal{F}_{i^*}) &\geq \Pr(\mathcal{F}_{i^*} \mid \mathcal{F}_{i^*-1}) \cdot \Pr(\mathcal{F}_{i^*-1} \mid \mathcal{F}_{i^*-2}) \cdots \Pr(\mathcal{F}_1 \mid \mathcal{F}_0) \cdot \Pr(\mathcal{F}_0) \\
&\geq (1 - 1/n^2)^{i^*} \\
&= 1 - o(1/n).
\end{aligned}$$

All that remains is to demonstrate that $\ln \ln n/\ln d - O(1)$ is indeed an appropriate choice for i^*. It suffices to show that $\gamma_i \geq 17 \ln n$ when i is $\ln \ln n/\ln d - O(1)$. From the recursions $\gamma_{i+1} = \gamma_i^d/(2^{i+3}n^{d-1})$, we find by a simple induction that

$$\gamma_i = \frac{n}{2^{\sum_{k=0}^{i-1}(i+2-k)d^k}}.$$

A very rough bound gives

$$\gamma_i \geq \frac{n}{2^{10d^{i-1}}}.$$

We therefore look for the maximum i such that

$$\frac{n}{2^{10d^{i-1}}} \geq 17 \ln n.$$

For n sufficiently large, we find that we can take i as large as $\ln \ln n / \ln d - O(1)$ by using the following chain of inequalities:

$$\frac{n}{2^{10d^{i-1}}} \geq 17 \ln n,$$

$$2^{10d^{i-1}} \leq \frac{n}{17 \ln n},$$

$$10d^{i-1} \leq \log_2 n - \log_2(17 \ln n),$$

$$d^{i-1} \leq \frac{1}{20} \ln n,$$

$$i \leq \frac{\ln \ln n}{\ln d} - O(1). \qquad \blacksquare$$

17.3. Applications of the Power of Two Choices

The balanced allocation paradigm has a number of interesting applications to computing problems. We elaborate here on two simple applications. When considering these applications, keep in mind that the $\ln \ln n / \ln d + O(1)$ bound we obtain for the balanced allocation paradigm generally corresponds to a maximum load of at most 5 in practice.

17.3.1. *Hashing*

When we considered hashing in Chapter 5, we related it to the balls-and-bins paradigm by assuming that the hash function maps the items being hashed to random entries in the hash table. Subject to this assumption, we proved that (a) when $O(n)$ items are hashed to a table with n entries, the expected number of items hashed to each individual entry in the table is $O(1)$, and (b) with high probability, the maximum number of items hashed to any entry in the table is $\Theta(\ln n / \ln \ln n)$.

These results are satisfactory for most applications, but for some they are not, since the expected value of the worst-case lookup time over all items is $\Theta(\ln n / \ln \ln n)$. For example, when storing a routing table in a router, the worst-case time for a lookup in a hash table can be an important performance criterion, and the $\Theta(\ln n / \ln \ln n)$ result is too large. Another potential problem is wasted memory. For example, suppose that we design a hash table where each bin should fit in a single fixed-size cache line of memory. Because the maximum load is so much larger than the average, we will have to use a large number of cache lines and many of them will be completely empty. For some applications, such as routers, this waste of memory is undesirable.

Applying the balanced allocation paradigm, we obtain a hashing scheme with $O(1)$ expected and $O(\ln \ln n)$ maximum access time. The 2-*way chaining* technique uses two random hash functions. The two hash functions define two possible entries in the table for each item. The item is inserted to the location that is least full at the time of insertion. Items in each entry of the table are stored in a linked list. If n items are sequentially inserted into a table of size n, the expected insertion and lookup time is still $O(1)$. (See Exercise 17.3.) Theorem 17.1 implies that with high probability the maximum time to find an item is $O(\ln \ln n)$, versus the $\Theta(\ln n / \ln \ln n)$ time when a single random hash function is used. This improvement does not come without cost. Since a search for an item now involves a search in two bins instead of one, the improvement in the expected maximum search time comes at the cost of roughly doubling the average search time. This cost can be mitigated if the two bins can be searched in parallel.

17.3.2. *Dynamic Resource Allocation*

Suppose a user or a process has to choose on-line between a number of identical resources (choosing a server to use among servers in a network; choosing a disk to store a directory; choosing a printer; etc.). To find the least loaded resource, users may check the load on all resources before placing their requests. This process is expensive, since it requires sending an interrupt to each of the resources. A second approach is to send the task to a random resource. This approach has minimal overhead, but if all users follow it then loads will vary significantly among servers. The balanced allocation paradigm suggests a more efficient solution. If each user samples the load of two resources and sends his request to the least loaded one, then the total overhead remains small while the load on the n resources varies much less.

17.4. Cuckoo Hashing

So far in this chapter we have considered balls-and-bins processes that correspond to multiple choice hashing schemes, where each item can be placed in one of d choices out of n total bins. Cuckoo hashing is a further variation on multiple choice hashing schemes that uses the following idea: suppose items not only have multiple choices of where they can be located, but even after we place an item, we can move it from one of its choices to another at a later point if needed. This should give us more power to place items in a way that balances the load. What can we say about cuckoo hashing schemes?

Let us start our investigation of cuckoo hashing by considering the setting where $d = 2$, so an item can be placed in one of two possible bins. We also start by assuming that each bin can hold only one item, so that our hash table can be kept as a simple array of m locations. How many items can be placed into such a table?

As a baseline, let us consider what happens when we cannot move items. Each item looks at its two choices, and is placed in the first if it is empty, or is placed in the second if it is empty and the first is not. (If the two choices are always made uniformly at random, and both choices are empty, it does not matter where the item is placed.)

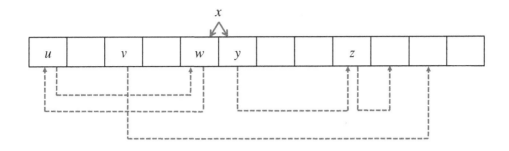

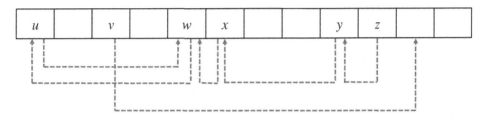

Figure 17.1: An example of a cuckoo hash table. For each placed item, the directed arrow shows the other location where that item can be moved to. In the initial configuration (top image), item x is inserted, but its choices contain items w and y. If x causes y to move and y causes z to move, then the resulting configuration (bottom image) can hold all items. In the original configuration, if the choices for x had been the locations containing items u and w, then x could not have been successfully placed.

As an exercise, you can check that without moves, when there are n bins, with high probability you can place only $O(n^{2/3})$ items before a new item being placed finds both its choices already hold another item. This is a simple variation of the birthday paradox.

Now let us consider the power that comes from moving items. If, on inserting an item x, there is no room for an item at either of its two choices, we instead move the item y in one of those bins to the other of its two choices. If the other bin for y is empty, then we are done – every item has a suitable place. However, there may be another item z in y's other location, in which case we may have to move z, and so on, until either we find an empty space, or we realize that there is no empty space to be found, which is a possibility. See Figure 17.1 for an example.

This approach is referred to as cuckoo hashing, taking the name from the cuckoo bird, which lays its eggs in the nests of other birds and whose young kick out the eggs or other young residing in the nest. We would like to understand various things about cuckoo hashing, namely:

- How many items can be successfully placed before an item cannot be placed?
- How long do we expect it to take to insert a new item?
- How can we know if we are in a situation where an item cannot be placed?

We address these issues by relating the cuckoo hashing process to a random graph process. Let us treat the bins as vertices, and the items being hashed as edges. That

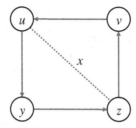

Figure 17.2: Items u, v, y, and z all reside in a bin, but their choices create a cycle in the cuckoo graph. Adding item x would create a component with two cycles (when considering the edges as undirected), which cannot be done. In simpler terms, a cuckoo hash table cannot store five items if all of their choices fall into four bins.

is, since each item hashes to two possible hash locations, we can view it as an edge connecting those two bins, or vertices, to which it hashes. As usual, we assume our hash values are completely random. In that case the resulting graph may have parallel edges, which are pairs of nodes connected by more than one edge, which occur when different items hash to the same two locations (vertices). The graph may also have self-loops, which are edges connecting a vertex to itself, which occur when both locations (vertices) chosen for an item are the same. We call this graph the *cuckoo graph*. We model the cuckoo graph corresponding to m items hashed into a table of n entries by a random graph with n nodes and m edges, where each of the two vertices of an edge is chosen independently and uniformly at random from the set of n nodes.

We remark that self-loops can be eliminated by partitioning the table into two subtables of equal size, and assigning each item a bin at random from each subtable. In that case we have a random bipartite graph with $n/2$ vertices on each side and m random edges, with each edge connecting two nodes, one chosen uniformly at random from each side. The differences arising from these variations is minimal.

The *load* of our cuckoo hash table will be m/n, the ratio of the number of items to the number of locations. Our main result is that if a cuckoo hash table with two choices has load less than and bounded away from $1/2$, placement will succeed with high probability.

A key approach in studying cuckoo hashing is to look at the connected components of the cuckoo graph. Recall that a connected component is simply a maximal group of vertices that are all connected, or reachable, by traversing edges in the graph. We show that as long as $m/n \leq (1 - \epsilon)/2$ for some constant $\epsilon > 0$, the maximum-sized connected component in the cuckoo graph has only $O(\log n)$ vertices with high probability, the expected number of vertices in a connected component for a given vertex v is constant, and all components are trees or contain a single cycle with high probability. (Here, a self-loop is considered a cycle on one vertex.) These facts about the cuckoo graph translate directly into answers to our questions about cuckoo hashing.

It should be clear that an item cannot be placed if it falls into a component that, after its placement, will have more items than bins to hold them, as shown by example in Figure 17.2. On the other hand, when all components are trees or have just a single cycle, every item can be placed successfully and efficiently. In fact we have the following lemma:

Lemma 17.7: *If an item is placed by cuckoo hashing so the resulting component is a tree or has a single cycle, the placement will occur successfully, and can be done in time proportional to the size of the component. If the resulting component has two or more cycles, the placement fails.*

Proof: If the number of edges, or items, exceeds the number of vertices, or bins, in the component, as is the case if there are two or more cycles, then an item cannot be placed.

To analyze the allocations of items to locations, it can help to think of each edge, or item, as being directed away from the vertex, or bin, in which it currently resides. Since each bin can store only one item, a proper allocation of items to bins must have no more than one edge directed out of each vertex. Keep in mind, however, that when we discuss cycles in components in our analysis, we are considering the undirected edges; the directed edges are just to help us keep track of how items can be moved.

It is clear that as long as all components are trees or have just a single cycle, the items *can* be placed successfully. For a tree, one can simply choose one vertex as a root, and orient all edges toward that root. That assignment has only one edge directed out of each vertex and the root of the tree is assigned no element. For a component with a cycle, the edges around the cycle have to be oriented consistently, and all other edges have to be directed toward the cycle.

Cuckoo hashing will place items if they can be placed, and each bin is visited at most twice during an insertion. There are three main cases to consider. When the item, or edge, is placed into a component that joins two existing tree components (one of which might be just a single vertex) so that the resulting component remains a tree, directed edges will be followed until we reach a vertex with no outgoing edge. When a directed edge is followed, it is reversed, corresponding to the replacement of the old item with the new item. (See Figure 17.3.)

When the item is placed so that both possible vertices already lie in the same component, the behavior is similar to the first case. There is a unique path to an empty vertex, corresponding to a bin that holds no item, and directed edges are followed and reversed until that vertex is reached.

The last case is when the item to be placed joins a component that has a cycle with a component that is a tree. It is possible in that case that placing the item will cause the process to follow edges around the cycle, reversing the cycle orientation as it goes. After going around the cycle and returning to the node where the new item was initially placed, the new item will be kicked out, and then a path is followed to the empty location in the tree component. It is important to see that while we can return once to the node the insertion started at, we traverse each edge at most twice, once in each direction. We never follow the same edge twice back into the cycle, because the edge will be flipped to point away from the cycle. (See Figure 17.4.)

In each case, placement takes time proportional to the component size. ∎

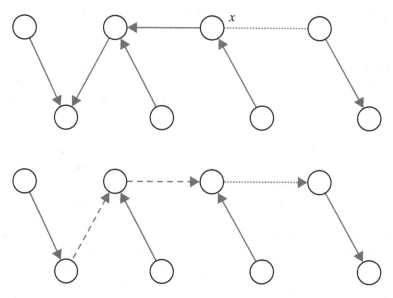

Figure 17.3: Item x is inserted into the cuckoo graph, and placed in the bin (or vertex) on the left (top image). It kicks out the item already there, moving the item to the neighboring bin in the graph. In terms of the graph, the vertex can only have one outgoing edge, so the other adjacent edge must reverse, and so on until the process terminates. In the bottom image, the reversed edges are shown as dashed.

Lemma 17.7 tells us that to understand how cuckoo hashing performs, we simply need to understand the component structure of the cuckoo graph. When we place a new item in the cuckoo hash table, we add a new edge to the graph, which lies in an existing component or joins two components. If we show the maximum component size is $O(\log n)$ with high probability, then we know from Lemma 17.7 that the maximum work needed to insert an item is $O(\log n)$ with high probability. Similarly, if we show that the expected size of a component is constant, then since the insertion of a new item joins two components, the expected time to insert an item is bounded by a constant. Of course, it is important to keep in mind that while insertion of a new item can take a logarithmic number of steps, a lookup of an item always takes constant time, since it is in one of two locations; this feature remains the key benefit of cuckoo hashing.

Finally, as we try to place an item by moving other items in the hash table, keeping track of the corresponding vertices visited in the cuckoo graph allows one to tell if the graph has a bad component with two cycles, in which case placement of a new item fails. Alternatively, because the maximum component size is $O(\log n)$ with high probability, in practice in implementations one often allows at most $c \log n$ replacements of items for a suitable constant c before declaring a failure. With this approach, one does not have to keep track of the vertices seen, avoiding the use of memory during placement.

We turn now to analyzing the connected component structure of a random cuckoo graph with n nodes and $m = (1 - \epsilon)n/2$ edges, for any constant $\epsilon > 0$. Based on our

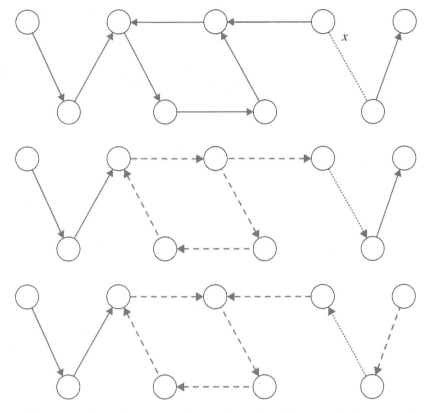

Figure 17.4: Item x is inserted into the cuckoo graph, and placed in the top bin (or vertex) of its two choices (top image). It kicks out the item already there, moving the item to the neighboring bin in the graph. In terms of the graph, the vertex can only have one outgoing edge, so the other adjacent edge must reverse, and so on. In this case, the process goes around the cycle and returns back to the original vertex where x was placed (middle image). The item x is itself kicked out to its other location, and the process terminates. Edges in the original graph that changed direction at least once are shown as dashed; an edge can only change direction at most twice.

analysis thus far, our task now is to analyze the maximum size and the expected size of connected components in the graph. Here size refers to the number of vertices in the component. Our proof is based on a branching processes technique.

Lemma 17.8: *Consider a cuckoo graph with n nodes and* $m = (1 - \epsilon)n/2$ *edges for some constant* $\epsilon > 0$.

(1) *With high probability the largest connected component in the cuckoo graph has size* $O(\log n)$.

(2) *The expected size of a connected component cuckoo in the graph is* $O(1)$.

Proof: We first focus on bounding the largest connected component. We observe that parallel edges and self-loops do not increase the size of a connected component. Thus, assuming a model in which the m edges are chosen uniformly at random with

447

no parallel edges or self-loops can only increase the probability of having a large connected component in the graph. This random graph model was introduced in Section 5.6 as the $G_{n,N}$ model. In our case the number of edges is $N = m$, and we refer to graphs with m uniformly chosen edges as being chosen from $G_{n,m}$.

Our second observation transforms the analysis to the related random graph model $G_{n,p}$, which we recall from Section 5.6 consists of graphs on n nodes with each of the possible $\binom{n}{2}$ edges included in the graph independently with probability p. We recall that having a connected component of size at least k for any value of k is a monotone increasing graph property; if a graph $G(V, E)$ has that property, then any graph $G' = (V, E')$ with $E \subseteq E'$ also has that property.

Since having a connected component of a given size is a monotone increasing graph property, we can use Lemma 5.14. In particular, for any $0 < \epsilon' < 1$, Lemma 5.14 allows us to conclude that the probability that a graph drawn from $G_{n,m}$ has a connected component of size at least k is within $e^{-O(m)}$ of the probability that a graph drawn from $G_{n,p}$ has a connected component of that size, where

$$p = (1 + \epsilon')\frac{m}{\binom{n}{2}} = \frac{(1 + \epsilon')(1 - \epsilon)}{n - 1} = \frac{1 - \gamma}{n - 1}.$$

This holds for any constant γ with $0 < \gamma < \epsilon$, by choosing a suitably small ϵ'. Thus, our problem is reduced to bounding the maximum size of a connected component in a graph drawn from $G_{n,p}$, with $p = (1 - \gamma)/n$.

Fix a vertex v. We explore the connected component containing vertex v by executing a breadth first search from v. We start by placing node v in a queue and look at the neighbors of v. We add these neighbors into a queue and look at the neighbors of these neighbors, adding any new vertices to the queue, and so on. More formally, after adding all the nodes at distance ℓ from the root v to the queue, we sequentially look at the neighbors of each of these nodes, adding to the queue neighbors at distance $\ell + 1$ from the root that are not yet in the queue. The process ends when there are no new neighbors to add to the queue. Clearly, when the process ends, the queue stores all the nodes in the connected component that includes v. Let $v = v_1, v_2, \ldots, v_k$ be the nodes in the queue at the termination of the process, in the order in which they entered the queue.

Let Z_i be the number of nodes added to the queue while looking at neighbors of v_i, i.e., Z_i counts the neighbors of v_i that are not neighbors of any node v_j, $j < i$. The key point in the analysis is that conditioning on the neighborhoods of $v_1, \ldots, v_{i-1}$, the distribution of Z_i is stochastically dominated by a binomial random variable distributed $B(n - 1, (1 - \gamma)/(n - 1))$.

Definition 17.1: *A random variable X stochastically dominates a random variable Y if for all a,*

$$\Pr(X \geq a) \geq \Pr(Y \geq a).$$

Equivalently, X stochastically dominates Y if for all a

$$F_X(a) \leq F_Y(a),$$

where F_X and F_Y are the cumulative distribution functions of X and Y, respectively.

To show this, we consider first the distribution of Z_1, the number of neighbors of node v. There are $n - 1$ other nodes, each connected to v with probability p, thus, Z_1 is distributed $B(n - 1, (1 - \gamma)/(n - 1))$. Consider now the distribution of Z_i, $i > 1$, where Z_i counts the neighbors of v_i that are not neighbors of any node v_j, $j < i$. Conditioned on the nodes that were already discovered by the breath first search process, there are no more than $n - i$ possible new nodes connected to v_i, and each of them is connected to v_i with probability p independent of any other edges. Thus, the distribution of Z_i, conditioned on the values of $Z_1, \ldots, Z_{i-1}$, is stochastically dominated by a random variable B_i with distribution $B(n - 1, (1 - \gamma)/(n - 1))$.

We bound the probability that our breadth first search found a component of size k. The breadth first search would have stopped with fewer than k vertices if

$$\sum_{j=1}^{k-1} Z_i < k - 1,$$

because then we would have found fewer than $k - 1$ additional vertices in exploring the first $k - 1$ vertices. So we must have

$$\sum_{j=1}^{k-1} Z_i \geq k - 1$$

for the breadth first search to reach k vertices. From our domination argument, the probability that our breadth first search reaches k vertices is bounded above by

$$\Pr\left(\sum_{j=1}^{k-1} Z_i \geq k - 1\right) \leq \Pr\left(\sum_{j=1}^{k-1} B_i \geq k - 1\right)$$
$$= \Pr(B((k - 1)(n - 1), (1 - \gamma)/(n - 1)) \geq k - 1).$$

Here we have used that the sum of binomials is itself binomial. We are now ready to apply the standard Chernoff bound (4.2). Let S be a binomial $B((k - 1)(n - 1), (1 - \gamma)/(n - 1))$ of mean $\mathbf{E}[S] = (1 - \gamma)(k - 1)$. Then

$$\Pr(S \geq k - 1) = \Pr\left(S \geq \frac{\mathbf{E}[S]}{1 - \gamma}\right)$$
$$\leq \Pr(S \geq \mathbf{E}[S](1 + \gamma))$$
$$\leq e^{-(k-1)(1-\gamma)\gamma^2/3}.$$

Here we have used that $1/(1 - \gamma) > (1 + \gamma)$. Setting $k \geq 1 + \frac{9}{\gamma^2(1-\gamma)} \ln n$, we have that the probability that v_1 is part of a connected component of size at least k is bounded above by $1/n^3$, and by a union bound the probability that any vertex is part of a connected component of size at least k is bounded above by $1/n^2$. Now applying Lemma 5.14, we can conclude that in the cuckoo graph with n nodes and m edges, the probability that there is connected component of size at least k is bounded above by $1/n^2 + e^{-O(m)} \leq 2/n^2$ for large enough n.

Next we bound the expected size of a connected component that includes a given node v. Consider first a graph chosen from $G_{n,p}$ with $p = (1 - \gamma)/(n - 1)$. Let X the size of the component that includes vertex v in that graph. As we have seen, for a graph chosen from $G_{n,p}$, we can view the breadth first search process as a branching process where the number of offspring of node v_i is Z_i, which is stochastically dominated by a random variable B_i distributed as $B(n - 1, (1 - \gamma)/(n - 1))$ and with expectation $1 - \gamma$. As we showed in Section 2.3, a branching process where the expected number of offspring of a node is bounded above by $1 - \gamma$ has an expected size of $1/\gamma$. Hence, in $G_{n,p}$, $\mathbf{E}[X] \leq 1/\gamma$.

Let Y be the size of the connected component that includes v in a graph chosen from $G_{n,m}$. Then, for any v,

$$\mathbf{E}[Y] = \sum_{i=1}^{n} \Pr(Y \geq k) \leq \sum_{k=1}^{n} \Pr(X \geq k) + ne^{-O(m)} \leq \frac{1}{\gamma} + ne^{-O(m)} = O(1),$$

where in the first inequality we applied Lemma 5.14 and in the second inequality we used the bound on $\mathbf{E}[X]$. ∎

Next we need to show that all connected components with more than one node in the cuckoo graph are either trees or have a single cycle.

Lemma 17.9: *Consider a cuckoo hashing graph with n nodes and $m = (1 - \epsilon)n/2$ edges. For any constant $\epsilon > 0$, with high probability all the connected components in the graph are either single vertices, trees, or unicyclic.*

Proof: For the proof, we need a bound on the number of ways k vertices can be a connected by a tree. We make use of the following combinatorial fact.

Lemma 17.10 [Cayley's Formula]: *The number of distinct labeled trees on k vertices is k^{k-2}.*

Here a labeled tree on k vertices is one where each vertex is given a distinct number from 1 to k, and trees that are isomorphic when taking into account the labels are considered the same. Hence there is one labeled tree on two vertices with one edge between them – there are two ways of labeling the vertices, but they are isomorphic. Similarly, there are three labeled trees on three vertices, with one tree for each assignment of a number to the vertex of degree 2. There are many proofs to Cayley's formula; one approach is given in Exercise 17.15.

A connected component that is not a tree or has more than one cycle must include a tree plus at least two additional edges. Let Y_k be a random variable denoting the number of components with k vertices and at least $k + 1$ edges. We determine a bound on $\mathbf{E}[Y_k]$ to bound the probability of the existence of such a component. We need only worry about values of k where $k = O(\log n)$ since we already proved that with high probability the graph has no larger connected components.

Given a set of k vertices that form a component, the k vertices must be connected by a tree. Suppose we choose a tree of $k - 1$ edges connecting those vertices. We require all of the edges in the tree to be part of the graph, and because we allow self-loops and multi-edges, each of the $m = (1 - \epsilon)n/2$ possible random edges will be a given specific edge of the tree with probability $2/n^2$. We then must have at least two additional edges within that component. The two additional edges fall within the component with probability k^2/n^2. Finally, all the $k(n - k)$ edges between vertices in the component and vertices not in the component must not be in the graph, or we would not have a component of size k. The following expression overcounts the number of components somewhat, as the same component may be counted multiple times.

$$\mathbf{E}[Y_k] \leq \binom{n}{k} k^{k-2} \binom{m}{k+1} \binom{k+1}{2} (k-1)! \left(\frac{2}{n^2}\right)^{k-1} \left(\frac{\binom{k}{2}}{\binom{n}{2}}\right)^2 \left(1 - \frac{2k(n-k)}{n^2}\right)^{m-k-1}.$$

That is, we first choose k vertices from the n vertices, we choose one of the k^{k-2} trees to connect these vertices, and we choose $k + 1$ of the m edges to form this tree and add two additional edges to the component, so there is more than one cycle.

$$\mathbf{E}[Y_k] \leq \binom{n}{k} k^{k-2} \binom{m}{k+1} \binom{k+1}{2} (k-1)! \left(\frac{2}{n^2}\right)^{k-1} \left(\frac{\binom{k}{2}}{\binom{n}{2}}\right)^2 \left(1 - \frac{2k(n-k)}{n^2}\right)^{m-k-1}$$

$$\leq \frac{n^k m^{k+1}}{2k!} k^{k-2} \left(\frac{2}{n^2}\right)^{k-1} \left(\frac{k^2}{n^2}\right)^2 e^{-2k(n-k)(m-k-1)/n^2}$$

$$\leq \frac{1}{n}(1 - \epsilon)^{k+1} \frac{k^2 e^k}{8} e^{-2k(n-k)(m-k-1)/n^2}$$

$$\leq \frac{1}{n}(1 - \epsilon)^{k+1} \frac{k^2}{8} e^{(kn^2 - 2k(n-k)(m-k-1))/n^2}$$

$$\leq \frac{k^2}{8n}(1 - \epsilon)^k e^{(kn^2 - 2knm)/n^2} e^{4k^2/n}$$

$$\leq \frac{k^2}{8n}(1 - \epsilon)^k e^{k\epsilon} e^{4k^2/n}$$

$$\leq \frac{k^2}{8n} e^{k(\epsilon + \ln(1-\epsilon))} e^{4k^2/n}.$$

To reach the second line in the equations above we have used that $\binom{n}{k} < n^k/k!$ and $1 - x \leq e^{-x}$; to reach the third line we have used $k^k/k! \leq e^k$. Because, from our previous argument, we can assume that $k = O(\log n)$, the final term $e^{4k^2/n}$ in the final line can be bounded above by 2 for large enough n. The key term in the final line is the $\epsilon + \ln(1 - \epsilon)$, which is negative, as can be seen using the expansion $\ln(1-\epsilon) = -\sum_{i=1}^{\infty} \epsilon^i/i$; the term $\epsilon + \ln(1 - \epsilon)$ is therefore $-\Theta(\epsilon^2)$ as ϵ goes to 0. The final expression therefore includes a term of the form $e^{-\Theta(k\epsilon^2)}$ that is geometrically decreasing in k. It follows that for any $z = O(\log n)$, $\sum_{k=1}^{z} \mathbf{E}[Y_k]$ is $O(1/n)$, and hence the probability that any component contains more than one cycle is $O(1/n)$. We can conclude that cuckoo hashing successfully places every item with high probability. ∎

One might wonder if we could do better. However, it is also easy to check that a cycle component occurs with probability $\Omega(1/n)$; for example, there is an $\Omega(1/n)$ probability that two items both choose the same bin for both its choices, or that three items choose the same distinct pair of bins. We consider ways one might improve this failure probability in Section 17.5.

Similarly, one might wonder if we could handle loads larger than $1/2$, or if the $1/2$ is just an outcome of our analysis. In fact, for cuckoo hashing as we have described it, $1/2$ is the limit. With $m = (1 + \epsilon)/2$ edges, the cuckoo graph looks very different; a constant fraction of the vertices become joined in a giant component of size $\Omega(n)$, and many of the vertices lie on cycles. We have seen similar threshold behaviors in random graphs before in Section 6.5.1; the threshold here corresponds directly to the load that can be handled by cuckoo hashing. However, higher loads are possible for more complex variations of cuckoo hashing, as we describe in Section 17.5.

Finally, it is worth mentioning that the analysis using Cayley's formula that we used to bound the number of components with two or more cycles could also be applied to bound the expected number of components of each size. There are some subtleties in the random graph model we have used here, but in Exercise 17.15, we show how to use this method rather than the branching process method to give an alternative proof that the largest component size is $O(\log n)$ in the $G_{n,p}$ random graph model.

17.5. Extending Cuckoo Hashing

17.5.1. *Cuckoo Hashing with Deletions*

It is worth noting that our analysis of cuckoo hashing depended only on the properties of the corresponding random graph. Because of this, our analysis for random hash functions holds even if we delete items, as long as the deletion process is also random, so that which items are deleted does not depend on the outcomes from the hash functions. For example, if items have lifetimes governed by a random distribution, then as long as there are always at most $m < n(1 - \epsilon)/2$ elements in the table, the probability we will fail on any specific configuration is only $O(1/n)$.

Indeed, we can actually show something slightly stronger; the addition of a new element causes a failure with probability only $O(1/n^2)$. This means we can delete and insert items for at least roughly a quadratic number of steps before a failure occurs. To see this, if we have m random edges in our cuckoo graph, we can bound the probability that a new item leads to the introduction of a double cycle. Suppose the new items creates a double cycle on exactly k vertices, where as before we can take k to be $O(\log n)$, as larger components are sufficiently unlikely that we can ignore them in our analysis. For this to happen, there must already be k edges among these k vertices. There are $\binom{n}{k}$ ways of choosing these vertices, and $\binom{m}{k}$ ways of choosing the items that correspond to the edges. After adding the new edge for the inserted item, the $k + 1$ edges must form a spanning tree, as well as two additional edges. Finally, there can be no other edges among the k vertices, or between those k vertices and the other $n - k$ vertices. Following the same analysis as we have used previously, if $\mathcal{E}$ is the event that the new vertex introduces a failure, we have

$$\Pr(\mathcal{E}) \leq \sum_k \binom{n}{k}\binom{m}{k}k^{k-2}\binom{k+1}{2}(k-1)!\left(\frac{2}{n^2}\right)^{k-1}\left(\frac{k^2}{n^2}\right)^2$$

$$\times \left(1 - \frac{k^2 + 2k(n-k)}{n^2}\right)^{m-k-1}$$

$$\leq \sum_k \frac{k^2(k+1)}{4n^2}\frac{k^k}{k!}\left(\frac{2m}{n}\right)^k e^{-(2k(n-k)+k^2)(m-k+1)/n^2}$$

$$\leq \sum_k \frac{k^2(k+1)}{4n^2}e^k(1-\epsilon)^k e^{-(2k(n-k)+k^2)(m-k+1)/n^2}$$

$$\leq \sum_k \frac{k^2(k+1)}{4n^2}e^k(1-\epsilon)^k e^{(kn^2-2knm)/n^2}e^{4k^2/n}$$

$$\leq \sum_k \frac{k^2(k+1)}{4n^2}(1-\epsilon)^k e^{k\epsilon}e^{4k^2/n}$$

$$\leq \sum_k \frac{k^2(k+1)}{4n^2}e^{k(\epsilon+\ln(1-\epsilon))}e^{4k^2/n}.$$

Again, we need only consider $k = O(\log n)$. The exponential term grows like $e^{-\Theta(\epsilon^2 k)}$, which gives that $\Pr(\mathcal{E})$ is $O(1/n^2)$.

Of course, deletion of an item in a cuckoo hash table, like insertion, only takes constant time.

17.5.2. *Handling Failures*

We have shown the failure probability of cuckoo hashing is $O(1/n)$ when inserting m items into $n > 2m$ bins. Unfortunately, that result is easily shown to be tight. As a first step, consider the following mode of failure: we find three balls with the same choices for the two bins. (To ease the calculations, we suppose that all three balls land in two distinct bins – no self-loops among the three.) The expected number of "triples" of balls with this property is

$$\binom{m}{3}\left(1-\frac{1}{n}\right)\left(\frac{2}{n^2}\right)^2.$$

This is because there are $\binom{m}{3}$ ways to choose the three balls. With probability $\left(1-\frac{1}{n}\right)$ the first ball did not choose a self-loop; the other two balls then each choose the same pair of bins with probability $2/n^2$. We easily observe that when $m = \Omega(n)$ this expectation is $\Omega(1/n)$. A calculation of the variance readily yields the probability that there is such a triple is also $\Omega(1/n)$, using the second moment method.

While the probability of failure for a cuckoo hash table is $o(1)$, the fact that it is $\Omega(1/n)$ remains concerning; this could be very high for many practical situations. One way to cope with this problem is to allow rehashing. If we ever reach a failure point, where either we find that we can't place an item because of cycles, or we simply find that a component is too large (over $c \log n$ for a suitable constant c), then we can choose a new hash function and rehash all the items into a new cuckoo hash table. A question is how much impact will rehashing have.

The amount of work to rehash using a new hash function for all items is $O(n)$, and we only have to do it with probability $O(1/n)$. Even if we have to rehash multiple times before we reach success, the expected work to hash m items can be bounded. Using order notation rather loosely, we find the total number of operations is

$$O(n) + \sum_{k=1}^{\infty} k \cdot O(n) \cdot (O(1/n))^k = O(n).$$

Hence the amortized amount of work per item due to rehashing is only constant in expectation, and also with high probability, since the probability of rehashing k or more times is $O(1/n^k)$. However, one can imagine that rehashing might not be a suitable solution in some practical settings, because it would be undesirable for the system to have to wait for a complete rehashing of the hash table.

An alternative approach to rehashing that generally does quite well is to set aside a small amount of memory for a *stash*. If an item cannot be placed because it creates a component with more than one cycle, it can be placed in the stash. Usually, the stash will be empty; however, when it is not empty, it will need to be checked on every lookup. (Further, if items are deleted, one should check whether an item in the stash can then be put back into the cuckoo hash table.) We have seen that the use of the stash should be rare, since the failure probability is only $O(1/n)$. Extending the previous analysis, one can show that failures behave "nearly independently"; the probability that j items need to be held in a stash falls like $O(1/n^j)$. Hence, even a very small stash, such as one that can hold four items, can greatly reduce the failure probability. The use of stashes is considered further in Exercise 17.17.

17.5.3. *More Choices and Bigger Bins*

There are many ways to vary or enhance cuckoo hashing. One way, as we have seen, is by using a stash. One can also slightly improve the performance using the following method: split the table into two subtables and make one choice randomly from each subtable for each item; when inserting an item, just place the new element in the first subtable, kicking out the element already there if needed; and finally, optimize the subtable sizes by making the first slightly larger, since now it will tend to hold more items. The slight asymmetry that arises from favoring the first subtable, both in placement and in size, can yield a small improvement in behavior, but the additional complexity may not be worthwhile for many applications.

However, more important variations of cuckoo hashing allow more than one item per bin, more than two choices per item, or both. Both of these approaches can significantly enhance the load that can be achieved, as well as reduce the probability of failure, at the expense of more complications in the insertion and lookup processes.

If each item has two choices but we allow $b > 1$ items per bin, then we continue to have a random graph problem, but now the question is whether cuckoo hashing can effectively find an orientation with at most b edges pointing away from a vertex. Allowing more than one item per bin can be very natural; for example, a bin may correspond to a fixed amount of memory, such as a cache line, that might correspond to the size of multiple items. One issue is how to choose which item to kick out of a bin when it is necessary to place an item into a full bin. Natural possibilities include breadth first search, or a "random walk" style search where at each step a random item is selected from the bin to be kicked out to make room for the existing element.

If each item has $d > 2$ choices but there is just one item per bin, then our problem involves random hypergraphs, rather than random graphs, where each edge is a collection of d vertices. When all choices for an item lead to a bin that already contains an item, we again face the issue of how to choose which item to kick out. One could again use approaches based on a breadth first search, or a "random walk" style search. A further variation is to allow different items differing number of choices, according to some distribution, where the number of choices is itself determined by a hash function on the item.

Of course, one can also combine more than two choices per item and more than one item per bin. With four choices and one item per bin, the maximum load that can be achieved with no failures with high probability (as n grows large) is over 0.97, much more than the 0.5 bound for two choices. Similarly, two choices with up to four items per bin allow loads over 0.98. Combining multiple choices with multiple items per bin yields even higher load factors.

The following theorem provides the form of the load threshold as the number of bin choices and the number of items per bin varies. Its proof is quite complex and beyond the scope of this book.

Theorem 17.11: *Consider a cuckoo hash table with n items, m/ℓ bins that each can hold up to ℓ items, and k choices per item. We consider a regime when n/m is held fixed, but $n, m \to \infty$. Let $\beta(c)$ denote the largest value of β so that*

$$\frac{1}{k} \frac{\beta}{(\Pr(Po(\beta) \geq \ell))^{k-1}} = c,$$

where $Po(x)$ refers to a discrete Poisson random variable with mean x. Define $c_{k,\ell}$ to be the unique value of c that satisfies

$$\frac{\beta(c) \cdot \Pr[Po(\beta(c)) \geq \ell]}{k \cdot \Pr[Po(\beta(c)) \geq \ell + 1]} = \ell.$$

The following results hold for any constant values $k \geq 3$ and $\ell \geq 1$, or for $k = 2$ and constant $\ell \geq 2$. For every $\epsilon > 0$, for large enough n, we have that if $n/m < c_{k,\ell} - \epsilon$, there is a way of placing the items in the hash table that respects their choices and the limits on the number of items per bin with probability $1 - o(1)$. If $n/m > c_{k,\ell} + \epsilon$, then there is no way to place the items that respects their choices and the limits on the number of items per bin with probability $1 - o(1)$.

455

17.6. Exercises

Exercise 17.1: (a) For Theorems 17.1 and 17.4, the statement of the proof is for the case that ties are broken randomly. Argue informally that, if the bins are numbered from 1 to n and if ties are broken in favor of the lower-numbered bin, then the theorems still hold.

(b) Argue informally that the theorems apply to any tie-breaking mechanism that has no knowledge of the bin choices made by balls that have not yet been placed.

Exercise 17.2: Consider the following variant of the balanced allocation paradigm: n balls are placed sequentially in n bins, with the bins labeled from 0 to $n - 1$. Each ball chooses a bin i uniformly at random, and the ball is placed in the least loaded of bins $i, i + 1 \bmod n, i + 2 \bmod n, \ldots, i + d - 1 \bmod n$. Argue that, when d is a constant, the maximum load grows as $\Theta(\ln n / \ln \ln n)$. That is, the balanced allocation paradigm does not yield an $O(\ln \ln n)$ result in this case.

Exercise 17.3: Explain why, with 2-way chaining, the expected time to insert an item and to search for an item in a hash table of size n with n items is $O(1)$. Consider two cases: the search is for an item that is in the table; and the search is for an item that is not in the table.

Exercise 17.4: Consider the following variant of the balanced allocation paradigm: n balls are placed sequentially in n bins. Each ball comes with d choices, chosen independently and uniformly at random from the n bins. When a ball is placed, we are also allowed to move balls among these d bins to equalize their load as much as possible. Show that the maximum load is still at least $\ln \ln n / \ln d - O(1)$ with probability $1 - o(1/n)$ in this case.

Exercise 17.5: Suppose that in the balanced allocation setup there are n bins, but the bins are not chosen uniformly at random. Instead, the bins have two types: $1/3$ of the bins are type A and $2/3$ of the bins are type B. When a bin is chosen at random, each of the type-A bins is chosen with probability $2/n$ and each of the type-B bins is chosen with probability $1/2n$. Prove that the maximum load of any bin when each ball has d bin choices is still at most $\ln \ln n / \ln d + O(1)$.

Exercise 17.6: Consider a parallel version of the balanced allocation paradigm in which we have n/k rounds, where k new balls arrive in each round. Each ball is placed in the least loaded of its d choices, where in this setting the load of each bin is the load at the end of the previous round. Ties are broken randomly. Note that the k new balls cannot affect each other's placement. Give an upper bound on the maximum load as a function of n, d, and k.

Exercise 17.7: We have shown that sequentially throwing n balls into n bins randomly, using two bin choices for each ball, yields a maximum load of $\ln \ln n / \ln 2 + O(1)$

with high probability. Suppose that, instead of placing the balls sequentially, we had access to all of the $2n$ choices for the n balls, and suppose we wanted to place each ball into one of its choices while minimizing the maximum load. In this setting, with high probability, we can obtain a maximum load that is constant.

Write a program to explore this scenario. Your program should take as input a parameter k and implement the following greedy algorithm. At each step, some subset of the balls are active; initially, all balls are active. Repeatedly find a bin that has at least one but no more than k active balls that have chosen it, assign these active balls to that bin, and then remove these balls from the set of active balls. The process stops either when there are no active balls remaining or when there is no suitable bin. If the algorithm stops with no active balls remaining, then every bin is assigned no more than k balls.

Try running your program with 10,000 balls and 10,000 bins. What is the smallest value of k for which the program terminates with no active balls remaining at least four out of five times? If your program is fast enough, try experimenting with more trials. Also, if your program is fast enough, try answering the same question for 100,000 balls and 100,000 bins.

Exercise 17.8: The following problem models a simple distributed system where agents contend for resources and back off in the face of contention. As in Exercise 5.12, balls represent agents and bins represent resources.

The system evolves over rounds. In the first part of every round, balls are thrown independently and uniformly at random into n bins. In the second part of each round, each bin in which at least one ball has landed in that round *serves* exactly one ball from that round. The remaining balls are thrown again in the next round. We begin with n balls in the first round, and we finish when every ball is served.

(a) Show that, with probability $1 - o(1/n)$, this approach takes at most $\log_2 \log_2 n + O(1)$ rounds. (*Hint:* Let b_k be the number of balls left after k rounds; show that $b_{k+1} \leq c(b_k)^2/n$, for a suitable constant c with high probability, as long as b_{k+1} is sufficiently large.)

(b) Suppose that we modify the system so that a bin accepts a ball in a round if and only if that ball was the *only* ball to request that bin in that round. Show that, again with probability $1 - o(1/n)$, this approach takes at most $\log_2 \log_2 n + O(1)$ rounds.

Exercise 17.9: The natural way to simulate experiments with balls and bins is to create an array that stores the load at each bin. To simulate 1,000,000 balls being placed into 1,000,000 bins would require an array of 1,000,000 counters. An alternative approach is to keep an array that records in the jth cell the number of bins with load j. Explain how this could be used to simulate placing 1,000,000 balls into 1,000,000 bins using the standard balls-and-bins paradigm and the balanced allocation paradigm with much less space.

Exercise 17.10: Write a program to compare the performance of the standard balls-and-bins paradigm and the balanced allocation paradigm. Run simulations placing n balls into n bins, with each ball having $d = 1, 2, 3$, and 4 random choices. You should try $n = 10,000$, $n = 100,000$, and $n = 1,000,000$. Repeat each experiment at least 100 times and compute the expectation and variance of the maximum load for each value of d based on your trials. You may wish to use the idea of Exercise 17.9.

Exercise 17.11: Write a simulation showing how the balanced allocation paradigm can improve performance for distributed queueing systems. Consider a bank of n FIFO queues with a Poisson arrival stream of customers to the entire bank of rate λn per second, where $\lambda < 1$. Upon entry a customer chooses a queue for service, and the service time for each customer is exponentially distributed with mean 1 second. You should compare two settings: (i) where each customer chooses a queue independently and uniformly at random from the n queues for service; and (ii) where each customer chooses two queues independently and uniformly at random from the n queues and waits at the queue with fewer customers, breaking ties randomly. Notice that the first setting is equivalent to having a bank of n $M/M/1$ FIFO queues, each with Poisson arrivals of rate $\lambda < 1$ per second. You may find the discussion in Exercise 8.27 helpful in constructing your simulation.

Your simulation should run for t seconds, and it should return the average (over all customers that have completed service) of the time spent in the system as well as the average (over all customers that have arrived) of the number of customers found waiting in the queue they selected for service. You should present results for your simulations for $n = 100$ and for $t = 10,000$ seconds, with $\lambda = 0.5, 0.8, 0.9$, and 0.99.

Exercise 17.12: Write a program to compare the performance of the following variation of the standard balls-and-bins paradigm and the balanced allocation paradigm. Initially n points are placed uniformly at random on the boundary of a circle of circumference 1. These n points divide the circle into n arcs, which correspond to bins. We now place n balls into the bins as follows: each ball chooses d points on the boundary of the circle, uniformly at random. These d points correspond to the arcs (or, equivalently, bins) that they lie on. The ball is placed in the least loaded of the d bins, breaking ties in favor of the smallest arc.

Run simulations placing n balls into n bins for the cases $d = 1$ and $d = 2$. You should try $n = 1,000$, $n = 10,000$, and $n = 100,000$. Repeat each experiment at least 100 times; for each run, the n initial points should be re-chosen. Give a chart showing the number of times the maximum load was k, based on your trials for each value of d.

You may note that some arcs are much larger than others, and therefore when $d = 1$ the maximum load can be rather high. Also, to find which bin each ball is placed in may require implementing a binary search or some other additional data structure to quickly map points on the circle boundary to the appropriate bin.

Exercise 17.13: There is a small but interesting improvement that can be made to the balanced allocation scheme we have described. Again we will place n balls into n bins. We assume here than n is even. Suppose that we divide the n bins into two groups of size $n/2$. We call the two groups the left group and the right group. For each ball, we independently choose one bin uniformly at random from the left and one bin uniformly at random from the right. We put the ball in the least loaded bin, but if there is a tie we

458

always put the ball in the bin from the left group. With this scheme, the maximum load is reduced to $\ln \ln n / 2 \ln \phi + O(1)$, where $\phi = (1 + \sqrt{5})/2$ is the golden ratio. This improves the result of Theorem 17.1 by a constant factor. (Note the two changes to our original scheme: the bins are split into two groups, and ties are broken in a consistent way; both changes are necessary to obtain the improvement we describe.)

(a) Write a program to compare the performance of the original balanced allocation paradigm with this variation. Run simulations placing n balls into n bins, with each ball having $d = 2$ choices. You should try $n = 10,000$, $n = 100,000$, and $n = 1,000,000$. Repeat each experiment at least 100 times and compute the expectation and variance of the maximum load based on your trials. Describe the extent of the improvement of the new variation.

(b) Adapt Theorem 17.1 to prove this result. The key idea in how the theorem's proof must change is that we now require two sequences, β_i and γ_i. Similar to Theorem 17.1, β_i represents a desired upper bound on the number of bins on the left with load at least i, and γ_i is a desired upper bound on the number of bins on the right with load at least i. Argue that choosing

$$\beta_{i+1} = \frac{c_1 \beta_i \gamma_i}{n^2} \quad \text{and} \quad \gamma_{i+1} = \frac{c_2 \beta_{i+1} \gamma_i}{n^2}$$

for some constants c_1 and c_2 is suitable (as long as β_i and γ_i are large enough that Chernoff bounds may apply).

Now let F_k be the kth Fibonacci number. Apply induction to show that, for sufficiently large i, $\beta_i \leq nc_3 c_4^{F_{2i}}$ and $\gamma_i \leq nc_3 c_4^{F_{2i+1}}$ for some constants c_3 and c_4. Following Theorem 17.1, use this to prove the $\ln \ln n / 2 \ln \phi + O(1)$ upper bound.

(c) This variation can easily be extended to the case of $d > 2$ choices by splitting the n bins into d ordered groups, choosing one bin uniformly at random from each group, and breaking ties in favor of the group that comes first in the ordering. Suggest what would be the appropriate upper bound on the maximum load for this case, and give an argument backing your suggestion. (You need not give a complete formal proof.)

Exercise 17.14: The birthday paradox (discussed in Section 5.1) shows that if balls are sequentially thrown randomly into n bins, with constant probability there will be a collision after $\Theta(\sqrt{n})$ balls are thrown.

(a) Suppose that balls are placed sequentially, each ball has two choices of where to be placed, and a ball will choose a bin that avoids a collision if that is possible. Show that there are constants c_1 and c_2 so that after $c_1 n^{2/3} - o(n^{2/3})$ balls are thrown no collision has occurred with probability at least $1/2$, and after $c_2 n^{2/3} + o(n^{2/3})$ balls are thrown at least one collision has occurred with probability at least $1/2$.

(b) How close can you make the constants c_1 and c_2?

(c) Extend your analyis for more than two choices. Specifically, show that if each ball has k choices for some constant k, there are constants $c_{1,k}$ and $c_{2,k}$ so that after $c_{1,k} n^{1-1/k} - o(n^{1-1/k})$ balls are thrown no collision has occurred with probability at least $1/2$, and after $c_{2,k}n^{1-1/k} + o(n^{1-1/k})$ balls are thrown at least one collision has occurred with probability at least $1/2$.

(d) How close can you make the constants $c_{1,k}$ and $c_{2,k}$?

Exercise 17.15: In our analysis for cuckoo hash tables we showed that the largest component size was $O(\log n)$ with high probability. Here we provide part of an alternative proof of this result in the $G_{n,p}$ model, using an analysis that makes use of Cayley's formula. Consider a random graph G chosen from $G_{n,p}$, with $p = c/n$ for a constant $c < 1$.

(a) Let X_k be the expected number of tree components on exactly k vertices for a random graph from $G_{n,p}$ with $p = c/n$ for a constant $c < 1$. A tree component on k vertices will be connected with $k - 1$ edges, and will have no edges to the other $n - k$ vertices. Show that

$$\mathbf{E}[X_k] = \binom{n}{k} k^{k-2} \left(\frac{c}{n}\right)^{k-1} \left(1 - \frac{c}{n}\right)^{kn-k(k+3)/2+1}.$$

(b) Show that for $1 \le k \le \sqrt{n}$,

$$\mathbf{E}[X_k] \le C \frac{n}{ck^2} e^{(1-c+\ln c)k}$$

for some constant C for large enough n.

(c) Using the expression for $\mathbf{E}[X_k]$, show that

$$\frac{\mathbf{E}[X_{k+1}]}{\mathbf{E}[X_k]} = (n - k)\left(1 + \frac{1}{k}\right)^{k-1} \frac{c}{n}\left(1 - \frac{c}{n}\right)^{n-k-2},$$

and in turn

$$\frac{\mathbf{E}[X_{k+1}]}{\mathbf{E}[X_k]} \le \left(1 - \frac{k}{n}\right) c e^{1-c(1-k/n)}\left(1 - \frac{c}{n}\right)^{-2}.$$

(d) Show that $xe^{1-x} \le 1$ for $x > 0$, and conclude that

$$\frac{\mathbf{E}[X_{k+1}]}{\mathbf{E}[X_k]} \le \left(1 - \frac{c}{n}\right)^{-2}.$$

(e) Using the above, argue that the probability that there is any tree component with more than $\sqrt{n}$ vertices in G is $o(1/n)$, and that therefore the maximum size of a tree component of G is $O(\log n)$ with probability $1 - o(1/n)$.

Exercise 17.16: Complete the argument from Section 17.5.2 to show that the failure probability for standard cuckoo hashing is at least $\Omega(1/n)$.

Exercise 17.17: Write code to implement the following experiment. You will build a cuckoo hash table using two choices per item and one item per bin, with an array of size 2^{20}, and you will insert 514,000 items into it. (This is a bit more than than 49% of 2^{20}.) You have to decide how many moves you will allow before deciding a failure has occurred; 200 should be sufficient. If during the insertion process an item cannot be inserted, place the item in a stash and continue inserting the remaining items.

Perform 100,000 trials. How often would you need a stash to hold an item? How often would a stash that can hold one item suffice? Two items?

Exercise 17.18: We show here one way to derive Cayley's formula. A directed rooted tree is a tree with a special root vertex, and all the edges in the tree are assigned a direction, with all edges directed away from the root. We count the number of *sequences* of directed edges that can lead to a directed rooted tree in two different ways, and use it to calculate an expression for $T(k)$, the number of distinct labeled trees on k vertices.

(a) We create an ordered triple as follows. We first choose a labeled but undirected tree. We next choose a vertex as a root, and now we can think of the tree as being a directed rooted tree. Finally, we choose one of the $(k-1)!$ possible permutations of the directed edges. We can think of our choices of labeled tree, root vertex, and edge permutation as an ordered triple.

   Show that there is a one-to-one correspondence between these ordered triples and sequences of directed edges on k vertices that lead to a directed rooted tree. Explain why this shows that the number of sequences of directed edges that can lead to a directed rooted tree on k vertices is $(k!) \cdot T(k)$.

(b) Now suppose instead we start with an empty graph, where we think of each vertex as initially its own rooted tree (with no edges), and add directed edges one at a time. At each step we will have a forest of directed edges. After ℓ steps the forest will have $k - \ell$ roots, so that after $k - 1$ edges are added, we will have a directed rooted tree. At each step we choose an edge to add by first choosing any of the k vertices in the graph. This vertex will be in one of the trees in the forest. We then choose a root from another tree to connect to, with the edge directed from the first vertex to the second. This removes one of the roots from consideration, so each step reduces the number of roots by one. Show that there is a one-to-one correspondence between sequences of directed edges that lead to a directed rooted tree and the sequences of edges that can be chosen in this manner, and show that there are $k^{k-1}(k-1)!$ ways of choosing the sequences of edges as above.

(c) Argue from the above steps that $T(k) = k^{k-2}$.

Exercise 17.19: Suppose we consider the effects of adding a stash that can hold a single item, with standard cuckoo hashing using two choices and one item per bin. In this case, we can consider two ways to fail; we might have a single component of k vertices with at least $k + 2$ edges, or we might have two disjoint components, one with k_1 vertices with at least $k_1 + 1$ edges and one with k_2 vertices with at least $k_2 + 1$ edges. By extending our previous analysis regarding components and edges, show that the probability of having a failure with cuckoo hashing when using a stash that can hold one item is $O(1/n^2)$.

Exercise 17.20: Write code to implement the following experiment. You will build a cuckoo hash table using four choices per item and one item per bin, with an array of size 2^{20}. If all choices are full, choose one of the items to kick out randomly. (You may, if you like, optimize after the first move on an insertion by not allowing yourself to choose to place an item in a bin that it has just been kicked out of at the last step.) You have to decide how many moves you will allow before deciding a failure has occurred; 200 should be sufficient. Load the table until you reach an item that cannot be placed. Record the load, or the fraction of the array that has been filled; that is, the number of items divided by 2^{20}. Repeat the experiment 1000 times. What load level seems safe with four choices? How does this compare to Theorem 17.11? (Theorem 17.11 is about the existence of a valid assignment, not about this placement algorithm, and is an asymptotic result. It is therefore not necessarily expected that the experiment should achieve the performance suggested by the theorem.)

Exercise 17.21: Modify your code above so that you can experiment with varying numbers of choices per item and varying numbers of items per bin. For different values of these parameters, determine (approximately) the load where the failure probability appears to be nontrivial and compare to Theorem 17.11.

Further Reading

N. Alon and J. Spencer, *The Probabilistic Method,* 2nd edn. Wiley, New York, 2000.

B. Bollobás, *Random Graphs,* 2nd edn. Academic Press, Orlando, FL, 1999.

T. H. Cormen, C. E. Leiserson, R. L. Rivest, and C. Stein, *Introduction to Algorithms,* 2nd edn. MIT Press / McGraw-Hill, Cambridge / New York, 2001.

T. M. Cover and J. A. Thomas, *Elements of Information Theory,* Wiley, New York, 1991.

W. Feller, *An Introduction to the Probability Theory, Vol. 1,* 3rd edn. Wiley, New York, 1968.

W. Feller, *An Introduction to the Probability Theory, Vol. 2.* Wiley, New York, 1966.

S. Har-Peled, *Geometric Approximation Algorithms*, AMS, Providence, RI, 2011.

M. Jerrum, *Counting, Sampling and Integrating: Algorithms and Complexity* (Lectures in Mathematics. ETH Zürich), Birkhäuser, Berlin, 2003.

S. Karlin and H. M. Taylor, *A First Course in Stochastic Processes,* 2nd edn. Academic Press, New York, 1975.

S. Karlin and H. M. Taylor, *A Second Course in Stochastic Processes.* Academic Press, New York, 1981.

M. Kearns, U. Vazirani, *An Introduction to Computational Learning Theory.* MIT Press, Cambridge, MA, 1994.

F. Leighton, *Parallel Algorithms and Architectures.* Morgan Kauffmann, San Mateo, CA, 1992.

R. Motwani and P. Raghavan, *Randomized Algorithms.* Cambridge University Press, Cambridge, UK, 1995.

S. Ross, *Stochastic Processes.* Wiley, New York, 1996.

S. Ross, *A First Course in Probability,* 6th edn., Prentice-Hall, Englewood Cliffs, NJ, 2002.

S. Ross, *Probability Models for Computer Science.* Academic Press, Orlando, FL, 2002.

S. Shalev-Shwartz and S. Ben-David, *Understanding Machine Learning: From Theory to Algorithms*, Cambridge University Press, Cambridge, UK, 2014.

J. H. Spencer, *Ten Lectures on the Probabilistic Method,* 2nd edn. SIAM, Philadelphia, 1994.

L. Valiant, *Probably Approximately Correct.* Basic Books, New York, 2013.

R. W. Wolff, *Stochastic Modeling and the Theory of Queues.* Prentice-Hall, Englewood Cliffs, NJ, 1989.

Index

Printed in the United States
by Baker & Taylor Publisher Services